foundations of operations management

second canadian edition

larry p. ritzman

Professor Emeritus at The Ohio State University and Boston College

lee j. krajewski

University of Notre Dame

manoj k. malhotra

University of South Carolina

robert d. klassen

University of Western Ontario

PEARSON

Prentice Hall

Toronto

Library and Archives Canada Cataloguing in Publication

Foundations of operations management/Larry P. Ritzman ... [et al.].—2nd Canadian ed.

Includes index.
Canadian ed. written by Larry P. Ritzman, Lee J. Krajewski, Robert D. Klassen.
ISBN-13: 978-0-13-227931-4
ISBN-10: 0-13-227931-2

1. Production management—Textbooks.   I. Ritzman, Larry P. Foundations of operations management.

TS155.F69 2007   658.5   C2006-902342-5

ISBN-10: 0-13-227931-2
ISBN-13: 978-0-13-227931-4

Editor-in-Chief: Gary Bennett
Executive Marketing Manager: Cas Shields
Executive Editor: Samantha Scully
Developmental Editors: Pamela Voves/John Polanszky
Production Editor: Marisa D'Andrea
Copy Editor: Valerie Adams
Proofreader: Marg Bukta
Production Coordinator: Andrea Falkenberg
Photo and Literary Permissions Researcher: Amanda McCormick
Indexer: Sheila Flavel
Page Layout: Gerry Dunn
Art Director: Julia Hall
Interior and Cover Design: Jennifer Stimson
Cover Image: John Lund/Getty Images

1 2 3 4 5   11 10 09 08 07

Dedicated with love to our families.

Barbara Ritzman

Karen and Matt; Kristin and Alayna

Lisa and Todd; Cody, Cole, Taylor, and Clayton

Kathryn and Paul

Mildred and Ray

Judie Krajewski

Gary

Lori and Dan; Aubrey, Madeline, and Amelia

Carrie and Jon; Jordanne and Alaina

Selena and Jeff

Virginia and Jerry

Virginia and Larry

Maya Malhotra

Vivek, Pooja, and Neha

Santosh and Ramesh Malhotra

Indra and Prem Malhotra; Neeti and Deeksha

Sadhana Malhotra

Leela and Mukund Dabholkar

Aruna and Harsha Dabholkar; Aditee

Mangala and Pradeep Gandhi; Priya and Medha

Lorraine Klassen

Nicholas

Benjamin

About the Authors

LARRY P. RITZMAN is the Thomas J. Galligan, Jr. Emeritus Professor in Operations and Strategic Management at Boston College, where he received the Distinguished Service Award from the School of Management. He is also a Professor Emeritus at The Ohio State University, where he served for 23 years. He received several awards at Ohio State for both teaching and research, including the Pace Setters' Club Award for Outstanding Research. He received his doctorate at Michigan State University, having had prior industrial experience at the Babcock and Wilcox Company. Over the years, he has been privileged to teach and learn more about operations management with numerous students at all levels—undergraduate, MBA, executive MBA, and doctorate.

Particularly active in the Decision Sciences Institute, Larry has served as council coordinator, publications committee chair, track chair, vice president, board member, executive committee member, doctoral consortium coordinator, and president. He was elected a Fellow of the Institute in 1987 and earned the Distinguished Service Award in 1996. He has received three best-paper awards. He is a frequent reviewer, discussant, and session chair for several other professional organizations.

Larry's areas of particular expertise are service processes, operations strategy, production and inventory systems, forecasting, multistage manufacturing, and layout. An active researcher, Larry's publications have appeared in such journals as *Decision Sciences, Journal of Operations Management, Production and Operations Management, Harvard Business Review*, and *Management Science*. He has served in various editorial capacities for several journals.

LEE J. KRAJEWSKI is the William R. and F. Cassie Daley Professor of Manufacturing Strategy at the University of Notre Dame. Prior to joining Notre Dame, Lee was a faculty member at The Ohio State University, where he received the University Alumni Distinguished Teaching Award and the College of Business Outstanding Faculty Research Award. He initiated the Center for Excellence in Manufacturing Management and served as its director for four years. In addition, he received the National President's Award and the National Award of Merit of the American Production and Inventory Control Society. He served as president of the Decision Sciences Institute and was elected a fellow of the Institute in 1988. He received the Distinguished Service Award in 2003.

Lee received his Ph.D. from the University of Wisconsin. Over the years, he has designed and taught courses at both graduate and undergraduate levels on topics such as operations strategy, introduction to operations management, operations design, project management, and manufacturing planning and control systems.

Lee served as the editor of *Decision Sciences*, was the founding editor of the *Journal of Operations Management*, and has served on several editorial boards. Widely published himself, Lee has contributed numerous articles to such journals as *Decision Sciences, Journal of Operations Management, Management Science, Harvard Business Review*, and *Interfaces*, to name just a few. He has received five best-paper awards. Lee's areas of specialization include operations strategy, manufacturing planning and control systems, supply chain management, and master production scheduling.

MANOJ K. MALHOTRA is the Jeff B. Bates Professor and Chairman of the Management Science Department at the Moore School of Business, University of South Carolina (USC), Columbia. He holds an engineering undergraduate degree from The Indian Institute of Technology (IIT) Kanpur, India, and a Ph.D. in operations management from The Ohio State University. He is certified as a Fellow of the American Production and Inventory Management Society (CFPIM), and has conducted seminars and consulted with such firms as John Deere, Metso Corporation, Phelps Dodge, Sonoco, UCB Chemicals, Milliken, and Verizon, among others.

Manoj's research has thematically focused on the deployment of flexible resources in manufacturing and service firms, and on the interface between operations and supply chain management and other functional areas of business. His work on these and related issues has been published in refereed journals, such as *Decision Sciences*, *European Journal of Operational Research*, *IIE Transactions*, *International Journal of Production Research*, *Journal of Operations Management*, *OMEGA*, and *Production and Operations Management Journal*. Manoj is currently an associate editor of *Decision Sciences* and *Journal of Operations Management*. He is a recipient of the Decision Sciences Institute's Outstanding Achievement Award for the Best Application Paper in 1990 and the Stan Hardy Award in 2002 for the best paper published in the field of operations management.

ROBERT D. KLASSEN is Professor of Operations Management and Hydro One Faculty Fellow in Environmental Management at the Richard Ivey School of Business, University of Western Ontario. He earned his doctorate from the University of North Carolina at Chapel Hill. He has also worked as an environmental engineer in the steel industry, following earlier experience in the consumer products and petroleum sectors.

Since joining Ivey in 1995, Robert has enjoyed interacting with students of all levels, including undergraduate, MBA, executive MBA, and doctoral students. He has developed and delivered courses in operations management, operations strategy, service management, management of technology, and most recently, sustainable development. He has also written more than two dozen teaching cases to help students bridge between research and teaching, concept and application, and theory and practice.

Robert's research interests focus on exploring the challenges for and linkages between manufacturing and the natural environment, encompassing innovations and supply chain management. His research has been published in *Management Science*, *Journal of Operations Management*, *Academy of Management Journal*, *Production and Operations Management*, *Manufacturing & Services Operations Management*, and *Decision Sciences,* among others. He has also served as the chair of the operations management division of the Academy of Management, and currently serves as an associate editor for the *Journal of Operations Management*, as well as on the editorial boards of several other journals.

Brief Contents

CD-ROM SUPPLEMENTS

Contents

ix

CD-ROM SUPPLEMENTS

Preface

NEW TO THE SECOND CANADIAN EDITION

As this second Canadian edition was developed, my primary emphasis was to expand and further refine three critical themes for operations management: effective process management, the importance of cross-functional integration, and the role of operations in the creation of customer value. Moreover, this edition further seeks to better capture and reinforce the importance of effective processes for service firms. Highlights of new sections and changes to the second Canadian edition are as follows:

- Chapter 1, "Competing with Operations," moves quickly from a brief introduction to highlight the value of effective process management for an advertising agency. The implications of global competition for operations also receive greater attention, with particular attention to how Canadian companies are leveraging service and manufacturing capabilities in India and China.

- Chapter 2, "Process Management," presents a new section and framework on customer involvement, which is particularly critical for service design. New conceptual figures have been added to illustrate the development of a consistent approach toward designing and improving processes.

- Chapter 3, "Managing Projects," presents an expanded treatment of different forms of project risk and measures of monitoring project progression.

- Chapter 4, "Capacity," offers new examples of assessing capacity in a service process and illustrating throughput time.

- Chapter 5, "Quality," in response to reviewer feedback, now includes an extensive discussion of the Six Sigma quality model, improvement process, and implementation. The presentation of sampling distributions, variation, and detection of out-of-control processes has been reworked.

- Chapter 7, "Location and Layout," is more contemporary and practice-oriented with the significant consideration of GIS-based location methods using Microsoft MapPoint 2004 (videos about the use of MapPoint 2004 are included on the Student CD-ROM that accompanies this text). A new Managerial Practice box has also been added.

- Chapter 8, "Forecasting," has a new opening vignette that illustrates Unilever's approach to customer demand planning. Based on reviewer feedback, this chapter now falls earlier in the book to provide the means to predict demand—one of several critical enablers for effective supply chain management.

- Chapter 9, "Supply Chain Management," now begins with a revised overview illustrating the supply chain complexity facing a typical Canadian retailer. In addition, the chapter also discusses recent trends toward outsourcing, offshoring, RFID tagging, and virtual supply chains.

- Chapter 10, "Lean Systems," has been expanded to cover the Five S concept and value stream mapping. These changes help tie together the first nine chapters of the book and reinforce the notion of viewing operations from a process management perspective at multiple levels, including facility, firm, and supply chain.

- Chapter 11, "Managing Technology," presents a new section on new service and product development.

MOTIVATION AND OBJECTIVES

As with the first Canadian edition, this edition endeavours to meet the growing demand in operations management for a brief book that has strong coverage of critical concepts and retains a rich set of pedagogical features. Most students who take an operations management course, either at the undergraduate or graduate level, are pursuing a major in functional areas other than operations, or seek to understand a general management perspective.

Business students need to understand the interrelated processes of a firm, which connect operations with all other functional areas of an organization. They need to understand how each part of an organization, not just the operations function, must design and manage processes and deal with quality, technology, and staffing issues. In addition, for courses that prefer a strong pedagogical structure, a number of instructional features clarify and reinforce student learning (clear, short definitions; step-by-step examples of quantitative techniques; numerous solved problems; and homework problems).

As a result, faculty need a concise book that conveys these essential ideas and techniques without the encyclopaedic volume of information found in many other textbooks. Yet it is very important to emphasize that the book is written to fit the perspectives and strengths of individual faculty. Consequently, many advanced concepts, tools, and topics that individual faculty may wish to explore in greater detail are included as full-length, full-colour supplements on the Student CD-ROM, along with experiential exercises, discussion questions, and cases.

As a starting point, this edition of *Foundations of Operations Management* draws much from the newly updated U.S. eighth edition. However, several shifts in emphasis and development are notable. First, the linkages between customer value and operations management are more strongly stressed and developed. Operations management *creates value* through the effective and efficient management of processes, including services, products, and process design.

Second, the *central importance of process management* has been expanded. To that end, a framework that conceptually links the three critical factors of capacity, variability, and inventory is introduced. Process choice—whether a project, batch, line or continuous process—implicitly combines these factors, with a change in any one factor having managerial implications for the other two. This framework serves to bring together traditional operations management topics of process choice, capacity, quality, lean systems, inventory, and supply chain management. As we explore these topics, I also frequently reinforce the notion that operations management involves cross-functional coordination, and tools can be used to help managers make *better operating decisions*.

Third, you may wonder why the vignettes focus on Canadian companies in such areas as quality, scheduling, lean operations, and process management. After all, don't the foundational principles of operations transcend the context of specific countries, geographies, and cultures? All too often, our students only see examples of U.S., Asian, or European companies building competitive capabilities through their well-designed operations and business processes. As a counterpoint, I present here a remarkable array of interesting Canadian companies that leverage their operations as an important competitive weapon as they battle in the global arena.

ORGANIZATION

The text is organized so that several basic strategic issues are covered before delving deeper into a range of tactical decisions.

Chapter 1, "Competing with Operations," sets the tone for the text. Organizations comprise many processes, and operations principles and techniques are particularly well suited for their management and analysis. A related message—the contribution of operations management and effective processes to the creation of customer value—is also introduced here. This perspective, which is carried forward throughout the text, appeals to students regardless of their academic major. This chapter also establishes the basic principles of operations strategy, with its primary purpose being the creation of customer value.

Chapter 2, "Process Management," provides more insight into the management and fundamental structure of processes. Using as a starting point the conceptual relationship between customization and volume, this chapter explores how various process-related decisions should be made. The form of customer interaction is particularly critical for service processes. It also provides a systematic approach to improving processes. Both service and manufacturing processes are highlighted here and elsewhere throughout the text.

Chapter 3, "Managing Projects," has substantial managerial material regarding project management. The material follows the introduction to projects as one type of process in Chapter 2. Both the basic qualitative and quantitative aspects of project management are considered. As noted above, an understanding of these issues by students is important regardless of their functional major, and project management tools will undoubtedly be used by many throughout their careers.

Chapter 4, "Capacity," begins our integrative development of critical process levers that every manager must understand. The process management triangle serves as the conceptual framework that links capacity, variability, and inventory, which are covered in this chapter and the two that follow. Process bottlenecks, economies and diseconomies of scale, capacity strategies, theory of constraints, and a systematic approach to capacity planning are also highlighted. At the end of this chapter, Supplement 4S bolsters the discussion on variability by specifically considering waiting lines. Finally, several supplements on the Student CD-ROM cover such related topics as decision making, financial analysis, work measurement, and learning curves.

Chapter 5, "Quality," begins with a quick overview of quality management through the lenses of three quality gurus, and underscores the multi-faceted definition of quality as an aspect of customer value. Quality includes both high performance design and conformance, which, when coupled with tight tolerances, yields services and products with low variability. Under the conceptual umbrella of total quality management, statistical process control techniques and a number of quality improvement tools are detailed. More advanced students can study acceptance sampling using the supplement on the Student CD-ROM.

Chapter 6, "Inventory Management," identifies the functions, costs, and managerial actions that can be taken to effectively use or reduce inventory. Basic inventory models and control systems are covered, and a number of quantitative examples walk students through the application of these concepts. More advanced inventory models are treated on the Student CD-ROM.

Chapter 7, "Location and Layout," continues the book's study of decisions that require long-term commitments about the process. Managers must help determine where to locate new facilities (including global operations) and how to organize the layout of the processes within a facility. New material has been added on the use of global positioning systems, which is particularly important for location planning and analysis. For interested instructors, topics such as linear programming and simulation are addressed on the Student CD-ROM.

Chapter 8, "Forecasting," spans the full range of forecasting approaches. Based on reviewer feedback, this chapter has been moved earlier in the sequence so that it could be covered before supply chain management. It begins with qualitative techniques and concludes with time series models. OM Tutors and Solvers are offered on the Student

CD-ROM to illustrate the use of computer modelling to understand and implement these models. This chapter also includes information on combination forecasts and focus forecasting.

Chapter 9, "Supply Chain Management," extends the consideration of operations beyond a single site or firm to operational linkages between firms. This chapter highlights several more recent developments within supply chains, such as e-purchasing, postponement, channel assembly, and green purchasing. It addresses order entry and order fulfillment processes, the impact of the Internet, and measures of supply chain performance. Both efficient and responsive supply chains are covered.

Chapter 10, "Lean Systems," draws together and reinforces concepts discussed in preceding chapters. The message is on integrating mutually supportive management approaches to develop highly efficient structures and methods for processes, individual firms, and supply chains. Quality at the source, small lot sizes, pull flow of materials, process visibility, and continuous improvement are linked together and illustrated in both manufacturing and service settings. These principles are relevant within a single facility, and are also relevant to coordination and improvement across a supply chain.

Chapter 11, "Managing Technology," has been newly expanded to cover additional concepts related to new service and product development. Other aspects related to developments in e-commerce have been retooled to reflect current business practices. More specific topics, such as computer-integrated manufacturing, are covered in greater detail on the Student CD-ROM.

Chapter 12, "Aggregate Planning and Scheduling," brings together planning for workforce levels across multiple service and product processes, and where possible, inventory holdings. The planning process is explored using straightforward spreadsheet tools. Scheduling in small batch processes, flow shops, and service operations are each treated in turn. For those wishing to push further, operations scheduling is included as a supplement on the Student CD-ROM. This approach allows students to understand the whole continuum of planning levels of output and workforce levels over time, as illustrated in the Air New Zealand vignette.

Chapter 13, "Resource Planning," focuses on materials requirements planning in manufacturing, although not to the exclusion of services. The concepts of dependent demand and a bill of resources are treated for service firms and virtual organizations. These later sections address resources such as financial assets, human resources, equipment, and inventories. Master production scheduling is further developed on the Student CD-ROM.

SPECIAL FEATURES OF THE BOOK

Many features are included to stress foundational concepts and to support the overall philosophy of any operations management course.

- **Streamlined.** The textbook is designed to have just 13 chapters with a supplemental Student CD-ROM that includes resources to support the basic text with commercial software, short cases, experiential exercises, and the like. For instructors who wish to explore particular topics in greater detail, such as work measurement and advanced inventory models, 11 supplemental chapters are also provided on the Student CD-ROM, along with a complete set of support materials.

- **Central Role of Processes.** The book focuses on processes—the fundamental unit of work in all organizations. It is all about processes! This unifying theme for service and manufacturing organizations builds bridges between chapters and opens up the topics in operations to all students, regardless of their majors or career paths. It creates a better "buy-in" for a course in operations management because students understand that processes underlie activities throughout the organization, not just in one functional area.

- **A Balanced Perspective.** An effective OM textbook should address both the "big picture" strategic issues and also the analytic tools that facilitate decision making. It is not just about "concepts" or just about "numbers"—it's about both dimensions. This text also offers a balanced treatment of services and manufacturing.

- **Pedagogical Structure.** Colourful and instructive formatting is used throughout the book and Student CD-ROM. Full-colour figures, clear explanations, step-by-step examples of quantitative techniques, solved problems, and numerous homework exercises assist students with identifying key concepts, understanding the linkages between concepts, solving problems, and using powerful decision-making tools.

- **Chapter-Opening Vignettes.** To help stimulate student interest, each chapter opens by profiling how real, world-class companies apply specific process issues. They highlight strong examples of best practices from notable Canadian and international firms.

- **Managerial Practices.** In each chapter, a major example illustrates how companies deal—either successfully or unsuccessfully—with the process issues they face as they run their operations. These updated features explore value creation in both service and manufacturing organizations.

- **Examples.** Numerous examples throughout each chapter are a popular feature and are designed to help students understand the quantitative material presented. Each concludes with a "Decision Point," which focuses on the decision implications for managers. Whenever a new technique is presented, an example is immediately provided to walk the student through the solution.

- **Across the Organization.** Each chapter begins and ends with a discussion of how the topic of the chapter is important to professionals throughout the organization, and how cross-functional connections link operations management to accounting, finance, human resources, marketing, and management information systems.

- **Margin Items.** Margin items have been simplified to focus on key definitions for quick student reference.

- **CD-ROM Resources.** Motivating students to learn and adjusting the course content to the student audience are important aspects for any successful course. For those who want the flexibility to expand or enrich their course, the CD-ROMs include application software (e.g., Microsoft MapPoint and Microsoft Project), cases, quantitative supplements, experiential exercises, and more.

  - *Application of commercial software tools.* Microsoft MapPoint, Extend, Microsoft Project, and OM Explorer collectively illustrate the use of software tools to complex management problems. For example, see Chapter 2 for SmartDraw, Chapter 3 for Microsoft Project, Chapter 4 for Extend, Chapter 7 for Microsoft MapPoint, and Chapter 12 for OM Explorer. The use of these tools is optional for students, based on the course time available to the instructor.

  - *Cases.* All chapters have at least one case that can either serve as a basis for classroom instruction or provide an important capstone problem to the chapter, challenging students to grapple with the issues of the chapter in a less structured and more comprehensive way. Many of the cases can be used as in-class exercises without prior student preparation.

- *The Big Picture and Tours.* Four full-colour, two-page spreads present the layout and operations issues facing four different organizations in health-care, steel, food products, and sporting entertainment industries.

- *Experiential Learning Exercises.* There are four experiential learning modules: Min-Yo Garment Company (Chapter 1), SPC with a Coin Catapult (Chapter 5), Swift Electronic Supply (Chapter 6), and Sonic Distributors (Chapter 9). Each of these experiences is an in-class exercise that actively involves students. Each has been thoroughly tested in class and proven to be a valuable learning tool.

- *Supplemental Chapters.* The Student CD-ROM also includes 11 supplemental chapters covering topics such as decision making and master production scheduling. These supplemental chapters are also covered by the various instructor's supplements that accompany the second Canadian edition of *Foundations of Operations Management*.

- **Solved Problems.** At the end of each chapter, detailed solutions demonstrate how to solve problems with the techniques presented in the chapter. These solved problems reinforce basic concepts and serve as models for students to refer to when doing the problems that follow.

ENHANCED INSTRUCTIONAL SUPPORT SYSTEM

INSTRUCTOR'S SOLUTIONS MANUAL

The Instructor's Solutions Manual, created by the authors so as to ensure its currency and accuracy, provides complete solutions to all discussion questions, problems, and notes for every case and experiential exercise. Each case includes a brief synopsis, a description of the purposes for using the case, recommendations for analysis and goals for student learning from the case, and detailed teaching suggestions for assigning and discussing the case with students. The Instructor's Solutions Manual is intended for instructors who may, in turn, choose to share parts of it with students. This supplement is available both through Pearson Education Canada's online catalogue at http://vig.pearsoned.ca and on the Instructor's Resource CD-ROM.

TESTGEN

A computerized testbank containing true/false, multiple-choice, short-answer, and problem questions for each textbook and supplemental chapter is available in the latest version of TestGen software. This software package allows instructors to custom design, save, and generate classroom tests. The test program permits instructors to edit, add, or delete questions from the test banks; edit existing graphics and create new graphics; analyze test results; and organize a database of tests and student results. It also provides many options for organizing and displaying tests, along with a search and sort feature. This TestGen testbank is available for download from Pearson Education Canada's online catalogue at http://vig.pearsoned.ca and on the Instructor's Resource CD-ROM.

POWERPOINT® PRESENTATIONS

This comprehensive set of slides illustrates and builds upon key concepts in the text. The PowerPoint slides are available for download from Pearson Education Canada's online catalogue at http://vig.pearsoned.ca and on the Instructor's Resource CD-ROM.

INSTRUCTOR'S RESOURCE MANUAL

New for the second Canadian edition of *Foundations of Operations Management*, the Instructor's Resource Manual features detailed instructor notes and teaching tips for all the textbook and supplemental chapters. The Instructor's Resource Manual is available for download from Pearson Education Canada's online catalogue at http://vig.pearsoned.ca and on the Instructor's Resource CD-ROM.

INSTRUCTOR'S RESOURCE CD-ROM

This valuable, time-saving resource provides instructors with electronic files for the complete Instructor's Solutions Manual, TestGen, PowerPoint Presentations, and Instructor's Resource Manual. Offering these materials as MS Word, PowerPoint, and PDF files (where appropriate) allows instructors to customize portions of the material to enhance their students' classroom learning experience.

COMPANION WEBSITE (WWW.PEARSONED.CA/RITZMAN)

This content-rich website offers students and instructors a range of valuable learning tools and resources, including an Interactive Study Guide with true/false, multiple-choice, and essay questions for each textbook and supplemental chapter, as well as a wealth of Internet activities and Internet tours.

ACKNOWLEDGMENTS

I wish to thank the people at Pearson Education Canada who inspired this project and made up the publishing team. My deep-felt thanks to Samantha Scully, who supervised the overall project, and Pamela Voves, who kept me moving forward on the manuscript revisions with many helpful suggestions and feedback. Thanks also to Marisa D'Andrea, Valerie Adams, Marg Bukta, Nadia Bhuiyan, Emma Gorst, Jennifer Stimson, Andrea Falkenberg, and Gerry Dunn for their work in producing this text.

I also wish to thank my Canadian colleagues who provided very useful feedback and guidance for this edition. They include the following:

F. A. Rick Burjaw, University of Western Ontario

Larry David, Centennial College

Cyril Foropon, University of Manitoba

Les Miscampbell, Centennial College

Mahesh Nagarajan, University of British Columbia

Robert A. Reyburn, Laurentian University

Morgan Ross, Red River College

David Sparling, University of Guelph

Finally, I am indebted to my colleagues at the University of Western Ontario, who have greatly influenced and developed my thinking on the teaching of operations management to business students. In particular, John Haywood-Farmer, Fraser Johnson, and Larry Menor, who provided much-needed discussion and feedback for this edition. Finally, I thank my family for their patience during the many long hours assembling this book. My wife, Lorraine, provided the love and encouragement that I needed in moving from the first edition to the second.

Robert D. Klassen
Ivey Business School
University of Western Ontario

A Great Way to Learn and Instruct Online

The Pearson Education Canada Companion Website is easy to navigate and is organized to correspond to the chapters in this textbook and the supplemental chapters on the Student CD-ROM. Whether you are a student in the classroom or a distance learner you will discover helpful resources for in-depth study and research that empower you in your quest for greater knowledge and maximize your potential for success in the course.

[www.pearsoned.ca/ritzman]

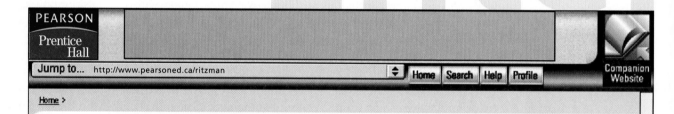

PEARSON Prentice Hall

Jump to... http://www.pearsoned.ca/ritzman | Home | Search | Help | Profile | Companion Website

Home >

Companion Website

Foundations of Operations Management, Second Canadian Edition, by Ritzman, Krajewski, Malhotra, and Klassen

Chapter Resources

The modules in this section provide students with tools for learning course material. These modules include:

- Across the Organization and Learning Goals
- True/False Quiz
- Multiple-Choice Quiz
- Essay Questions
- Internet Activities
- Internet Exercises
- Glossary Flashcards

In the quiz modules students can send answers to the grader and receive instant feedback on their progress through the Results Reporter. Coaching comments and references to the textbook may be available to ensure that students take advantage of all available resources to enhance their learning experience.

Instructor Resources

A link to this book on the Pearson Education Canada online catalogue (vig.pearsoned.ca) provides instructors with additional teaching tools. Downloadable PowerPoint Presentations and an Instructor's Manual are just some of the materials that may be available. The catalogue is password protected. To get a password, simply contact your Pearson Education Canada Representative or call Faculty Sales and Services at 1-800-850-5813.

1 Competing with Operations

Across the Organization

Competitive operations is important to:

- **accounting**, which prepares financial and cost accounting information that aids operations managers in designing and operating production systems.
- **finance**, which manages the cash flows and capital investment requirements that are created by the operations function.
- **human resources**, which hires and trains employees to match process needs, location decisions, and planned production levels.
- **management information systems**, which develop information systems and decision support systems for operations managers.
- **marketing**, which helps create the demand that operations must satisfy, link customer demand with staffing and production plans, and keep the operations function focused on satisfying customers' needs.
- **operations**, which designs and operates processes to give the firm a sustainable competitive advantage.

Learning Goals

After reading this chapter, you will be able to:

1. describe operations in terms of inputs, processes, outputs, information flows, suppliers, and customers.
2. define how operations can contribute to customer value.
3. describe operations as a function alongside finance, accounting, marketing, and human resources.
4. explain how operations management is fundamental to both manufacturers and service providers.
5. explain how operations strategy is a pattern of decisions directed at processes, systems, and facilities in order to achieve specific competitive priorities.
6. distinguish among different types of operations strategies in manufacturing and service organizations.
7. explain how to link marketing strategy to operations strategy through the use of competitive priorities.
8. give examples of how operations can be used as a competitive weapon.

With continued strong expansion in Canada, the United States, and Europe, Palliser Furniture is Canada's largest manufacturer of upholstered, leather, and wood furniture, and 13th largest in North America. Revenues for this Winnipeg, Manitoba-based company—named after a nineteenth-century explorer of western Canada—have grown to over $400 million. Yet although strong financial performance remains critical to continued investment in better technology and its workforce, Palliser's president and CEO, Arthur DeFehr, also stresses community both inside and outside the firm for the 4000 employees, who come from 70 nations and speak 40 languages.

New product styling at Palliser Furniture reflects evolving customer value and is matched with manufacturing processes in smaller, focused plants.

Palliser's mission statement focuses on leadership in design, service, and customer value. Looking back, DeFehr observes that it is remarkable that the company was able to establish itself in a location with a small market and few resources. Moreover, the recent rapid rise in the Canadian dollar has created intense pressure to further improve competitiveness through lower costs and improved service. Despite these challenges, good people combined with strong manufacturing techniques have consistently produced high-quality products. More than 50 years after its founding, Palliser now has manufacturing facilities in Canada, the United States, Mexico, Indonesia, and Lithuania.

Customer value, including such aspects as product design and quality, has changed significantly for furniture over the years. Ten years ago, leather products made up only a small fraction of the upholstery market. Management saw an opportunity to differentiate Palliser's product line, and wisely chose to emphasize that as a major product line. This focus on leather also prompted Palliser to redefine its manufacturing processes.

For example, as the number of employees increased, more managers were needed to direct production employees, which in turn could have hampered improvement in such areas as quality. To shift some of this responsibility for work practices to employees, management decided to implement cellular manufacturing, where a team of 25 people produce an entire item. Both product and process changes have proven very successful—the company is now the second-largest leather furniture producer in North America.

Recently, this concept of cellular manufacturing has been extended to an operations strategy that embraces focused factories. Smaller factories of two hundred to three hundred people focus on a narrow product range targeted at a particular segment of customers. By doing so, specific customer needs can be better matched with process capabilities. And responsiveness to the customer and communications within the plant improve.

First implemented in the Upholstery Division, focused factories have since been applied to other divisions. This focus on a few specific, customer-driven priorities has enabled another division to reposition itself with a new generation of ready-to-assemble products that offer more contemporary styling with lighter-coloured woods, steel, and tempered glass.

Driven by these new products, Palliser's operations have been extended into retail settings, where new company-owned stores sell this partially assembled, easily transported furniture. Management views this forward integration as critical to showcasing Palliser's broad product range and guaranteeing access in key markets. As with focused factories, a single retail location can house two distinctly different stores: one catering to established customers with more traditional styles, and the other to first-time buyers looking for up-to-date styling that is easy to move.

Other process changes continue to better integrate operations with the large-volume retail customers. Working with FurnishNet (www.

→

furnishnet.com), Palliser expects to continue improving the flow of information from retailers through warehouses to manufacturing. Electronic orders, invoicing, and shipment notices then can speed the flow of furniture from manufacturing to retailer. Thus, whether in manufacturing or retail services, Palliser is relying on its operations to compete successfully and deliver customer value in a highly competitive, dynamic environment.

Source: Adapted with permission from: J. E. Watson, "Entrepreneur of the Year: Palliser's International Success Is a Team Effort," *Manitoba Business*, vol. 22 (2000), no. 4, pp. 7–11. © Jim E. Watson, Manitoba Business Magazine (1996) Ltd. Additional information from: B. Carroll, "Palliser Looking to Boost Store EDI with FurnishNet," *Furniture Today*, vol. 27, no. 2, p. 40; P. Scott, "Palliser's Looking Forward to New Era with Expansion," *Winnipeg Free Press*, March 24, 2001, p. f4; "FP 500—2004: The Rankings," *National Post Business*, June 2004, p. 75; and corporate Web site.

Operations management deals with processes that produce goods and services that people use every day. *Processes* are the fundamental activities that organizations use to do work and achieve their goals. Every organization, whether public or private, manufacturing or service, must manage processes and the operations where these processes are performed.

The changes at Palliser Furniture provide one example of designing processes for competitive operations. Processes must be created for each major type of furniture, as well as for the expanding retail operations of this company. In some areas, managers move to automate and speed the processes—for example, order taking and invoicing—and in other areas changes must be made to redesign products and focus on specific attributes. However, all of these processes involve coordination across all functional areas of the firm.

In essence, operations management is really about creating customer value through the effective and efficient management of processes, including product, service, and process design. Throughout this book, we explore with you the role of managing processes within the total organization. We explain what managers of processes do, the decisions they make, and some of the tools and concepts that they can use. By developing a sound operations strategy and using appropriate techniques, managers can design and operate processes to give companies a competitive edge. Helping you understand how to make operations a competitive weapon begins with this chapter and continues throughout the book.

A PROCESS VIEW

process Any activity or group of activities that takes one or more inputs, transforms and adds value to them, and provides one or more outputs for its customers.

An organization is only as effective as its processes. A **process** is any activity or group of activities that takes one or more inputs, transforms and adds value, and generates one or more outputs for its customers. The type of processes can vary significantly. For example, a primary process in a factory could be a physical or chemical change of raw materials, like wood and leather, into physical products, such as furniture. But there also are many nonmanufacturing processes at a factory, such as order fulfillment, making due-date promises to customers, and inventory control. In contrast, the primary process for an airline would be the movement of passengers and their luggage from one location to another. Here, too, processes are needed for making reservations, checking in passengers, serving meals, and scheduling crews.

As Figure 1.1 illustrates, processes have inputs and customer outputs. Inputs include human resources (workers and managers), capital (equipment and facilities), energy, and purchased materials and services including information. The numbered circles represent operations through which services, products, and customers pass and where activities are performed. The arrows represent flows and can cross because one

FIGURE 1.1

*Processes and
Operations*

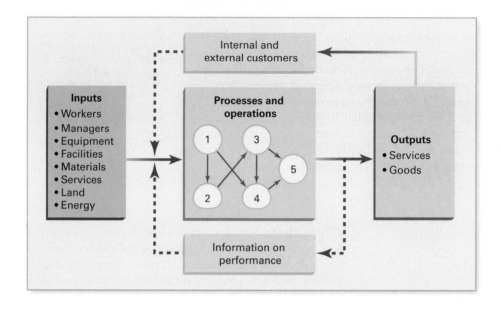

FIGURE 1.1

*Processes and
Operations*

customer can have different requirements (and thus, a different flow pattern) from another customer. Processes provide outputs—often services, which can take the form of information—to their "customers."

Both manufacturing and service organizations now realize that every process and every person in an organization has customers. Some are **external customers,** who may be either end users or intermediaries (such as manufacturers, wholesalers, or retailers) buying the firm's finished products and services. Others are **internal customers** who may be one or more other employees who rely on inputs from earlier processes in order to perform processes in the next office, shop, or department. Either way, processes must be managed with the right customer in mind.

Figure 1.1 can represent a whole firm, a department or small group, or even a single individual. Each one has inputs and uses processes at various operations to provide outputs. The dashed lines represent two special types of input: participation by customers and information on performance from both internal and external sources. Participation by customers occurs not only when they receive outputs but also when they take an active part in the processes, such as when students participate in a class discussion. Information on performance includes internal reports on customer service or inventory levels and external information from market research, government reports, or telephone calls from suppliers. Managers need all types of information to manage processes most effectively.

external customers End users or intermediaries, such as manufacturers, wholesalers, or retailers, who buy a firm's products and services.

internal customers One or more employees who use outputs from earlier, upstream processes to perform processes in the next office, shop, or department.

HOW PROCESSES WORK

Let's take a look at what happens at an ad agency. Suppose a client contacts her account executive (AE) about her need for a memorable ad campaign for the upcoming National Hockey League (NHL) Stanley Cup series. The AE gathers the pertinent information and passes it along to a creative design team and a media planning team that prepare an ad layout and a media exposure plan acceptable to the client. The AE also gives the information to the accounting department, which prepares an account for billing purposes. The creative design team passes the layout design to a production team, which prepares the final layout for publication and delivers it to the selected media outlets according to the schedule developed by the media team and approved by the client. The design team, media team, and production team send their billable hours

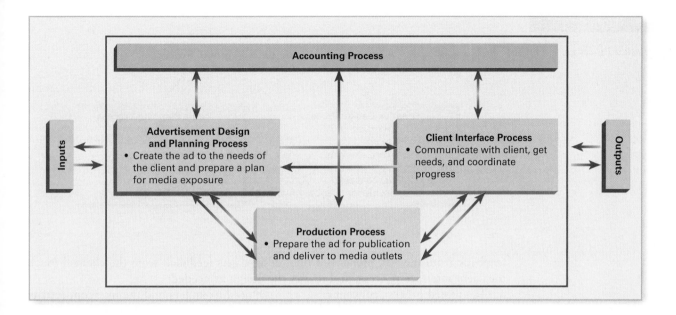

Process View of an Ad Agency

nested process A process within a process.

and expense items to the accounting department, which prepares an invoice that is approved by the AE and then sent to the client for payment.

Figure 1.2 shows a process view of the ad agency at two levels. The red-outlined box represents the ad agency as an aggregate process. Viewed at this level, the ad agency requires inputs from external sources and produces outputs, which are advertisements for external clients. The inputs from external sources are resources used by the ad agency's processes and include employees, managers, money, equipment, facilities, materials, services, land, and energy. The output is the NHL ad campaign for the client. However, inside the red box we see a more detailed process view: The client interface process includes the AE and her interactions with the client. The advertisement design and planning process creates the ad and plans its exposure during the Stanley Cup series. The production process acquires the actors, prepares the production set and props, coordinates the schedules of all involved in the production of the ad, films the content, prepares a video, and delivers the ad to the media outlets on time. The arrows in the diagram indicate information and work flows between the processes, along with feedback on performance.

NESTED PROCESSES

Processes can be broken down into subprocesses, which can in turn be broken down into still more subprocesses. We refer to this concept of a process within a process as a **nested process**. One part of a process can be separated from another for several reasons. One person or one department may be unable to do all parts of the process, or different segments in the process may require different skills. Some segments of the process may be standardized for all customers, making high-volume operations possible. Other segments may be customized, requiring processes best suited to flexible, low-volume operations.

If we peel away a few more layers of our process view of the ad agency, we can focus on the advertisement design and planning process. Figure 1.3 shows that two separate processes are involved. The creative design process starts with a work order from the AE, after which the creative design director assembles the team. The work order includes the ad's objective, the overall message, the evidence supporting the claims, and the intended audience. The design team comes up with several designs, gets

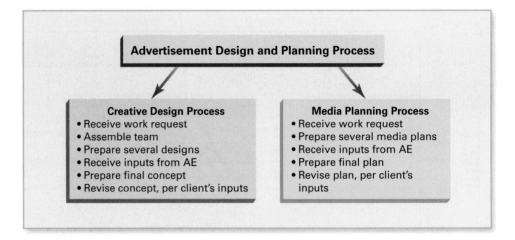

feedback from the AE, prepares a final design, gets feedback from the client through the client interface process, and revises the design as needed.

The nested process concept reinforces the need to understand the interconnectivity of activities within a business and the nature of each process's inputs and outputs. Sometimes, nested processes must be performed sequentially; in other cases, they can be performed independently of one another. However, all activities nested within a process must be performed to provide the full set of services.

WHAT IS OPERATIONS MANAGEMENT?

operations management
The systematic design, direction, and control of processes that transform inputs into services and products for internal, as well as external, customers.

The term **operations management** refers to the systematic design, direction, and control of processes that transform inputs into services and products for internal, as well as external, customers. Broadly speaking, operations management underlies all departments in a business because departments carry out many processes. If you aspire to manage a department or a particular process in your discipline, or if you just want to understand how the process you are a part of fits into the overall fabric of the business, you need to understand the principles of operations management. From this perspective, at least a little bit of operations management lives with all of us.

Narrowly interpreted, the operations management *function* or department is typically one of several functions in an organization, although it may have other labels depending on the industry, such as customer service, order fulfillment, or manufacturing. As such, it is responsible for the actual transformation of inputs to outputs. Each function, as depicted in Figure 1.4, specializes by having its own knowledge and skill areas, primary responsibilities, processes, and decision domains.

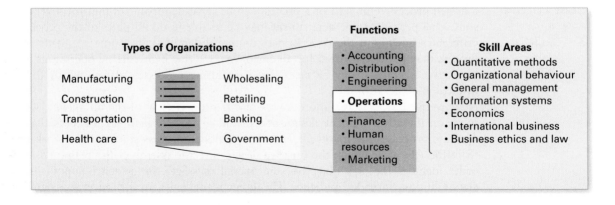

Business and government leaders increasingly recognize the importance of involving the whole organization in making strategic decisions. Operations plays an important role in meeting global competition. Foreign competition and the explosion of new technologies increase the awareness that a firm competes not only through creative marketing and skillful finance, but also through its unique competencies in operations, new services and products, and sound management of core processes. The organization that offers superior services and products at lower prices is a formidable competitor.

OPERATIONS MANAGEMENT AS A SET OF DECISIONS

Here, we preview the types of decisions that operations managers make. These decisions define both the scope and content of operations management (OM) and the organization of this book. Some decisions are strategic in nature; others are tactical. Strategic plans are developed further into the future than tactical plans. Thus, strategic decisions are less structured and have long-term consequences, whereas tactical decisions are more structured, routine, and repetitive and have short-term consequences. Strategic choices also tend to focus on the entire organization, cutting across departmental lines; tactical decisions tend to focus on departments, teams, and tasks. In general, operations management decisions may be divided into four categories: strategic choices; process-related choices, including capacity, quality, and inventory; supply chain management; and detailed operating decisions. This text follows that flow of decisions.

TRENDS IN OPERATIONS MANAGEMENT

Several business trends are currently having a great impact on operations management: the growth of the service sector; productivity changes; global competitiveness; and environmental, ethical, and diversity issues. In this section, we briefly overview these trends, as well as their implications for operations managers.

SERVICE SECTOR GROWTH

The service sector of the Canadian economy is significant and covers a broad range of diverse activities, including transportation, public utilities, communication, health, financial services, education, government, real estate, repair services, and retail sales. This sector has also been the primary engine for growth in total employment, although manufacturing employment has increased somewhat too, as shown in Figure 1.5. Between 1958 and 1999, the number of Canadian jobs in service-producing industries rose from 51 percent to 73 percent of total employment, now accounting for more than 10 million jobs. Similar increases in the percentage of the workforce in service jobs are taking place in the other industrial countries. For example, the share of the workforce in service jobs is well above 60 percent in the United Kingdom, the United States, France, and Japan.

Retail and wholesale trade, health and social services, and education are the largest service sector employers. Not surprisingly, employment in the service sector is much more likely to be part time, with 23 percent of employees being part time, versus only 8 percent in the goods-producing sector. However, recent data indicate that the stability of jobs (i.e., turnover) in the service sector is very similar (Crompton and Vickers, 2000).

The service and manufacturing sectors of the economy are complementary. For example, the outputs of many service firms are required by other firms as inputs, with manufacturing firms buying services such as express mail and consulting services. Just as important, many services depend on the outputs from manufacturing firms. For example, trucks are purchased by transportation firms and telecommunication

FIGURE 1.5

Service Sector in Canada Has Experienced Significant Growth

Source: Adapted from: M. Crompton and S. Vickers, "One Hundred Years of Labour Force," *Canadian Social Trends*, Catalogue No. 11-008 (Summer 2000), Ottawa: Statistics Canada, p. 8.

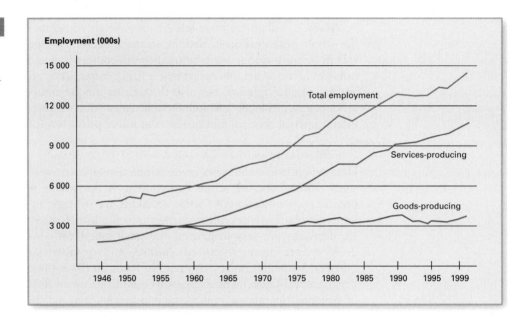

equipment is used extensively for financial services. Consulting firms also regularly engage manufacturing firms as clients—for example, to improve competitiveness, develop new operations strategies, upgrade technology, and relocate operations globally. Finally, many firms, such as Palliser Furniture noted at the beginning of the chapter, are developing important competitive benefits from extending their operations into both manufacturing and services. As a result, in this text, the term "operations" includes both service and manufacturing processes.

PRODUCTIVITY IMPROVEMENT

productivity The value of outputs (goods and services) produced divided by the values of input resources.

Productivity is the value of outputs (goods and services) produced divided by the values of input resources (wages, cost of equipment, and the like) used:

$$\text{Productivity} = \frac{\text{Output}}{\text{Input}}$$

Many measures of productivity are possible, and all are rough approximations. For example, the value of output can be measured by what the customer pays or simply by the number of units produced or customers served. The value of inputs can be judged by their cost or simply by the number of hours worked.

Managers usually pick several reasonable measures and monitor trends to spot areas needing improvement. For example, a manager at an insurance firm might measure office productivity as the number of insurance policies processed per employee each week. A manager at a carpet company might measure the productivity of installers as the number of square metres of carpet installed per hour. Both of these measures reflect *labour productivity*, which is an index of the output per person or hour worked. Similar measures may be used for *machine productivity*, where the denominator is the number of machines. Accounting for several inputs simultaneously is also possible. *Multifactor productivity* is an index of the output provided by more than one of the resources used in production. For example, it may be the value of the output divided by the sum of labour, materials, and overhead costs. When developing such a measure, you must convert the quantities to a common unit of measure, typically dollars.

The way processes are managed plays a key role in productivity improvement. Labour and multifactor productivity measures can provide a means to monitor improvement over time; however, they can be deceptive. For example, a firm can decide to transfer some of its work to outside suppliers and lay off some of its own workforce. Labour productivity will increase considerably, because the value of the firm's total sales (the numerator) remains unchanged while the number of employees (the denominator) drops. Also, because many processes only have internal customers, it is often difficult to assign a dollar value to the value of process outputs. Thus, productivity measures are often a good starting point, but insufficient in isolation. Just as importantly, managers must monitor performance measures on quality, inventory levels, capacity utilization, on-time delivery, employee satisfaction, customer satisfaction, and the like. The smart manager monitors *multiple* measures of performance, setting goals for the future and seeking better ways to design and operate processes.

It is interesting and even surprising to break down productivity improvements between the manufacturing and services sectors. Although employment in the service sector has grown rapidly in Canada, productivity gains have historically been much lower. For example, during the 1990s, labour productivity improved by almost 20 percent in manufacturing versus only 15 percent in the service sector. Major trading partners such as the United States, Japan, and Germany have experienced a similar challenge.

However, there are recent signs of improvement, as an increasing number of service firms are using technology to raise productivity and deliver services directly to customers, often using the Internet. Greater international competition, in areas such as financial services, is also motivating service firms to accelerate improvements in the efficiency of their processes. More recently, productivity growth for Canadian businesses grew 1.5 percent annually from 2000 to 2003 and most of that was generated by the service sector (Statistics Canada, 2005a).

GLOBAL COMPETITION

Today, businesses accept the fact that, to prosper, they must view customers, suppliers, facility locations, and competitors in global terms. Most products today are global composites of materials and services from around the world. Your Gap polo shirt may be sewn in Honduras from cloth cut in the United States. Sitting in the theatre, you munch a Nestlé's Crunch bar (Swiss) while watching a Columbia Pictures movie (Japanese) at a Cineplex theatre (Canadian).

Different locations around the world offer important advantages for operations. Wages for comparable skills can vary dramatically throughout the world, with two notable examples of low-cost labour being China and India. In China, foreign companies opened as many as 60 000 new factories between 2000 and 2003. These companies include many technology companies, such as Celestica, Nokia, Motorola, and IBM, and nearly all of the big footwear and clothing brands. The implications for Canadian firms are enormous. Those that want to continue to compete on low price are shifting significant parts of their manufacturing operations either internally or through outsourcing to China and other parts of Asia. Others that maintain large operations in North America, like Palliser

Foreign companies have opened thousands of new factories in China in recent years. Labour costs are low in China, and its workforce is educated and disciplined.

Furniture from the opening vignette, are adjusting to compete on the basis of fast delivery and small production runs.

What China is to manufacturing, India is to service. As with the manufacturing companies, the cost of labour is a key factor. A programmer in India receives a fraction of the wages of a programmer in Canada with comparable skills and experience. And Indian software companies have grown very sophisticated in their applications. For example, to remain competitive, Electronic Data Systems increased its staff in India by almost tenfold over just three years. Back-office support operations are also affected for the same reason. Many firms are using Indian companies for customer-support call-centres, accounting and bookkeeping, preparing tax returns, and processing insurance claims.

Operations in these countries can extend into research and development (R&D), with a number of Canadian high-tech companies opening, acquiring, or expanding significant development capabilities in India. For example, ATI Technologies acquired a subsidiary located in Hyderabad to both gain access to a strong talent pool and cut development costs. The Indian subsidiary now creates software to compress and decompress audio and video data for hand-held game and mobile phone developers (Holloway, 2005).

Strong global competition affects industries everywhere. Regional trading blocs such as the North American Free Trade Agreement (NAFTA) and the European Union (EU) further change the competitive landscape in both services and manufacturing. As a result, Canadian manufacturers have been under increasing competitive pressures in domestic and international markets in areas such as financial services, steel, appliances and household durable goods, machinery, and chemicals. The recent rise in the Canadian dollar relative to U.S. and European currencies has added another challenge for exporters. Yet, managers must continue to build operational capabilities through investment in human resources, quality, and product and process technologies.

ETHICS, WORKFORCE DIVERSITY, AND THE NATURAL ENVIRONMENT

Businesses face more ethical quandaries than ever before, intensified by an increasing global presence and rapid technological change. Companies are locating new operations, and have more suppliers and customers, in other countries. Potential ethical dilemmas arise when business can be conducted by different rules. Some countries are more sensitive than others about lavish entertainment, conflicts of interest, bribery, discrimination against minorities and women, poverty, minimum-wage levels, unsafe workplaces, and workers' rights. Managers must decide in such cases whether to design and operate processes that do more than just meet local standards that are lower than those back home. In addition, technological change brings debates about data protection and customer privacy, such as on the Internet. In an electronic world, businesses are geographically far from their customers, and a reputation for trust may become even more important.

Environmental and social issues such as toxic wastes, poisoned drinking water, poverty, air quality, and global warming are getting more emphasis. In the past, many people viewed environmental problems as quality-of-life issues; now many people see them as risk management and a matter of survival. Economically developed nations have a particular burden because their combined populations, representing only 25 percent of the global population, con-

Leading companies have found that workforce diversity can provide a forum for unique perspectives and solutions.

sume 70 percent of all resources. In particular, greenhouse gas emissions have received a great deal of attention recently as many countries have moved to adopt the Kyoto Protocol. Just seven nations, including the United States, produce almost half of all these emissions. Although Canada contributes only about 2 percent to global emissions, it is one of the highest per capita emitters, which is largely the result of our resource-based economy, our climate, and our geographical size (Environment Canada, 2002).

In 2002, Canadian businesses incurred about $3.8 billion in annual operating expenses for environmental protection, 40 percent of that being directed at pollution control and waste management (Statistics Canada, 2005b). During the same year, capital investment for environmental protection reached about $3 billion. Compared to other developed countries, Canada spends only about 1.1 percent of gross domestic product (GDP) on pollution control—much less than other countries such as the United States, Germany, and Japan, which spend about 1.5 percent (OECD, 2002, 2005).

In a promising change of direction, managers are increasingly shifting their attention away from pollution control to prevention. Prevention can take the form of changes to the product or service, modifications to the process, or new management systems (Klassen and Whybark, 1999). In manufacturing, examples include new wood finishes cured by UV light, thereby preventing the release of harmful organic solvents, and paper bleached using alternatives to elemental chlorine. Similarly, service firms have worked with customers to reduce the environmental impact of their processes. For example, hotels have reduced laundry needs by asking customers to reuse towels and financial institutions have shifted the flow of some information from paper-based mail to electronic delivery.

The message is clear: consideration of ethics, workforce diversity, and the natural environment is becoming part of every manager's job. When designing and operating processes, managers should consider integrity, respect for the individual, and respect for the customer along with more conventional performance measures such as productivity, quality, cost, and profit.

DEVELOPING A CUSTOMER-DRIVEN OPERATIONS STRATEGY

The trends in operations management present a dynamic environment within which firms must find their competitive niche. Operations can be used as a competitive weapon; however, the firm must have a sound operations strategy that focuses on creating and contributing to customer value. Developing a customer-driven operations strategy begins with corporate strategy, which, in turn, identifies and analyzes the markets that will be served. Based on a clear definition of customer value, managers can emphasize specific competitive priorities around which to formulate an effective operations strategy. Because operations cannot be all things to all customers, specialized capabilities must be acquired, developed, or expanded to meet particular customer needs. This basic strategic process is illustrated in Figure 1.6.

CORPORATE STRATEGY

Corporate strategy determines which customers the firm serves, which new goods or services are introduced to the market, which responses are taken to changes in its business and socioeconomic environment, and how expansion is undertaken to compete in international markets. In essence, corporate strategy specifies the business that the company will pursue, and how a firm can differentiate itself from competitors. For example, choices could include producing standardized products versus customized products or competing on the basis of cost advantage versus responsive delivery.

Competitive Priorities: Link Between Corporate Strategy and Functional Area Strategies

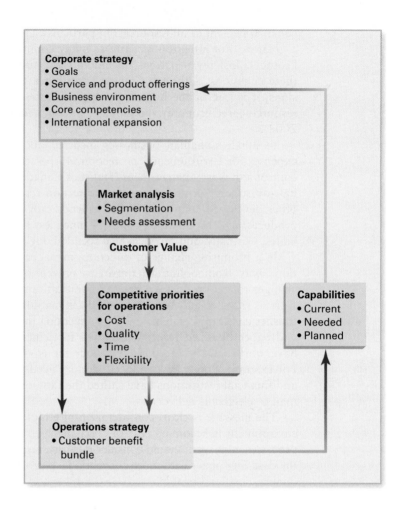

Corporate strategy provides the overall direction and framework for developing an operations strategy. In addition to setting goals or objectives, three aspects are critical for operations: monitoring and adjusting to changes in the business environment, identifying and developing the firm's core competencies, and developing a global perspective.

BUSINESS ENVIRONMENT. The external business environment in which a firm competes changes continually and an organization needs to adapt to those changes. Adaptation begins with *environmental scanning*, the process by which managers monitor trends in the socioeconomic environment, including the industry, the marketplace, and society, for potential opportunities or threats. A crucial reason for environmental scanning is to stay ahead of the competition. Competitors may be gaining an edge by broadening product lines, improving quality, or lowering costs. New entrants into the market or competitors that offer substitutes for a firm's product or service may threaten continued profitability. Other important environmental concerns are economic trends, technological changes, political conditions, social changes (such as attitudes toward work), the availability of vital resources, and the collective power of customers or suppliers.

CORE COMPETENCIES. Corporate strategy must address changes in the business environment and continually look for new opportunities. Firms succeed by taking advantage of what they do particularly well—that is, the organization's unique strengths.

core competencies The unique resources and processes that an organization's management can leverage when formulating and implementing strategy.

Core competencies are the unique resources and processes that an organization's management can leverage when formulating and implementing strategy. They reflect the collective learning of the organization, especially in how to coordinate diverse processes and integrate multiple technologies. These competencies include such resources as facilities and people, and processes such as product development.

It is important to recognize that competencies extend beyond a single product to multiple products and markets (Prahalad and Hamel, 1990). For example, Honda has a strong competency in the design and manufacture of small internal combustion engines. This competency has been very well applied in a wide range of products and markets, including automobiles, lawn mowers, watercraft, and motorcycles. Most recently, Honda has turned this competency toward the small aircraft sector, where it plans to introduce a new, very fuel-efficient jet engine, which has the potential to dramatically reshape this market. Thus, new business opportunities are possible by continuing to extend the reach of a core competency while creating deep expertise that is difficult to buy or copy. This is particularly crucial as global competition increases and competitors move quickly to copy basic product and service features.

GLOBAL PERSPECTIVE. Identifying opportunities and threats today requires a global perspective. International expansion of operations may include buying foreign parts or services, combating threats from foreign competitors, or planning ways to enter markets beyond traditional national boundaries. Although warding off threats from global competitors is necessary, firms should also actively seek to penetrate foreign markets.

Two effective approaches for international expansion are strategic alliances and locating abroad. A *strategic alliance* is an agreement with another firm that may take one of three forms. A *collaborative effort* often arises when one firm has core competencies that another needs but is unwilling or unable to duplicate. Such relationships are common in buyer–supplier relationships. Another form of strategic alliance is the *joint venture* in which two firms agree to produce a product or service jointly. This leverages the expertise of the partner to reduce the risks of operating in a new business environment. Finally, *technology licensing* is an agreement in which one company licenses its product or process methods to another.

Another way to enter global markets is to locate operations in a foreign country. However, managers must recognize that what works well in their home country might not work well elsewhere. For example, McDonald's is known for the consistency of its products—a Big Mac tastes the same anywhere in the world. However, a family-owned chain, Jollibee Foods Corporation, has become the dominant fast-food chain in the Philippines. Jollibee caters to a local preference for sweet-and-spicy flavours, which it incorporates into its fried chicken, spaghetti, and burgers. Jollibee's strength is its understanding of local tastes, and the company claims its burger is similar to the one a Filipino would cook at home. McDonald's responded by introducing its own Filipino-style spicy burger, but competition is stiff. The experience of McDonald's demonstrates that, to be successful, corporate strategies must recognize customs, preferences, and economic conditions in other countries.

MARKET ANALYSIS

A key to success in formulating a customer-driven operations strategy that offers superior value is understanding what the customer wants and how to provide it better than the competition does. *Market analysis* first divides the firm's customers into market segments and then identifies the needs of each segment. A sound marketing program can then be devised and an effective operating strategy developed to support it.

MARKET SEGMENTATION. Market segmentation seeks to identify particular groups or sub-groups of customers from a larger population that have enough common needs to justify designing and offering distinct products or services. In general, the characteristics that differentiate segments, including demographic, psychological, and industry factors, must be identified. Management's ability to target increasingly smaller, more specialized market segments has improved with new applications of information technology, such as loyalty programs like Air Miles, and more flexible manufacturing and service processes, such as the recent introduction of train scheduling for freight shipments at Canadian National Railway.

NEEDS ASSESSMENT. The second step in market analysis is to make a *needs assessment*, which identifies the requirements of each segment and assesses how well competitors are addressing those requirements. This assessment provides the important information that allows operations to differentiate the company from its competitors by offering greater value. Each market segment has market needs that can be related to product/service, process, or demand attributes. For operations management, market needs may be grouped as follows:

- *Product* or *service needs*. Attributes of the product or service, such as price, quality, and degree of customization desired.

- *Delivery system needs*. Attributes of the processes and the supporting systems and resources, such as availability, convenience, courtesy, safety, accuracy, reliability, delivery speed, and delivery dependability.

- *Volume needs*. Attributes of the demand for the product or service, such as high or low volume, and the variability and predictability in volumes.

- *Other needs*. Other attributes, such as reputation, after-sale technical support, competent legal services, and product or service design capability.

CUSTOMER VALUE AND COMPETITIVE PRIORITIES

customer value The combination of quality, time, and flexibility relative to price for the customer benefit bundle of goods and services. Price translates into cost for operations management.

customer benefit bundle A package of a core good or service along with a set of peripheral products or services.

For operations management, we focus on aspects of **customer value** that are driven by processes that relate to the product or service itself, to its delivery system, and to related volume factors. Customer value includes both the tangible and the intangible product attributes and features that a customer desires (Collier, 1994). These attributes and features, which can be termed a **customer benefit bundle**, consist of a core good and/or service and a set of peripheral goods and services. For example, when you purchase an automobile, the core product is the car itself—its features and qualities. However, the peripheral services offered by the dealer play a key role in whether you will buy the car. They include the manner in which you are treated by the salesperson, the availability of financing, and the quality of after-sales service at the dealership. Thus, the customer benefit bundle is the automobile plus the services provided by the dealership. Customers won't be completely satisfied unless they receive a well-integrated benefit bundle that addresses all of their needs.

In general, there are four broad dimensions of customer value that collectively create the customer benefit bundle: quality, time, flexibility, and price. Conceptually, customer value is defined as a ratio:

$$\text{Customer value} = \frac{\text{(Quality, time, flexibility)}}{\text{Price}}$$

Because price is usually determined by the market and other competitive forces, operations must work to improve *cost* (rather than price), relative to quality, time, and flexibility. An operations strategy is only sustainable if price exceeds cost, as many bankrupt firms have tragically discovered.

For operations management to effectively and efficiently create customer value, a clear understanding of the organization's long-term goals is needed, as embodied in its corporate strategy. Thus, customer value vividly underscores that operations management cannot succeed in isolation, but must be strongly linked both strategically and tactically to other functional areas. At the foundation is a cross-functional effort by marketing and operations to understand the needs of each market segment and to specify the operating advantages that the firm needs to outperform competitors. These critical operating advantages must then be translated into and related to each of the firm's processes. The relative emphasis or weighting of the dimensions of customer value that operations management must possess to outperform its competitors is called **competitive priorities**.

competitive priorities
The relative weighting of the dimensions of customer value that operations management must possess to out-perform its competitors.

More specifically, we can dissect the four dimensions of customer value into eight possible competitive priorities for processes:

Cost	1. Low-cost operations
Quality	2. High-performance design
	3. Consistency (i.e., conformance)
Time	4. Fast delivery time
	5. On-time delivery
	6. New service and product development speed
Flexibility	7. Customization and variety
	8. Volume flexibility

Numerous challenges hinder the translation of customer value into competitive priorities and effective processes. Most customers view a business as a single aggregate process that accepts orders for products or services and then delivers them in a fashion that satisfies customers' needs. Yet multiple processes, often nested with other processes, must be coordinated with the firm and between functional areas to provide the desired customer benefit package. In addition, many processes may serve more than one market segment, further complicating management's task. The challenge for managers is to match the appropriate competitive priorities with specific process designs and investments that create value, as defined by each of the firm's market segments.

COST

Lowering prices can increase demand for products or services, but it also reduces profit margins if the product or service cannot be produced at lower cost. To compete effectively on the basis of price, operations managers must control the cost of labour, materials, scrap, overhead, and other factors. Collectively, improvements in design and management of operations must create a system that lowers the cost per unit of the product or service. Often, lowering cost requires additional investment in automated facilities and equipment. The Managerial Practice feature shows how Costco uses its operations strategy to lower costs and increase margins.

QUALITY

Quality is a complex dimension of a product or service that is often related to both tangible and perceptual aspects defined by the customer. Today, more than ever, quality has important market implications. As for operations, two competitive priorities deal with quality: high-performance design and consistent quality.

high-performance design
The level of functionality or particular attributes that is specified for operations to make a product or perform a service.

HIGH-PERFORMANCE DESIGN. The first priority, **high-performance design**, focuses on the level of particular attributes such as superior features, close tolerances, and greater durability; helpfulness, courteousness, and availability of service employees; convenience of access to service locations; and safety of products or services. High-performance design determines the level of functionality that operations must achieve to make a product or perform a service. To do so, customer needs must be

MANAGERIAL PRACTICE
Using Operations for Profit at Costco

Looking for bargains on items ranging from watermelons to symphonic baby grand pianos? One company addressing those needs is Costco (www.costco.com), a wholesale club with 66 warehouse stores in Canada. With 471 warehouses worldwide, revenues were $52 billion in 2005, generating profits of over $1 billion, and capital investment exceeded $1 billion. Individual and business customers pay Costco a relatively small annual fee for a membership and the privilege of buying staple items in bulk quantities and other select items at big discounts.

What makes Costco so successful? It has linked the needs of its customers to its operations by developing a customer-driven operations strategy that supports its retailing concept. Costco's competitive priorities are low-cost operations, quality, and flexibility. A visit to one of Costco's stores will show how these competitive priorities manifest themselves.

Shoppers checking out the bargains that they found at one of Costco's wholesale clubs. Costco operates member-centred discount warehouse outlets in North America and Asia.

Low-Cost Operations
Customers come to Costco because of low prices, which are possible because processes are designed for efficiency. The store is actually a warehouse where products are stacked on pallets with little signage. Only a limited selection is carried in each product category, reducing inventory and handling. New products can replace old products efficiently. In addition, Costco managers are tough price negotiators with suppliers because they buy in high volumes. Suppliers are expected to change factory runs to produce specially built packages that are bigger but cheaper per unit. Costco's profit margins are low, but annual profits are high because of the volume.

Quality
Customers are not looking for high levels of customer service, but they are looking for high value. In addition to low prices, Costco backs everything it sells with a return-anything-at-any-time guarantee. Customers trust Costco, which has generated

an 86 percent membership renewal rate—the highest in the industry. To support the need for high value, operations must ensure that products are of high quality and undamaged when placed in the store.

Flexibility
One of the key aspects of Costco's operations is the fact that it carries only 4000 carefully selected items in a typical store, while superstores of competitors might carry 125 000 items. However, items change frequently to provide return customers with a "surprise" aspect to the shopping experience. Processes must be flexible to accommodate a dynamic store layout. In addition, the supply chain must be carefully managed because the products are constantly changing.

Source: "Inside the Cult of Costco," *Fortune*, September 6, 1999, pp. 184–190; Annual Report, 2005.

accurately assessed and then translated into a product or service design that reaches the higher end of these specifications.

consistent quality The frequency with which the product or service meets design specifications.

CONSISTENT QUALITY. The second quality priority, **consistent quality**, measures the frequency with which the service and product meets design specifications. Customers want services or products that consistently meet the specifications they contracted for, have come to expect, or saw advertised. To compete on the basis of consistent quality, managers need to design and monitor operations to reduce errors. A firm that does not have consistent quality creates uncertainty in the minds of customers (even those that don't need high-performance design), and tends to be viewed based on the lowest level it achieves. As a result, firms with poor consistency tend to struggle as competition increases.

TIME

As the saying goes, "Time is money." Some companies do business at "Internet speed," while others thrive on consistently meeting delivery promises. Three competitive priorities deal with time: fast delivery time, on-time delivery, and development speed.

fast delivery time The elapsed time between receiving a customer's order and filling it, sometimes termed *lead time*.

FAST DELIVERY TIME. The first time priority, **fast delivery time**, is the elapsed time between receiving a customer's order and filling it, sometimes termed *lead time* by industrial buyers. An acceptable delivery time can be a year for a complex, customized machine, several weeks for elective surgery, and minutes for an ambulance. Manufacturers can shorten delivery times by storing inventory. Service providers and manufacturers can also reduce lead times by having excess capacity, so that customers or customer orders do not have to wait in long queues.

on-time delivery Measurement of the frequency with which delivery-time promises are met.

ON-TIME DELIVERY. The second time priority, **on-time delivery**, measures the frequency with which delivery-time promises are met. Manufacturers measure on-time delivery as the percentage of customer orders shipped when promised, with 95 percent often considered the goal. Similar measures apply to distributors, where management monitors how often an item is not available for immediate purchase. Other service providers, such as supermarkets, might measure on-time delivery as the percentage of customers who wait in the express checkout lines for less than three minutes.

development speed Measurement of how quickly a new product or service is introduced, covering the elapsed time from idea generation through design to production.

DEVELOPMENT SPEED. The third time priority, **development speed**, measures how quickly a new product or service is introduced, covering the elapsed time from idea generation through final design to market introduction. Contributing to this priority is the ability of managers to innovate, on the basis of either recognition of evolving market needs or new technology developments. Repeatedly getting new products and services to market first gives the firm an edge on the competition that is difficult to overcome. Firms that have rapid development speed are often identified as market leaders. This third time priority is especially important in the electronics, entertainment, and fashion apparel industries.

time-based competition Defining the steps and time needed to deliver a product or service, and then critically analyzing each step to determine whether time can be reduced without hurting quality.

TIME-BASED COMPETITION. Many companies leverage the combined competitive priorities of development speed and fast delivery time. With **time-based competition**, managers carefully define the steps and time needed to deliver a product or service and then critically analyze each step to determine whether they can save time without hurting quality.

FLEXIBILITY

Flexibility is a characteristic of a firm's operations that enables it to react to customer needs quickly and efficiently. Some firms give top priority to two types of flexibility: customization and volume flexibility.

customization The ability to satisfy the unique needs of each customer by changing product or service designs and systems.

CUSTOMIZATION. Many customers require a unique or customized product or service. **Customization** typically implies that the operating system must be flexible to receive individualized customer orders, adjust designs accordingly, and create the requested product or service.

volume flexibility The ability to quickly accelerate or decelerate the rate of production or service to handle large fluctuations in demand.

VOLUME FLEXIBILITY. To handle large fluctuations in demand, **volume flexibility** is often needed to quickly accelerate or decelerate the rate of production or service. This important capability often supports the achievement of other competitive priorities (e.g., development speed or fast delivery times). The time between peaks may be years, as with cycles in the home-building industry or political campaigns; it may be months, as with ski resorts or the manufacture of lawn fertilizers; it may even be hours, as with the systematic swings in demand at a large postal facility where mail is received, sorted, and dispatched.

SELECTING COMPETITIVE PRIORITIES

You might wonder why firms have to choose among competitive priorities. Why not compete in all areas at once and dramatically improve your competitive position? In certain situations, firms *can* improve on all competitive priorities simultaneously. For example, in a manufacturing firm, scrap from mistakes in operations and the need to rework defective parts and products sometimes account for a quarter of a product's cost. By reducing defects and improving quality, the firm can reduce costs, improve productivity, and cut delivery time—all at the same time.

order winner A criterion customers use to differentiate the services or products of one firm from those of another.

At some point, though, further improvements in one area may require a trade-off with one or more of the others. For example, a survey of manufacturers indicated that raising the degree of customization or producing high-performance design products is linked with both higher costs and higher prices (Safizadeh et al., 1996). Therefore, firms must select a subset of competitive priorities to emphasize with operations processes and systems. In any given market, one particular dimension of customer value often transcends others to influence purchase behaviour between competing products. This dimension is called an **order winner** (Hill, 2000). For example, consistent quality is an order winner for many of Toyota's automobiles.

order qualifier A demonstrated level of performance of an order winner that is required for a firm to do business in a particular market segment.

Sometimes the minimum level of a particular dimension of customer value has become a requirement for doing business in a specific market segment. Such a requirement is called an **order qualifier**. In such situations, customers will not place orders for products or services unless a certain level of performance can be demonstrated. Fulfilling the order qualifier will not ensure competitive success in a market; it will only position the firm to compete. For example, for television sets, one measure of quality is product reliability. Customers expect to purchase a set that will not require repairs for many years. Products that do not live up to that level of quality do not last long in the market. In the electronics industry in general, product reliability is rapidly becoming an order qualifier.

operations strategy The pattern of decisions and investments in products, services, and processes used to implement an organization's corporate strategy and to create customer value.

OPERATIONS STRATEGY AS A PATTERN OF DECISIONS

Competitive priorities provide a basis for the design of processes and the formulation of an effective and sustainable **operations strategy**. An operations strategy is not a single initiative, such as a quality improvement program, more automated machinery, or even a new facility located abroad, but rather a pattern of decisions and investments over time that develop operating advantages. These decisions include both the "hardware" and "software" of business processes. Hardware is relatively easy to identify as the physical components, and includes such areas as plant capacity, service facilities, telecommunications equipment, and product technology. In contrast, software is sometimes more difficult to identify as infrastructural components of processes. It is just as important, and includes such areas within operations as human resources and training, organizational structure, and quality systems.

Collectively, an operations strategy must reflect a clear understanding of the firm's long-term goals as embodied in its corporate strategy. Corporate strategy provides the umbrella for key operations management decisions as shown in Figure 1.7. This strategy determines how the firm's processes are organized to handle the volume and variety of products or services for each market segment. This initial choice sets in motion a series of other decisions that governs the design of the processes, systems, and procedures that support the operations strategy. These decisions are not static; they must be constantly re-evaluated according to the dynamics of the marketplace.

From a strategic perspective, operations managers are responsible for making the decisions that ensure the firm has the capability to address the competitive priorities of new and existing market segments as they evolve. Furthermore, the pattern of decisions for one organization may be quite different from that of another, even if they are both in the same industry, because of differences in core competencies, market segments served, and extent of international operations. Each process must be analyzed from the perspective of the customers it serves, be they external or internal.

FIGURE 1.7

Connection Between Corporate Strategy and Key Operations Management Decisions

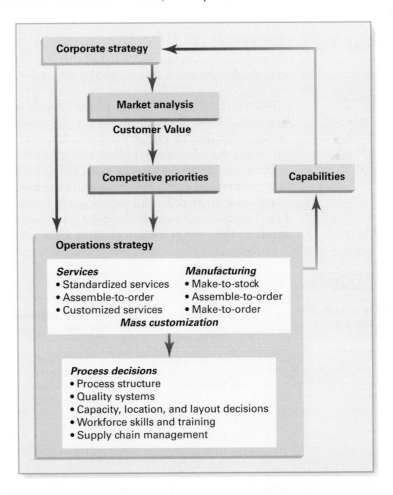

COMBINING GOODS AND SERVICES

Many firms make general distinctions between being a manufacturing or service organization. Although both have processes with many similarities, three primary characteristics tend to differentiate goods-producing processes from service-producing processes (Figure 1.8). First, customers tend to be highly involved in the production process for services, particularly those that are experience-based, such as an amusement park. Although tangible facilities might be part of that experience, the output of the process is the enjoyment and memories of the customer. Second, outputs that are physical goods often can be produced in advance, and then held in inventory until needed by the customer. In contrast, because service processes usually require the customer to be directly involved, they cannot be produced in advance. Third, the quality of goods can often be monitored using physical measures of specific characteristics, with little ambiguity. However, the outputs of many service operations tend to have perceptual characteristics, such as whether a movie was "exciting." Distinctions between manufacturing and service outputs must be reflected in the operations strategies chosen by an organization.

Today, few firms place themselves at either end of the continuum, with manufacturing firms moving into service offerings, and services selling physical goods. For example, some manufacturing firms such as Palliser Furniture are working to develop showcase retail stores, and Lexus is strongly committed to outstanding after-sales service support through its dealer network. Moving in the opposite direction, Disney produces and licenses an increasing number of goods related to its cast of characters. As a result, firms must explicitly design and manage a set of processes that collectively deliver both goods and services that form a *coherent, consistent customer benefit bundle.*

GENERAL SERVICE STRATEGIES

Standardized services, assemble-to-order services, and customized-services strategies are used for processes devoted to the delivery of services.

STANDARDIZED SERVICES. Processes that provide services with little variety in high volumes tend to use the **standardized-services strategy.** Typical competitive priorities are consistent quality, on-time delivery, and low cost. Because of the high volume, processes providing the primary service can be organized so that the flow of customers follows a linear pattern in the facility. For example, Canada Post uses standardized-services strategies for the letter mail process and the parcel process. The millions of letters and parcels that arrive daily for processing are sorted by destination and loaded into trucks. Parcel processing is separate from letter processing because of the different market segments and because of the nature of the automated sorting equipment required for each

standardized-services strategy A strategy that provides low-variety, homogeneous services at high volumes.

FIGURE 1.8

Continuum of Service and Manufacturing Process Outputs

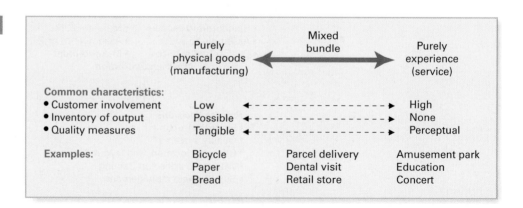

type of item. The tasks required of the employees and equipment are repetitive and routine, ideal for the standardized-services strategy. Banking at ING Direct in Canada also uses a standardized-services strategy with relatively few banking services offered from one physical location.

ASSEMBLE-TO-ORDER SERVICES. The **assemble-to-order services** strategy amounts to designing operations to include processes that produce a set of standardized services, as well as other downstream processes that assemble these standardized offerings into a bundle tailored to a specific customer's needs. The assembly processes must be flexible so that the correct bundle can be assembled for the customer. Typical competitive priorities are customization and fast delivery time. For example, long-distance telephone service providers offer customized service packages to retain customers in a highly competitive industry. Internet access, cellular phone service, credit cards, satellite broadcast service, personal 800 numbers, and cable TV are among the list of options. The assembly process could be automated, as on a Web page, or personalized through telemarketing. Companies such as Bell work with the customer to assemble the appropriate mix of services and provide a billing service that combines all charges on one itemized bill.

CUSTOMIZED SERVICES. Processes designed to provide individualized services tend to use a **customized-services strategy.** Typical competitive priorities include high-performance design and customization. Volume, in terms of service requirements per customer, is low. Nested processes tend to be grouped by the function they perform, and customers are routed from process to process until the service is completed. This strategy enables the production of a high variety of customized services while providing reasonable utilization of the processes. For example, Figure 1.9 shows the flow pattern of patients through a health clinic process. Although there are five processes providing services, any one customer may not need all of them. The customers may have to compete for the resources: note that all patients must see the doctor. Many different routing patterns may exist in a facility employing a customized-services strategy.

GENERAL MANUFACTURING STRATEGIES
Manufacturing strategies differ from those in services because of the ability to use inventories. However, you will also notice a number of elements in common with service strategies. Make-to-stock, assemble-to-order, and make-to-order strategies address the competitive priorities of processes devoted to manufacturing.

assemble-to-order services A strategy with processes that produce a set of standardized services, followed by other processes that assemble a package of standardized offerings for a specific customer's needs.

customized-services strategy A strategy that provides individualized services.

FIGURE 1.9

Health Clinic Process

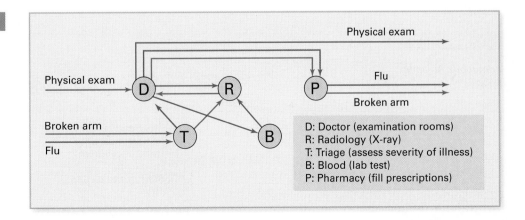

make-to-stock manufacturing strategy
A manufacturing strategy that involves holding items in stock for immediate delivery, thereby minimizing customer delivery times.

mass production The approach used by firms that employ a make-to-stock strategy.

assemble-to-order manufacturing strategy
An approach to producing customized products from relatively few assemblies and components after customer orders are received.

make-to-order manufacturing strategy
A strategy used by manufacturers that make products to customer specifications in low volumes.

MAKE-TO-STOCK MANUFACTURING. Manufacturing firms that hold items in stock for immediate delivery, thereby minimizing customer delivery times, use a **make-to-stock manufacturing strategy**. This strategy is feasible for standardized products with high volumes and reasonably accurate forecasts. For example, in Figure 1.10, which depicts a final automobile assembly process, both the midsize six-cylinder and the compact four-cylinder models are assembled on the same line. Collectively, the volume of the two models is sufficient to warrant a make-to-stock strategy for the facility. The routing pattern for the two products is straightforward, with four processes devoted to the two products. This strategy is also applicable to situations in which the firm is producing a unique product for a specific customer if the volumes are high enough, such as suppliers of automotive parts for specific model cars.

The term **mass production** is often used to characterize firms using a make-to-stock strategy. Because their environment is relatively stable and predictable, mass-production firms typically have a bureaucratic organization, and workers repeat narrowly defined tasks. The competitive priorities for these companies typically are consistent quality and low costs.

ASSEMBLE-TO-ORDER MANUFACTURING. The **assemble-to-order manufacturing strategy** is an approach to producing customized products from relatively few assemblies and components after customer orders are received. Typical competitive priorities are customization and fast delivery time. The assemble-to-order strategy involves assembly processes and fabrication processes. Because they are devoted to manufacturing standardized components and assemblies in high volumes, the fabrication processes focus on creating appropriate amounts of inventories for the assembly processes. Stocking finished products would be economically prohibitive because the numerous possible options make forecasting relatively inaccurate. For example, a manufacturer of upscale upholstered furniture can produce hundreds of a particular style of sofa, no two alike, to meet customers' selections of fabric and wood. Once the specific order from the customer is received, the assembly processes create the product from the standardized components and assemblies produced by the fabrication processes. The fabrication processes should be efficient to keep costs low, while the assembly processes should be flexible to produce the varied products demanded by the customers.

MAKE-TO-ORDER MANUFACTURING. Manufacturers that make products to customer specifications in low volumes tend to use a **make-to-order manufacturing strategy**. With this strategy, a firm is viewed as a set of processes that can be used in many different ways to satisfy the unique needs of customers. This strategy provides a high degree of customization, which is a major competitive priority for these manufacturers. Because

FIGURE 1.10

Automobile Assembly Process

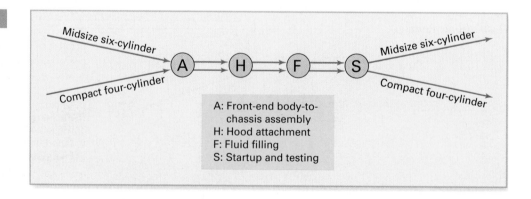

A: Front-end body-to-chassis assembly
H: Hood attachment
F: Fluid filling
S: Startup and testing

most products, components, and assemblies are custom-made, the manufacturing process must be flexible to accommodate the variety. Specialized medical equipment, castings, and expensive homes are suited to the make-to-order strategy.

MASS CUSTOMIZATION

mass customization
An assemble-to-order strategy whereby a firm's flexible processes generate customized products or services in high volumes at reasonably low costs.

Combining the assemble-to-order strategy with mass production yields **mass customization**, whereby a firm's flexible processes generate customized products or services in high volumes at reasonably low costs. Mass customizers attempt to provide the variety inherent in an assemble-to-order strategy but often focus on relatively high-volume markets. A key to being a successful mass customizer is postponing the task of differentiating a product or service for a specific customer until the latest possible moment. Doing so allows the greatest application of standard modules of the product or service before specific customization. Hewlett-Packard (HP) provides a good example of mass customization. HP postpones assembly of the printer with the country-specific power supply and packaging of the appropriate manuals until the last link in the process—the distributor in the region where the printer is being delivered. Being a successful mass customizer such as HP may require redesign of products or services and processes. We will have more to say about postponement in Chapter 9, "Supply Chain Management."

PRODUCT OR SERVICE IMPLICATIONS. A product or service should be designed so that it consists of independent modules that can be assembled into different forms easily and inexpensively. For instance, on any given night, Starwood's many hotels (including the well-known brand, Sheraton) receive such guests as leisure travellers and businesspeople, including those who plan to attend conventions. Until recently, each individual hotel had its own approach to convention planning; for example, paperwork for confirming program details and food requirements differed between properties, and technology available for meeting rooms varied widely.

After significant process redesign, consistency was introduced into the convention planning process, including an extensive list of separate, standardized services. Every hotel property now has the same paperwork and can share it electronically between locations. In addition, each convention has a "Star Meeting Concierge" whose sole responsibility is to anticipate and fulfill the particular needs of customers during the event.

Each convention is assigned a Star Meeting Concierge within a standardized process. This concierge coordinates the specific services, program details, and rooms needed.

PROCESS IMPLICATIONS. Processes should be designed so that they can be used to meet a wide variety of needs. We discuss process management in more detail in Chapter 2; however, one key to supporting mass customization is to design processes as independent modules that can be arranged to provide customization at the latest possible moment, as Hewlett-Packard did with its printers. Benetton adopted a similar approach in its sweater manufacturing process. Rather than dyeing the yarn before manufacturing the sweater, Benetton reversed the dyeing and knitting processes so that sweaters were dyed after the customer had placed an order or the colour preferences of consumers for the upcoming season had been determined. By rearranging the processes, Benetton saved millions of dollars in write-offs for obsolete inventory.

INTERNET IMPLICATIONS. The Internet has been a valuable technology for mass-customization strategies. Web pages can be designed to attract customers and allow them to configure their own products or services easily and quickly. Customers of Amazon.ca fill baskets of goods from a vast array of possibilities, each one different from the next customer's. Dell sells computers through a Web page that allows consumers to configure their own computers from a large variety of options. CIBC offers investment services along with its banking services for its Internet customers. Each of these ventures gives customers an enormous amount of choice in the products or services they buy, but they also put a lot of pressure on the processes that must produce them. Flexibility and short response times are prized qualities for mass-customization processes.

OPERATIONS MANAGEMENT ACROSS THE ORGANIZATION

We have described operations management as designing and operating processes (in both manufacturing and services) as a set of decisions and as one of several functional areas within an organization. In this final section, we describe operations management as an interfunctional imperative and a competitive weapon for organizations.

OPERATIONS MANAGEMENT AS AN INTERFUNCTIONAL IMPERATIVE

Operations managers need to build and maintain solid relationships both interorganizationally and intraorganizationally. Here, our focus is on intraorganizational relationships, which call for cross-functional coordination (see Chapter 9, "Supply Chain Management," for interorganizational relationships). Too often, managers allow artificial barriers to be erected between functional areas and departments. In these situations, jobs or tasks move sequentially from marketing through engineering to operations. The result is often slow or poor decision making because each department bases its decisions solely on its own limited perspective, not the organization's overall perspective. Greater cross-functional coordination and flatter organizational structures are now being actively pursued in many organizations.

CROSS-FUNCTIONAL COORDINATION. Regardless of how organizational lines are drawn, departments and functions are always linked together through processes. Consequently, operations managers need to build and maintain solid relationships both inside and outside the organization. Too often, managers create or face various barriers between functional areas and departments. Customer orders or tasks move sequentially from marketing to engineering to operations, often resulting in slow or poor decision making because each department bases its decisions on its own limited perspective, not the organization's overall goals.

Cross-functional coordination is essential to effective management. Consider how other functional areas interact with operations. To begin, perhaps the strongest connection is with the marketing function, which determines the need for new services and products and the demand for existing ones. Operations managers must bring together human and capital resources to handle demand effectively. The operations manager must consider facility locations and relocations to serve new markets, and the design of layouts for service organizations must match the image that marketing wants to convey to the customer. Marketing and sales make delivery promises to customers, which must be related to current operations capabilities. The combination of effective marketing and focused operations is critical for customer satisfaction.

The operations manager also needs feedback from the accounting and finance functions to understand current performance. These functions help to monitor labour and material costs, and influence investment decisions in new technology, layout redesign, capacity expansion, and even inventory levels. Similarly, human resources interacts with operations to hire and train workers and aids in changeovers related to new process and job designs. Finally, engineering can also have a big impact on operations. In designing new services or products, engineering needs to consider technical trade-offs and to ensure that the designs do not create costly specifications or exceed capabilities.

ACHIEVING CROSS-FUNCTIONAL COORDINATION. Several approaches may be used to achieve cross-functional coordination. Each organization should select some blend of them to get everyone pulling in the same direction.

- A unified strategy should be developed by management as a starting point, giving each department a vision of what it must do to help fulfill the overall organizational strategy.

- The organizational structure and management hierarchy can be redesigned to promote cross-functional coordination. Drawing departmental lines around areas of specialization may work against integration by creating insular views and "turf battles." Another option is to organize around major product lines or processes.

- The goal-setting process and reward systems can encourage cross-functional coordination. So can bringing people together from different functional areas—through task forces or committees—to make decisions and solve problems.

- Improvements to information systems also can boost coordination. In part, information must be tailored to the needs of each functional manager. However, sharing information helps harmonize the efforts of managers from different parts of the organization and enables them to make decisions consistent with organizational goals.

- Informal social systems are another device that can be used to encourage better understanding across functional lines. Joint cafeteria facilities, exercise rooms, and social events can help build a sense of camaraderie, as can corporate training and development programs.

- Employee selection and promotion also can help foster more cross-functional coordination by encouraging broad perspectives and common goals. Of course, employees must first be competent in their own skill areas.

The best mix of approaches depends on the organization. Some organizations need more coordination than others. The need is greatest when functions are dispersed (owing to organizational structure or geographical distance), organizations are large, and many products or services are customized. The need is crucial in service organizations that have high customer contact and provide services directly to customers.

OPERATIONS MANAGEMENT AS A COMPETITIVE WEAPON

In this global era, business and government leaders are increasingly recognizing the importance of involving the whole organization in making strategic decisions. Because the organization usually commits the bulk of its human and financial assets to operations, operations is an important function in meeting global competition. Too often, operations policies covering capacity, inventory levels, and schedules reflect incorrect assumptions about customer value and corporate strategy—ultimately working at cross-purposes to a firm's strategic goals. This lack of understanding can waste a firm's resources for years.

Due to an increasing array of competitors and an explosion of new technologies, recognition is growing that a firm competes not only by offering new products and services, creative marketing, and skillful finance but also by having unique competencies in operations. The organization that can offer superior products and services produced at lower cost is a formidable competitor.

EQUATION SUMMARY

1. Productivity is the ratio of output to input, or:

$$\text{Productivity} = \frac{\text{Output}}{\text{Input}}$$

CHAPTER HIGHLIGHTS

- Every organization must manage processes and the operations by which these processes are performed. Processes are the fundamental means by which organizations perform work and achieve their goals. Processes transform inputs into outputs, and are ideally designed to create customer value. Inputs include human resources (workers and managers), capital resources (equipment and facilities), purchased materials and services, land, and energy. Outputs are goods and services that firms combine into a customer benefit bundle.

- Conceptually, for operations management, customer value is defined as the ratio of equality, time, and flexibility to cost.

- The concept of processes applies not just to an entire organization but also to the work of each department and individual. Each has work processes and customers (whether internal or external).

- A process can be broken down into subprocesses, which in turn can be broken down still further. A process within a process is known as a nested process.

- Types of decisions with which operations managers are involved include strategic choices (operations strategy); process (capacity, quality, inventory, and location and layout); supply chain management (including lean systems); and operating decisions (technology, forecasting, aggregate planning and scheduling, and resource planning).

- Decisions within operations should be linked. For example, quality, process, capacity, and inventory decisions affect one another and should not be made independently. Strategy (long-range plans) and tactical analysis (for short-range decision making) should complement each other.

- Operations management requires utilization of a variety of skills and technologies. It plays a key role in determining productivity, which is the prime determinant of profitability and, in the aggregate, a nation's standard of living.

- Smart managers use multiple performance measures to monitor and improve performance.

- Several trends are at work in operations management: service sector employment is growing; productivity is a major concern, particularly in the service sector; and a global perspective must be encouraged. The pursuit of better quality, competition based on time, and rapid technological change are also important trends. The importance of the natural environmental, ethics, and workforce diversity is increasing.

- Operations managers must deal with both intraorganizational and interorganizational relationships. For operations to be used successfully as a competitive weapon, it must address interfunctional concerns. As a result, concepts and issues from operations management must be understood by managers in every functional area.

- Corporate strategy involves monitoring and adjusting to changes in the external business environment and exploiting core competencies. Firms expanding and competing internationally may form strategic alliances through collaborative efforts, joint ventures, or licensing of technology.

- Market analysis is key to formulating a customer-driven operations strategy. Market segmentation and needs assessment are methods of pinpointing elements of a product or service that satisfy customers.

- Customer-driven operations strategy requires translating market needs into specific operating advantages, called competitive priorities. There are four basic dimensions that cover eight priorities: low-cost operations; quality, including high-performance design and consistent quality; time, including fast delivery time, on-time delivery, and new product and service development; and flexibility, including customization and volume flexibility. Management must decide on which dimensions the firm's processes should excel, sometimes requiring difficult trade-offs.

- With time-based competition, managers seek to significantly reduce time in the various steps required to deliver a product or service.

- Operations strategy is a pattern of decisions and investments in products, services, and processes used to implement an organization's corporate strategy and to create customer value.

- The outputs from manufacturing and service processes range from pure goods to pure experience. Three primary characteristics tend to differentiate goods-producing processes from service-producing processes: customer involvement, potential inventory of outputs, and measurement of quality. These differences must be reflected in the operations strategy used by an organization.

- Processes devoted to producing services choose one of the following three operations strategies: standardized services, which facilitate low-cost operations, consistent quality, and on-time delivery; assemble-to-order services, which facilitate customization and fast delivery time; and customized services, which facilitate high-performance design and customization.

- Processes devoted to manufacturing choose one of the following three operations strategies: make-to-stock, which facilitates low costs, consistent quality, and fast delivery time; assemble-to-order, which facilitates fast delivery time and customization; and make-to-order, which facilitates customization and low volumes.

- Mass customization is an extreme form of the assemble-to-order strategy, whereby a firm uses both flexible and standard processes to produce customized products or services in high volumes at reasonable costs.

 ## CD-ROM RESOURCES

The Student CD-ROM that accompanies this text contains the following resources, which allow you to further practise and apply the concepts presented in this chapter.

- **Equation Summary**: All the equations for this chapter can be found in one convenient location.

- **Discussion Questions**: These questions challenge your understanding of the role of operations management and operations strategy.

- **Cases**:
  - *Chad's Creative Concepts*. How should Chad Thomas, traditionally a custom manufacturer, cope with the new move into standard products sold by retail outlets?
  - *BSB, Inc.: The Pizza Wars Come to Campus*. How should Renee Kershaw react to product proliferation?

- **OM Explorer Tutors**: OM Explorer contains one tutor program that will help you explore productivity measures.

- **Tours**: See how the *Lower Florida Keys Health System* community hospital uses a customized-services strategy and how *Chaparral Steel* designed its processes for competitive operations.

- **Supplement A**: *Decision Making*. This supplement provides the background to use break-even analysis, preference matrices, decision theory, and decision trees.

REFERENCES AND FURTHER READINGS

Berry, W. L., C. Bozarth, T. Hill, and J. E. Klompmaker. "Factory Focus: Segmenting Markets from an Operations Perspective." *Journal of Operations Management*, vol. 10 (1991), no. 3, pp. 363–387.

Blackburn, Joseph. *Time-Based Competition: The Next Battleground in American Manufacturing*. Homewood, IL: Business One Irwin, 1991.

Bowen, David E., Richard B. Chase, Thomas G. Cummings, and Associates. *Service Management Effectiveness*. San Francisco: Jossey-Bass, 1990.

Buchholz, Rogene A. "Corporate Responsibility and the Good Society: From Economics to Ecology." *Business Horizons*, July/August 1991, pp. 19–31.

Collier, David A. *The Service Quality Solution*. Milwaukee: ASQC Quality Press, and Burr Ridge, IL: Irwin Professional Publishing, 1994.

Crompton, S., and Vickers, M. "One Hundred Years of Labour Force." *Canadian Social Trends*, Catalogue No. 11-008 (Summer 2000). Ottawa: Statistics Canada.

Environment Canada, Greenhouse Gas Division. Web site, 2002 <www.ec.gc.ca/pdb/ghg/ghg_home_e.cfm>, accessed March 26, 2003.

Feitzinger, Edward, and Hau L. Lee. "Mass Customization at Hewlett-Packard: The Power of Postponement." *Harvard Business Review*, vol. 75 (1997), no. 1, pp. 116–121.

Fitzsimmons, James A., and Mona Fitzsimmons. *Service Management for Competitive Advantage*. New York: McGraw-Hill, 1994.

Gilmore, James H., and B. Joseph Pine II. "The Four Faces of Mass Customization." *Harvard Business Review*, vol. 75 (1997), no. 1, pp. 91–101.

Hammer, Michael, and Steven Stanton. "How Process Enterprises Really Work." *Harvard Business Review*, November/December 1999, pp. 108–120.

Hayes, Robert H., and Gary P. Pisano. "Beyond World-Class: The New Manufacturing Strategy." *Harvard Business Review*, January/February 1994, pp. 77–86.

Heskett, James L., and Leonard A. Schlesenger. "The Service-Driven Service Company." *Harvard Business Review*, September/October 1991, pp. 71–81.

Hill, Terry. *Manufacturing Strategy: Text and Cases*, 3rd ed. Homewood, IL: Irwin/McGraw-Hill, 2000.

Holloway, A. "Hand-Helds across the Water," *Canadian Business*, vol. 78, no. 13 (2005), pp. 63–65.

"The Horizontal Corporation." *Business Week*, December 20, 1993, pp. 76–81.

Jones, N., and R. D. Klassen. "Managing Pollution Prevention: Integrating Environmental Technologies in Manufacturing." In Sarkis, J. (ed.), *Green Manufacturing and Operations: From Design to Delivery and Back*. Sheffield, UK: Greenleaf Publishing, 2001, pp. 56–68.

Kaplan, Robert S., and David P. Norton. *Balanced Scoreboard*. Boston, MA: Harvard Business School Press, 1997.

Klassen, R. D., and D. C. Whybark. "The Impact of Environmental Technologies on Manufacturing Performance." *Academy of Management Journal*, vol. 40 (1999), no. 6, pp. 599–615.

Organisation for Economic Co-operation and Development (OECD). "OECD in Figures: Statistics on Member Countries." *OECD Observer*, 2002, 2005/Supplement 1. Paris: OECD, 2002, 2005.

O'Reilly, Brian. "They've Got Mail!" *Fortune*, February 7, 2000, pp. 101–112.

Pine, B. Joseph II, Bart Victor, and Andrew C. Boynton. "Making Mass Customization Work." *Harvard Business Review*, September/October 1993, pp. 108–119.

Post, James E. "Managing As If the Earth Mattered." *Business Horizons*, July/August 1991, pp. 32–38.

Prahalad, C. K., and G. Hamel. "The Core Competence of the Corporation." *Harvard Business Review*, May/June 1990, pp. 79–91.

Prahalad, C. K., and V. Ramaswamy. "Co-opting Customer Competence." *Harvard Business Review*, January–February 2000, pp. 79–87.

Roth, Aleda V., and Marjolijn van der Velde. "Operations as Marketing: A Competitive Service Strategy." *Journal of Operations Management*, vol. 10 (1993), no. 3, pp. 303–328.

Safizadeh, H. M., L. P. Ritzman, D. Sharma, and C. Wood. "An Empirical Analysis of the Product-Process Matrix." *Management Science*, vol. 42 (1996), no. 11, pp. 1576–1591.

Schmenner, Roger W. *Service Operations Management*. Englewood Cliffs, NJ: Prentice-Hall, 1995.

"Service Exports and the U.S. Economy." *International Trade Association*. U.S. Government.

Skinner, Wickham. "Manufacturing—Missing Link in Corporate Strategy." *Harvard Business Review*, May/June 1969, pp. 136–145.

Skinner, Wickham. "Manufacturing Strategy on the 'S' Curve." *Production and Operations Management*, vol. 5 (1996), no. 1, pp. 3–14.

Statistics Canada. *The Canadian Productivity Accounts Data 2003*, Catalogue No. 15-003-XIE. Ottawa: Statistics Canada, 2005a.

Statistics Canada. *The Canadian Productivity Accounts Data 2003*, Catalogue No. 16-201-XIE. Ottawa: Statistics Canada, 2002.

Statistics Canada. *Human Activity and the Environment*, Catalogue No. 16-201-XIE. Ottawa: Statistics Canada, 2005b.

"Time for a Reality Check in Asia." *Business Week*, December 2, 1996, pp. 58–66.

van Biema, Michael, and Bruce Greenwald, "Managing Our Way to Higher Service-Sector Productivity." *Harvard Business Review*, July/August 1997, pp. 87–95.

Ward, Peter T., Deborah J. Bickford, and G. Keong Leong. "Configurations of Manufacturing Strategy, Business Strategy, Environment and Structure." *Journal of Management*, vol. 22 (1996), no. 4, pp. 597–626.

Wheelwright, Steven C., and H. Kent Bowen. "The Challenge of Manufacturing Advantage." *Production and Operations Management*, vol. 5 (1996), no. 1, pp. 59–77.

Womack, James P., Daniel T. Jones, and Daniel Roos. *The Machine That Changed the World*. New York: HarperPerennial, 1991.

2 Process Management

Across the Organization

Process management is important to:

- **accounting,** which seeks better ways to perform its work processes and provides cost analyses of process improvement proposals.
- **finance,** which seeks better processes to perform its work, does financial analyses of new process proposals, and looks for ways to raise funds to finance automation.
- **human resources,** which melds process and job design decisions into an effective whole.
- **management information systems,** which identify how information technologies can support the exchange of information.
- **marketing,** which seeks better processes to perform its work and explores opportunities to expand market share by encouraging ongoing customer dialogue.
- **operations,** which designs and manages production and service processes in order to maximize customer value and enhance a firm's core competencies.

Learning Goals

After reading this chapter, you will be able to:

1. describe each of the four major process decisions and how they must relate to customer value.
2. describe how each of the basic forms of process structure are best suited to particular levels of market-based customization and volume.
3. discuss how customer involvement influences the processes of service providers.
4. define capital intensity and calculate the break-even volume to compare processes of different capital intensity.
5. discuss the meaning of automation and economies of scope.
6. explain the concept of focused factories and how it applies to service providers.
7. analyze a process for key areas of improvement by constructing flow diagrams and process charts.
8. describe the key elements of process re-engineering.

Chris Griffiths, president of Garrison Guitars in Mount Pearl, Newfoundland (www.garrison guitars.com), has developed innovative products and processes that have translated into multi-million-dollar sales since the firm's inception in 2000. Yet, despite having manufacturing operations in Canada, only a small percentage of the 12 000 guitars produced annually are sold here. Most are exported to the United States, the United Kingdom, Austria, Australia, Japan, and China.

The design and construction of musical instruments is usually a labour-intensive process, undertaken by craftspeople with years of experience. Attention to detail contributes to high quality in both aesthetics and sound.

Garrison has taken a very different, revolutionary approach. Although the guitars are still hand-assembled in a plant that employs 63 people, Griffiths has redesigned the manufacture of critical steps of the process— all while implementing new technologies to improve the sound, lower the costs, and increase the product consistency.

New product and process designs have created a strong competitive advantage.

It all began with a fundamental re-examination of the basic design and manufacturing process for high-quality guitars. Griffiths observed that significant improvements might be possible by combining many of the small pieces of wood inside the guitar into a single piece that braces the outer thinwood veneers. Creating such a complex shape might be possible using a single glass-fibre, injection-moulded piece. This critical insight took six years to realize, along with a $4 million investment to start up production. Design innovations included a glass-fibre neck and end blocks that interlock with the bracing system to create a highly resonant frame for the hardwood exterior.

The result: patents for active bracing and blocking systems that reduce the number of total internal parts from 34 individually machined and installed pieces to just eight. The redesigned instrument was stronger and had an enhanced ability to vibrate, which translated directly into improved sound quality for musicians.

This new design did not require the traditional craft approach to producing guitars. Instead, a designer was responsible for specifying precision-moulded components, and each guitar could be assembled more easily, in far less time. No longer would many individual pieces need to be adjusted and fine-tuned by a highly skilled person.

To match the precise dimensions of the injection-moulded bracing system and ensure a perfect fit, Garrison's process needed similar accuracy in the remaining wood components. A state-of-the-art laser cuts the solid wood tops, back, and sides of the instrument to very precise tolerances. The guitar's neck is also precision-carved using a three-axis computer numerically controlled (CNC) milling machine, turning out one neck in about five minutes. Finally, finishing operations employ coatings that dry in under a minute when exposed to UV light, preventing the release of harmful solvents into the environment.

These efforts to redesign and simplify the manufacturing process have reduced the traditional production time of a guitar body by 90 percent, to a total of 12 minutes. In addition, the physical space required for assembly is reduced by about 70 percent. Yet CEO Griffiths stresses that the changes were not about taking a shortcut in the manufacturing process; the key was delivering musicians a superior product. Effective process management linked to innovative product design created significant competitive advantages.

Source: "Garrison Guitars," *Music Trades,* vol. 149 (2001), no. 6; C. Lynds, "Marrying Technology with Craftsmanship: Innovative Design and Automation Produce Premium-Quality Guitars," *Plant,* vol. 60 (2001), no. 16, pp. 14–15; J. Oganda, "Guitar Assembly with No Strings Attached," *Design News,* vol. 56 (2001), no. 15; R. Simone, "Young Guitar Maker's Invention Has Revolutionized the Industry," *Kitchener-Waterloo Record,* April 27, 2002, p. F2.

Essential issues in the design of processes are deciding how to make products and how to provide services, the results of which are often presented to the customer as a customer benefit bundle. Deciding on processes involves many different choices in selecting human resources, equipment, and materials. Processes are involved in how marketing prepares a market analysis, how accounting bills customers, how a retail store provides services on the sales floor, and how a manufacturing plant performs its assembly operations. Process decisions affect an organization's ability to compete over the long run.

Process decisions are also strategic in nature. As we saw in Chapter 1, they should further a company's long-term competitive goals. In making process decisions, managers focus on controlling such competitive priorities as quality, flexibility, time, cost, and innovation. For example, firms can improve their ability to compete on the basis of time by examining each step of their processes and finding ways to respond more quickly to their customers. Productivity (and, therefore, cost) is affected by choices made when processes are designed. Process management is an ongoing activity, with the same principles applying to both first-time and redesign choices. Thus, the processes at Garrison Guitars must change and evolve with new technology and customer demands.

We begin by defining four basic process decisions: process structure, customer involvement, resource flexibility, and capital-intensity. We discuss these decisions for both service and manufacturing processes, and methods of focusing operations. We pay particular attention both to ways in which service strategy, capital-intensity, and customer involvement affect service operations and to methods for focusing operations. We then present a systematic approach to designing processes, using flow diagrams, process charts, and simulation. We conclude with two basic philosophies of analyzing and modifying processes—re-engineering and process improvement.

WHAT IS PROCESS MANAGEMENT?

A process involves the use of an organization's resources to provide something of value. No product can be made and no service provided without a process, and no process can exist without a product or service.

process management
The selection of the inputs, operations, work flows, and methods that transform inputs into outputs.

Process management is the design and selection of the inputs, operations, work flows, and methods that transform inputs into outputs. Input selection begins by deciding which processes are to be done in-house and which processes are to be done outside and purchased as materials and services. Process decisions also deal with the proper mix of human skills and equipment and which parts of the processes are to be performed by each. Decisions about processes must be consistent with competitive priorities and the organization's ability to obtain the resources necessary to support them.

Process decisions must be made when:

- A new or substantially modified product or service is being offered.

- Quality must be improved.

- Competitive priorities have changed.

- Demand for a product or service is changing.

- Current performance is inadequate.

- The cost or availability of inputs has changed.

- Competitors are gaining by using a new process.

- New technologies are available.

Not all such situations lead to changes in current processes. Process decisions must also take into account and will alter other aspects of operations, such as quality, capacity, layout, and inventory. Moreover, managers must consider advances in technology and changing competitor capabilities. The impact on the environment is another consideration. A good example is McDonald's. It made subtle changes in the processes used to package food, reducing waste by more than 30 percent since 1990 and becoming a leading buyer of recycled materials. The greening of McDonald's entailed replacing "clamshell" boxes with special lightweight paper, introducing shorter napkins, and relying less on plastics in straws, dining trays, and playground equipment. McDonald's is now looking at a plan to turn waste into fertilizer, so that eating out could generate less waste than eating at many homes.

There are three major principles concerning process decisions that are particularly important:

1. The key to successful process design is to make choices that both make sense for the competitive situation and cohesively fit together. They should not work at cross-purposes, with one process optimized at the expense of other processes. A more effective process is one that matches major process decisions and has close strategic alignment with customer value (see Figure 2.1).

2. Although this section focuses on individual processes, they are the building blocks that eventually create the firm's whole value chain. The cumulative effect on customer value and competitive advantage is huge.

FIGURE 2.1

Major Process Decisions

Process Structure
• customization-volume positioning
• customer, product, and information flows

Customer Involvment
• customer contact
• multiple modes of interaction

Major Process Decisions

Resource Flexibility
• specialized or general-purpose
• workforce and equipment

Capital Intensity
• economies of scale
• degree of automation

Strategic Alignment

Customer Value
• cusomer benefit bundle: cost, quality, time, flexibility, innovation

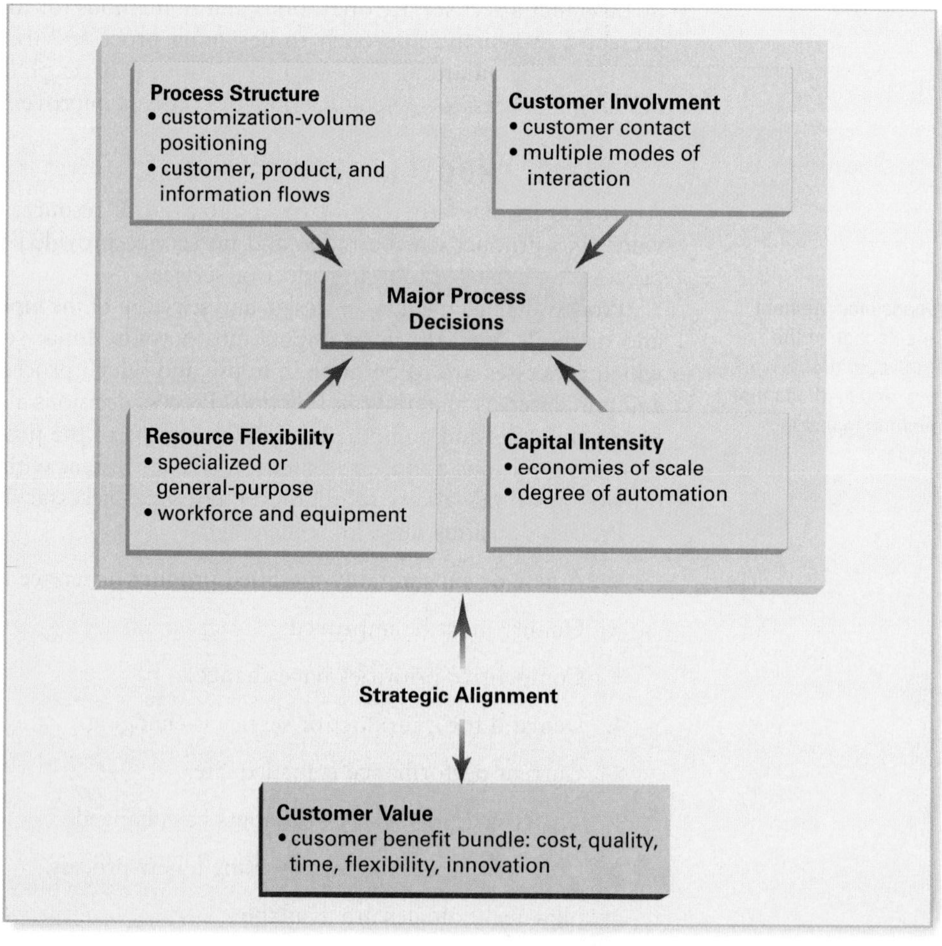

3. Whether processes in the value chain are performed internally or by outside suppliers, managers must pay particular attention to the interfaces between processes that connect the firm to suppliers and customers (see Chapter 9, "Supply Chain Management"). Having to deal with these interfaces underscores the need for cross-functional coordination.

Four

MAJOR PROCESS DECISIONS

Process decisions directly affect the process itself and indirectly affect the products and services that it provides. Whether dealing with processes for offices, service providers, or manufacturers, operations managers must consider four common process decisions: *process structure, customer involvement, resource flexibility,* and *capital-intensity.* Process decisions act as building blocks that are used in different ways to implement operations strategy, which collectively must be aligned to offer customer value, as depicted in Figure 2.1.

PROCESS STRUCTURE

One of the first decisions a manager makes in designing a well-functioning process is the **process structure**, which determines whether resources are organized around products or processes. The structure is strongly influenced by the competitive priorities (see Chapter 1, "Competing with Operations") given to the process. However, what is emphasized for the overall facility or product line is not necessarily what should be emphasized for each of the processes or subprocesses that contribute to creating the customer benefit bundle. The manager has four basic process structures, which form a continuum, to choose from: project, batch, line, and continuous flow.

Figure 2.2 shows that these types of processes are found in service and manufacturing organizations alike. The fundamental message in Figure 2.2 is that the best choice for a process depends on the volume and degree of customization required of the process. A process choice might apply to an entire process or just one subprocess within it. For example, one of a service facility's processes might best be characterized as a batch process and another process as a line process. Because our definition of a process in Chapter 1 provides a basic understanding of processes in general, we now concentrate on the differences among the four process structures.

PROJECT PROCESS. Examples of a project process are building a shopping centre, installing new enterprise resource planning (ERP) software, planning a major event, running a political campaign, putting together a comprehensive training program, doing management consulting work, or developing a new technology or product. A **project process** is characterized by a high degree of job customization, the large scope of each project, and the release of substantial resources once a project is completed (see Chapter 3, "Managing Projects").

A project process lies at the high-customization, low-volume end of the process-choice continuum. The sequence of operations and the process involved in each are unique to the project, creating one-of-a-kind products or services made specifically to customer order. Although some projects may look similar, each is unique. Project processes are valued on the basis of their capabilities to do certain kinds of work rather than on their ability to produce specific products or services. Projects tend to be complex, take a long time, and be large. Many interrelated tasks must be completed, requiring close coordination. Resources needed for a project are assembled and then released for further use after the project is finished. Projects typically make heavy use of certain skills and resources at particular stages and then have little use for them the rest of the time. With a project process, work flows are redefined with each new project.

process structure A process decision that determines whether resources are organized around products or processes.

project process A process characterized by a high degree of job customization, the large scope of each project, and the release of substantial resources once a project is completed.

*The Influence of
Customization and
Volume on Process
Structure*

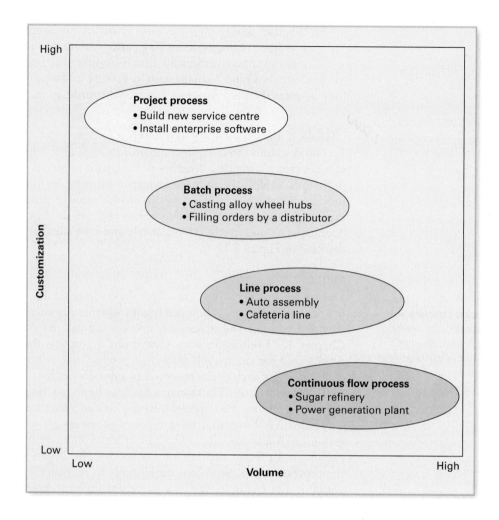

batch process A process
with the flexibility needed
to produce a wide variety
of services and products
in small to moderate
quantities. Resources
such as workers and
equipment are usually
grouped by task.

BATCH PROCESS. Next on the continuum of process choices is the **batch process**. Batches
can range in size from very small to much larger in size. Smaller batch processes, sometimes termed a *job shop* in manufacturing, include machining a metal casting for a customized order, providing emergency room care, handling special-delivery mail, and
making customized cabinets. In contrast, larger batch processes might include scheduling
air travel for a tour group, making components that feed an assembly line, processing a
group of similar mortgage loans, and manufacturing large earthmoving equipment.

The batch process creates the flexibility needed to produce a variety of products or
services in significant quantities. Customization is relatively high and volume for any
one product or service is low. However, volumes are not as low as for a project process,
which by definition does not produce in quantity. For manufacturing, products in small
batches tend to be produced as needed (i.e., make-to-order) and not ahead of time. The
specific needs of the next customer are unknown, and the timing of repeat orders from
the same customer is unpredictable.

A batch process tends to have resources grouped or organized by task rather than
allocating them to specific products and services. Thus, equipment and workers capable of certain types of work are located together, and these resources are more flexible
than the line process (described next) and handle various tasks. Because of customization, parts, orders, and customers will follow different routings between individual
process steps, as needed.

As batches become larger, the service and product range created by a batch process will decrease, and dominant routings emerge between process steps. Also, the greater volumes allow some components or products to be processed in advance or held in stock to improve process speed. Variety is achieved more through an assemble-to-order strategy than a make-to-order strategy.

line process A process with linear movement of materials, information, or customers from one operation to the next according to a fixed sequence. Volumes are relatively high, allowing resources to be organized around standardized services and products.

LINE PROCESS. Products created by a line process include automobiles, appliances, and toys. Services based on a line process are fast-food restaurants and cafeterias. A **line process** lies between the batch and continuous processes on the continuum; volumes are high and products or services are standardized, which allows resources to be organized around a product or service. There are line flows, with little inventory held between operations. Each operation performs the same process over and over, with little variability in the products or services provided.

Production orders are not directly linked to customer orders, as is the case with project and small batch processes. Service providers with a line process follow a standardized-services strategy. Manufacturers with line processes often follow a make-to-stock strategy, with standard products held in inventory so that they are ready when a customer places an order. This use of a line process is sometimes called *mass production*, which is what the popular press commonly refers to as a manufacturing process.

However, the assemble-to-order strategy and *mass customization* (see Chapter 1, "Competing with Operations") are other possibilities with line processes. Either of these process choices, which can employ new technologies such as flexible automation or modular product designs, expand this "bubble" upward on Figure 2.2. Product variety is possible by careful control of the addition of standard options to the main product or service.

continuous flow process The extreme end of high-volume, standardized production with rigid line flows.

CONTINUOUS FLOW PROCESS. Examples of companies that use continuous flow processes are petroleum refineries, chemical plants, and plants making beer, steel, and food (such as Lantic Sugar's large refinery operations in Montreal). Firms with such facilities are also referred to as the *process industry*. An electric generation plant represents one of the few continuous processes found in the service sector. A **continuous flow process** is the extreme end of high-volume, standardized production with rigid line flows. Its name derives from the way materials move through the process. Usually, one primary material, such as a liquid, gas, or powder, moves without stopping through the facility. The processes seem more like separate entities than a series of connected operations. The process is often capital-intensive and operated round the clock to maximize utilization and to avoid expensive shutdowns and startups.

CUSTOMER INVOLVEMENT

customer involvement The ways in which customers become part of the process and the extent of their participation.

The second significant process decision deals with **customer involvement**, the ways in which customers become part of the process and the extent of their participation. This is particularly important in services, as the customer is frequently being transformed by the process. A good way to begin increasing customer involvement is by making more of the process visible to the customer. Letting customers see what normally is hidden from them is part of the service design at Harvey's, a fast-food restaurant. There you can see workers in a sanitary and neat workplace grilling your meat, and you can pick the kinds and quantities of toppings desired as they assemble your hamburger.

To be sure, customer involvement also affects manufacturing firms, and is increasingly being used to improve competitiveness. Customers can provide detailed specifications used to customize products ranging from home furnishings to automobiles. One luxury manufacturer is taking customer involvement a significant step further.

BMW is launching a new initiative, BMW Welt ("World" in English), that will offer personalized delivery service of new vehicles directly from the manufacturer to their new owners. Approximately 170 vehicles each day are expected to be picked up by customers at the manufacturing plant in Munich by 2006.

What is effective customer involvement in one circumstance may provide little customer value in another. A quick, streamlined process with little customer interaction might work very well for a fast-food restaurant, yet be totally inappropriate for a five-star restaurant, where customers seek a leisurely dining experience with very attentive servers. Moreover, even within the same industry such as food service, firms can find very different, yet profitable, ways to involve customers.

Two dimensions are important to consider for customer involvement, particularly in service processes. First, management can choose to vary the extent of customer interaction or contact during the service process (Chase, 1981). Second, and just as critical, the amount of time that the customer interacts with the process, termed the **service encounter**, can vary significantly even within an industry (Schmenner, 2004). The service encounter begins when the customer and service process first meet, and continues until the customer completes the process. However, it should be stressed that the customer need not actually be transformed in the process, as with auto repair.

There are five factors that gauge the level of **customer interaction**, each of which forms a continuum: physical presence, what is being processed, intensity, personal attention, and mode of delivery (see Figure 2.3). The first factor is the extent to which the customer is *physically present* during the process. This can be approximated as the percentage of the total time the customer is at the process, relative to the total time to complete the service. When physical presence is required, either the customer comes to the facility, or the service providers and equipment travel to meet the customer.

The second factor is *what is being processed*, which could include the customer, the customer's possessions, or information. People-processing services involve tangible actions to people, such as transportation on an airline or filling a cavity. Naturally, these services require a customer to be present for at least part of the service. Possession-

service encounter The time during which a customer is in contact with a service process, starting from when the customer and process first meet, and finishing when the customer completes the process.

customer interaction The extent to which the customer is present, is actively engaged, and receives personalized, face-to-face attention during the process.

FIGURE 2.3

Factors for Assessing Customer Interaction

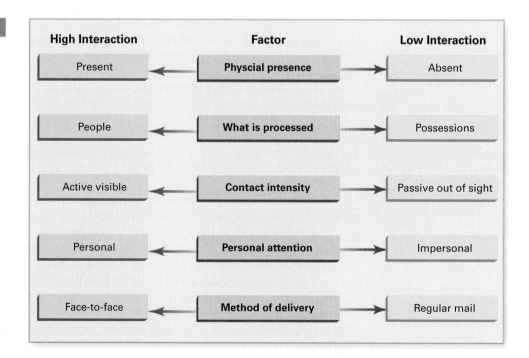

High Interaction	Factor	Low Interaction
Present	Physcial presence	Absent
People	What is processed	Possessions
Active visible	Contact intensity	Passive out of sight
Personal	Personal attention	Impersonal
Face-to-face	Method of delivery	Regular mail

processing services provide a transformation for a person, such as pet grooming or auto repair. The object must be present, but the customer may not be until the service is completed. Finally, information processing collects, analyzes, and transmits data, possibly with new insights, either using facts or opinions supplied by the customer or others. Financial planning, education, and legal services are examples of such services.

The *intensity* of contact goes beyond physical presence to examine the degree of

MANAGERIAL PRACTICE
Service Processes at the Ritz-Carlton

The Ritz-Carlton Hotel Company (www.ritzcarlton.com) targets the top 1 to 3 percent of luxury travellers, and so gives top quality a huge emphasis as a competitive priority. With its Montreal location being one of only 57 hotels and resorts worldwide, the goal is to not just exceed guests' expectations, but also staff expectations. Every employee carries a card with eight business-card-sized panels describing Ritz-Carlton's Gold Standards, which include an elegant and simple motto: "We are ladies and gentlemen serving ladies and gentlemen." There is a passion to have its people and processes behave in extraordinary ways, both toward their guests (external customers) and toward each other (often internal customers). They pay remarkable attention to every occasion during the customer encounter as an opportunity to either delight or disappoint customers, called "customer touch points." By one calculation, the average guest represents 1100 touch points each day, but not all of those touch points involve the customer's physical presence with an employee. Many of those points occur out of sight, such as in the kitchen, offices, or garage. Eventually, these are points that affect guests positively or negatively. Emphasis on high quality is codified and integrated into processes at each touch point.

The Ritz-Carlton manages details like few other organizations do. It is strongly process-driven, and sophisticated systems measure virtually every aspect of performance. It has an almost fanatical determination to drive quality improvements through all of its operations. It begins with hiring the right people for the 120 hotel-specific job positions. Current employees are involved in the interviewing process of new applicants, so that everyone feels responsible. After finding the right people, there is very extensive orientation and continuing education. Job certification is task-specific, depending on the processes that a person will perform.

A "daily lineup" is required of everyone, every day. These lineups feature typical announcements on new policies, recognitions, and so on. Most interesting are the stories of excep-

The Ritz-Carlton's sophisticated processes allow it to manage details like few other hotels do. Employees are encouraged to treat not only guests graciously, but each other, too.

tional behaviour toward guests. In every daily lineup, employees are encouraged to share stories of exceptional customer care. The great stories are remembered and repeated, communicating not only what's possible but what's expected. When employees encounter situations where guests' needs are not being met, they are expected to take charge of the problem and follow it through to resolution. They are empowered to spend up to $2000 per guest to resolve complaints or problems. Customers with complaints are not passed along to "the person who can help you." Part of the job is to take responsibility for getting such problems fixed. Employees and the processes they perform seek to "enliven the senses, instill well-being, and fulfill even the unexpressed wishes of their guests."

Source: Bacon, Terry R., and David G. Pugh. "Ritz-Carlton and EMC: The Gold Standards in Operational Behavioral Differentiation." *Journal of Organizational Excellence* (Spring 2004), pp. 61–76; www.ritzcarlton.com/corporate/about_us/ (accessed October 7, 2005).

interaction between the service provider and the customer. Active contact means that the customer is very much part of the creation of the service and affects the service process itself. The process is also very visible to the customer. Passive contact means that the customer is not interacting with the process, but instead may simply be waiting in line. Passive processes can include public transportation or theatres.

A fourth factor is the extent of *personal attention* offered. Highly attentive processes tend to be more intimate, with a higher degree of trust and richer range of information exchanged. As a result, the customer often experiences the service rather than simply receiving it. For example, highly personalized service is critical for enabling the Ritz-Carlton hotel in Montreal to exceed its customers' expectations (see the Managerial Practice feature). Impersonal contact at times can translate into customers feeling as if they are merely numbers in the system, as may be the case when waiting in line for government services.

The final factor of customer contact is the *mode of delivery*. A high-interaction mode would use face-to-face or telephone contact (with a human operator), assuring more clarity in identifying and satisfying customer needs. Low-interaction modes might include postal mail and billboard advertising.

Customer interaction and service encounter time combine to form a wide range of service processes, even within the same industry (see Figure 2.4). At one extreme, we have services that are factory-like, such as a fast-food restaurant or cheque-clearing operation in a bank, where the service encounter is very short and interaction is low. At the other extreme, professional services, such as a gourmet restaurant or design by an architect, require interaction with highly skilled staff over a relatively longer period of time. Two other categories, service shop or mass service, capture either more interaction or a longer service encounter when compared to the service factory. However, both scales really form a continuous spectrum, and service processes should usually be compared relative to each other within the same industry. Overall, productivity improves as a service process shifts toward the lower-right quadrant (Schmenner, 2004).

FIGURE 2.4

*Customer Involvement
for Service Processes*

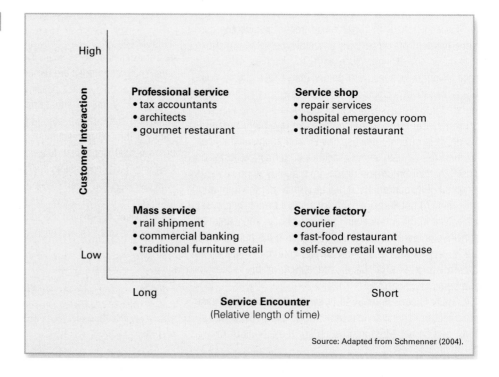

SERVICE FACTORY. The service factory has low customer interaction and a short service encounter. The work tends to be standardized and routine, with line flows from one operation to another until the service is completed. An example is the monthly production of client fund balance reports for a mutual fund company. The process doesn't vary, is repeated frequently, and requires very little attention. Because these processes usually occur behind the scenes and are not visible to the customer, the term "back office" is sometimes used. The primary emphasis here is often cost efficiency, and not surprisingly, these processes also tend to be highly automated. The typical process structure is a line or continuous flow process.

SERVICE SHOP. The service shop tends to have a higher level of customer interaction than the service factory because the service must be at least partially customized to meet the unique needs of individuals or small groups (i.e., small batches). Workstations and equipment tend to be organized by task with various routings between them. The work is reasonably complex, possibly involving skilled professionals for at least part of the process, such as a hospital emergency room or auto repair, but the overall time for the service encounter remains relatively short. Moreover, some steps may be performed ahead of time (e.g., preparation of medical instruments), while other steps, such as the doctor–patient diagnosis, must be tailored to the individual. Thus, some efficiency may be sacrificed to improve overall effectiveness in meeting individual needs.

MASS SERVICE. In contrast to the service shop, mass services tend to have much less interaction to improve efficiency and cost. As a result, the service encounter tends to be longer with little customization. Also, to improve productivity, many mass services, such as education and public transit, handle large groups of customers simultaneously (i.e., large batches). Customers follow the same ordering of steps through the process, although the particular product or service may vary. Web-based retailing is typically a mass service, with relatively little interaction with customers (although new designs and customer tracking capabilities are increasing this process), and additional time required for the service encounter. While different products are purchased by customers, they all follow the same basic steps: visit the retail Web site, search for merchandise, add to shopping cart, make payment, assemble and ship the order, and receive delivery.

PROFESSIONAL SERVICE. Finally, both high customer interaction and long service encounters characterize a professional service, with the service provider working directly with the customer. The service is usually adjusted and tailored to individual customer needs, with a wide variety of options. The process is complex and steps may be followed in a flexible order to suit individual requirements. Rather than focus on low cost, professional services emphasize effectiveness, including high quality, timely responsiveness, and flexibility. Examples include law offices and tax accountants. Here, the process structure tends to be oriented toward project or small batch process.

INTERNET-BASED INVOLVEMENT. The Internet, including such technologies as Web browsers, search engines, and e-mail, has added a rich new mode of customer interaction. Collectively, these technologies offer the potential to greatly expand the scope, flexibility, location, and variety in the service or manufacturing process. Both whole processes and subprocesses nested within them can be conducted over the Internet for either business-to-business (B2B) or business-to-consumer (B2C) markets. Internet-based customer involvement offers process managers much more than simply automating the buying and selling of goods electronically. Firms can significantly improve their processes to yield competitive advantages by cutting costs, improving quality, and increasing speed and flexibility.

At first glance, managers might be tempted to think that Web-enabled processes only work to increase customer involvement by reducing the time for the service encounter, by expanding access and variety, and by increasing customization. However, managers can use the Web to either increase *or* decrease the level of customer involvement depending on the service strategy. Processes that traditionally had high-contact modes, such as telephone contact with a staff member or physical presence in a retail branch, can be altered to lower Web-based interaction. Banking is one such service, where customers can now do virtually all of their banking over the Internet rather than in a physical bank branch. However, other services such as billing and monthly statements have been moved from a low-contact mode with slow postal mailings to the immediate delivery of e-mail statements.

The Internet also enables companies to engage in an active dialogue with customers and make them partners in creating value. Customers can become a new source of competence for such processes. To harness customer competencies, companies must involve customers in an ongoing dialogue. For example, Wal-Mart does more than just distribute Procter and Gamble's products—it shares daily sales information that managers at Procter and Gamble can use in planning and production.

RESOURCE FLEXIBILITY

resource flexibility The ease with which employees and equipment can handle a wide variety of products, output levels, duties, and functions.

The choices that management makes concerning competitive priorities determine the degree of flexibility required of a company's resources—its employees, facilities, and equipment. **Resource flexibility** is the ease with which employees and equipment can handle a wide variety of products, output levels, duties, and functions. For example, when a process handles products and services with short life cycles or high customization, employees need to perform a broad range of duties and equipment must be general-purpose. Otherwise, resource utilization will be too low for economical operation.

flexible workforce A workforce whose members are capable of doing many tasks, either at their own workstations or as they move from one workstation to another.

WORKFORCE. Operations managers must decide whether to have a flexible workforce. Members of a **flexible workforce** are capable of doing many tasks, either at their own workstations or as they move from one workstation to another. However, such flexibility often comes at a cost, requiring greater skills and, thus, more training and education. Nevertheless, benefits can be large: worker flexibility can be one of the best ways to achieve reliable customer service and alleviate capacity bottlenecks. Resource flexibility helps to absorb the feast-or-famine workloads in individual operations that are caused by low-volume production, varied routings, and fluid scheduling.

The type of workforce required also depends on the need for volume flexibility. When conditions allow for a smooth, steady rate of output, the likely choice is a permanent workforce that expects regular full-time employment. If the process is subject to hourly, daily, or seasonal peaks and valleys in demand, the use of part-time or temporary employees to supplement a smaller core of full-time employees may be the best solution. However, this approach may not be practical if knowledge and skill requirements are too high for a temporary worker to grasp quickly. Controversy continues to grow over the practice of replacing full-time workers with temporary or part-time workers.

EQUIPMENT. When products or services have a short life cycle and a high degree of customization, low volumes mean that process managers should select flexible, general-purpose equipment. Figure 2.5 illustrates this relationship by showing the total cost lines for two different types of equipment that can be chosen for a process. Each line

FIGURE 2.5

Relationship Between Process Costs and Product Volume

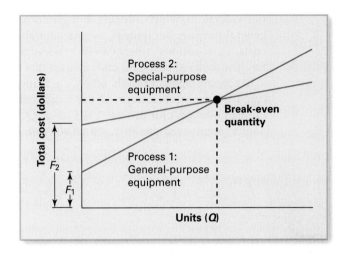

represents the total annual cost of the process at different volume levels. It is the sum of fixed costs and variable costs. When volumes are low (because customization is high), process 1 is the better choice. It calls for inexpensive general-purpose equipment, which keeps investment in equipment low and makes fixed costs (F_1) small. Its variable unit cost is high, which gives its total cost line a relatively steep slope. However, volumes are not high enough for the high variable costs to outweigh the benefit of low fixed costs.

Conversely, process 2 is the better choice when volumes are high and customization is low. Its advantage is low variable unit cost, as reflected in the flatter total cost line. This efficiency is possible when customization is low because the equipment can be designed for a narrow range of products or tasks. Its disadvantage is high equipment investment and, thus, high fixed costs (F_2). When the annual volume produced is high enough, spreading these fixed costs over more units produced, the advantage of low variable costs more than compensates for the high fixed costs.

CAPITAL-INTENSITY

capital-intensity The mix of equipment and human skill in a process.

For either the design of a new process or the redesign of an existing one, an operations manager must determine the amount of capital-intensity required. **Capital-intensity** is the mix of equipment and human skills in a process; the greater the relative cost of equipment, the greater the capital-intensity. As the capabilities of technology increase and its costs decrease, managers face an ever-widening range of choices, from operations utilizing very little automation to those requiring task-specific equipment and very little human intervention. **Automation** is a system, process, or piece of equipment that is self-acting and self-regulating. Although automation is often thought to be necessary to gain competitive advantage, it has both advantages and disadvantages. Thus, the automation decision requires careful examination.

automation A system, process, or piece of equipment that is self-acting and self-regulating.

One advantage of automation is that adding capital-intensity can significantly increase productivity and improve quality. One big disadvantage of capital-intensity can be the prohibitive investment cost for low-volume operations. Generally, capital-intensive operations must have high utilization to be justifiable. Also, automation does not always align with an organization's competitive priorities. If a firm offers a unique product or high-quality service, competitive priorities may indicate the need for skilled servers, hand labour, and individual attention rather than new technology.

Look again at Figure 2.5. Financially, this decision about capital-intensity involves a trade-off between fixed and variable costs. By comparing total cost, we can identify the volume at which process 1 is preferred over process 2. Process 1, which uses general-purpose equipment, is not capital-intensive and, therefore, has small fixed costs, F_1. Customer orders can be processed in smaller batches. In contrast, process 2, has greater fixed costs, F_2, and involves more continuous processing. However, process 1 has much higher variable costs, v_1, than process 2 with variable costs, v_2, as indicated by the steeper slope of the total cost line. Thus, the total cost to produce Q (annual quantity) for process 1 is $F_1 + v_1Q$, and for process 2 is $F_2 + v_2Q$. To find the annual break-even quantity, we set the two cost functions equal and solve for Q:

$$F_1 + v_1Q = F_2 + v_2Q$$

$$Q = \frac{F_1 - F_2}{v_2 - v_1}$$

EXAMPLE 2.1   *Break-Even Analysis for Two Process Configurations*

A county elections officer is considering installing new voting equipment to replace antiquated equipment. Two options are being considered. The first uses the latest in voting technology with electronic voting terminals. Cast ballots could be processed, checked, and tallied continuously using terminals similar to an ATM. The officer estimates the fixed cost for all the necessary terminals is $131 500 and variable costs total $0.20 per ballot. The second, more traditional process technology uses a centralized optical vote-card reader to process the ballots in a single batch. Ballots would be shipped to the central location from individual polling stations after closing. Estimated costs of this option are $46 800 for new equipment, and $2.40 per vote cast. The officer expects that, on average, a total of 25 000 ballots will be cast in various local, provincial, and federal elections in the county each year.

What is the break-even quantity?

SOLUTION

The formula for the break-even quantity yields:

$$Q = \frac{F_1 - F_2}{v_2 - v_1}$$

$$= \frac{131\ 500 - 46\ 800}{2.40 - 0.20} = 38\ 500$$

where:

F_1 = Fixed cost for process 1
v_1 = Variable cost per unit for process 1
F_2 = Fixed cost for process 2
v_2 = Variable cost per unit for process 2

The break-even quantity is 38 500 cast ballots. As the 25 000-vote forecast is less than this amount, the centralized optical vote-card reader is preferred. Only if the county expected to have more than 38 500 ballots cast each year would the use of electronic voting terminals be better financially. However, other factors to consider might include monitoring vote quality (including overvoting, in which too many candidates are selected on the ballot), flexibility, and ease of completion.

Decision Point The elections officer chose the traditional process technology with a centralized optical vote-card reader and batch processing. Voter education for proper completion of the ballots was also implemented. A deciding factor was that the annual volume was well below the 38 500-ballot break-even point.

FIXED AUTOMATION. Manufacturers use two types of automation: fixed and flexible (or programmable). Particularly appropriate for line and continuous process choices, **fixed automation** produces one type of part or product in a fixed sequence of simple operations. Until the mid-1980s, many automobile plants were dominated by fixed automation—and some still are. Chemical processing plants and oil refineries also utilize this type of automation.

Operations managers favour fixed automation when demand volumes are high, product designs are stable, and product life cycles are long. These conditions compensate for the process's two primary drawbacks: large initial investment cost and relative inflexibility. However, fixed automation maximizes efficiency and yields the lowest variable cost per unit if volumes are high.

FLEXIBLE AUTOMATION. **Flexible (or programmable) automation** can be changed easily to handle various products. The ability to reprogram machines is useful for both low-customization and high-customization processes. In the case of high customization, a machine that makes a variety of products in small batches can be programmed to alternate between products. When a machine has been dedicated to a particular product or family of products, as in the case of low customization and a line flow, and the product is at the end of its life cycle, the machine can simply be reprogrammed with a new sequence of operations for a new product. However, such flexibility comes at a price, as the operating speed might be slower or the capital cost higher than for fixed automation.

Canada is one of the industrialized-world leaders in applying flexible automation, on the basis of robots per capita. Throughout the 1990s, much of this technology in

fixed automation A manufacturing process that produces one type of part or product in a fixed sequence of simple operations.

flexible (or programmable) automation A manufacturing process that can be changed easily to handle various products.

Flexible automation is used to sort milk containers at a dairy in Denmark.

North America was applied in the automotive sector. However, an increasing number of applications have been developed in the food, pharmaceutical, and electronics industries, particularly with materials handling (Guidoni, 2000). For example, ABB Flexible Automation offers systems that can palletize loads to specific customer orders, which reduces the cost of distribution. Another new direction is laser cutting and trimming, as noted with Garrison Guitars at the beginning of this chapter. Regardless of the application, the president of FANUC Robotics Canada stressed, "The critical element is understanding the process flow."

STRATEGIC ALIGNMENT

The process manager should understand how these four process decisions—process structure, customer involvement, resource flexibility, and capital-intensity—must tie together, so as to spot ways of improving poorly designed processes. Two common elements in these relationships are volume and product/service variety, which in turn are derived from an underlying operations strategy.

Figure 2.6 summarizes the general relationship between volume and process decisions, and applies to all operations. However, customer involvement is often particularly critical for service processes.

High volumes typically translate into all of the following:

1. *A line or continuous flow process.* Standardized flows are preferred, with customers or products moving through a consistent series of steps. Each customer

FIGURE 2.6

Volume and the Major Process Decisions

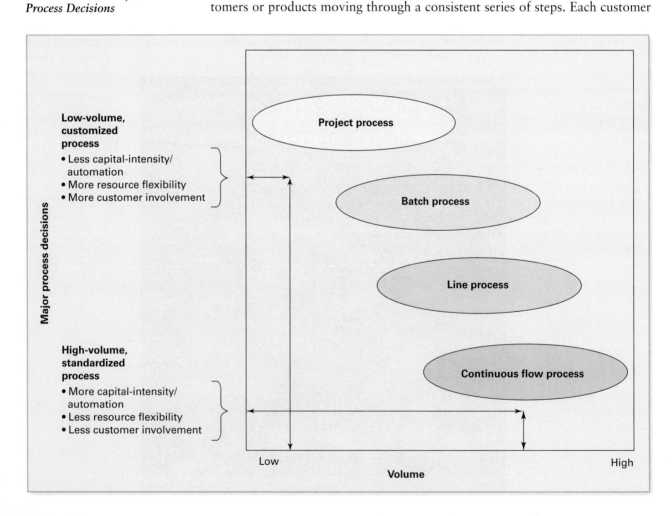

gets the same basic service, and service specifications are tightly controlled. Standardized products increase volumes and process repeatability. One example is the front-end process of a cafeteria line, where the customer moves from one station to the next, making food selections and then paying at the end of the line. Other examples include processes in public transportation; auto assembly; backroom processes in banking, insurance, and postal service; oil refining; and airport baggage handling.

2. *Less customer involvement.* For services, customers may not be present because the process has little variation, as with the backroom operations of financial institutions. Less contact occurs between employees and customers, and customized orders and requests are difficult to accommodate. If the customer is involved in the process, it is in performing self-service activities to get lower prices or in selecting from standard product options rather than getting unique customized treatment.

3. *Less resource flexibility.* High process volumes and repetition create less need for resource flexibility, which is usually more expensive. Instead, specialization and simplification is possible, which reduces capital and labour costs. Resources are dedicated to each standardized product or service, and personnel can focus on a narrower set of tasks repeated more frequently.

4. *More capital-intensity and automation.* High volumes justify large fixed costs and increase repetition, which can improve the efficiency of operations. Because customers are usually less involved with the process, automation possibilities increase. Capital-intensity is high, with much less labour content needed to deliver the product. Of course, there can be exceptions to always automating processes for standardized high-volume goods and services. Examples are wholesalers and full-service retailers. In such cases, capital-intensity is low because the nature of the work being done makes it difficult to achieve automation for these processes.

Low volumes typically mean all of the following:

1. *A project or small batch process.* Customized treatment means a low-volume process, and each customer requires different changes in the process itself. Examples are processes for management consultants, physicians, gourmet restaurants, and construction. Each customer has individual needs that must be understood and accounted for in the process.

2. *More customer involvement.* Front-line employees interact more frequently with customers, often on a one-to-one basis, to understand and diagnose each customer's individual needs. They must be able to relate well to their customers, not merely possess technical skills. Exercising judgment as they provide new or unique products and services—often termed "solutions"—is commonplace.

3. *More resource flexibility.* Employees and equipment must be trained and able to handle new or unique services as demand occurs and changes. Thus, they must be versatile and flexible and able to handle a wide array of customer requests. Skill levels are high and the scope of activities is enlarged, often with a great deal of operating discretion.

4. *Less capital-intensity and automation.* Because of an almost infinite variability of problems and customer specifications, the process is difficult to automate,

although flexible automation might be possible. Generally, capital-intensity is low, which means high labour-intensity. It should be noted that some low-volume processes are capital-intensive because particular equipment is needed regardless of the volume (e.g., medical diagnostics). With specialized processes, such as product design and health care, employee skill levels are very high and expensive.

Of course, these are general tendencies rather than rigid prescriptions. Exceptions can be found, but these relationships provide a way of understanding how process decisions can be linked coherently.

ECONOMIES OF SCOPE

Note that capital-intensity and resource flexibility vary inversely in Figure 2.6. If capital-intensity is high, resource flexibility is low. In certain types of manufacturing operations, such as machining and assembly, programmable automation breaks this inverse relationship between resource flexibility and capital-intensity. It makes possible both high capital-intensity and high resource flexibility, creating economies of scope. **Economies of scope** reflect the ability to produce multiple products more cheaply in combination than separately. In such situations, two conflicting competitive priorities—customization and low price—become more compatible. However, taking advantage of economies of scope requires that a family of parts or products have enough collective volume to utilize equipment fully. Adding a product to the family results in one-time programming (and sometimes fixture) costs. (*Fixtures* are reusable devices that maintain exact tolerances by holding the product firmly in position while it is processed.)

economies of scope Economies that reflect the ability to produce multiple products more cheaply in combination than separately.

Economies of scope also apply to service processes. Consider, for example, Disney's approach to the Internet. When the company's managers entered the volatile Internet world, their businesses were only weakly tied together. They wanted plenty of freedom to evolve in and even shape emerging markets. They wanted flexibility and agility, not control, in these fast-moving markets. Disney's Infoseek business, in fact, was not even fully owned. However, once its Internet markets became more crystallized, managers at Disney moved to reap the benefits of economies of scope. They aggressively linked their Internet processes with one another and with other parts of Disney. They bought the rest of the Infoseek business and then combined it with Internet businesses such as Disney Travel Online into a single business (Go.com). They made their content Web sites accessible from a single portal (Go Network) and created new links to established businesses like ESPN. A flexible technology that handles many services together can be less expensive than handling each one separately, particularly when the markets are not too volatile.

GAINING FOCUS

Before 1970, many firms were willing to endure the additional complexity that went with size. New products or services were added to a facility in the name of better utilizing fixed costs and keeping everything under the same roof. The result was a jumble of competitive priorities, process choices, and technologies. In the effort to do everything, nothing was done well.

focused factories The result of a firm's splitting large plants that produced all the company's products into several specialized smaller plants.

FOCUSED FACTORIES. Canada's Palliser Furniture, Venmar Ventilation, and Magna International, the U.S.'s Hewlett-Packard and SC Johnson, Japan's Ricoh and Mitsubishi, and Britain's Imperial Chemical Industries PLC are some of the firms that have created **focused factories**, splitting large plants that produced all the company's products into several specialized smaller plants. The theory is that narrowing the range of demands on a facility will lead to better performance because management can concentrate on fewer tasks and lead a workforce toward a single goal. In some situations, a plant that used to produce all the components of a product and assemble them may split into one that produces the components and one that assembles them so that each can focus on its own individual process technology.

FOCUS BY PROCESS SEGMENTS. A facility's process often can neither be characterized nor actually designed for one set of competitive priorities and one process choice. At a services facility, some parts of the process might seem like a job process and other parts like a line process. Such arrangements can be effective, provided that sufficient focus is given to each process. **Plants within plants (PWPs)** are different operations within a facility with individual competitive priorities, processes, and workforces under the same roof. Boundaries for PWPs may be established by physically separating subunits or simply by revising organizational relationships. At each PWP, customization, capital-intensity, volume, and other relationships are crucial and must be complementary. The advantages of PWPs are fewer layers of management, greater ability to rely on team problem solving, and shorter lines of communication among departments.

Another way of gaining focus is with the use of cells. A **cell** is a group of two or more dissimilar workstations located close to each other that process a limited number of parts or models with similar process requirements. A cell has line flows, even though the operations around it may have flexible flows (see Chapter 7, "Location and Layout"). The small size of focused factories, PWPs, and cells offers a flexible, agile system that competes better on the basis of short lead times.

FOCUSED SERVICE OPERATIONS. Service industries have also implemented the concepts of focus, PWPs, and cells. For example, Toronto's Rogers Centre has executive boxes with unique services and equipment that operate within the same facility and for the same entertainment events as customers purchasing basic tickets. Air Canada also differentiates between first- and economy-class customers with particular service processes. Finally, specialty retailers, such as the Gap, have opened stores that have smaller, more accessible spaces. These focused facilities have generally chipped away at the business of large department stores. Using the same philosophy, some department stores are focusing on specific customers or products, with remodelled interiors creating the effect of many small boutiques under one roof.

PROCESS ANALYSIS

The four main process decisions encompass broad, strategic issues. The next critical concern in process management is determining exactly how each process is performed. We begin with a structured approach to analyzing a process, spotting areas for improvement, developing ways to improve them, and implementing the desired changes. The following section offers two different but complementary philosophies for developing better processes: process re-engineering and process improvement.

A SYSTEMATIC APPROACH

Managers or teams might use process re-engineering or process improvement, but process analysis should follow a systematic procedure. Here is a six-step procedure that can pay off with improvements:

1. *Describe the strategic dimensions of the process.* How is customer value defined and what is the customer benefit bundle? What are the competitive

plants within plants (PWPs) Different operations within a facility with individual competitive priorities, processes, and workforces under the same roof.

cell A group of two or mor dissimilar workstations located close to each other that process a limited number of parts or models with similar process requirements.

priorities, operations strategy, process structure, and other major process decisions that apply?

2. *Identify the inputs, outputs, and customers of the process.* Make a comprehensive list so that the value-added capability of the process can be evaluated. Consider both internal and external customers.

3. *Identify the important performance measures, sometimes called "metrics," of the process.* These should be specifically tied to dimensions of customer value. Possible performance measures could be multiple measures of quality, customer satisfaction, throughput time, cost, errors, safety, environmental measures, on-time delivery, flexibility, and the like.

4. *Document the process.* Use "as is" for an ongoing process and "as proposed" for a process being designed for the first time. Be particularly alert for one or more of the following characteristics:

   ● Customers are dissatisfied with the value of the product or service that they receive from the process.

   ● The process introduces too many quality problems or errors.

   ● The process is slow in responding to customers.

   ● The process is costly.

   ● The process is often a bottleneck (see Chapter 4, "Capacity"), with work piling up waiting to go through it.

   ● The process creates disagreeable work, pollution, waste, or adds little value.

   Collect information on each part of the process and for each of the performance measures selected in step 3. Whenever possible, benchmark against similar processes within or external to the firm to expose areas of substandard performance.

5. *Critically question how the process might create better customer value.* In order to do so, the manager or team should ask six questions:

   a. *What* is being done?
   b. *When* is it being done?
   c. *Who* is doing it?
   d. *Where* is it being done?
   e. *How* is it being done?
   f. *How well* does it do on the various performance measures?

Xerox has invested significantly to create 4100 jobs in two new facilities in Ireland. Benchmarking has helped Xerox create state-of-the-art facilities. Here, teams of technicians explore ways to improve products.

Answers to these questions are challenged by asking still another series of questions. *Why* is the process even being done? *Why* is it being done where it is being done? *Why* is it being done when it is being done? Such questioning often leads to creative answers and breakthroughs in process design. Once again, benchmarking against processes elsewhere, either inside or outside the organization, can pay off with new ideas and substantial improvements.

6. *Evaluate the changes and implement those that appear to give the best payoffs on the various performance measures selected in step 3.* Later on, after the process has been changed, check to see whether the changes worked. Go back to step 1 as needed.

DOCUMENT THE PROCESS

Documenting the process requires a detailed understanding of all of the tasks that happen within a process, including both value-added and non–value-added activities. Doing so allows the manager to "lift the lid" and peer inside how an organization does its work. You see how a process operates at any level of detail, and how well it is performing. Trying to construct one of these diagrams or charts also may reveal that there is no established process! When breaking down the process into the specific steps performed, the degree of customer involvement and process complexity become much clearer.

Three techniques are effective for documenting and evaluating processes: flow diagrams, process charts, and simulation. Later, we will expand these three techniques to consider additional tools that focus on quality improvement (see Chapter 5, "Quality"). These techniques involve the systematic observation and recording of process details to allow better assessment. They also lend themselves to brainstorming the process for improvements, which is step 5. Finally, they are useful for performing step 6 because they should be reapplied to the newly proposed process, along with information on how performance measures are affected. Thus, they provide a "before" and "after" look at the process. Important inputs to these three techniques are time estimates of how long it takes to do various tasks.

flow diagram A diagram that traces the flow of information, customers, employees, equipment, or materials through a process.

FLOW DIAGRAMS. A **flow diagram** traces the flow of information, customers, employees, equipment, or materials through a process. There is no precise format, and the diagram can be drawn simply with boxes, lines, and arrows. Figure 2.7 is a diagram of an automobile repair process, beginning with the customer's call for an appointment and ending with the customer's pickup of the car and departure. In this figure, the dotted *line of visibility* divides activities that are directly visible to the customers from those that are not visible. Such information is particularly valuable for service operations involving considerable customer contact. Operations that are essential to success and where failure occurs most often are identified. Other formats are just as acceptable, and it is often helpful to list important performance metrics beside each step, such as total elapsed time, quality losses, error rate, capacity, and cost.

Sometimes flow diagrams are overlaid on a facility's layout. To make this special kind of flow diagram, the analyst first does a rough sketch of the area in which the process is performed. On a grid, the analyst plots the path followed by the person, material, or equipment, using arrows to indicate the direction of movement or flow.

process chart An organized way of documenting all the activities performed on a customer or product by a person, a group of people, equipment, or a workstation.

PROCESS CHARTS. A **process chart** is an organized way of documenting the purpose of all the activities performed on a subject by a person, a group of people, equipment, or a workstation. The subject can be a customer, possession, product, or data. For example, a process chart may track a patient with an ankle injury moving through an emer-

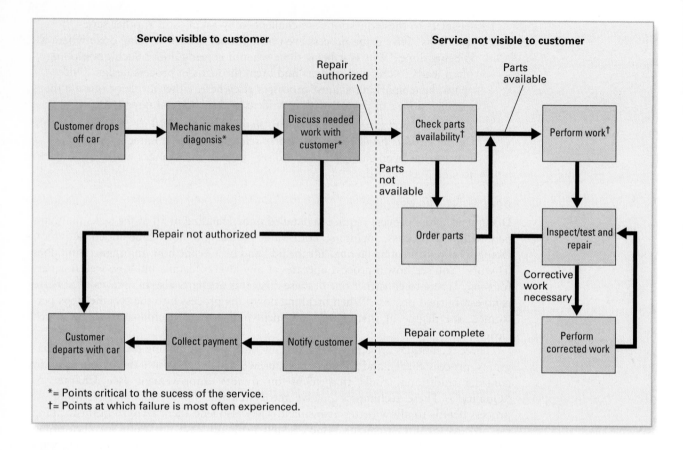

FIGURE 2.7

Flow Diagram for Automobile Repair (Created with SmartDraw)

gency room. Data are presented in a tabular form, and can summarize a rich set of information on each step in the process. Often data are used to drill down to the job level for an individual person, a team, or a focused nested process. Here we group the type of activities for a typical process into five categories:

- *Operation.* Changes, creates, or adds something. Drilling a hole and serving a customer are examples of operations.

- *Transportation.* Moves the study's subject from one place to another (sometimes called *materials handling*). A customer walking from one end of a counter to the other, a crane hoisting a steel beam to a location, and a conveyor carrying a partially completed product from one workstation to the next are examples of transportation.

- *Inspection.* Checks or verifies something but does not change it. Checking for blemishes on a surface, weighing a product, and taking a temperature reading are examples of inspections.

- *Delay.* Occurs when the subject is held up awaiting further action. Time spent waiting for materials or equipment, cleanup time, and time that workers, machines, or workstations are idle because there is nothing for them to do are examples of delays.

- *Storage.* Occurs when something is put away until a later time. Supplies unloaded and placed in a storeroom as inventory, equipment put away after use, and papers put in a file cabinet are examples of storage.

Depending on the situation, other categories can be used. For example, subcontracting for outside services might be a category, or temporary storage and permanent storage might be two separate categories. Choosing the right category for each activity requires taking the perspective of the subject charted. A delay for the equipment could be inspection or transportation for the operator.

To complete a chart for a new process, the analyst must identify each step performed. If the process is an existing one, the analyst can actually observe the steps, categorizing each one according to the subject being studied. The analyst then records the distance travelled and the time taken to perform each step. After recording all the activities and steps, the analyst summarizes the number of steps, the times, and the distances data. Figure 2.8 shows a process chart prepared for a patient with a twisted ankle being treated at a hospital. The process begins at the entrance and ends with the patient exiting after picking up the prescription.

After a process is charted, the analyst sometimes estimates the annual cost of the entire process. It becomes a benchmark against which other methods for performing the process can be evaluated. Annual labour cost can be estimated by finding the

FIGURE 2.8

Process Chart for Emergency Room Admission (Created with OM Explorer)

Solver - Process Charts

Enter data in yellow shaded areas.

Process: Emergency room admission

Subject: Ankle injury patient

Beginning: Enter emergency room

Ending: Leave Hospital

Insert Step

Append Step

Remove Step

Summary

Activity		Number of Steps	Time (min)	Distance (m)
Operation	●	5	23.00	
Transport	➡	9	11.00	255
Inspect	■	2	8.00	
Delay	▶	3	8.00	
Store	▼	--	--	

Step No.	Time (min)	Distance (m)	●	➡	■	▶	▼	Step Description
1	0.50	5.0			X			Enter emergency room, approach patient window
2	10.00		X					Sit down and fill out patient history
3	0.75	15.0			X			Nurse escorts patient to ER triage room
4	3.00					X		Nurse inspects injury
5	0.75	15.0			X			Return to waiting room
6	1.00						X	Wait for available bed
7	1.00	20.0			X			Go to ER bed
8	4.00						X	Wait for doctor
9	5.00					X		Doctor inspects injury and questions patient
10	2.00	60.0			X			Nurse takes patient to radiology
11	3.00		X					Technician x-rays patient
12	2.00	60.0		X				Return to bed in ER
13	3.00						X	Wait for doctor to return
14	2.00		X					Doctor provides diagnosis and advice
15	1.00	20.0		X				Return to emergency entrance area
16	4.00		X					Check out
17	2.00	50.0		X				Walk to pharmacy
18	4.00		X					Pick up prescription
19	1.00	10.0			X			Leave the building

product of (1) time in hours to perform the process each time, (2) variable costs per hour, and (3) number of times the process is performed each year:

$$\text{Annual labour cost} = \left(\begin{array}{c}\text{Time to perform}\\ \text{the process}\end{array}\right)\left(\begin{array}{c}\text{Variable costs}\\ \text{per hour}\end{array}\right)\left(\begin{array}{c}\text{Number of times process}\\ \text{performed per year}\end{array}\right)$$

In the case of the patient in Figure 2.8, this conversion wouldn't be necessary, with total patient time being sufficient. What is being tracked is the patient's time, not the time and costs of the service providers.

SIMULATION MODELS. A flow diagram is a simple but powerful tool for understanding each of the activities that make up a process and how they tie together. A process chart provides information similar to a table rather than a diagram but also provides time and cost information for the process. A simulation model goes one step further by showing how the process performs dynamically over time. **Simulation** is an act of reproducing the behaviour of a process using a model that describes each step of the process. Once the current process is modelled, the analyst can make changes in the process to measure the impact on certain performance measures, such as response time, waiting lines, resource utilization, and the like. To learn more about how simulation works, see Supplement G, "Simulation," on the Student CD-ROM.

ROBUST DESIGN. One goal of documenting the process is to assess the robustness of the process. A **robust process design** continues to effectively deliver customer value, despite uncertainty, changes, and problems. As part of the design process, managers and engineers must specify targets for inputs and operating conditions. However, minor variations from these ideal targets often cause the process to operate poorly, generating waste or creating customer dissatisfaction. Instead, careful process design and improvement can reduce the sensitivity of the process to small changes from "ideal." For example, a supplier might occasionally ship flour to a cookie bakery with higher or lower moisture content than is ideal. However, a process design that monitors the moisture level of the dough and baked cookies in real time allows the process to adapt to this variation, and continue to produce high-quality products with little change in waste and cost.

DEVELOPING A BETTER PROCESS

Process analysis and documentation are really means to an end: a better process with greater customer value (effectiveness) and less waste (efficiency). Generally speaking, waste is a poor use of process resources. Processes can be designed or redesigned using two different approaches: process re-engineering and process improvement (see Figure 2.9). In general, process re-engineering should be viewed as radical, dramatic change; something to be undertaken only occasionally. In contrast, process improvement is an ongoing necessity as customer needs evolve, competitors adapt, and the marketplace develops. We begin with process re-engineering, which is getting considerable attention today in management circles.

PROCESS RE-ENGINEERING

Re-engineering is the fundamental rethinking and radical redesign of processes to improve performance dramatically in terms of cost, quality, service, and speed. Process re-engineering is about reinvention rather than incremental improvement. It is strong medicine and not always needed or successful. Pain, in the form of layoffs and large

simulation The act of reproducing the behaviour of a process using a model that describes each step of the process.

robust process design A process that is less sensitive to or accommodates variation in inputs or operating conditions while maintaining customer value.

re-engineering The fundamental rethinking and radical redesign of processes to improve performance dramatically in terms of cost, quality, service, and speed.

FIGURE 2.9

Developing a Better Process

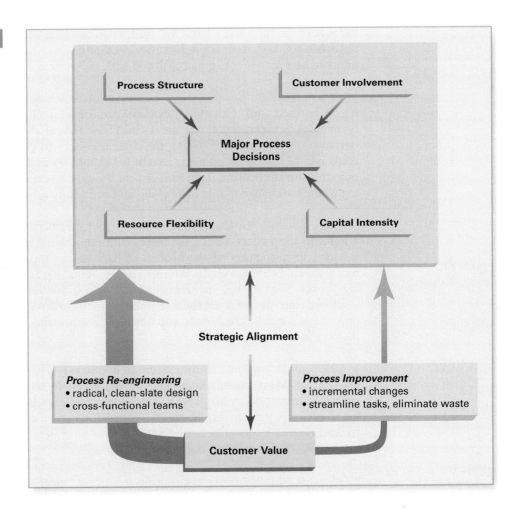

cash outflows for investments in information technology, almost always accompanies massive change. However, re-engineering processes can have big payoffs. For example, Nestlé Canada re-engineered its supply chain, with the objectives of streamlining internal and external information flows and explicitly linking initial consumer demand planning with the final purchase. "The only way that we can compete is if each Nestlé employee takes responsibility to reduce non-value-added costs at every step of our operation," said Nestlé's chairman and CEO (Gahbauer, 1998). To create improvement, cross-functional teams applied four core elements: systematic identification of cost drivers, focus on root causes (see Chapter 5, "Quality"), standardized use of best practices, and ongoing measurement of results. After three years of effort, waste was reduced by 35 percent, range of products by 50 percent, and inventory by 40 percent.

A process selected for re-engineering should be a core process, such as a firm's order-fulfillment activities. Re-engineering then requires focusing on that process, often using cross-functional teams, information technology, leadership, and process analysis. Let us examine each element of the overall approach.

CRITICAL PROCESSES. The emphasis of re-engineering should be on core business processes, as done by Nestlé Canada, rather than on functional departments such as purchasing or marketing. By focusing on processes, managers may spot opportunities to eliminate unnecessary work and supervisory activities rather than worry about defending turf.

Because of the time and energy involved, re-engineering should be reserved for essential processes, such as new product development or customer service. Normal process-improvement activities can be continued with the other processes.

STRONG LEADERSHIP. Senior executives must provide strong leadership for re-engineering to be successful. Otherwise, cynicism, resistance ("We tried that before."), and boundaries between functional areas can block radical changes. Managers can help overcome resistance by providing the clout necessary to ensure that the project proceeds within a strategic context. Executives should set and monitor key performance objectives for the process. Top management should also create a sense of urgency, making a case for change that is compelling and constantly refreshed.

CROSS-FUNCTIONAL TEAMS. A team, consisting of members from each functional area affected by the process change, is charged with carrying out a re-engineering project. For instance, in re-engineering the process of handling an insurance claim, three departments should be represented: customer service, adjusting, and accounting. Re-engineering works best at high-involvement workplaces, where self-managing teams and employee empowerment are the rule rather than the exception. Top-down and bottom-up initiatives can be combined—top-down for performance targets and bottom-up for deciding how to achieve them.

INFORMATION TECHNOLOGY. Information technology is a primary enabler of process engineering. Most re-engineering projects design processes around information flows such as customer order fulfillment. The process owners who will actually be responding to events in the marketplace need information networks and computer technology to do their jobs better. The re-engineering team must determine who needs the information, when they need it, and where they need it.

CLEAN-SLATE PHILOSOPHY. Re-engineering requires a "clean-slate" philosophy—that is, starting with the way the customer wants to deal with the company. To ensure a customer orientation, teams begin with internal and external customer objectives for the process. Often teams first establish a price target for the product or service, deduct profits desired, and then find a process that provides what the customer wants at the price the customer will pay. Re-engineers start from the future and work backward, unconstrained by current approaches.

Like many new techniques and concepts in operations management, re-engineering was highly touted in the early 1990s, almost as a recipe for instant competitive advantage. It has led to many successes and will continue to do so. However, actual experience gives a better picture of the method. It is not simple or easily done, nor is it appropriate for all processes or all organizations. Many firms can't invest the time and resources to implement a radical, clean-slate approach. Moderate gains that better fit corporate strategy and culture might give greater cumulative results than the pursuit of breakthroughs. Significant process improvements that have nothing to do with information technology can be realized. A firm must not only improve cross-functional processes but also the processes within each functional area. Finally, the best understanding of a process, and how to improve it, often lies with the people who perform the work every day, not cross-functional teams or top management.

process improvement
The systematic study of the activities and flows of each process to improve its performance.

PROCESS IMPROVEMENT

The systematic study of the activities and flows of each process both precedes and underpins any effective effort at **process improvement**. Only after a process is really understood can it really be improved. Analysis also helps to identify the critical points in the process where the majority of time is wasted, materials are lost, equipment is needlessly idle, and workers are hampered by unavailable resources.

After a process has been systematically considered, this information becomes the basis for brainstorming about opportunities to achieve better performance. Using flow diagrams, process charts, or other tools, a team must look for ways to streamline tasks, cut expensive materials or services, improve the environment, or make jobs safer. The process analysis also indicates which activities take the most time. The emphasis is on identifying and improving the critical few areas where significant gains can be achieved (sometimes with very little investment).

During this creative part, the team must ask the what, when, who, where, how long, and how questions, challenging each of the steps of the process. To make a process more efficient, the team should question each delay and assess which steps can be combined, rearranged, or eliminated. There is always a better way, but someone must identify a specific problem, and then the team can develop a better way. Improvements in productivity, quality, time, and flexibility can be significant. Unlike process re-engineering, process improvement must be continually and actively pursued—it's an ongoing competitive necessity.

PROCESS MANAGEMENT ACROSS THE ORGANIZATION

Processes are everywhere and are the basic unit of work. They are found in accounting, finance, human resources, management information systems, marketing, and operations. Managers in all departments must make sure that their processes are adding as much customer value as possible. They must be open to change in their processes, whether coming from a major re-engineering effort or simply from an ongoing effort at process improvement. Managers must also understand that enterprise processes cut across organizational lines, regardless of whether the firm is organized along functional, product, regional, or process lines.

An increasing number of firms are explicitly stressing process management, with senior management identifying "process owners" for broad business issues that cross traditional departmental boundaries. In this role, managers must take overall accountability for designing, implementing, and monitoring processes that address critical customer needs. For example, the process owner of an "after-sales service" process at a farm equipment manufacturer must encompass order confirmation, order status, delivery of goods, accounts receivable, technical support, and warranty service. Focusing on process management with cross-functional coordination further blurs any line between manufacturing and service; instead, the need to deliver a bundle of goods and services that creates customer satisfaction is stressed.

EQUATION SUMMARY

1. Break-even analysis:

$$Q = \frac{F_1 - F_2}{V_2 - V_1}$$

2. Annual labour cost estimated from process chart:

$$\text{Annual labour cost} = \begin{pmatrix} \text{Time to perform} \\ \text{the process} \end{pmatrix} \begin{pmatrix} \text{Variable costs} \\ \text{per hour} \end{pmatrix} \begin{pmatrix} \text{Number of times process} \\ \text{performed per year} \end{pmatrix}$$

CHAPTER HIGHLIGHTS

- Process management deals with *how* to make a product or service. Many choices must be made concerning the best mix of human resources, equipment, and materials.

- Process management is of strategic importance and is closely linked to a firm's long-term success. It involves the selection of inputs, operations, work flows, and methods used to produce goods and services.

- Process decisions are made in the following circumstances: a new product is to be offered or an existing product modified, quality improvements are necessary, competitive priorities are changed, demand levels change, current performance is inadequate, competitor capabilities change, new technology is available, or cost or availability of inputs changes.

- The four major process decisions are process structure, customer involvement, resource flexibility, and capital-intensity. Basic process structures are project, batch, line, and continuous flow processes. Customer involvement is the extent to which customers interact with the process during the service encounter. Resource flexibility is the degree to which equipment is general-purpose and individuals can handle a wide variety of work. Capital-intensity is the mix of capital equipment and human skills in a process.

- Fixed automation maximizes efficiency for high-volume products with long life cycles, but flexible (programmable) automation provides economies of scope. Flexibility is gained and setups are minimized because the machines can be reprogrammed to follow new instructions.

- A basic variable underlying the relationships among the four major process decisions is volume, which in turn is shaped by operations strategy. For example, high volume is associated with a line or continuous flow process, little resource flexibility, little customer involvement, and high capital-intensity.

- Customer involvement is central to understanding and categorizing service processes, both between industries and within an industry. Based on the two dimensions of customer interaction and the time for the service encounter, services can be described as professional service, service shop, mass service, and service factory. Process efficiency tends to increase as both the interaction and encounter time decrease. Internet-based involvement offers many options to increase or decrease customer involvement, depending on the need for greater interaction or improved efficiency.

- Focusing operations avoids confusion among competitive priorities, process choices, and technologies. Focused facilities, plants within plants, and cells are ways to achieve focus in both manufacturing and service operations.

- Three basic techniques for analyzing process activities and flows are flow diagrams, process charts, and simulation. They are ways to organize the detailed study of process components.

- Process re-engineering uses cross-functional teams to rethink the design of critical processes. Process improvement is a systematic analysis of activities and flows that occurs continuously.

SOLVED PROBLEM 1

An automobile service is having difficulty providing oil changes in the 29 minutes or less mentioned in its advertising. You are to analyze the process of changing automobile engine oil. The subject of the study is the service mechanic. The process begins when the mechanic directs the customer's arrival and ends when the customer pays for the services.

SOLUTION

Figure 2.10 shows the completed process chart. The process is broken into 21 steps. A summary of the times and distances travelled is shown in the upper right-hand corner of the process chart. The times add up to 28 minutes, which does not allow much room for error if the 29-minute guarantee is to be met and the mechanic travels a total of 128 m.

FIGURE 2.10

*Process Chart for
Changing Engine Oil*

Solver - Process Charts

Enter data in yellow-shaded areas.

Process: *Changing engine oil*

Subject: *Mechanic*

Beginning: *Direct customer arrival*

Ending: *Total charges, receive paym*

[Insert Step]

[Append Step]

[Remove Step]

Summary

Activity	Number of Steps	Time (min)	Distance (m)
Operation ●	7	16.50	
Transport ➡	8	5.50	131
Inspect ■	4	5.00	
Delay ▶	1	0.70	
Store ▼	1	0.30	

Step No.	Time (min)	Distance (m)	●	➡	■	▶	▼	Step Description
1	0.80	15.0		X				Direct customer into service bay
2	1.80		X					Record name and desired service
3	2.30				X			Open hood, verify eng. type, inspect hoses & fluids
4	0.80	10.0		X				Walk to customer in waiting area
5	0.60		X					Recommend additional services
6	0.70					X		Wait for customer decision
7	0.90	22.0		X				Walk to storeroom
8	1.90		X					Look up filter number(s), find filter(s)
9	0.40				X			Check filter number(s)
10	0.60	15.0		X				Carry filter(s) to service pit
11	4.20		X					Perform under-car services
12	0.70	12.0		X				Climb from pit, walk to automobile
13	2.70		X					Fill engine with oil, start engine
14	1.30				X			Inspect for leaks
15	0.50	12.0		X				Walk to pit
16	1.00				X			Inspect for leaks
17	3.00		X					Clean and organize work area
18	0.70	25.0		X				Return to auto, drive from bay
19	0.30						X	Park the car
20	0.50	20.0		X				Walk to customer waiting area
21	2.30		X					Total charges, receive payment

What improvement can you make in the process shown in Figure 2.10?

SOLUTION

Your analysis should verify the following three ideas for improvement. You may also find others.

1. *Move step 17 to step 21.* Customers shouldn't have to wait while the mechanic cleans the work area.

2. *Store small inventories of frequently used filters in the pit.* Step 7 involves travel to the storeroom. If the filters are moved to the pit, a copy of the reference material must also be placed in the pit. The pit will have to be organized and well lighted.

3. *Use two mechanics.* Steps 10, 12, and 15 involve running up and down the steps to the pit. Much of this travel could be eliminated. The service time could be shortened by having one mechanic in the pit working simultaneously with another working under the hood.

CD-ROM RESOURCES

The Student CD-ROM that accompanies this text contains the following resources, which allow you to further practise and apply the concepts presented in this chapter.

- **Equation Summary**: All the equations for this chapter can be found in one convenient location.
- **Discussion Questions**: Three questions will expand your thinking on the ethical, environmental, and political dimensions of designing processes.
- **Cases**: *Custom Molds, Inc.* How should the Millers design their processes, given the changing environment?
- **Experiential Exercise**: *Min-Yo Garment Company.* Experience the challenges of matching markets to the capability of your manufacturing process in this exciting in-class simulation.
- **The Big Picture**: Process structure at *King Soopers Bakery*. See how three different process structures are used under the same roof, depending on volume and the degree of product customization.
- **OM Explorer Tutors**: OM Explorer contains two tutor programs that will help you learn about break-even analysis applied to equipment selection and process charts.
- **OM Explorer Solvers**: OM Explorer has one program that will help with the general use of process charts.
- **Extend LT**: A student version is included to develop and use simulation models. *Artistic Glass* is considering changes to its process structure, and a simulation exercise and model is included.
- **Supplement A:** *Decision Making.* Learn about break-even analysis applied to process decisions.
- **Supplement B:** *Financial Analysis.* Learn about several tools for evaluating revised processes that involve large capital investments.
- **Supplement C:** *Work Measurement.* Learn about several tools for estimating the time it takes for each step in a process.
- **Supplement D:** *Learning Curve Analysis.* Learn about how to account for learning effects when estimating time requirements for new or revised processes.
- **Supplement E:** *Computer-Integrated Manufacturing.* Read about how complex computer systems can give manufacturers more resource flexibility.
- **Supplement G:** *Simulation.* Learn how to simulate a process and understand how it performs dynamically over time.

PROBLEMS

1. Your class has volunteered to assist with publicizing the campaign of a candidate. The campaign includes assembling 10 000 yard signs (preprinted water-resistant paper signs to be glued and stapled to a wooden stake) on a Saturday. Construct a flow diagram and a process chart for yard sign assembly. What inputs in terms of materials, human effort, and equipment are involved? Estimate the number of volunteers and staples, and the amount of glue, equipment, lawn and garage space, and pizza required.

2. Prepare a flow diagram for a process of your choice.

3. Diagrams of two self-service gasoline stations, both located on corners, are shown in Figure 2.11(a) and (b). Both have two rows of four pumps and a booth at which an attendant receives payment for the gasoline. At neither station is it necessary for the customer to pay in advance. The exits and entrances are marked on the diagrams. Analyze the flows of cars and people through each station.

   a. Which station has the more efficient flows from the standpoint of the customer?
   b. Which station is likely to lose more potential customers who cannot gain access to the pumps because another car is headed in the other direction?
   c. At which station can a customer pay without getting out of the car?

4. The management of the Just Like Home restaurant has asked you to analyze some of its processes. One of these processes is making a single-scoop ice cream cone. Cones can be ordered by a server (for table service) or by a customer (for takeout). Figure 2.12 illustrates the process chart for this operation.

   - The ice cream counter server earns $10 per hour (including variable fringe benefits).
   - The process is performed 10 times per hour (on average).
   - The restaurant is open 363 days a year, 10 hours a day.

   a. Complete the summary (top right) portion of the chart.
   b. What is the total labour cost associated with the process?
   c. How can this operation be made more efficient? Draw a process chart of the improved process. What are the annual labour savings if this new process is implemented?

5. Dr. Gulakowicz is an orthodontist. She estimates that adding two new chairs will increase fixed costs by $150 000, including the annual equivalent cost of the capital investment and the salary of one more technician. Each new patient is expected to bring in $3000 per year in additional revenue, with variable costs estimated at $1000 per patient. The two new chairs will allow her to expand her practice by as many as 200 patients annually. How many patients would have to be added for the new process to break even?

FIGURE 2.11

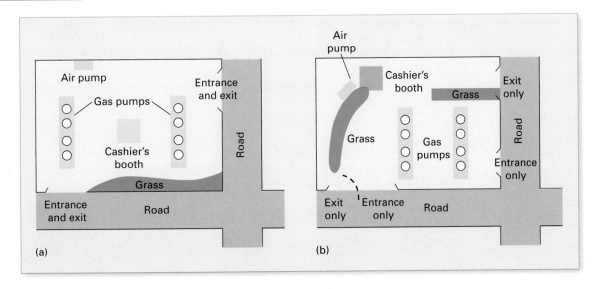

(a)

(b)

FIGURE 2.12

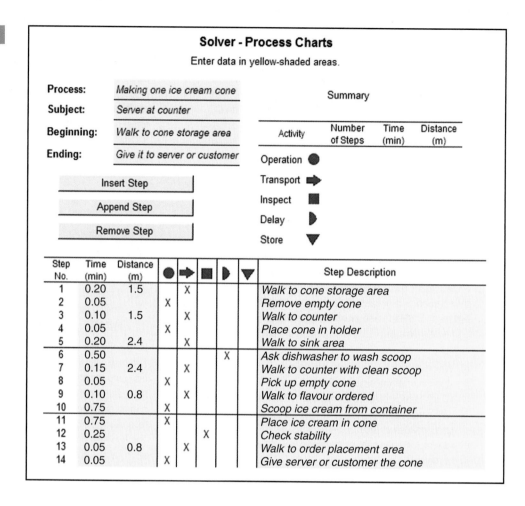

Solver - Process Charts

Enter data in yellow-shaded areas.

Process:	Making one ice cream cone
Subject:	Server at counter
Beginning:	Walk to cone storage area
Ending:	Give it to server or customer

Insert Step

Append Step

Remove Step

Summary

Activity	Number of Steps	Time (min)	Distance (m)
Operation ●			
Transport ➡			
Inspect ■			
Delay ▶			
Store ▼			

Step No.	Time (min)	Distance (m)	●	➡	■	▶	▼	Step Description
1	0.20	1.5		X				Walk to cone storage area
2	0.05		X					Remove empty cone
3	0.10	1.5		X				Walk to counter
4	0.05		X					Place cone in holder
5	0.20	2.4		X				Walk to sink area
6	0.50						X	Ask dishwasher to wash scoop
7	0.15	2.4		X				Walk to counter with clean scoop
8	0.05		X					Pick up empty cone
9	0.10	0.8		X				Walk to flavour ordered
10	0.75		X					Scoop ice cream from container
11	0.75		X					Place ice cream in cone
12	0.25				X			Check stability
13	0.05	0.8		X				Walk to order placement area
14	0.05		X					Give server or customer the cone

6. Two different manufacturing processes are being considered for making a new product. The first process is less capital-intensive, with fixed costs of only $50 000 per year and variable costs of $700 per unit. The second process has fixed costs of $400 000 but variable costs of only $200 per unit.

   a. What is the break-even quantity, beyond which the second process becomes more attractive than the first?
   b. If the expected annual sales for the product is 800 units, which process would you choose?

REFERENCES AND FURTHER READINGS

Brown, Donna. "Outsourcing: How Corporations Take Their Business Elsewhere." *Management Review*, February 1992, pp. 16–19.

Chase, R. B. "The Customer Contact Approach to Services: Theoretical Bases and Practical Extensions." *Operations Research*, vol. 29 (1981), no. 4, pp. 698–706.

Dixon, J. Robb, Peter Arnold, Janelle Heineke, Jay S. Kim, and Paul Mulligan. "Business Process Reengineering: Improving in New Strategic Directions." *California Management Review*, Summer 1994, pp. 1–17.

Gahbauer, S. "Nestlé Freshens Up Supply Chain Performance." *Modern Purchasing*, vol. 40 (1998), no. 5, p. 26.

Grover, Varun, and Manoj K. Malhotra. "Business Process Reengineering: A Tutorial on the Concept, Evolution, Method, Technology and Application." *Journal of Operations Management*, vol. 15 (1997), no. 3, pp. 194–213.

Guidoni, G. "Robotic Renaissance: Auto Sector Still Leading the Way in North American Industry's Unfolding Love Affair with Robotic Technologies." *Canadian Packaging*, vol. 53 (2000), no. 4, pp. 17–18.

Hall, Gene, Jim Rosenthal, and Judy Wade. "How to Make Reengineering Really Work." *Harvard Business Review*, November/December 1993, pp. 119–131.

Hammer, M. "The Superefficient Company." *Harvard Business Review*, vol. 79 (2001), no. 8, pp. 82–91.

Hammer, Michael, and James Champy. *Reengineering the Corporation: A Manifesto for Business Revolution*. New York: HarperBusiness, 1993.

Hammer, M., and S. Stanton. "How Process Enterprises Really Work." *Harvard Business Review*, vol. 77 (1999), no. 6, pp. 108–118.

Harrigan, K. R. *Strategies for Vertical Integration*. Lexington, MA: D. C. Heath, 1983.

Malhotra, Manoj K., and Larry P. Ritzman. "Resource Flexibility Issues in Multistage Manufacturing." *Decision Sciences*, vol. 21 (1990), no. 4, pp. 673–690.

"Process, Process, Process." *Planning Review* (special issue), vol. 22 (1993), no. 3, pp. 1–56.

Safizadeh, M. Hossen, Larry P. Ritzman, and Debasish Mallick. "Revisiting Alternative Theoretical Paradigms in Manufacturing." *Production and Operations Management*, vol. 9 (2000), no. 2, pp. 111–127.

Schmenner, R. W. "Service Businesses and Productivity." *Decision Sciences*, vol. 35 (2004), no. 3, pp. 333–347.

Tonkin, Lea A. P. "Outsourcing: A Tool, Not a Solution." *Target*, vol. 15 (1999), no. 2, pp. 44–45.

3 Managing Projects

Across the Organization

Managing project processes is important to:

- **finance,** which uses project processes for financing new business acquisitions.
- **human resources,** which uses project processes for initiating new training and development programs.
- **management information systems,** which uses project processes for designing new information systems to support re-engineered processes.
- **marketing,** which uses project processes to design and execute new product advertising campaigns.
- **operations,** which uses project processes to manage the introduction of new technologies for the production of goods and services.

Learning Goals

After reading this chapter, you will be able to:

1. define the major activities associated with organizing, planning, monitoring, and controlling projects.
2. diagram the network of interrelated activities in a project.
3. identify the sequence of critical activities that determines the duration of a project.
4. describe the factors that managers must consider when assessing risks in a project and calculate the probability of completing a project on time.
5. explain how to determine a minimum-cost project schedule.

When engineers at Kinetics Inc., in Toronto, are designing factory equipment on their computers, they can almost feel their big pharmaceutical customers breathing down their necks. Nobody is there with them, but the designers do let clients see works-in-progress right from the start—in animated 3D over the Internet. It's part of an online collaborative design initiative the firm undertook to speed up projects.

It worked. Over a two-year implementation period, the time required for a typical project of designing and building a purification module was reduced by almost 40 percent, to about 20 weeks. The more design time is compressed, the faster the equipment is built and shipped out the door. As productivity increases, additional revenue and profit are generated.

Similar benefits are being reported in traditional, large-scale construction projects. EllisDon Construction, a Canadian firm with projects around the world, including major facilities at the 2004 Olympics in Greece, developed its own Web-based system in-house. Senior managers view online project management tools as contributing to overall value, not just reducing cost.

Across a diverse range of industries, firms are increasingly attracted to online project management tools to collaborate on design and monitor progress. Users can share centrally stored design drawings and 3D models while talking on the phone or videoconferencing with other members of a design team. These technologies help reduce the traditional delays in sending communications to and getting design approvals from distant clients.

For example, Kinetics and its customers meet online on prearranged dates, play with a 3D model of the product on their computer screens while talking on the phone, and come to a decision on the spot about how to proceed. The technology also helps bring together geographically dispersed teams and automates work flow. When a preliminary drawing is completed, for example, the software

From conceptual engineering and design to fabrication, Kinetics Inc. uses computer-aided design technologies to improve project management, which ultimately allows customers to bring new products to market faster.

automatically forwards it to a supervisor for approval, an engineer who checks it, or to purchasing staff to begin sourcing required materials. Not only is design time reduced by days or weeks, but it also helps ensure a higher-quality finished project.

With major construction projects, building owners can log on to EllisDon's Web site from anywhere in the world and monitor the progress of their projects, including viewing pictures taken every 15 minutes at the building site. Financial statements are also online in real time and can be accessed instantaneously. "It speeds up how our people work and our clients love it because they get their information when they need it." The various architects, engineers, suppliers, and subcontractors have different levels of clearance on the site so they can gauge when their supplies or workers will be needed.

But for all its benefits, online design collaboration still has significant challenges and there are roadblocks to mass adoption. Initial startup costs remain quite high for both hardware and software. Moreover, even enthusiastic and relatively seasoned users admit it can take massive organizational adjustments. For example, if there is a history of adversarial relationships between customers and suppliers, a project manager must decide how much information should be shared. Customers must also be willing to work in new ways, such as not nitpicking preliminary designs. Yet, despite the necessary changes in the process of managing projects, online collaboration delivers significant competitive advantages, with the potential for further gains as learning continues.

Source: Adapted with permission from: Copyright 2002, G. Blackwell, "Industrial Design of the Times: Online Collaboration Cuts Costs, Speeds Engineering Process," *The Globe and Mail*, February 28, 2002, p. B13. Mr. Blackwell is a freelance technology writer based in London, Ontario. *Other sources:* D. Procter, "Builders Cyber Ignorant?" *Toronto Construction News*, March 2001; S. Lawson, "System Gives EllisDon 'edge,'" *London Free Press*, March 2, 2001.

project An interrelated set of activities with a definite starting and ending point, which results in a unique outcome for a specific allocation of resources.

Companies such as Kinetics and EllisDon are experts at managing projects. They have mastered the ability to schedule activities and monitor progress within strict time, cost, and performance guidelines. A **project** is an interrelated set of activities with a definite starting and ending point, which results in a unique outcome for a specific allocation of resources. Typical competitive priorities for such processes include on-time delivery and customization (see Chapter 2, "Process Management"). A project process is the mechanism for completing a project.

Project processes can be complex and challenging to manage. Projects often cut across organizational lines, because they need the skills of multiple professions and organizations. Furthermore, each project is unique, even if it has some routine elements, requiring new combinations of skills and resources in the project process. Uncertainties, such as the advent of new technologies or the activities of competitors, can change the character of projects and require responsive countermeasures. Finally, project processes themselves are temporary, because personnel, materials, and facilities are organized to complete a project within a specified time frame and then disbanded.

In this chapter, we discuss three major activities associated with managing project processes: organizing projects, planning projects, and monitoring and controlling projects.

ORGANIZING PROJECTS

Successful projects begin with a clear definition of scope, objectives, and tasks. However, a successful project *process* begins with a clear understanding of its organization and how personnel are going to work together to complete the project. In this section, we will address two important activities in this initial phase of managing projects: defining the objectives and scope, and selecting the project manager and team.

DEFINING THE OBJECTIVES AND SCOPE

Before a project is undertaken, it is important to clearly identify both the purpose and goals that are expected. These might be driven by firm-level strategy, gaps in existing business processes, or opportunities to increase customer value. A thorough statement of the project scope, time frame, and allocated resources is essential to managing the project process. The scope provides a succinct statement of project objectives and captures the essence of the desired project outcomes in the form of major deliverables, which are concrete outcomes of the project process. These deliverables become the focus of management attention during the life of the project. Each of the deliverables requires activities to achieve it; therefore, it is important to avoid many changes to the scope of the project once it is under way. Changes to the scope of a project inevitably increase costs and delay completion. Changes to scope—collectively called **scope creep**—in sufficient quantity are primary causes of failed projects.

scope creep Many small incremental changes to project objectives, which in total significantly expand the scope.

The time frame for a project should be as specific as possible. For example, "by the first quarter, 2007" is too vague for most purposes. Some people could interpret it as the beginning and others as the end of the quarter. Even though it should be considered only a target at this early stage of the project plan, the time frame should be much more specific, as in "the billing process re-engineering project should be completed by January 1, 2007."

Although specifying an allocation of resources to a project may be difficult at the early stages of planning, it is important for managing the project process. The allocation could be expressed as a dollar figure or as full-time equivalents of personnel time. For example, the allocated resources in a project might be $250 000. Avoid statements such as "with available resources," because they are too vague and imply that there are sufficient resources to complete the project when there may not be. A specific statement of allocated resources makes it possible to make adjustments to the scope of the project as it proceeds.

SELECTING THE PROJECT MANAGER AND TEAM

Once the project is defined, a project manager must be chosen. Project managers should be good motivators, teachers, and communicators. They should be able to organize a set of disparate activities and work with personnel from a variety of disciplines. These qualities are important because project managers have the responsibility to see that their projects are completed successfully. The project manager is responsible for establishing the project goals and providing the means to achieve them. The project manager must also specify how the work will be done and ensure that any necessary training is conducted. Finally, the project manager evaluates progress and takes appropriate action when schedules are in jeopardy.

The project team is a group of people led by the project manager. Members of the project team may represent entities internal to the firm, such as marketing, finance, accounting, or operations, or entities external to the firm, such as customers or suppliers. A clear definition of who is on the team is essential, as is a clear understanding of their specific roles and responsibilities, such as helping to create the project plan, performing specific tasks, and reporting progress and problems. Everyone performing work for the project should be a part of the project team. Consequently, the size and makeup of the team may fluctuate during the life of the project.

PLANNING PROJECTS

Once the project has been defined and the project process organized, the team must formulate a plan that identifies the specific tasks to be accomplished and a schedule for their completion. Planning projects involves five steps:

1. Defining the work breakdown structure

2. Diagramming the network

3. Developing the schedule

4. Analyzing cost–time trade-offs

5. Assessing risks

DEFINING THE WORK BREAKDOWN STRUCTURE

work breakdown structure (WBS) A statement of all work that has to be completed.

The **work breakdown structure (WBS)** is a statement of all work that has to be completed. Perhaps the single most important contributor to delay is the omission of work that is germane to the successful completion of the project. The project manager must work closely with the team to identify all work tasks. Typically, in the process of accumulating work tasks, the team generates a hierarchy of the work breakdown. Major work components are broken down to smaller tasks by the project team. Care must be taken to include all important tasks in the WBS; otherwise, project delays are possible. For example, a project for improving the delivery of groceries directly to consumers might have as a major activity "build a warehouse," which might be further refined to a host of construction-related tasks including "pour a foundation" and "wire for electrical service." Easily overlooked, however, are tasks such as "getting final approval for the warehouse" or "preparing final reports," which can take considerable time and can affect the completion date of the project.

activity The smallest unit of work effort consuming both time and resources that the project manager can schedule and control.

An **activity** is the smallest unit of work effort consuming both time and resources that the project manager can schedule and control. Each activity in the work breakdown structure must have an "owner" who is responsible for doing the work. *Task ownership* avoids confusion in the execution of activities and assigns responsibility for timely completion. The team should have a defined procedure for assigning tasks to team members, which can be democratic (by consensus of the team) or autocratic (by the project manager).

DIAGRAMMING THE NETWORK

Network planning methods can help managers monitor and control projects. These methods treat a project as a set of interrelated activities that can be visually displayed in a **network diagram**, which consists of nodes (circles) and arcs (arrows) that depict the relationships between activities. Two network planning methods were developed in the 1950s. The **program evaluation and review technique (PERT)** was created for the U.S. Navy's Polaris missile project, which involved 3000 separate contractors and suppliers. The **critical path method (CPM)** was developed as a means of scheduling maintenance shutdowns at chemical processing plants. Although early versions of PERT and CPM differed in their treatment of activity-time estimates, today the differences between PERT and CPM are minor. For purposes of our discussion, we refer to them collectively as PERT/CPM. These methods offer several benefits to project managers, including the following:

1. Considering projects as networks forces project teams to identify and organize the data required and to identify the interrelationships of activities. This process also provides a forum for managers of different functional areas to discuss the nature of the various activities and their resource requirements.

2. Networks enable project managers to estimate the completion time of projects, an advantage that can be useful in planning other events and in conducting contractual negotiations with customers and suppliers.

3. Reports highlight the activities that are crucial to completing projects on schedule. They also highlight the activities that may be delayed without affecting completion dates, thereby freeing up resources for more critical activities.

4. Network methods enable project managers to analyze the time and cost implications of resource trade-offs.

ESTABLISHING PRECEDENCE RELATIONSHIPS. Diagramming the project as a network requires establishing the precedence relationships among activities. A **precedence relationship** determines a sequence for undertaking activities; it specifies that one activity cannot start until a preceding activity has been completed. For example, brochures announcing a conference for executives must first be designed by the program committee (activity A) before they can be printed (activity B). In other words, activity A must *precede* activity B. For large projects, this task is essential because incorrect or omitted precedence relationships will result in costly delays. The precedence relationships are represented by a network diagram.

ACTIVITY-ON-NODE (AON) NETWORKS. A networking approach useful for creating a network diagram is the **activity-on-node (AON) network**, in which nodes represent activities and arcs represent the precedence relationships among them. This approach is *activity-oriented*. Here, precedence relationships require that an activity not begin until all preceding activities have been completed. Arrows represent the precedence relationships, and the direction of an arrow represents the sequence of activities. In AON networks, when there are multiple activities with no predecessors, it is usual to show them ema-

---

network diagram A diagram that depicts the relationships between activities, which consists of nodes (circles) and arcs (arrows).

program evaluation and review technique (PERT) A network planning method created for the U.S. Navy's Polaris missile project.

critical path method (CPM) A network planning method initially developed as a means of scheduling maintenance shutdowns at chemical processing plants.

precedence relationship A relationship that determines a sequence for undertaking activities; it specifies that one activity cannot start until a preceding activity has been completed.

activity-on-node (AON) network An approach used to create a network diagram, in which nodes represent activities and arcs represent the precedence relationships among them.

nating from a common node called Start. When there are multiple activities with no successors, it is usual to show them connected to a node called Finish. We will use AON networks later to describe assembly lines (see Chapter 7, "Location and Layout").

EXAMPLE 3.1   *Diagramming a Hospital Project*

In the interest of better serving the public, St. Adolf's Hospital has decided to relocate to a new, larger facility. The move will involve constructing a new building nearby and making it operational. Judy Kramer, executive director of the board of St. Adolf's, must prepare for two meetings, scheduled for next week, before the hospital's board of directors on the proposed project. The meetings will address the specifics of the total project, including time and cost estimates for its completion.

With the help of her team, Kramer has developed a work breakdown structure consisting of 11 major project activities. The team also has specified the immediate predecessors (those activities that must be completed before a particular activity can begin) for each activity, as shown in the following table.

ACTIVITY	DESCRIPTION	IMMEDIATE PREDECESSOR(S)
A	Select administrative and medical staff.	—
B	Select site and do site survey.	—
C	Select equipment.	A
D	Prepare final construction plans and layout.	B
E	Bring utilities to the site.	B
F	Interview applicants and fill positions in nursing, support staff, maintenance, and security.	A
G	Purchase and take delivery of equipment.	C
H	Construct the hospital.	D
I	Develop an information system.	A
J	Install the equipment.	E, G, H
K	Train nurses and support staff.	F, I, J

Using the 11 activities and their precedence relationships, we can now draw the network diagram for the hospital project, as shown in Figure 3.1. It depicts activities as circles, with arrows indicating the sequence in which they are to be performed. The numbers represent estimated times in weeks for each activity. Activities A and B emanate from a *start* node because they have no immediate predecessors. The arrows connecting activity A to activities C, F, and I indicate that all three require completion of activity A before they can begin. Similarly, activity B must be completed before activities D and E can begin, and so on. Activity K connects to a *finish* node because no activities follow it. The start and finish nodes do not actually represent activities. They merely provide beginning and ending points for the network.

Modelling a large project as a network forces the project team to identify the necessary activities and recognize the precedence relationships. If this preplanning is skipped, unexpected delays often occur.

DEVELOPING THE SCHEDULE
Next, the project team must make time estimates for activities. When the same type of activity has been done many times before, time estimates are apt to have a relatively high degree of certainty. There are several ways to get time estimates in such an environment. First, statistical methods can be used if the project team has access to data on actual activity times experienced in the past. Second, if activity times improve with the

Network for the St. Adolf's Hospital Project, Showing Activity Times

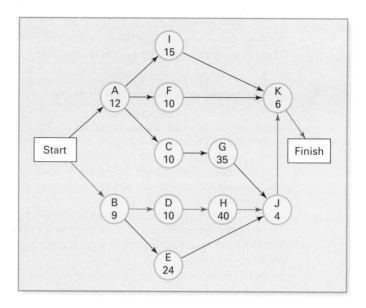

number of replications, the times can be estimated using learning curve models (see Supplement D, "Learning Curve Analysis," in the Student CD-ROM). Finally, the times for first-time activities are often estimated using managerial opinions on the basis of similar prior experiences. However, if there is a high degree of uncertainty in the estimates, probability distributions for activity times can be used. We discuss two approaches for incorporating uncertainty in project networks when we address risk assessment later. For now, we assume that the activity times are known, and we will use the estimated time for each activity noted in Figure 3.1.

A crucial aspect of project management is estimating the time of completion. If each activity in relocating the hospital were done in sequence, with work proceeding on only one activity at a time, the time of completion would equal the sum of the times for all the activities, or 175 weeks. However, Figure 3.1 indicates that some activities can be carried on simultaneously given adequate resources. We call each sequence of activities between the project's start and finish a **path**. The network describing the hospital relocation project has five paths: A–I–K, A–F–K, A–C–G–J–K, B–D–H–J–K, and B–E–J–K. The **critical path** is the sequence of activities between a project's start and finish that takes the longest time to complete. Thus, the activities along the critical path determine the completion time of the project; that is, if one of the activities on the critical path is delayed, the entire project will be delayed. The estimated times for the paths in the hospital project network are shown in the following table:

path The sequence of activities between a project's start and finish.

critical path The sequence of activities between a project's start and finish that takes the longest time to complete.

PATH	ESTIMATED TIME (WEEKS)
A–I–K	33
A–F–K	28
A–C–G–J–K	67
B–D–H–J–K	69
B–E–J–K	43

The activity string B–D–H–J–K is estimated to take 69 weeks to complete. As the longest, it constitutes the critical path and is shown in red in Figure 3.1.

Because the critical path defines the completion time of the project, Judy Kramer and the project team should focus on these activities. However, projects can have more than one critical path. If activity A, C, or G were to fall behind by two weeks, the string A–C–G–J–K would become a second critical path. Consequently, the team should be aware that delays in activities not on the critical path could cause delays in the entire project.

Manually finding the critical path in this way is easy for small projects; however, computers must be used for large projects. Computers calculate activity slack and prepare periodic reports, enabling managers to monitor progress. **Activity slack** is the maximum length of time that an activity can be delayed without delaying the entire project. Activities on the critical path have zero slack. Constantly monitoring the progress of activities with little or no slack enables managers to identify activities that need to be expedited to keep the project on schedule. Activity slack is calculated from four times for each activity: earliest start time, earliest finish time, latest start time, and latest finish time.

activity slack The maximum length of time that an activity can be delayed without delaying the entire project.

EARLIEST START AND EARLIEST FINISH TIMES. The earliest start and earliest finish times are obtained as follows:

earliest start time (ES) The earliest finish time of the preceding activity.

earliest finish time (EF) An activity's earliest start time plus its estimated duration, t, or $EF = ES + t$.

1. The **earliest start time (ES)** for an activity is the earliest finish time of the preceding activity. For activities with more than one preceding activity, ES is the latest of the earliest finish times of the preceding activities.

2. The **earliest finish time (EF)** of an activity equals its earliest start time plus its estimated duration, t, or $EF = ES + t$.

To calculate the duration of the entire project, we determine the EF for the last activity on the critical path.

LATEST START AND LATEST FINISH TIMES. To obtain the latest start and latest finish times, we must work backward from the finish node. We start by setting the latest finish time of the project equal to the earliest finish time of the last activity on the critical path.

latest finish time (LF) The latest start time of the activity that immediately follows.

latest start time (LS) The latest finish time of an activity minus its estimated duration, t, or $LS = LF - t$.

1. The **latest finish time (LF)** for an activity is the latest start time of the activity following it. For activities with more than one activity immediately following, LF is the earliest of the latest start times of those activities.

2. The **latest start time (LS)** for an activity equals its latest finish time minus its estimated duration, t, or $LS = LF - t$.

EXAMPLE 3.2

Calculating Start and Finish Times for the Activities

Using the activity times and precedence relationships noted in Figure 3.1, we can now calculate the start and finish times for all activities, as well as the project as a whole.

To compute the earliest start and earliest finish times, we begin at the start node at time zero. Because activities A and B have no predecessors, the earliest start times for these activities are also zero. The earliest finish times for these activities are:

$$EF_A = 0 + 12 = 12 \quad \text{and} \quad EF_B = 0 + 9 = 9$$

Because the earliest start time for activities I, F, and C is the earliest finish time of activity A:

$$ES_I = 12, \quad ES_F = 12, \quad \text{and} \quad ES_C = 12$$

Similarly:

$$ES_D = 9 \quad \text{and} \quad ES_E = 9$$

After placing these ES values on the network diagram as shown in Figure 3.2, we determine the EF times for activities I, F, C, D, and E:

$$EF_I = 12 + 15 = 27, \quad EF_F = 12 + 10 = 22, \quad EF_C = 12 + 10 = 22,$$
$$EF_D = 9 + 10 = 19, \quad \text{and} \quad EF_E = 9 + 24 = 33$$

The earliest start time for activity G is the latest EF time of all immediately preceding activities. Thus:

$$
\begin{aligned}
ES_G &= EF_C & \qquad ES_H &= EF_D \\
&= 22 & &= 19
\end{aligned}
$$

$$
\begin{aligned}
EF_G &= ES_G + t & \qquad EF_H &= ES_H + t \\
&= 22 + 35 & &= 19 + 40 \\
&= 57 & &= 59
\end{aligned}
$$

Because activity J has several predecessors, the earliest time that activity J can begin is the latest of the EF times of any of its preceding activities: EF_G, EF_H, EF_E. Thus, $ES_J = 59$, and $EF_J = 59 + 4 = 63$. Similarly, $ES_K = 63$ and $EF_K = 63 + 6 = 69$. Because activity K is the last activity on the critical path, the earliest the project can be completed is week 69. The earliest start and finish times for all activities are shown in Figure 3.2.

Network for the Hospital Project, Showing Data Needed for Activity Slack Calculation

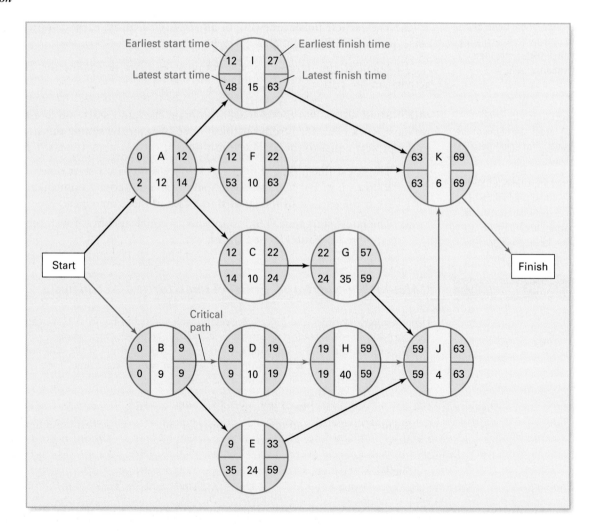

To compute the latest start and latest finish times, we begin by setting the latest finish activity time of activity K at week 69, its earliest finish time. Thus, the latest start time for activity K is:

$$LS_K = LF_K - t = 69 - 6 = 63$$

If activity K is to start no later than week 63, all its predecessors must finish no later than that time. Consequently:

$$LF_I = 63, \quad LF_F = 63, \quad \text{and} \quad LF_J = 63$$

The latest start times for these activities are shown in Figure 3.2 as:

$$LS_I = 63 - 15 = 48, \quad LS_F = 63 - 10 = 53, \quad \text{and} \quad LS_J = 63 - 4 = 59$$

After obtaining LS_J, we can calculate the latest start times for the immediate predecessors of activity J:

$$LS_G = 59 - 35 = 24, \quad LS_H = 59 - 40 = 19, \quad \text{and} \quad LS_E = 59 - 24 = 35$$

Similarly, we can now calculate latest start times for activities C and D:

$$LS_C = 24 - 10 = 14 \quad \text{and} \quad LS_D = 19 - 10 = 9$$

Activity A has more than one immediately following activity: I, F, and C. The earliest of the latest start times is 14 for activity C. Thus:

$$LS_A = 14 - 12 = 2$$

Similarly, activity B has two immediate followers, D and E. Because the earliest of the latest start times of these activities is 9:

$$LS_B = 9 - 9 = 0$$

Decision Point   The earliest or latest start dates can be used for developing a project schedule. For example, Kramer should start activity B immediately, because the latest start date is 0; otherwise, the project will not be completed by week 69. When the LS is greater than the ES for an activity, that activity could be scheduled for any date between ES and LS. Such is the case for activity E, which could be scheduled to start anytime between week 9 and week 35, depending on the availability of resources. The earliest start and earliest finish times and the latest start and latest finish times for all activities are shown in Figure 3.2.

PROJECT SCHEDULE.   The project manager, often with the assistance of computer software, creates the project schedule by superimposing project activities, with their precedence relationships and estimated duration times, on a time line. The resulting diagram is called a **Gantt chart**. Figure 3.3 shows a Gantt chart for the hospital project created with Microsoft Project, a popular software package. The critical path is shown in red. The chart clearly shows which activities can be undertaken simultaneously and when they should be started. In this example, the schedule calls for all activities to begin at their earliest start times. Gantt charts are popular because they are intuitive and easy to construct.

Gantt chart A project schedule, usually created by the project manager using computer software, that superimposes project activities, with their precedence relationships and estimated duration times, on a time line.

ACTIVITY SLACK.   Information on slack can be useful because it highlights activities that need close attention. In this regard, activity slack is the amount of schedule slippage that can be tolerated for an activity before the entire project will be delayed. Activities on the critical path have zero slack. Slack in an activity is reduced when the estimated duration of an activity is exceeded or when the scheduled start time for the activity must be delayed because of resource considerations. For example, activity G in the hospital project is estimated to have two weeks of slack. Suppose that the orders for the new equipment are placed in week 22, the activity's earliest start date. If the supplier informs the project team that it will have a two-week delay in the normal delivery time,

FIGURE 3.3

MS Project Gantt Chart for the Hospital Project Schedule

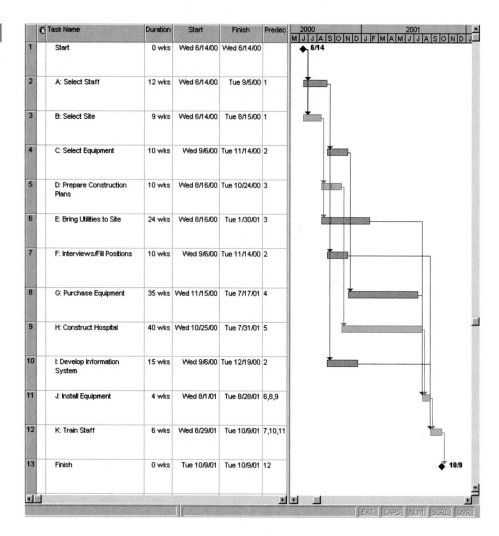

	Task Name	Duration	Start	Finish	Predec
1	Start	0 wks	Wed 6/14/00	Wed 6/14/00	
2	A: Select Staff	12 wks	Wed 6/14/00	Tue 9/5/00	1
3	B: Select Site	9 wks	Wed 6/14/00	Tue 8/15/00	1
4	C: Select Equipment	10 wks	Wed 9/6/00	Tue 11/14/00	2
5	D: Prepare Construction Plans	10 wks	Wed 8/16/00	Tue 10/24/00	3
6	E: Bring Utilities to Site	24 wks	Wed 8/16/00	Tue 1/30/01	3
7	F: Interviews/Fill Positions	10 wks	Wed 9/6/00	Tue 11/14/00	2
8	G: Purchase Equipment	35 wks	Wed 11/15/00	Tue 7/17/01	4
9	H: Construct Hospital	40 wks	Wed 10/25/00	Tue 7/31/01	5
10	I: Develop Information System	15 wks	Wed 9/6/00	Tue 12/19/00	2
11	J: Install Equipment	4 wks	Wed 8/1/01	Tue 8/28/01	6,8,9
12	K: Train Staff	6 wks	Wed 8/29/01	Tue 10/9/01	7,10,11
13	Finish	0 wks	Tue 10/9/01	Tue 10/9/01	12

the activity time becomes 37 weeks, consuming all the slack and making activity G critical. Management must carefully monitor the delivery of the equipment to avoid delaying the entire project.

Sometimes managers can manipulate slack to overcome scheduling problems. Slack information helps the project team make decisions regarding the reallocation of resources. When resources can be used on several different activities in a project, they can be taken from activities with slack and given to activities that are behind schedule until the slack is used up.

total slack Slack shared by other activities; calculated as LS − ES or LF − EF.

There are two types of activity slack. **Total slack** for an activity is a function of the performance of activities leading to it. It can be calculated in one of two ways for any activity:

$$S = LS - ES \quad \text{or} \quad S = LF - EF$$

free slack The amount of time that an activity's earliest finish time can be delayed without delaying the earliest start time of any activity immediately following it.

Free slack is the amount of time that an activity's earliest finish time can be delayed without delaying the earliest start time of any activity immediately following it. The distinction between the two types of slack is important for making resource allocation decisions. If an activity has total slack but no free slack, any slippage in its start date will affect the slack of other activities. However, the start date for an activity with free slack can be delayed without affecting the schedules of other activities.

EXAMPLE 3.3	*Calculating Activity Slack*

We can now calculate the slack for the activities in the hospital project based on the data in Figure 3.2 on page 70.

Figure 3.4 from Microsoft Project 2000 shows the total slack and free slack for each activity. It shows activities B, D, H, J, and K are on the critical path because they have zero slack.

FIGURE 3.4

Schedule Table Showing Activity Slacks for the Hospital Project

	Task Name	Start	Finish	Late Start	Late Finish	Free Slack	Total Slack
1	Start	Wed 6/14/00	Wed 6/14/00	Wed 6/14/00	Wed 6/14/00	0 wks	0 wks
2	A: Select Staff	Wed 6/14/00	Tue 9/5/00	Wed 6/28/00	Tue 9/19/00	0 wks	2 wks
3	B: Select Site	Wed 6/14/00	Tue 8/15/00	Wed 6/14/00	Tue 8/15/00	0 wks	0 wks
4	C: Select Equipment	Wed 9/6/00	Tue 11/14/00	Wed 9/20/00	Tue 11/28/00	0 wks	2 wks
5	D: Prepare Constructi	Wed 8/16/00	Tue 10/24/00	Wed 8/16/00	Tue 10/24/00	0 wks	0 wks
6	E: Bring Utilities to Site	Wed 8/16/00	Tue 1/30/01	Wed 2/14/01	Tue 7/31/01	26 wks	26 wks
7	F: Interviews/Fill Posit	Wed 9/6/00	Tue 11/14/00	Wed 6/20/01	Tue 8/28/01	41 wks	41 wks
8	G: Purchase Equipme	Wed 11/15/00	Tue 7/17/01	Wed 11/29/00	Tue 7/31/01	2 wks	2 wks
9	H: Construct Hospital	Wed 10/25/00	Tue 7/31/01	Wed 10/25/00	Tue 7/31/01	0 wks	0 wks
10	I: Develop Information	Wed 9/6/00	Tue 12/19/00	Wed 5/16/01	Tue 8/28/01	36 wks	36 wks
11	J: Install Equipment	Wed 8/1/01	Tue 8/28/01	Wed 8/1/01	Tue 8/28/01	0 wks	0 wks
12	K: Train Staff	Wed 8/29/01	Tue 10/9/01	Wed 8/29/01	Tue 10/9/01	0 wks	0 wks
13	Finish	Tue 10/9/01	Tue 10/9/01	Tue 10/9/01	Tue 10/9/01	0 wks	0 wks

Decision Point The total slack in an activity depends on the performance of activities leading to it. If the project team decides to schedule activity A to begin in week 2 instead of immediately, the total slack for activities C and G would be zero. Thus, total slack is shared among all activities on a particular path. The table also shows that several activities have free slack. For example, activity G has two weeks of free slack. If the schedule goes as planned to week 22 when activity G is scheduled to start, and the supplier for the equipment asks for a two-week extension on the delivery date, the project team knows that the delay will not affect the schedule for the other activities. Nonetheless, activity G would be on the critical path.

ANALYZING COST–TIME TRADE-OFFS

Keeping costs at acceptable levels is almost always as important as meeting schedule dates. The reality of project management is that there are always time and cost trade-offs. For example, a project can often be completed earlier than scheduled by hiring more workers or running extra shifts. Such actions could be advantageous if savings or additional revenues accrue from completing the project early.

Total project costs are the sum of direct costs, indirect costs, and penalty costs. These costs are dependent either on activity times or on project completion time. Direct costs include labour, materials, and any other costs directly related to project activities. Managers can shorten individual activity times by using additional direct resources such as overtime, personnel, or equipment. Indirect costs include administration, depreciation, financial, and other variable overhead costs that can be avoided by reducing total project time: the shorter the duration of the project, the lower the indirect costs will be. Finally, a project may incur penalty costs if it extends beyond some specific date, whereas a bonus may be provided for early completion. The Managerial Practice feature on page 74 shows how substantial delays and cost overruns can be often driven by the overall novelty or complexity of the project.

A project manager may consider *crashing*, or expediting, some activities on the critical path (or paths) to reduce overall project completion time. However, reducing the time of an activity comes at an extra cost, termed the **crash cost**, in addition to the normal activity cost. For example, if a particular construction activity was on the critical

crash cost The additional cost associated with reducing an activity time.

MANAGERIAL PRACTICE
Despite Project Delays, Bridge Retrofit a Modern-Day Miracle

The project went about $25 million over budget and inflicted more than two years of delays on commuters when it finished 18 months behind schedule. But the buzz on the soon-to-be completed reconstruction of Vancouver's Lions Gate Bridge is that a minor engineering miracle was performed high above Burrard Inlet. During that time, construction crews have been rebuilding this suspension bridge, which connects Vancouver's North Shore to the downtown, piece by piece. The bridge now has wider lanes and sidewalks, features viewing platforms, and can withstand a major earthquake.

The technological marvel in all this was that the retrofit project was done without closing the bridge to weekday traffic. The idea to keep the crossing open during the reconstruction came from the bridge's owner, the Province of British Columbia. Aging bridges that need to be rebuilt are usually closed for two or three months, during which crews work around the clock replacing panels, section by section. That wasn't an option with the Lions Gate, because closing it would have meant gridlock for commuters, as it is one of only two bridges connecting the downtown to the North Shore, with up to 70 000 cars crossing every day.

That meant the work was done on the weekends and at night, during ten-hour periods between 8 p.m. and 6 a.m.—an engineering feat never before attempted on a bridge that size. "You're into major, technical calculations with a project like this," noted one engineering expert. "This has never been done on a major suspension bridge."

But what looked like a doable and daring project on paper ran aground with glitches, delays, and soaring costs. Assistant project manager Carson Carney noted that task was more difficult than first thought. Delays developed early on, as problems arose with the assembly plan to rebuild the bridge in short time bursts. At night, workers were required to perform a tightly choreographed construction dance, which, on some evenings, called on them to dismantle a 10- or 20-metre section of the bridge, lower it onto a barge, hoist a new panel into place, then splice it to the existing deck using 800 bolts—all before morning rush hour. However, removing an entire section of a suspension bridge changes its shape. To prevent the bridge from buckling

The retrofit project for the Lions Gate Bridge in Vancouver, B.C., was done without closing the bridge to weekday traffic.

when a section was removed, engineers were constantly adjusting the pressure on the bridge's suspended hangers.

"Certainly, it is an engineering first, and in that respect it is a success," Mr. Carney said. "The fact that it was done, that it was able to be done, is really a marvel of modern engineering."

Source: Jane Armstrong, "Bridge Retrofit a Modern Miracle," *The Globe and Mail*, January 7, 2002, p. A8. Reprinted with permission from *The Globe and Mail*.

path, overtime might be used to accelerate its completion. Alternatively, for activities *not* on the critical path, savings might be possible if their times can be extended. For example, materials might be shipped by ground freight rather than air freight, if critical activities are not delayed.

MINIMIZING COSTS. The objective of this cost analysis is to determine the project schedule that minimizes total project costs. In determining the **minimum-cost schedule**, we start with the normal time schedule and crash activities along the critical path—the length of which is the total time of the project. We want to determine by how much we can reduce the time of critical activities, until the crash costs exceed the savings in indirect and penalty costs. The procedure involves the following steps:

minimum-cost schedule
A schedule determined by crashing activities along the critical path (or paths) such that the costs of crashing do not exceed the savings from penalty and indirect costs. Non-critical activities also may be extended.

- *Step 1.* Determine the project's critical path(s).
- *Step 2.* Find the activity or activities on the critical path(s) with the lowest cost of crashing per week.
- *Step 3.* Reduce the time for this activity until (a) it cannot be further reduced, (b) another path becomes critical, or (c) the increase in direct costs exceeds the savings that result from shortening the project. If more than one path is critical, the time for an activity on each path may have to be reduced simultaneously.
- *Step 4.* Repeat this procedure until the increase in direct costs is larger than the savings generated by shortening the project.

EXAMPLE 3.4

Finding a Minimum-Cost Schedule

For the St. Adolf's Hospital project, indirect costs have been estimated at $8000 per week. However, after week 65, if the hospital is not fully operational, provincial government regulators will impose a penalty cost of $20 000 per week. With the current critical path completion time of 69 weeks, the hospital faces large penalty costs unless the schedule is changed. For every week that the project is shortened—to week 65—the hospital saves one week of penalty and indirect costs, or $28 000. For reductions beyond week 65, the savings are only the weekly indirect costs of $8000.

To determine the minimum-cost schedule for the St. Adolf's Hospital project, we need to use the information in Table 3.1 and Figure 3.2 (on page 70).

Without changes, the projected completion time of the project is 69 weeks. The project costs for that schedule are $1 992 000 in direct costs from Table 3.1, 69($8000) = $552 000 in indirect costs based on the total project time, and (69 − 65)($20 000) = $80 000 in penalty costs. In total, the project costs are $2 624 000.

TABLE 3.1

Direct Cost and Time Data for the Hospital Project

ACTIVITY	NORMAL ACTIVITY TIME (WEEKS)	NORMAL COST ($)	MINIMUM ACTIVITY TIME (WEEKS)	CRASH COST ($ PER WEEK)
A	12	$ 12 000	11	$10 000
B	9	50 000	7	7 000
C	10	4 000	5	6 000
D	10	16 000	8	2 500
E	24	120 000	14	8 000
F	10	10 000	6	1 500
G	35	500 000	25	7 000
H	40	1 200 000	35	12 000
I	15	40 000	10	2 500
J	4	10 000	1	3 000
K	6	30 000	5	9 000
Total		$1 992 000		

STAGE 1

- *Step 1.* As noted in Figure 3.2, the critical path is B–D–H–J–K.
- *Step 2.* The cheapest activity on the critical path to crash per week is D at $2500,

which is much less than the savings in indirect and penalty costs of $28 000 per week.

- *Step 3.* Crash activity D by only 2 weeks, because now a second critical path is present. Now, as depicted in Figure 3.5, the two critical paths are:

  A–C–G–J–K: 67 weeks, and B–D–H–J–K: 67 weeks

FIGURE 3.5

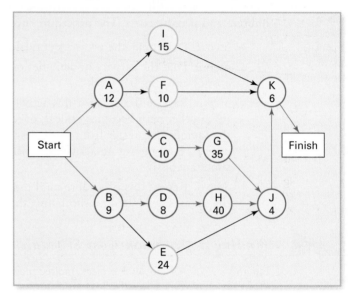

The net savings are 2($28 000) − 2($2500) = $51 000. The total project costs are now $2 624 000 − $51 000 = $2 573 000.

STAGE 2

- *Step 1.* Because we now have two critical paths, both critical paths must now be shortened to realize any savings in indirect project costs. If one is shortened and the other is not, the length of the project remains unchanged.

- *Step 2.* Our alternatives are to crash one of the following combinations of activities—(A, B), (A, D), (A, H), (C, B), (C, D), (C, H), (G, B), (G, D), (G, H)—or to crash either activity J or K, which are on both critical paths.

- *Step 3.* The lowest-cost alternative is to crash J at a cost of $3000 per week for 3 weeks, which is the greatest extent possible for J. As shown in Figure 3.6, updated critical path times are:

  A–C–G–J–K: 64 weeks B–D–H–J–K: 64 weeks

As we are now less than the required 65 weeks, penalty costs are saved for only two weeks, not three. However, indirect costs are saved for all three weeks. As a result, the net savings are 2($28 000) + $8000 − 3($3000) = $55 000. Total project costs are $2 573 000 − $55 000 = $2 518 000.

Decision Point The lowest-cost alternative to crash is now the combination of (C, D) at a cost of $8500 per week. Because this exceeds weekly indirect costs, any other combination of activities will result in a net increase in total project costs.

The minimum-cost schedule is 64 weeks, with a total cost of $2 518 000. To obtain this schedule, the project team must crash activity D to 8 weeks and activity J to its minimum of 1 week. The other activities remain at their normal times. This schedule costs $106 000 less than the normal-time schedule.

If a noncritical activity can be extended without creating a path longer than the existing critical paths, further cost savings are possible. For example, if activity I could be extended from a normal time of 15 weeks to 21 weeks by using part-time instead of full-time staff, further sav-

FIGURE 3.6

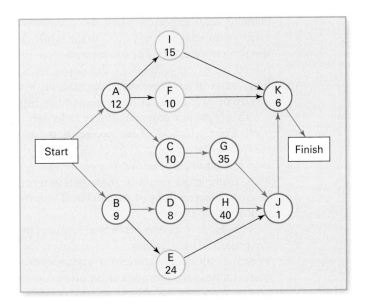

ings might be possible. (Recall from Figure 3.4 that the free slack is 36 weeks.) If the savings were $2000 per week, the total project costs would be reduced to $2 518 000 − (6)($2000) = $2 506 000.

ASSESSING RISKS

Risk is a measure of the probability and consequence of not reaching a defined project goal. Risk involves the notion of uncertainty as it relates to project timing and costs. Often project teams must deal with uncertainty caused by labour shortages, weather, supply delays, or the outcomes of critical tests. A major responsibility of the project manager at the start of a project is to develop a **risk-management plan**. Team members should have an opportunity to describe the key risks to the project's success and pre-scribe ways to circumvent them, either by redefining key activities or by developing con-tingency plans in the event problems occur. A good risk-management plan will quantify the risks and predict their impact on the project. For each risk, the outcome is either acceptable or unacceptable, depending on the project manager's tolerance level for risk.

risk-management plan
A plan that identifies the key risks to a project's success and prescribes ways to circumvent them.

Project risks can be grouped into four categories: strategic alignment, new service or product attributes, team capability, and execution. First, the risk of poor *strategic alignment* can occur when projects work at cross-purposes to each other, or do not fit together to support the broader goals of the firm. Instead, a set of projects, called a program or *portfolio*, should be aligned around a common strategic purpose and col-lectively enhance customer value. For example, a financial services firm might under-take a set of four related projects: (1) determine what the competition offers in the way of financial reports; (2) design new reporting services; (3) implement changes to the reporting process to reduce customer errors and improve delivery speed; and (4) develop a new Web interface to reach out to new customers. These projects must be integrated in terms of both purpose and timing, and as additional proposals come for-ward, management must assess and prioritize these based on the fit with the existing portfolio.

Second, many projects involve introducing *new service or product attributes*. Market risk is embedded in project objectives that specify particular market share or sales volumes. Competitive actions, either in parallel to or in response to the project, may weaken the market, or economic conditions may change, resulting in lower demand than expected when the project was initially approved. Technological risk arises from scientific advances made while the project is underway, possibly rendering the project obsolete. For example, a new cell phone under development may be displaced by a new technology developed by a competitor. Also, legal risks, such as liability suits or environmental legislation, may require a change in the design of the service or product after development has begun.

Third, project *team capability* risks are concerns associated with the project team itself. Poor selection of the project manager and team members can compromise the completion of a project. The complexity of the project, relative to what the team or the firm has attempted before, is usually also a good indicator of the likelihood of problems. Complexity might be measured in terms of budget size, number of individuals or groups involved, mix of internal and external resources, and lack of related technological experience.

Finally, project *execution* risk captures potential problems related to implementing the project. The accuracy of information for the work breakdown schedule is critical, as well as all data required for assessing progress, completion times of activities, and costs. Ineffective communication often can contribute to delays. Problems that impede progress must be quickly identified, action items developed, and responsibility clearly assigned.

PERT/CPM networks can be used to quantify risks associated with project timing. Often the uncertainty associated with an activity can be reflected in the activity's time duration. For example, an activity in a new-product development project might be developing the enabling technology to manufacture it, an activity that may take from eight months to a year. To incorporate uncertainty into the network model, probability distributions of activity times can be used. There are two approaches: computer simulation and statistical analysis. With simulation, the time for each activity is randomly chosen from its probability distribution. The critical path of the network is determined and the completion date of the project computed. The procedure is repeated many times, which results in a probability distribution for the completion date.

The statistical analysis approach requires that activity times be stated in terms of three reasonable time estimates:

optimistic time The shortest time in which an activity can be completed, if all goes exceptionally well.

most likely time The probable time required to perform an activity.

pessimistic time The longest estimated time required to perform an activity.

1. The **optimistic time** (*a*) is the shortest time in which the activity can be completed, if all goes exceptionally well.

2. The **most likely time** (*m*) is the probable time required to perform the activity.

3. The **pessimistic time** (*b*) is the longest estimated time required to perform the activity.

In the remainder of this section, we will discuss how to calculate activity statistics using these three time estimates and how to analyze project risk using probabilities.

CALCULATING TIME STATISTICS. With three time estimates—the optimistic, most likely, and pessimistic—the project manager has enough information to estimate the probability that a project will be completed on schedule.

To do so, the project manager must first calculate the mean and variance of a probability distribution for each activity. In PERT/CPM, each activity time is treated as though it were a random variable derived from a beta probability distribution. This distribution can have various shapes, allowing the most likely time estimate or mode (*m*) to fall anywhere between the pessimistic (*b*) and optimistic (*a*) time estimates.

Two other key assumptions are required. First, we assume that *a*, *m*, and *b* can be estimated accurately, and represent a reasonable time range negotiated between the project manager and the team members responsible for the activities. Second, we assume that the standard deviation, σ, of the activity time is one-sixth the range $b - a$. Thus, the chance that actual activity times will fall between a and b is high.

The mean of the beta distribution can be estimated by using the following weighted average of the three time estimates:

$$t_e = \frac{a + 4m + b}{6}$$

The variance of the beta distribution for each activity is estimated as:

$$\sigma_e^2 = \left(\frac{b - a}{6}\right)^2$$

ANALYZING PROBABILITIES. Because time estimates for activities involve uncertainty, project managers are interested in determining the probability of meeting project completion deadlines. To develop the probability distribution for project completion time, we assume that the duration time of one activity does not depend on that of any other activity. This assumption enables us to estimate the mean and variance of the probability distribution of the time duration of the entire project by summing the duration times and variances of the activities along the critical path. However, if one work crew is assigned two activities that can be done at the same time, the activity times will be interdependent. In addition, if other paths in the network have small amounts of slack, one of them might become the critical path before the project is completed. In such a case, we should calculate a probability distribution for those paths.

Because of the assumption that the activity duration times are independent random variables, we can make use of the central limit theorem, which states that the sum of a group of independent, identically distributed random variables approaches a normal distribution as the number of random variables increases. The mean of the normal distribution is the sum of the expected activity times on the path. In the case of the critical path, it is the earliest expected completion time for the project, T_E:

$$T_E = \Sigma \text{ (Activity times, } t_e\text{, on the critical path)}$$

Similarly, because of the assumption of activity time independence, we use the sum of the variances of the activities along the path as the variance of the time distribution for that path. That is:

$$\sigma^2 = \Sigma \text{ (Variances of activities, } \sigma_e\text{, on the critical path)}$$

To analyze probabilities of completing a project by a certain date using the normal distribution, we use the z-transformation formula:

$$z = \frac{T - T_E}{\sqrt{\sigma^2}}$$

where:

T = Due date for the project

The procedure for assessing the probability of completing any activity in a project by a specific date is similar to the one just discussed. However, instead of the critical path, we would use the longest time path of activities from the start node to the activity node in question. See the Solved Problem on page 85 for an example of calculating the probability of completing a project on time.

MONITORING AND CONTROLLING PROJECTS

Once project planning is over, the challenge becomes keeping the project on schedule within the budget of allocated resources. In this section, we discuss how to monitor project status and resource usage. In addition, we identify the features of project management software useful for monitoring and controlling projects.

PROJECT STATUS

A good tracking system will help the project team accomplish its project goals. Often the very task of monitoring project progress motivates the team as it sees the benefits of its planning efforts come to fruition. It also focuses attention on the decisions that must be made as the project unfolds. Effective tracking systems collect information on three topics: open issues, risks, and schedule status.

OPEN ISSUES AND RISKS. One of the duties of the project manager is to make sure that issues that have been raised during the project actually get resolved in a timely fashion. The tracking system should remind the project manager of due dates for open issues and who was responsible for seeing that they are resolved. Likewise, it should provide the status of each risk to project delays specified in the risk-management plan so that the team can review them at each meeting. The project manager should also enter new issues or risks into the system as they arise. To be effective, the tracking system requires team members periodically to update information regarding their respective responsibilities. Although the tracking system can be computerized, it can also be as simple as using e-mail, voice mail, or meetings to convey the necessary information.

SCHEDULE STATUS. Even the best-laid project plans can go awry. Monitoring slack time in the project schedule can help the project manager control activities along the critical path. Suppose in the hospital project that activity A is completed in 16 weeks rather than the anticipated 12 weeks and that activity B takes 10 weeks instead of the expected 9 weeks. Table 3.2 shows how these delays affect slack times as of the 16th week of the project. Activities A and B are not shown because they have already been completed.

Negative slack occurs when the assumptions used to compute planned slack are invalid. Activities C, G, J, and K, which depend on the timely completion of activities A and B, show negative slack because they have been pushed beyond their planned latest start dates. The activities at the top of Table 3.2 are more critical than those at the bottom, because they are the furthest behind schedule and affect the completion time of the entire project. To meet the original completion target of week 69, the project manager must try to make up two weeks of time somewhere along path C–G–J–K. Moreover, one week will have to be made up along path D–H. If that time is made up, there will be

TABLE 3.2				

Slack Calculations After Activities A and B Have Been Completed

Activity	Duration	Earliest Start	Latest Start	Slack
C	10	16	14	−2
G	35	26	24	−2
J	4	61	59	−2
K	6	65	63	−2
D	10	10	9	−1
H	40	20	19	−1
E	24	10	35	25
I	15	16	48	32
F	10	16	53	37

two critical paths: C–G–J–K and D–H–J–K. Many project managers work with computer scheduling programs that generate slack reports like the one shown in Table 3.2.

PROJECT RESOURCES

The resources allocated to a project are consumed at an uneven rate that is a function of the timing of the schedules for the project's activities. Projects have a *life cycle* that consists of four major phases: organization, planning, execution, and closeout. Figure 3.7 shows that each of the four phases requires different resource commitments.

FIGURE 3.7

Project Life Cycle

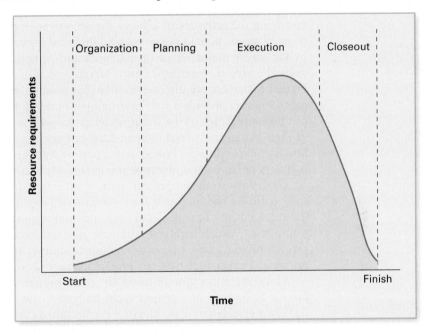

We have already discussed the activities associated with the project organization and project planning phases. The phase that takes the most resources is the *execution phase*, during which managers focus on activities pertaining to deliverables. The project schedule becomes very important, because it shows when each resource devoted to a given activity will be required. Monitoring the progress of activities throughout the project is important in order to avoid potential overloading of resources. Problems arise when a specific resource, such as a construction crew or staff specialist, is required on several activities with overlapping schedules. Project managers have several options to alleviate resource problems, including:

- *Resource levelling*, which is an attempt to reduce the peaks and valleys in resource needs by shifting the schedules of conflicting activities within their earliest and latest start dates. If an activity must be delayed beyond its latest start date, the completion date of the total project will be delayed unless activities on the critical path can be reduced to compensate.

- *Resource allocation*, which is an attempt to shift resources from activities with slack to those on the critical path where resources are overloaded. A slack report such as the one in Table 3.2 identifies potential candidates for resource shifting. However, efficiency can be compromised if shifted employees do not have all the skills required for their new assignments.

- *Resource acquisition*, which simply adds more of an overloaded resource to maintain the schedule of an activity.

The project *closeout* is an activity that many project managers forget to include in their consideration of resource usage. The purpose of this final phase in the project life cycle is to write final reports and complete remaining deliverables. A very important aspect of this phase, however, is compiling the team's recommendations for improving the project process of which they were a part. Many team members will be assigned to other projects where they can apply what they learned.

CONTROLLING PROJECTS

Project managers must account for the effective use of the firm's resources as well as managing the activities to achieve the objectives of the project. Resources include the physical assets, human resources, and financial resources. Physical assets are controlled by the timely maintenance of machines and equipment so that their failure does not delay the project. Inventories must be received, stored for future use, and replenished. Project managers are also responsible for human resource deployment and development. Projects provide a rich environment to develop future leaders; project managers can take advantage of the situation by assigning team members important tasks to aid in their managerial development. Last but not least, project managers must control financial expenditures. Project management software assists with accounting reports, budget reports, capital investment controls, and cash flow reports.

Deviations from the project plan, often referred to as *variances*, must be periodically reported and analyzed for their causes. Project managers can exert control over the achievement of the project's time and quality goals by routine monitoring of exception reports, which highlight variances that fall outside specified limits. Unacceptable project progress can trigger levelling, allocation, or acquisition decisions. Industry norms and experience help the project manager know when to take action.

Three measures can be used to guide project managers (Mantel et al., 2005). *Earned value* (EV) of a project is the budgeted cost of the work actually completed to date. It is calculated by multiplying the budgeted cost of each activity by its percentage of completion and summing all activities in the project. *Actual cost* (AC) is the real cost of the work performed to date. Finally, *planned cost* (PC) is the budgeted cost of the work that was scheduled to have been completed to date in the original project plan. These measures can be used to calculate two indices for assessing project progress at any particular date during the project:

$$\text{Cost Performance Index (CPI)} = \frac{\text{EV}}{\text{AC}}$$

$$\text{Schedule Performance Index (SPI)} = \frac{\text{EV}}{\text{PC}}$$

The CPI tells you how actual project expenditures relate to the original project budget. The SPI tells you whether progress on the project's many activities is ahead or behind the project plan. The critical value for each index is 1.0. Values less than 1.0 are undesirable and, if low enough, would trigger action.

For example, suppose that as of today your project has EV = \$14 000, AC = \$20 000, and PC = \$19 000. Consequently,

$$\text{CPI} = \frac{\$14\ 000}{\$20\ 000} = 0.70$$

$$\text{SPI} = \frac{\$14\ 000}{\$19\ 000} = 0.74$$

The indices tell you that you have spent more than the original project plan allowed, and for the amount that you have spent so far, you have not progressed very well in the project schedule. This revelation would prompt you to re-examine your resource decisions to see why the schedule has slipped and review the expenditure history to see why project costs are exceeding the planned costs for the progress so far.

Monitoring and controlling projects are ongoing activities throughout the execution phase of the project life cycle. The project **close out**, however, is an activity that many project managers forget to include in their consideration of resource usage. The purpose of this final phase in the project life cycle is to write final reports and complete remaining deliverables. An important aspect of this phase, however, is compiling the team's recommendations for improving the project process of which they were a part. Many team members will be assigned to other projects where they can apply what they learned.

close out An activity that includes writing final reports, completing remaining deliverables, and compiling the team's recommendations for improving the project process.

MANAGING PROJECTS ACROSS THE ORGANIZATION

Projects are big and small. They are contained within a single department or cut across several departments. Many organizations have several projects going on at any one time, addressing issues of concern to finance, marketing, accounting, human resources, information systems, or operations. Regardless of the scope, projects are completed with the use of a project process. The size of the project team may be small and the need for project management software marginal, but successful projects will use the principles discussed in this chapter regardless of the discipline the project addresses.

The applicability of project processes is pervasive across all types of organizations and disciplines. Managers often find themselves working with counterparts from other departments. For example, consider a project to develop a corporate database at a bank. Because no department knows exactly what services a customer is receiving from the other departments, the project will consolidate information about corporate customers from many areas of the bank into one corporate database. From this information corporate banking services could be designed not only to better serve the corporate customers but also to provide a basis for evaluating the prices that the bank charges. Marketing is interested in knowing all the services a customer is receiving so that it can package and sell other services that the customer may not be aware of. Finance is interested in how "profitable" a customer is to the bank and whether provided services are appropriately priced. The project team should consist of representatives from marketing, the finance departments with a direct interest in corporate clients, and management information systems. Projects such as this one are becoming more common as companies take advantage of the Internet to provide services and products directly to the customer.

EQUATION SUMMARY

1. Start and finish times:

$$ES = \max [\text{EF times of all activities immediately preceding activity}]$$
$$EF = ES + t$$
$$LF = \min [\text{LS times of all activities immediately following activity}]$$
$$LS = LF - t$$

2. Activity total slack:

$$S = LS - ES \quad \text{or} \quad S = LF - EF$$

3. Activity time statistics:

$$t_e = \frac{a + 4m + b}{6} \quad \text{(expected activity time)}$$

$$\sigma_e^2 = \left(\frac{b - a}{6}\right)^2 \quad \text{(variance of activity time)}$$

4. *z*-transformation formula:

$$z = \frac{T - T_E}{\sqrt{\sigma^2}}$$

where:

T = Due date for the project

$T_E = \Sigma$ (expected activity times on the critical path) $= \Sigma t_e$

$\sigma^2 = \Sigma$ (variances of activities on the critical path) $= \Sigma \sigma_e^2$

5. Monitoring project progress:

$$CPI = \frac{EV}{AC}$$

$$SPI = \frac{EV}{PC}$$

where:

CPI = cost performance index

SPI = schedule performance index

EV = earned value, or budgeted cost of the work actually completed to date

AC = actual cost of the work performed to date

PC = planned cost of the work that was scheduled to have been completed to date

CHAPTER HIGHLIGHTS

- A project is an interrelated set of activities that often transcends functional boundaries. A project process is the organization and management of the resources dedicated to completing a project. Managing project processes involves organizing, planning, and monitoring and controlling the project.

- Project planning involves defining the work breakdown structure, diagramming the network, developing a schedule, analyzing cost–time trade-offs, and assessing risks.

- Project planning and scheduling focus on the critical path: the sequence of activities requiring the greatest cumulative amount of time for completion. Delay in critical activities will delay the entire project.

- A project manager may consider crashing, or expediting, some activities on the critical path (or paths) to reduce overall project completion time. However, reducing the time of an activity comes at an extra cost, termed the crash cost, in addition to the normal activity cost.

- Risks associated with the completion of activities on schedule can be incorporated in project networks by recognizing three time estimates for each activity and then calculating expected activity times and variances. The probability of completing the schedule by a certain date can be computed with this information.

- Monitoring and controlling the project involves the use of activity-time slack reports and reports on actual resource usage. Overloads on certain resources can be rectified by resource levelling, allocation, or acquisition.

CD-ROM RESOURCES

The Student CD-ROM that accompanies this text contains the following resources, which allow you to further practise and apply the concepts presented in this chapter.

- **Equation Summary**: All the equations for this chapter can be found in one convenient location.

- **Discussion Questions**: Three questions will challenge your understanding of the role of project management by asking you to reflect on your experiences.

- **Microsoft Project**: A student version is included to develop project plans.

- **Case**: *The Pert Studebaker.* Will Vikky Roberts complete the project on time and within budget?

- **The Big Picture**: *Coors Field Baseball Stadium Project.* See how a major-league baseball stadium is constructed and how project leader John Lehigh and his team coped with the many unforeseen events.

- **OM Explorer Solvers**: OM Explorer has two spreadsheets designed to solve project planning problems with uncertainty, and another to assist with budgeting.

- **Extend LT**: *Connect Telecom* must improve its process for new product introductions.

- **Supplement C:** *Work Measurement.* This supplement presents several tools for estimating the time to perform predictable or repetitive project tasks after learning effects have worn off.

- **Supplement D:** *Learning Curve Analysis.* This supplement provides the background to estimate the time or resources required to perform an activity consisting of the production of a given number of identical units.

SOLVED PROBLEM

An advertising project manager has gathered the activity information for a new advertising campaign as shown in the accompanying table. The project deadline is 23 weeks. What is the probability of completing the project by that time?

ACTIVITY	TIME ESTIMATES (weeks)			IMMEDIATE PREDECESSOR(S)
	OPTIMISTIC	MOST LIKELY	PESSIMISTIC	
A	1	4	7	—
B	2	6	7	—
C	3	3	6	B
D	6	13	14	A
E	3	6	12	A, C
F	6	8	16	B
G	1	5	6	E, F

SOLUTION

The expected time and variance for each activity are calculated as follows:

$$t_e = \frac{a + 4m + b}{6}, \quad \sigma_e^2 = \left(\frac{b - a}{6}\right)^2$$

ACTIVITY	EXPECTED TIME (WEEKS)	VARIANCE
A	4.0	1.00
B	5.5	0.69
C	3.5	0.25
D	12.0	1.78
E	6.5	2.25
F	9.0	2.78
G	4.5	0.69

Now we need to calculate the earliest start, latest start, earliest finish, and latest finish times for each activity. Starting with activities A and B, we proceed from the beginning of the network and move to the end, calculating the earliest start and finish times, on the basis of the expected activity times. The earliest finish for the project is week 20, when activity G has been completed. This is shown graphically in Figure 3.8. Using that as a target date, we can work backward through the network, calculating the latest start and finish times (also in Figure 3.8).

Network Diagram with All Time Estimates Needed to Calculate Slack

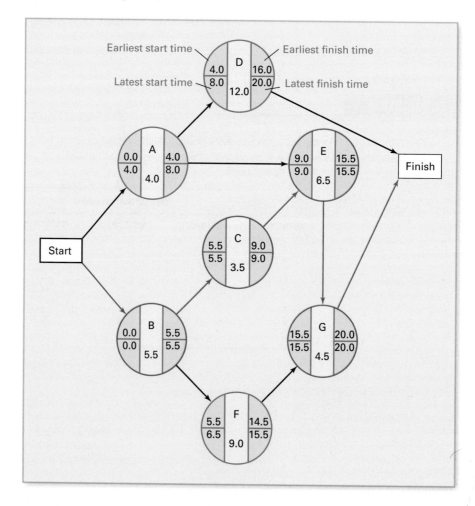

The activities on the critical path can now be identified based on having no slack (i.e., LS − ES = 0). Here the critical path is B–C–E–G, with a total expected time of 20 weeks. The variance of this path is $(0.69 + 0.25 + 2.25 + 0.69) = 3.88$.

To find the probability of completing the project in 23 weeks or less, we first calculate the z-value:

$$z = \frac{T - T_E}{\sqrt{\sigma^2}} = \frac{23 - 20}{\sqrt{3.88}} = 1.52$$

Using the Normal Distribution appendix, we find that the probability of completing the project in 23 weeks or less is 0.9357. In other words, the probability that the project will exceed 23 weeks is 6 percent. However, the length of path B–F–G, at 19 weeks, is very close to that of the critical path and also has a large variance of 4.16. This path might well become the critical path as the project proceeds. The probability that this path might exceed 23 weeks, for which $z = 1.96$, is 5 percent.

PROBLEMS

1. A project has the following precedence relationships and activity times:

ACTIVITY	ACTIVITY TIME (weeks)	IMMEDIATE PREDECESSOR(S)
A	4	—
B	10	—
C	5	A
D	15	B, C
E	12	B
F	4	D
G	8	E
H	7	F, G

   a. Draw the network diagram.

   b. Calculate the total slack for each activity. Which activities are on the critical path?

2. Consider the following project information.

ACTIVITY	ACTIVITY TIME (weeks)	IMMEDIATE PREDECESSOR(S)
A	4	—
B	3	—
C	5	—
D	3	A, B
E	6	B
F	4	D, C
G	8	E, C
H	12	F, G

   a. Draw the network diagram for this project.

   b. Specify the critical path.

   c. Calculate the total slack for activities A and D.

   d. What happens to the slack for D if A takes five weeks?

3. Recently, you were assigned to manage a project for your company. You have constructed a network diagram depicting the various activities in the project (Figure 3.9). In addition,

you have asked your team to estimate the amount of time that they would expect each of the activities to take. Their responses are shown in the following table.

ACTIVITY	TIME ESTIMATES (days)		
	OPTIMISTIC	MOST LIKELY	PESSIMISTIC
A	5	8	11
B	4	8	11
C	5	6	7
D	2	4	6
E	4	7	10

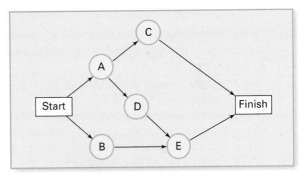

FIGURE 3.9   **Project Diagram**

   a. What is the expected completion time of the project?

   b. What is the probability of completing the project in 21 days or less?

   c. What is the probability of completing the project in 17 days or less?

4. The director of continuing education at Bluebird University has just approved the planning for a sales training seminar. Her administrative assistant has identified the various activities that must be done and their relationships to each other, as shown in Table 3.3.

TABLE 3.3 *Activities for the Sales Training Seminar*

ACTIVITY	DESCRIPTION	IMMEDIATE PREDECESSOR(S)
A	Design brochure and course announcement.	—
B	Identify prospective teachers.	—
C	Prepare detailed outline of course.	—
D	Send brochure and student applications.	A
E	Send teacher applications.	B
F	Select teacher for course.	C, E
G	Accept students.	D
H	Select text for course.	F
I	Order and receive texts.	G, H
J	Prepare room for class.	G

Because of the uncertainty in planning the new course, the assistant also has supplied time estimates for each activity.

ACTIVITY	TIME ESTIMATES (days)		
	OPTIMISTIC	MOST LIKELY	PESSIMISTIC
A	5	7	8
B	6	8	12
C	3	4	5
D	11	17	25
E	8	10	12
F	3	4	5
G	4	8	9
H	5	7	9
I	8	11	17
J	4	4	4

The director wants to conduct the seminar 47 working days from now. What is the probability that everything will be ready in time?

5. Jason Ritz, district manager for Gumfull Foods, Inc., is in charge of opening a new fast-food outlet. His major concern is the hiring of a manager and a cadre of hamburger cooks, assemblers, and dispensers. He also has to coordinate the renovation of a building that was previously owned by a pet-supplies retailer. He has gathered the data shown in Table 3.4.

Top management has told Ritz that the new outlet is to be opened as soon as possible. Every week that the project can be shortened will save the firm $1200 in lease costs. Ritz thought about how to save time during the project and came up with two possibilities. One was to employ Arctic, Inc., a local employment agency, to locate some good prospects for the manager's job. This approach would save three weeks in activity A and cost Gumfull Foods $2500. The other was to add a few workers to shorten the time for activity B by two weeks at an additional cost of $2700.

Help Jason Ritz by answering the following questions:

a. How long is the project expected to take?
b. Suppose that Ritz has a personal goal of completing the project in 14 weeks. What is the probability that this will happen?
c. What additional expenditures should be made to reduce the project's duration? Use the expected time for each activity as though it were certain.

6. Reliable Garage is completing production of the J2000 kit car. The following data are available for the project.

ACTIVITY	ACTIVITY TIME (Weeks)	IMMEDIATE PREDECESSOR(S)
A	2	—
B	6	A
C	4	B
D	5	C
E	7	C
F	5	C
G	5	F
H	3	D, E, G

a. Draw the network diagram for the project.
b. Determine the project's critical path and duration.
c. What is the total slack for each activity?

7. Information about a project is summarized in Table 3.5. The project must be shortened by three weeks (assume that project indirect costs and penalty costs are negligible). Identify which activities to crash while minimizing the crash costs.

TABLE 3.4 *Data for the Fast-Food Outlet Project*

ACTIVITY	DESCRIPTION	IMMEDIATE PREDECESSOR(S)	TIME (weeks) a	m	b
A	Interview for new manager.	—	2	4	6
B	Renovate building.	—	5	8	11
C	Place ad for employees and interview applicants.	—	7	9	17
D	Have new-manager prospects visit.	A	1	2	3
E	Purchase equipment for new outlet and install.	B	2	4	12
F	Check employee applicant references and make final selection.	C	4	4	4
G	Check references for new manager and make final selection.	D	1	1	1
H	Hold orientation meetings and do payroll paperwork.	E, F, G	2	2	2

TABLE 3.5 *Project Activity and Cost Data*

ACTIVITY	NORMAL TIME (days)	MINIMUM ACTIVITY TIME (days)	CRASH COST ($ per day)	IMMEDIATE PREDECESSOR(S)
A	7	6	200	—
B	12	9	250	—
C	7	6	250	A
D	6	5	300	A
E	1	1	—	B
F	1	1	—	C, D
G	3	1	200	D, E
H	3	2	350	F
I	2	2	—	G

a. What is the project's duration if only normal times are used?

b. What is the minimum-cost schedule?

c. What is the critical path for the minimum-cost schedule?

9. The project manager of Good Public Relations has gathered the data shown in Table 3.7 for a new advertising campaign.

a. How long is the project likely to take?

b. What is the probability that the project will take more than 38 weeks?

c. Consider the path A–E–G–H–J. What is the probability that this path will exceed the expected project duration?

8. A manager has compiled the information for a planned project in Table 3.6. Indirect project costs amount to $250 per day, and the company will incur a $100 per day penalty for each day the project lasts beyond day 14.

TABLE 3.6 *Project Activity and Cost Data*

ACTIVITY	NORMAL TIME (days)	NORMAL COST ($)	MINIMUM ACTIVITY TIME (days)	CRASH COST ($ per day)	IMMEDIATE PREDECESSOR(S)
A	5	1000	4	200	—
B	5	800	3	600	—
C	2	600	1	300	A, B
D	3	1500	2	500	B
E	5	900	3	150	C, D
F	2	1300	1	100	E
G	3	900	3	0	E
H	5	500	3	200	G

TABLE 3.7 *Activity Data for Advertising Project*

ACTIVITY	TIME ESTIMATES (days) Optimistic	Most Likely	Pessimistic	IMMEDIATE PREDECESSOR(S)
A	8	10	12	—
B	5	8	17	—
C	7	8	9	—
D	1	2	3	B
E	8	10	12	A, C
F	5	6	7	D, E
G	1	3	5	D, E
H	2	5	8	F, G
I	2	4	6	G
J	4	5	8	H
K	2	2	2	H

REFERENCES AND FURTHER READINGS

Branston, Lisa. "Construction Firms View the Web as a Way to Get Out from Under a Mountain of Paper." *The Wall Street Journal*, November 15, 1999.

Cleland, David I., and Lewis R. Ireland. *Project Management: Strategic Design and Implementation*, 4th ed. New York: McGraw-Hill, 2002.

IPS Associates. *Project Management Manual*. Boston: Harvard Business School Publishing, 1996.

Kerzner, Harold. *Applied Project Management: Best Practices on Implementation*. New York: John Wiley & Sons, 2000.

Kerzner, Harold. *Project Management: A Systems Approach to Planning, Scheduling and Controlling*, 6th ed. New York: John Wiley & Sons, 1998.

Mantel, Samuel J., Jr., Jack R. Meredith, Scott M. Shafer, and Margaret M. Sutton. *Project Management in Practice*, 2nd ed. New York: John Wiley & Sons, 2005.

Meredith, Jack R., and Samuel J. Mantel. *Project Management: A Managerial Approach*, 5th ed. New York: John Wiley & Sons, 2005.

Pellegrinelli, Sergio, and Cliff Bowman. "Implementing Strategy through Projects." *Long Range Planning*, vol. 27, no. 4 (1994), pp. 125–132.

"Project Management Body of Knowledge." Available from the Project Management Institute at <www.pmi.org>.

4 Capacity

Across the Organization

Capacity is important to:

- **accounting**, which prepares the cost accounting information needed to evaluate capacity expansion decisions.
- **finance**, which performs the financial analysis of proposed capacity expansion investments and raises funds to support them.
- **human resources**, which must hire and train employees to support capacity plans.
- **management information systems**, which design databases used in determining work standards that help in calculating capacity gaps.
- **marketing**, which provides demand forecasts needed to identify capacity gaps.
- **operations**, which must select capacity strategies that provide the capacity levels to meet future demand most effectively.
- **purchasing**, which obtains outside capacity that is outsourced.

Learning Goals

After reading this chapter, you will be able to:

1. describe different ways to measure capacity, establish process capacity, and calculate capacity utilization.
2. understand the linkages between capacity, inventory, and variability for process management.
3. identify bottlenecks, and discuss short- and long-term strategies to expand bottlenecks (related to the concept of the theory of constraints).
4. identify sources and forms of variability and understand the implications for process capacity.
5. explain the reasons for economies and diseconomies of scale.
6. discuss strategic issues such as capacity cushions, timing and sizing options, and linkages with other decisions.
7. identify a systematic approach to capacity planning.
8. describe how waiting-line models, simulation, and decision trees can assist capacity decisions.

In addition to making garbage trucks, Wittke Waste Equipment Ltd. used to manufacture three-quarters of the dumpster bins used in western Canada. Unfortunately, by the mid-1990s, the Medicine Hat, Alberta, plant's increasingly high-tech line of garbage trucks had hit the ditch and five general managers had come and gone in five years. To complicate matters, North America's waste sector was roiling through massive consolidations.

At that time, a new general manager, Pat Ross, in his mid-thirties, arrived and immediately began to reshape operations. Ross recalled, "We manufactured 15 models of vehicles, a ridiculously large number for a small outfit. We got dribbles of sales for esoteric vehicles in places like Singapore and Saudi Arabia but the business usually dried up when Ottawa's export financing ran out."

Nor was Wittke's capacity for making garbage trucks central to the plans of its Toronto-based parent, Northside Group Inc. Instead, corporate management had a vision that Northside would become a continental-scale parts supplier to heavy truck manufacturers. In Kelowna, B.C., Northside had a plant making sleeper cabs, bumpers, and many other components for a major customer, Western Star Trucks. A newly constructed plant in Virginia produced aluminum and steel fuel tanks for Volvo trucks. Another plant acquired in Vulcain, Quebec, made parts for Paccar/Kenworth Trucks and Bombardier. As the truck sector boomed into the late 1990s, garbage vehicles from Medicine Hat seemed a mere corporate sideline.

Immediately after arriving, Ross began to develop Wittke's people, eliminate dealers, and sell direct. These changes contributed to a breakthrough concept conceived by a long-term employee and a Canadian customer, which would prove crucial to Wittke's future growth and expansion. Garbage truck bodies typically weigh 9 to 10 tonnes, but Wittke developed an equally strong

Wittke Waste Equipment's production capacity for garbage trucks has increased dramatically in response to soaring demand.

body weighing just over 7 tonnes. Because it was lighter, the hydraulic tilting mechanisms on dumpster-handling trucks speeded up by as much as 20 percent, and the vehicles could load 15 to 20 percent more trash by weight without breaking road limits.

As a result of this breakthrough, Wittke's annual production soared over five years from a money-losing 220 trucks to a profitable 800. Plant payroll now tops 400. Waste Management, Inc., which handles 28 percent of North America's solid waste, recently placed an order for a minimum of 2100 trucks (worth an average of $250 000 apiece) over the next three years. Now, two-thirds of all front-end loading trash vehicles purchased in California today are made by Wittke.

The timing has worked out well too. "Heavy truck manufacturing has tanked badly. There's just too much manufacturing capacity," says Mr. Ross, who was made Northside's president a year ago. Wittke, not Western Star Trucks, is now the largest customer of the Kelowna parts manufacturing plant. In response, the Medicine Hat plant has embarked on a series of plant expansions that will, at minimum, double capacity. A third assembly line will increase capacity by approximately 500 units per year. A fourth assembly line has been "roughed in" and will be added when demand dictates.

For Wittke, capacity expansion has been nicely linked with product and process changes, allowing operations to provide a strong competitive advantage.

Source: Adapted with permission: M. Byfield, "Wittke, Medicine Hat's Biggest Employer Makes the World's Most Efficient Dumpster-Handling Vehicles," *Report Newsmagazine*, vol. 28 (2001), no. 13, pp. 35–36. Reprinted with permission of *Report Newsmagazine*. Additional information from Wittke Inc. Website at www.wittke.com, accessed April 4, 2003.

capacity The maximum
rate of output for a
process.

After deciding what products or services should be offered and how they should be made, management must plan the capacity of its processes. The experience of Wittke Waste Equipment demonstrates how important capacity planning and adjustments are to an organization's future. **Capacity** is the maximum rate of output for a process. The operations manager must provide the capacity to meet current and future demand; otherwise, the organization will miss opportunities for growth and profits.

Capacity planning is made at two levels. Long-term capacity plans, which we describe in this chapter, deal with investments in new facilities and equipment. These plans cover at least two years into the future, but construction lead times alone can force much longer time horizons. Canadian firms invest more than $80 billion annually in *new* facilities, plants, and equipment. Service industries account for about three-quarters of this investment. Such sizable investments require top-management participation and approval because they are not easily reversed. Short-term capacity plans focus on workforce size, overtime budgets, inventories, and other types of decisions that we explore in later chapters.

CAPACITY AND PROCESS CHOICE

Managerial decisions about process choice have significant implications for planning and managing process capacity (see Chapter 2, "Process Management" and Figure 2.1, p. 32). Process choice—whether a project, batch, line, or continuous flow process—implicitly combines three process factors: capacity utilization, inventory, and variability. These three factors are related, as a change in any one factor has managerial implications for the other two (Lovejoy, 1998). In a very practical sense, lower capacity utilization, greater inventory, and less variability are substitutes for each other (Figure 4.1). The basic management issues for each factor are first introduced, with a more detailed discussion in later chapters about the management of variability and inventory.

FIGURE 4.1

Process Management Triangle

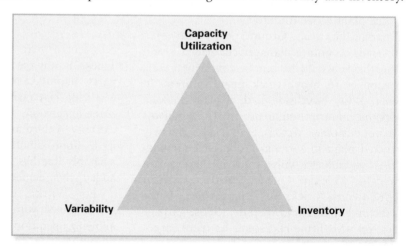

MEASURING CAPACITY

No single capacity measure is applicable to all types of situations. However, each measure is related to a maximum rate that captures items per unit time, either explicitly or implicitly. For example, an automobile assembly line might be able to produce 62 cars per hour. By way of comparison, a retailer might measure capacity as annual sales dollars generated per square metre per week, an airline as available seat-miles (ASMs) per month, and a small batch process as number of machine hours. Even if a theatre states its capacity as number of seats, time must be implicitly included based on the number of shows per day. In general, capacity can be expressed in one of two ways: output measures and input measures.

Output measures are the usual choice for high-volume processes that produce only a limited range of similar products or services, usually expressed in terms of output over a period of time (Statistics Canada, 2001). For example, capacity could be number of customers per day, cars per hour, or litres of water per minute. Naturally, the actual output rate of a process might be much less than the capacity because of inefficiencies or lack of demand.

Measuring output is preferred when the firm provides a relatively small number of standardized products and services, or when applied to individual processes within the overall firm. For example, a restaurant may be able to handle 100 takeout customers *or* 50 sitdown customers per hour. It might also handle 50 takeout *and* 25 sitdown customers or many other combinations of the two types of customers. However, as the range of products and services or degree of customization increases, translating each output into a common metric becomes very challenging. For example, a bank would have one capacity measure for processes that serve customers with the Internet and another measure for customers served with traditional "bricks-and-mortar" facilities.

Input measures are the usual choice for low-volume, flexible processes. For example, in a photocopy centre, capacity can be measured in machine-hours or number of machines. Just as product mix can complicate output capacity measures, so too can demand complicate input measures. Demand, which invariably is expressed as an output rate, must be converted to an input measure. Only after making the conversion can a manager compare demand requirements and capacity on an equivalent basis. For example, the manager of a copy centre must convert its annual demand from different clients for copies to the number of machine-hours required.

As noted in Chapter 1, "Competing with Operations," these measures of output and input can be combined to calculate the ratio of productivity for a process. Comparisons then can be made to industry benchmarks or competitors, and managers can also track internal improvement over time.

UTILIZATION. Capacity planning requires a knowledge of the current capacity of a process, as well as the degree to which a process or resource is actually being used to produce goods and services. **Capacity utilization**, or the degree to which equipment, space, or labour is currently being used, is expressed as a percentage:

capacity utilization The degree to which capacity is currently being used to generate products or services.

$$\text{Capacity utilization} = \frac{\text{Output}}{\text{Effective capacity}} \times 100\%$$

Capacity utilization is an important indicator that helps operations managers decide whether adding extra capacity or eliminating unneeded capacity might improve competitiveness. As technology increases productivity, the product- and service-mix changes, and workers develop and learn better methods, capacity utilization at individual operations can change quite dramatically.

Both output and effective capacity must be measured in the same terms, such as customers per hour, units, minutes, or dollars. Usually, output is based on the *actual* quantity of goods or services produced by the process. However, in some circumstances when the market demand exceeds process capacity, output is better expressed in terms of *required* quantity. The greatest difficulty in calculating capacity utilization lies in defining effective capacity, the denominator in the ratio.

effective capacity The maximum output that a process or firm can reasonably sustain under normal conditions.

EFFECTIVE CAPACITY. The maximum output that a process or firm can reasonably sustain under *normal conditions* is its **effective capacity**. In some organizations, effective capacity implies a one-shift operation; in others, it implies a three-shift operation. The critical issue is identifying the greatest level of output a process can reasonably sustain by using realistic employee work schedules and the equipment currently in place.

PEAK CAPACITY. The maximum output that a process or facility can achieve under *ideal conditions* is called **peak capacity**. When capacity is measured relative to equipment alone, the appropriate measure is rated capacity: an engineering assessment of maximum annual output, assuming continuous operation except for an allowance for normal maintenance and repair downtime. Peak capacity can be sustained for only a short time, such as a few hours in a day or a few days in a month. A process reaches it by using marginal methods of production, such as excessive overtime, extra shifts, temporarily reduced maintenance activities, overstaffing, and subcontracting. Although they can help with temporary peaks, these options cannot be sustained for long. Employees do not want to work excessive overtime for extended periods; overtime and night-shift premiums drive up costs and quality drops.

When operating at close to peak capacity, a firm can make minimal profits or even lose money despite high sales levels. Cummins Engine Company reacted a few years ago to an unexpected demand surge caused by the weakened dollar by working at peak capacity: the plant operated three shifts, often seven days a week. Overtime soared and exhausted workers dragged down productivity. Productivity suffered when Cummins called back less-skilled workers, laid off during an earlier slump. These factors caused Cummins to report a quarterly loss of $6.2 million, even as sales jumped.

CALCULATING PROCESS CAPACITY. Most processes involve multiple operations, and their effective capacities are not usually identical. Within a process, a **bottleneck** is an operation that has the lowest effective capacity of any operation in the process and, thus, limits the system's output. Alternatively, if customer demand exceeds process capacity, a bottleneck is any operation with capacity utilization greater than 100 percent.

For example, let's consider a simplified process for making a wooden drawer that becomes part of a computer desk. Four basic operations are required (Figure 4.2). First, the basic pieces of a drawer (two sides, front, and back) are put together by two people in drawer fabrication. Next, the drawers are moved to an automated operation that nails and glues the sides and bottom of the drawer. Third, another person performs some touchup sanding and places the drawer on a conveyor. Last, the drawer has a clear finish sprayed on as it moves through a spray booth. The effective capacities are noted in Figure 4.2.

peak capacity The maximum output that a process or facility can achieve under ideal conditions.

bottleneck An operation that has the lowest effective capacity of any operation in the process and, thus, limits the output rate of the process. Alternatively, a bottleneck is any operation with capacity utilization greater than 100 percent.

FIGURE 4.2

Identifying the Capacity Bottleneck

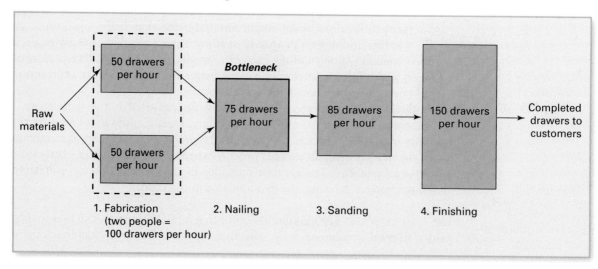

If each operation works without breakdowns or quality problems, the second operation (Nailing) is the bottleneck operation that limits the process output to 75 drawers per hour. In effect, the entire drawer manufacturing *process* can produce only as fast as the slowest operation. So the process capacity is set by this bottleneck, specifically 75 drawers per hour. Expansion of the overall process capacity occurs only when capacity at the bottleneck operation is increased.

COMPLEX PROCESSES. Many service and manufacturing firms offer multiple products in small volumes, each of which may have a different sequence of operations or workstations. For example, project or small batch processes do not enjoy the simple line flows shown in Figure 4.2. Even if a similar sequence is followed, the operations time may be unique for each customer or product. However, process capacity and bottlenecks can still be identified by computing the average utilization of each operation across a group of projects, customers, or products, as we see in Example 4.1.

EXAMPLE 4.1	*Identifying Capacity in a Service Process*

Speedy Loan, a financial services company, promises fast turnaround on loan applications. It offers three basic types of loans: (A) new mortgage applications; (B) mortgage renewals; and (C) car loans. Loan applications are processed through five different workstations (V, W, X, Y, and Z). Except for workstation X, which has two workers, all workstations are staffed by one worker.

Different types of loan applications require different steps to cross-reference the applicant's financial background, assess the applicant's risk profile, and compile the final loan authorization for signature. The flowcharts in Figure 4.3 note the order of steps and processing times per type of application. (Inverted triangles at the beginning of each process represent the inbox or queue of applications waiting for processing.) Workers are currently available for 35 hours per week.

FIGURE 4.3

Flowcharts for Speedy Loan

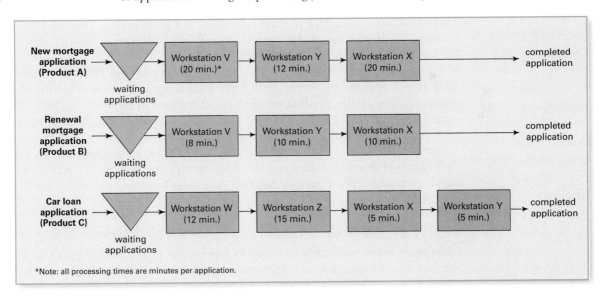

Customer demand currently is 60 new mortgage applications, 80 mortgage renewals, and 100 car loans. Which operation is the bottleneck, limiting the process capacity for Speedy Loan?

SOLUTION

For capacity utilization, the total workload (i.e., required output) for each workstation is based on the overall mix of applications, and processing time requirements for each application. Output is most easily expressed here as time required per week (i.e., minutes). The customer

TABLE 4.1 demand for each application, listed as Products A, B, and C, is converted into workload, and then summed across all three for each workstation, as noted in the sixth column of Table 4.1.

WORKSTATION	WORKERS (NUMBER)	WORKLOAD (MINUTES)				EFFECTIVE CAPACITY (MINUTES)	CAPACITY UTILIZATION (PERCENT)
		PRODUCT A	PRODUCT B	PRODUCT C	TOTAL		
V	1	60 × 20 = 1200	80 × 8 = 640	0	1840	2100	88
W	1	0	0	100 × 12 = 1200	1200	2100	57
X	2	60 × 20 = 1200	80 × 10 = 800	100 × 5 = 500	2500	4200	60
Y	1	60 × 12 = 720	80 × 10 = 800	100 × 5 = 500	2020	2100	96
Z	1	0	0	100 × 15 = 1500	1500	2100	71

The effective capacity is based on the number of workers and the number of available hours for each worker. Thus, effective capacity for each workstation is 35 hours or 2100 minutes per week, except for workstation X, which has two people, yielding 4200 minutes (see Table 4.1). So now capacity utilization is calculated as the ratio of required output to effective capacity for each workstation (last column).

Decision Point   The process capacity is set by the slowest operation, workstation V. This workstation needs the most total time to process all customer demand for the week. If customer demand increases even marginally, Speedy Loan will not be able to meet market requirements. Both workstations V and Y are bottlenecks to fully meet demand, and adding more capacity must be considered.

MARKET DEMAND.   More generally, market demand is also an important factor to consider when looking for bottlenecks. If demand exceeds the effective capacity of any individual operation, *each* of these operations is a bottleneck to creating satisfied customers. A clear signal of this unmet demand is to calculate a capacity utilization of greater than 100 percent for any operation.

For example, if the market requires 90 drawers per hour from the drawer manufacturing process, two operations have a capacity utilization of greater than 100 percent. Specifically, Nailing would have utilization of 90 ÷ 75 × 100 = 120 percent; for Sanding, utilization is 90 ÷ 85 × 100 = 106 percent. Both operations are bottlenecks; to fulfill all market demand, the effective capacity of both operations must be increased. So when identifying bottlenecks, it is important to keep two perspectives in mind: internally, the operation(s) that establishes process capacity, and externally, the operation(s) that has insufficient capacity to meet market demand.

INVENTORY

Inventory is any stock of items used to support the production of goods and services or satisfy customer demand. Further details are provided in Chapter 6, "Inventory Management," so it is sufficient at this point to recognize that items include any materials, orders, information, and people that flow through a process.

For purposes of process choice, inventory has two critical implications: cost and time. First, increasing the amount of inventory adds to the cost of producing goods and services. For example, if a copy centre holds a stock of raw paper between weekly deliveries from a supplier, the firm must pay for the related direct costs, such as working capital and handling. Even people waiting in line at a restaurant have a cost—for the physical space, customer aggravation, and potentially lost business.

Second, the amount of inventory is related to the time that customers or products take to move through a process. A waiting line at a bank offers a simple example; as the average number of people waiting in line in front of each teller increases, the average overall service time increases. The same principle applies to both manufacturing and services, where items are typically waiting in front of several operations. Thus, the total time that a typical item spends in any process, termed **throughput time**, increases as the average level of inventory in that process increases.

throughput time Total time for an item to move through a process from the first operation to the last, including operations time, movement time between operations, and wait time.

Inventory level and throughput time can be related mathematically using Little's Law (Little, 1992). The *average* throughput time for items in a process is related to both average work-in-process (WIP) inventory and actual output rate. (The first and last operation for the process must be clearly defined.)

$$\text{Throughput time} = \frac{\text{WIP inventory}}{\text{Output rate}}$$

Note that for this calculation, output rate must always be expressed as "items per time" (unlike capacity utilization, where both output and effective capacity can be expressed in any identical units). Thus, if a copy centre had an average of 80 customer orders waiting for or in various stages of production (e.g., layout, printing, and packaging) and serviced 200 customers each five-day week, an order is expected to take, on average, $80 \div 200 = 0.4$ weeks or two days to complete.

The throughput time for a *specific* item as it moves through a process can also be found by summing all the time for individual operations and activities:

$$\text{Throughput time} = \text{Operations time} + \text{Movement time} + \text{Wait time}$$

Wait time captures many sources of delay, including machine setup, waiting for resources (such as people, equipment, and information), and other delays. A summary of the relationships among these process measures is depicted in Figure 4.4. For example, throughput time includes both operation and wait time, and is a function of work-in-process inventory and actual production rate.

FIGURE 4.4

Measuring Process Performance

Source: Adapted from: R. B. Chase, N. J. Aquilano, and F. R. Jacobs, *Operations Management for Competitive Advantage* (New York: McGraw-Hill/ Irwin, 2001), p. 100.

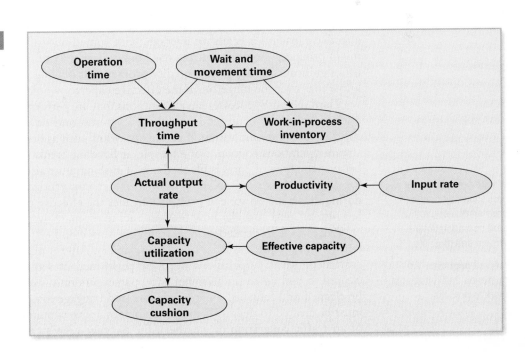

If increasing inventory adds to cost and throughput time, why do managers allow inventory to be in a process? This critical question returns us to the process management triangle (see Figure 4.1 on page 92). Inventory can smooth the flow of customers, parts, or materials through the process, which in turn necessitates less investment in capacity or serves as a buffer to accommodate greater variability.

VARIABILITY

Unfortunately, in practice, designing and evaluating process capacity is rarely as straightforward as illustrated in Figure 4.2 (page 94). Products, people, and equipment change from minute to minute, day to day, and year to year. Variation is really a measure of how much something changes. Many managers have a general intuition about the average production or demand rates for a process, usually based on observing a process over an extended period of time. Variability is much less intuitive.

For example, Bombardier's sales of a particular model of Sea-Doo watercraft in a particular region might average 27 units per day, based on sales during the previous year. A simple approach might be to install capacity to produce exactly 27 units per day. However, the product manager would quickly point out that exactly 27 units are not sold each and every day. Instead, sales tend to be much higher before the summer season, and much lower (if any) during the remainder of the year.

This variability affects Bombardier's entire process. Suppliers, manufacturing, assembly, logistics, and sales support, to name just a few subprocesses, must be designed to take into account this seasonal rise and fall in sales. Managers can choose to build a very large assembly plant to accommodate peak demand (i.e., greater capacity), or, more commonly, manufacture extra units ahead of peak season (i.e., greater inventory). If insufficient capacity or inventory is ready for the peak season, another, much less attractive option is to turn away customers! In essence, this last option reduces variability by lowering the maximum demand filled by operations.

IMPLICATIONS FOR PROCESS CAPACITY. If we return to our simple process in Figure 4.2, how is process capacity related to variability? First, it is important to clearly differentiate between the capacity of individual operations and the overall capacity of the process.

Second, if each individual operation has some variability, then its output rate (i.e., effective capacity) is really an average, with some hour-to-hour variation. So Nailing might produce 77 drawers during one hour and then 71 drawers the next hour because of a significant breakdown or quality problems. If Nailing were working by itself, we know that over the longer term the effective capacity would be 75 drawers per hour.

Third, because processes have operations that are performed in sequence, each operation is linked to, or depends on, those upstream and downstream. These are called *dependent operations*. Variation in one operation, such as breakdowns, can force downstream operations to stop. For example, if Sanding breaks down, Nailing must stop, because the flow of parts is **blocked**, and Finishing must also stop because it is **starved** for drawers. As a result, Nailing (bottleneck) cannot produce the expected 75 drawers during that hour. So we can't simply consider the effective capacity of each *operation*, but instead must consider how they interact to estimate overall process capacity.

Processes with dependent operations are very common. Air Canada offers another example where process delays create variability. After a plane arrives in Halifax with customers, several operations must be performed in sequence. The plane must be cleared to pull up to the terminal gate, passengers must be unloaded, the plane must be cleaned and refuelled, new passengers and baggage must be loaded, and the plane must be cleared to depart. If too many planes arrive simultaneously (possibly because of air traffic congestion or weather), the baggage crew's capacity will be overloaded,

blocked operation An operation that cannot pass work along to the next operation downstream and must stop.

starved operation An operation that runs out of work to process.

resulting in delays in unloading some planes. Processing a full plane also takes longer for some operations than a half-empty plane.

For our furniture manufacturing process to produce 75 drawers per hour, management has two basic options to accommodate the variability in Nailing and Sanding:

1. *Add capacity* to the Nailing bottleneck, so that the *process* is capable of producing the expected 75 parts per hour, even when breakdowns in Sanding occur. The extra capacity needed depends on the variability of Sanding. For example, an effective capacity of 79 drawers per hour at Nailing may be sufficient to accommodate the variability at Sanding (Figure 4.5(a)).

2. *Add inventory* between Nailing and Sanding, so that Nailing can continue to produce when a breakdown occurs in Sanding (Figure 4.5(b)). Because Sanding has a higher capacity, it will eventually catch up. For similar reasons, inventory could also be added ahead of the Nailing operation to accommodate variability in Fabrication and ensure that Nailing is never starved for parts. However, the allowable inventory ahead of Nailing must be limited; otherwise, the faster production of Fabrication will far outpace Nailing.

Naturally, as indicated by the process management triangle, a combination of additional capacity and inventory also would accommodate process variability. As the variability of Sanding increases further, additional capacity and inventory are necessary to maintain an average *process* output rate of 75 parts per hour. Again, the emphasis must be on the overall process capacity, not just on individual operations.

Maintaining Process Output Rate with Variability

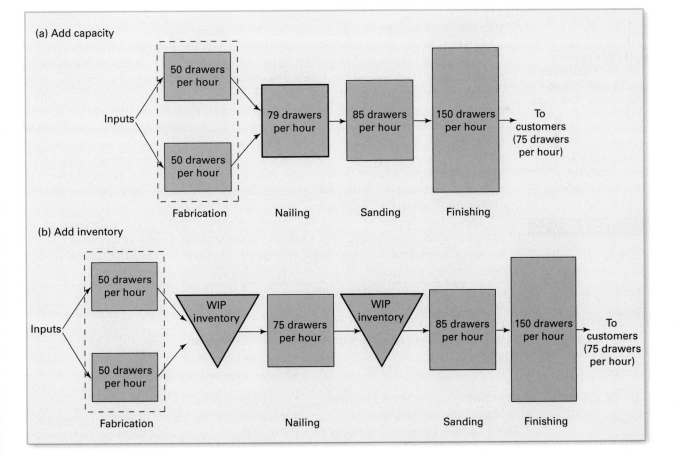

For Air Canada, variability in passenger loads or poor weather creates delays, which adds to work-in-process inventory in the form of passengers (although people undoubtedly dislike being termed "inventory"). To estimate how much additional capacity or inventory is needed, managers must measure variability by gathering data on the frequency and pattern of variability—which then can be translated into the right mix of capacity and inventory. One tool to assist with this analysis is computer simulation (see Supplement G on the Student CD-ROM, "Simulation").

MEASURING VARIABILITY. For operation processes, variability can occur in the operations time needed by an X-ray technician, the reliability of a laser printer, or the time needed for an airline check-in process. One basic measure for comparing variability between operations or processes is the *coefficient of variation* (cv). This measure is simply a ratio of the standard deviation (a common statistical measure of variation) to the average.

$$\text{Coefficient of variation} = \frac{\text{Standard deviation}}{\text{Average}}$$

The higher that process variability is, the more expensive and difficult the process is to manage. So how high is the cv for a process with high variability? It really depends on both the time horizon and the relative stability of process alternatives. For example, researchers have suggested a high variability process has a cv of greater than 1.33 (Hopp and Spearman, 2001). High process variability is present in situations, for example, where machine breakdowns require long repair times and customer demand fluctuates dramatically.

TWO FORMS OF VARIABILITY. It is important to recognize that variability is not simply uncertainty. When we consider the many ways variability is introduced into a process, it becomes clear that variability takes on two general forms with different implications for managers: random and predictable variation. **Random variation** is introduced by chance and results from small changes or differences in equipment operations, people's behaviour, or environmental conditions. This form corresponds to uncertainty. In contrast, **predictable variation** is determined by specific, usually larger-scale causes, often driven by natural cycles related to time of day, day of week, season of year, or even multiyear economic cycles. Many management decisions also create predictable variation. For example, scheduling preventive maintenance on an aircraft engine reduces the fleet capacity available at that time to serve customers. Examples of each form of variability are illustrated in Table 4.2.

These two forms of variability often combine, making the management of processes quite complicated. For example, a manager at a copy centre might know from past sales data that there is an average of 200 customers per five-day week, but

random variation
Uncertainty that results from chance related to small changes or differences in equipment operations, people's behaviour, or environmental conditions.

predictable variation
Changes determined by specific, usually larger-scale causes, often driven by natural cycles such as time of day. Many management decisions, such as preventive maintenance, also create predictable variation.

TABLE 4.2

Examples of Variability

Source	Form of Variability	
	Random	**Predictable**
Internal (e.g., process)	• Quality defects from a metal stamping press • Equipment breakdowns • Worker absenteeism	• Setup time for a packaging operation • Preventive maintenance • Number of models of an automobile
External (e.g., market)	• Arrival of individual customers at a hair salon • Transit time for local delivery of package • Medical treatments needed for emergency patient	• Daily pattern of demand for fast-food restaurant • Seasonal demand for printing of annual reports • More technical support immediately after new product launch

that sales tend to be higher at the end of the week (i.e., Thursday and Friday) with correspondingly lower figures at the beginning of the week (i.e., predictable variation). Yet, even for sales at the end of the week, the process must accommodate the random arrivals of particular customers, each with different copying needs. Customers (and orders) must wait longer for assistance, or more staff and copy machines must be scheduled.

Although both forms of variability can hurt the efficiency of a process, random variability is much more difficult for managers to adjust to—often at significant cost to the firm or the customer. In the short term, random variability must usually be accommodated, possibly by adding extra capacity, coping with longer waiting lines (see Supplement 4S in this book, "Waiting Lines"), or maintaining inventory of extra products (see Chapter 6, "Inventory Management"). Managers can take specific actions over the longer term to reduce random process variability, such as reducing poor-quality raw materials (see Chapter 5, "Quality"), scheduling the arrival of customers or the availability of equipment and parts (see Chapter 13, "Resource Planning"), or upgrading process technology (see Chapter 11, "Managing Technology").

Because predictable variability is linked to specific cycles or particular management practices, managers can plan and act with greater confidence. Preventive maintenance can be shifted to the weekend, additional staff can be added for service at lunchtime, or larger batches can be produced of a standard, frequently requested item. Predictable customer behaviour can also be modified to some degree, possibly through the use of incentives. Discounts can be offered to customers to shift demand in a relatively predictable manner.

If we return to our earlier discussion of bottlenecks, variability in workload for individual operations along a process can create *floating bottlenecks*. One week the particular mix of work may make Nailing a bottleneck, and the next week it may make Sanding appear to be the bottleneck. This type of variability increases the complexity of day-to-day scheduling. In this situation, management prefers lower utilization rates, which allow greater slack to absorb unexpected surges in demand.

Finally, variability should not be viewed as always bad. In fact, customers may desire a broad range of options. If a competitive priority of the firm is to respond to this market need, an operations manager should not be pushing for lower variability! Instead, operations can respond with greater flexibility and customization, which requires greater capacity (i.e., lower capacity utilization). Thus, whether good or bad, variability must be actively managed.

SIZING PROCESS CAPACITY

Planning for the right amount of capacity is central to the long-term success of an organization. Often, industry-level transformations may push managers to invest in new capacity, driven by changes in product and process technologies, as the Managerial Practice feature demonstrates. Moreover, too little capacity can often be as painful (in terms of lost opportunities) as too much capacity. When choosing a capacity strategy, managers have to consider such questions as the following: How much of a cushion do we need to handle variable, uncertain demand? Should we expand capacity before the demand is there or wait until demand is more certain? A systematic approach is needed to answer these and similar questions and to develop a capacity strategy appropriate for each situation.

MANAGERIAL PRACTICE
Costs and Benefits of Bank Mergers

Frequent discussions about possible mergers of large Canadian banks have fuelled much speculation about both costs and competitive benefits. One touted benefit is a better alignment of capacity with technology and market changes, in addition to cost savings. For example, in 2000, Toronto-Dominion Bank completed its acquisition of Canada Trust to create TD Bank Financial Group, with assets of $258 billion, a 20 percent increase. However, management expected to shed 4900 jobs and eventually close 275 retail branches following the acquisition.

Such a dramatic increase of capacity is by no means unique, as the global banking industry is in the biggest wave of consolidation in its history. Similar bank mergers have been carried out in other places, including Europe, Japan, and the United States, even on a larger scale. Over several years, a number of major mergers created JPMorgan Chase (www.jpmorganchase.com). By 2000, the combined operations of this financial institution had assets of US$660 billion and employed more than 100 000 people. Here, too, capacity consolidation was expected to streamline operations, with 12 000 job cuts and US$1.5 billion savings in annual expenses.

In addition to economies-of-scale benefits, acquisitions can also strengthen operational capabilities in targeted areas. One acquisition by Chase expanded capacity for investment banking through the addition of more than 300 highly trained professional staff. In this industry, where it is often said, "The assets go home at night," management estimates that it costs about US$250 000 per person to recruit, train, and retain such professionals.

In part, consolidation is a sensible response to excess capacity. Banking also has become a technology-driven business. More than ever, financial products and services, from loans to credit cards, are marketed through computers and telephones instead of through bank branches. Banks able to make large investments in technology gain an unparalleled ability to reach customers in Canada, the United States, and around the world. Unprecedented capital investments create the need to spread costs over a broader customer base.

Greater use of electronic and Web-based technologies also undermines a bank's traditional role as intermediary between borrowers and savers, making it easier for both kinds of customers to get together directly. Lower profit margins in retail banking encourage moves into wholesale business, such as investment banking, where size and large capacity can, to

The headquarters of TD Bank Financial Group in Toronto. Consolidation of operations not only can lead to cost savings but also provides economies-of-scale benefits in an increasingly technology-driven industry.

some extent, be equated with strength. Dealing with a product—money—that moves across borders electronically, banks are quick to feel the forces of globalization and technological change.

Although these reasons for large size can be impressive, there are concerns about capacity getting too big. When that happens, customers may withdraw their accounts and turn to smaller banks that meet a variety of personal and business banking needs. Small banks are generally more accustomed to giving a high degree of personalized service. To protect revenue, large banks must strive to offer the same exceptional service that small banks offer.

Source: S. Lipin and E. S. Browning, "Is the New Chase the Bank of the Future?" *The Wall Street Journal*, September 14, 2000; S. Morrison, "Toronto-Dominion to Buy Canada Trust," *Financial Times*, August 4, 1999; "The Bank-Merger Splurge," *The Economist*, August 28, 1999; and corporate Web sites.

THEORY OF CONSTRAINTS

Before expanding the capacity of any process, it is critical to ensure that existing resources are used efficiently and effectively. The fundamental idea underlying the **theory of constraints (TOC)** is to focus on bottleneck resources because increasing their output increases the output of the entire process (and financial performance). The bottleneck resources must be kept as busy as practical.

theory of constraints (TOC) An approach to management that focuses on whatever impedes progress toward the goal of maximizing the flow of total value-added funds or sales less discounts and variable costs. Also referred to as the drum-buffer-rope method.

To do so, managers should minimize the idle time lost at bottlenecks because jobs or customers are delayed at upstream operations in the process or because the necessary materials or tools are temporarily unavailable. They should also minimize the time spent unproductively for **setup time**, which is changing over from one product or service to another. When a changeover is made at a bottleneck operation, the number of units or customers processed before the next changeover should be large compared to the number processed at less critical operations. Maximizing the number processed per setup means that there will be fewer setups per year, and thus less total time lost to setups.

setup time The time required to change an operation from making one type of product or service to making another.

With TOC, sometimes referred to as the drum-buffer-rope method, managers must focus on scheduling around bottlenecks that impede progress toward the goal of making money. (TOC further defines making money as simultaneously improving net profit, return on investment, and cash flow.) The bottlenecks might be overloaded processes such as order entry, new-product development, or a manufacturing operation. The bottleneck becomes the "drum" for the rest of the process, setting the pace. Inputs are only pulled into the process at that pace (i.e., rope), and extra inventory is placed around the bottleneck so that it is never starved or blocked (i.e., buffer). Minimal inventory is allowed elsewhere in the process to minimize throughput time.

For example, let's return to our drawer manufacturing example (see Figure 4.5b). Suppose that the delivery commitments for all styles of computer desk drawers for the next month indicate that Nailing has a capacity utilization of 105 percent. The other three operations will have capacity utilization of less than 100 percent. According to TOC, Nailing is the only bottleneck resource, whereas the Fabrication, Sanding, and Finishing are nonbottleneck resources. Any idle time at Nailing is a lost opportunity to generate total value-added funds. To maximize the output rate of the drawer manufacturing system, managers should focus on Nailing's schedule.

APPLYING TOC. The theory of constraints focuses management's attention and action on the bottleneck, and involves the following steps:

1. *Identify the system bottleneck(s).* For the drawer manufacturing example, the bottleneck is Nailing because it is restricting the firm's ability to meet the schedules of subsequent processes. Bottlenecks also can often be identified by looking for the operation with the largest queue of parts being delayed or longest line of customers waiting for service.

2. *Exploit the bottleneck(s).* Create schedules that maximize the throughput of the bottleneck(s). For the drawer manufacturing example, schedule Nailing to maximize its utilization while meeting other commitments to the extent possible. Also make sure that only good-quality parts are passed on to the bottleneck from other operations.

3. *Subordinate all other decisions to step 2.* Nonbottleneck resources should be scheduled to support the schedule of the bottleneck and not produce more than it can handle. That is, Fabrication should not produce more than Nailing can handle, and the activities of Sanding and subsequent operations should be based on the output rate of Nailing.

4. *Elevate the bottleneck(s).* After the scheduling improvements in steps 1–3 have been exhausted and the bottleneck is still a constraint to throughput, management should consider increasing the capacity of the bottleneck. For example, if Nailing is still a constraint after exhausting schedule improvements, consider increasing its capacity by adding another shift or other resources.

5. *Do not let inertia set in.* Actions taken in steps 3 and 4 will improve Nailing's capacity and may alter the loads on other processes. Consequently, the system constraint(s) may have shifted. Then the steps need to be repeated in order to identify and manage the new set of constraints.

Over the longer term, capacity of bottleneck operations can be expanded in various ways. Investments can be made in new equipment and in bricks-and-mortar facility expansions. The bottleneck's capacity also can be expanded by operating it more hours per week, such as going from a one-shift operation to multiple shifts, or going from five workdays per week to six or seven workdays per week. Investing in new information technology can help highly skilled workers service more customers. Managers also might relieve the bottleneck by redesigning the process, through either process re-engineering or process improvement (see Chapter 2, "Process Management").

Details on the scheduling method used in TOC can be found in Simons and Simpson (1997). Large and small corporations have applied the principles of the theory of constraints; these include Delta Airlines, National Semiconductor, ITT, Dresser Industries, Allied-Signal, Bethlehem Steel, United Airlines, Johnson Controls, and Rockwell Automotive. General Motors' automotive trim plant in Windsor, Ontario, has reported inventory reductions of 68 percent and throughput time reductions of 94 percent over a two-year period. Just as important, output increased by 16.8 percent and annual costs fell by $23 million.

STRATEGICALLY LOCATING THE BOTTLENECK. So where would a thoughtful manager ideally want the bottleneck to be located in a process? The natural inclination of many managers is to try to achieve a perfectly balanced process to reduce total investment, where each operation has the same capacity. Alternatively, to simplify the task of coordinating the process, a manager could position the bottleneck as the first operation in a process.

However, the primary objective of any process is not to simplify scheduling or minimize investment, but instead to maximize *customer value* as discussed in Chapter 1, "Competing with Operations." As we saw in Figure 4.5 (page 99), variability requires managers to add both capacity and inventory to produce the average output rate demanded by customers. The logical action is to add both selectively, particularly to those stations where capacity is least expensive. Taking this a few steps further and continuing to add small amounts of capacity to accommodate variability, we soon see that the most expensive operation is the last place that we want to add capacity—which creates a bottleneck for the process. Then, on the basis of the drum-rope-buffer method, inventory must be added judiciously ahead of the bottleneck, with minimal inventory elsewhere in the process.

Thus, the most expensive operation should be our bottleneck (if it isn't, we have a significant opportunity for improvement!). But the most expensive operation is not necessarily the most expensive piece of equipment. In a software firm such as Corel Corporation, the developer of WordPerfect, the most expensive resource is highly skilled people, such as software engineers. These individuals should never be forced to be idle because they are waiting for other process operations, such as testing for bugs.

CAPACITY CUSHION

Average utilization rates should not get too close to 100 percent. When they do, that is usually a signal to increase capacity or decrease order acceptance so as to avoid declining productivity and maintain customer service. The **capacity cushion** is the amount of reserve capacity a firm maintains to handle sudden increases in demand or temporary losses of production capacity; it measures the amount by which the average capacity utilization falls below 100 percent. Specifically:

Capacity cushion = 100% − Capacity utilization (%)

Businesses find large cushions appropriate when variability increases. In certain service industries (e.g., groceries), demand on some days of the week is predictably higher than on other days, and there are even hour-to-hour patterns. Long customer waiting times are not acceptable, because customers grow impatient if they have to wait in a supermarket checkout line for more than a few minutes. Prompt customer service requires supermarkets to maintain a capacity cushion large enough to handle peak demand.

Similar issues arise if long-term future demand is uncertain, particularly if resource flexibility is low. Another type of demand uncertainty occurs with a changing product mix, possibly due to new product introductions or customized orders. Though total demand might remain stable, the load can shift unpredictably from one work centre to another as the mix changes. Supply uncertainty also favours large capacity cushions. Firms need to build in excess capacity to allow for employee absenteeism, vacations, holidays, and any other delays. Penalty costs for overtime and subcontracting can create the need for further increases in capacity cushions.

In general, capacity, inventory, and variability are strongly related to process choice, as depicted in Figure 4.6, with project and batch processes having higher variability, lower capacity utilization (and capital-intensity), and higher work-in-process

capacity cushion The amount of reserve capacity a firm maintains to handle variability in the process or demand. It measures the amount by which the average utilization falls below 100 percent.

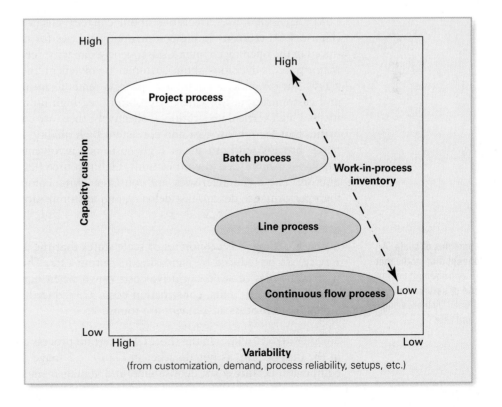

FIGURE 4.6

Matching Process Variability and Capacity Cushion

inventories. At the other end of the spectrum, continuous processes have lower variability, higher capacity utilization, and lower work-in-process inventory.

Over the past ten years, Canadian manufacturers have maintained an average cushion of 18 percent. However, given the linkage between process choice and capacity cushion, it is important to recognize that the average size of the cushion varies by industry. Moreover, for some industries, capacity comes in large, expensive increments, so expanding even by the minimum amount possible may create a large cushion. For example, a new paper plant is sized to capture economies of scale, and adding an airline route often requires flying a minimum number of flights, which can create overcapacity.

The argument in favour of small cushions is simple: unused capacity costs money. For capital-intensive firms, minimizing the capacity cushion is vital, as a low return on investment tends to occur if the utilization is low. As a result, managers in capital-intensive industries such as paper, chemicals, or steel prefer cushions of about 10 percent or lower. Small cushions have other advantages; they reveal inefficiencies that may be masked by capacity excesses—problems with absenteeism, for example, or unreliable suppliers. Once managers and workers have identified such problems, they often can find ways to correct them. However, these industries have great difficulty adjusting capacity to match peaks and valleys in market demand.

In more labour-intensive industries, where the number of workers can be easily adjusted, a larger capacity cushion is possible, because the lower investment in equipment makes high utilization less critical. For example, the less capital-intensive leather goods industry has a much larger cushion that averages about 26 percent in Canada. This industry can more easily accommodate changes in demand by varying the size of the workforce. Similar challenges arise in service firms. The hotel industry breaks even with 60 percent to 70 percent utilization (40 percent to 30 percent cushion) and begins to suffer customer service problems when the cushion drops to 20 percent.

COMPETITIVE PRIORITIES. Decisions about capacity cushions, inventory, and variability (Figure 4.6) return us to the competitive priorities for operations management introduced in the opening chapter. Consequently, capacity decisions cannot be isolated from major process decisions about customer involvement and resource flexibility, to name a few. For example, a continuous process tends to mean little customer involvement and customization, low capacity cushion (i.e., high utilization), low resource flexibility, and high vertical integration. Collectively, these are consistent with competitive priorities that favour low cost and consistent high quality. In contrast, a project or small batch process tends to mean high customer involvement and customization, high capacity cushion (i.e., low utilization), high resource flexibility, and little vertical integration. These characteristics are consistent with competitive priorities that favour high-performance design, fast delivery, and customization.

ECONOMIES OF SCALE

economies of scale A concept that states that the average unit cost of a good or service can be reduced by increasing its output rate.

A concept known as **economies of scale** states that the average unit cost of a good or service can be reduced by increasing its output rate. There are four principal reasons why economies of scale can drive costs down when output increases: fixed costs are spread over more units, construction costs are reduced, costs of purchased materials are cut, and process advantages are found.

SPREADING FIXED COSTS. In the short term, certain process costs do not vary with changes in the output rate, as noted earlier in Figure 2.2 (page 34). These fixed costs include equipment, heating costs, debt service, and management salaries. Depreciation of plant and equipment already owned is also a fixed cost in the accounting sense. When the output rate—and, therefore, the facility's utilization rate—increase, the average unit cost drops, because fixed costs are spread over more units.

REDUCING CONSTRUCTION COSTS. Certain activities and expenses are required in building small and large facilities alike: building permits, architects' fees, rental of building equipment, and the like. Doubling the size of the facility usually does not double construction costs.

CUTTING COSTS OF PURCHASED MATERIALS. Higher volumes can reduce the costs of purchased materials and services. They give the purchaser a better bargaining position and the opportunity to take advantage of quantity discounts. Retailers such as Zellers reap significant economies of scale because their national stores sell huge volumes of each item. Producers that rely on a vast network of suppliers (e.g., General Motors) and food processors (e.g., Kraft General Foods) also can buy inputs for less because of the potential for competitive bidding and the large quantities that they purchase.

FINDING PROCESS ADVANTAGES. High-volume production provides many opportunities for cost reduction. At a higher output rate, the process shifts toward a line or continuous process, with resources dedicated to individual products. Firms may be able to justify the expense of more efficient technology or more specialized equipment. The benefits of dedicating resources to individual products or services may include speeding up the learning effect, lowering inventory, improving process and job designs, and reducing the number of changeovers. Alternatively, flexible technology and mass customization can allow higher utilization and lower cost.

DISECONOMIES OF SCALE

diseconomies of scale
When the average cost per unit increases as the facility's size increases.

As a service or manufacturing facility continues to grow, it is possible for it to become so large that **diseconomies of scale** set in; that is, the average cost per unit increases as the facility's size increases. The reason is that excessive size can bring complexity, loss of focus, and inefficiencies that raise the average unit cost of a product or service. There may be too many layers of employees and bureaucracy, and management may lose touch with employees and customers. The organization is less agile and loses the flexibility needed to respond to changing demand. Many large companies become so involved in analysis and planning that they innovate less and avoid risks. The result is that small companies outperform corporate giants in numerous industries.

Figure 4.7 illustrates the transition from economies of scale to diseconomies of scale. The 500-bed hospital shows economies of scale because the average unit cost at

FIGURE 4.7

Economies and Diseconomies of Scale

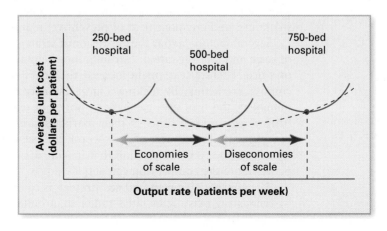

its *best operating level*, represented by the blue dot, is less than that of the 250-bed hospital. However, further expansion to a 750-bed hospital leads to higher average unit costs and diseconomies of scale. One reason the 500-bed hospital enjoys greater economies of scale than the 250-bed hospital is that the cost of building and equipping it is less than twice the cost for the smaller hospital. The 750-bed facility would enjoy similar savings. Its higher average unit costs can be explained only by diseconomies of scale, which outweigh the savings realized in construction costs.

However, this analysis does not mean that the optimal size for all hospitals is 500 beds. Optimal size depends on the number of patients per week to be served. On the one hand, a hospital serving a small community would have lower costs by choosing a 250-bed capacity rather than the 500-bed capacity. On the other hand, assuming the same cost structure, a large community will be served more efficiently by two 500-bed hospitals than by one 1000-bed facility.

TIMING OF EXPANSION

A basic concern for any long-term planning of capacity is when to expand and by how much. Figure 4.8 illustrates two extreme strategies: the *expansionist strategy*, which involves large, infrequent jumps in capacity, and the *wait-and-see strategy*, which involves smaller, more frequent jumps. The first strategy relies on capacity expansion ahead of demand (i.e., lead), while the second favours trailing demand (i.e., lag).

FIGURE 4.8

Two Capacity Strategies

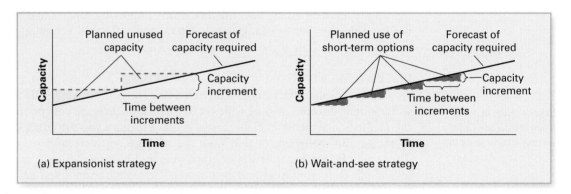

(a) Expansionist strategy

(b) Wait-and-see strategy

The timing and sizing of expansion are related; that is, if demand is increasing and the time between increments increases, the size of the increments must also increase. The expansionist strategy, which stays ahead of demand, minimizes the chance of sales lost to insufficient capacity. The wait-and-see strategy lags behind demand, relying on short-term options such as the use of overtime, temporary workers, subcontractors, stockouts, and postponement of preventive maintenance to meet any shortfalls.

Several factors favour the expansionist strategy. Expansion may result in economies of scale and a faster rate of learning, thus helping a firm reduce its costs and compete on price. This strategy might increase the firm's market share or act as a form of pre-emptive marketing. By making a large capacity expansion or announcing that one is imminent, the firm uses capacity to pre-empt expansion by other firms. These other firms must sacrifice some of their market share or risk burdening the industry with overcapacity. To be successful, however, the pre-empting firm must have the credibility to convince the competition that it will carry out its plans—and it must signal its plans before the competition can act.

The conservative wait-and-see strategy is to expand in smaller increments, such as by renovating existing facilities rather than building new ones. Because the wait-and-see strategy follows demand, it reduces the risks of overexpansion based on overly optimistic demand forecasts, obsolete technology, or inaccurate assumptions regarding the competition.

However, this strategy has its own risks, such as being pre-empted by a competitor or being unable to respond if demand is unexpectedly high. The wait-and-see strategy has been criticized as a short-term strategy typical of some U.S. management styles. Managers on the fast track to corporate advancement tend to take fewer risks. They earn promotions by avoiding the big mistake and maximizing short-term profits and return on investment. The wait-and-see strategy fits this short-term outlook, but it can erode market share over the long run.

Management may choose one of these two strategies or one of the many between these extremes. With strategies in the more moderate middle, firms may expand more frequently (on a smaller scale) than with the expansionist strategy but do not always lag behind demand as with the wait-and-see strategy. An intermediate strategy could be to *follow the leader*, expanding when others do. If others are right, so are you, and nobody gains a competitive advantage. If they make a mistake and overexpand, so have you, but everyone shares in the agony of overcapacity.

A SYSTEMATIC APPROACH TO CAPACITY DECISIONS

Theory of Constraints (TOC), along with other process management and scheduling approaches, looks at how best to manage existing capacity within an existing process, but long-term decisions still must be made to plan for capacity as market demand expands, varies over time, and possibly declines. Such planning typically includes how many machines should be bought for a given department, or how many workers staffed for a given process. Once ordered, equipment can take up to a year, or longer in some instances, to be delivered. Hence a systematic approach is needed to plan for long-term capacity decisions, while the firm invokes TOC principles to manage day-to-day operations.

Although every situation is somewhat different, a four-step procedure generally can help managers make sound capacity decisions. In describing this procedure, we assume that management has already performed the preliminary step of determining existing capacity:

1. Estimate future capacity requirements.

2. Identify gaps by comparing requirements with available capacity.

3. Develop alternative plans for filling the gaps.

4. Evaluate each alternative, both qualitatively and quantitatively, and make a final choice.

STEP 1: ESTIMATE CAPACITY REQUIREMENTS

capacity requirement The process capacity needed for some future time period to meet the demand of customers, given the firm's desired capacity cushion.

planning horizon The set of consecutive time periods considered for planning purposes.

A process's **capacity requirement** is what its capacity should be for some future time period to meet the demand of the firm's customers (external or internal), given the firm's desired capacity cushion. Larger requirements are practical for processes or workstations that could potentially be bottlenecks in the future, and management may even plan for larger cushions than normal.

The foundation for estimating the needed capacity over the long term is forecasts of demand, productivity, competition, and technological change. These forecasts normally need to be made for several time periods in a **planning horizon**, which is the set of consecutive time periods considered for planning purposes. Long-term capacity plans need to consider more of the future (perhaps a whole decade) than do short-term plans. Unfortunately, the farther ahead you look, the more chance you have of making an inaccurate forecast.

The demand forecast has to be converted to a number that can be compared directly with the capacity measure being used. Suppose that capacity is expressed as the number of available stations at an operation (e.g., people, equipment, etc.). When just one product (service) is being processed, the number of stations required, M, is:

$$\text{Number of stations required} = \frac{\text{Processing time required to meet demand}}{\substack{\text{Time available from one station,} \\ \text{after deducting desired cushion}}}$$

$$M = \frac{Dp}{N[1 - (C/100)]}$$

where:

D = Forecast demand (e.g., customers per year)

p = Processing time (e.g., hours per customer)

N = Total time during which the station operates (e.g., hours per year)

C = Desired capacity cushion (e.g., $0.18 = 18\%$)

The processing time, p, in the numerator depends on the process and methods selected to do the work. Estimates of p come from established work standards or equipment specifications. The denominator, N, considers the total availability of the station, using the same time interval over which we developed the forecast demand, such as a year. N is then multiplied by a proportion that accounts for the desired capacity cushion, C. The proportion is simply $1 - C$, where C is converted from a percentage to a proportion by dividing by 100.

As noted before, other managerial decisions and problems that create variability can reduce the capacity cushion, including scheduled maintenance, breakdowns, and changing from one product to another (i.e., setup time). **Setup time** is the additional time needed to change over from one service or product to the next, which in turn increases the overload at the workstation being changed over. The setup time needed is found by dividing the forecast demand by the total number of batches produced over a particular time period, which gives the number of setups per year, and then multiplying by the time per setup.

For example, if the monthly demand for a particular wood drawer size is 1200 units, and the average order size is 160, there is an average of $1200/160 = 7.5$ setups per month. If each setup takes 50 minutes, we must account for $(7.5 \times 50) \div 60 = 6.25$ hours lost to setups each month. Accounting for both processing and setup time when there are multiple products and services (remember that time must be expressed consistently in terms of hour, month, year, etc.), we get:

$$\text{Number of stations required} = \frac{\substack{\text{Processing } and \text{ setup time required to} \\ \text{meet demand, summed over all products}}}{\substack{\text{Time available from one station,} \\ \text{after deducting desired cushion}}}$$

$$M = \frac{[Dp + (D/Q)s]_{\text{product 1}} + [Dp + (D/Q)s]_{\text{product 2}} + \cdots + [Dp + (D/Q)s]_{\text{product } n}}{N[1 - (C/100)]}$$

where:

Q = Number of units in each batch

s = Setup time per batch

setup time The time required to change or readjust a process or an operation from one service or product to another.

Always round up the fractional part unless it is cost-efficient to use short-term options such as overtime or stockouts to cover any shortfalls.

EXAMPLE 4.2

Estimating Requirements

A copy centre in an office building prepares bound reports for two large clients. The centre makes multiple copies (the batch size) of each report. The processing time to run, collate, and bind each copy depends on, among other factors, the number of pages. The centre operates 250 days per year, with one eight-hour shift. Management believes that a capacity cushion of 15 percent (beyond the allowance built into time standards) is best. It currently has three copy machines. On the basis of the following table of information, determine how many machines are needed at the copy centre.

ITEM	CLIENT X	CLIENT Y
Annual demand forecast (copies)	2000	6000
Standard processing time (hour/copy)	0.5	0.7
Average lot size (copies per report)	20	30
Standard setup time (hours)	0.25	0.40

SOLUTION

$$M = \frac{[Dp + (D/Q)s]_{\text{product 1}} + [Dp + (D/Q)s]_{\text{product 2}}}{N[1 - (C/100)]}$$

$$= \frac{[2000(0.5) + (2000/20)(0.25)]_{\text{client X}} + [6000(0.7) + (6000/30)(0.40)]_{\text{client Y}}}{[(250 \text{ days/year})(1 \text{ shift/day})(8 \text{ hours/shift})](1.0 - 15/100)}$$

$$= \frac{5305}{1700} = 3.12$$

Rounding up to the next integer gives a requirement of four machines for these two clients.

Decision Point The copy centre's capacity is being stretched and no longer has the desired 15 percent capacity cushion. Not wanting customer service to suffer, management decided to use overtime as a short-term solution to handle past-due orders. If demand continues at the current level or grows, it will acquire a fourth machine.

STEP 2: IDENTIFY GAPS

capacity gap Any difference (positive or negative) between projected demand and current capacity.

A **capacity gap** is any difference (positive or negative) between projected demand and current capacity. Identifying gaps requires the use of the correct capacity measure. Complications arise when multiple operations and several resource inputs are involved. Expanding the capacity of some operations may increase overall capacity. However, if one operation is a bottleneck, capacity can be expanded only if the capacity of the bottleneck operation is expanded.

STEP 3: DEVELOP ALTERNATIVES

base case The act of doing nothing and losing orders from any demand that exceeds current capacity.

The next step is to develop alternative plans to cope with projected gaps. One alternative, called the **base case**, is to do nothing and simply lose orders from any demand that exceeds current capacity. Other alternatives are various timing and sizing options for adding new capacity, including the expansionist and wait-and-see strategies illustrated in Figure 4.8 (page 108). Additional possibilities include expanding at a different location and using short-term options such as overtime, temporary workers, and subcontracting.

STEP 4: EVALUATE THE ALTERNATIVES

In this final step, the manager evaluates each alternative, both quantitatively and qualitatively.

QUALITATIVE CONCERNS. Qualitatively, the manager has to look at how each alternative fits the overall capacity strategy and other aspects of the business not covered by the financial analysis. Of particular concern might be uncertainties about demand, competitive reaction, technological change, and cost estimates. Some of these factors cannot be quantified and have to be assessed on the basis of judgment and experience. Others can be quantified, and the manager can analyze each alternative by using different assumptions about the future. One set of assumptions could represent a worst case, in which demand is less, competition is greater, and construction costs are higher than expected. Another set of assumptions could represent the most optimistic view of the future. This type of "what if" analysis allows the manager to get an idea of each alternative's implications before making a final choice.

cash flow The difference between the flows of funds into and out of an organization over a period of time, including revenues, costs, and changes in assets and liabilities.

QUANTITATIVE CONCERNS. Quantitatively, the manager estimates the change in cash flows for each alternative over the forecast time horizon compared to the base case. **Cash flow** is the difference between the flows of funds into and out of an organization over a period of time, including revenues, costs, and changes in assets and liabilities. The manager is concerned here only with calculating the cash flows attributable to the project.

A good example of capacity's impact on revenues is a steakhouse restaurant in Lexington, Kentucky. Customers liked the neon signs that dotted the wall, the blaring jukebox, and the way they could throw peanut shells on the floor. However, they had to wait as long as two hours to be seated, and the choice of items on the menu was limited. The restaurant expanded capacity by adding more seats and enlarging the kitchen to handle larger volumes and offer more choices. Within months, the restaurant started to bring in $80 000 a week, a 60 percent increase. This facility became the prototype for Logan's Roadhouse, Inc., the Nashville-based dining chain that was one of the fastest-growing companies in 1996. Logan's has since opened ten restaurants in Indiana, Kentucky, and Tennessee. Each one costs $2.2 million to build, but high volume yields a sales average of some $3.8 million a year.

| EXAMPLE 4.3 | *Evaluating the Alternatives* |

Grandma's Chicken Restaurant is experiencing a boom in business. The owner expects to serve a total of 80 000 meals this year. Although the kitchen is operating at 100 percent capacity, the dining room can handle a total of 105 000 diners per year. Forecast demand for the next five years is 90 000 meals for the next year, followed by a 10 000-meal increase in each of the succeeding years.

One alternative is to expand both the kitchen and the dining room now, bringing their capacities up to 130 000 meals per year. The initial investment would be $200 000, made at the end of this year (year 0). The average meal is priced at $10, and the incremental before-tax profit margin is 20 percent. The 20 percent figure was arrived at by determining that, for each $10 meal, $8 covers variable costs. The remaining $2 goes to pre-tax profit.

What are the pre-tax cash flows from this project for the next five years compared to those of the base case of doing nothing?

SOLUTION

Recall that the base case of doing nothing results in losing all potential sales beyond 80 000 meals. With the new capacity, the cash flow would equal the extra meals served by having a 130 000-meal capacity, multiplied by a profit of $2 per meal. In year 0, the only cash flow is −$200 000 for the initial investment. In year 1, the 90 000-meal demand will be completely satisfied by the expanded capacity, so the incremental cash flow is (90 000 − 80 000)(2) = $20 000.

For subsequent years, the figures are as follows:

Year 2:   Demand = 100 000; Cash flow = (100 000 – 80 000)$2 = $40 000
Year 3:   Demand = 110 000; Cash flow = (110 000 – 80 000)$2 = $60 000
Year 4:   Demand = 120 000; Cash flow = (120 000 – 80 000)$2 = $80 000
Year 5:   Demand = 130 000; Cash flow = (130 000 – 80 000)$2 = $100 000

If the new capacity were smaller than the expected demand in any year, we would subtract the base case capacity from the new capacity (rather than the demand).

Decision Point Before deciding on this capacity alternative, the owner should account for the time value of money, applying such techniques as the present value or internal rate of return methods (see Supplement B, "Financial Analysis," on the Student CD-ROM). The owner should also examine the qualitative concerns. For example, the homey atmosphere that the restaurant has projected may be lost with expansion. Furthermore, other alternatives should be considered (see Solved Problem 2 on page 117).

TOOLS FOR CAPACITY PLANNING

Long-term capacity planning requires demand forecasts for an extended period of time. Unfortunately, forecast accuracy declines as the forecasting horizon lengthens. In addition, anticipating what competitors will do increases the uncertainty of demand forecasts. Finally, demand during any period is not evenly distributed; peaks and valleys of demand may (and often do) occur within the period. These realities necessitate the use of capacity cushions. In this section, we introduce three tools that deal more formally with demand uncertainty and variability: waiting-line models, simulation, and decision trees. Waiting-line models and simulation account for the random, independent behaviour of many customers, in terms of both their time of arrival and their processing needs. Decision trees allow anticipation of events such as competitors' actions.

WAITING-LINE MODELS

Waiting-line models often are useful in capacity planning. Waiting lines tend to develop in front of a work centre, such as an airport ticket counter, a machine centre, or a central computer. The reason is that the arrival time between orders or customers varies and the processing time may vary from one customer to the next. Waiting-line models use probability distributions to provide estimates of average customer delay time, average length of waiting lines, and utilization of the work centre. Managers can use this information to choose the most cost-effective capacity, balancing customer service and the cost of adding capacity.

Supplement 4S in this book, "Waiting Lines," which follows this chapter, provides a fuller treatment of these models. It introduces formulas for estimating important characteristics of a waiting line, such as average customer waiting time and average facility utilization, for different facility designs. For example, a facility might be designed to have one or multiple lines at each operation and to route customers through one or multiple operations. Given the estimating capability of these formulas and cost estimates for waiting and idle time, managers can select cost-effective designs and capacity levels that also provide the desired level of customer service.

SIMULATION

More complex waiting-line problems must be analyzed with simulation. This tool helps to identify a process's bottlenecks and appropriate capacity cushions, even for complex processes with random demand patterns and/or with predictable surges in demand during a typical day. Building and working with simulation models is treated in greater detail in Supplement G, "Simulation," on the Student CD-ROM.

DECISION TREES

The decision tree method is a general approach to a wide range of decisions, such as product planning, process management, capacity, and location. A decision tree can be particularly valuable for evaluating different capacity expansion alternatives when demand is uncertain and sequential decisions are involved. For example, the owner of Grandma's Chicken Restaurant (see Example 4.3) may expand the restaurant now only to discover in a few years that demand growth is much higher than forecast. In that case, she needs to decide whether to expand further. In terms of construction costs and down-time, expanding twice is likely to be much more expensive than building a large facility from the outset. However, making a large expansion now when demand growth is low means poor facility utilization. Much depends on the demand.

decision tree A schematic model of alternatives available to the decision maker, along with their possible consequences.

A **decision tree** is a schematic model of alternatives available to the decision maker, along with their possible consequences. The name derives from the tree-like appearance of the model. It consists of a number of square *decision nodes*, representing decision points, that sprout *branches*, which depict multiple alternatives (which should be read from left to right). Branches also come out of circular *event nodes*, which represent chance points where more than one event is possible that influences the decision. The probability of each chance event is shown above each branch. The probabilities for all branches leaving a event node must add up to exactly one. Finally, the payoff at the end of each branch is conditional on a specific alternative-event combination, and is given only at the outset, before the analysis begins. Payoffs are often expressed as the present value of net costs or profits.

After drawing a decision tree, we solve it by working from right to left, calculating the *expected payoff* for each node as follows:

1. For an event node, we multiply the payoff of each event branch by the event's probability. We add these products to get the event node's expected payoff.

2. For a decision node, we pick the alternative that has the best expected payoff. If an alternative leads to an event node, its payoff is equal to that node's expected payoff (already calculated). We "saw off," or "prune," the other branches not chosen by marking two short lines through them. The decision node's expected payoff is the one associated with the single remaining unpruned branch.

We continue this process until the leftmost decision node is reached. The unpruned branch extending from it is the best alternative to pursue. If multistage decisions are involved, we must await subsequent events before deciding what to do next. If new probability or payoff estimates are obtained, we repeat the process.

Figure 4.9 shows a decision tree for this view of the problem with new information provided. Demand growth can be either low or high, with probabilities of 0.4 and 0.6, respectively. The initial expansion in year 1 (square node 1) can either be small or

FIGURE 4.9

A Decision Tree for Capacity Expansion (payoffs in thousands of dollars)

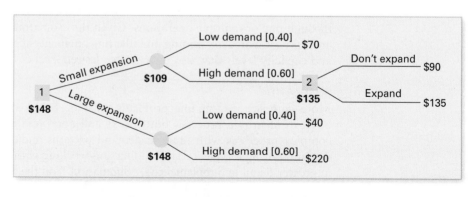

large. The second decision node (square node 2), whether to expand at a later date, is reached only if the initial expansion is small and demand turns out to be high. If demand is high and if the initial expansion was small, a decision must be made about a second expansion in year 4. Payoffs for each branch of the tree are estimated. For example, if the initial expansion is large, the financial benefit is either $40 000 or $220 000, depending on whether demand is low or high. Weighting these payoffs by the probabilities yields an expected value of $148 000. This expected payoff is higher than the $109 000 payoff for the small initial expansion, so the better choice is to make a large expansion in year 1.

MANAGING CAPACITY ACROSS THE ORGANIZATION

Managers make capacity choices at the organization level, as illustrated by Wittke Waste Equipment in our chapter opener. They also must make capacity decisions at the individual-process level in accounting, finance, human resources, information technology, marketing, and operations. Capacity issues can cut across departmental lines, because relieving a bottleneck in one part of an organization does not have the desired effect unless a bottleneck in another part of the organization is also addressed. Managers everywhere must understand capacity measures, economies and diseconomies of scale, capacity cushions, timing-and-sizing strategies, capacity cushions, and trade-offs between customer service and capacity utilization. They must also understand how such capacity decisions link with other decisions that have to be made about their processes.

EQUATION SUMMARY

1. Capacity utilization, expressed as a percent:

$$\text{Capacity utilization} = \frac{\text{Output}}{\text{Effective capacity}} \times 100\%$$

2. Capacity cushion, C, expressed as a percent:

$$C = 100\% - \text{Capacity utilization (\%)}$$

3. Throughput time for a process:

$$\text{Throughput time} = \frac{\text{WIP inventory}}{\text{Output rate}}$$

$$\text{Throughput time} = \text{Operations time} + \text{Movement time} + \text{Wait time}$$

4. Coefficient of variation (cv):

$$cv = \frac{\text{Standard deviation}}{\text{Average}}$$

5. a. Capacity requirement for one product:

$$M = \frac{Dp}{N[1 - (C/100)]}$$

b. Capacity requirement for multiple products:

$$M = \frac{[Dp + (D/Q)s]_{\text{product 1}} + [Dp + (D/Q)s]_{\text{product 2}} + \cdots + [Dp + (D/Q)s]_{\text{product } n}}{N[1 - (C/100)]}$$

CHAPTER HIGHLIGHTS

- Operations managers plan for timely acquisition, use, and disposition of capacity.

- Long-term capacity planning is crucial to an organization's success because it often involves large investments in facilities and equipment and because such decisions are not easily reversed.

- Capacity can be stated in terms of either input or output measures. Output measures giving the number of products or services completed in a time period are useful when a firm provides *standardized* products or services. However, a statement of the number of *customized* products or services completed in a time period is meaningless because the work content per unit varies. Demand for customized products and services must be translated into input measures, such as labour hours, machine hours, and material requirements.

- Operating at peak capacity calls for extraordinary effort, using marginal production methods, and is usually not sustainable. Maximum output under normal conditions is called effective capacity. The operation having the lowest effective capacity is called a bottleneck and limits the capacity of the entire system. Variable workloads and changing product mixes complicate measuring capacity and can cause different operations to become bottlenecks under varying circumstances. Such floating bottlenecks make determining a firm's effective capacity difficult.

- Focusing capacity and scheduling decisions on bottleneck resources with an approach called the theory of constraints (TOC) can help maximize the flow of total value-added funds.

- The desirable amount of capacity cushion varies, depending on competitive priorities, cost of unused capacity, resource flexibility, supply uncertainties, shelf life, variability and uncertainty of demand, and other factors.

- Economies of scale derive from spreading fixed costs, reducing construction costs, reducing purchased materials costs, and obtaining process advantages. Diseconomies of scale cause some firms to focus their operations and move to smaller, rather than larger, facilities.

- Three capacity strategies are expansionist, wait and see, and follow the leader. The expansionist strategy is attractive when there are economies of scale, learning effects, and a chance for pre-emptive marketing. The wait-and-see strategy minimizes risk by relying more on short-term options. The follow-the-leader strategy maintains the current balance between competitors.

- Capacity choices must be linked to other operations management decisions.

- The four steps in capacity planning are (1) estimate capacity requirements, (2) identify gaps, (3) develop alternatives, and (4) evaluate the alternatives.

- Waiting-line models help the manager choose the capacity level that best balances customer service and the cost of adding more capacity. As waiting-line problems involve more servers, mathematical models quickly become very complex. Simulation is used to analyze most multiple-server waiting-line situations. Decision trees are schematic models that can be helpful in evaluating different capacity expansion alternatives when demand is uncertain and sequential decisions are involved.

SOLVED PROBLEM 1

You have been asked to put together a capacity plan for a critical bottleneck operation at the Surefoot Sandal Company. Your capacity measure is number of machines. Three products (men's, women's, and children's sandals) are manufactured. On average, about 10 000 sandals are in various stages of production. The time standards (processing and setup), lot sizes, and demand forecasts are given in the following table. The firm operates two eight-hour shifts, five days per week, fifty weeks per year. Experience shows that a capacity cushion of 5 percent is sufficient.

PRODUCT	TIME STANDARDS		LOT SIZE (pairs/lot)	DEMAND FORECAST (pairs/year)
	PROCESSING (h/pair)	SETUP (h/lot)		
Men's sandals	0.05	0.5	240	80 000
Women's sandals	0.10	2.2	180	60 000
Children's sandals	0.02	3.8	360	120 000

a. How long does a typical pair of sandals take to move through the manufacturing process?

b. How many machines are needed?

c. If the operation currently has two machines, what is the capacity gap?

SOLUTION

a. Using Little's Law:

$$\text{Throughput time} = \frac{\text{WIP inventory}}{\text{Output rate}}$$

$$= \frac{10\,000 \text{ sandals}}{(80\,000 + 60\,000 + 120\,000) \text{ sandals per year}}$$

$$= 0.038 \text{ year}$$

Given that Surefoot Sandal operates 250 days per year, this throughput time translates into 9.6 days, or slightly less than two weeks.

b. The number of hours of operation per year, N, is:

$N = (2 \text{ shifts/day}) (8 \text{ hours/shift}) (250 \text{ days/machine-year})$

$\quad = 4000 \text{ hours/machine-year}$

The number of machines required, M, is the sum of machine-hour requirements for all three products divided by the number of productive hours available for one machine:

$$M = \frac{[Dp + (D/Q)s]_{men} + [Dp + (D/Q)s]_{women} + [Dp + (D/Q)s]_{children}}{N[1 - (C/100)]}$$

$$= \frac{\begin{array}{c}[80\,000(0.05) + (80\,000/240)0.5] + [60\,000(0.10) + (60\,000/180)2.2] \\ + [120\,000(0.02) + (120\,000/360)3.8]\end{array}}{4000[1 - (5/100)]}$$

$$= \frac{14\,567 \text{ hours/year}}{3800 \text{ hours/machine-year}} = 3.83 \quad \text{or} \quad 4 \text{ machines}$$

c. The capacity gap is 1.83 machines (3.83 − 2). Two more machines should be purchased, unless management decides to use short-term options to fill the gap.

SOLVED PROBLEM 2

The base case for Grandma's Chicken Restaurant (see Example 4.3 on page 112) is to do nothing. The capacity of the kitchen in the base case is 80 000 meals per year. A capacity alternative for Grandma's Chicken Restaurant is a two-stage expansion. This alternative expands the kitchen at the end of year 0, raising its capacity from 80 000 meals per year to that of the dining area (105 000 meals per year). If sales in years 1 and 2 live up to expectations, the capacities of both the kitchen and the dining room will be expanded at the *end* of year 3 to 130 000 meals per year. The initial investment would be $80 000 at the end of year 0 and an additional investment of $170 000 at the end of year 3. The pre-tax profit is $2 per meal. What are the pre-tax cash flows for this alternative through year 5, compared with the base case?

SOLUTION

Table 4.3 shows the cash inflows and outflows. The year 3 cash flow is unusual in two respects. First, the cash inflow from sales is $50 000 rather than $60 000. The increase in sales over the base is 25 000 meals (105 000 − 80 000) instead of 30 000 meals (110 000 − 80 000), because the restaurant's capacity falls somewhat short of demand. Second, a cash outflow of $170 000 occurs at the end of year 3, when the second-stage expansion occurs. The net cash flow for year 3 is $50 000 − $170 000 = −$120 000.

TABLE 4.3 *Project Activity and Cost Data*

YEAR	PROJECTED DEMAND (meals/year)	PROJECTED CAPACITY (meals/year)	CALCULATION OF INCREMENTAL CASH FLOW COMPARED TO BASE CASE (80 000 meals/year)	CASH INFLOW (OUTFLOW)
0	80 000	80 000	Increase kitchen capacity to 105 000 meals =	($80 000)
1	90 000	105 000	90 000 − 80 000 = (10 000 meals)($2/meal) =	$20 000
2	100 000	105 000	100 000 − 80 000 = (20 000 meals)($2/meal) =	$40 000
3	110 000	105 000	105 000 − 80 000 = (25 000 meals)($2/meal) =	$50 000
			Increase total capacity to 130 000 meals =	($170 000)
				($120 000)
4	120 000	130 000	120 000 − 80 000 = (40 000 meals)($2/meal) =	$80 000
5	130 000	130 000	130 000 − 80 000 = (50 000 meals)($2/meal) =	$100 000

SOLVED PROBLEM 3

A retailer must decide whether to build a small or a large facility at a new location. Demand at the location can be either low or high, with probabilities estimated to be 0.4 and 0.6, respectively. If a small facility is built and demand proves to be high, the manager may choose not to expand (payoff is $223 000) or to expand (payoff is $270 000). If a small facility is built and demand is low, there is no reason to expand and the payoff is $200 000. If a large facility is built and demand proves to be low, the choice is to do nothing ($40 000) or to stimulate demand through local advertising. The response to advertising may be either modest or sizable, with their probabilities estimated to be 0.3 and 0.7, respectively. If it is modest, the payoff is estimated to be only $20 000; the payoff grows to $220 000 if the response is sizable. Finally, if a large facility is built and demand turns out to be high, the payoff is $800 000.

Draw a decision tree. Then analyze it to determine the expected payoff for each decision and event node. Which alternative—building a small facility or building a large facility—has the higher expected payoff?

SOLUTION

The decision tree in Figure 4.10 shows the event probability and the payoff for each of the seven alternative-event combinations. The first decision is whether to build a small or a large facility. Its node is shown first, to the left, because it is the decision the retailer must make now. The second decision node—whether to expand at a later date—is reached only if a small facility is built and demand turns out to be high. Finally, the third decision point—whether to advertise—is reached only if the retailer builds a large facility and demand turns out to be low.

Analysis of the decision tree begins with calculation of the expected payoffs from right to left, shown on Figure 4.10 beneath the appropriate event and decision nodes.

1. For the event node dealing with advertising, the expected payoff is 160, or the sum of each event's payoff weighted by its probability [0.3(20) + 0.7(220)].

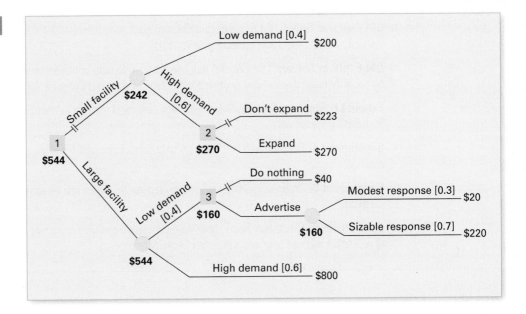

FIGURE 4.10

Decision Tree for Retailer

2. The expected payoff for decision node 3 is 160, because *Advertise* (160) is better than *Do nothing* (40). Prune the *Do nothing* alternative.

3. The payoff for decision node 2 is 270, because *Expand* (270) is better than *Do not expand* (223). Prune *Do not expand*.

4. The expected payoff for the event node dealing with demand, assuming that a small facility is built, is 242 [or 0.4(200) + 0.6(270)].

5. The expected payoff for the event node dealing with demand, assuming that a large facility is built, is 544 [or 0.4(160) + 0.6(800)].

6. The expected payoff for decision node 1 is 544, because the large facility's expected payoff is largest. Prune *Small facility*.

Decision Point The retailer should build the large facility, given the large expected payoff of $544 000. This initial decision is the only one made now. Subsequent decisions are made after learning whether demand actually is low or high.

CD-ROM RESOURCES

The Student CD-ROM that accompanies this text contains the following resources, which allow you to further practise and apply the concepts presented in this chapter.

- **Equation Summary**: All the equations for this chapter can be found in one convenient location.

- **Discussion Questions**: Four questions expand your thinking on economies of scale, safety issues, and capacity cushions.

- **Case**: *Fitness Plus, Part A.* How should Fitness Plus measure its capacity, and what capacity strategy is best?

- **Experiential Exercise**: *Min-Yo Garment Company.* Experience the challenges of matching markets to the capacity of your manufacturing process in this exciting in-class simulation.

- **OM Explorer Tutors**: OM Explorer contains two tutor programs that will help you learn about capacity (capacity requirements and projecting cash flows).

- **OM Explorer Solvers**: OM Explorer has one program to help with general capacity planning problems on capacity requirements, and another for the *Min-Yo Garment Company* experiential exercise.

- **Extend LT**: *Provincial Automobile License Renewals* must identify the bottleneck and improve its process for handling customers.

- **Supplement A:** *Decision Making.* See how to construct decision trees for uncertain, sequential capacity decisions.

- **Supplement C:** *Work Measurement.* See how processing times can be estimated as inputs to capacity planning.

- **Supplement G:** *Simulation.* Read about how simulation can give important insights on the performance of processes and can help make the right capacity decisions.

PROBLEMS

1. Trim Tailor Shop has two general types of customers, labelled A and B, that require custom tailoring and alterations. The process flowcharts for each are shown in Figure 4.11. After step T1, Type A customers proceed to step T2 and then to any of the three workstations at T3, followed by step T4, and then step T7. After step T1, Type B customers proceed to step T5 and then steps T6 and T7. The numbers in parentheses are the minutes it takes to process a customer.

   a. What is the effective capacity of Trim Tailor Shop in terms of the numbers of Type A customers who can be served in an hour? Assume no customers are waiting at steps T1 or T7.

   b. If 30 percent of the customers are Type A customers and 70 percent are Type B customers, what is the effective capacity of Trim Tailor Shop in customers per hour?

   c. Where would you expect Type A customers to experience waiting lines, assuming no Type B customers in the shop? Where would the Type B customers have to wait, assuming no Type A customers?

2. Sterling Motors is a telephone or mail-order dealer in British auto parts. Sterling has six telephones for receiving orders. Order takers answer the telephones, check inventory availability and prepare picking tickets for the warehouse stock pickers. One order may consist of several lines, with a different part or multiple of a part ordered on each line. Each order

---

FIGURE 4.11

Flowcharts for Trim Tailor Shop

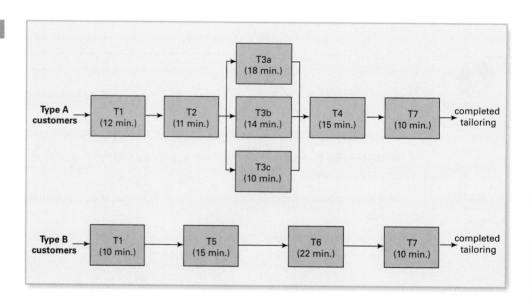

taker can prepare picking tickets at a rate of one line every three minutes. The telephones are normally answered weekdays from 6 a.m. to 4 p.m., Pacific time. Stock pickers can fill and package parts at a rate of one line every five minutes. Sterling employs eight stock pickers, who normally work weekdays from 8 a.m. to 5 p.m. (except for lunch hours).

a. What is the effective capacity of order taking in lines per week? stock picking?

b. For three weeks after the spring catalogue is mailed in May, the eight warehouse employees work 10 hours per day between 7 a.m. and 6 p.m., six days per week. What is the peak capacity of the system in lines per week?

c. During the second week of May, Sterling filled 5000 order lines. What is the capacity utilization?

3. The Clip Joint operates four barber's chairs in the student centre. During the week before semester break and the week before graduation, the Clip Joint experiences peak demands. Military-style haircuts take 5 minutes each, and other styles require 20 minutes each. Operating from 9 a.m. to 6 p.m. on the six days before semester break, the Clip Joint completes 500 military-style haircuts and 400 other haircuts. During a comparable six-day week before graduation, the Clip Joint completes 700 military-style haircuts and 300 other haircuts. In which week is utilization higher?

4. Up, Up, and Away is a producer of kites and wind socks. Relevant data on a bottleneck operation in the shop for the upcoming fiscal year are given in the following table:

ITEM	KITES	WIND SOCKS
Demand forecast	30 000 units/year	12 000 units/year
Lot size	20 units	70 units
Standard processing time	0.3 h/unit	1.0 h/unit
Standard setup time	3.0 h/lot	4.0 h/lot

The shop works two shifts per day, eight hours per shift, 200 days per year. There currently are four machines, and a 25 percent capacity cushion is desired. How many machines should be purchased to meet the upcoming year's demand without resorting to any short-term capacity solutions?

5. Tuff-Rider, Inc., manufactures touring bikes and mountain bikes in a variety of frame sizes, colours, and component combinations. Identical bicycles are produced in lots of 100. The projected demand, lot size, and time standards are shown in the following table:

ITEM	TOURING	MOUNTAIN
Demand forecast	5000 units/year	10 000 units/year
Lot size	100 units	100 units
Standard processing time	0.25 h/unit	0.5 h/unit
Standard setup time	2 h/lot	3 h/lot

The shop currently works eight hours a day, five days a week, 50 weeks a year. It has five workstations, each producing one bicycle in the time shown in the table. The shop maintains a 15 percent capacity cushion. How many workstations will be required next year to meet expected demand without using overtime and without decreasing the firm's current capacity cushion?

6. Worcester Athletic Club is considering expanding its facility to include two adjacent suites. The owner will remodel the suites in consideration of a seven-year lease. Expenditures for rent, insurance, utilities, and exercise equipment leasing would increase by $45 000 per year. This expansion would increase Worcester's lunchtime rush-hour capacity from the present 150 members to 225 members. A maximum of 30 percent of the total membership attends the Athletic Club during any one lunch hour. Therefore, Worcester's facility can presently serve a total membership of 500. Membership fees are $40 per month. On the basis of the following membership forecasts, determine what before-tax cash flows the expansion will produce for the next several years:

YEAR	1	2	3	4	5	6	7
MEMBERSHIP	450	480	510	515	530	550	600

7. Beta World amusement park has the opportunity to expand its size now (the end of year 0) by purchasing adjacent property for $250 000 and adding attractions at a cost of $550 000. This expansion is expected to increase attendance by 30 percent over projected attendance without expansion. The price of admission is $30, with a $5 increase planned for the beginning of year 3. Additional operating costs are expected to be $100 000 per year. Estimated attendance for the next five years, *without expansion*, follows:

YEAR	1	2	3	4	5
ATTENDANCE	30 000	34 000	36 250	38 500	41 000

a. What are the pre-tax combined cash flows for years 0 through 5 that are attributable to the park's expansion?

b. Ignoring tax, depreciation, and the time value of money, determine how long it will take to recover (pay back) the investment.

8. Kim Epson operates a full-service car wash, which operates from 8 a.m. to 8 p.m., seven days a week. The car wash has two stations: an automatic washing and drying station and a manual interior cleaning station. The automatic washing and drying station can handle 30 cars per hour. The interior cleaning station can handle 200 cars per day. On the basis of a recent year-end review of operations, Kim estimates that future demand for the interior cleaning station for the seven days of the week, expressed in average number of cars per day, would be as follows:

DAY	Mon.	Tues.	Wed.	Thurs.	Fri.	Sat.	Sun.
CARS	160	180	150	140	280	300	250

By installing additional equipment (at a cost of $50 000), Kim can increase the capacity of the interior cleaning station to 300 cars per day. Each car wash generates a pre-tax contribution of $4. Should Kim install the additional equipment if she expects a pre-tax payback period of three years or less?

9. A manager is trying to decide whether to buy one machine or two. If only one machine is purchased and demand proves to be excessive, the second machine can be purchased later. Some sales would be lost, however, because the lead time for delivery of this type of machine is six months. In addition, the cost per machine will be lower if both machines are purchased at the same time. The probability of low demand is estimated to be 0.30 and that of high demand to be 0.70. The after-tax net present value of the benefits (NPV) from purchasing two machines together is $90 000 if demand is low and $170 000 if demand is high.

If one machine is purchased and demand is low, the NPV is $120 000. If demand is high, the manager has three options: doing nothing, which has an NPV of $120 000; subcontracting, with an NPV of $140 000; and buying the second machine, with an NPV of $130 000.

a. Draw a decision tree for this problem.

b. What is the best decision and what is its expected payoff?

10. Acme Steel Fabricators has experienced booming business for the past five years. The company fabricates a wide range of steel products, such as railings, ladders, and light structural steel framing. The current manual method of materials handling is causing excessive inventories and congestion. Acme is considering the purchase of an overhead rail-mounted hoist system or a forklift truck to increase capacity and improve manufacturing efficiency.

The annual pre-tax payoff from the system depends on future demand. If demand stays at the current level, the probability of which is 0.50, annual savings from the overhead hoist will be $10 000. If demand rises, the hoist will save $25 000 annually because of operating efficiencies in addition to new sales. Finally, if demand falls, the hoist will result in an estimated annual loss of $65 000. The probability is estimated to be 0.30 for higher demand and 0.20 for lower demand.

If the forklift is purchased, annual payoffs will be $5000 if demand is unchanged, $10 000 if demand rises, and −$25 000 if demand falls.

a. Draw a decision tree for this problem and compute the expected value of the payoff for each alternative.

b. Which is the best alternative, based on the expected values?

REFERENCES AND FURTHER READINGS

Bakke, N. A., and R. Hellberg. "The Challenges of Capacity Planning." *International Journal of Production Economics*, 31–30 (1993), pp. 243–264.

Chase, R. B., N. J. Aquilano, and F. R. Jacobs. *Operations Management for Competitive Advantage*, 9th ed. New York: Irwin/McGraw-Hill, 2001.

Goldratt, E. Y., and J. Cox. *The Goal*. New York: North River, 1984.

Hammesfahr, J.R.D., J. A. Pope, and A. Ardalan. "Strategic Planning for Production Capacity." *International Journal of Operations and Production Management*, vol. 13 (1993), no. 5, pp. 41–53.

Hopp, W. J., and M. L. Spearman. *Factory Physics: Foundations in Manufacturing Management*, 2nd ed. New York: Irwin/McGraw-Hill, 2001.

"How Goliaths Can Act Like Davids." *Business Week/Enterprise*, 1993, pp. 192–200.

Little, John D. C. "Tautologies, Models, and Theories: Can We Find 'Laws' of Manufacturing?" *IIE Transactions*, vol. 24 (1992), no. 3, pp. 7–13.

Lovejoy, W. S. "Integrated Operations: A Proposal for Operations Management Teaching and Research." *Production and Operations Management*, vol. 7 (1998), no. 2, pp. 106–124.

Ritzman, L. P., and M. H. Safizadeh. "Linking Process Choice with Plant-Level Decisions About Capital and Human Resources." *Production and Operations Management*, vol. 8 (1999), no. 4, pp. 374–392.

Simons, J., Jr., and W. P. Simpson III. "An Exposition of Multiple Constraint Scheduling as Implemented in the Goal System (formerly Disaster™)." *Production and Operations Management*, vol. 6, no. 1 (Spring 1997), pp. 3–22.

Statistics Canada. *The Daily*. Ottawa: Statistics Canada, 2001.

4S Waiting Lines

Learning Goals

After reading this supplement, you will be able to:

1. recognize the elements of a waiting-line problem in a real situation.
2. use waiting-line models to estimate the operating characteristics of a system.
3. know when to use the single-server, multiple-server, and finite-source models.
4. describe how waiting-line models can be used to make managerial decisions.

waiting line or **queue**
One or more customers or items waiting for service. Materials, equipment, or products can also form a queue as they wait for further operations.

Anyone who has had to wait at a stoplight, Tim Hortons, or a provincial licence office has experienced the dynamics of queues or waiting lines. Perhaps one of the best examples of effective management of waiting lines is that of Walt Disney World. One day there may be only 25 000 customers, but on another day there may be 90 000. Careful analysis of process flows, technology for people-mover (materials handling) equipment, capacity, and layout keeps the waiting times for attractions at acceptable levels.

The analysis of waiting lines is of concern to managers because it affects design, capacity planning, layout planning, inventory management, and scheduling. However, waiting lines include more than just people. A **waiting line** is one or more customers or items queued for an operation, which can include people waiting for service, materials waiting for further processing, equipment waiting for maintenance, and sales orders waiting for delivery. In a general sense, these items also represent inventory, which is discussed further in Chapter 6, "Inventory Management."

In this supplement we discuss why waiting lines form, the structure of waiting-line models, and the uses of these models in operations management. We also discuss the decisions managers address with the models. In addition, waiting lines can also be analyzed using computer simulation (see Supplement G, "Simulation," on the Student CD-ROM for more details).

WHY HAVE WAITING LINES?

Although people rarely enjoy waiting, waiting lines can serve several managerial purposes to improve the performance of the system, and under some circumstances, even improve the customer experience. However, the primary purpose of waiting lines is to balance two types of costs: capacity and waiting. For capacity-related costs, waiting lines allow managers to accommodate short surges in demand with less capacity—provided that at a minimum, average capacity exceeds average demand.

Scheduling fewer workers at a fast-food restaurant, running a limited number of cars on a public transit system, and installing less IT server capacity for a Web service improves the utilization of resources and lowers investment or operating costs. In contrast, as additional capacity is installed, lines will be shorter, but capacity-related investment and operating costs increase.

Although capacity costs decrease with longer average waiting lines, customer-related waiting costs increase as the average number of people, materials, machines, or products in the waiting line increases, as depicted in Figure 4S.1. For example, customer satisfaction can decrease, which in turn reduces the likelihood of future, repeat business. In extreme cases, customers may leave the line before being served or cancel their order (this is called *reneging*). Also, as discussed in greater detail in Chapter 6, "Inventory Management," having more materials or equipment waiting to be processed requires higher levels of investment.

Managing the Trade-off Between Capacity and Waiting Costs

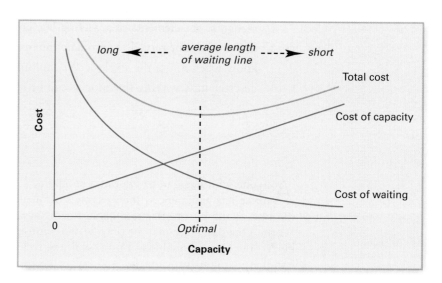

Costs may not be the only management concern. Managers must consider not only the physical arrangement of any waiting line, but in many situations also the customer's perception. Some customer experiences actually benefit from the psychological impact of waiting lines. For example, a short period of waiting in a theme park can contribute to heightening the anticipation and excitement of a thrill ride, such as a roller coaster. Similarly, a queue outside a night club can signal desirability and exclusivity. Through intelligent design, managers can reduce the negative aspects of waiting lines, and improve customer service, as described in Table 4S.1.

WHY WAITING LINES FORM

A waiting line forms because of a temporary imbalance between demand and capacity of the system to process customers or items. In most real-life waiting-line problems, the demand rate varies; that is, customers arrive at unpredictable intervals. The rate of service also varies, depending on individual customer needs.

For example, suppose bank customers arrive at an average rate of 15 per hour throughout the day and the bank can process an average of 20 customers per hour. Why would a waiting line ever develop? The answers are that the customer arrival rate varies and the time required to process a customer can vary. During the noon hour, 30 customers may arrive at the bank. Some of them may have complicated transactions,

TABLE 4S.1

Managing Waiting Lines

Source: Adapted from: K. L. Katz, B. M. Larson, and R. C. Larson, "Prescription for Waiting-in-Line Blues: Entertain, Enlighten, and Engage," *Sloan Management Review*, vol. 32 (1991), no. 2, pp. 44–53.

1. **Determine the acceptable waiting time for customers.**
   Customer expectations for a reasonable waiting time can be affected by competition, the value of the service provided, and customers' perception of the value of their time.

2. **Segment customers based on value or type of service.**
   Using "express" service lanes can shorten the wait for customers requiring minimal assistance or those customers willing to pay extra for faster service. However, clear, easy-to-monitor criteria for express service must be established, and well-trained people are essential for the express service.

3. **Use distractions to entertain or physically involve the customer.**
   Visual information, possibly presented using TV screens, can distract customers, particularly if light and humorous. In addition, if the customer must provide information as part of the service, install facilities to allow for this while waiting in line. An employee may also assist with pre-processing during peak times.

4. **Move customers out of lines.**
   Reservation systems can smooth demand patterns, and automation, such as Web-based delivery, can encourage self-service.

5. **If customers tend to overestimate waiting times, provide feedback on actual waiting times.**
   Although posting the current wait times for short, relatively predictable wait times (e.g., for fast food) may not be helpful, customers appreciate receiving information for longer, less predictable wait times (e.g., for airline takeoff when there is a delay).

6. **Change customer behaviour.**
   Inform customers about peak times or provide other incentives to shift demand away from peak times.

7. **Resources that are not serving customers should be out of sight.**
   Staff or equipment not directly involved with serving customers should be moved to back rooms. Idle resources signal to customers that they are not the first priority.

8. **Adopt a long-term perspective.**
   For frequently used services, customers expect consistent, predictable waiting times.

9. **Train staff to take the initiative.**
   If a staff member observes an unusual situation developing in line, such as a screaming child, all customers may perceive better service if this situation is dealt with immediately.

10. **Emphasize good service at the front of the line!**
    Managers also must not overlook the primary objective—good service when the front of the line is finally reached. A friendly, attentive employee providing helpful service, along with well-designed equipment and facilities, may overcome any negative impressions of waiting and leave an excellent final impression.

requiring above-average process times. The waiting line may grow to 15 customers for a period of time before it eventually disappears. Even though the bank manager provided for more than enough capacity on average, waiting lines can still develop.

Waiting lines can develop even if the time to process a customer is constant. For example, a subway train is computer-controlled to arrive at stations along its route. Each train is programmed to arrive at a station, say, every 15 minutes. Even with the constant operations time, waiting lines develop while riders wait for the next train or cannot get on a train because of the size of the crowd at a busy time of the day. Consequently, variability in the rate of demand determines the sizes of the waiting lines in this case. In general, if there is no variability in the demand and operations rates and enough capacity has been provided, no waiting lines form.

USES OF WAITING-LINE THEORY

Waiting-line theory applies to both service and manufacturing firms, relating customer or item arrival and process characteristics to output characteristics. It also provides a basis for Little's Law, presented in Chapter 4, "Capacity" (Lovejoy, 1998). Waiting-line models apply to a wide variety of process stuctures, including project, batch, and line processes. In our discussion, we will frequently use the term *customer*, although these principles apply equally well to items waiting ahead of a workstation or operation. The process might be hair cutting at a hair salon, satisfying customer complaints, or processing a production order of parts on a certain machine. Other examples of customers and services include lines of theatregoers waiting to purchase tickets, trucks waiting to be unloaded at a warehouse, machines waiting to be repaired by a maintenance crew, and patients waiting to be examined by a physician. Regardless of the situation, waiting-line problems have several common elements, discussed in the next section.

STRUCTURE OF WAITING LINES

Analyzing waiting-line problems begins with a description of the situation's basic elements. Each specific situation will have different characteristics, but four elements are common to all situations:

customer population
An input that generates potential customer demand.

1. An input of customers or items, here termed simply **customer population**, that generates potential demand

2. A waiting line of customers or items

3. A workstation or operation, consisting of a person (or crew), a machine (or group of machines), or both necessary to perform one or more activities

priority rule A rule that selects the next customer to be served at the service facility.

4. A **priority rule**, which selects the next customer to be served or item to be transformed by a workstation or operation

Figure 4S.2 shows these basic elements. The **queuing configuration** describes the number of lines and the arrangement of the workstations or operations. After the service has been performed, the served customers or transformed items leave the system.

queuing configuration
The number of lines and the arrangement of the facilities.

Basic Elements of Waiting-Line Models

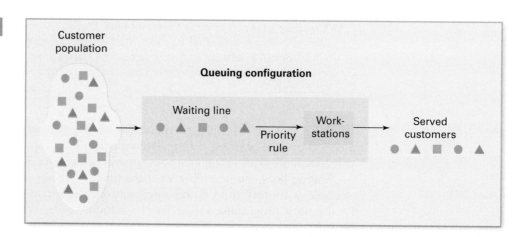

CUSTOMER POPULATION

A customer population is the source of input to the system. An infinite customer population is one in which the number of customers in the system does not affect the rate at which the population generates new customers. For example, consider a mail-order operation for which the customer population consists of shoppers who have received a catalogue of products sold by the company. Because the customer population is so large and only a small fraction of the shoppers place orders at any one time, the number of new orders it generates is not appreciably affected by the number of orders waiting for service or being processed. For this case, the customer population is assumed to be infinite.

In contrast, if the potential number of new customers appreciably affects the number of customers in the system, the input source is said to be finite. For example, suppose that a maintenance crew is assigned to repair five machines. The customer population for the maintenance crew is five machines in good working order. If one of these fails, the available population is clearly affected. In this supplement, we only consider analysis for waiting lines with an infinite customer population.

Customers in waiting lines may be *patient* or *impatient*, which has nothing to do with the colourful language a customer may use while waiting in line for a long time on a hot day. In the context of waiting-line problems, a patient customer is one who enters the system and remains there until being served; an impatient customer is one who either decides not to enter the system (*balks*) or leaves the system before being served (*reneges*). For the methods used in this supplement, we make the simplifying assumption that all customers are patient.

QUEUING CONFIGURATAION

The queuing configuration may be described by the number of lines and the arrangement of the workstations.

NUMBER OF LINES. Waiting lines may be designed to be a *single line* or *multiple lines*. Figure 4S.3 shows an example of each arrangement. Generally, single lines are utilized at airline counters, inside banks, and at some fast-food restaurants, whereas multiple lines are utilized in grocery stores, at drive-in bank operations, and in discount stores.

FIGURE 4S.3

Waiting-Line Arrangements

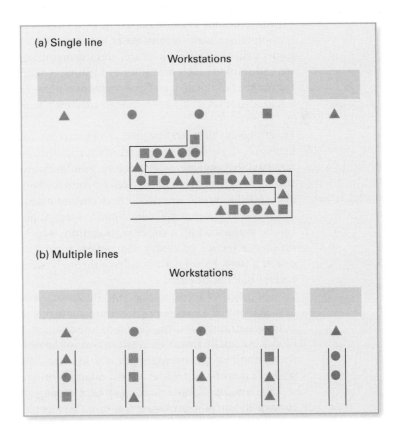

Weary tourists wait to check in at a hotel registration desk.

When multiple workstations are available and each can handle general transactions, the single-line arrangement keeps each workstation uniformly busy and gives customers a sense of fairness. Customers believe that they are being served on the basis of when they arrived, not how well they guessed their waiting time when selecting a particular line. The multiple-line design is best when some of the workstations provide a limited set of services. In this arrangement, customers select the services they need and wait in the line where that service is provided, such as at a grocery store where there are special express lanes for customers paying with cash or having fewer than ten items.

Sometimes waiting lines are not organized neatly. Machines that need repair at a customer's site may be left in place, and the maintenance crew comes to them. Nonetheless, we can think of such machines as forming a single line or multiple lines, depending on the number of repair crews and their specialties. Likewise, passengers who telephone for a taxi also form a line even though they may wait at different locations.

ARRANGEMENT OF WORKSTATIONS. Workstations consist of the personnel and equipment necessary to perform an operation for the customer. Figure 4S.4 shows examples of the five basic arrangements. Managers should choose an arrangement based on customer volume and the nature of services performed. Some processes require only a single step, also called a **phase**, whereas others require a sequence of steps.

phase A single step in the process.

In the *single-channel, single-phase* system, all operations demanded by a customer can be performed by a single workstation, which is also called a single-server configuration for service processes. Customers form a single line and go through the process one at a time. Examples are a drive-through car wash and a machine that must process several batches of parts.

The *single-channel, multiple-phase* arrangement is used when several operations are best performed in sequence by more than one workstation, yet customer volume or other constraints limit the design to one channel. Customers form a single line and proceed sequentially from one workstation to the next, with a waiting line between phases. An example of this arrangement is a McDonald's drive-through, where the first workstation takes the order, the second takes the money, and the third provides the food.

The *multiple-channel, single-phase* arrangement is used when demand is large enough to warrant providing the same service at more than one workstation or when

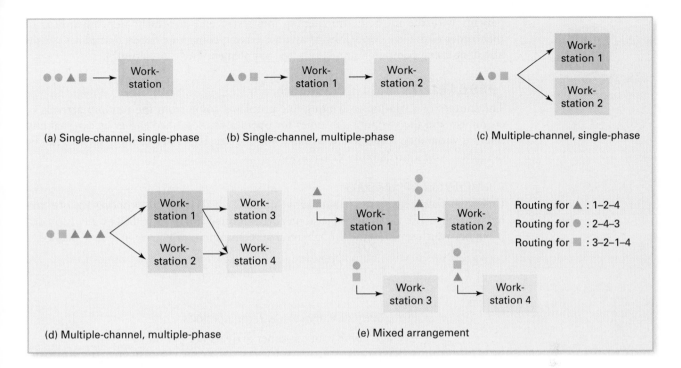

FIGURE 4S.4

Examples of Workstation Arrangements

the services offered by the workstations are different. Customers form one or more lines, depending on the design. In the single-line design, customers are served by the first available server, as in the lobby of a bank. If each channel has its own waiting line, customers wait until the server for their line can serve them, as at a bank's drive-through facilities.

The *multiple-channel, multiple-phase* arrangement occurs when customers can be served by one of the first-phase workstations but then require another operation from a second-phase workstation, and so on. In some cases, customers cannot switch channels after service has begun; in others they can. An example of this arrangement is a laundromat. Washing machines are the first-phase workstations, and dryers are the second-phase workstations. Some of the washing machines and dryers may be designed for extra-large loads, thereby providing the customer a choice of channels.

The most complex waiting-line problem involves customers who have unique sequences of required services; consequently, service cannot be described neatly in phases. A *mixed* arrangement is used in such a case. In the mixed arrangement, waiting lines can develop in front of each workstation, where each customized order may require the use of various machines and different routings.

PRIORITY RULE

The priority rule determines which customer or item to serve next. Most queuing configurations that you encounter use the first-come, first-served (FCFS) rule. The customer at the head of the waiting line has the highest priority, and the customer who arrived last has the lowest priority. Other priority disciplines might take the customer with the earliest promised due date (EDD) or the customer with the shortest expected processing time (SPT). We focus on FCFS in this supplement and discuss EDD and SPT elsewhere (see Chapter 12, "Aggregate Planning and Scheduling").

pre-emptive discipline
A rule that allows a customer of higher priority to interrupt the service of another customer.

A **pre-emptive discipline** is a rule that allows a customer of higher priority to interrupt the service of another customer. For example, in a hospital emergency room, patients with the most life-threatening injuries receive treatment first, regardless of their order of arrival. Modelling of systems having complex priority disciplines is usually done using computer simulation (see Supplement G, "Simulation").

PROBABILITY DISTRIBUTIONS

The sources of variation in waiting-line problems come from the random arrivals of customers and the variations in times for operations, described earlier as external and internal variability, respectively, in Table 4.2 on page 100. Each of these sources can be described with a probability distribution.

DISTRIBUTION OF ARRIVALS

Unless scheduled, customers tend to arrive randomly; recall that this is one source of external variability. The variability of customer arrivals often can be described by a Poisson distribution, which specifies the probability that n customers will arrive in T time periods:

$$P(n) = \frac{(\lambda T)^n}{n!} \, e^{-\lambda T} \qquad \text{for } n = 0, 1, 2, \ldots$$

where:

$P(n)$ = Probability of n arrivals in T time periods

λ = Average number of customer arrivals per period

e = 2.7183

The mean of the Poisson distribution is λT, and the variance also is λT. The Poisson distribution is a discrete distribution; that is, the probabilities are for a specific number of arrivals per unit of time.

| EXAMPLE 4S.1 | *Calculating the Probability of Arrivals* |

Management is redesigning the customer service process in a large department store. Accommodating four customers is important. Customers arrive at the desk at the rate of two customers per hour. What is the probability that four customers will arrive during any hour?

SOLUTION
In this case λ = 2 customers per hour, T = 1 hour, and n = 4 customers. The probability that four customers will arrive in any hour is:

$$P(4) = \frac{[2(1)]^4}{4!} \, e^{-2(1)} = \frac{16}{24} \, e^{-2} = 0.090$$

Decision Point The manager of the customer service desk can use this information to determine the space requirements for the desk and waiting area. There is a relatively small probability that four customers will arrive in any hour. Consequently, seating capacity for two or three customers should be more than adequate unless the time to service each customer is lengthy. Further analysis on service times is warranted.

interarrival times The
time between customer
arrivals.

Another way to specify the arrival distribution is to do it in terms of customer **interarrival times**—that is, the time between customer arrivals. If the customer population generates customers according to a Poisson distribution, the *exponential distribution* describes the probability that the next customer will arrive in the next T time periods. The exponential distribution can also be used to describe the time to complete an operation; we discuss the details of this distribution in the next section.

DISTRIBUTION OF OPERATIONS TIME

operations time The time required to complete all activities or tasks at a workstation. Also called *service time* or *processing time*.

The exponential distribution describes the probability that the **operations time** (sometimes labelled *service time*) at a particular workstation will be no more than a target time (*T*). The probability can be calculated by using the formula:

$$P(t \leq T) = 1 - e^{-\mu T}$$

where:

μ = Mean number of customers completing service per period

t = Service time of the customer

T = Target service time

The mean of the operations time distribution is $1/\mu$, and the variance is $(1/\mu)^2$. As *T* increases, the probability that the operations time will be less than *T* approaches 1.0. For simplicity, let us look at a single-channel, single-phase arrangement.

EXAMPLE 4S.2 *Calculating the Service Time Probability*

The management of the large department store in Example 4S.1 must determine whether more training is needed for the customer service clerk. The clerk at the customer service desk can serve an average of three customers per hour. What is the probability that a customer will require less than 10 minutes of service?

SOLUTION

We must have all the data in the same time units. Because μ = 3 customers per *hour*, we convert minutes of time to hours, or *T* = 10 minutes = 10/60 hour = 0.167 hour. Then:

$$P(t \leq T) = 1 - e^{-\mu T}$$
$$P(t \leq 0.167 \text{ hour}) = 1 - e^{-3(0.167)} = 1 - 0.61 = 0.39$$

Decision Point The probability that the customer will require only 10 minutes or less is not very high, which leaves the possibility that customers may experience lengthy delays. Management should consider additional training for the clerk so as to reduce the time it takes to process a customer request.

Some characteristics of the exponential distribution do not always conform to an actual situation. The exponential distribution model is based on the assumption that each operations time is independent of those that preceded it. In real life, however, productivity may improve as human workers learn about the work. Another assumption underlying the model is that very small, as well as very large, operations times are possible. However, real-life situations often require a fixed-length startup time, some cutoff on total operations time, or nearly constant operations time, similar to an assembly line.

USING WAITING-LINE MODELS TO ANALYZE OPERATIONS

As noted at the beginning of this supplement, operations managers can use waiting-line models to trade off the costs of waiting against any gains that might be made by minimizing capacity investment in the service system. Managers should therefore be concerned about the following performance characteristics of the system:

1. *Line length.* The number of customers in the waiting line reflects one of two conditions. Short queues could mean either good customer service or too much

capacity. Similarly, long queues could indicate either low server efficiency or the need to increase capacity.

2. *Number of customers in the system.* The number of customers in the queue and being served also relates to process efficiency and capacity. A large number of customers in the system causes congestion and may result in customer dissatisfaction, unless more capacity is added.

3. *Waiting time in line.* Long lines do not always mean long waiting times. If the service rate is fast, a long line can be served efficiently. However, when waiting time seems long, customers perceive the quality of service to be poor. Managers may try to change the arrival rate of customers or design the system to make long wait times seem shorter than they really are, as noted in Table 4S.1 on page 125.

4. *Total time in the system.* The total elapsed time from entry into the system until exit from the system may indicate problems with customers, server efficiency, or capacity. If some customers are spending too much time in the service system, there may be a need to change the priority discipline, increase productivity, or adjust capacity in some way.

5. *Capacity utilization.* The utilization of the process or individual operations reflects the percentage of time that they are busy. Management's goal is to maintain high utilization and profitability without adversely affecting the other operating characteristics.

The best method for analyzing a waiting-line problem is to relate the five operating characteristics and their alternatives to dollars. However, placing a dollar figure on certain characteristics (such as the waiting time of a shopper in a grocery store) is difficult. In such cases, an analyst must weigh the cost of implementing the alternative under consideration against a subjective assessment of the cost of *not* making the change.

We now present two models and some examples showing how waiting-line models can help operations managers make decisions. We analyze problems requiring the single-server and multiple-server models, both of which are single-phase. References to more advanced models are cited at the end of this supplement.

SINGLE-WORKSTATION MODEL

The simplest waiting-line model involves a single workstation and a single line of customers. In service processes, this model is often termed a *single-server* model. To further specify the model, we make the following assumptions:

1. The customer population is infinite and all customers are patient.

2. The customers arrive according to a Poisson distribution with a mean arrival rate of λ.

3. The operations time distribution is exponential with a mean processing rate of μ.

4. Customers are served on a first-come, first-served basis.

5. The length of the waiting line is unlimited.

With these assumptions we can apply various formulas to describe the operating characteristics of the system:

$$\rho = \text{Average capacity utilization of the system}$$
$$= \frac{\lambda}{\mu}$$

$$P_n = \text{Probability that } n \text{ customers are in the system}$$
$$= (1 - \rho)\rho^n$$

$$L = \text{Average number of customers in the system}$$
$$= \frac{\lambda}{\mu - \lambda}$$

$$L_q = \text{Average number of customers in the waiting line}$$
$$= \rho L$$

$$W = \text{Average time spent in the system, including}$$
$$\text{waiting time and operations time}$$
$$= \frac{1}{\mu - \lambda}$$

$$W_q = \text{Average waiting time in line}$$
$$= \rho W$$

Calculating the Operating Characteristics of a Single-Channel, Single-Phase System

EXAMPLE 4S.3

The manager of a grocery store in the retirement community of Sunnyville is interested in providing good service to the senior citizens who shop in his store. Presently, the store has a separate checkout counter for senior citizens. On average, 30 senior citizens per hour arrive at the counter, according to a Poisson distribution, and are served at an average rate of 35 customers per hour, with exponential service times. Find the following operating characteristics:

a. Probability of zero customers in the system
b. Utilization of the checkout clerk
c. Number of customers in the system
d. Number of customers in line
e. Time spent in the system
f. Waiting time in line

SOLUTION

The checkout counter can be modelled as a single-channel, single-phase system.

a. To begin, utilization must be calculated before estimating the probability that no customers are in the waiting line.

Utilization is:

$$\rho = \frac{\lambda}{\mu} = \frac{30}{35} = 0.857$$

Next, the probability is estimated, where $n = 0$:

$$P_n = (1 - \rho)\rho^n$$
$$= (1 - 0.857)(0.857)^0$$
$$= 0.143$$

b. The utilization is calculated above as 0.857.

c. The average number of customers can be calculated as:

$$L = \frac{\lambda}{\mu - \lambda}$$
$$= \frac{30}{35 - 30} = 6 \text{ customers}$$

d. The average number of customers waiting in line is:

$$L_q = \rho L$$
$$= 0.857 \times 6 = 5.142 \text{ customers}$$

e. Average time spent by customers in the system is:

$$W = \frac{1}{\mu - \lambda}$$
$$= \frac{1}{35 - 30} = 0.2 \text{ hours}$$

f. Finally, the average time spent by customers waiting in line is:

$$W_q = \rho W$$
$$= 0.857 \times 0.2 = 0.171 \text{ minutes}$$

Both the average waiting time in the system (W) and the average time spent waiting in line (W_q) are expressed in hours. To convert the results to minutes, simply multiply by 60 minutes/hour. For example, $W = 0.2(60) = 12$ minutes, and $W_q = 0.171(60) = 10.26$ minutes.

EXAMPLE 4S.4   *Analyzing Service Rates with the Single-Server Model*

The manager of the Sunnyville grocery in Example 4S.3 wants answers to the following questions:

a. What processing rate would be required to have customers average only eight minutes in the system?

b. For that processing rate, what is the probability of having more than four customers in the system?

c. What processing rate would be required to have only a 10 percent chance of exceeding four customers in the system?

SOLUTION

a. We use the equation for the average time in the system and solve for μ.

$$W = \frac{1}{\mu - \lambda}$$

$$8 \text{ minutes} = 0.133 \text{ hour} = \frac{1}{\mu - 30}$$

$$0.133\mu - 0.133(30) = 1$$

$$\mu = 37.52 \text{ customers/hour}$$

b. The probability that there will be more than four customers in the system equals 1 minus the probability that there are four or fewer customers in the system.

$$P = 1 - \sum_{n=0}^{4} P_n$$

$$= 1 - \sum_{n=0}^{4} (1 - \rho)\rho^n$$

and:

$$\rho = \frac{30}{37.52} = 0.80$$

Then:

$$P = 1 - 0.2(1 + 0.8 + 0.8^2 + 0.8^3 + 0.8^4)$$
$$= 1 - 0.672 = 0.328$$

Therefore, there is a nearly 33 percent chance that more than four customers will be in the system.

c. We use the same logic as in part (b), except that μ is now a decision variable. The easiest way to proceed is to find the correct average utilization first and then solve for the processing rate.

$$P = 1 - (1 - \rho)(1 + \rho + \rho^2 + \rho^3 + \rho^4)$$
$$= 1 - (1 + \rho + \rho^2 + \rho^3 + \rho^4) + \rho(1 + \rho + \rho^2 + \rho^3 + \rho^4)$$
$$= 1 - 1 - \rho - \rho^2 - \rho^3 - \rho^4 + \rho + \rho^2 + \rho^3 + \rho^4 + \rho^5$$
$$= \rho^5$$

or:

$$\rho = P^{1/5}$$

If $P = 0.10$:

$$\rho = (0.10)^{1/5} = 0.63$$

Therefore, for a capacity utilization of 63 percent, the probability of more than four customers in the system is 10 percent. For $\lambda = 30$, the mean processing rate must be:

$$\frac{30}{\mu} = 0.63$$

$$\mu = 47.62 \text{ customers/hour}$$

Decision Point The processing rate would only have to modestly increase to achieve the eight-minute target. However, the probability of having more than four customers in the system is too high. The manager must now find a way to increase the processing rate from 35 per hour to approximately 48 per hour. He can increase this rate in several different ways, ranging from employing a high-school student to help bag the groceries to installing electronic point-of-sale equipment that reads the prices from bar-coded information on each item.

MULTIPLE-WORKSTATION MODEL

With the multiple-workstation model, also labelled the *multiple-server model* for services, customers form a single line and choose one of s workstations when one is available. The system has only one phase. We make the following assumption in addition to those for the single-workstation model: There are s identical workstations, and the distribution of the operations time for each workstation is exponential, with a mean operations time of $1/\mu$.

With these assumptions, we can apply several formulas to describe the operating characteristics of the system:

ρ = Average utilization of the system

$$= \frac{\lambda}{s\mu}$$

P_0 = Probability that zero customers are in the system

$$= \left[\sum_{n=0}^{s-1} \frac{(\lambda/\mu)^n}{n!} + \frac{(\lambda/\mu)^s}{s!}\left(\frac{1}{1-\rho}\right)\right]^{-1}$$

P_n = Probability that n customers are in the system

$$= \begin{cases} \dfrac{(\lambda/\mu)^n}{n!}P_0, & 0 < n < s \\[2ex] \dfrac{(\lambda/\mu)^n}{s!s^{n-s}}P_0, & n \geq s \end{cases}$$

L_q = Average number of customers waiting in line

$$= \frac{P_0(\lambda/\mu)^s\rho}{s!(1-\rho)^2}$$

W_q = Average waiting time of customers in line

$$= \frac{L_q}{\lambda}$$

W = Average time spent in the system, including waiting and operations time

$$= W_q + \frac{1}{\mu}$$

L = Average number of customers in the system

$$= \lambda W$$

EXAMPLE 4S.5

Estimating Idle Time and Hourly Operating Costs with the Multiple-Workstation Model

The managers of a Canada Post terminal in New Brunswick are concerned about the amount of time the delivery trucks are idle, waiting to be unloaded. The terminal operates with four unloading bays. Each bay requires a crew of two employees, and each crew costs $30 per hour. The estimated cost of an idle truck is $50 per hour. Trucks arrive at an average rate of three per hour, according to a Poisson distribution. On average, a crew can unload a semi-trailer rig in one hour, with exponential service times. What is the total hourly cost of operating the system?

SOLUTION

The *multiple-workstation model* is appropriate. To find the total cost of labour and idle trucks, we must calculate the average number of trucks in the system.

First, we must calculate capacity utilization, ρ:

$$\rho = \frac{\lambda}{s\mu} = \frac{3 \text{ trucks per hour}}{4 \text{ bays} \times 1 \text{ hour per truck per bay}} = 0.75$$

To estimate the average number of trucks in the system, L, we must calculate (in order) the following, P_0, L_q, W_q, and W:

$$P_0 = \left[\sum_{n=0}^{s-1} \frac{(\lambda/\mu)^n}{n!} + \frac{(\lambda/\mu)^s}{s!} \left(\frac{1}{1-\rho} \right) \right]^{-1}$$

$$= \left[1 + 3 + \frac{3^2}{2} + \frac{3^3}{6} + \frac{3^4}{24} \times \left(\frac{1}{1-0.75} \right) \right]^{-1}$$

$$= \frac{1}{1 + 3 + 4.5 + 4.5 + 13.5} = 0.03774$$

$$L_q = \frac{P_0(\lambda/\mu)^s \rho}{s!(1-\rho)^2}$$

$$= \frac{0.03774 \times (3/1)^4 \times 0.75}{24 \times (1-0.75)^2} = 1.528 \text{ trucks}$$

$$W_q = \frac{L_q}{\lambda}$$

$$= \frac{1.528}{3} = 0.509 \text{ hours}$$

$$W = W_q + \frac{1}{\mu}$$

$$= 0.529 + 1 = 1.529 \text{ hours}$$

We can now estimate the average number of trucks in the system:

$$L = \lambda W$$

$$= 3 \times 1.529 = 4.53 \text{ trucks}$$

Thus, the results show that the four-bay design will be utilized 75 percent of the time and that the average number of trucks either being serviced or waiting in line is 4.53 trucks. We can now calculate the hourly costs of labour and idle trucks:

Labour cost:	$30(s) = \$30(4)$	$= \$120.00$
Idle truck cost:	$50(L) = \$50(4.53)$	$= \underline{226.50}$
	Total hourly cost	$= \$346.50$

Decision Point Management must now assess whether $346.50 per day for this operation is acceptable. Attempting to reduce costs by eliminating crews will only increase the waiting time of the trucks, which is more expensive per hour than the crews. However, if the service rate can be increased through better work methods, for example, L can be reduced and daily operating costs will be less.

DECISION AREAS FOR MANAGEMENT

After analyzing a waiting-line problem, management can improve the service system by making changes in one or more of the following areas:

1. *Arrival rates.* Management often can affect the rate of customer arrivals, λ, through advertising, special promotions, or differential pricing. For example, a telephone company uses differential pricing to shift residential long-distance calls from daytime hours to evening hours.

2. *Number of service facilities.* By increasing the number of workstations, such as tool cribs, toll booths, or bank tellers, or by dedicating some workstations in a phase to a unique set of services, management can increase system capacity.

3. *Number of phases.* Managers can decide to allocate tasks to sequential phases if they determine that two sequential workstations may be more efficient than one. For instance, in the assembly-line problem discussed in Chapter 7, "Location and Layout," the decision concerns the number of phases needed along the assembly line. Determining the number of workers needed on the line also involves assigning a certain set of work elements to each one. Changing the arrangement of workstations can increase the processing rate, μ, of each workstation and the capacity of the system.

4. *Number of servers per workstation.* Managers can influence the processing rate by assigning more than one person to a workstation.

5. *Worker efficiency.* By adjusting the capital-to-labour ratio, devising improved work methods, or instituting incentive programs, management can increase the efficiency of workers assigned to a workstation. Such changes are reflected in μ.

6. *Priority rule.* Managers set the priority rule to be used, decide whether to have a different priority rule for each workstation, and decide whether to allow pre-emption (and, if so, under what conditions). Such decisions affect the waiting times of the customers and the utilization of workstations.

7. *Line arrangement.* Managers can influence customer waiting times and the utilization of individual workstations by deciding whether to have a single line or multiple lines in a given phase of service.

Obviously, these factors are interrelated. An adjustment in the customer arrival rate, λ, might have to be accompanied by an increase in the processing rate, μ, in some way. Decisions about the number of workstations, the number of phases, and waiting-line arrangements also are related.

For each of the problems we analyzed with the waiting-line models, the arrivals had a Poisson distribution (or exponential interarrival times), the processing times had an exponential distribution, the workstations had a simple arrangement, and the priority discipline was first come, first served. Waiting-line theory has been used to develop other models in which these criteria are not met, but these models are very complex.

Many times the nature of the customer population, the constraints on the line, the priority rule, the distribution of operations time, and the arrangement of workstations are such that waiting-line theory is no longer useful. In these cases, simulation often is used (see Supplement G, "Simulation").

EQUATION SUMMARY

1. Customer arrival Poisson distribution: $P_n = \dfrac{(\lambda T)^n}{n!} e^{-\lambda T}$

2. Operations-time exponential distribution: $P(t \leq T) = 1 - e^{-\mu T}$

	SINGLE-SERVER MODEL	MULTIPLE-SERVER MODEL
Average capacity utilization of the system	$\rho = \dfrac{\lambda}{\mu}$	$\rho = \dfrac{\lambda}{s\mu}$
Probability that n customers are in the system	$P_n = (1 - \rho)\rho^n$	$P_n = \begin{cases} \dfrac{(\lambda/\mu)^n}{n!} P_0, & 0 < n < s \\ \dfrac{(\lambda/\mu)^n}{s! \, s^{n-s}} P_0, & n \geq s \end{cases}$
Probability that zero customers are in the system	$P_0 = 1 - \rho$	$P_0 = \left[\displaystyle\sum_{n=0}^{s-1} \dfrac{(\lambda/\mu)^n}{n!} + \dfrac{(\lambda/\mu)^s}{s!}\left(\dfrac{1}{1-\rho}\right) \right]^{-1}$
Average number of customers in the system	$L = \dfrac{\lambda}{\mu - \lambda}$	$L = \lambda W$
Average number of customers in the waiting line	$L_q = \rho L$	$L_q = \dfrac{P_0(\lambda/\mu)^s \rho}{s!(1 - \rho)^2}$
Average time spent in the system, including waiting and operations time	$W = \dfrac{1}{\mu - \lambda}$	$W = W_q + \dfrac{1}{\mu}$
Average waiting time in line	$W_q = \rho W$	$W_q = \dfrac{L_q}{\lambda}$

SUPPLEMENT HIGHLIGHTS

- Waiting lines form when customers or items arrive at a faster rate than they are being served or processed. Because customer arrival rates vary, long waiting lines may occur even when the system's designed processing rate is substantially higher than the average customer arrival rate.

- Waiting-line models have been developed for use in analyzing service and manufacturing systems. If the assumptions made in creating a waiting-line model are consistent with an actual situation, the model's formulas can be solved to predict the performance of the system with respect to capacity utilization, average customer waiting time, and the average number of customers in the system.

- Four elements are common to all waiting-line problems: a customer population, a waiting line, a queuing configuration, and a priority rule for determining which customer is to be served next.

CD-ROM RESOURCES

The Student CD-ROM that accompanies this text contains the following resources, which allow you to further practise and apply the concepts presented in this supplement.

- **Equation Summary**: All the equations for this supplement can be found in one convenient location.

- **OM Explorer Tutors**: OM Explorer contains two tutor programs that will help you learn how to use the single-server and multiple-server models.

- **OM Explorer Solvers**: OM Explorer has a program that can be used to solve general problems involving waiting lines.

- **Extend LT**: *Security Inspection at the Randville Plant*. The chief of security must explore options to cut delays with employees passing through the security checkpoint.

SOLVED PROBLEM 1

A photographer at the post office takes passport pictures at an average rate of 20 pictures per hour. The photographer must wait until the customer blinks or scowls, so the time to take a picture is exponentially distributed. Customers arrive at a Poisson-distributed average rate of 19 customers per hour.

   a. What is the capacity utilization of the photographer?

   b. How much time will the average customer spend at the photograph step of the passport issuing process?

SOLUTION

   a. The assumptions in the problem statement are consistent with a single-server model. Utilization is:

$$\rho = \frac{\lambda}{\mu} = \frac{19}{20} = 0.95$$

   b. The average customer time spent at the photographer's station is:

$$W = \frac{1}{\mu - \lambda} = \frac{1}{20 - 19} = 1 \text{ hour}$$

SOLVED PROBLEM 2

The Mega Multiplex Movie Theatre has three concession clerks serving customers on a first-come, first-served basis. The processing time per customer is exponentially distributed with an average of 2 minutes per customer. Concession customers wait in a single line in a large lobby, and arrivals are Poisson distributed with an average of 81 customers per hour. Previews run for 10 minutes before the start of each show. If the average time in the concession area exceeds 10 minutes, customers become dissatisfied.

   a. What is the average capacity utilization of the concession clerks?

   b. What is the average time spent in the concession area?

SOLUTION

a. The problem statement is consistent with the multiple-server model, and the average utilization rate is:

$$\rho = \frac{\lambda}{s\mu} = \frac{81 \text{ customers/hour}}{(3 \text{ servers})\left(\dfrac{60 \text{ minutes/server hour}}{2 \text{ minutes/customer}}\right)} = 0.90$$

The concession clerks are busy 90 percent of the time.

b. The average time spent in the system, W, is

$$W = W_q + \frac{1}{\mu}$$

Here:

$$W_q = \frac{L_q}{\lambda} \qquad L_q = \frac{P_0(\lambda/\mu)^s\rho}{s!(1-\rho)^2} \qquad \text{and} \qquad P_0 = \left[\sum_{n=0}^{s-1}\frac{(\lambda/\mu)^n}{n!} + \frac{(\lambda/\mu)^s}{s!}\left(\frac{1}{1-\rho}\right)\right]^{-1}$$

We must solve for P_0, L_q, and W_q, in that order, before we can solve for W:

$$P_0 = \left[\sum_{n=0}^{s-1}\frac{(\lambda/\mu)^n}{n!} + \frac{(\lambda/\mu)^s}{s!}\left(\frac{1}{1-\rho}\right)\right]^{-1}$$

$$= \frac{1}{1 + \dfrac{(81/30)}{1} + \dfrac{(2.7)^2}{2} + \left[\dfrac{(2.7)^3}{6}\left(\dfrac{1}{1-0.9}\right)\right]}$$

$$= \frac{1}{1 + 2.7 + 3.645 + 32.805} = \frac{1}{40.15} = 0.0249$$

$$L_q = \frac{P_0(\lambda/\mu)^s\rho}{s!(1-\rho)^2} = \frac{0.0249\,(81/30)^3(0.9)}{3!(1-0.9)^2} = \frac{0.4411}{6(0.01)} = 7.352 \text{ customers}$$

$$W_q = \frac{L_q}{\lambda} = \frac{7.352 \text{ customers}}{81 \text{ customers/hour}} = 0.0908 \text{ hour}$$

$$W = W_q + \frac{1}{\mu} = 0.0908 \text{ hour} + \frac{1}{30} \text{ hour} = (0.1241 \text{ hour})\left(\frac{60 \text{ minutes}}{\text{hour}}\right)$$

$$= 7.45 \text{ minutes}$$

With three concession clerks, customers will spend an average of 7.45 minutes in the concession area.

PROBLEMS

1. The Solomon law firm produces many legal documents that must be typed for clients and the firm. Requests average 8 pages of documents per hour, and they arrive according to a Poisson distribution. The secretary can type 10 pages per hour on average according to an exponential distribution.

   a. What is the average capacity utilization of the secretary?

   b. What is the probability that more than 4 pages are waiting or being typed?

   c. What is the average number of pages waiting to be typed?

2. Moore, Aiken, and Leung is a dental clinic serving the needs of the general public on a first-come, first-served basis. The clinic has three dental chairs, each staffed by a dentist. Patients arrive at the rate of five per hour, according to a Poisson distribution, and do not balk or renege. The average time required for a dental checkup is 30 minutes, according to an exponential distribution.

   a. What is the probability that no patients are in the clinic?

   b. What is the probability that six or more patients are in the clinic?

   c. What is the average number of patients waiting?

   d. What is the average total time that a patient spends in the clinic?

3. Fantastic Styling Salon is run by two stylists, Jenny Perez and Bill Sloan, each capable of serving five customers per hour, on average. Eight customers, on average, arrive at the salon each hour.

   a. If all arriving customers wait in a common line for the next available stylist, how long would a customer wait in line, on average, before being served?

   b. Suppose that 50 percent of the arriving customers want to be served only by Perez and that the other 50 percent want only Sloan. How long would a customer wait in line, on average, before being served by Perez? By Sloan? What is the average customer waiting time in the line?

   c. Do you observe a difference in the answers to parts (a) and (b)? If so, why? Explain.

4. You are the manager of a local bank where three tellers provide services to customers. On average, each teller takes 3 minutes to serve a customer. Customers arrive, on average, at a rate of 50 per hour. Having recently received complaints from some customers that they have had to wait for a long time before being served, your boss asks you to evaluate the service system. Specifically, you must provide answers to the following questions:

   a. What is the average capacity utilization of the three-teller service system?

   b. What is the probability that no customers are being served by a teller or are waiting in line?

   c. What is the average number of customers waiting in line?

   d. On average, how long does a customer wait in line before being served?

   e. On average, how many customers would be at a teller's station and in line?

5. Tram Tweet hosts a psychology talk show on CTPG radio. Tram's advice averages 8 minutes per caller but varies according to an exponential distribution. The average time between calls is 20 minutes, exponentially distributed. Generating calls in this local market is difficult, so Tram doesn't want to lose any calls to busy signals. The radio station has only three telephone lines. What is the probability that a caller receives a busy signal?

6. The supervisor at the Precision Machine Shop wants to determine the staffing policy that minimizes total operating costs. The average arrival rate at the tool crib, where tools are dispensed to the workers, is eight machinists per hour. Each machinist's pay is $20 per hour. The supervisor can staff the crib either with a junior attendant who is paid $5 per hour and can process 10 arrivals per hour or with a senior attendant who is paid $12 per hour and can process 16 arrivals per hour. Which attendant should be selected, and what would be the total estimated hourly cost?

7. You are in charge of a quarry that supplies sand and stone aggregates to your company's construction sites. Empty trucks from construction sites arrive at the quarry's huge piles of sand and stone aggregates and wait in line to enter the station, which can load either sand or aggregate. At the station, they are filled with material, weighed, checked out, and proceed to a construction site. Currently, nine empty trucks arrive per hour, on average. Once a truck has entered a loading station, it takes 6 minutes for it to be filled, weighed, and checked out.

   Concerned that trucks are spending too much time waiting and being filled, you are evaluating two alternatives to reduce the average time the trucks spend in the system. The first alternative is to add side boards to the trucks (so that more material could be loaded) and to add a helper at the loading station (so that filling time could be reduced) at a total cost of $50 000. The arrival rate of trucks would change to six per hour, and the filling time would be reduced to four minutes. The second alternative is to add another loading station at a cost of $80 000. The trucks would wait in a common line and the truck at the front of the line would move to the next available station.

   Which alternative would you recommend if you want to reduce the current average waiting time in the system?

REFERENCES AND FURTHER READINGS

Cooper, Robert B. *Introduction to Queuing Theory*, 2nd ed. New York: Elsevier–North Holland, 1980.

Hillier, F. S., and G. S. Lieberman. *Introduction to Operations Research*, 2nd ed. San Francisco: Holden-Day, 1975.

Lovejoy, W. S. "Integrated Operations: A Proposal for Operations Management Teaching and Research," *Production and Operations Management*, vol. 7 (1998), no. 2, pp. 106–124.

Moore, P. M. *Queues, Inventories and Maintenance*. New York: John Wiley & Sons, 1958.

Saaty, T. L. *Elements of Queuing Theory with Applications*. New York: McGraw-Hill, 1961.

Quality

Across the Organization

Quality is important to:

- **accounting,** which must measure and estimate the costs of poor quality and provide error-free data to its internal customers.
- **finance,** which must assess the cash flow implications of total quality management (TQM) programs and provide defect-free financial reports to its internal customers and shareholders.
- **human resources,** which recruits, motivates, and trains employees who value quality work.
- **management information systems,** which design the systems for tracking productivity and quality performance.
- **marketing,** which uses quality and performance data for promotional purposes.
- **operations,** which designs and implements TQM programs.

Learning Goals

After reading this chapter, you should be able to:

1. define *quality* from the customer's perspective.
2. discuss the four major cost categories of quality.
3. describe the principles and elements of TQM and Six Sigma programs, and how they contribute to improved quality and productivity.
4. distinguish among the various tools for improving quality and explain how each should be used.
5. discuss how control charts are developed and used to determine whether a process is out of statistical control.
6. assess whether a process is capable of producing a product or service to specifications.

Blue Mountain Resorts, located north of Toronto, is one of Ontario's most popular ski resorts, with 20 percent of the Ontario skier and snowboarder market. Since its founding in 1941 by Czechoslovakian immigrant Jozo Weider, Blue Mountain has expanded dramatically from the Schuss trail, which was serviced by a lift that used two sleds and a cable powered by an old truck engine. Property development and expansion now include a four-star resort hotel, a conference centre, retail shops, a condominium development, and a highly rated golf course. With a year-round staff of 330, and an additional 1200 winter seasonal employees, Blue Mountain hosts more than 555 000 skier visits annually.

In 1991, Blue Mountain Resorts started what senior management later termed a "quality service journey" to build and expand the business. One of the first issues uncovered was the negative impact of poor employee morale on service quality, which in turn was driven by a number of factors ranging from working conditions to frustration with the historical level of quality. It was clearly evident that the service quality problems were not going to be an easy fix—it would involve difficult changes and a long-term commitment from senior management.

Starting with a challenging vision, "To be the best resort in Canada at exceeding customer expectations," an orientation toward high-quality service was developed through a series of expanding initiatives: basic, supporting, and, finally, enhanced services. Part of the senior management commitment involved designating a service quality coordinator and targeting quality improvement at both internal and external customers.

Although Blue Mountain had been collecting basic operational information for several years, the new emphasis on service quality forced management to gather and act on more specific customer data. Early on, targets were set and linked to

Many factors contribute to customers' perception of quality at Blue Mountain Resorts. Over the last decade, quality initiatives have grown and service has improved dramatically.

employee bonuses for improvements in customer survey ratings. Hiring practices were changed to involve front-line staff and to more closely match job demands with employee capabilities. Annual service quality reports also served to communicate employee successes and new quality initiatives.

After the first three years, management felt that there wasn't enough being done to "wow" the customer. So they turned their attention to enhanced service, which unfortunately came at the expense of other process fundamentals that were essential for high-quality service. For example, during that holiday season, staff was added on the ski hill to handle complaints and to answer questions from guests. Other staff provided unexpected services—such as handing out hot chocolate drinks and hors d'oeuvres on silver platters. However, other basic service elements faltered, with more than 1000 calls being lost in the call centre in one month alone and poor signage hampering the arrival of new customers. In essence, Blue Mountain was trying to achieve high levels of service without adequate processes and systems—ultimately with disastrous financial results.

As attention was redirected to process management, the journey shifted to focus on continuous improvement. Cross-functional process improvement teams identified poor quality and service failure points, looked for root causes, and made recommendations for corrective action based on data analysis. For example, rather than treating the call centre as an order desk, quality improvement initiatives resulted in new formal training, new communications technology, and processes to support one-stop service. To assess performance, the number of abandoned calls is monitored, and targets of 80 percent of calls being answered within 20 seconds were established.

Customers reacted very positively! During the first few years of the quality journey, the percentage of customers indicating that Blue Mountain was better than other Canadian resorts increased from 19 percent to more than 50 percent. Consequently, a new measure was established—the percentage of customers that ranked staff friendliness as a 10 on a ten-point scale. In 1995, 17 percent of customers reported 10 on the staff friendliness question. Targets have been steadily increasing since that time.

Although people and processes are both critical to quality, management also realized that building quality requires capital investment. By 2000, the ski hill had the capacity to handle 7500 skiers comfortably during any particular day, while night skiing handled an additional 3000. Because management can't control the weather, hill grooming and snowmaking help to improve the quality of the customer experience. Blue Mountain has the

largest snowmaking capacity in Canada, which uses about 45 000 litres of water per minute and incorporates the latest computer technology to optimize coverage of the terrain. High quality also translated into a wider variety of services being offered to skiers and snowboarders. Among the most important is the ski school, employing 180 professionals, making it one of the largest ski and snowboarding schools in Canada.

Over this ten-year period, the journey for Blue Mountain to build service quality became a multifaceted and tightly coupled system of continuous improvement, employee involvement, redesigned business processes, and new capital investment.

Source: Adapted with permission from: P. F. Johnson, *Blue Mountain Resorts: The Quality Service Journey*, 9B00D016 (London, ON: Ivey Publishing, 2000). Ivey Publishing will not grant permission for further use of this adapted version.

total quality management (TQM) A philosophy that stresses three principles: customer satisfaction, employee involvement, and continuous improvements in quality.

The challenge for business today is to produce quality products or services efficiently. Blue Mountain Resorts is but one example of a company that has met the challenge and is using quality as a competitive weapon. This chapter explores the competitive implications of quality, focusing on the philosophy and tools of total quality management, which many firms have embraced. **Total quality management (TQM)** stresses three principles: customer satisfaction, employee involvement, and continuous improvements in quality. As Figure 5.1 indicates, TQM also integrates other areas essential to quality, including benchmarking, product and service design,

FIGURE 5.1

TQM Wheel

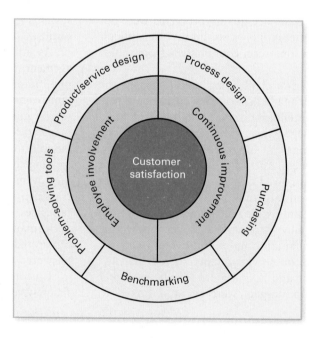

process design, purchasing, and problem-solving tools. Statistical process control forms a foundational set of techniques to appraise and monitor quality in processes and operating systems.

QUALITY: A MANAGEMENT PHILOSOPHY

We previously identified two competitive priorities that deal with quality: high-performance design and consistent quality (see Chapter 1, "Competing with Operations"). These priorities characterize an organization's competitive thrust. Strategic plans that recognize quality as an essential competitive priority must be based on some operational definition of quality. In this section, we discuss individuals who have shaped the management of quality. We also consider various definitions of quality and emphasize the importance of bridging the gap between consumer expectations of quality and operating capabilities.

GURUS OF QUALITY MANAGEMENT

Many individuals have contributed to the development of quality management over the last 80 years, beginning with Walter Shewhart's development of statistical tools. The distinctive perspectives of three people, Deming, Juran, and Crosby, help us to understand the basis for many of the different approaches and tools in wide use today to monitor and improve quality. That is not to say that others have not been instrumental in shaping the way we conceptualize quality, such as Armand Feigenbaum with his concept of total quality control, and Taguchi with his emphasis on designing in quality through engineering, discussed near the end of this chapter. However, Deming, Juran, and Crosby provide important philosophical starting points for a deeper understanding of how to effectively manage quality.

W. EDWARDS DEMING. The foundation to Deming's philosophy to quality management is statistical process control (SPC). SPC, described in much greater detail later in this chapter, uses statistical methods to monitor the quality of output from individual operations along a process. Although Deming initially introduced these techniques to U.S. managers, it was only later, in the 1950s, that his methods proved far more influential with Japanese management. He became a major figure in the Japanese quality movement, where at times he is referred to as the father of quality control. In recognition, the highest industrial award for excellence in Japan has been named the Deming Prize.

In a nutshell, Deming's philosophy advocates continuous improvement of the production process to achieve conformance to specifications and reduce variability. As noted in Chapter 4, "Capacity," higher variability requires additional investment in capacity and inventory. Extensive final inspection and testing comes too late in the process to get rid of poor quality. To reduce variability, Deming's approach to process improvement focuses on two actions: reduce *common* causes of quality problems, such as poor design and inadequate employee training; and reduce *special* causes, such as specific short-term equipment problems or a particular operational practice. Statistical techniques are critical to identifying and reducing both types of causes.

Deming's 14 points, listed in Table 5.1, go beyond SPC to address management's central role in total quality management. Primary responsibility for quality improvement lies with management, as he argued that 85 percent of quality problems can be attributed to managers or the systems they put in place. His rationale was that management is responsible for designing the system, for leading efforts to improve the system, and for empowering employees. However, employees were not ignored; they must monitor quality throughout the process and systematically analyze and implement improvements using a four-step approach. This approach, termed the Deming wheel, or Plan-Do-Check-Act (PDCA) cycle, is discussed in greater detail in the later section titled "Continuous Improvement" (see also Figure 5.2 on page 157).

(see also Figure 5.2 on page 157)

TABLE 5.1

Deming's 14 Points for Improving Quality

Source: Adapted from: W. E. Deming, "Transformation of Today's Management," *Executive Excellence*, vol. 4 (1987), no. 12, p. 8.

1. Create constancy of purpose toward improvement of product and service.
2. Adopt a new philosophy, with management leading change.
3. Cease dependence on inspection to achieve quality—build quality into the product.
4. Stop awarding business on the basis of price; instead minimize total cost.
5. Constantly improve the system of production and service.
6. Institute training on the job.
7. Institute leadership, the aim of which is to help people and equipment do a better job.
8. Drive out fear so that everyone can work effectively.
9. Break down barriers between departments.
10. Eliminate slogans, exhortations, and targets, which only create adversarial relationships.
11. Eliminate quotas, and management by objective and by numbers—substitute leadership.
12. Remove barriers that rob people of their right to pride in their work.
13. Institute a vigorous program of education and self-improvement.
14. Put everybody in the company to work to accomplish the transformation.

JOSEPH M. JURAN. Like Deming, Joseph Juran served as a consultant to Japanese industry. However, Juran defined quality in terms of the customer—as fitness for use. He also advocated that the costs of quality can be better understood by explicitly recognizing specific categories: prevention, appraisal, and failure costs. These categories are explained in detail later in this chapter. However, only by examining all of these can a complete and accurate picture of the implications of poor quality be understood, which then serves as the basis for delivering optimal levels of quality.

To effectively manage quality, Juran emphasized the critical importance of three interrelated managerial processes: quality planning, control, and improvement. According to Juran, "Quality does not happen by accident; it has to be planned." The planning process, driven by senior managers and experts, ensures that customer needs are well understood, and that systems are designed to attain the particular quality characteristics deemed necessary by the customer. Management sets goals and priorities, assesses the results of previous plans, and coordinates quality objects with other company goals. For this reason, quality training must start at the top of the organization with management.

Quality control is about maintaining a stable, predictable level of quality. To do so, actual performance must be evaluated, comparisons are made to objectives, and, where discrepancies are found, corrective action is initiated. Finally, quality improvement uses project teams to achieve periodic "breakthroughs" with dramatic gains to address chronic quality problems. Improvement processes must also establish and support the necessary infrastructure, such as employee training and other resources for project teams. Many individual quality improvement projects are under way throughout an organization at any given time. Collectively, these three processes of planning, control, and improvement form what Juran referred to as the *quality trilogy.*

PHILIP CROSBY. A third leader in quality management, Philip Crosby, further explored the costs of poor quality, which he argued are greatly misunderstood and underestimated. The cost of poor quality must include lower productivity, lost sales, equipment downtime and poor service, to name just a few outcomes. His book *Quality Is Free* stresses that the trade-off between tolerating versus preventing poor quality should always favour prevention and improvement. In Crosby's view, a company's objective must be *zero defects*. Quality excellence is achieved through clear goals and standards (rather than statistical data), strong organizational commitment, redesigned processes to remove error-causing situations, and open communication between management and employees.

To summarize, the views of these three quality gurus are compared in Table 5.2.

	Deming	Juran	Crosby
Definition of quality	A predictable degree of uniformity and dependability at low cost and suited to the market	Customer-defined: fitness for use	Conformance to requirements
Senior management responsibility	Responsible for 85% of quality problems; management designs system	Source of more than 80% of quality problems; management plans and reviews improvement projects	Responsible for quality
General philosophy	Reduce variability by continuous improvement; cease mass inspection	Multifaceted management of quality, especially human elements	Prevention, not inspection
Basic structure	14 points for management; PDCA cycle	Quality trilogy: planning, ongoing control, and breakthrough improvement projects	14 steps to quality improvement
Basis for improvement	Continuous to reduce variation; eliminate goals without methods	Project-by-project team approach; set goals	A process, not a program; improvement goals
Costs of quality	No optimum; continuous improvement	Quality is not free; there is an optimum	Quality is free; cost of nonconformance
Performance standard/motivation	Many quality metrics; use statistics to assess performance; critical of zero defects	Avoid campaigns to do perfect work	Zero defects, less emphasis on statistics
Statistical process control (SPC)	Statistical methods of quality control must be used	Recommends SPC but warns that it can lead to tool-driven approach	Rejects statistically acceptable levels of quality
Teamwork	Employee participation in decision making; break down barriers between departments	Quality council and project teams	Quality improvement teams; quality councils
Purchasing and goods received	Statistical evidence and control charts required, as inspection is too late and allows defects to enter system	Problems are complex; carry out formal surveys	State requirements; supplier is extension of business; most faults due to purchasers themselves
Vendor rating	No, critical of most systems	Yes, but help supplier improve using quality trilogy	Rate buyers and suppliers, as both contribute to material faults
Single sourcing of supply	Yes	No, can neglect to sharpen competitive edge	No

TABLE 5.2

Views of Three Quality Gurus

Source: Adapted from: J. S. Oakland, *Total Quality Management* (London, Eng.: Heinemann Professional Publishing Ltd., 1989), pp. 292–293; M. M. Davis, N. J. Aquilano, and R. B. Chase, *Fundamentals of Operations Management*, 4th ed. (Burr Ridge, IL: McGraw-Hill Irwin, 2003), p. 216.

CUSTOMER SATISFACTION: DEFINITIONS OF QUALITY

Quality is one of the key dimensions of customer value; however, customers define quality in various ways, partly depending on whether the customers are internal or external to the firm. In a general sense, **quality** may be defined as meeting or exceeding the expectations of the customer. For practical purposes, it is necessary to be more precise and identify particular facets or components (Garvin, 1987; Parasuraman et al., 1986) that apply to the customer benefit bundle of goods and services being produced. Like a diamond, quality looks somewhat different depending on the shape of the bundle, and which facet is presented to the customer. Broadly speaking, the two competitive priorities of high-performance design and conformance relate quality to customer value. Managers can monitor and improve specific quality dimensions, one or more of which may apply at any one time.

quality The degree of excellence based on meeting or exceeding the expectations of the customer, including both high-performance design and conformance.

HIGH-PERFORMANCE DESIGN

High-performance design includes basic performance, supplemental features, reliability, durability, support, and psychological impressions.

BASIC PERFORMANCE. Customers generally expect products or services to offer key characteristics or technical capabilities. These characteristics are measurable and well understood, allowing customers to make direct comparisons between competitive products. For example, performance characteristics for a computer might include computing power and speed, memory, disk storage, Internet connectivity, and footprint (i.e., the area it takes up on your desk). Unfortunately, such a complex product might require trade-offs in performance, with a larger size being needed to accommodate additional memory and storage. For home delivery of newspapers, performance might include delivering a clean, dry newspaper, even in inclement weather.

SUPPLEMENTAL FEATURES. In addition to key characteristics, customers consider secondary, less important aspects, sometimes termed "bells and whistles," that are merely nice to have. Supplemental features often make the product easier to use or service more pleasant. For example, the layout and backlighting of the keyboard on a laptop computer can make it easier to use in low-light conditions. Setting up water stations for thirsty golfers at several locations around a golf course enhances the experience, particularly during hot weather.

RELIABILITY. The likelihood of a product working properly or service being performed during a specified period is termed reliability. Because any measure of reliability is expected to be very high, firms often report reliability in terms of failure, for example, mean time between failures, failure rate per month, or average percent late. For example, Seagate, a disk drive manufacturer, advertised that a particular disk drive had a "mean time between failures" of 1.2 million hours. Reliability is particularly critical for customers when the costs of failure or downtime are high, such as with the telecommunications industry. Equipment reliability is critical for service providers, where customers can be immediately aware of any downtime.

DURABILITY. In contrast to reliability, durability measures the lifespan of a product before it begins to deteriorate or no longer functions at an acceptable level. For simple products such as fluorescent lights, this might be measured in hours of expected service. However, for other, more expensive capital goods, such as automobiles, durability also captures the costs of repair relative to replacement. Finally, for many high-technology products, durability also can include how long the product is useful before it becomes obsolete. For example, a computer may "work" for ten years, yet still be obsolete for all but the simplest functions in less than five years. Durability reflects the ease with which the computer can be upgraded to maintain compatibility with current standards for software.

SUPPORT. Often the support provided by the company after the initial sale of the product or service is as important to customers as the quality of the basic product or service itself. Customers get upset with a company if financial statements are incorrect, responses to warranty claims are delayed, or advertising is misleading. Serviceability is also very important, as it adds to the overall life-cycle cost of the product. For example, many products need occasional repair, such as the brakes on an automobile. If this can be done quickly and inexpensively, customers perceive higher quality. At times, good product serviceability and support also can reduce the consequences of poor quality.

For example, if you had just had brake service done for your car, you would be upset if the brakes began squealing again a week later. If the manager of the brake shop offers to redo the work at no additional charge, the company's intent to satisfy the customer is clear.

PSYCHOLOGICAL IMPRESSIONS. People often evaluate the quality of a product or service on the basis of psychological impressions: atmosphere, image, craftsmanship, or aesthetics. In the provision of services, where the customer is in close contact with the provider, the appearance and actions of the provider are very important. Nicely dressed, courteous, friendly, and sympathetic employees can affect the customer's perception of service quality. For example, rumpled, discourteous, or grumpy waiters can undermine a restaurant's best efforts to provide high-quality service. Also, some patients may judge a dentist's quality of service on the basis of the age of her equipment, because new dental technology greatly reduces the discomfort associated with visits to the dentist. In manufacturing, product quality often is judged on the basis of the knowledge and personality of salespeople, as well as the product image presented in advertisements.

CONFORMANCE

On the basis of customer expectations, a firm must develop specifications for product and service design, as well as any associated operating characteristics. These specifications describe high-performance design in detail, including such aspects as basic performance, supplemental features, and reliability. Conformance captures the consistency with which the firm meets these specifications.

In general, high conformance quality coupled with tight tolerances for specifications yields consistent products with low variability. For example, all the components of the disk drive must conform to particular specifications for size, speed of access, failure rate, and drop distance (i.e., resistance to breakage) to achieve the desired quality of the finished product. In service systems, conformance to specifications is also important, even though tangible outputs may not be created. For example, one specification for a service operation might be response time. Bell Canada measures the performance of its operators in Ontario by the length of time it takes to process a telephone call ("handle time"). In the past, if the group average time exceeded a standard of 23 seconds, managers worked with the operators to reduce it.

QUALITY AS A COMPETITIVE WEAPON

Consumers are much more quality-minded now than in the past, yet attaining quality in all areas of a business is a difficult task. To make things even more difficult, consumers change their perceptions of quality. In general, a business's success depends on the accuracy of its perceptions of consumer expectations and its ability to bridge the gap between those expectations and operating capabilities. Good quality can pay off in higher profits. In many markets, high-quality products and services can be priced higher than comparable lower-quality ones.

Higher quality (i.e., greater consistency and less variability) can also translate into lower costs, which yield a greater return for the same sales dollar. Consistent quality is particularly critical in commodity-based industries, such as mining and forest products, where the price is set by broad market forces. Poor quality erodes the firm's ability to compete in the marketplace and increases the costs of producing its product or service.

For example, poor-quality service has been a frequent complaint about Air Canada to Canada's federal Air Travel Complaints Commissioner. In contrast, relatively few complaints have been received about WestJet's service quality—well below what might be expected given its second-place market share. These reports, which are often published in the media, can contribute to losses in market share for a firm with poor quality, as well as to higher costs associated with resolving those complaints. Similarly, Toyota consistently dominates quality surveys of new-car buyers, such as the Initial Quality Survey by J. D. Power, which in turn influences the purchase decisions of other new customers. Big Rock Brewery, a regional brewery based in Calgary, Alberta, attributes its continued growth and success against much larger, dominant firms to offering high-quality products. Collectively, high quality means that management is better able to compete on both price and quality, yielding significantly better customer value.

COSTS OF QUALITY

Many companies spend significant time, effort, and expense on systems, training, and organizational changes to improve the performance and quality of their processes. They believe that it is important to be able to gauge current levels of performance so that any process gaps can be determined. Gaps reflect potential dissatisfied customers and additional costs for the firm.

Experts have estimated that the losses from the costs of poor quality range from 20 percent to 30 percent of gross sales for defective or unsatisfactory products. Four major categories of costs are associated with quality management: prevention, appraisal, internal failure, and external failure.

PREVENTION COSTS

prevention costs Costs associated with preventing defects before they happen.

Prevention costs are associated with avoiding defects before they happen. They include the costs of redesigning the process to remove the causes of poor quality, redesigning the product to make it simpler to manufacture, training employees in the methods of continuous improvement, and working with suppliers to increase the quality of purchased items or contracted services. In order to improve quality, firms have to invest additional time, effort, and money. Later in this chapter we further explore these costs and methods to prevent poor quality.

APPRAISAL COSTS

appraisal costs Costs incurred in assessing the level of quality attained by the operating system.

Appraisal costs are incurred to assess and inspect the level of quality attained by the operating system. Appraisal helps management identify quality problems. As preventive measures improve quality, appraisal costs decrease, because fewer resources are needed for quality inspections and the subsequent search for causes of any problems that are detected.

INTERNAL FAILURE COSTS

internal failure costs Costs resulting from defects that are discovered during the production of a product or service.

Internal failure costs result from defects that are discovered during the production of a product or service. They fall into two major cost categories: *yield losses*, which are incurred if a defective item must be scrapped, and *rework costs*, which are incurred if the item is rerouted to some previous operation(s) to correct the defect or if the service must be performed again. For example, if the final inspector at an automobile paint shop discovers that the paint on a car has a poor finish, the car may have to be completely resanded and repainted. The additional time spent correcting such a mistake results in lower productivity for the sanding and painting departments. In addition, the car may not be finished by the date on which the customer is expecting it. Continuous improvement projects can work on identifying the causes of these defects and implementing changes to prevent them.

EXTERNAL FAILURE COSTS

External failure costs arise when a defect is discovered *after* the customer has received the product or service. For instance, suppose that you have the oil changed in your car and that the oil filter is improperly installed, causing the oil to drain onto your garage floor. You might insist that the company pay for the car to be towed and restore the oil and filter immediately. External failure costs to the company include the towing and additional oil and filter costs, as well as the loss of future revenue because you decide never to take your car back there for service. Dissatisfied customers talk about bad service or products to their friends, who in turn tell others. If the problem is bad enough, consumer protection groups alert the media. The potential impact on future profits is difficult to assess, but without doubt external failure costs erode market share and profits. Encountering defects and correcting them after the product is in the customer's hands is costly.

External failure costs also include warranty service and litigation costs. A **warranty** is a written guarantee that the producer will replace or repair defective parts or perform the service to the customer's satisfaction. Usually, a warranty is given for some specified period. For example, television repairs might be guaranteed for 90 days and new automobiles for five years or 100 000 kilometres, whichever comes first. Warranty costs must be considered in the design of new products or services, particularly as they relate to reliability.

EMPLOYEE INVOLVEMENT

One of the important elements of TQM is employee involvement, as shown in Figure 5.1. A program in employee involvement includes changing organizational culture and encouraging teamwork.

CULTURAL CHANGE

The challenge of quality management is to instill an awareness of the importance of quality in all employees, and to motivate them to improve product quality efficiently and effectively. With TQM, everyone is expected to contribute to the overall improvement of quality—from the administrator who finds cost-saving measures, to the salesperson who learns of a new customer need, to the engineer who designs a product with fewer parts, to the manager who communicates clearly with other department heads. In other words, TQM involves all the functions that are involved in creating a product or service.

One of the main challenges in developing the proper culture for TQM is to define *customer* for each employee. As noted earlier, customers can be either internal or external. External customers are the people or firms who buy the product or service. In this sense, the entire firm is a single unit that must do its best to satisfy external customers. However, communicating customers' concerns to everyone in the organization is difficult. Some employees, especially those having little contact with external customers, may have difficulty seeing how their jobs contribute to the whole effort. However, each employee also has one or more internal customers—other employees in the firm who rely on that individual's output. For example, a machinist who drills holes in a component and passes it on to a welder has the welder as her customer. Even though the welder is not an external customer, he will have many of the same definitions of quality as an external customer, except that they will relate to the component instead of a complete product.

All employees must do a good job of serving their internal customers if external customers ultimately are to be satisfied. The concept of internal customers works if each *internal* customer demands only value-added activities of their internal suppliers—that is, activities that the external customer will recognize and pay for. The notion of internal customers applies to all parts of a firm and enhances cross-functional coordination. For example, accounting must prepare accurate and timely reports for management, and purchasing must provide high-quality materials on time for operations.

In TQM, everyone in the organization must share the view that high quality is an end in itself. Errors or defects should be caught and corrected at the source, not passed along to an internal customer. This philosophy is called *quality at the source*. In addition, firms should avoid trying to "inspect quality into the product" by using inspectors to weed out defective products or unsatisfactory services after all operations have been performed. In some manufacturing firms, workers have the authority to stop a production line if they spot quality problems.

TEAMS

teams Small groups of people who have a common purpose, set their own performance goals and approaches, and hold themselves accountable for success.

Employee involvement is a key tactic for improving quality and competitiveness. One way to achieve employee involvement is by the use of **teams**, which are small groups of people who have a common purpose, set their own performance goals and approaches, and hold themselves accountable for success. Teams differ from the more typical "working group" in the following ways:

- Members have a common commitment to an overarching purpose that all believe in and that transcends individual priorities.
- Leadership roles are shared rather than held by a single, strong leader.
- Performance is judged not only by individual contributions but also by collective "work products" that reflect the joint efforts of all the members.
- Open-ended discussion, rather than a managerially defined agenda, is prized at meetings.
- Members of the team do real work together, rather than delegating to subordinates.

employee empowerment An approach to teamwork that moves responsibility for decisions farther down the organizational chart—to the level of the employee actually doing the job.

The three approaches to teamwork most often used are problem-solving teams, special-purpose teams, and self-managing teams. All three use some amount of **employee empowerment**, which shifts responsibility for decisions farther down the organizational chart—to the level of the employee actually doing the job. See the Managerial Practice feature for a look at how employee empowerment in the hotel industry contributes to superior service quality.

quality circles Another name for problem-solving teams—small groups of supervisors and employees who meet to identify, analyze, and solve production and quality problems.

PROBLEM-SOLVING TEAMS. First introduced in the 1920s, problem-solving teams, also called **quality circles**, only became popular in the late 1970s after the Japanese used them successfully. These teams are small groups of supervisors and employees who meet to identify, analyze, and solve production and quality problems. The philosophy behind this approach is that the people who are directly responsible for making the product or providing the service will be best able to consider ways to solve a problem. Also, employees take more pride and interest in their work if they are allowed to help shape it. The teams typically consist of five to twelve volunteers, drawn from different areas of a department or from a group of employees assigned to a particular task, such as automobile assembly or credit application processing. The teams meet several hours a week to work on quality and productivity problems and make suggestions to management. Such teams are used extensively by Japanese-managed firms in North America. The Japanese philosophy is to encourage input from employees while maintaining close control over their job activities. Although problem-solving teams can successfully reduce costs and improve quality, they quickly die if management fails to implement many of the suggestions generated.

MANAGERIAL PRACTICE
Employees Are Central to Quality at Crowne Plaza Christchurch

The Crowne Plaza Christchurch, a luxury hotel in Christchurch, New Zealand, has 297 guest rooms, three restaurants, three lounges, and 338 employees to serve 2250 guests each week who purchase an average of 2450 meals. Even though the operation is complex, service quality gets top priority at the Crowne Plaza, because customers demand it. Customers have many opportunities to evaluate the quality of service they are receiving. For example, prior to the guest's arrival, the reservation staff has gathered a considerable amount of information about his or her particular likes and dislikes. This information (e.g., a preference for firm pillows or extra towels) is distributed to housekeeping and other hotel operations and is used to customize the service. Upon arrival, a guest is greeted by a porter who opens the car door and unloads the luggage. Then he or she is escorted to the receptionist, who registers him or her and assigns the room. Finally, when the guest goes to dinner, servers and cooks must also live up to the high standard of quality that distinguishes the Crowne Plaza from its competitors.

How can such a level of quality be sustained? The Crowne Plaza has empowered employees to take preventive and, if necessary, corrective action without management approval. Also, management and employees use line charts, histograms, and other graphs to track performance and identify areas needing improvement. In the restaurants, photos of finished dishes remind employees of presentation and content. Finally, in this service business with high customer contact, employee recruit-

The Crowne Plaza Christchurch offers the utmost in quality for its guests. The Café offers a wide variety of dishes that must live up to the reputation of the hotel.

ing, training, and motivation are essential for achieving and sustaining high levels of service quality.

Source: Operations Management in Action Video Series (Upper Saddle River, NJ: Prentice-Hall, 2000).

---

special-purpose teams
Groups that address issues of paramount concern to management, labour, or both.

SPECIAL-PURPOSE TEAMS. Special-purpose teams, an outgrowth of the problem-solving teams, address issues of paramount concern to management, labour, or both. For example, management may form a special-purpose team to design and introduce new work policies or new technologies, or to address customer service problems. Essentially, this approach gives workers a voice in high-level decisions.

self-managing team A small group of employees who work together to produce a major portion, or sometimes all, of a product or service.

SELF-MANAGING TEAMS. The **self-managing team** approach takes worker participation to its highest level: a small group of employees work together to produce a major portion, or sometimes all, of a product or service. Members learn all the tasks involved in the operation, rotate from job to job, and take over managerial duties such as work and vacation scheduling, ordering supplies, and hiring. In some cases, team members design the process and have a high degree of latitude as to how it takes shape. Self-managing teams essentially change the way work is organized, because employees have control over their jobs. Only recently have self-managing teams begun to catch on in North America, where they have increased productivity by 30 percent or more in some firms.

CONTINUOUS IMPROVEMENT

continuous improvement
The philosophy of continually seeking ways to improve operations, based on a Japanese concept called *kaizen*.

Continuous improvement, based on a Japanese concept called *kaizen*, is the philosophy of continually seeking ways to improve operations. Continuous improvement involves identifying benchmarks of excellent practice and instilling a sense of employee ownership in the process. The focus can be on reducing the length of time required to process requests for loans at a bank, the amount of scrap generated at a soldering machine, or the number of employee injuries at a construction site. Continuous improvement also can focus on problems with customers or suppliers, such as customers who request frequent changes in shipping quantities and suppliers who fail to maintain high quality. The bases of the continuous improvement philosophy are the beliefs that virtually any aspect of an operation can be improved and that the people most closely associated with an operation are in the best position to identify the changes that should be made. The idea is not to wait until a massive problem occurs before acting.

GETTING STARTED WITH CONTINUOUS IMPROVEMENT

Instilling a philosophy of continuous improvement in an organization may be a lengthy process, and several steps are essential to its eventual success:

1. Train employees in the methods of statistical process control (SPC) and other tools for improving quality and performance.

2. Establish clear quality-related metrics and make SPC methods a normal aspect of daily operations.

3. Build work teams and employee involvement.

4. Utilize problem-solving tools within the work teams.

5. Develop a sense of operator ownership in the process.

Note that employee involvement is central to the philosophy of continuous improvement. However, the last two steps are crucial if the philosophy is to become part of everyday operations. Problem solving addresses the aspects of operations that need improvement and evaluates alternatives for achieving improvements. A sense of operator ownership emerges when employees feel as though they own the processes and methods they use, and they take pride in the quality of the product or service they produce. It comes from participation on work teams and in problem-solving activities, which instill in employees a feeling that they have some control over their workplace and tasks.

PROBLEM-SOLVING PROCESS

plan-do-check-act cycle
A cycle, also called the Deming Wheel, used by firms actively engaged in continuous improvement to train their work teams in problem solving.

Most firms actively engaged in continuous improvement train their work teams to use the Deming Wheel, which uses a **plan-do-check-act cycle** for problem solving. Figure 5.2 shows this cycle, which lies at the heart of the continuous improvement philosophy. The cycle comprises the following steps:

1. *Plan.* The team selects a process (e.g., activity, method, machine, or policy) that needs improvement. The team then documents the selected process, usually by analyzing data (using the tools we discuss later in the chapter); sets qualitative goals for improvement; and discusses various ways to achieve

FIGURE 5.2

Plan-Do-Check-Act Cycle

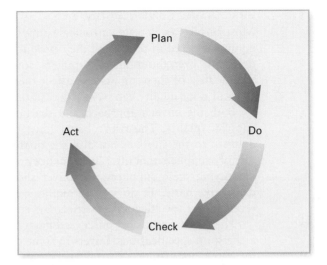

the goals. After assessing the benefits and costs of the alternatives, the team develops a plan with quantifiable measures for improvement.

2. *Do.* The team implements the plan and monitors progress. Data are collected continuously to measure the improvements in the process. Any changes in the process are documented, and further revisions are made as needed.

3. *Check.* The team analyzes the data collected during the *do* step to find out how closely the results correspond to the goals set in the *plan* step. If major shortcomings exist, the team may have to re-evaluate the plan or stop the project.

4. *Act.* If the results are successful, the team documents the revised process so that it becomes the standard procedure for all who may use it. The team may then instruct other employees in the use of the revised process.

Problem-solving projects often focus on reducing or eliminating those aspects of operations that do not add value to the product or service. Value is added during operations such as machining a part or serving a customer using a Web page. No value is added in activities such as inspecting parts for quality defects or routing requests for loan approvals to several different departments. Continuous improvement seeks to reduce these wasteful activities. For example, suppose that a firm has identified three non-value-added activities in the manufacture of its products: inspection of each part, repair of defects, and handling of materials between operations. The time that parts spend in each activity is not adding value to the product, and hence is not generating revenue for the firm. Continuous improvement projects might focus on reducing materials handling time by rearranging machine locations to minimize the distances travelled by materials, or by improving the methods for producing the parts to reduce the need for inspection and rework.

IMPROVING QUALITY THROUGH TQM

Programs of employee involvement and continuous improvement are aimed at improving quality in a general sense. TQM focuses on processes such as purchasing, product and service design, and process design, and utilizes tools such as quality function deployment, benchmarking, and data analysis.

PURCHASING CONSIDERATIONS

Most businesses depend on outside suppliers for some of the materials, services, or equipment used in producing their products and services. Large companies have hundreds and even thousands of suppliers, some of which supply the same types of parts. The quality of these inputs can affect the quality of the firm's work, and purchased parts of poor quality can have a devastating effect.

Both the buyer's approach and the buyer's specifications are keys to controlling supplier quality. The firm's buyer must emphasize not only the cost and speed of delivery to the supplier but also the quality of the product. A competent buyer will identify suppliers that offer high-quality products or services at a reasonable cost. After identifying these suppliers, the buyer should work with them to obtain essentially defect-free parts. To do so may require examining and evaluating trade-offs between receiving off-specification materials and seeking corrective action.

The specifications for purchased parts and materials must be clear and *realistic*. As a check on specifications, buyers in some companies initiate *process capability studies* for important products, a topic we address later in this chapter. These studies amount to trial runs of small product samples to ensure that all components, including the raw materials and purchased parts, work together to form a product that has the desired quality level at a reasonable cost. Analysis of study results may identify unrealistic specifications and the need for design changes.

PRODUCT AND SERVICE DESIGN

Because design changes often require changes in methods, materials, or specifications, they can increase defect rates. Change invariably increases the risk of making mistakes, so stable product and service designs can help reduce internal quality problems. However, stable designs may not be possible when a product or service is sold in markets globally. Although changed designs have the potential to increase market share, management must be aware of possible quality problems resulting from any changes. If a firm needs to make design changes to remain competitive, it should carefully test new designs and redesign the product or service and the process with a focus on the market and customer expectations. Simulation can improve the quality of new designs. Implementing both strategies involves a trade-off: higher quality and increased competitiveness potentially are exchanged for added time and cost.

reliablity The probability that a product will be functional when used.

Another dimension of quality related to product design is **reliability**, which refers to the probability that the product will be functional when used. Products often consist of a number of components that all must be operative for the product to perform as intended. Sometimes products can be designed with extra components (or subsystems) so that if one component fails, another can be activated.

Suppose that a product has several modules, components or subsystems, each with its own reliability measure (the probability that it will operate when called upon). The reliability of each module contributes to the quality of the total system; that is, the reliability of the complete product equals the product of all the reliabilities of the modules, or:

$$r_s = (r_1)(r_2)...(r_i)...(r_n)$$

where:

r_s = Reliability of the complete product

n = Number of modules, components, or subsystems

r_i = Reliability of each module, component, or subsystem i

This measure of reliability is based on the assumption that the reliability of each component or subsystem is independent of the others.

Suppose that a small portable radio designed for joggers has three components: a motherboard with a reliability of 0.99, a housing assembly with a reliability of 0.90, and a headphone set with a reliability of 0.85. The reliabilities are the probabilities that each component will still be operating two years from now. The reliability of the portable radio is:

$$r_s = (0.99)(0.90)(0.85) = 0.76$$

The poor headsets and housings hurt the reliability of this product. Suppose that new designs resulted in a reliability of 0.95 for the housing and 0.90 for the headsets. Product reliability would improve to:

$$r_s = (0.99)(0.95)(0.90) = 0.85$$

Manufacturers must be concerned about the quality of every component, because the product fails when any component fails.

PROCESS DESIGN

The design of the process used to produce a product or service greatly affects its quality. Managers at the First National Bank noticed that customers' requests for a letter of credit took four days to go through dozens of steps involving nine employees before a letter of credit would be issued. To improve the process and shorten the waiting time for customers, the bank trained letter-of-credit issuers to do all the required tasks so that the customer could deal with just one person. In addition, customers were given the same employee each time they requested a letter. The bank now issues letters of credit in less than a day.

The purchase of new machinery can help prevent or overcome potential quality problems. For example, many worker tasks can be very repetitious and prone to error, such as manual data entry. Others may require high skills, such as precision welding, yet those skills may be in short supply locally. Finally, others require intense worker concentration at fast operating speeds, such as bottle inspection after packaging. For each of these situations, automated equipment may dramatically improve quality.

One of the keys to obtaining high quality is concurrent engineering (see Chapter 1, "Competing with Operations"), in which operations managers and designers work closely together in the initial phases of product or service design to ensure that production requirements and process capabilities are synchronized. The result is much better quality and shorter development time. NCR makes ATMs and terminals for checkout counters, and has plants located around the world, including one in Waterloo, Ontario. Using concurrent engineering, NCR developed a new terminal model in 22 months, half the usual time. The terminal had 85 percent fewer parts and could be assembled in only two minutes. Quality rejects and engineering changes dropped significantly. The U.S. National Institute of Standards and Technology has estimated that manufacturing firms using concurrent engineering for electronic components need 30 percent to 70 percent less development time, require 20 percent to 90 percent less time to market, and produce 200 percent to 600 percent better-quality products.

QUALITY FUNCTION DEPLOYMENT

quality function deployment (QFD) A means of translating customer requirements into the appropriate technical requirements for each stage of product or service development and production.

A key to improving quality through TQM is linking the design of products or services to the processes that produce them. **Quality function deployment (QFD)**, first described in 1978 by Yoji Akao and Shigeru Mizuno, is a means of translating customer requirements ("voice of the customer") into the appropriate technical requirements ("voice of the engineer") for each aspect of a service or component of a product.

Customer requirements and technical specifications are compared to both competitive offerings and the firm's.

These relationships and trade-offs can be presented as a "house of quality" (Hauser and Clausing, 1988). The competitive analysis provides a place to start looking for ways to gain a competitive advantage. Then the relationships between customer needs and engineering attributes need to be specified. Finally, the fact that improving one performance measure may detract from another must be recognized.

The QFD approach provides a way to set targets and debate their effects on product quality. Engineering uses the data to focus on significant product design features. Marketing uses this input for determining marketing strategies. Operations uses the information to identify the processes that are crucial to improving product quality as perceived by the customer. As a result, QFD encourages interfunctional communication for the purpose of improving the quality of products and services. Many companies around the world have used the approach, including Toyota, Hewlett-Packard, Samsung, Procter & Gamble, Polaroid, and Deere & Company.

BENCHMARKING

benchmarking A continuous, systematic procedure that measures a firm's products, services, and processes against those of industry leaders.

Benchmarking is a continuous, systematic procedure that measures a firm's products, services, and processes against those of industry leaders, both in the same industry and outside. Companies use benchmarking to understand better how outstanding companies do things so that they can improve their own operations. Typical measures used in benchmarking include cost per unit, service upsets (breakdowns) per customer, processing time per unit, customer retention rates, revenue per unit, return on investment, and customer satisfaction levels. Those involved in continuous improvement efforts rely on benchmarking to formulate goals and targets for performance.

Competitive benchmarking is based on comparisons with a direct industry competitor. *Functional* benchmarking compares areas such as administration, customer service, and sales operations with those of outstanding firms in any industry. For instance, Xerox benchmarked its distribution function against L. L. Bean's because Bean is renowned as a leading retailer in distribution efficiency and customer service.

Internal benchmarking involves using an organizational unit with superior performance as the benchmark for other units. This form of benchmarking can be advantageous for firms that have several business units or divisions. All forms of benchmarking are best applied in situations in which a long-term program of continuous improvement is needed.

TOOLS FOR DATA ANALYSIS

The first step in improving the quality of an operation is data collection. Data can help uncover operations requiring improvement and the extent of remedial action needed. There are nine tools for organizing and presenting data to identify areas for quality and performance improvement: flow diagrams, process charts, checklists, histograms and bar charts, Pareto charts, scatter diagrams, cause-and-effect diagrams, graphs, and control charts. We discussed flow diagrams and process charts in Chapter 2, "Process Management," and we discuss control charts in depth later when we address statistical process control. In this section we demonstrate the use of the other six methods to emphasize the breadth of applications possible.

checklist A form used to record the frequency of occurrence of certain product or service characteristics related to quality.

CHECKLISTS. Data collection through the use of a checklist is often the first step in the analysis of quality problems. A **checklist** is a form used to record the frequency of occurrence of certain product or service characteristics related to quality. The characteristics may be measurable on a continuous scale (e.g., weight, diameter, time, or length) or on a yes-or-no basis (e.g., paint discolouration, odours, rude servers, or too much grease).

HISTOGRAMS AND BAR CHARTS. The data from a checklist often can be presented succinctly and clearly with histograms or bar charts. A **histogram** summarizes data measured on a continuous scale, showing the frequency distribution of some quality characteristic (in statistical terms, the central tendency and dispersion of the data). Often the mean of the data is indicated on the histogram. A **bar chart** is a series of bars representing the frequency of occurrence of data characteristics measured on a yes-or-no basis. The bar height indicates the number of times a particular quality characteristic was observed.

PARETO CHARTS. When managers discover several quality problems that need to be addressed, they have to decide which should be attacked first. Vilfredo Pareto, a nineteenth-century Italian scientist whose statistical work focused on inequalities in data, proposed that most of an "activity" is caused by relatively few of its factors. In a restaurant quality problem, the activity could be customer complaints and the factor could be "discourteous waiter." For a manufacturer, the activity could be product defects and a factor could be "missing part." Pareto's concept, called the 80-20 rule, is that 80 percent of the defects are caused by 20 percent of the factors. By concentrating on the 20 percent of the factors (the "vital few"), managers can solve most of the quality problems.

The few vital factors can be visually identified with a **Pareto chart**, a bar chart on which the factors are plotted in decreasing order of frequency along the horizontal axis. The chart has two vertical axes, the one on the left showing frequency (as in a histogram) and the one on the right showing the cumulative percentage of frequency. The cumulative frequency curve identifies the few vital factors that warrant immediate managerial attention.

SCATTER DIAGRAMS. Sometimes managers suspect but are not sure that a certain factor is causing a particular quality problem. A **scatter diagram**, which is a plot of two variables showing whether they are related, can be used to verify or negate the suspicion. Each point on the scatter diagram represents one data observation. For example, the manager of a castings shop may suspect that casting defects are a function of the diameter of the casting. A scatter diagram could be constructed by plotting the number of defective castings found for each diameter of casting produced. After the diagram is completed, any relationship between diameter and number of defects could be observed.

CAUSE-AND-EFFECT DIAGRAMS. An important aspect of TQM is linking each aspect of quality prized by the customer to the inputs, methods, and process steps that build a particular attribute into the product. One way to identify a design problem that needs to be corrected is to develop a **cause-and-effect diagram** that relates a key quality problem to its potential causes. The diagram, first developed by Kaoru Ishikawa, helps management trace customer complaints directly to the operations involved. Operations that have no bearing on a particular defect are not shown on the diagram for that defect.

The cause-and-effect diagram sometimes is called a *fishbone diagram*. The main quality problem (effect) is labelled as the fish's "head," the major categories of potential causes as structural "bones," and the likely specific causes as "ribs." When constructing and using a cause-and-effect diagram, an analyst identifies all the major categories of potential causes for the quality problem. For example, these might be People,

histogram A summarization of data measured on a continuous scale, showing the frequency distribution of some quality characteristic (in statistical terms, the central tendency and dispersion of the data).

bar chart A series of bars representing the frequency of occurrence of data characteristics measured on a yes-or-no basis.

Pareto chart A bar chart on which factors are plotted in decreasing order of frequency along the horizontal axis.

scatter diagram A plot of two variables showing whether they are related.

cause-and-effect diagram A diagram that relates a key quality problem to its potential causes.

Machines, Materials, and Process. For each major category, the analyst lists all the likely causes of the quality problem. For example, under People might be listed "lack of training," "poor communication," and "absenteeism." Each cause can be further explored by asking "Why?" For example, "absenteeism" might be caused by poor morale or "out of specification" might be caused by adopting a new supplier. Brainstorming helps the analyst identify and properly classify all suspected causes. The analyst then systematically investigates the causes listed on the diagram for each major category, updating the chart as new causes become apparent. The process of constructing a cause-and-effect diagram calls management and worker attention to the primary factors affecting product or service quality.

graphs Representations of data in a variety of pictorial forms, such as line graphs and pie charts.

GRAPHS. **Graphs** represent data in a variety of pictorial formats, such as line graphs and pie charts. *Line graphs* represent data sequentially with data points connected by line segments to highlight trends in the data. Line graphs are used in control charts and forecasting (see Chapter 8, "Forecasting"). Pie charts represent quality factors as slices of a pie; the size of each slice is in proportion to the number of occurrences of the factor. Pie charts are useful for showing data from a group of factors that can be represented as percentages totalling 100.

Each of the tools for improving quality that we have just discussed may be used independently, but their power is greatest when they are used together. In solving a quality problem, managers often must act as detectives, sifting data to clarify the issues involved and deducing the causes. We call this process *data snooping*. Example 5.1 demonstrates how four of the tools for improving quality can be used for data snooping.

| EXAMPLE 5.1 | *Identifying Causes of Poor Headliner Quality* |

The Wellington Fibreboard Company produces headliners, the fibreglass components that form the inner roof of passenger cars. Management wanted to identify which defects were most prevalent and to find the cause.

SOLUTION
Figure 5.3 shows the sequential application of several tools for improving quality:

- *Step 1.* A checklist of different types of defects was constructed from last month's production records.
- *Step 2.* A Pareto chart prepared from the checklist data indicated that broken fibreboard accounted for 72 percent of the quality defects. The manager decided to dig further into the problem of broken fibreboard.
- *Step 3.* A cause-and-effect diagram for broken fibreboard identified several potential causes for the problem. The one strongly suspected by the manager was employee training.
- *Step 4.* The manager reorganized the production reports only for broken fibreboard occurrences into a Pareto chart by shift because the personnel on the three shifts had different levels of experience.

Decision Point The second Pareto chart (Step 4) indicated that the second shift, with the least experienced workforce, had the most defects. Further investigation revealed that workers were not using proper procedures for stacking the fibreboards after the press operation, causing cracking and chipping. The manager initiated additional training sessions focused on board handling after the press operation. Although the second shift was not responsible for all the defects, finding the source of many defects enabled the manager to improve the quality of her operations.

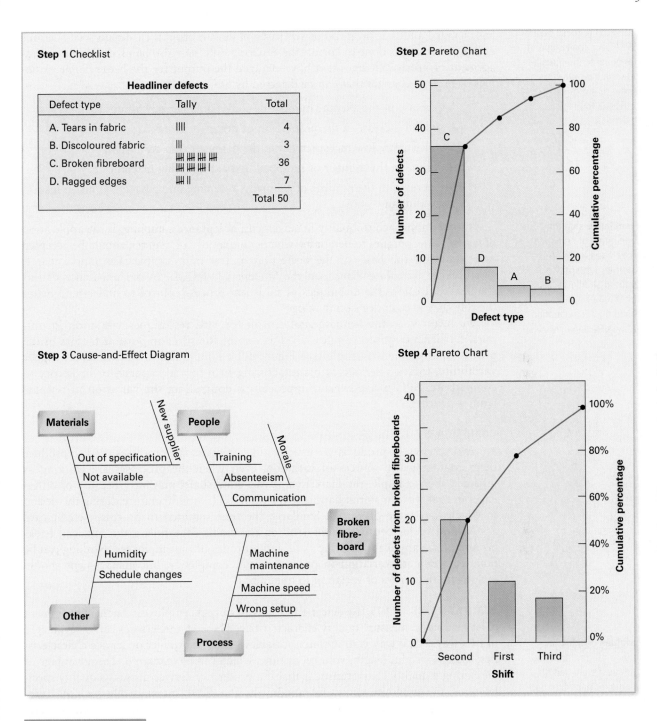

Step 1 Checklist

Headliner defects

Defect type	Tally	Total
A. Tears in fabric	IIII	4
B. Discoloured fabric	III	3
C. Broken fibreboard	IIII IIII IIII IIII IIII IIII IIII I	36
D. Ragged edges	IIII II	7
	Total	50

Step 2 Pareto Chart

Step 3 Cause-and-Effect Diagram

Step 4 Pareto Chart

FIGURE 5.3

Application of the Tools for Improving Quality

STATISTICAL PROCESS CONTROL (SPC)

Statistical process control (SPC), another data analysis tool, is the application of statistical techniques to determine whether the output of a process conforms to the product or service design. In SPC, tools called control charts are used primarily to detect production of defective products or services or to indicate that the production process

statistical process control (SPC) The application of statistical techniques to determine whether the output of a process conforms to the product or service design.

has changed and that products or services will deviate from their design specifications unless something is done to correct the situation. SPC can also be used to inform management of process changes that have changed the output for the better. Some examples of process changes that can be detected by SPC are:

- A decrease in the average number of complaints per day at a hotel
- A sudden increase in the proportion of defective gearboxes
- A consistently low measurement in the diameter of a crankshaft
- A decline in the number of scrapped units at a milling machine
- An increase in the number of claimants receiving late payment from an insurance company

acceptance sampling The application of statistical techniques to determine whether a quantity of material should be accepted or rejected based on the inspection or test of a sample.

Another approach to quality management, **acceptance sampling**, is the application of statistical techniques to determine whether a quantity of material should be accepted or rejected on the basis of the inspection or test of a sample (see Supplement F, "Acceptance Sampling Plans" on the Student CD-ROM). In the remainder of this chapter, we explore the techniques of statistical process control to understand better the role they play in decision making.

We begin with the fundamental reason for SPC techniques: variation in outputs. Earlier, variation was described as one of the three important factors in the process management triangle (see Figure 4.1). Poor quality, which creates higher variability, forces a service or manufacturing firm to add capacity or inventory to compensate. SPC is a powerful approach to controlling the variation in outputs from a process.

VARIATION OF OUTPUTS

No two services or products are exactly alike, because the processes used to produce them contain many sources of variation, even when the processes are working as intended. For example, the diameters of two crankshafts may vary because of differences in tool wear, material hardness, operator skill, or temperature during the period in which they were produced. Similarly, the time required to process a credit card application varies because of the load on the credit department, the financial background of the applicant, and the skills and attitudes of the employees. Nothing can be done to eliminate variation in process output completely, but management should investigate the *causes* of variation to minimize it.

variables Product or service characteristics, such as weight, length, volume, or time, that can be measured.

QUALITY MEASUREMENTS. To detect variations in output, employees or their equipment must be able to measure quality characteristics. These characteristics can be evaluated in two ways. One way is to monitor **variables**—that is, product or service characteristics, such as weight, length, volume, or time, which can be *measured*. The advantage of measuring a quality characteristic is that if a product or service misses its quality specifications, the employee knows by how much. The disadvantage is that such measurements typically involve special equipment, employee skills, exacting procedures, and time and effort.

attributes Product or service characteristics that can be quickly counted for acceptable quality.

Another way to evaluate quality is to measure **attributes**—that is, product or service characteristics that can be quickly *counted* for acceptable quality. The method allows employees to make a simple yes-or-no decision about whether a product or service meets the specifications. Attributes are often used when quality specifications are complex and measuring by variables is difficult or costly. Some examples of attributes that can be counted are the number of insurance forms containing errors that cause underpayments or overpayments and the proportion of washing machines failing final inspection. The advantage of attribute counts is that less effort and fewer resources are needed than for measuring variables. The disadvantage is that, even though attribute counts can reveal that quality of performance has changed, they may not be of much use in indicating by how much.

SAMPLING. The most thorough approach to inspection is to inspect each product or service at each stage of the process for quality. This method, called *complete inspection*, is used when the costs of passing defects to the next workstation or to external customers outweigh the inspection costs. Firms often use automated inspection equipment that can record, summarize, and display data, particularly in a technology-intensive industry, like electronics. Many companies have found that automated inspection equipment can pay for itself in a reasonably short time.

A well-conceived **sampling plan** can approach the same degree of protection as complete inspection. A sampling plan specifies a **sample size**, which is a quantity of randomly selected observations of process outputs; the time between successive samples; and decision rules that determine when action should be taken. Sampling is appropriate when inspection costs are high because of the special knowledge, skills, procedures, or expensive equipment required to perform the inspections or when testing is destructive.

sampling plan A plan that specifies a sample size, the time between successive samples, and decision rules that determine when action should be taken.

sample size A quantity of randomly selected observations of process outputs.

SAMPLING DISTRIBUTIONS. A process will produce output that can be assessed using particular measures, either variables or attributes. Each of these can be described with a process distribution, which can be characterized by its location, spread, and shape. The mean of the distribution indicates location, while spread is described by the range or standard deviation. Relatively small values for the range or the standard deviation imply that the observations are clustered near the mean. The shape can be simply described as either symmetric or skewed. A symmetric distribution has the same shape above and below the mean (i.e., a mirror image), while a skewed distribution does not.

The mean and variance of the process distribution will be known with 100 percent accuracy only with a complete inspection. The purpose of sampling, however, is to estimate the variable or attribute measure for the output of the process without doing complete inspection. That measure is then used to assess the performance of the process itself.

For example, the time required by a laboratory to analyze patient specimens and report the results to an intensive care unit lab in a hospital (a variable measure) will vary; this is one dimension of service quality (i.e., reliability). If you measured the time to complete an analysis of a large number of patients and plotted the results, the data would form a pattern that is the process distribution. With sampling, we try to estimate the parameters of the process distribution using statistics such as the sample mean and the sample range or standard deviation.

These sample statistics have their own distribution, called a sampling distribution, which is different from the process distribution. For example, in the laboratory, suppose that the process distribution for analyzing and reporting has a mean of 25 minutes. A lab technician who periodically takes a sample of the time required for five analyses and calculates the sample mean could determine how well the process is currently performing. Plotting a large number of these *sample means* would show that they have their own distribution with a mean centred on 25 minutes, as does the process distribution mean, but with *much less* variability. The reason is that the highs and lows of individual times in each sample of five are offset when averaged within each sample.

Some distributions of sample means (e.g., for means with sample sizes of 4 or more and proportions with sample sizes of 20 or more) can be approximated by the *normal* distribution, allowing the use of the normal table if both the mean and standard deviation are known. We can determine the probability that any particular sample mean will fall outside certain limits. The ability to assign probabilities to sample results is important for the construction and use of control charts.

COMMON CAUSES. For SPC, there are two basic categories of variation in output: common causes and assignable causes. These are related to the random and predictable variability described with the process management triangle (recall Figure 4.1). However, the terms common cause and assignable cause are narrower in scope. They focus specifically on service or product quality related to a particular process, rather than other forms of variation such as demand volume, transit times, or setup times.

Common causes of variation are the purely random, unidentifiable sources of variation that are unavoidable with the current process. If process variability results solely from common causes of variation, a typical assumption is that the distribution is symmetric, with most observations near the centre.

ASSIGNABLE CAUSES. The second category of variation, **assignable causes of variation**, also known as special causes, includes any variation-causing factors that can be identified and eliminated. Assignable causes of variation include an employee needing training or a machine needing repair.

Let us return to the example of the laboratory process. Figure 5.4 shows how assignable causes can change the distribution of output, namely time for analysis. The green curve is the process distribution when only common causes of variation are present. The red lines depict a change in the distribution because of assignable causes. In Figure 5.4(a), the red line indicates that the process took more time than planned in many of the cases, thereby increasing the average time of analysis. In Figure 5.4(b), an increase in the variability of the time for each case affected the spread of the distribution. Finally, in Figure 5.4(c), the red line indicates that the process produced a preponderance of the tests in less than average time. Such a distribution is skewed, or no longer symmetric to the average value. A process is said to be in statistical control when the location, spread, or shape of its distribution does not change over time. After the process is in statistical control, managers use SPC procedures to detect the onset of assignable causes so that they can be eliminated.

common causes of variation The purely random sources of variation inherent in a process and generally considered unavoidable.

assignable causes of variation Any variation-causing factors that can be identified and eliminated.

FIGURE 5.4

Effects of Assignable Causes on the Process Distribution for the Lab Analysis Process

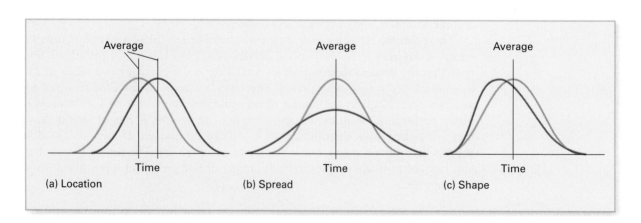

(a) Location   (b) Spread   (c) Shape

DIAGNOSING VARIATION WITH CONTROL CHARTS

control chart A time-ordered diagram used to determine whether observed variations are abnormal.

To determine whether observed variations are abnormal, we can measure and plot the quality characteristic taken from the sample on a time-ordered diagram called a **control chart**. A control chart has a central line, which is the mean of the sample distribution, and two control limits based on the sampling distribution of the quality measure. The control limits are used to judge whether action is required. The larger value represents the *upper control limit* (UCL), and the smaller value represents the *lower control limit* (LCL). Figure 5.5 shows how the control limits relate to the sampling distribution. A sample statistic that falls between the UCL and the LCL indicates that the process is exhibiting common causes of variation; a statistic that falls outside the control limits indicates that the process is exhibiting assignable causes of variation.

In practice, the question then becomes how far away from the central line to draw the process control limits. Too close to the central line, and too many observations might be considered abnormal, resulting in needless diagnostics and adjustments. Too far, and critical corrections are overlooked and not implemented. On the basis of this trade-off, the process control limits are usually drawn at three standard deviations from the mean. These limits are used because the likelihood of finding a sample outside these limits due to random chance is very small (about 0.3%).

Observations falling outside the control limits do not always mean poor quality. For example, in Figure 5.5 the assignable cause may be a new billing process introduced to reduce the number of incorrect bills sent to customers. If the proportion of incorrect bills, the quality statistic from a sample of bills, falls *below* the LCL of the control chart, the new procedure has likely changed the billing process for the better and a new control chart should be constructed.

Managers or employees responsible for monitoring a process can use control charts in the following ways:

1. Take a random sample from the process, measure the quality characteristic, and calculate a variable or attribute measure.

2. If the statistic falls outside the chart's control limits, look for an assignable cause.

FIGURE 5.5

Relationship of Control Limits to Sampling Distribution and Observations from Three Samples

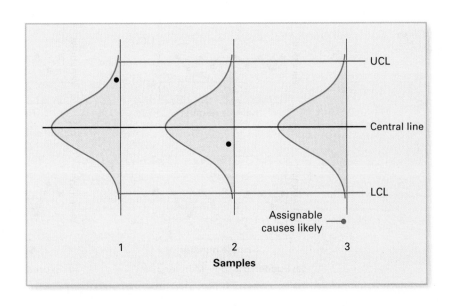

3. Eliminate the cause if it degrades quality; incorporate the cause if it improves quality. Reconstruct the control chart with new data.

4. Repeat the procedure periodically.

Sometimes problems with a process can be detected even though the control limits have not been exceeded. There are several rules for detecting the presence of assignable causes (Wheeler, 1995). A lack of control is indicated when:

Rule 1: A point falls outside a control limit.

Rule 2: Two-of-three successive points are on the same side of the central line and more than two standard deviations away from the central line.

Rule 3: Four-of-five successive values are on the same side of the central line and more than one standard deviation away from the central line.

Rule 4: Eight consecutive values fall on the same side of the central line.

In practice, only (1) and (4) are generally used. Figure 5.6 contains four examples of control charts. Chart (a) shows a process that is in statistical control. No action is needed. However, chart (b) shows a pattern called a *run*, and so violates Rule 4. Here, nine observations are below the central line and show a downward trend. The probability is low that such a result could take place by chance.

Chart (c) shows that the process takes a sudden change from its normal pattern. The last four observations are unusual: three rising toward the UCL and the fourth remaining above the nominal value. A manager should monitor processes with such sudden changes even though the control limits have not been exceeded. Finally, chart (d) violates Rule 1; the process went out of control twice because two sample results fell outside the control limits. The probability that the process distribution has changed is high. We discuss more implications of being out of statistical control when we discuss process capability later in this chapter.

Control charts are not perfect tools for detecting shifts in the process distribution because they are based on sampling distributions. Two types of error are possible with the use of control charts. A **type I error** occurs when the employee concludes that the

type I error An error that occurs when the employee concludes that the process is out of control based on a sample result that falls outside the control limits, when in fact it was due to pure randomness.

FIGURE 5.6

Control Chart Examples

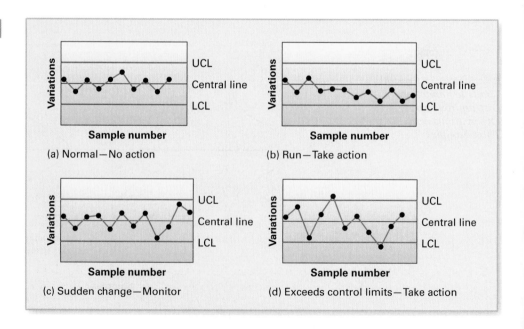

(a) Normal—No action

(b) Run—Take action

(c) Sudden change—Monitor

(d) Exceeds control limits—Take action

type II error An error that occurs when the employee concludes that the process is in control and only randomness is present, when actually the process is out of statistical control.

process is out of control based on a sample result that falls outside the control limits, when in fact it was due to pure randomness. A **type II** error occurs when the employee concludes that the process is in control and only randomness is present, when actually the process is out of statistical control.

Management can control these errors by the choice of control limits. The choice would depend on the costs of looking for assignable causes when none exist versus the cost of not detecting a shift in the process. For example, setting control limits at three standard deviations from the mean reduces the type I error because chances are quite small that a sample result will fall outside of the control limits unless the process is out of statistical control. However, the type II error may be significant because more subtle shifts in the nature of the process distribution will go undetected because of the wide spread in the control limits. Alternatively, the spread in the control limits can be reduced to two standard deviations, thereby increasing the likelihood of sample results falling outside of the control limits. Now the type II error is smaller, but the type I error is larger because employees are likely to search for assignable causes when the sample result occurred solely by chance. As a general rule, managers will use wider limits when the cost for searching for assignable causes is large relative to the cost of not detecting a shift in the process distribution.

CONSTRUCTING SPC CHARTS

Statistical process control (SPC) methods are useful for both measuring the current quality of products or services and detecting whether the process itself has changed in a way that will affect quality. In this section, we first discuss mean and range charts for variables and then consider control charts for product or service attributes.

CONTROL CHARTS FOR VARIABLES

The two basic measures of quality, variables and attributes, require different methods to sample and chart, as well as diagnose common versus special causes. Control charts for variables consist of two parts, described next, and are used to monitor the mean and the variability of the process distribution.

R-chart A chart used to monitor changes in process variability.

R-CHARTS. A range chart, or **R-chart,** is used to monitor process variability. To calculate the range of a set of sample data, the analyst subtracts the smallest from the largest measurement in each sample. If any of the data fall outside the control limits, the process variability is not in control.

The control limits for the R-chart are:

$$\text{UCL}_R = D_4\overline{R} \quad \text{and} \quad \text{LCL}_R = D_3\overline{R}$$

where:

$\overline{R}$ = Average of several past R values and the central line of the control chart

D_3, D_4 = Constants that provide three standard deviation (three-sigma) limits for a given sample size

Values for D_3 and D_4 are contained in Table 5.3 and change as a function of the sample size. Note that the spread between the control limits narrows as the sample size increases. This change is a consequence of having more information on which to base an estimate for the process range.

x̄-chart A chart used to monitor changes in the sample mean.

x̄-CHARTS. An $\overline{x}$-chart (read "x-bar chart") is used to monitor changes in the mean. When the assignable causes of process variability have been identified and the process

TABLE 5.3	Size of Sample (*n*)	Factor for UCL and LCL for x̄-Charts (*A₂*)	Factor for LCL for *R*-Charts (*D₃*)	Factor for UCL for *R*-Charts (*D₄*)
	2	1.880	0	3.267
Factors for Calculating Three-Sigma Limits for the x̄-Chart and R-Chart	3	1.023	0	2.575
	4	0.729	0	2.282
	5	0.577	0	2.115
Source: 1950 Reprinted with permission from: American Society for Testing Materials, *Manual on Quality Control of Materials*. Copyright American Society for Testing Materials.	6	0.483	0	2.004
	7	0.419	0.076	1.924
	8	0.373	0.136	1.864
	9	0.337	0.184	1.816
	10	0.308	0.223	1.777

variability is in statistical control, the analyst can construct an -chart to control the process average. The control limits for the x̄-chart are:

$$\text{UCL}_{\bar{x}} = \bar{\bar{x}} + A_2\overline{R} \qquad \text{and} \qquad \text{LCL}_{\bar{x}} = \bar{\bar{x}} - A_2\overline{R}$$

where:

$\bar{\bar{x}}$ = Central line of the chart and either the average of past sample means or a target value set for the process

A_2 = Constant to provide three-sigma limits for the sample mean

The values for A_2 are contained in Table 5.3. Note that the control limits use the value of $\overline{R}$; therefore, the x̄-chart must be constructed *after* the process variability is in control.

Analysts can develop and use x̄- and R-charts in the following way:

Step 1. Collect data on the variable quality measurement (such as weight, diameter, or time) and organize the data by sample number. Preferably, at least 20 samples should be taken for use in constructing a control chart.

Step 2. Compute the range for each sample and the average range, $\overline{R}$, for the set of samples.

Step 3. Use Table 5.3 to determine the upper and lower control limits of the R-chart.

Step 4. Plot the sample ranges. If all are in control, proceed to step 5. Otherwise, find the assignable causes, correct them, and return to step 1.

Step 5. Calculate $\bar{x}$ for each sample and the central line of the chart, $\bar{\bar{x}}$.

Step 6. Use Table 5.3 to determine the parameters for $\text{UCL}_{\bar{x}}$ and $\text{LCL}_{\bar{x}}$ and construct the x̄-chart.

Step 7. Plot the sample means. If all are in control, the process is in statistical control in terms of the process average and process variability. Continue to take samples and monitor the process. If any are out of control, find the assignable causes, correct them, and return to step 1. If no assignable causes are found after a diligent search, assume that the out-of-control points represent common causes of variation and continue to monitor the process.

EXAMPLE 5.2	*Using $\bar{x}$- and R-Charts to Monitor a Process*

The management of West Allis Industries is concerned about the production of a special metal screw used by several of the company's largest customers. The diameter of the screw is critical. Data from five samples are shown in the accompanying table. The sample size is 4. Is the process in control?

SOLUTION

Step 1. For simplicity we have taken only five samples. In practice, more than 20 samples would be desirable. The data are shown in the following table.

Data for the $\bar{x}$- and R-Charts: Observations of Screw Diameter (cm)

SAMPLE NUMBER	OBSERVATION				R	$\bar{x}$
	1	2	3	4		
1	0.5014	0.5022	0.5009	0.5027	0.0018	0.5018
2	0.5021	0.5041	0.5024	0.5020	0.0021	0.5027
3	0.5018	0.5026	0.5035	0.5023	0.0017	0.5026
4	0.5008	0.5034	0.5024	0.5015	0.0026	0.5020
5	0.5041	0.5056	0.5034	0.5047	0.0022	0.5045
				Average	0.0021	0.5027

Step 2. Compute the range for each sample by subtracting the lowest value from the highest value. For example, in sample 1 the range is $0.5027 - 0.5009 = 0.0018$ centimetres. Similarly, the ranges for samples 2, 3, 4, and 5 are 0.0021, 0.0017, 0.0026, and 0.0022 centimetres, respectively. As shown in the table, $\bar{R} = 0.0021$ centimetres.

Step 3. To construct the R-chart, select the appropriate constants from Table 5.3 for a sample size of 4. The control limits are:

$$UCL_R = D_4R = 2.282(0.0021) = 0.00479 \text{ cm}$$

$$LCL_R = D_3R = 0(0.0021) = 0 \text{ cm}$$

Step 4. Plot the ranges on the R-chart, as shown in Figure 5.7. None of the sample ranges falls outside the control limits. Consequently, the process variability is in statistical control. If any of the sample ranges had fallen outside of the limits, or an unusual pattern had appeared (see Figure 5.6 on page 168), we would have had to search for the causes of the excessive variability, correct them, and repeat step 1.

FIGURE 5.7	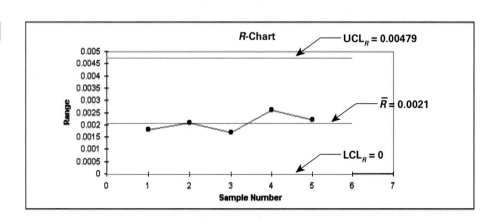

Range Chart from the OM Explorer and $\bar{x}$- and R-Chart Solver for the Metal Screw, Showing That the Process Variability Is in Control

Step 5. Compute the mean for each sample. For example, the mean for sample 1 is:

$$\frac{0.5014 + 0.5022 + 0.5009 + 0.5027}{4} = 0.5018 \text{ cm}$$

Similarly, the means of samples 2, 3, 4, and 5 are 0.5027, 0.5026, 0.5020, and 0.5045 centimetres, respectively. As shown in the table, $\bar{\bar{x}} = 0.5027$ centimetres.

Step 6. Now construct the $\bar{x}$-chart for the process average. The average screw diameter is 0.5027 cm and the average range is 0.0021 cm, so use $\bar{\bar{x}} = 0.5027$, $\bar{R} = 0.0021$, and A_2 from Table 5.3 for a sample size of 4 to construct the control limits:

$$\text{LCL}_x = \bar{\bar{x}} + A_2\bar{R} = 0.5027 + 0.729(0.0021) = 0.5042 \text{ cm}$$

$$\text{LCL}_x = \bar{\bar{x}} - A_2\bar{R} = 0.5027 - 0.729(0.0021) = 0.5012 \text{ cm}$$

Step 7. Plot the sample means on the control chart, as shown in Figure 5.8.

FIGURE 5.8

The $\bar{x}$-Chart from the OM Explorer $\bar{x}$- and R-Chart Solver for the Metal Screw, Showing That Sample 5 Is Out of Control

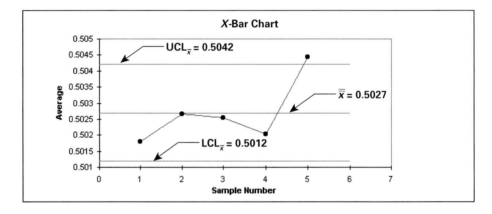

The mean of sample 5 falls above the upper control limit, indicating that the process average is out of control and that assignable causes must be explored, perhaps using a cause-and-effect diagram.

Decision Point A mechanical part in the lathe machine that makes the screw had become damaged on the day the sample was taken. Management initiated maintenance to replace the worn part. Subsequent samples showed that the process was back in statistical control.

If the standard deviation of the process distribution is known, another form of the $\bar{x}$-chart may be used:

$$\text{UCL}_{\bar{x}} = \bar{\bar{x}} + z\sigma_{\bar{x}} \quad \text{and} \quad \text{LCL}_{\bar{x}} = \bar{\bar{x}} - z\sigma_{\bar{x}}$$

where:

$\sigma_{\bar{x}} = \sigma/\sqrt{n} =$ Standard deviation of sample means

$\sigma =$ Standard deviation of the process distribution

$n =$ Sample size

$\bar{\bar{x}} =$ Average of sample means or a target value set for the process

$z =$ Normal deviate; usually $z = 3$ for control charts

The analyst can use an R-chart to be sure that the process variability is in control before constructing the $\bar{x}$-chart. The advantage of using this form of the $\bar{x}$-chart is that the analyst can adjust the spread of the control limits by changing the value of z.

CONTROL CHARTS FOR ATTRIBUTES

Two charts commonly used for quality measures based on product or service attributes are the *p*- and *c*-charts. The *p*-chart is used for controlling the proportion of defective products or services generated by the process. The *c*-chart is used for controlling the number of defects when more than one defect can be present in a product or service.

p-chart A chart used for controlling the proportion of defective products or services generated by the process.

p-CHARTS. The *p*-chart is a commonly used control chart for attributes. The quality characteristic is counted rather than measured, and the entire item or service can be declared good or defective. For example, in the banking industry, the attributes counted might be the number of non-endorsed deposits or the number of incorrect financial statements sent. The method involves selecting a random sample, inspecting each item in it, and calculating the sample proportion defective, *p*, which is the number of defective units divided by the sample size.

Sampling for a *p*-chart involves a yes-or-no decision: the item or service either is or is not defective. The underlying statistical distribution is based on the binomial distribution. However, for large sample sizes, the normal distribution provides a good approximation to it. The standard deviation of the distribution of proportion defective, σ_p, is:

$$\sigma_p = \sqrt{\bar{p}(1 - \bar{p})/n}$$

where:

n = Sample size

$\bar{p}$ = Historical average population proportion defective or target value and central line on the chart

The central line on the *p*-chart may be the average of the past sample proportion defective or a target that management has set for the process. We can use σ_p to arrive at the upper and lower control limits for a *p*-chart:

$$\text{UCL}_p = \bar{p} + z\sigma_p \quad \text{and} \quad \text{LCL}_p = \bar{p} - z\sigma_p$$

where:

z = Normal deviate (number of standard deviations from the average)

The chart is used in the following way. Periodically, a random sample of size *n* is taken, and the number of defective products or services is counted. The number of defectives is divided by the sample size to get a sample proportion defective, *p*, which is plotted on the chart. When a sample proportion defective falls outside the control limits, the analyst assumes that the proportion defective generated by the process has changed and searches for the assignable cause. Observations falling below the LCL_p indicate that the process may actually have improved. The analyst may find no assignable cause because there is always a small chance that an "out of control" proportion will have occurred randomly. However, if the analyst discovers assignable causes, those sample data should not be used to calculate the control limits for the chart. See Solved Problem 3 on page 188 for a detailed solution to a problem requiring the use of the *p*-chart.

c-chart A chart used for controlling the number of defects when more than one defect can be present in a product or service.

c-CHARTS. Sometimes products have more than one defect per unit. For example, a roll of carpeting may have several defects, such as tufted or discoloured fibres or stains from the production process. Other situations in which more than one defect may occur include defects in a television picture tube face panel, accidents at a particular intersection, and complaints at a hotel. When management is interested in reducing the number of defects per unit, another type of control chart, the *c*-chart, is useful.

The underlying sampling distribution for a *c*-chart is the Poisson distribution. It is based on the assumption that defects occur over a continuous region and that the probability of two or more defects at any one location is negligible. The mean of the distribution is $\bar{c}$ and the standard deviation is $\sqrt{\bar{c}}$. A useful tactic is to use the normal approximation to the Poisson so that the control limits are:

$$\text{UCL}_c = \bar{c} + z\sqrt{\bar{c}} \quad \text{and} \quad \text{LCL}_c = \bar{c} - z\sqrt{\bar{c}}$$

See Solved Problem 4 on page 189 for a detailed example of the use of a *c*-chart.

PROCESS CAPABILITY

process capability The ability of the process to meet the design specifications for a product or service.

nominal value A target for design specifications.

tolerance An allowance above or below the nominal value.

Statistical process control techniques help managers achieve and maintain a process distribution that does not change in terms of its mean and variance. The control limits on the control charts signal when the mean or variability of the process changes. However, a process that is in statistical control may not be producing products or services according to their design specifications, because the control limits are based on the mean and variability of the *sampling distribution*, not the design specifications. **Process capability** refers to the ability of the process to meet the design specifications for a product or service. Design specifications often are expressed as a **nominal value**, or target, and a **tolerance**, or allowance above or below the nominal value. For example, design specifications for the useful life of a light bulb might have a nominal value of 1000 hours and a tolerance of 200 hours. This tolerance gives an *upper specification* of 1200 hours and a *lower specification* of 800 hours. The process producing the bulbs must be capable of doing so within these design specifications; otherwise, it will produce a certain proportion of defective bulbs. Management also is interested in detecting occurrences of light bulb life exceeding 1200 hours because something might be learned that can be built into the process in the future.

Process capability also applies to services. For example, McDonald's can monitor service quality using SPC tools to measure variables such as drive-through service time. According to a recent pilot test in Canada, the design specification for drive-through service is a maximum of 30 seconds from payment to order completion. This provides the upper specification. The capability of the drive-through process at each restaurant can be assessed for its ability to satisfy customer quality expectations before launching a national campaign.

DEFINING PROCESS CAPABILITY

Figure 5.9 shows the relationship between a process distribution and the upper and lower specifications for the process of producing light bulbs under two conditions. In Figure 5.9(a), the process is capable because the extremes of the process distribution fall within the upper and lower specifications. In Figure 5.9(b) the process is not capable because it produces too many bulbs with short lives.

Figure 5.9 shows clearly why managers are so concerned with reducing process variability. As variability decreases—as seen by a lower standard deviation—poor quality output is produced less frequently. Figure 5.10 shows what reducing variability does for the output of a process with a normal probability distribution. The firm with two-sigma quality (Tolerance limits = Process mean ± 2 standard deviations) produces 4.56 percent defective parts, or 45 600 defective parts per million. The firm with four-sigma quality produces only 0.0063 percent defectives, or 63 defective parts per million. Finally, the firm with six-sigma quality produces only 0.0000002 percent defectives, or 0.002 defective parts per million.

How can a manager determine quantitatively whether a process is capable? Two measures are commonly used in practice to assess capability: process capability ratio and process capability index.

FIGURE 5.9

FIGURE 5.9

*Relationship Between
Process Distribution
and Specifications*

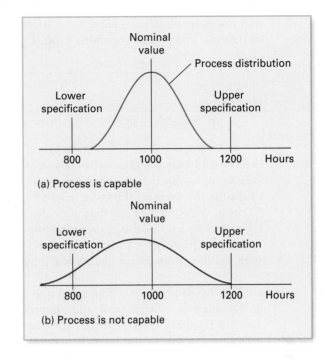

(a) Process is capable

(b) Process is not capable

FIGURE 5.10

*Effects of Reducing
Variability on Process
Capability*

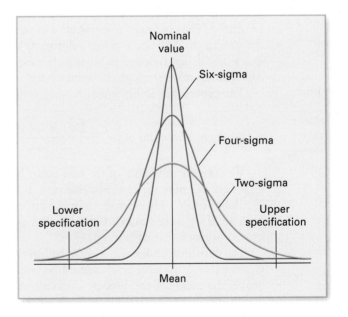

PROCESS CAPABILITY RATIO. A process is *capable* for a particular measure of quality if it has a process distribution whose extreme values fall within the upper and lower specifications for a product or service. How do we know which extreme values are likely to occur? As a general rule, most values of any process distribution fall within ±3 standard deviations of the mean. For example, if the distribution is normal, 99.74 percent of the values fall within ±3 standard deviations, for a total range of approximately 6 standard deviations. Hence, if a process is capable, the difference between the upper

process capability ratio, C_p The tolerance width divided by six standard deviations (process variability).

and lower specification, called the *tolerance width*, must be greater than 6 standard deviations. The **process capability ratio, C_p,** is defined as:

$$C_p = \frac{\text{Upper specification} - \text{Lower specification}}{6\sigma}$$

where:

σ = Standard deviation of the process distribution

A C_p value of 1.0 implies that the firm is producing three-sigma quality (0.26 percent defects) and that the process is consistently producing outputs within specifications even though some defects are generated. C_p values greater than 1.0 imply higher levels of quality achievement. Firms striving to achieve greater than three-sigma quality use a critical value for the ratio that is greater than 1.0. For example, a firm targeting six-sigma quality will use 2.0, a firm targeting five-sigma quality will use 1.67, and a firm striving for four-sigma quality will use 1.33. Processes producing products or services with less than three-sigma quality will have C_p values less than 1.0.

PROCESS CAPABILITY INDEX. The process is capable only when the capability ratio is greater than the critical value and the process distribution is centred on the nominal value of the design specifications. For example, the bulb-producing process may have a process capability ratio greater than 1.33. However, if the mean of the distribution of process output, $\bar{\bar{x}}$, is closer to the lower specification, defective bulbs may still be generated. Likewise, if $\bar{\bar{x}}$ is closer to the upper specification, very good bulbs may be generated. Thus, we need to compute a capability index that measures the potential for the process to generate outputs relative to either upper or lower specifications. This index also is appropriate to situations with only one specification limit, such as the McDonald's drive-through 30-second limit for good service quality.

process capability index, C_{pk} An index that measures the potential for a process to generate defective outputs relative to either upper or lower specifications.

The **process capability index, C_{pk},** is defined as:

$$C_{pk} = \text{Minimum of}\left[\frac{\bar{\bar{x}} - \text{Lower specification}}{3\sigma}, \frac{\text{Upper specification} - \bar{\bar{x}}}{3\sigma}\right]$$

We take the minimum of the two ratios because it gives the *worst-case* situation. If C_{pk} is greater than the critical value (say, 1.33 for four-sigma quality) and the process capability ratio is also greater than the critical value, we can finally say the process is capable. If C_{pk} is less than 1.0, the process average is close to one of the tolerance limits and is generating defective output.

The capability index will always be less than or equal to the capability ratio. When C_{pk} equals C_p, the process is centred between the upper and lower specifications and, hence, the mean of the process distribution is centred on the nominal value of the design specifications. See Solved Problem 5 on page 190 for a detailed example of the process capability ratio and the process capability index.

IMPROVEMENT USING PROCESS CAPABILITY

To determine the capability of a process to produce within the tolerances, use the following steps:

Step 1. Collect data on the process output, and calculate the mean and the standard deviation of the process output distribution.

Step 2. Use the data from the process distribution to compute process control charts, such as an $\bar{x}$- or an R-chart.

Step 3. Take a series of random samples from the process and plot the results on the control charts. If at least 20 consecutive samples are within the control limits of the charts, the process is in statistical control. If the process is not in statistical control, look for assignable causes and eliminate them. Recalculate the mean and standard deviation of the process distribution and the control limits for the charts. Continue until the process is in statistical control.

Step 4. Calculate the process capability ratio and the process capability index. If the results are acceptable, document any changes made to the process and continue to monitor the output by using the control charts. If the results are unacceptable, further explore assignable causes for reducing the variance in the output or centring the process distribution on the nominal value. As changes are made, recalculate the mean and standard deviation of the process distribution and the control limits for the charts and repeat step 3.

QUALITY ENGINEERING

quality engineering An approach that involves combining engineering and statistical methods to reduce costs and improve quality by optimizing product design and process characteristics.

Quality engineering, originated by Genichi Taguchi, is an approach that involves combining engineering and statistical methods to reduce costs and improve quality by optimizing product design simultaneously with process characteristics. Statistical methods can be applied to create a product or service design that is insensitive to small variations in the process, increasing the consistency for meeting customer expectations. This design approach is termed *robust design.*

quality loss function The rationale that a product or service that barely conforms to the specifications is more like a defective product or service than a perfect one.

Taguchi also argued that unwelcome costs are associated with any deviation from a quality characteristic's target value. These costs form a **quality loss function.** Taguchi's view is that the value of the quality loss function is zero when the quality characteristic of the product or service is exactly on the target value. As the quality characteristic gets closer to the tolerance limits, the value of the loss function rises exponentially. The rationale is that a product or service that barely conforms to the specifications is more like a defective product or service than a perfect one. By looking at quality in this way, Taguchi emphasizes the need for managers to continually search for ways to reduce *all* variability from the target value in the production process and not be content with merely meeting specification limits.

SIX SIGMA

We have seen how TQM and SPC can improve process performance and quality. Another approach, relying heavily on the principles and tools of TQM, has gained in popularity in recent years. **Six Sigma** is a comprehensive and flexible system for achieving, sustaining, and maximizing business success by minimizing defects and variability in processes. Six Sigma is driven by a close understanding of customer needs; the disciplined use of facts, data, and statistical analysis; and diligent attention to managing, improving, and reinventing business processes. Although many of the principles and tools of Six Sigma are similar to those of TQM, the approach has more formality than TQM.

Six Sigma A comprehensive and flexible system for achieving, sustaining, and maximizing business success by minimizing defects and variability in processes.

Motorola is credited with developing Six Sigma more than 20 years ago to improve its manufacturing capability in a world marketplace that was becoming increasingly competitive. Management noticed that some customers were complaining about the quality of Motorola's products and that competitor products were outperforming its products. Motorola initially responded by setting higher goals for each of its processes so as to reduce the number of defects to one-tenth the previous level of performance. To achieve such a goal required that they work smarter, not just harder.

Motorola began by soliciting new ideas from its employees and benchmarking its competitors. What followed were extensive changes to employee compensation and reward programs, training programs, and critical processes. The results were impressive. At one plant, after 10 months the defect rate improved 70 percent and the yield improved 55 percent.

The procedures for achieving those impressive results were documented and refined and became known as Six Sigma. Its name relates to the goal of achieving low rates of defective output even if the mean of process shifts 1.5 standard deviations. The 1.5 standard deviation value is a fudge factor used to account for the shift and drift in the mean of a process's outputs due to assignable causes over the long term. Motorola found that this variation normally fell between 1.4 and 1.6 standard deviations. Under this assumption, a process achieving six-sigma quality would likely produce 3.4 defects per million opportunities over the long term.

General Electric views Six Sigma as a strategy, a discipline, and a set of tools. It is a strategy because it focuses on what the customer wants, whether the customer is internal or external, and it aims at total customer satisfaction. Consequently, Six Sigma leads to better business results as measured by market share, revenue, and profits. It is a discipline because it has a formal sequence of steps, called the Six Sigma Improvement Model, to accomplish the desired improvement in process performance. The goal is to simplify processes and close the gaps between a process's competitive priorities and its competitive capabilities. Finally, it is a set of tools because it makes use of powerful tools such as those discussed in this chapter and in Chapter 2, "Process Management." The tools help detect whether process performance has gone astray, and they provide a means to monitor performance on an ongoing basis.

Although Six Sigma was rooted in an effort to improve manufacturing processes, General Electric popularized applying this to a wide range of services and support processes such as sales, human resources, customer service, and financial services. The concept of eliminating defects is the same, although the definition of "defect" depends on the process involved. For example, a human resource department's failure to meet a hiring target counts as a defect. Applying Six Sigma to service processes is more challenging than applying it to manufacturing processes for the following reasons:

1. The "work product" is much more difficult to see because it often consists of information, requests, orders, proposals, presentations, meetings, invoices, designs, and ideas. Service processes are often involved with computers and networks, sometimes international, that make the process "virtual" and difficult to document. This virtual aspect makes it difficult for people working in diverse functional areas such as sales, marketing, and software development to understand that they are actually part of a process that needs analysis.

2. Service processes can be changed quickly. Responsibilities can be shifted, forms revised, and new steps added without capital investment. Service processes in many companies evolve, adapt, and grow almost continuously.

3. Precise data on service process performance is often difficult to collect. Those that do exist tend to be often anecdotal or subjective. Large piles of unprocessed documents in a department's inbox are often easy to see; however, measuring backlogs, rework, delays, and the costs of working on them is difficult. For example, streamlining a loan closure process is complicated because the process may involve many different people, each only devoting a small slice of his or her workday.

Despite the challenges, Six Sigma has been successfully applied to a host of service processes, including financial services, human resource processes, marketing processes, and health-care administrative processes.

SIX SIGMA IMPROVEMENT MODEL

The Six Sigma Improvement Model is a five-step procedure designed to generate significant improvements in quality and process performance. The model can be applied to projects involving incremental improvements to processes, or to projects requiring major changes, such as redesigning of an existing process or developing a new process.

1. *Define.* Determine the characteristics of the process's output that are critical to customer satisfaction and identify any gaps between these characteristics and the process's capabilities. These gaps—whether a mismatch in the process's structure relative to customization and volume (see Figure 2.2 on page 34), poor positioning on customer involvement (see Figure 2.4 on page 38), or weak design uncovered through quality functional deployment—provide opportunities for improvement. To start, the current process should be documented using flowcharts and process charts. (See Chapter 2, "Process Management.")

2. *Measure.* Quantify the work the process does that affects the gap. Select what to measure, identify data sources, and prepare a data collection plan.

3. *Analyze.* Use data to fully characterize and understand the process. Useful tools include Pareto charts, scatter diagrams, and cause-and-effect diagrams, along with statistical process control tools to determine where improvements are necessary. Whether or not major redesign is necessary, establish procedures to make the desired outcome routine.

4. *Improve.* Modify or redesign existing methods to meet the new performance objectives. Implement the changes.

5. *Control.* Monitor the process to make sure that high performance levels are maintained. Once again, data analysis tools such as Pareto charts, bar charts, scatter diagrams, as well as the statistical process control tools can be used to control the process.

Successful users of Six Sigma have found that it is essential to rigorously follow the steps in the Six Sigma Improvement Model, which is sometimes referred to as the *DMAIC process*, using the first letter of each step in the model.

IMPLEMENTATION

Implementing a successful Six Sigma program begins with an understanding that Six Sigma is not a product you can buy—it requires time and commitment. Here are some lessons that Motorola, General Electric, and other leaders in Six Sigma learned about implementing the program:

- *Top-down commitment.* Corporate leaders must show their commitment to the program and take a visible role in auditing processes and searching for ways to improve the business. They must set an example for everyone in the organization.

- *Measurement systems to track progress.* Management must be committed to providing the means to track results and, along with employees, use those means to measure process performance.

- *Tough goal setting.* Establish the highest standards for the organization by regularly benchmarking "best-in-class" companies to assess the critical dimensions of customer satisfaction.

- *Education.* Employees must be trained in the "whys" and the "how-tos" of quality and what it means to customers, both internal and external. This learning is accomplished with "train-the-trainer" programs. Successful firms using Six Sigma develop a cadre of internal teachers who then are responsible for teaching and assisting teams involved in a process improvement project. These teachers have different titles depending on their experience and level of achievement. **Green Belts** devote part of their time to teaching and helping teams with their projects and the rest of their time to their normally assigned duties. **Black Belts** are full-time teachers and leaders of teams involved in Six Sigma projects. Finally, **Master Black Belts** are full-time teachers who review and mentor Black Belts. Selection criteria for Master Black Belts are quantitative skills and the ability to teach and mentor. According to the Six-Sigma Academy, a typical Black Belt can spearhead five to six projects a year, with average savings in the range of US$175 000 per project.

● *Communication.* Successes are as important to understand as failures. Communicating organizational successes is a critical step in ensuring that the firm can build upon them in the future.

● *Customer priorities.* Never lose sight of the customer's priorities, which are translated into competitive priorities for the firm's processes. Identify where gaps exist.

Successful firms using Six Sigma are mindful of these lessons; however, they are never satisfied. Continuous improvement or redesign of existing processes must be on the minds of all employees.

INTERNATIONAL QUALITY CERTIFICATION

Once a company has gone through the effort of making its processes capable, it must document its level of quality so as to better market its products or services. This is especially important in international trade. However, if each country had its own set of standards, companies selling in international markets would have difficulty complying with quality documentation standards in the countries where they did business. To overcome this problem, the International Organization for Standardization (www.iso.ch) devised a set of standards called ISO 9000 for companies doing business in the European Union and internationally. Subsequently, a new set of documentation standards, ISO 14000, was devised for environmental management systems.

ISO 9000 QUALITY DOCUMENTATION STANDARDS

ISO 9000 is really a family of standards that govern the way that quality is managed and documented within an organization. Now in its third revision, the primary changes since 1987 are a simplified documentation and an expanded emphasis on customers, the role of top management, and continuous improvement (West, 2001).

The primary standard, ISO 9001:2000, has the broadest scope and ensures a rigorous quality management system is in place. Unlike Six Sigma discussed earlier, ISO certification says *nothing* about the actual quality specifications of a final product or service. Instead, the 2000 structure adopts a process approach where each quality process is clearly mapped, individual responsibilities are clearly defined, and interactions between processes, managers, employees, and customers are delineated. The company must specifically document and ensure that processes are in place to guarantee top management commitment and involvement, good design practices, monitoring of quality, and customer satisfaction. Companies become certified by demonstrating to a qualified *external* examiner that they consistently follow their documented processes. Once certified, companies are listed in a directory and can promote themselves to

Green Belt An employee who has achieved the first level of training in a Six Sigma program and spends part of his or her time teaching and helping teams with their projects.

Black Belt An employee who has reached the highest level of training in a Six Sigma program and spends all of his or her time teaching and leading teams involved in Six Sigma projects.

Master Black Belt Full-time teachers and mentors to several Black Belts.

ISO 9000 A family of standards governing the development and documentation of a quality program.

potential customers as being certified according to a particular standard. Recertification is required every three years.

The other two major quality standards do not require examination by an external third party. ISO 9004:2000 establishes guidelines for organizations seeking to build a quality management system that includes processes to improve performance, including continuous improvement. Finally, ISO 9000:2000 is an overview descriptive document that provides guidelines and fundamental definitions for use in the other two standards.

ISO 14000—ENVIRONMENTAL MANAGEMENT

ISO 14000 A family of standards governing environmental management of products and processes, including material use, recycling, and disposal of waste.

The **ISO 14000** family of standards addresses a broad range of issues related to the way a firm manages environmental issues. Like ISO 9001, ISO 14001:2004 does not specify particular outputs or pollutant emission levels, but instead requires companies to prepare a plan for ongoing improvement in their environmental performance. To maintain their certification, companies must be inspected by outside, private auditors on a regular basis.

Of the family of standards, several of the most important areas covered include:

- *Environmental management system (14001:2004).* Certifies that a management system is in place to monitor and improve environmental performance, including resource consumption, pollutant emissions, and waste generation.
- *Environmental labelling (14020 series).* Defines terms such as *recyclable*, *energy-efficient*, and *safe for the ozone layer*, as well as the principles and procedures for environmental claims.
- *Environmental performance evaluation (14030 series).* Specifies guidelines for the certification of companies.
- *Life-cycle assessment (14040 series).* Evaluation of the lifetime environmental impact from the manufacture, use, and disposal of a product.
- *Design for the environment (14062).* Incorporating environmental performance in product design and development.

Collectively, this family of standards is structured around the plan-do-check-act cycle of quality improvement discussed earlier (see Figure 5.2 on page 157).

BENEFITS OF ISO CERTIFICATION

Completing the ISO 9001 certification process can take as long as 18 months and involve many hours of management and employee time. The cost of certification can exceed $1 million for large companies. Despite the expense and commitment involved in ISO certification and other quality awards, they bestow significant external and internal benefits. The external benefits come from the potential sales advantage that companies in compliance have. Companies looking for a supplier will likely select a company that has demonstrated compliance with ISO documentation standards, all other factors being equal. Registered companies report an average of a 48 percent increased profitability and a 76 percent improvement in marketing. Consequently, more and more firms are seeking certification to gain a competitive advantage. Hundreds of thousands of manufacturing sites worldwide are ISO 9001 certified.

Internal benefits relate directly to the firm's TQM program. The British Standards Institute, a leading third-party auditor, estimates that most ISO 9001-registered companies experience a 10 percent reduction in the cost of producing a product because of the quality improvements they make while striving to meet the documentation requirements. Certification requires a company to analyze and document its procedures, which is necessary in any event for implementing continuous improvement, employee involvement, and similar programs. The internal benefits can be significant. The guidelines and requirements of the ISO documentation standards provide companies with a jumpstart in pursuing TQM programs.

NATIONAL QUALITY AWARDS

A number of national governments and international organizations have created widely recognized quality awards, including the Baldrige National Quality Award in the United States (www.quality.nist.gov), the Deming Prize in Japan (www.deming.org/demingprize), the European Quality Awards (www.efqm.org), and the Canada Awards for Excellence (www.nqi.ca).

By way of example, the Canadian award promotes, recognizes, and publicizes quality strategies and achievements, and the application and review process is typical of those of other countries. A rigorous three-stage review process is based on seven major criteria, criteria that often help private and public sector companies define what quality means for them:

1. *Leadership* (10% weight for judging private sector applicants). Leadership system, values, expectations, and commitment to continuous improvement

2. *Planning* (8%). The effectiveness of strategic and business planning and deployment of plans, focusing on key improvement issues and analysis

3. *Customer focus* (9%). How the company defines the customer, determines customer and market requirements, and achieves customer satisfaction

4. *People focus* (14%). The success of efforts to realize the full potential of the workforce to create a high-performance organization, including a participative environment, continuous learning, and employee satisfaction

5. *Process management* (11%). The effectiveness of systems to control and improve key processes to ensure the quality of products and services

6. *Supplier/partner focus* (6%). The effectiveness of methods to select and partner with key suppliers to cooperatively improve supplier capabilities and quality

7. *Overall business performance* (42%). Service and product quality and operational results in customer satisfaction, employee satisfaction, and financial performance

Customer satisfaction underpins these seven criteria. As the award criteria have evolved, the last criterion, organizational performance, has been given increasing weight in selecting winners. This change implies that strong quality performance positively affects the bottom line, and the marketplace is the ultimate jury for rewarding high quality. Past award winners include Delta Hotels, British Columbia Transplant Society, Dana Canada, British Columbia Transplant Society, Telus (B.C.), Honeywell Water Controls, 3M Canada, and Telus.

TQM ACROSS THE ORGANIZATION

Total quality management is a philosophy that must permeate the entire organization if it is to be successful. The payoffs can be great; however, everyone must be involved. TQM has value for both manufacturing and service organization. For example, the Dana Spicer Driveshaft facility, located in Thorold, Ontario, received the 2001 Canada Award for Excellence Quality Trophy. The plant manufactures driveshafts used in commercial and light vehicles and the 200 employees generate more than $58 million in sales. Dana uses an internally developed quality leadership process to evaluate and continually improve the performance of its key operations. This system is thoroughly embedded throughout the parent division, which won a U.S. Malcolm Baldrige National Quality Award the previous year.

The plant's efforts and programs in the area of continuous quality improvement revolve around three key "people" areas: the customer, the investor, and the employee. The company uses cross-functional teams to focus its efforts on continuous improvement. These teams include internal people from all areas of expertise as well as customers. A flexible, decentralized system of management provides an open forum for the discussion and development of new ideas. "The sharing of ideas and experiences provides a broad base of knowledge that allows us to better serve the customer," says Shane Smith, plant manager. "Building relationships with customers and Dana people promotes a much stronger platform of understanding across the board. Open communication comes in the form of customer contacts and is then passed on to employees during monthly meetings" (Smith, 2001).

EQUATION SUMMARY

1. The reliability of a product: $r_s = (r_1)(r_2)\ldots(r_n)$

2. Control limits for variable process control charts:

   a. *R*-chart, range of sample:

   Upper control limit $= \text{UCL}_R = D_4\bar{R}$

   Lower control limit $= \text{LCL}_R = D_3\bar{R}$

   b. $\bar{x}$-chart, sample mean:

   Upper control limit $= \text{UCL}_{\bar{x}} = \bar{\bar{x}} + A_2\bar{R}$

   Lower control limit $= \text{LCL}_{\bar{x}} = \bar{\bar{x}} - A_2\bar{R}$

   c. When the standard deviation of the process distribution, σ, is known:

   Upper control limit $= \text{UCL}_{\bar{x}} = \bar{\bar{x}} + z\sigma_{\bar{x}}$

   Lower control limit $= \text{LCL}_{\bar{x}} = \bar{\bar{x}} - z\sigma_{\bar{x}}$

   where: $\sigma_{\bar{x}} = \dfrac{\sigma}{\sqrt{n}}$

3. Control limits for attribute process control charts:

   a. *p*-chart, proportion defective:

   Upper control limit $= \text{UCL}_p = \bar{p} + z\sigma_p$

   Lower control limit $= \text{LCL}_p = \bar{p} - z\sigma_p$

   where: $\sigma_p = \sqrt{\bar{p}(1 - \bar{p})/n}$

   b. *c*-chart, number of defects:

   Upper control limit $= \text{UCL}_c = \bar{c} + z\sqrt{\bar{c}}$

   Lower control limit $= \text{LCL}_c = \bar{c} - z\sqrt{\bar{c}}$

4. Process capability ratio: $C_p = \dfrac{\text{Upper specification} - \text{Lower specification}}{6\sigma}$

5. Process capability index:

$$C_{pk} = \text{Minimum of} \left[\frac{\bar{\bar{x}} - \text{Lower specification}}{3\sigma}, \frac{\text{Upper specification} - \bar{\bar{x}}}{3\sigma} \right]$$

CHAPTER HIGHLIGHTS

- Total quality management stresses three principles: a customer-driven focus, employee involvement, and continuous improvements in quality.

- The consumer's view of quality may be defined in a variety of ways. The customer may make a quantitative judgment about whether a product or service meets specified design and operating characteristics (conformance). In other situations, assessment of the performance, features, reliability, durability, product or service support, and psychological impressions, such as aesthetics, may take on greater importance. TQM requires firms to listen to customers and report their changing perceptions of quality.

- Quality can be used as a competitive weapon. High-performance design and consistent quality are competitive priorities associated with quality. World-class competition requires businesses to produce quality products or services efficiently.

- Responsibility for quality is shared by all employees in the organization. Employee involvement programs include leadership in changing organizational culture, individual development, awards and incentives, and teamwork.

- Continuous improvement involves identifying benchmarks of excellent practice and instilling a sense of ownership in employees so that they will continually identify product, services, and process improvements that should be made.

- Quality management is important because of its impact on market share, price, and profits and because of the costs of poor quality. The four main categories of costs associated with quality management are prevention, appraisal, internal failure, and external failure. If quality is to be improved, prevention costs must increase. Appraisal, internal failure, and external failure costs all decline as quality is improved through preventive measures.

- Benchmarking is a comparative measure. It is used to establish goals for continuous improvement. Forms of benchmarking include competitive, functional, and internal.

- Concurrent engineering improves the match between product design and production process capabilities. The higher quality and shorter product-development times associated with concurrent engineering are competitive advantages.

- Quality improvement requires close cooperation among functions (design, operations, marketing, purchasing, and others). Quality function deployment (QFD) encourages interfunctional planning and communication.

- Keys to controlling supplier quality are the buyer's approach and specification management. The buyer must consider quality, delivery, and cost. Specifications must be clear and realistic. Improved communication between purchasing and other departments is needed.

- Approaches to organizing and presenting quality improvement data include checklists, histograms and bar charts, Pareto charts, scatter diagrams, cause-and-effect diagrams, graphs, and control charts.

- A key to meeting design specifications in a product or service is to reduce output variability. When a process is in a state of statistical control, outputs subject to common causes of variation follow a stable probability distribution. When assignable causes of variation are present, the process is out of statistical control. Statistical process control (SPC) methods are used to detect the presence of assignable causes of variation.

- Statistical process control charts are useful for measuring the current quality generated by the process and for detecting whether the process has changed to the detriment of quality. Thus, R-charts are used to monitor process variability, $\bar{x}$- and p-charts identify abnormal variations in the process average, and c-charts are used for controlling the number of defects when a product or service process could result in multiple defects per unit of output. The presence of abnormal variation triggers a search for assignable causes.

- Process variability should be in control before process average control charts are constructed. The reason is that the average range is used in the calculation of control limits for process average control charts. Crucial decisions in the design of control charts are sample size and control limits.

- The central line of a control chart is the average of past averages of the quality measurement. The spread in control limits affects the chances of detecting a shift in the process average or range, as well as the chances of searching for assignable causes when none exist.

- A process can be in statistical control but still not be capable of producing all of its output within design specifications. The process capability ratio and the process capability index are quantitative measures used to assess the capability of a process.

- The Canadian Award for Excellence promotes, recognizes, and publicizes the quality strategies and achievements of outstanding companies.

- ISO 9000 is a family of standards governing the development and documentation of quality processes. Companies can be certified by external examiners for ISO 9001:2000. Similarly, ISO 14001:2004 requires companies seeking certification to develop management systems that track materials use, waste generation, and pollutant emissions. Processes that foster improvement in environmental performance are also necessary.

CD-ROM RESOURCES

The Student CD-ROM that accompanies this text contains the following resources, which allow you to further practise and apply the concepts presented in this chapter.

- **Equation Summary**: All the equations for this chapter can be found in one convenient location.

- **Discussion Questions**: Five questions will challenge your understanding of the importance of quality for competitive operations.

- **Cases**:

  - *Cranston Nissan*. Analyze the many instances of service quality breakdown that one of the authors of this text experienced.

  - *José's Authentic Mexican Restaurant*. How can quality be improved at this restaurant?

- **Experiential Exercise**: *Statistical Process Control with a Coin Catapult*. Experience the gathering of data and the development of control charts for variable or attribute measures in this entertaining in-class exercise.

- **OM Explorer Tutors**: OM Explorer contains five tutor programs to enhance your understanding of Pareto charts, *x*-bar charts, *p*-charts, *c*-charts, and process capability.

- **OM Explorer Solvers**: OM Explorer contains five programs designed to solve general problems with multiple types of quality charts and process capability.

- **Extend LT**: *Service Quality at Best Burger*. Service quality of the drive-through-window operations must be improved.

- **Tours**: See how the management of *Lower Florida Keys Health System* community hospital designs its processes to achieve quality and how *Chaparral Steel* builds quality into its products at each step of manufacturing.

- **Supplement F: Acceptance Sampling Plans**. Use this supplement to learn how to design single-sampling plans and estimate the average outgoing quality of your plan.

SOLVED PROBLEM 1

Vera Johnson and Merris Williams manufacture vanishing cream. The following are the operations and reliabilities of their packaging operation. The reliabilities are the probabilities that each operation will be performed to the desired specifications.

OPERATION	RELIABILITY
Mix	0.99
Fill	0.98
Cap	0.99
Label	0.97

Johnson and Williams ask their spouses to keep track of and analyze reported defects. They find the following:

DEFECT	FREQUENCY
Lumps of unmixed product	7
Over- or underfilled jars	18
Jar lids did not seal	6
Labels rumpled or missing	29
Total	60

a. What is the reliability of the packaging operation?

b. Draw a Pareto chart to identify the vital defects.

SOLUTION

a. The formula is:

$$r_s = (r_1)(r_2)...(r_n)$$

Substituting $r_1 = 0.99$, $r_2 = 0.98$, ..., gives:

$$r_s = (0.99)(0.98)(0.99)(0.97)$$
$$= 0.9317, \text{ or about 93\% reliability}$$

b. Defective labels account for 48.33% of the total number of defects:

$$\frac{29}{60} \times 100\% = 48.33\%$$

Improperly filled jars account for 30% of the total number of defects:

$$\frac{18}{60} \times 100\% = 30.00\%$$

The cumulative percentage for the two most frequent defects is:

$$48.33\% + 30.00\% = 78.33\%$$

Lumps represent $\dfrac{7}{60} \times 100\% = 11.67\%$ of defects

the cumulative percentage is: $78.33\% + 11.67\% = 90.00\%$

Defective seals represent $\frac{6}{60} \times 100\% = 10\%$ of defects

the cumulative percentage is: $10\% + 90\% = 100.00\%$

The Pareto chart is shown in Figure 5.11.

FIGURE 5.11

Pareto Chart

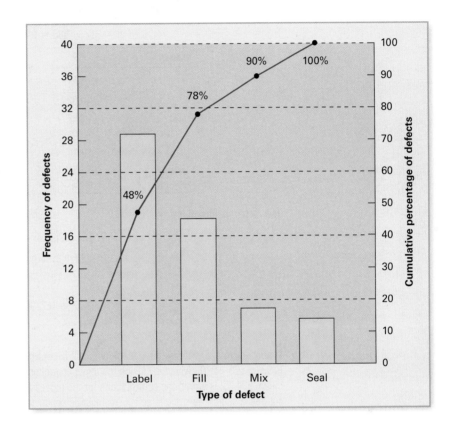

SOLVED PROBLEM 2

The Watson Electric Company produces incandescent light bulbs. The following data on the number of lumens for 40-watt light bulbs were collected when the process was in control.

SAMPLE	OBSERVATION			
	1	2	3	4
1	604	612	588	600
2	597	601	607	603
3	581	570	585	592
4	620	605	595	588
5	590	614	608	604

a. Calculate control limits for an *R*-chart and an $\bar{x}$-chart.

b. Since these data were collected, some new employees were hired. A new sample obtained the following readings: 570, 603, 623, and 583. Is the process still in control?

SOLUTION

a. To calculate $\bar{x}$, compute the mean for each sample. To calculate R, subtract the lowest value in the sample from the highest value in the sample. For example, for sample 1:

$$\bar{x} = \frac{604 + 612 + 588 + 600}{4} = 601$$

$$R = 612 - 588 = 24$$

SAMPLE	$\bar{X}$	R
1	601	24
2	602	10
3	582	22
4	602	32
5	604	24
Total	2991	112
Average	$\bar{\bar{x}} = 598.2$	$\bar{R} = 22.4$

The R-chart control limits are:

$$UCL_R = D_4\bar{R} = 2.282(22.4) = 51.12$$

$$LCL_R = D_3\bar{R} = 0(22.4) = 0$$

The $\bar{x}$-chart control limits are:

$$UCL_x = \bar{\bar{x}} + A_2\bar{R} = 598.2 + 0.729(22.4) = 614.53$$

$$LCL_x = \bar{\bar{x}} - A_2\bar{R} = 598.2 - 0.729(22.4) = 581.87$$

b. First check to see whether the variability is still in control on the basis of the new data. The range is 53 (or $623 - 570$), which is outside the upper control limit for the R-chart. Even though the sample mean, 594.75, is within the control limits for the process average, process variability is not in control. A search for assignable causes must be conducted.

SOLVED PROBLEM 3

The data processing department of Confederation Bank has five data entry clerks. Each day their supervisor verifies the accuracy of a random sample of 250 records. A record containing one or more errors is considered defective and must be redone. The results of the last 30 samples are shown in the table. All were checked to make sure that none was out of control.

SAMPLE	NUMBER OF DEFECTIVE RECORDS	SAMPLE	NUMBER OF DEFECTIVE RECORDS	SAMPLE	NUMBER OF DEFECTIVE RECORDS
1	7	11	18	21	17
2	5	12	5	22	12
3	19	13	16	23	6
4	10	14	4	24	7
5	11	15	11	25	13
6	8	16	8	26	10
7	12	17	12	27	14
8	9	18	4	28	6
9	6	19	6	29	11
10	13	20	11	30	9
				Total	300

a. Based on these historical data, set up a *p*-chart using $z = 3$.

b. Samples for the next four days showed the following:

SAMPLE	NUMBER OF DEFECTIVE RECORDS
31	17
32	15
33	22
34	21

What is the supervisor's assessment of the data-entry process likely to be?

SOLUTION

a. From the table, the supervisor knows that the total number of defective records is 300 out of a total sample of 7500 (equal to 30 × 250). Therefore, the central line of the chart is:

$$\bar{p} = \frac{300}{7500} = 0.04$$

The control limits are:

$$UCL_p = \bar{p} + z\sqrt{\frac{\bar{p}(1-\bar{p})}{n}} = 0.04 + 3\sqrt{\frac{0.04(0.96)}{250}} = 0.077$$

$$LCL_p = \bar{p} - z\sqrt{\frac{\bar{p}(1-\bar{p})}{n}} = 0.04 - 3\sqrt{\frac{0.04(0.96)}{250}} = 0.003$$

b. Samples for the next four days showed the following:

SAMPLE	NUMBER OF DEFECTIVE RECORDS	PROPORTION
31	17	0.068
32	15	0.060
33	22	0.088
34	21	0.084

Samples 33 and 34 are out of control. The supervisor should look for the problem and, upon identifying it, take corrective action.

SOLVED PROBLEM 4

The Minnow County Highway Safety Department monitors accidents at the intersection of Routes 123 and 14. Accidents at the intersection have averaged three per month.

a. Which type of control chart should be used? Construct a control chart with three-sigma control limits.

b. Last month, seven accidents occurred at the intersection. Is this sufficient evidence to justify a claim that something has changed at the intersection?

SOLUTION

a. The safety department cannot determine the number of accidents that did *not* occur, so it has no way to compute a proportion defective at the intersection. Therefore, the administrators must use a *c*-chart for which:

$$\text{UCL}_c = \bar{c} + z\sqrt{\bar{c}} = 3 + 3\sqrt{3} = 8.20$$

$$\text{LCL}_c = \bar{c} - z\sqrt{\bar{c}} = 3 - 3\sqrt{3} = -2.196$$

There cannot be a negative number of accidents, so the lower control limit in this case is adjusted to zero.

b. The number of accidents last month falls within the upper and lower control limits of the chart. We conclude that no assignable causes are present and that the increase in accidents was due to chance.

SOLVED PROBLEM 5

Pioneer Chicken advertises "lite" chicken with 30 percent fewer calories. (The pieces are 33 percent smaller.) The process average distribution for "lite" chicken breasts is 420 calories, with a standard deviation of the population of 25 calories. Pioneer randomly takes samples of six chicken breasts to measure calorie content.

a. Design an $\bar{x}$-chart, using the process standard deviation.

b. The product design calls for the average chicken breast to contain 400 ± 100 calories. Calculate the process capability ratio (target = 1.33) and the process capability index. Interpret the results.

SOLUTION

a. For the process standard deviation of 25 calories, the standard deviation of the sample mean is:

$$\sigma_{\bar{x}} = \frac{\sigma}{\sqrt{n}} = \frac{25}{\sqrt{6}} = 10.2 \text{ calories}$$

$$\text{UCL}_{\bar{x}} = \bar{\bar{x}} + z\sigma_{\bar{x}} = 420 + 3(10.2) = 450.6 \text{ calories}$$

$$\text{LCL}_{\bar{x}} = \bar{\bar{x}} - z\sigma_{\bar{x}} = 420 - 3(10.2) = 389.4 \text{ calories}$$

b. The process capability ratio is:

$$C_p = \frac{\text{Upper specification} - \text{Lower specification}}{6\sigma} = \frac{500 \text{ calories} - 300 \text{ calories}}{6(25)} = 1.333$$

The process capability index is:

$$C_{pk} = \text{Minimum of} \left[\frac{\bar{\bar{x}} - \text{Lower specification}}{3\sigma}, \frac{\text{Upper specification} - \bar{\bar{x}}}{3\sigma} \right]$$

$$= \text{Minimum of} \left[\frac{420 - 300}{3(25)} = 1.60, \frac{500 - 420}{3(25)} = 1.07 \right] = 1.07$$

Because the process capability ratio is greater than 1.33, the process should be able to produce the product reliably with four-sigma quality. However, the process capability index is 1.07, so the current process is not centred properly for four-sigma quality. The mean of the process distribution is too close to the upper specification.

PROBLEMS

1. Contented Airlines (CA) is reluctant to begin service at the new Delayed Indefinitely Airport (DIA) until the automated baggage-handling system can transport luggage to the correct location with at least 99 percent reliability for any given flight. Lower reliability will result in damage to CA's reputation for quality service. The baggage system will not deliver to the right location if any of its subsystems fail. The subsystems and their reliability for satisfactory performance during operation for any given flight are shown in the following table.

SUBSYSTEM	RELIABILITY
Power supply	70.0% surge-free
Scanner reading	99.8% accurate
Computer software	98.2% glitch-free
Mechanical systems	97.5% jam-free
Operators	96.0% error-free

a. What is the reliability of the luggage system for any given flight?

b. When the passenger shuttle system operates, power surges trip the motors on the baggage system. Each of the luggage system motors must then be manually reset. Installing surge protectors increases power supply reliability to 99.9 percent. What is the reliability of the luggage system?

c. What could be done to improve the reliability of the luggage system?

2. Smith, Schroeder, and Torn (SST) is a short-haul household furniture moving company. SST's labour force is temporary and part-time. SST is concerned with recent complaints, as tabulated on the following tally sheet.

COMPLAINT	TALLY
Broken glass	### ### ///
Delivered to wrong address	### ////
Furniture rubbed together while on truck	### ### ### ###
Late delivery	###
Late arrival for pickup	### ### ### ///
Missing items	### ### ### ### ### /
Nicks and scratches from rough handling	### ###
Soiled upholstery	### ///

a. Draw a bar chart and a Pareto chart to identify the most serious moving problems.

b. Use a cause-and-effect diagram to identify potential causes of complaints.

3. Regina Fibreboard makes roof liners for the automotive industry. The manufacturing manager is concerned about product quality. She suspects that one particular defect, tears in the fabric, is related to production-run size. An assistant gathers the following data from production records.

RUN	SIZE	DEFECTS (%)	RUN	SIZE	DEFECTS (%)
1	1000	3.5	11	6500	1.5
2	4100	3.8	12	1000	5.5
3	2000	5.5	13	7000	1.0
4	6000	1.9	14	3000	4.5
5	6800	2.0	15	2200	4.2
6	3000	3.2	16	1800	6.0
7	2000	3.8	17	5400	2.0
8	1200	4.2	18	5800	2.0
9	5000	3.8	19	1000	6.2
10	3800	3.0	20	1500	7.0

a. Draw a scatter diagram for these data.

b. Does there appear to be a relationship between run size and percent defects? What implications does this have for Regina Fibreboard's business?

4. The operations manager for Superfast Airlines at Macdonald International Airport noticed an increase in the number of delayed flight departures. She brainstormed possible causes with her staff:

- Aircraft late to gate
- Acceptance of late passengers
- Passengers arrive late at gate
- Passenger processing delays at gate
- Late baggage to aircraft
- Other late personnel or unavailable items
- Mechanical failures

Draw a cause-and-effect diagram to organize the possible causes of delayed flight departures into the following major categories: equipment, personnel, material, procedures, and "other factors" beyond managerial control. Provide a detailed set of causes for each major cause identified by the operations manager and incorporate them into your cause-and-effect diagram.

5. At Conner Company, a custom manufacturer of printed circuit boards, the finished boards are subjected to a final inspection prior to shipment to its customers. As Conner's quality assurance manager, you are responsible for making a presentation to management on quality problems at the beginning of each month. Your assistant has analyzed the reject memos for all the circuit boards that were rejected during the past month. He has given you a summary statement listing the reference number of the circuit board and the reason for rejection from one of the following categories:

A = Poor electrolyte coverage

B = Improper lamination

C = Low copper plating

D = Plating separation

E = Improper etching

For 50 circuit boards that had been rejected last month, the summary statement showed the following:

C B C C D E C C B A D A C C C B C A C D C A C C B A C A C
B C C A C A A C C D A C C C E C C A B A C

a. Prepare a tally sheet (or checklist) of the different reasons for rejection.

b. Develop a Pareto chart to identify the more significant types of rejection.

c. Examine the causes of the most significant type of defect, using a cause-and-effect diagram.

6. The Marlin Company produces plastic bottles to customer order. The quality inspector randomly selects four bottles from the bottle machine and measures the outside diameter of the bottle neck, a critical quality dimension that determines whether the bottle cap will fit properly. The dimensions (in centimetres) from the last six samples are:

	BOTTLE			
SAMPLE	1	2	3	4
1	0.604	0.612	0.588	0.600
2	0.597	0.601	0.607	0.603
3	0.581	0.570	0.585	0.592
4	0.620	0.605	0.595	0.588
5	0.590	0.614	0.608	0.604
6	0.585	0.583	0.617	0.579

a. Assume that only these six samples are sufficient and use the data to determine control limits for an R- and an $\bar{x}$-chart.

b. Suppose that the specification for the bottle neck diameter is 0.600 ± 0.050 centimetres. If the population standard deviation is 0.012 centimetres, and if management has targeted three-sigma quality, is the process capable of producing the bottle?

7. A textile manufacturer wants to set up a control chart for irregularities (e.g., oil stains, shop soil, loose threads, and tears) per 10 square metres of carpet. The following data were collected from a sample of twenty 10-square-metre pieces of carpet.

Sample	1	2	3	4	5	6	7	8	9	10
Irregularities	11	8	9	12	4	16	5	8	17	10

Sample	11	12	13	14	15	16	17	18	19	20
Irregularities	11	5	7	12	13	8	19	11	9	10

a. Using these data, set up a c-chart with $z = 3$.

b. Suppose that the next five samples had 15, 18, 12, 22, and 21 irregularities. What do you conclude?

8. The production manager at Sunny Soda, Inc., is interested in tracking the quality of the company's 300 millilitre bottle filling line. The bottles must be filled within the tolerances set for this product, because the dietary information on the label shows 300 millilitres as the serving size. The design standard for the product calls for a fill level of 300.00 ± 2.5 millilitres. The manager collected the following sample data (millilitres per bottle) on the production process:

	OBSERVATION			
SAMPLE	1	2	3	4
1	300.00	299.25	302.50	302.00
2	297.75	298.50	302.50	299.00
3	297.25	300.50	299.25	299.75
4	302.50	302.25	301.25	298.75
5	302.00	298.00	303.00	301.25
6	298.50	299.50	301.50	302.00
7	302.25	300.00	300.00	300.75
8	300.25	301.00	299.75	298.75
9	300.00	299.00	299.25	300.75
10	298.00	298.50	302.25	300.00
11	297.75	299.75	301.25	302.50
12	300.25	300.00	301.50	299.25
13	299.50	299.75	301.50	300.75
14	300.50	300.00	301.25	298.75
15	300.00	301.25	300.25	299.25

a. Are the process average and range in statistical control?

b. If management wants three-sigma quality, is the process capable of meeting the design standard? Explain.

9. Management at Webster Chemical Company is concerned as to whether caulking tubes are being properly capped. If a significant proportion of the tubes are not being sealed, Webster is placing its customers in a messy situation. Tubes are packaged in large boxes of 144. Several boxes are inspected, and the following numbers of leaking tubes are found:

SAMPLE	TUBES	SAMPLE	TUBES	SAMPLE	TUBES
1	3	8	6	15	5
2	5	9	4	16	0
3	3	10	9	17	2
4	4	11	2	18	6
5	2	12	6	19	2
6	4	13	5	20	1
7	2	14	1	Total	72

Calculate p-chart three-sigma control limits to assess whether the capping process is in statistical control.

10. The Precision Machining Company makes handheld tools on an assembly line that produces one product every minute. On one of the products, the critical quality dimension is the diameter of a very small hole bored in one of the assemblies. Management considers the process to be in control. Historically, the mean diameter has been 0.0150 centimetres and the average range has been 0.002 centimetres. Design an $\bar{x}$-chart to control this process, with the control limits set at three-sigma from the centre line.

Management has provided the results of 80 minutes of output from the production line, as shown in Table 5.4. During this 80 minute period, the process average changed once. All measurements are in thousandths of a centimetre.

a. Set up an $\bar{x}$-chart with $n = 4$. The frequency should be sample four, then skip four. Thus, your first sample would be for minutes 1–4, the second would be for minutes 9–12, and so on. When would you stop the process to check for a change in the process average?

b. Set up an $\bar{x}$-chart with $n = 8$. The frequency should be sample eight, then skip four. When would you stop the process now? What can you say about the desirability of large samples on a frequent sampling interval?

11. The plant manager at Northern Pines Brewery has decided to gather data on the number of defective bottles generated on the line. Every day a random sample of 250 bottles was inspected for fill level, cracked bottles, bad labels, and poor seals. Any bottle failing to meet the standard for any of these criteria was counted as a reject. The study lasted 30 days and yielded the data in Table 5.5. From the data, what can you tell the manager about the quality of the bottling line? Do you see any nonrandom behaviour in the bottling process? If so, what might cause this behaviour?

12. Red Baron Airlines serves hundreds of cities every day, but competition is increasing from smaller companies affiliated with major carriers. One of the key competitive priorities is on-time arrivals and departures. Red Baron defines *on time* as any arrival or departure that takes place within 15 minutes of the scheduled time. To stay on top of the market, management has set the high standard of 98 percent on-time performance. The operations department was put in charge of monitoring the performance of the airline. Each week, a random sample of 300 flight arrivals and departures was checked for schedule performance. Table 5.6 contains the numbers of arrivals and departures over the last 30 weeks that did not meet Red Baron's definition of on-time service. What can you tell management about the quality of service? Can you identify any nonrandom behaviour in the process? If so, what might cause the behaviour?

TABLE 5.4 *Sample Data for Precision Machining Company*

MINUTES	DIAMETER (thousandths of cm)										
1–12	15	16	18	14	16	17	15	14	14	13	16	17
13–24	15	16	17	16	14	14	13	14	15	16	15	17
25–36	14	13	15	17	18	15	16	15	14	15	16	17
37–48	18	16	15	16	16	14	17	18	19	15	16	15
49–60	12	17	16	14	15	17	14	16	15	17	18	14
61–72	15	16	17	18	13	15	14	14	16	15	17	18
73–80	16	16	17	18	16	15	14	17				

TABLE 5.5 *Sample Data for Northern Pines Brewery*

SAMPLES	NUMBER OF REJECTED BOTTLES IN SAMPLE OF 250									
1–10	4	9	6	12	8	2	13	10	1	9
11–20	4	6	8	10	12	4	3	10	14	5
21–30	13	11	7	3	2	8	11	6	9	5

TABLE 5.6 *Sample Data for Red Baron Airlines*

SAMPLES	NUMBER OF LATE PLANES IN SAMPLE OF 300 ARRIVALS AND DEPARTURES									
1–10	3	8	5	11	7	2	12	9	1	8
11–20	3	5	7	9	12	5	4	9	13	4
21–30	12	10	6	2	1	8	4	5	8	2

REFERENCES AND FURTHER READINGS

Barnard, William, and Thomas F. Wallace. *The Innovation Edge.* Essex Junction, VT: Oliver Wight Publications, Inc., 1994.

Besterfield, Dale. *Quality Control,* 6th ed. Upper Saddle River, NJ: Prentice-Hall, 2001.

Brown, Ed. "The Best Business Hotels." *Fortune,* March 17, 1997, pp. 204–205.

Collier, David A. *The Service Quality Solution.* New York: Irwin Professional Publishing; Milwaukee: ASQC Quality Press, 1994.

Crosby, Philip B. *Quality Is Free: The Art of Making Quality Certain.* New York: McGraw-Hill, 1979.

Deming, W. Edwards. *Out of the Crisis.* Cambridge, MA: Massachusetts Institute of Technology Center for Advanced Engineering Study, 1986.

Denton, D. Keith. "Lessons on Competitiveness: Motorola's Approach." *Production and Inventory Management Journal,* Third Quarter 1991, pp. 22–25.

Duncan, Acheson J. *Quality Control and Industrial Statistics,* 5th ed. Homewood, IL: Irwin, 1986.

Feigenbaum, A. V. *Total Quality Control: Engineering and Management,* 3rd ed. New York: McGraw-Hill, 1983.

Garvin, David A. "Competing on the Eight Dimensions of Quality." *Harvard Business Review,* vol. 65 (1987), no. 6, pp. 101–109.

Hauser, John R., and Don Clausing. "The House of Quality." *Harvard Business Review,* May/June 1988, pp. 63–73.

Juran, Joseph M., and A. Blanton Godfrey. *Juran's Quality Handbook,* 5th ed. New York: McGraw-Hill, 1999.

Katzenbach, Jon R., and Douglas K. Smith. "The Discipline of Teams." *Harvard Business Review,* March/April 1993, pp. 111–120.

Lindsay, William M., and Joseph A. Petrick. *Total Quality and Organizational Development.* Delray Beach, FL: St. Lucie Press, 1997.

Logothetis, N. *Managing for Total Quality: From Deming to Taguchi and SPC.* New York: Prentice Hall, 1992.

Miller, Bill. "ISO 9000 and the Small Company: Can I Afford It?" *APICS—The Performance Advantage,* September 1994, pp. 45–46.

Mitra, Amitava. *Fundamentals of Quality Control and Improvement,* 2nd ed. Upper Saddle River, NJ: Prentice-Hall, 1998.

Nakhai, Benham, and Joao S. Neves. "The Deming, Baldrige, and European Quality Awards." *Quality Progress,* April 1994, pp. 33–37.

Neves, Joao S., and Benham Nakhai. "The Evolution of the Baldrige Award." *Quality Progress,* June 1994, pp. 65–70.

Oakland, John S. *Total Quality Management.* London: Heinemann Professional Publishing Ltd., 1989.

Parasuraman, A., V. A. Zeithaml, and L. L. Berry. *SERVQUAL: A Multiple Item Scale for Measuring Perceptions of Service Quality.* Cambridge, MA: Marketing Science Institute, 1986.

Pletsch, Adam. "Ford St. Thomas Performs Great Six Sigma." *Plant,* vol. 61, no. 9, 2002, p. 21.

Prahalad, C. K., and M. S. Krishnan. "The New Meaning of Quality in the Information Age." *Harvard Business Review,* September/October 1999, pp. 109–118.

Rabbitt, John T., and Peter A. Bergh. *The ISO 9000 Book.* White Plains, NY: Quality Resources, 1993.

Roelofsen, Mike. "Searching for Business Perfection." *London Free Press,* September 16, 2002, pp. 12–13.

Roth, Daniel. "Motorola Lives!" *Fortune,* September 27, 1999, pp. 305–306.

Rust, Roland T., Timothy Keiningham, Stephen Clemens, and Anthony Zahorik. "Return on Quality at Chase Manhattan Bank." *Interfaces,* vol. 29, no. 2 (March/April 1999), pp. 62–72.

Sanders, Lisa. "Going Green with Less Red Tape." *Business Week,* September 23, 1996, pp. 75–76.

Smith, Shane. Quoted in National Quality Institute, "Recipient Profiles." National Quality Institute site <www.nqi.ca/english/profiles_2001.htm&mt>; accessed April 7, 2003.

Sullivan, Lawrence P. "The Power of Taguchi Methods." *Quality Progress,* vol. 20 (1987), no. 6, pp. 76–79.

"Want EC Business? You Have Two Choices." *Business Week,* October 19, 1992, pp. 58–59.

West, John E. "Implementing ISO 9001:2000." *Quality Progress,* vol. 34 (2001), no. 5, pp. 65–68.

Wheeler, Donald J. *Advanced Topics in Statistical Process Control.* Knoxville, TN: SPC Press, Inc., 1995.

"Why Online Browsers Don't Become Buyers." *Computerworld,* November 29, 1999, p. 14.

Across the Organization

Inventory management is important to:

- **accounting,** which provides the cost estimates used in inventory control, pays suppliers, and bills customers.
- **finance,** which deals with the implications of interest or investment opportunity costs on inventory management and anticipates how best to finance inventory and the cash flows related to inventory.
- **management information systems,** which develop and maintain the technology for tracking and controlling inventories.
- **marketing and sales,** which create the need for inventory systems and rely on inventories to satisfy customers.
- **operations,** which has the responsibility to establish the firm's inventory policies and control inventories.

Learning Goals

After reading this chapter, you will be able to:

1. describe the cost and service trade-offs involved in inventory decisions.
2. distinguish among the different types of inventory and know how to manage their quantities.
3. compute the economic order quantity and apply it in various situations.
4. develop policies for both continuous review and periodic review inventory control systems.
5. identify ways to maintain accurate inventory records.

Although new products are expected to drive future growth at Xerox Canada, it must be supported by strong service of products already in the field. Slow fulfillment of a worn part or needed supplies costs customers time and money. That makes the management of Xerox's inventory of replacement parts absolutely critical. However, managers have also had to make bold cuts in inventory and operating costs to improve financial performance. In the words of Al Gallina, director of logistics, "It has been a delicate balancing act."

First, a forecasting system has proven instrumental in reducing Canadian inventory. Statistical methods are used for a first pass, and then the logistics team meets monthly with sales and marketing to further refine the forecast. Doing so has shifted Xerox away from building and shipping to inventory, with its associated "just-in-case" inefficiencies. Instead, the emphasis is on build-to-order and just-in-time, which require better information flow, as well as greater supply chain speed and flexibility. The net result: with lower inventories, leased warehouse space was reduced by 4500 square metres.

Second, a complete rethinking of how to best deliver critical parts and supplies to Xerox's field technicians was also undertaken. Although technicians travel with much of the inventory in their service vehicles (the target service level is 85 percent for in-the-field repairs), a rapid delivery network is essential for other critical parts. This massive network had grown to two warehouses and 19 depots that shipped more than 1.5 million pieces annually—ranging from fusers and rollers to complete plug-and-play modules—with a targeted service level of 95 percent.

Although service expectations were generally met, Xerox had some glaring inefficiencies in smaller centres. Some satellite locations needed only half a person to manage the volume, yet two

Achieving a balance between inventories in centralized or satellite locations can improve customer service, while still reducing overall costs.

people would be staffed for safety reasons, sick days, and vacation. Maintaining consistency across multiple carriers was also very challenging, with their varying procedures, delivery times, and formal reporting capabilities.

Xerox employed a two-pronged approach. To begin, the parts ordering system was centralized in a St. John, N.B., call centre. Next, Xerox went looking for a strategic partner to manage the depot network. By outsourcing, labour and facility costs for each depot could be spread across several firms to make such a vast network economically feasible. Xerox's partner was Progistix, and the contract included gain sharing—as Progistix added clients to its network, the Xerox share of total costs for the depot network was reduced.

Now, technicians looking for critical parts check in with the central call centre and provide the shipping address. Once Xerox's mainframe identifies the closest depot with the part, it sends the order by EDI link to Progistix, which, in turn, prints out the order at the appropriate depot. Because inventory accuracy is vitally important to maintain service, inventory variances between Xerox and its outsourcing partner are compared and resolved daily. Xerox also tracks the time between when the order came in and delivery.

The results speak for themselves: Canadian inventory has been cut in half in just 12 months, and the service level has risen to 98 percent. Gallina adds, "But we're not completely satisfied yet and we are going to continue to look for further reductions. That's obviously going to be a challenge, so we need to be thinking how we can do things differently."

Source: Lou Smyrlis, "Mission Critical," *Canadian Transportation & Logistics*, vol. 105, no. 5, pp. 20–22, 36. Reprinted with permission of Lou Smyrlis, Editorial Director, *Canadian Transportation & Logistics*.

Inventory management is an important concern for managers in all types of businesses. **Inventory** is a stock of items used to satisfy customer demand or support the production of goods or services. For companies that operate on relatively low profit margins, poor inventory management can seriously undermine the business. The challenge is not to pare inventories to the bone to reduce costs or to have plenty around to satisfy all demands, but to have the right amount to achieve the competitive priorities for the business most efficiently. In this chapter, we first introduce the basic concepts of inventory management for all types of businesses and then discuss inventory control systems appropriate for retail and distribution inventories.

inventory A stock of items, including materials, orders, information, and people, that flow through or are used in a process to satisfy customer demand.

INVENTORY CONCEPTS

Inventory is created when items, including materials, parts, or finished goods are received faster than they are disbursed. Considered more generally, items can also include customer orders waiting to be processed, called an *order backlog*, or customers waiting in a service process (see Supplement 4S, "Waiting Lines"). In this section, the focus is on materials, and we identify the pressures for high and low inventories, define the different types of inventory, discuss tactics that can be used to reduce inventories when appropriate, identify the trade-offs involved in making manufacturing inventory placement decisions, and discuss how to identify the inventory items needing the most attention.

PRESSURES FOR LOW INVENTORIES

An inventory manager's job is to balance the conflicting costs and pressures that argue for both low and high inventories and determine appropriate inventory levels. There are two primary reasons for keeping inventories low. First, inventory represents a temporary monetary investment in goods on which a firm must pay (rather than receive) interest. Second, as inventory in a process increases, the total time required for items to pass through the process, called *throughput time*, increases (Chapter 4, "Capacity"). As a result, customer responsiveness slows for service processes or make-to-order products.

inventory holding cost The variable cost of keeping items on hand, including interest, storage and handling, taxes, insurance, and shrinkage.

Inventory holding cost or carrying cost is the variable cost of keeping items on hand, including interest, storage and handling, taxes, insurance, and shrinkage. When these components change with inventory levels, so does the holding cost. Companies usually state an item's holding cost per period of time as a percent of its value. The annual cost to maintain one unit in inventory typically ranges from 20 percent to 40 percent of its value. Suppose that a firm's holding cost is 30 percent. If the average value of total inventory is 20 percent of sales, the average annual cost to hold inventory is 0.30(0.20) = 6 percent of total sales. This cost is sizable in terms of gross profit margins, which often are less than 10 percent. Thus, the components of holding cost create pressures for low inventories.

COST OF CAPITAL. The cost of capital is the opportunity cost of investing in an asset relative to the expected return on assets of similar risk. Inventory is an asset; consequently, we should use a cost measure that adequately reflects the firm's approach to financing assets. Most firms use the *weighted average cost of capital (WACC)*, which is the average of the required return on a firm's stock equity and the interest rate on its debt, weighted by the proportion of equity and debt in its portfolio. The cost of capital usually is the largest component of holding cost, and is as high as 15 percent, depending on the particular capitalization portfolio of the firm. Firms typically update the WACC on an annual basis because it is used to make many financial decisions.

STORAGE AND HANDLING COSTS. Inventory takes up space and must be moved into and out of storage. Storage and handling costs may be incurred when a firm rents space on either a long- or a short-term basis. There also is an opportunity cost for storage when a firm could use storage space productively in some other way.

TAXES, INSURANCE, AND SHRINKAGE. More taxes are paid if end-of-year inventories are high, and insurance on assets increases when there is more to insure. Shrinkage takes three forms. Pilferage, or theft of inventory by customers or employees, is a significant percentage of sales for some businesses. Obsolescence occurs when inventory cannot be used or sold at full value, owing to model changes, engineering modifications, or unexpectedly low demand. Obsolescence is a big expense in retail clothing, where drastic discounts on seasonal clothing must be offered at the end of a season. Finally, deterioration through physical spoilage or damage results in lost value. Food and beverages, for example, lose value and might even have to be discarded when their shelf life is reached. When the rate of deterioration is high, building large inventories may be unwise.

PRESSURES FOR HIGH INVENTORIES

Given the costs of holding inventory, why not eliminate it altogether? Let us look briefly at the pressures related to maintaining inventories.

CUSTOMER SERVICE. Creating finished goods inventory can speed delivery and improve on-time delivery. Inventory reduces the potential for stockouts and backorders, which are key concerns of wholesalers and retailers. A **stockout** occurs when an item that is typically stocked is not available to satisfy a demand the moment it occurs, resulting in loss of the sale. A **backorder** is a customer order that cannot be filled when promised or demanded but is filled later. Customers may be willing to wait for a backorder, but next time they may take their business elsewhere. Sometimes customers are given discounts for the inconvenience of waiting.

ORDERING COST. Each time a firm places a new order, it incurs an **ordering cost,** or the cost of preparing a purchase order for a supplier or a production order for the shop. For the same item, the ordering cost is the same, regardless of the order size: the purchasing agent must take the time to decide how much to order and, perhaps, select a supplier and negotiate terms. Time also is spent on paperwork, followup, and receiving. In the case of a production order for a manufactured item, a blueprint and routing instructions often must accompany the shop order. The Internet can help streamline the order process and reduce the costs of placing orders.

SETUP COST. The cost involved in changing over an operation to produce a different component or item is the **setup cost.** It includes labour and time to make the changeover, cleaning, and new tools or fixtures. Scrap or rework costs can be substantially higher at the start of the run. Generally, setup cost also is independent of order size, so there is pressure to order a large supply of the component and hold it in inventory. Setup costs also are present in services, where, for example, an airline must set up each aircraft for each batch of customers taking a new flight.

LABOUR AND EQUIPMENT UTILIZATION. By creating more inventory, management can increase workforce productivity and facility utilization in three ways, all of which are related to reducing variability (see Chapter 4, "Capacity"). First, placing larger, less frequent production orders reduces the number of unproductive setups, which add no

stockout An item that is typically stocked is not available to satisfy a demand the moment it occurs, resulting in the loss of the sale.

backorder A customer order that cannot be filled when promised or demanded but is filled later.

ordering cost The cost of preparing a purchase order for a supplier or a production order for the shop.

setup cost The cost involved in changing over an operation to produce a different component, item, or service.

value to a product or service. Second, holding inventory reduces the chance of costly rescheduling of production orders, because the components needed to make the product are not in inventory. Third, building inventories improves resource utilization by stabilizing the output rate for industries when demand is cyclical or seasonal. The firm uses inventory built during slack periods to handle extra demand in peak seasons and minimizes the need for extra shifts, hiring, layoffs, overtime, and additional equipment.

TRANSPORTATION COST. Sometimes outbound transportation cost can be reduced by increasing inventory levels. Having inventory on hand allows more full-load shipments and minimizes the need to expedite shipments by more expensive modes of transportation. Forward placement of inventory can also reduce outbound transportation cost, even though the pooling effect is lessened and more inventory is necessary. Inbound transportation cost also may be reduced by creating more inventory. Sometimes several items are ordered from the same supplier. Combining these orders and placing them at the same time may lead to rate discounts, thereby decreasing the costs of transportation and raw materials.

PAYMENTS TO SUPPLIERS. A firm often can reduce total payments to suppliers if it can tolerate higher inventory levels. Suppose that a firm learns that a key supplier is about to increase prices. It might be cheaper for the firm to order a larger quantity than usual—in effect delaying the price increase—even though inventory will increase temporarily. Similarly, a firm can take advantage of quantity discounts. A **quantity discount**, whereby the price per unit drops when the order is sufficiently large, is an incentive to order larger quantities. Quantity discounts are frequently offered by suppliers to reduce their ordering and setup costs.

quantity discount A drop in the price per unit when the order is sufficiently large.

FUNCTIONS OF INVENTORY

Another perspective on inventory is to classify it by how and why it is created. In this context, there are five functions of inventory for an item: safety stock, decoupling, anticipation, cycle, and pipeline. They cannot be identified physically; that is, a manager can't look at a pile of half-assembled computers or customers and see any difference between items that function as cycle inventory or as safety stock inventory. However, conceptually, each of the five types comes into being in an entirely different way. Once you understand these differences, you can prescribe different ways to reduce inventory, which we discuss in the next section.

safety stock inventory Inventory held to protect against uncertainties and random variation in demand, lead time, processing time, quality, and supply.

SAFETY STOCK INVENTORY. To avoid customer service problems and the hidden costs of unavailable components, companies hold safety stock to act as a buffer. **Safety stock inventory** protects against unexpected variation or uncertainty in demand, lead time, processing time, and supply. Safety stocks are desirable when suppliers fail to deliver the desired quantity on the specified date with acceptable quality or when manufactured items have significant amounts of scrap or rework. In addition, safety stock also accommodates random variability that happens with individual operations. For example, a machine may break down or an employee be may be required to handle a particularly difficult customer. Having safety stock as a buffer is critical ahead of a process bottleneck, as discussed in Chapter 4, "Capacity," to maintain process output. Safety stock inventory ensures that upstream and downstream operations are not disrupted when such problems occur, allowing operations to continue.

To create safety stock, one option is to place an order for delivery earlier than when the item is typically needed. The replenishment order, therefore, arrives ahead of time, giving a cushion against uncertainty. For example, suppose that the average lead time from a supplier is three weeks but a firm orders five weeks in advance just to be safe. This policy creates a safety stock equal to a two weeks' supply $(5 - 3)$. Another option is to order or hold extra items based on the degree of variability.

decoupling inventory
Inventory held to accommodate different rates or patterns of production between two operations.

DECOUPLING INVENTORY. To accommodate the different processing rates of individual operations in a process, **decoupling inventory** can be used to smooth the flow of items. These different processing rates are reasonably certain and may occur because of the "lumpiness" of investing in capacity at any individual operation. Other factors include the scheduling of preventive maintenance or changes in process choice (e.g., changing from batch process in fabrication to line process for final assembly). Unlike safety stock, decoupling inventory accommodates predictable variation. For example, a plastic moulding machine produces 100 parts per hour, but people assemble the final product at 50 parts per hour. As a result, parts are held between operations to balance production rates and moulding is shut down periodically.

anticipation inventory
Inventory used to absorb uneven, but predictable, rates of demand or supply.

ANTICIPATION INVENTORY. Inventory used to absorb predictable, uneven rates of demand or supply, which businesses often face, is referred to as **anticipation inventory**. Seasonal demand patterns lend themselves to the use of anticipation inventory. Manufacturers of air conditioners, for example, can experience 90 percent of their annual demand during just three months of a year. Such uneven demand may lead a manufacturer to stockpile anticipation inventory during periods of low demand so that output levels do not have to be increased much when demand peaks. Smoothing output rates with inventory can increase productivity because varying output rates and workforce size can be costly. Anticipation inventory also can help when supply, rather than demand, is uneven. A company may stock up on a certain purchased item if its suppliers are threatened with a strike or have severe capacity limitations.

cycle inventory The portion of total inventory that varies directly with lot size.

lot sizing The determination of how frequently and in what quantity to order inventory.

CYCLE INVENTORY. The portion of total inventory that varies directly with lot size is called **cycle inventory**. Determining how frequently to order, and in what quantity, is called **lot sizing**. The quantity ordered or produced is called a *lot* or *batch*. Two principles apply:

1. The lot size, Q, varies directly with the elapsed time (or cycle) between orders. If a lot is ordered every five weeks, the average lot size must equal five weeks' demand.

2. The longer the time between orders for a given item, the greater the cycle inventory must be.

At the beginning of the interval, the cycle inventory is at its maximum, or Q. At the end of the interval, just before a new lot arrives, cycle inventory drops to its minimum, or 0. The average cycle inventory is the average of these two extremes:

$$\text{Average cycle inventory } = \frac{Q + 0}{2} = \frac{Q}{2}$$

This formula is exact only when the demand rate is constant and uniform. However, it does provide a reasonably good estimate even when demand rates are not constant. Factors other than the demand rate (e.g., scrap losses) also may cause estimating errors when this simple formula is used.

pipeline inventory
Inventory moving from point to point in the materials flow system.

PIPELINE INVENTORY. Items moving from point to point in a process are called **pipeline inventory**. Materials move from suppliers to a plant, from one operation to the next in the plant, from the plant to a distribution centre or customer, and from the distribution centre to a retailer. Pipeline inventory consists of orders that have been placed but not yet received. For example, a manufacturer of decorative glass panels in British Columbia uses glass and parts produced in China and India. Although shipments arrive periodically at the plant, the transportation lead time requires a pipeline inventory of parts en route from the international locations at all times. Pipeline inventory between two points, for crashing transportation or production, can be measured as the average demand during lead time, $\overline{D}_L$, which is the average demand for the item per period (d) times the number of periods in the item's lead time (L) to move between the two points, or:

$$\text{Pipeline inventory} = \overline{D}_L = dL$$

Note that the lot size does not directly affect the average level of the pipeline inventory. Increasing Q inflates the size of each order, so if an order has been placed but not received, there is more pipeline inventory for that lead time. But that increase is cancelled by a proportionate decrease in the number of orders placed per year. The lot size can *indirectly* affect pipeline inventory, however, if increasing Q causes the lead time to increase. Here $\overline{D}_L$ and, therefore, pipeline inventory will increase. See Solved Problem 1 on page 225 for a detailed example of how to estimate the various types of inventory.

INVENTORY REDUCTION TACTICS

Managers always are eager to find cost-effective ways to reduce inventory. Later in this chapter, we examine various ways of finding optimal lot sizes (see also Supplement H, "Special Inventory Models," on the Student CD-ROM). Here we discuss something more fundamental—the basic tactics (which we call *levers*) for reducing inventory. A primary lever is one that must be activated if inventory is to be reduced. A secondary lever reduces the penalty cost of applying the primary lever and the need for having inventory in the first place.

SAFETY STOCK INVENTORY. The primary lever for reducing safety stock inventory is to reduce random variation, including the uncertainty found in demand, supply, delivery, and operations. Four secondary levers can be used:

1. Improve demand forecasts so that fewer surprises come from customers. Customers also can be encouraged to order items before they need them.

2. Cut lead times of purchased or produced items to reduce demand uncertainty during lead time. For example, local suppliers with short lead times could be selected whenever possible.

3. Reduce supply uncertainties. Suppliers may be more reliable if production plans are shared with them, permitting them to make more realistic forecasts. Analyzing supplier risk may allow reductions where low risks are present. Surprises from unexpected scrap or rework can be reduced by improving manufacturing processes. Preventive maintenance can minimize unexpected downtime caused by equipment failure.

4. Rely more on a capacity cushion of equipment and labour, including more flexible equipment and cross-trained workers. These cushions are particularly critical in services where customers are willing to wait only a very short time.

DECOUPLING INVENTORY. The primary lever for reducing decoupling inventory is to reduce predictable variation. Secondary levers emphasize better coordination and adjusting the output rate of individual operations.

1. More closely aligned schedules can be implemented. This usually translates into taking more frequent, but shorter, reductions in output from a higher-capacity operation. For example, rather than simply scheduling an entire shift for preventive maintenance while other operations continue, more frequent but shorter periods of preventive maintenance reduce the quantity amount of decoupling inventory needed.

2. The production rate of individual, higher-output operations might be slowed to more closely match the overall output rate of the system. This may also improve quality at the higher-capacity operations, as people and equipment are not required to work at the maximum output rate.

ANTICIPATION INVENTORY. The primary lever for reducing anticipation inventory is to better match the demand and production rates. Secondary levers are used to level customer demand in one of the following ways:

1. Add new products with different demand cycles so that a peak in the demand for one product compensates for the seasonal low in another.

2. Provide off-season promotional campaigns.

3. Offer seasonal pricing plans.

CYCLE INVENTORY. The primary lever is simply to reduce the lot size. Methods of lean systems (see Chapter 10, "Lean Systems") use small lots relative to traditional lot sizes, which might equal several weeks' (or even months') supply. However, making such reductions in Q without making any other changes can be devastating. For example, setup costs can skyrocket, which leads to use of the two secondary levers.

1. Streamline methods for placing orders and making setups, which reduces ordering and setup costs and allows Q to be reduced.

repeatability The degree to which the same work can be done again.

2. Increase repeatability to eliminate the need for changeovers. **Repeatability** is the degree to which the same work can be done again. It can be increased through high product demand; use of specialization; devoting resources exclusively to a product; using the same part in many different products; flexible automation; the one-worker, multiple-machines concept; or group technology (see Chapter 2, "Process Management" and Chapter 7, "Location and Layout"). Increased repeatability may justify new setup methods, reduce transportation costs, and allow quantity discounts from suppliers.

PIPELINE INVENTORY. An operations manager has direct control over lead time but not demand rate. Because pipeline inventory is a function of demand during lead time, the primary lever is to reduce the lead time. Two secondary levers can help managers cut lead times:

1. Find more responsive suppliers and select new carriers for shipments between stocking locations or improve materials handling within the plant. Introducing a computer system could overcome information delays between a distribution centre and retailer.

2. Decrease Q, at least in those cases in which lead time depends on lot size. Smaller jobs generally require less time to complete.

PLACEMENT OF MANUFACTURING INVENTORIES

The positioning of a firm's inventories supports its competitive priorities. Inventories can be held at the raw materials, work-in-process, and finished goods levels. In general, managers make inventory placement decisions on the basis of two basic factors: process structure and product characteristics. Naturally, these factors are related, and their interaction creates unique challenges and opportunities for individual companies. It must be emphasized that placement refers to the *relative allocation* of inventory across a process, as there are still other pressures that drive managers to increase or decrease overall inventory levels.

Recall that process structure is related to the degree of product customization. In general, a product may be considered to be a *special* or a *standard*. A **special** is an item made to order or, if purchased, bought to order. Just enough of the item is ordered or processed to cover the latest customer request. In contrast, a **standard** is an item made to stock and normally available when needed. When a company makes more of its items as standards, particularly at the finished goods level, it tends to place inventory closer to the customer. Inventory held toward the finished goods level means short delivery times—but a higher dollar investment in inventory. Alternatively, holding inventory at the raw materials level would reduce the cost of carrying inventory—but at the expense of the quick customer response time.

Product characteristics also influence inventory management in a company. If a process has few raw materials and creates many finished goods, such as a petroleum refinery, managers prefer to hold inventory in raw materials as long as possible. In contrast, if many raw materials are used to produce only a few final products, such as automobile assembly, shifting inventory to finished goods improves customer responsiveness. Finally, if a small number of modules (each of which has many raw materials) is needed to create a wide variety of products, the largest allocation of inventory is usually in intermediate modules. For example, computer manufacturing relies on the assembly of a relatively small number of modules. The rationale behind these allocations is based on inventory pooling, where variability from demand is reduced.

Inventory placement can change over time as an operations strategy develops and process choice evolves. For example, McDonald's recently changed from a make-to-stock process, where finished hamburgers were held in inventory, to an assemble-to-order process, where cooked hamburger patties are held in inventory. This new placement enables greater customization and delivery of fresher final products.

IDENTIFYING CRITICAL INVENTORY ITEMS WITH ABC ANALYSIS

Thousands of items are held in inventory by a typical organization, but only a small percentage of them deserves management's closest attention and tightest control. **ABC analysis** divides items into three classes according to their dollar usage so that managers can focus on items that have the highest dollar value. This method is the equivalent of creating a *Pareto chart* except that it is applied to inventory rather than process defects. As Figure 6.1 shows, class A items typically represent only about 20 percent of the items but account for 80 percent of the dollar usage. Class B items account for another 30 percent of the items but only 15 percent of the dollar usage. Finally, 50 percent of the items fall in class C, representing a mere 5 percent of the dollar usage. The goal of ABC analysis is to identify the inventory levels of class A items and enable management to control them tightly by using the levers just discussed.

The analysis begins by multiplying the annual demand rate for one item by the dollar value (cost) of one unit to determine its dollar usage. After ranking the items on the basis of dollar usage and creating the Pareto chart, the analyst looks for "natural" changes in slope. The dividing lines in Figure 6.1 between classes are only approximate.

special An item made to order; if purchased, it is bought to order.

standard An item made to stock and normally available when needed.

ABC analysis The method of dividing items into three classes according to their dollar usage so that managers can focus on items that have the highest dollar value.

FIGURE 6.1

Typical Chart from ABC Analysis

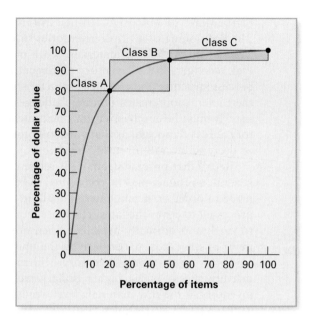

Class A items could be somewhat higher or lower than 20 percent of all items, but normally account for the bulk of the dollar usage.

A manager can direct that class A items be reviewed frequently to reduce the average lot size and keep inventory records current. Class B items are candidates for systems where purchase or replenishment decisions can be programmed. Finally, a stockout of a class C item can be as crucial as for a class A or B item, but the inventory holding cost of class C items tends to be low. These features suggest that higher inventory levels can be tolerated and that more safety stock, larger lot sizes, and perhaps even a visual system, which we discuss later, may suffice for class C items. See Solved Problem 2 on page 225 for a detailed example of ABC analysis.

ECONOMIC ORDER QUANTITY

economic order quantity (EOQ) The lot size that minimizes total annual inventory holding and ordering costs.

Recall that managers face conflicting pressures to keep inventories low enough to avoid excess inventory holding costs but high enough to reduce the frequency of orders and setups. A good starting point for balancing these conflicting pressures and determining the best cycle-inventory level for an item is finding the **economic order quantity (EOQ)**, which is the lot size that minimizes total annual inventory holding and ordering costs. The approach to determining the EOQ is based on the following assumptions:

1. The demand rate for the item is constant (e.g., always 10 units per day) and known with certainty.

2. There are no constraints (e.g., truck capacity or materials handling limitations) on the size of each lot.

3. The only two relevant costs are the inventory holding cost and the fixed cost per lot for ordering or setup.

4. Decisions for one item can be made independently of decisions for other items (i.e., no advantage is gained in combining several orders going to the same supplier and the demand for one item is not directly linked to another item).

5. There is no uncertainty in lead time or supply. The lead time is constant (e.g., always 14 days) and known with certainty. The amount received is exactly what was ordered and it arrives all at once rather than piecemeal.

The economic order quantity will be optimal when the five assumptions are satisfied. In reality, few situations are so simple and well behaved. In fact, different lot-sizing approaches are needed to reflect quantity discounts, uneven demand rates, or interactions between items (see Supplement H, "Special Inventory Models," on the Student CD-ROM). However, the EOQ is often a reasonable first approximation of average lot sizes, even when one or more of the assumptions do not quite apply.

CALCULATING THE EOQ

We begin by formulating the total cost for any lot size, Q. Next, we derive the EOQ, which is the Q that minimizes total cost. Finally, we describe how to convert the EOQ into a companion measure, the elapsed time between orders.

When the EOQ assumptions are satisfied, cycle inventory behaves as shown in Figure 6.2. A cycle begins with Q units held in inventory, which happens when a new order is received. During the cycle, on-hand inventory is used at a constant rate and, because demand is known with certainty and the lead time is a constant, a new lot can be ordered so that inventory falls to 0 precisely when the new lot is received. Because inventory varies uniformly between Q and 0, the average cycle inventory equals half the lot size, Q.

FIGURE 6.2

Cycle Inventory Levels

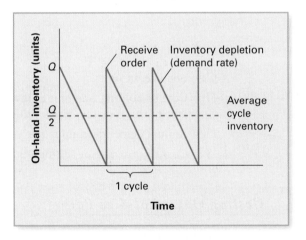

The annual holding cost for this amount of inventory, which increases linearly with Q, as Figure 6.3(a) shows, is:

Annual holding cost = (Average cycle inventory)(Unit holding cost)

The annual ordering cost is:

Annual ordering or setup cost = (Number of orders/year)(Ordering or setup cost)

The average number of orders per year equals annual demand divided by Q. For example, if 1200 units must be ordered each year and the average lot size is 100 units, then 12 orders will be placed during the year. The annual ordering or setup cost decreases nonlinearly as Q increases, as shown in Figure 6.3(b), because fewer orders are placed.

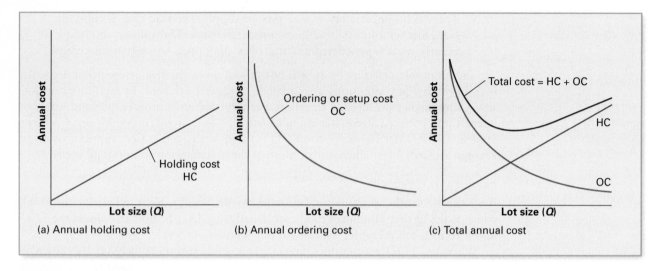

FIGURE 6.3

Total Inventory Cost

The total annual cost,[1] as graphed in Figure 6.3(c), is the sum of the two cost components:[2]

Total annual cost = Annual holding cost + Annual ordering or setup cost

$$C = \frac{Q}{2}\,(H) + \frac{D}{Q}\,(S)$$

where:

C = Total cost per year

Q = Lot size, in units

H = Cost of holding one unit in inventory for a year, often calculated as a proportion of the item's value

D = Annual demand, in units per year

S = Cost of ordering or setting up one lot, in dollars per lot

EXAMPLE 6.1

Costing Out a Lot-Size Policy

A museum of natural history opened a gift shop two years ago. Managing inventories has become a problem, however. Low inventory turnover is squeezing profit margins and causing cash-flow problems.

One of the top-selling items in the container group at the museum's gift shop is a birdfeeder. Sales are 18 units per week, and the supplier charges $60 per unit. The cost of placing an order with the supplier is $45. Annual holding cost is 25 percent of a feeder's value, and the museum operates 52 weeks per year. Managment chose a 390-unit lot size so that new orders could be placed less frequently. What is the annual cost of the current policy of using a 390-unit lot size? Would a lot size of 468 be better?

---

[1]Expressing the total cost on an annual basis usually is convenient (though not necessary). Any time horizon can be selected, as long as D and H cover the same time period. If the total cost is calculated on a monthly basis, D must be monthly demand and H must be the cost of holding a unit for one month.

[2]The number of orders actually placed in any year is always a whole number, although the formula allows the use of fractional values. However, rounding is not needed, because what is being calculated is an average for multiple years. Such averages need not be integers.

SOLUTION

We begin by computing the annual demand and holding cost as

$$D = (18 \text{ units/week})(52 \text{ weeks/year}) = 936 \text{ units}$$

$$H = 0.25(\$60/\text{unit}) = \$15 \text{ per unit per year}$$

The total annual cost for the current policy is

$$C = \frac{Q}{2}(H) + \frac{D}{Q}(S)$$

$$C = \frac{390}{2}(\$15) + \frac{936}{390}(\$45) = \$2925 + \$108 = \$3033$$

The total annual cost for the alternative lot size is

$$C = \frac{468}{2}(\$15) + \frac{936}{468}(\$45) = \$3510 + \$90 = \$3600$$

Decision Point The lot size of 468 units, which is a half-year supply, would be a more expensive option than the current policy. The savings in order costs are more than offset by the increase in holding costs. Management should use the total annual cost equation to explore other lot-size alternatives.

Taken a few steps further, Figure 6.4 displays the impact of using several Q values for the birdfeeder. Eight different lot sizes were evaluated in addition to the current one. Both holding and ordering costs were plotted, but their sum—the total cost curve—is the important feature. The graph shows that the best lot size, namely the EOQ, is the lowest point on the total cost curve, or between 50 and 100 units. Obviously, reducing the current lot-size policy ($Q = 390$) can result in significant savings.

A more efficient approach is to use the EOQ formula:

$$\text{EOQ} = \sqrt{\frac{2DS}{H}}$$

FIGURE 6.4

Total Inventory Cost Function for Birdfeeder

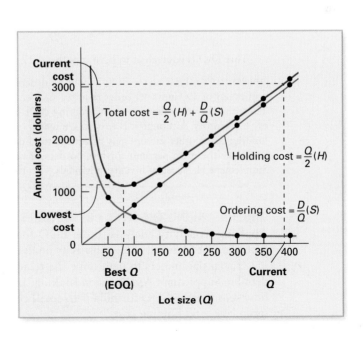

Using basic calculus, we obtain the EOQ from the minimum of the total cost formula. (Take the first derivative of the total cost function with respect to Q, set it equal to 0, and solve for Q.) As Figure 6.4 indicates, the EOQ is the order quantity for which annual holding cost equals annual ordering cost. This is mirrored in Figure 6.4; when the annual holding cost for any Q exceeds the annual ordering cost, as with the 390-unit order, we can immediately conclude that Q is too big. A smaller Q reduces holding cost and increases ordering cost, bringing them into balance. Similarly, if the annual ordering cost exceeds the annual holding cost, Q should be increased.

time between orders (TBO) The average elapsed time between receiving (or placing) replenishment orders.

Sometimes inventory policies are based on the time between replenishment orders, rather than on the number of units in the lot size. The **time between orders (TBO)** is the average elapsed time between receiving (or placing) replenishment orders. For a particular lot size, Q, the TBO_Q is simply Q divided by annual demand. However, the TBO can be stated in any period of time, as demonstrated in Example 6.2, by using demand over that time period.

When we use the EOQ, the TBO is:

$$\text{TBO}_{\text{EOQ}} = \frac{\text{EOQ}}{D}$$

EXAMPLE 6.2

Finding the EOQ, Total Cost, and TBO

Using information about the birdfeeder (Example 6.1), calculate the EOQ and its total cost. How frequently will orders be placed if the EOQ is used?

SOLUTION

Using the formulas for EOQ and annual cost, we get:

$$\text{EOQ} = \sqrt{\frac{2DS}{H}} = \sqrt{\frac{2(936)(45)}{15}} = 74.94 \quad \text{or} \quad 75 \text{ units}$$

When the EOQ is used, the time between orders (TBO) can be expressed in various ways for the same time period.

$$\text{TBO}_{\text{EOQ}} = \frac{\text{EOQ}}{D} = \frac{75}{936} = 0.080 \text{ year}$$

This TBO is equivalent to 0.96 months, 4.17 weeks, and 29.25 days.

Decision Point Using the EOQ, about 12 orders per year will be required. In contrast, the current policy of 390 units per order requires an average of 2.4 orders each year (every five months). Thus, the current policy saves on ordering costs but incurs a much larger cost for carrying the cycle inventory. Although it is easy to see which option is best on the basis of total ordering and holding costs, other factors may affect the final decision. For example, if the supplier is willing to reduce the price per unit for large orders, it may be better to order the larger quantity (see Supplement H, "Special Inventory Models," on the Student CD-ROM).

UNDERSTANDING THE EFFECT OF CHANGES

Applying sensitivity analysis to the EOQ formula can yield valuable insights into the management of inventories. Sensitivity analysis is a technique for systematically changing crucial parameters to determine the relative effects of change (discussed in greater detail in Supplement A, "Decision Making"). In essence, this technique allows us to see how sensitive the EOQ formula is to small changes, errors or uncertainties in demand, setup cost, and holding cost.

CHANGE IN THE DEMAND RATE. Because D is in the numerator, the EOQ (and, therefore, the best cycle-inventory level) increases in proportion to the square root of the annual demand. Therefore, when demand rises, the lot size also rises, but at a much slower rate than demand. For example, a 50 percent increase in demand translates into only a 22 percent increase in the EOQ.

CHANGE IN THE SETUP COSTS. As with demand, S is in the numerator, so increasing S increases the EOQ and, consequently, the average cycle inventory. Conversely, reducing S reduces the EOQ, allowing smaller lot sizes to be produced economically. This relationship explains why manufacturers are so concerned about cutting setup time and costs. When weeks of supply decline, inventory turns increase. When setup cost and setup time become trivial, a major impediment to small-lot production is removed.

CHANGE IN THE HOLDING COSTS. Because H is in the denominator, the EOQ declines when H increases. Conversely, when H declines, the EOQ increases. Larger lot sizes are justified by lower holding costs.

ERRORS IN ESTIMATING *D, H,* AND *S.* Total cost is fairly insensitive to errors, even when the estimates are wrong by a large margin. The reasons are that errors tend to cancel each other out and that the square root reduces the effect of the error. Suppose that we incorrectly estimate the holding cost to be double its true value—that is, we calculate EOQ using 2H, instead of H. For Example 6.2, this 100 percent error increases total cost by only 6 percent, from $1124 to $1192. Thus, the EOQ lies in a fairly large zone of acceptable lot sizes, allowing managers to deviate somewhat from the EOQ to accommodate supplier contracts or storage constraints. See Solved Problems 3 and 4 (pages 226 and 227) for two examples demonstrating the sensitivity of order quantity decisions and total annual costs in the face of parameter estimation errors.

INVENTORY CONTROL SYSTEMS

The EOQ and other lot-sizing methods (see Supplement H, "Special Inventory Models," on the Student CD-ROM) answer the important question: How much should we order? Another important question that needs an answer is: When should we place the order? An inventory control system responds to both questions. In selecting an inventory control system for a particular application, the nature of the demands imposed on the inventory items is crucial. An important distinction between types of inventory is whether an item is subject to dependent or independent demand. Retailers and distributors must manage **independent demand items**—that is, items for which demand is influenced by market conditions and is not related to the inventory decisions for any other item held in stock. Independent demand inventory includes:

independent demand items Items for which demand is influenced by market conditions and is not related to the inventory decisions for any other item held in stock.

1. Wholesale and retail merchandise, as described for Source Medical in the Managerial Practice feature

2. Service industry inventory, such as stamps and mailing labels for post offices, office supplies for law firms, and laboratory supplies for research universities

3. End-item and replacement-part distribution inventories

4. Maintenance, repair, and operating (MRO) supplies—that is, items that don't become part of the final product or service, such as employee uniforms, fuel, paint, and machine repair parts

MANAGERIAL PRACTICE
Inventories Are Critical to Patient Care

Source Medical is Canada's largest national distributor of medical and surgical products, and strives to provide value as a "one-stop" shop for many hospitals and health-care providers. Using more than 400 suppliers, the company is able to fulfill approximately 85 percent of a hospital's medical and surgical product requirements for everything from bandages to operating tables. In 2001, more than 600 employees handled $600 million of product through its automated information and warehouse systems.

A two-year initiative has focused on making inventory and service improvements in their warehousing operations. Although revenues have experienced double-digit growth during that time, inventory has been reduced by 15 percent and service levels have improved. For example, the number of items supplied when first ordered has risen by 8 percent.

Essentially, the company went back to the basics to achieve these inventory and service improvements. "We really took a hard look at what our inventory requirements were. We wanted a certain amount of inventory that would ride the small bumps," says Brian Cox, vice-president. "We also wanted our inventory to be able to absorb the demand fluctuations. The next step was to understand the exceptions that are outside of those two operating parameters—either too much inventory or low inventory. So, we established an exception management process ... to find failures in the supply chain."

Today, Source Medical distributes its product items to customers nationally through nine regional warehouses. The largest warehouse, located in Mississauga, Ontario, is more than 23 000 square metres in area and operates 24 hours per day with three shifts. Approximately 30 to 35 full truckloads and 50 to 60 less-than-truckload shipments arrive every day. In total, the facility has about 30 000 individual items.

The warehouse makes extensive use of inventory profiling—based on ABC analysis—using sales volume, item value, and physical size. This analysis quickly identified the need for two very different areas in one warehouse. About 2000 high-volume, full-case items are held in one area, and another 28 000 "must have" items in another. Finally, there are a number of "direct buy" items that aren't stored in the warehouse at all, but instead are matched with an in-out

High-reach lift trucks are used to store and retrieve medical supplies.

document, cross-docked, and turned around for immediate delivery.

Inside the warehouse, a radio frequency system and bar-code scanners are used to manage receiving, replenishment, and order picking, which is based on customer delivery routes. To reduce costs and achieve a high level of customer satisfaction, picking performance must be closely monitored, and overall accuracy is close to 99.8 percent. Pickers are also assigned to a specific section of the facility on the basis of their product knowledge and individual abilities. This helps expedite picking and ensures fast product replenishment, both of which are critical to having the right supplies available for patient care.

As Source Medical strives to be at the forefront of services for Canada's health-care industry, effective inventory management offers a core competitive advantage.

Source: Adapted with permission: Robert Robertson, "Saving Lives," *Materials Management and Distribution,* vol. 47, no. 5 (July 1, 2002), pp. 14–20; Additional information from company Web site (www.sourcemedical.com), accessed April 7, 2003.

Managing independent demand inventory can be tricky, because demand is influenced by external factors. For example, the owner of a bookstore may not be sure how many copies of the latest bestseller customers will purchase during the coming month. As a result, she may decide to stock extra copies as a safeguard. Independent demand such as the demand for various book titles must be forecasted. The chapter opener illustrates how Xerox Canada made significant inventory reductions through improved forecasting.

In this chapter, we focus on inventory control systems for independent demand items, which is the type of demand the bookstore owner, other retailers, and distributors face. Even though demand from any one customer is difficult to predict, low demand from some customers is often offset by high demand from others. Thus, total demand for any independent demand item may follow a relatively smooth pattern, with some random fluctuations. *Dependent demand items* are those required as components or inputs to a product or service. Dependent demand exhibits a pattern very different from that of independent demand and must be managed with different techniques (see Chapter 13, "Resource Planning").

In this section, we discuss and compare two inventory control systems: the continuous review system, called a Q system, and the periodic review system, called a P system. We close with a look at hybrid systems, which incorporate features of both the P and the Q systems.

CONTINUOUS REVIEW (Q) SYSTEM

continuous review (Q) system *or* **reorder point (ROP) system** A system designed to track the remaining inventory of an item every time a withdrawal is made to determine whether it is time to replenish.

inventory position (IP) The net quantity of an item available to satisfy future demand.

scheduled receipts (SR) Orders that have been placed but not yet received. Also termed *open orders*.

reorder point (R) The predetermined minimum level that an inventory position must reach before a fixed quantity Q of the item is ordered.

A **continuous review (Q) system**, sometimes called a **reorder point (ROP) system** or *fixed order-quantity system*, tracks the remaining inventory of an item every time a withdrawal is made to determine whether it is time to reorder. In practice, these reviews are done frequently (e.g., daily) or continuously (after every withdrawal). The advent of computers and electronic cash registers linked to inventory records has made continuous reviews easy. At each review a decision is made about an item's inventory position; if it is judged to be too low, the system triggers a new order. The **inventory position (IP)** measures the net quantity of an item available to satisfy future demand. It includes **scheduled receipts (SR)**, which are orders that have been placed but not yet received, plus on-hand inventory (OH) minus backorders (BO). Sometimes scheduled receipts are called **open orders**. More specifically:

Inventory position = On-hand inventory + Scheduled receipts − Backorders

$$IP = OH + SR - BO$$

When the inventory position reaches a predetermined minimum level, called the **reorder point (R)**, a fixed quantity Q of the item is ordered. In a continuous review system, although the order quantity Q is fixed, the time between orders can vary. Hence, Q can be based on the EOQ, a price break quantity (the minimum lot size that qualifies for a quantity discount), a container size (such as a truckload), or some other quantity selected by management.

SELECTING THE REORDER POINT WHEN DEMAND IS CERTAIN. To demonstrate the concept of a reorder point, suppose that the demand for feeders at the museum gift shop in Example 6.1 is always 18 per week, the lead time is a constant two weeks, and the supplier always ships on time the exact amount ordered. With both demand and lead time certain, the museum's buyer can wait until the inventory position drops to 36 units, or (18 units/week) $\times$ (2 weeks), to place a new order. Thus, in this case, the reorder point, R, equals the *demand during lead time*, with no added allowance for safety stock.

Figure 6.5 shows how the system operates when demand and lead time are constant. The downward-sloping line represents the on-hand inventory, which is being depleted at a constant rate. When it reaches reorder point *R* (the horizontal line), a new order for *Q* units is placed. The on-hand inventory continues to drop throughout lead time *L* until the order is received. At that time, which marks the end of the lead time, on-hand inventory jumps by *Q* units. A new order arrives just when inventory drops to 0. The time between orders (TBO) is the same for each cycle.

The inventory position, IP, shown in Figure 6.5 corresponds to the on-hand inventory, except during the lead time. Just after a new order is placed, at the start of the lead time, IP increases by *Q*, as shown by the dashed line. The IP exceeds OH by this same margin throughout the lead time.[3] At the end of the lead time, when the scheduled receipts convert to on-hand inventory, IP = OH once again. The key point here is to compare IP, not OH, with *R* in deciding whether to reorder. A common error is to ignore scheduled receipts or backorders.

FIGURE 6.5

Q System When Demand and Lead Time Are Constant and Certain

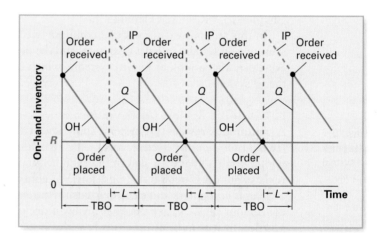

SELECTING THE REORDER POINT WHEN DEMAND IS UNCERTAIN. In reality, demand and lead times are not always predictable. For instance, the museum's buyer knows that *average* demand is 18 feeders per week and that the *average* lead time is two weeks. That is, a variable number of feeders may be purchased during the lead time, with an average demand during lead time of 36 feeders (assuming that each week's demand is identically distributed). This situation gives rise to the need for safety stocks. Suppose that the buyer sets *R* at 46 units, thereby placing orders before they typically are needed. This approach will create a safety stock, or stock held in excess of expected demand, of 10 units (46 − 36) to buffer against uncertain demand. In general:

Reorder point = Average demand during lead time + Safety stock

Figure 6.6 shows how the *Q* system operates when demand is variable and uncertain. We assume that the variability in lead times is negligible and, therefore, can be treated as a constant, as we did in the development of the EOQ model. The wavy downward-sloping line indicates that demand varies from day to day. Its slope is steeper in the second cycle, which means that the demand rate is higher during this time period. The changing demand rate means that the time between orders changes,

---

[3]A possible exception is the unlikely situation when more than one scheduled receipt is open at the same time because of long lead times.

FIGURE 6.6

Q *System When Demand Is Uncertain*

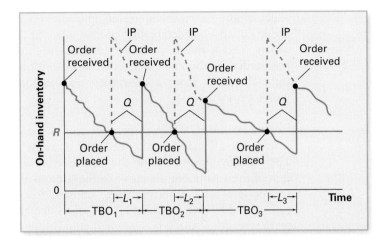

so $TBO_1 \neq TBO_2 \neq TBO_3$. Because of uncertain demand, sales during lead time are unpredictable, and safety stock is added to hedge against lost sales. This addition is why R is higher in Figure 6.6 than in Figure 6.5. It also explains why the on-hand inventory usually doesn't drop to 0 by the time a replenishment order arrives. The greater the safety stock and, thus, the higher reorder point R, the less likely a stockout.

Because the average demand during lead time is variable and uncertain, the real decision to be made when selecting R concerns the safety stock level. Deciding on a small or large safety stock is a trade-off between customer service and inventory holding costs. Cost minimization models can be used to find the best safety stock, but they require estimates of stockout and backorder costs, which are usually difficult to make with any precision. The usual approach for determining R is for management—based on judgment—to set a reasonable service-level policy for the inventory and then determine the safety stock level that satisfies this policy.

CHOOSING AN APPROPRIATE SERVICE-LEVEL POLICY. Managers must weigh the benefits of holding safety stock against the cost of holding it when developing a policy for service level. One way to determine the safety stock is to set a **cycle-service level**—the desired probability of not running out of stock in any one *ordering cycle*, which begins at the time an order is placed and ends when it arrives in stock. In a bookstore, the manager may select a 90 percent service level for a book. In other words, the probability is 90 percent that demand will not exceed the supply *during the lead time*. The probability of running short during the lead time, creating a stockout or backorder, is only 10 percent (100 − 90). This stockout risk, which occurs only during the lead time in the Q system, is greater than the overall risk of stockout because the risk is nonexistent outside the ordering cycle.

To translate this policy into a specific safety stock level, we must know how demand during the lead time is distributed. If demand varies little around its average, safety stock can be small. Conversely, if demand during lead time varies greatly from one order cycle to the next, the safety stock must be large. Variability is measured with probability distributions, which are specified by a mean and a variance.

Another measure of customer service is the fraction of total demand met from on-hand inventory. Fill rate can be expressed at several levels, depending on the needs of the customer. If measured for individual items, the **item fill rate** is the quantity of a particular item that is delivered from inventory, relative to the total demand for that item. At a more general level, customers that frequently order multiple items per

cycle-service level The desired probability of not running out of stock in any one ordering cycle, which begins at the time an order is placed and ends when it arrives in stock.

item fill rate Percentage of demand for an item that is met from on-hand inventory, relative to the total demand for that item.

order might be more interested in *order fill rate*, which captures the number of orders filled completely (no partly filled or backordered items) relative to total orders. This is the most challenging measure and can be appropriate when all items are needed by the customer. For example, a photo finishing shop must have all the right chemicals from a distributor to develop photographs—having most simply won't work.

FINDING THE SAFETY STOCK. When selecting the safety stock, the inventory planner often assumes that demand during lead time is normally distributed, as shown in Figure 6.7. The average demand during the lead time is the centreline of the graph, with 50 percent of the area under the curve to the left and 50 percent to the right. Thus, if a cycle-service level of 50 percent were chosen, reorder point R would be the quantity represented by this centreline. As R equals demand during the lead time plus the safety stock, the safety stock is 0 when R equals this average demand. Demand is less than average 50 percent of the time and, thus, having no safety stock will be sufficient only 50 percent of the time.

FIGURE 6.7	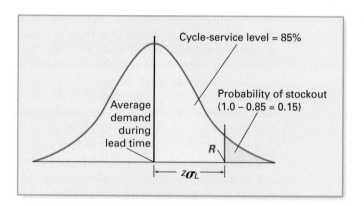

Finding Safety Stock with a Normal Probability Distribution for an 85 Percent Cycle-Service Level

To provide a service level above 50 percent, the reorder point must be greater than average demand during the lead time. In Figure 6.7, that requires moving the reorder point to the right of the centreline so that more than 50 percent of the area under the curve is to the left of R. An 85 percent cycle-service level is achieved in Figure 6.7, with 85 percent of the area under the curve to the left of R and only 15 percent to the right. We compute the safety stock by multiplying the number of standard deviations from the mean needed to implement the cycle-service level, z, by the standard deviation of demand during lead time probability distribution,[4] σ_L:

$$\text{Safety stock} = z\sigma_L$$

The higher the value of z, the higher the safety stock and the cycle-service level should be. If $z = 0$, there is no safety stock, and stockouts will occur during 50 percent of the order cycles.

---

[4]Some inventory planners using manual systems prefer to work with the mean absolute deviation (MAD) rather than the standard deviation, because it is easier to calculate. (MAD is discussed in Chapter 8, "Forecasting.") To approximate the standard deviation you simply multiply the MAD by 1.25. Then proceed to calculate the safety stock.

EXAMPLE 6.3	*Finding the Safety Stock and* **R**

Records show that the demand for dishwasher detergent during the lead time is normally distributed, with an average of 250 boxes and $\sigma_L = 22$. What safety stock should be carried for a 99 percent cycle-service level? What is R?

SOLUTION

The first step is to find z, the number of standard deviations to the right of average demand during the lead time that places 99 percent of the area under the curve to the left of that point (0.9900 in the Appendix to this book, "Normal Distribution"). The closest number in the table is 0.9901, which corresponds to 2.3 in the row heading and .03 in the column heading. Adding these values gives a z of 2.33. With this information, you can calculate the safety stock and reorder point:

$$\text{Safety stock} = z\sigma_L = 2.33(22) = 51.3, \quad \text{or} \quad 51 \text{ boxes}$$

$$\begin{aligned} \text{Reorder point} &= \text{Average demand during lead time} + \text{Safety stock} \\ &= 250 + 51 = 301 \text{ boxes} \end{aligned}$$

We rounded the safety stock to the nearest whole number. In this case, the theoretical cycle-service level will be less than 99 percent. Raising the safety stock to 52 boxes will yield a cycle-service level greater than 99 percent.

Decision Point Management can control the quantity of safety stock by choosing a service level. Another approach to reducing safety stock is to reduce the standard deviation of demand during the lead time, which can be accomplished by closer coordination with major customers through information technology.

Finding the appropriate reorder point and safety stock in practice requires estimating the demand distribution for the lead time. Sometimes average demand during the lead time and the standard deviation of demand during the lead time, σ_L, are not directly available and must be calculated by combining information on the demand rate with information on the lead time. There are two reasons for this additional calculation:

1. Developing estimates first for demand and then for the lead time may be easier. Demand information comes from the customer, whereas lead times come from the supplier.

2. Records are not likely to be collected for a time interval that is exactly the same as the lead time. The same inventory control system may be used to manage thousands of different items, each with a different lead time. For example, if demand is reported *weekly*, records can be used directly to compute the average and the standard deviation of demand during the lead time if the lead time is exactly one week. However, the average and standard deviation of demand during the lead time for a lead time of three weeks are more difficult to determine.

We can get at the more difficult case by making some reasonable assumptions (e.g., probability distributions of demand for each time interval are identical and independent of each other). In general, the standard deviation of several periods is equal to the square root of the sum of the variances of those periods. If the time periods are of identical length, t, and total lead time for an order is L:

$$\sigma_L = \sqrt{\sigma_t^2 L} = \sigma_t \sqrt{L}$$

Figure 6.8 shows how the demand distribution for the lead time is developed from the individual distributions of weekly demands ($t = 1$ week), where $d = 75$, $\sigma_t = 15$, and $L = 3$ weeks. In this case, average demand during the lead time is $(75)(3) = 225$ units and $\sigma_L = 15\sqrt{3} = 25.98$, or 26. More complex formulas or simulation must be used when both demand and the lead time are variable or when the supply is uncertain. However, in such cases the safety stock must be larger than otherwise.

FIGURE 6.8

Development of Demand Distribution for the Lead Time

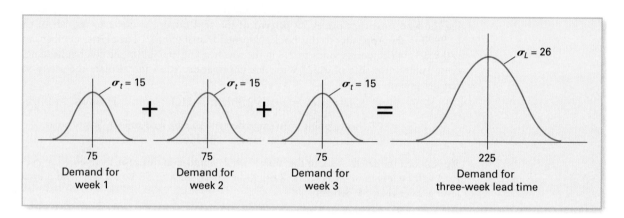

CALCULATING TOTAL Q SYSTEM COSTS. Total costs for the continuous review (Q) system is the sum of three cost components:

Total Q system cost = Annual cycle inventory holding cost + Annual ordering cost + Annual safety stock holding cost

$$C = \frac{Q}{2}(H) + \frac{D}{Q}(S) + Hz\sigma_L$$

The annual cycle inventory holding cost and annual ordering costs are the same equations we used for computing the annual cost for the EOQ. The annual cost of holding the safety stock is computed under the assumption that the safety stock is on hand all the time. Referring to Figure 6.6 on page 213, in each order cycle, sometimes, we will have experienced a demand greater than the average demand during lead time, and sometimes we will have experienced less. On average over the year, we can assume the safety stock will be on hand.

EXAMPLE 6.4

Finding the Safety Stock and R When the Demand Distribution for the Lead Time Must Be Developed

Let's return to the birdfeeder example. Suppose that the average demand is 18 units per week with a standard deviation of 5 units. The lead time is constant at two weeks. Determine the safety stock and reorder point if management wants a 90 percent cycle-service level. What is the total cost of the Q system?

SOLUTION
In this case, $t = 1$ week, $d = 18$, and $L = 2$, so:

$$\sigma_L = \sigma_t\sqrt{L} = 5\sqrt{2} = 7.1$$

Consult the body of the normal table for 0.9000, which corresponds to a 90 percent cycle-service level. The closest number is 0.8997, which corresponds to a z value of 1.28. With this information, we calculate the safety stock and reorder point as follows:

$$\text{Safety stock} = z\sigma_L = 1.28(7.1) = 9.1, \quad \text{or} \quad 9 \text{ units}$$
$$\text{Reorder point} = dL + \text{Safety stock}$$
$$= 18(2) + 9 = 45 \text{ units}$$

Hence, the Q system for the birdfeeder operates as follows: Whenever the inventory position reaches 45 units, order 75 units. The total Q system cost for the birdfeeder is:

$$C = \frac{75}{2}(\$15) + \frac{936}{75}(\$45) + 9(\$15) = \$562.50 + \$561.60 + \$135 = \$1259.10$$

Decision Point Various order quantities and safety stock levels can be used in the Q system. For example, management could specify a different order quantity (because of shipping constraints) or a different safety stock (because of storage limitations). The total costs of such systems can be calculated, and the trade-off between costs and service levels could be assessed.

---

visual system A system that allows employees to place orders when inventory visibly reaches a certain marker.

TWO-BIN SYSTEM. The concept of a Q system can be incorporated in a **visual system**, that is, a system that allows employees to place orders when inventory visibly reaches a certain marker. Visual systems are easy to administer, because records are not kept on the current inventory position. The historical usage rate can simply be reconstructed from past purchase orders. Visual systems are intended for use with low-value items that have a steady demand, such as nuts and bolts or office supplies. Overstocking is common, but the extra inventory holding cost is minimal because the items have relatively little value.

two-bin system A visual system version of the Q system, in which an item's inventory is stored at two different locations.

A visual system version of the Q system is the **two-bin system** in which an item's inventory is stored at two different locations. Inventory is first withdrawn from one bin. If the first bin is empty, the second bin provides backup to cover demand until a replenishment order arrives. An empty first bin signals the need to place a new order. Filled-in order forms placed near the bins let workers send one to purchasing or even directly to the supplier. When the new order arrives, the second bin is restored to its normal level and the rest is put in the first bin. The two-bin system operates like a Q system, with the normal level in the second bin being the reorder point R. The system also may be implemented with just one bin by marking the bin at the reorder point level.

PERIODIC REVIEW (*P*) SYSTEM

periodic review (*P*) system A system in which an item's inventory position is reviewed periodically rather than continuously.

An alternative inventory control system is the **periodic review (*P*) system**, sometimes called a *fixed interval reorder system* or *periodic reorder system*, in which an item's inventory position is reviewed periodically rather than continuously. Such a system can simplify delivery scheduling because it establishes a routine, although the quantity ordered each time varies. A new order is always placed at the end of each review, and the time between orders (TBO) is fixed at P. Demand is a random variable, so total demand between reviews varies. In a P system, the lot size, Q, may change from one order to the next, but the time between orders is fixed. An example of a periodic review system is that of a soft-drink supplier making weekly rounds of grocery stores. Each week the supplier reviews the store's inventory of soft drinks and restocks the store with enough items to meet demand and safety stock requirements until the next week.

Four of the original EOQ assumptions are maintained: (1) no constraints on the size of the lot; (2) only holding and ordering costs are relevant; (3) decisions for one item are independent of decisions for other items; and (4) no uncertainty in lead times or supply quantities. However, demand uncertainty is again allowed for. Figure 6.9 shows the periodic review system under these assumptions. The downward-sloping line again represents on-hand inventory. When the predetermined time, P, has elapsed since the last review, an order is placed to bring the inventory position, represented by the dashed line, up to the target inventory level, T. The lot size for the first review is Q_1, or the difference between inventory position IP_1 and T. As with the continuous review system, IP and OH differ only during the lead time. When the order arrives, at the end of the lead time, OH and IP again are identical. Figure 6.9 shows that lot sizes vary from one order cycle to the next. Because the inventory position is lower at the second review, a greater quantity is needed to achieve an inventory level of T.

P *System When Demand Is Uncertain*

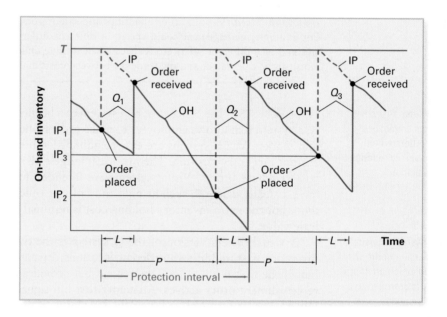

SELECTING THE TIME BETWEEN REVIEWS. To run a P system, managers must make two decisions: the length of time between reviews, P, and the target inventory level, T. Let us first consider the time between reviews, P. It can be any convenient interval, such as each Friday or every other Friday. Another option is to base P on the cost trade-offs of the EOQ. In other words, P can be set equal to the average time between orders for the economic order quantity, or TBO_{EOQ}. Because demand is variable, some orders will be larger than the EOQ and some will be smaller. However, over an extended period of time, the average lot size should equal the EOQ. If other models are used to determine the lot size (e.g., those described in Supplement H, "Special Inventory Models," on the Student CD-ROM), we divide the lot size chosen by the annual demand, D, and use this ratio as P. It will be expressed as the fraction of a year between orders, which can be converted into months, weeks, or days as needed.

SELECTING THE TARGET INVENTORY LEVEL. Now let us consider how to calculate the target inventory level, T. Figure 6.9 reveals that an order must be large enough to make the inventory position, IP, last beyond the next review, which is P time periods away. At that time a new order is placed, but it does not arrive until after the lead time, L.

protection interval The time interval for which inventory must be planned when each new order is placed.

Therefore, as Figure 6.9 shows, a **protection interval** of $P + L$ periods is needed, or the time interval for which inventory must be planned when each new order is placed. A fundamental difference between the Q and P systems is the length of time needed for stockout protection. A Q system needs stockout protection only during the lead time because orders can be placed as soon as they are needed and will be received L periods later. A P system, however, needs stockout protection for the longer $P + L$ protection interval because orders are placed only at fixed intervals and the inventory isn't checked until the next designated review time.

As with the Q system, we need to develop the appropriate distribution of demand during the protection interval to specify the system fully. In a P system, we must develop the distribution of demand for $P + L$ time periods. The target inventory level T must equal the expected demand during the protection interval of $P + L$ periods, plus enough safety stock to protect against demand uncertainty over this same protection interval. We use the same statistical assumptions that we made for the Q system. Thus, the average demand during the protection interval is $d(P + L)$, or:

$$T = d(P + L) + \text{Safety stock for protection interval}$$

We compute safety stock for a P system much as we did for the Q system. However, the safety stock must cover demand uncertainty for a longer period of time. When using a normal probability distribution, we multiply the desired standard deviations to implement the cycle-service level, z, by the standard deviation of demand during the protection interval, σ_{P+L}. Thus:

$$\text{Safety stock} = z\sigma_{P+L}$$

Based on our earlier logic for calculating σ_L, we know that the standard deviation of the distribution of demand during the protection interval is:

$$\sigma_{P+L} = \sigma_t \sqrt{P + L}$$

Because a P system requires safety stock to cover demand uncertainty over a longer time period than a Q system, a P system requires more safety stock; that is, σ_{P+L} exceeds σ_L. Hence, to gain the convenience of a P system requires that overall inventory levels be somewhat higher than those for a Q system.

CALCULATING TOTAL *P* SYSTEM COSTS. The total costs for the P system are the sum of the same three cost elements as for the Q system. The differences are in the calculation of the order quantity and the safety stock. Referring to Figure 6.9, the average order quantity will be the average consumption of inventory during the P periods between orders. Consequently, $Q = dP$. Total costs for the P system are:

$$C = \frac{dp}{2}(H) + \frac{D}{dp}(S) + Hz\sigma_{P+L}$$

EXAMPLE 6.5	*Calculating* P *and* T

Again let us return to the birdfeeder example. Recall that demand for the birdfeeder is normally distributed with a mean of 18 units per week and a standard deviation in weekly demand of 5 units. The lead time is 2 weeks, and the business operates 52 weeks per year. The Q system developed in Example 6.4 called for an EOQ of 75 units and a safety stock of 9 units for a cycle-service level of 90 percent. What is the equivalent P system? What is the total cost? Answers are to be rounded to the nearest integer.

SOLUTION

We first define D and then P. Here P is the time between reviews, expressed as a multiple (or fraction) of time interval t ($t = 1$ week, because the data are expressed as demand *per week*):

$$D = (18 \text{ units/week})(52 \text{ weeks/year}) = 936 \text{ units}$$

$$P = \frac{\text{EOQ}}{D}(52) = \frac{75}{936}(52) = 4.2, \quad \text{or} \quad 4 \text{ weeks}$$

With $d = 18$ units per week, we can also calculate P by dividing the EOQ by d to get $75/18 = 4.2$, or 4 weeks. Hence, we would review the birdfeeder inventory every 4 weeks. We now find the standard deviation of demand over the protection interval ($P + L = 6$):

$$\sigma_{P+L} = \sigma_t\sqrt{P + L} = 5\sqrt{6} = 12 \text{ units}$$

Before calculating T, we also need a z value. For a 90 percent cycle-service level, $z = 1.28$ (see the Appendix to this book, "Normal Distribution"). We now solve for T:

$$T = \text{Average demand during the protection interval} + \text{Safety stock}$$
$$= d(P + L) + z\sigma_{P+L}$$
$$= (18 \text{ units/week})(6 \text{ weeks}) + 1.28(12 \text{ units}) = 123 \text{ units}$$

Every 4 weeks we would order the number of units needed to bring inventory position IP (counting the new order) up to the target inventory level of 123 units. The safety stock for this P system is $1.28(12) = 15$ units.

The total P system cost for the birdfeeder is:

$$C = \frac{4(18)}{2}(\$15) + \frac{936}{4(18)}(\$45) + 15(\$15) = \$540 + \$585 + \$225 = \$1350$$

Decision Point The P system requires 15 units in safety stock, while the Q system only needs 9 units. If cost were the only criterion, the Q system would be the choice for the birdfeeder. As we discuss in the next section, other factors may sway the decision in favour of the P system.

---

single-bin system A system of inventory control in which a maximum level is marked on the storage shelf or bin on a measuring rod, and the inventory is brought up to the mark periodically.

SINGLE-BIN SYSTEM. The concept of a P system can be translated into a simple visual system of inventory control. In the **single-bin system**, a maximum level is marked on the storage shelf or bin on a measuring rod, and the inventory is brought up to the mark periodically—say, once a week. The single bin may be, for example, a gasoline storage tank at a service station or a storage bin for small parts at a manufacturing plant.

COMPARATIVE ADVANTAGES OF THE Q AND P SYSTEMS

Neither the Q nor the P system is best for all situations. Three P-system advantages must be balanced against three Q-system advantages. The advantages of one system are implicitly disadvantages of the other one. The primary advantages of P systems are the following:

1. Administration of the system is convenient, because replenishments are made at fixed intervals. Employees can regularly set aside a day or part of a day to concentrate on this particular task. Fixed replenishment intervals also allow for standardized pickup and delivery times.

2. Orders for multiple items from the same supplier may be combined into a single purchase order. This approach reduces ordering and transportation costs and may result in a price break from the supplier.

3. The inventory position, IP, needs to be known only when a review is made (not continuously, as in a Q system). However, this advantage is moot for firms using computerized record-keeping systems, in which a transaction is reported upon each receipt or withdrawal. When inventory records are always current, the system is called a **perpetual inventory system**.

The primary advantages of Q systems are the following:

1. The review frequency of each item may be individualized. Tailoring the review frequency to the item can reduce total ordering and holding costs.

2. Fixed lot sizes, if large enough, may result in quantity discounts. Physical limitations such as truckload capacities, materials handling methods, and furnace capacities also may require a fixed lot size.

3. Lower safety stocks result in savings.

In conclusion, the choice between Q and P systems is not clear-cut. Which one is better depends on the relative importance of its advantages in various situations. Management must weigh each alternative carefully in selecting the best system.

HYBRID SYSTEMS

Various hybrid inventory control systems merge some but not all the features of the P and Q systems. We briefly examine two such systems: optional replenishment and base stock.

OPTIONAL REPLENISHMENT SYSTEM. Sometimes called the optional review, min-max, or (s, S) system, the **optional replenishment system** is much like the P system. It is used to review the inventory position at fixed time intervals and, if the position has dropped to (or below) a predetermined level, to place a variable-sized order to cover expected needs. The new order is large enough to bring the inventory position up to a target inventory, similar to T for the P system. However, orders are not placed after a review unless the inventory position has dropped to the predetermined minimum level. The minimum level acts as reorder point R does in a Q system. If the target is 100 and the minimum level is 60, the minimum order size is 40 (or $100 - 60$). The optional review system avoids continuous reviews and so is particularly attractive when both review and ordering costs are significant.

BASE-STOCK SYSTEM. In its simplest form, the **base-stock system** issues a replenishment order, Q, every time a withdrawal is made, for the same amount as the withdrawal. This one-for-one replacement policy maintains the inventory position at a base-stock level equal to expected demand during the lead time plus safety stock. The base-stock level, therefore, is equivalent to the reorder point in a Q system. However, order quantities now vary to keep the inventory position at R at all times. Because this position is the lowest IP possible that will maintain a specified service level, the base-stock system may be used to minimize cycle inventory. More orders are placed but each is smaller. This system is appropriate for very expensive items, such as replacement engines for jet airplanes. No more inventory is held than the maximum demand expected until a replacement order can be received. The base-stock system is used in just-in-time systems (see Chapter 10, "Lean Systems").

---

perpetual inventory system A system of inventory control in which the inventory records are always current.

optional replenishment system A system used to review the inventory position at fixed time intervals and, if the position has dropped to (or below) a predetermined level, to place a variable-sized order to cover expected needs.

base-stock system An inventory control system that issues a replenishment order, Q, each time a withdrawal is made, for the same amount as the withdrawal.

INVENTORY RECORD ACCURACY

cycle counting An inventory control method whereby storeroom personnel physically count a small percentage of the total number of items each day, correcting errors that they find.

Regardless of the inventory system in use, record accuracy is crucial to its success. One method of achieving and maintaining accuracy is to assign responsibility to specific employees for issuing and receiving materials and accurately reporting each transaction. A second method is to secure inventory behind locked doors or gates to prevent unauthorized or unreported withdrawals. This method also guards against storing new receipts in the wrong locations, where they can be lost for months. **Cycle counting** is a third method, whereby storeroom personnel physically count a small percentage of the total number of items every day, correcting errors that they find. Class A items are counted most frequently. A final method for computerized systems is to make logic error checks on each transaction reported and fully investigate any discrepancies. Discrepancies may include (1) actual receipts when there is no record of scheduled receipts, (2) disbursements that exceed the current on-hand balance, and (3) receipts with an inaccurate (nonexistent) part number.

These methods can keep inventory record accuracy within acceptable bounds. Accuracy pays off mainly through better customer service, although some inventory reductions can be achieved by improving accuracy. A side benefit is that auditors may not require end-of-year counts if records prove to be sufficiently accurate.

INVENTORY MANAGEMENT ACROSS THE ORGANIZATION

Inventories are important to all types of organizations and their employees. Inventories affect everyday operations because they must be counted, paid for, used in operations, used to satisfy customers, and managed. Inventories require an investment of funds, as does the purchase of a new machine. Monies invested in inventory are not available for investment in other things; thus, they represent a drain on the cash flows of an organization. Carrying that notion to its extreme, one may conclude that inventories should be eliminated. Not only is that idea impossible but it is also hazardous to the financial health of an organization.

We have focused on independent demand inventories in this chapter. These inventories are often found in retail and distribution operations, service industries, maintenance supplies, and finished goods. Consequently, independent demand inventories are often the last stocking point before the consumer. Companies concerned with customer service know that availability of products is a key selling point in many markets. Earlier we discussed how at least one manufacturer has improved financial performance by outsourcing some of the inventory management. However, inventory management can be a strong source of competitive advantage, as is the case with Source Medical. This is particularly true when viewed across a supply chain, as we will explore further in Chapter 9, "Supply Chain Management."

Is inventory a boon or a bane? Certainly, profitability is reduced if there is too much inventory, and customer confidence is damaged if there is too little inventory. The objective is not to simply minimize inventory or to maximize customer service, but rather to have the right amount to support the competitive priorities of the company. Even within the same industry, different competitive priorities, which translate into different process choices, influence how managers must design their inventory systems.

EQUATION SUMMARY

1. Cycle inventory $= \dfrac{Q}{2}$

2. Pipeline inventory $= dL$

3. Total annual cost = Annual holding cost + Annual ordering or setup cost

   $$C = \frac{Q}{2}(H) + \frac{D}{Q}(S)$$

4. Economic order quantity: $\text{EOQ} = \sqrt{\dfrac{2DS}{H}}$

5. Time between orders for EOQ, expressed in weeks: $\text{TBO}_{\text{EOQ}} = \dfrac{\text{EOQ}}{D}$ (52 weeks/year)

6. Inventory position = On-hand inventory + Scheduled receipts − Backorders

   $$\text{IP} = \text{OH} + \text{SR} - \text{BO}$$

7. Continuous review system:

   Reorder point (R) = Average demand during lead time + Safety stock

   $$= dL + z\sigma_L$$

   Protection interval = Lead time (L)

   Standard deviation of demand during the lead time $= \sigma_L = \sigma_t\sqrt{L}$

   Order quantity = EOQ

   Replenishment rule: Order EOQ units when: $\text{IP} \leq R$

   Total Q system cost: $C = \dfrac{Q}{2}(H) + \dfrac{D}{Q}(S) + Hz\sigma_L$

8. Periodic review system:

   Target inventory level (T) = Average demand during the protection interval + Safety stock

   $$= d(P + L) + z\sigma_{P+L}$$

   Protection interval = Time between orders + Lead time = $P + L$

   Review interval = Time between orders = P

   Standard deviation of demand during the protection interval $= \sigma_{P+L} = \sigma_t\sqrt{P + L}$

   Order quantity = Target inventory level − Inventory position = $T - \text{IP}$

   Replenishment rule: Every P time periods order $T - \text{IP}$ units

   Total P system cost: $C = \dfrac{dP}{2}(H) + \dfrac{D}{dP}(S) + Hz\sigma_{P+L}$

CHAPTER HIGHLIGHTS

- Inventory decisions involve trade-offs among the conflicting objectives of low investment, good customer service, and high resource utilization. Benefits of good customer service and high resource utilization may be outweighed by the cost of carrying large inventories, including interest or opportunity costs, storage and handling costs, taxes, insurance, shrinkage, and obsolescence. Order quantity decisions are guided by a trade-off between the cost of holding inventories and the combined costs of ordering, setup, transportation, and purchased materials.

- Safety stock, decoupling, anticipation, cycle, and pipeline inventories vary in size with random and predictable variability, production rate flexibility, order quantity, and lead time, respectively.

- Inventory placement at the plant level depends on process choice and product characteristics. These include whether an item is a standard or a special and the trade-off between short customer response time and low inventory costs.

- ABC analysis helps managers focus on the few significant items that account for the bulk of investment in inventory.

- Class A items deserve the most attention, with less attention justified for class B and class C items.

- Independent demand inventory management methods are appropriate for wholesale and retail merchandise, service industry supplies, finished goods and service parts replenishment, and maintenance, repair, and operating supplies.

- A basic inventory management question is whether to order large quantities infrequently or to order small quantities frequently. The EOQ provides guidance for this choice by indicating the lot size that minimizes (subject to several assumptions) the sum of holding and ordering costs over some period of time, such as a year.

- In the continuous review (Q) system, the buyer places orders of a fixed lot size Q when the inventory position drops to the reorder point. In the periodic review (P) system, every P fixed time interval the buyer places an order to replenish the quantity consumed since the last order. Visual systems, such as single-bin and two-bin systems, are adaptations of the P and Q systems that eliminate the need for records.

- The base-stock system minimizes cycle inventory by maintaining the inventory position at the base-stock level.

CD-ROM RESOURCES

The Student CD-ROM that accompanies this text contains the following resources, which allow you to further practise and apply the concepts presented in this chapter.

- **Equation Summary**: All the equations for this chapter can be found in one convenient location.

- **Discussion Questions**: Three questions will challenge your understanding of practical inventory management.

- **Case**: *Parts Emporium.* Analyze the situation for two parts, develop the appropriate inventory system for each one, and estimate the savings relative to current practice.

- **Experiential Exercise**: *Swift Electronic Supply Inc.* Design an inventory system and test it under actual conditions in this interactive simulation.

- **OM Explorer Tutors**: OM Explorer contains five tutor programs that will help you learn how to estimate inventory levels, perform ABC analysis, calculate EOQs and total costs, determine the safety stock and reorder point for Q systems, and calculate the review period and target inventory level for P systems.

- **OM Explorer Solver**: OM Explorer has three programs that can be used to solve general problems involving inventory level estimation, Q or P system development, economic production lot size calculation, quantity discount analysis, and one-period inventory decisions.

- **Extend LT**: *Inventory Management at Ready Hardware.* Inventory replenishment.

- **Supplement A:** *Decision Making.* Use this supplement to get background information on how to do sensitivity analysis.

- **Supplement G:** *Simulation.* Learn how to conduct simulations and keep track of the results.

- **Supplement H:** *Special Inventory Models.* See how to apply additional inventory tools, including the economic production lot size model, the analysis of quantity discounts, and the one-period inventory model.

SOLVED PROBLEM 1

A distribution centre (DC) experiences an average weekly demand of 50 units for one of its items. The product is valued at $650 per unit. Average inbound shipments from the factory warehouse average 350 units. Average lead time (including ordering delays and transit time) is 2 weeks. The DC operates 52 weeks per year, it carries a 1-week supply of inventory as safety stock, and it has no anticipation inventory. What is the average aggregate inventory being held by the DC?

SOLUTION

TYPE OF INVENTORY	CALCULATION OF AVERAGE INVENTORY QUANTITY	
Cycle	$\frac{Q}{2} = \frac{350}{2} =$	175 units
Safety stock	1-week supply $=$	50 units
Anticipation	None	
Pipeline	$dL = (50 \text{ units/week})(2 \text{ weeks}) =$	100 units
	Total average aggregate inventory $=$	325 units

SOLVED PROBLEM 2

Booker's Book Bindery divides inventory items into three classes according to their dollar usage. Calculate the usage values of the following inventory items and determine which is most likely to be classified as an A item.

PART NUMBER	DESCRIPTION	QUANTITY USED PER YEAR	UNIT VALUE ($)
1	Boxes	500	3.00
2	Cardboard (square metres)	18 000	0.02
3	Cover stock	10 000	0.75
4	Glue (litres)	300	10.00
5	Inside covers	20 000	0.05
6	Reinforcing tape (metres)	3 000	0.15
7	Signatures	150 000	0.45

SOLUTION

PART NUMBER	DESCRIPTION	QUANTITY USED PER YEAR		UNIT VALUE ($)		ANNUAL DOLLAR USAGE ($)
1	Boxes	500	×	3.00	=	1 500
2	Cardboard (square metres)	18 000	×	0.02	=	360
3	Cover stock	10 000	×	0.75	=	7 500
4	Glue (litres)	300	×	10.00	=	3 000
5	Inside covers	20 000	×	0.05	=	1 000
6	Reinforcing tape (metres)	3 000	×	0.15	=	450
7	Signatures	150 000	×	0.45	=	67 500
					Total	81 310

The annual dollar usage for each item is determined by multiplying the annual usage quantity by the value per unit as shown in Figure 6.10. The items are sorted by annual dollar usage, in declining order. Finally, A–B and B–C class lines are drawn roughly according to the guidelines presented in the text. Here, class A includes only one item (signatures), which represents only 1/7, or 14 percent, of the items but accounts for

83 percent of annual dollar usage. Class B includes the next two items, which taken together represent 28 percent of the items and account for 13 percent of annual dollar usage. The final four, class C, items represent more than half the number of items but only 4 percent of total annual dollar usage.

FIGURE 6.10

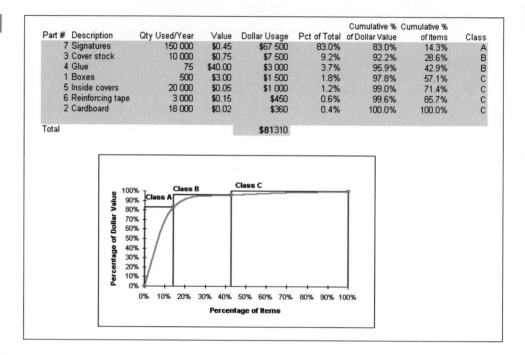

Part #	Description	Qty Used/Year	Value	Dollar Usage	Pct of Total	Cumulative % of Dollar Value	Cumulative % of Items	Class
7	Signatures	150 000	$0.45	$67 500	83.0%	83.0%	14.3%	A
3	Cover stock	10 000	$0.75	$7 500	9.2%	92.2%	28.6%	B
4	Glue	75	$40.00	$3 000	3.7%	95.9%	42.9%	B
1	Boxes	500	$3.00	$1 500	1.8%	97.8%	57.1%	C
5	Inside covers	20 000	$0.05	$1 000	1.2%	99.0%	71.4%	C
6	Reinforcing tape	3 000	$0.15	$450	0.6%	99.6%	85.7%	C
2	Cardboard	18 000	$0.02	$360	0.4%	100.0%	100.0%	C
Total				$81310				

SOLVED PROBLEM 3

In Example 6.2 (page 208), the economic order quantity, EOQ, is 75 units when annual demand, D, is 936 units/year, setup cost, S, is $45, and holding cost, H, is $15/unit/year. Suppose that we mistakenly estimate inventory holding cost to be $30/unit/year.

a. What is the new order quantity, Q, if D = 936 units/year, S = $45, and H = $30/unit/year?

b. What is the change in order quantity, expressed as a percentage of the economic order quantity (75 units)?

SOLUTION

a. The new order quantity is:

$$EOQ = \sqrt{\frac{2DS}{H}} = \sqrt{\frac{2(936)(\$45)}{\$30}} = \sqrt{2808} = 52.99, \quad \text{or} \quad 53 \text{ units}$$

b. The percentage change is:

$$\left(\frac{53 - 75}{75}\right)(100) = -29.33\%$$

The new order quantity (53) is about 29 percent smaller than the correct order quantity (75).

SOLVED PROBLEM 4

In Example 6.2, the total cost, C, is $1124/year.

a. What is the annual total cost when $D = 936$ units/year, $S = \$45$, $H = \$15$/unit/year, and Q is the result from Solved Problem 3(a)?

b. What is the percentage change in total cost?

SOLUTION

a. With 53 as the order quantity, the annual cost is:

$$C = \frac{Q}{2}(H) + \frac{D}{Q}(S) = \frac{53}{2}(\$15) + \frac{936}{53}(\$45) = \$397.50 + \$794.72$$

$$= \$1192.22$$

b. The percentage change is:

$$\left(\frac{\$1192 - \$1124}{\$1124}\right)(100) = 6.05\%$$

A 100 percent error in estimating the holding cost caused the order quantity to be 29 percent too small, and that in turn increased annual costs by about 6 percent.

SOLVED PROBLEM 5

A regional warehouse purchases hand tools from various suppliers and then distributes them on demand to retailers in the region. The warehouse operates five days per week, 52 weeks per year. Only when it is open can orders be received. The following data are estimated for 10 millimetre hand drills with double insulation and variable speeds:

Average daily demand = 100 drills
Standard deviation of daily demand (σ_t) = 30 drills
Lead time (L) = 3 days
Holding cost (H) = \$9.40/unit/year
Ordering cost (S) = \$35/order
Cycle-service level = 92%

The warehouse uses a continuous review (Q) system.

a. What order quantity, Q, and reorder point, R, should be used?

b. If on-hand inventory is 40 units, there is one open order for 440 drills, and there are no backorders, should a new order be placed?

SOLUTION

a. Annual demand is:

$$D = (5 \text{ days/week})(52 \text{ weeks/year})(100 \text{ drills/day}) = 26\,000 \text{ drills/year}$$

The order quantity is:

$$EOQ = \sqrt{\frac{2DS}{H}} = \sqrt{\frac{2(26\,000)(\$35)}{\$9.40}} = \sqrt{193\,167} = 440.02, \quad \text{or} \quad 440 \text{ drills}$$

and the standard deviation is:

$$\sigma_L = \sigma_t\sqrt{L} = (30 \text{ drills}) \sqrt{3} = 51.96, \quad \text{or} \quad 52 \text{ drills}$$

A 92 percent cycle-service level corresponds to $z = 1.41$ (see the Appendix, "Normal Distribution"). Therefore:

$$\text{Safety stock} = z\sigma_L = 1.41(52 \text{ drills}) = 73.38, \quad \text{or} \quad 73 \text{ drills}$$
$$\text{Average demand during the lead time} = 100(3) = 300 \text{ drills}$$
$$\text{Reorder point} = \text{Average demand during the lead time} + \text{Safety stock}$$
$$= 300 \text{ drills} + 73 \text{ drills} = 373 \text{ drills}$$

With a continuous review system, $Q = 440$ and $R = 373$.

b. Inventory position = On-hand inventory + Scheduled receipts − Backorders:

$$IP = OH + SR - BO = 40 + 440 - 0 = 480 \text{ drills}$$

IP (480) exceeds R (373); do not place a new order.

SOLVED PROBLEM 6

Suppose that a periodic review (P) system is used at the warehouse, but otherwise the data are the same as in Solved Problem 5.

a. Calculate the P (in workdays, rounded to the nearest day) that gives approximately the same number of orders per year as the EOQ.

b. What is the value of the target inventory level, T? Compare the P system to the Q system in Solved Problem 5.

c. It is time to review the item. On-hand inventory is 40 drills; there is a scheduled receipt of 440 drills and no backorders. How much should be reordered?

SOLUTION

a. The time between orders is:

$$P = \frac{EOQ}{D} (260 \text{ days/years}) = \frac{440}{26\ 000}(260) = 4.4, \quad \text{or} \quad 4 \text{ days}$$

b. Before calculating T, we must estimate the standard deviation of demand over the protection interval:

$$\sigma_{P+L} = \sigma_t\sqrt{P + L} = 30\sqrt{4 + 3} = 79.4 \text{ drills}$$

As with Solved Problem 5, for a cycle-service level of 92%, $z = 1.41$.

$$T = \text{Average demand during the protection interval} + \text{Safety stock}$$
$$= d(P + L) + z\sigma_{P+L}$$
$$= 100(4 + 3) + 1.41 \times 79.4$$
$$= 812 \text{ drills}$$

c. Inventory position is the amount on hand plus scheduled receipts minus backorders, or:

$$IP = OH + SR - BO = 40 + 440 - 0 = 480 \text{ drills}$$

The order quantity is the target inventory level minus the inventory position, or:

$$Q = T - \text{IP} = 812 \text{ drills} - 480 \text{ drills} = 332 \text{ drills}$$

In a periodic review system, the order quantity for this review period is 332 drills.

PROBLEMS

1. A part is produced in lots of 1000 units. It is assembled from two components worth $50 total. The value added in production (for labour and variable overhead) is $60 per unit, bringing total costs per completed unit to $110. The average lead time for the part is six weeks and annual demand is 3800 units. There are 50 business weeks per year.

   a. How many units of the part are held, on average, in cycle inventory? What is the dollar value of this inventory?

   b. How many units of the part are held, on average, in pipeline inventory? What is the dollar value of this inventory? *Hint:* Assume that the typical part in pipeline inventory is 50 percent completed. Thus, half the labour and variable overhead costs have been added, bringing the unit cost to $80, or $50 + $60/2.

2. Lockwood Industries is considering the use of ABC analysis to focus on the most critical items in its inventory. For a random sample of 8 items, the following table shows the annual dollar usage. Rank the items and assign them to the A, B, or C class.

ITEM	DOLLAR VALUE	ANNUAL USAGE
1	$0.01	1 200
2	$0.03	120 000
3	$0.45	100
4	$1.00	44 000
5	$4.50	900
6	$0.90	350
7	$0.30	70 000
8	$1.50	200

3. Yellow Press, Inc., buys slick paper in 700-kilogram rolls for textbook printing. Annual demand is 2500 rolls. The cost per roll is $800, and the annual holding cost is 15 percent of the cost. Each order costs $50.

   a. How many rolls should Yellow Press order at a time?

   b. What is the time between orders?

4. At Dot Com, a large retailer of popular books, demand is constant at 32 000 books per year. The cost of placing an order to replenish stock is $10, and the annual cost of holding is $4 per book. Stock is received 5 working days after an order has been placed. No backorders are allowed. Assume 300 working days a year.

   a. What is Dot Com's optimal ordering quantity?

   b. What is the optimal number of orders per year?

   c. What is the optimal interval (in working days) between orders?

   d. What is demand during the lead time?

   e. What is the reorder point?

   f. What is the inventory position immediately after an order has been placed?

5. Sam's Cat Hotel operates 52 weeks per year, 6 days per week, and uses a continuous review inventory system. It purchases kitty litter for $11.70 per bag. The following information is available about these bags:

   > Demand = 90 bags/week
   > Order cost = $54/order
   > Annual holding cost = 27% of cost
   > Desired cycle-service level = 80%
   > Lead time = 3 weeks (18 working days)
   > Standard deviation of weekly demand = 15 bags

   Current on-hand inventory is 320 bags, with no open orders or backorders.

   a. What is the EOQ? What would be the average time between orders (in weeks)?

   b. What should R be?

   c. An inventory withdrawal of 10 bags was just made. Is it time to reorder?

   d. The store currently uses a lot size of 500 bags (i.e., $Q = 500$). What is the annual holding cost of this policy? Annual ordering cost? Without calculating the EOQ, how can you conclude from these two calculations that the current lot size is too large?

   e. What would be the annual cost saved by shifting from the 500-bag lot size to the EOQ?

6. Consider again the kitty litter ordering policy for Sam's Cat Hotel in Problem 5.

   a. Suppose that the weekly demand forecast of 90 bags is incorrect and actual demand averages only 60 bags per week. How much higher will total costs be, owing to the distorted EOQ caused by this forecast error?

   b. Suppose that actual demand is 60 bags but that ordering costs are cut to only $6 by using the Internet to automate order placing. However, the buyer does not tell anyone, and the EOQ isn't adjusted to reflect this reduction in *S*. How much higher will total costs be, compared to what they could be if the EOQ were adjusted?

7. Petromax Enterprises uses a continuous review inventory control system for one of its inventory items. The following information is available on the item. The firm operates 50 weeks in a year.

> Demand = 50 000 units per year
> Ordering cost = $35 per order
> Holding cost = $2 per unit per year
> Average lead time = 3 weeks
> Standard deviation of weekly demand = 125 units

a. What is the economic order quantity for this item?

b. If Petromax wants to provide a 90 percent cycle-service level, what should be the safety stock and the reorder point?

8. Suppose that Sam's Cat Hotel in Problem 5 uses a *P* system instead of a *Q* system. The average daily demand is 15 bags (90/6), and the standard deviation of *daily* demand is 6.124 bags (15/$\sqrt{6}$).

a. What *P* (in working days) and *T* should be used to approximate the cost trade-offs of the EOQ?

b. How much more safety stock is needed than with a *Q* system?

c. It's time for the periodic review. How much should be ordered?

9. Your firm uses a continuous review system and operates 52 weeks per year. One of the items handled has the following characteristics:

> Demand (*D*) = 20 000 units/year
> Ordering cost (*S*) = $40/order
> Holding cost (*H*) = $2/unit/year
> Lead time (*L*) = 2 weeks
> Cycle-service level = 95%

Demand is normally distributed, with a standard deviation of *weekly* demand of 100 units. Current on-hand inventory is 1040 units, with no scheduled receipts and no backorders.

a. Calculate the item's EOQ. What is the average time, in weeks, between orders?

b. Find the safety stock and reorder point that provide a 95 percent cycle-service level.

c. For these policies, what are the annual costs of (i) holding the cycle inventory and (ii) placing orders?

d. A withdrawal of 15 units just occurred. Is it time to reorder? If so, how much should be ordered?

10. Suppose that your firm uses a periodic review system, but otherwise the data are the same as in Problem 9.

a. Calculate the *P* that gives approximately the same number of orders per year as the EOQ. Round your answer to the nearest week.

b. Find the safety stock and the target inventory level that provide a 95 percent cycle-service level.

c. How much larger is the safety stock than with a *Q* system?

11. A company begins a review of ordering policies for its continuous review system by checking the current policies for a sample of items. Following are the characteristics of one item (assume 52 weeks per year):

> Demand (*D*) = 64 units/week
> Ordering and setup cost (*S*) = $50/order
> Holding cost (*H*) = $13/unit/year
> Lead time (*L*) = 2 weeks
> Standard deviation of *weekly* demand = 12 units
> Cycle-service level = 88%

a. What is the EOQ for this item?

b. What is the desired safety stock?

c. What is the reorder point?

d. What are the cost implications if the current policy for this item is *Q* = 200 and *R* = 180?

12. Using the same information as in Problem 11, develop the best policies for a periodic review system.

a. What value of *P* gives the same approximate number of orders per year as the EOQ? Round to the nearest week.

b. What safety stock and target inventory level provide an 88 percent cycle-service level?

13. Wood County Hospital consumes 1000 boxes of bandages per week. The price of bandages is $35 per box, and the hospital operates 52 weeks per year. The cost of processing an order is $15, and the cost of holding one box for a year is 15 percent of the value of the material.

a. The hospital orders bandages in lot sizes of 900 boxes. What *extra cost* does the hospital incur, which it could save by using the EOQ method?

b. Demand is normally distributed, with a standard deviation of weekly demand of 100 boxes. The lead time is 2 weeks. What safety stock is necessary if the hospital uses a continuous review system and a 97 percent cycle-service level is desired? What should be the reorder point?

c. If the hospital uses a periodic review system, with *P* = 2 weeks, what should be the target inventory level, *T*?

14. The West Coast Lighting Centre stocks more than 3000 lighting fixtures, including chandeliers, swags, wall lamps, and track lights. The store sells at retail, operates 6 days per week, and advertises itself as the "brightest spot in the

city." One expensive fixture is selling at an average rate of 5 units per day. The reorder policy is $Q = 40$ and $R = 15$. A new order is placed on the day the reorder point is reached. The lead time is 3 business days. For example, an order placed on Monday will be delivered on Thursday. Simulate the performance of this Q system for the next 3 weeks (18 workdays). Any stockouts result in lost sales (rather than backorders). The beginning inventory is 19 units, and there are no scheduled receipts. Table 6.1 simulates the first week of operation. Extend Table 6.1 to simulate operations for the next 2 weeks if demand for the next 12 business days is 7, 4, 2, 7, 3, 6, 10, 0, 5, 10, 4, and 7. (See Supplement G, "Simulation," on the Student CD-ROM.)

   a. What is the average daily ending inventory over the 18 days?

   b. How many stockouts occurred?

15. Simulate Problem 14 again, but this time use a P system with $P = 8$ and $T = 55$. Let the first review occur on the first Monday. As before, the beginning inventory is 19 units, and there are no scheduled receipts. (See Supplement G, "Simulation," on the Student CD-ROM.)

   a. What is the average daily ending inventory over the 18 days?

   b. How many stockouts occurred?

TABLE 6.1 *First Week of Operation*

WORKDAY	BEGINNING INVENTORY	ORDERS RECEIVED	DAILY DEMAND	ENDING INVENTORY	INVENTORY POSITION	ORDER QUANTITY
1. Monday	19	—	5	14	14	40
2. Tuesday	14	—	3	11	51	—
3. Wednesday	11	—	4	7	47	—
4. Thursday	7	40	1	46	46	—
5. Friday	46	—	10	36	36	—
6. Saturday	36	—	9	27	27	—

REFERENCES AND FURTHER READINGS

American Production and Inventory Control Society, Inc. *Inventory Management Reprints*. Falls Church, VA: APICS Professional Bookstore, 1993.

Berlin, Bob. "Solving the OEM Puzzle at Valleylab." *APICS—The Performance Advantage*, March 1997, pp. 58–63.

Callioni, Gianpaolo, Xavier de Montgros, Regine Slagmulder, Luk N. Van Wassenhove, and Linda Wright. "Inventory-Driven Costs." *Harvard Business Review*, March 2005, pp. 135–141.

Chikan, A., A. Milne, and L. G. Sprague. "Reflections on Firm and National Inventories." Budapest: International Society for Inventory Research, 1996.

Greene, James H. *Production and Inventory Control Handbook*, 3rd ed. New York: McGraw-Hill, 1997.

Krupp, James A. G. "Are ABC Codes an Obsolete Technology?" *APICS—The Performance Advantage*, April 1994, pp. 34–35.

Silver, Edward A. "Changing the Givens in Modeling Inventory Problems: The Example of Just-In-Time Systems." *International Journal of Production Economics*, vol. 26 (1996), pp. 347–351.

Silver, Edward A., D. F. Pyke, and Rein Peterson. *Inventory Management, Production Planning and Scheduling*, 3d ed. New York: John Wiley & Sons, 1998.

Tersine, Richard J. *Principles of Inventory and Materials Management*, 4th ed. Upper Saddle River, NJ: Prentice-Hall, 1994.

Timme, Stephen G., and Christine Williams-Timme. "The Real Cost of Holding." *Supply Chain Management Review*, July–August 2003, pp. 30–37.

7 Location and Layout

Across the Organization

Location and layout are important to:

- **accounting,** which prepares cost estimates for changing layouts and operating at new locations.
- **distribution,** which seeks warehouse layouts that make materials handling easier and make customer response times shorter.
- **engineering,** which considers the impact of product design choices on layout.
- **finance,** which performs the financial analysis for investments in new layouts or in facilities at new locations.
- **human resources,** which hires and trains employees to support new or relocated operations.
- **management information systems,** which provide information technologies that link operations at different locations.
- **marketing,** which assesses how new locations and revised layouts will appeal to customers.
- **operations,** which seeks facility locations and layouts that best balance multiple performance criteria.

Learning Goals

After reading this chapter, you will be able to:

1. discuss the managerial challenges in global operations.
2. describe the factors affecting location choices, in both manufacturing and services.
3. apply the load-distance method and break-even analysis to single-site location problems.
4. describe the four basic layout types and when each is best used.
5. identify the types of performance criteria that are important in evaluating layouts.
6. explain how cells can help create hybrid layouts.
7. recommend how to design flexible-flow and line-flow layouts.

A 35-year-old mother may not know it, but the Internet has made her trips to the mall a little easier. In 2000, RiverTown Crossings (www.rivertowncrossings.com) located a new facility in Grandville, Michigan. Since then she rarely ventures beyond just one section of the RiverTown Crossings Mall—the one with Abercrombie Kids, Gap Kids, Gymboree, and other kids' clothing stores. She can shop in that wing and find almost everything she needs. In an effort to compete with the allure of online shopping, the mall owner, General Growth Properties, Inc. (www.generalgrowth.com), selected a layout that runs counter to decades of retailing wisdom: it clustered competing stores together. Shoppers were asking for such clusters long before Web retailing took off, and General Growth began experimenting with the idea three years ago. Now, all its new malls will have clusters.

Worried about a future when shoppers point and click instead of park and walk and wait in line, developers are finally trying to make it more convenient to shop in malls. Some owners are revising their existing layouts by removing large fixtures, such as planters and fountains, to clear sightlines to storefronts. Others are adding directories that are easier to understand than current mall maps. A few malls in the design stages are opting to put anchor department stores closer together—a layout that cuts down on walking. A few malls are trying to offer shoppers elements of the Web using high-tech directories. At the Dayton Mall, in Ohio, sleek electronic kiosks give shoppers e-mail access

The Internet has revolutionized the way traditional businesses design their processes, even to the point of layout design. RiverTown Crossings Mall has clustered company stores to improve comparison shopping, a convenience that Web retailing already offers online customers.

and let them search for names of stores carrying types of merchandise, such as "sweaters." The kiosks also have printers that can generate a map with a store's location highlighted.

Beneath the new layout designs is an old retailing secret: the traditional mall was designed to be difficult. This planned inconvenience forced customers who wanted to comparison-shop to walk from one end of the mall to the other, so that they had every opportunity to make impulse purchases on their way. Many developers left little to chance in directing the traffic flow to their advantage, using plants, carpeting, and other fixtures to set winding routes past stores.

Revising the layout of existing malls to make them more convenient is costly. Most of them are jungles of escalators, fountains, and play areas—and those are the easy obstacles. The tougher problem is figuring out how to rearrange similar stores that are probably operating on long leases. After all, a mall developer cannot simply order four shoe store tenants to pick up and move. And many retailers still prefer to keep their distance from competitors. RiverTown's Hallmark Gold Crown store is located on the first level on the north end of the mall, while an American Greetings store is on the second level on the south end. Hallmark Cards' location strategy calls for space between its stores and those of competitors.

Source: "Making Malls (Gasp!) Convenient," *Wall Street Journal*, February 8, 2000, pp. B1, B4.

Every year in Canada, manufacturing firms and service providers build and remodel innumerable plants, stores, office buildings, warehouses, and other facilities. Choosing where to locate new manufacturing facilities, service outlets, or branch offices, and how to lay them out, have both strategic and tactical dimensions. The location and layout of a business's facilities have significant impacts on the company's operating costs, the prices it charges for goods and services, and its ability to compete in the marketplace.

Analyzing location patterns to discover a firm's underlying strategy is fascinating. For example, White Castle, a U.S. hamburger chain started in 1921, locates restaurants near manufacturing plants. This is consistent with the firm's strategy to cater to blue-collar workers. As a result, restaurants tend to be located near the target population and away from competitors such as Wendy's and McDonald's, and are open around the clock. In contrast, why do competing new-car sales showrooms deliberately cluster near one another? In this case, customers prefer to do their comparison shopping in one area. For either industry, management's location decision reflects a particular strategy.

Recognizing the strategic impact of location decisions, we first examine the most important trend in location patterns: the globalization of operations. We then consider qualitative factors that influence location choices. Next we present some analytic techniques for making single- or multiple-facility location decisions. Finally, we turn to facility layout, beginning with strategic issues and then describing ways to design effective layouts.

THE GLOBALIZATION AND GEOGRAPHIC DISPERSION OF OPERATIONS

globalization Businesses' deployment of facilities and operations around the world.

The term **globalization** describes businesses' deployment of facilities and operations around the world. Globalization results in more exports to and imports from other countries. Worldwide exports now account for more than 30 percent of worldwide gross national product, up from 12 percent in 1962. Exports from Canada's manufacturing sector are slightly higher, averaging about 33 percent of total sales. In addition, the volume of corporate voice, data, and teleconferencing traffic between countries is growing at an annual rate of 15 to 20 percent, offering one indication of how businesses are increasingly bridging national boundaries. A global orientation is not limited to large companies: smaller Canadian companies can also be heavily oriented toward international markets. For example, Trojan Technologies, a growing manufacturer of ultraviolet disinfection systems for municipal wastewater and drinking water, generates about 90 percent of its revenues abroad.

Globalization of services is also widespread. The value of world trade in services is roughly 20 percent of total world trade. Banking, law, information services, airlines, education, consulting, and restaurant services are particularly active globally. For example, EllisDon Construction, based in London, Ontario, was awarded the contract for construction of two major facilities for the 2004 Olympics in Greece. McDonald's opened a record 220 restaurants in foreign countries in just one year. Wal-Mart Stores, the world's largest retailer, paid $10.8 billion in 1999 for the United Kingdom's Asda Group PLC, whose large stores and selection of goods closely mirror its own. The purchase is part of Wal-Mart's push to expand across Europe; 6200 facilities are now located around the world.

DISADVANTAGES TO GLOBALIZATION

Of course, operations in other countries can have disadvantages. A firm may have to relinquish proprietary technology if it turns over some of its component manufacturing to offshore suppliers or if suppliers need the firm's technology to achieve desired quality and cost goals.

There may be political risks. Each nation can exercise its sovereignty over the people and property within its borders. The extreme case is nationalization, in which a government may take over a firm's assets without paying compensation. Also, a firm may alienate customers at home if jobs are lost to offshore operations.

Employee skills may be lower in foreign countries, requiring additional training time. Korean firms moved much of their sports shoe production to low-wage Indonesia and China, but they still manufacture hiking shoes and in-line roller skates in Korea because of the greater skills required.

When a firm's operations are scattered, customer response times can be longer. Effective cross-functional connections also may be more difficult if face-to-face discussions are needed.

MANAGING GLOBAL OPERATIONS

All the concepts and techniques described in this book apply to operations throughout the world. However, location decisions involve added complexities when a firm sets up facilities abroad. One study revealed that the most important barrier to effective global manufacturing operations is that many firms do not take a global view of their market opportunities and competitors (Klassen and Whybark, 1994). Global markets impose new standards on quality and time. Managers should not think about domestic markets first and then global markets later, if at all. Also, they must have a good understanding of their competitors, which requires greater appraisal capabilities when the competitors are global rather than domestic. Other important challenges of managing multinational operations include other languages and customs, different management styles, unfamiliar laws and regulations, and different costs.

OTHER LANGUAGES. The ability to communicate effectively is important to all organizations. Although English is sometimes referred to as the international language of business, working in the customer's (or supplier's) native language can often avoid costly mistakes. Canadian managers are increasingly able to do business in multiple languages, partly because of the diverse range of cultural backgrounds represented here. Software tools are also becoming more sophisticated to assist with basic translations.

DIFFERENT NORMS AND CUSTOMS. Several franchisers, such as Century 21 Real Estate, Levi Strauss, and Quality Inns International, found that even when the same language is spoken, different countries have unique norms and customs that shape their business values. The goals, attitudes toward work, customer expectations, desire for risk taking, and other business values can vary dramatically from one part of the world to another. For example, a survey showed that more than two-thirds of Japanese managers believed that business should take an active role in environmental protection, whereas only 25 percent of Mexican managers agreed.

WORKFORCE MANAGEMENT. Employees in different countries prefer different management styles. Managers moving to operations in another country must often re-evaluate their on-the-job behaviours (e.g., superior–subordinate relationships), assumptions about workers' attitudes, and hiring and promotion practices. Practices that work well in one country may be ineffective in another.

UNFAMILIAR LAWS AND REGULATIONS. Managers in charge of overseas plants must deal with unfamiliar labour laws, tax laws, and regulatory requirements. The after-tax consequences of an automation project, for instance, can be quite different from country

Radisson Hotels International's opening of the upscale Radisson Slavjanskaya in Moscow experienced difficulties with language, workforce norms, and regulations, to name just a few challenges.

to country because of different tax laws. Legal systems also differ, both in terms of written rules and enforcement. Some policies and practices that are illegal in one country might be acceptable or even mandated elsewhere in the world.

UNEXPECTED COST MIX. Firms may shift some of their operations to another country because of lower inventory, labour, materials, and real estate costs. However, these same differences may mean that policies that worked well in one economic environment—such as automating a process—might be a mistake in the new environment.

In dealing with global operations, managers must decide how much of the firm's operations to shift overseas and how much control the home office should retain. At one extreme, firms can rely on their home offices for strategic direction and remain highly centralized. At the other extreme, firms can have a worldwide vision but allow each subsidiary to operate independently. Here the manager must be able to manage highly decentralized organizations that have a complex mix of product strategies, cultures, and consumer needs.

FACTORS AFFECTING LOCATION DECISIONS

facility location The process of determining a geographic site for a firm's operations.

Facility location is the process of determining a geographic site for a firm's operations. Managers of both service and manufacturing organizations must weigh many factors when assessing the desirability of a particular site, including proximity to customers and suppliers, labour costs, and transportation costs. Managers can divide location factors into dominant and secondary factors. Dominant factors are those derived from competitive priorities (cost, quality, time, and flexibility) and have a particularly strong impact on sales or costs. For example, favourable labour climate, workforce language skills, and monetary incentives are dominant factors when locating call centres in New Brunswick. Secondary factors also are important, but management may downplay or even ignore some of them. Thus, for GM's Saturn plant in the U.S., which makes many parts on-site, inbound transportation costs were considered to be a secondary factor.

DOMINANT FACTORS IN MANUFACTURING

Six groups of factors dominate location decisions for new manufacturing plants: (1) labour climate; (2) proximity to markets; (3) quality of life; (4) proximity to suppliers and resources; (5) proximity to the firm's other facilities; and (6) utilities, taxes, and real estate costs.

LABOUR CLIMATE. A favourable labour climate may be the most important factor for labour-intensive firms in industries such as textiles, furniture, and consumer electronics. Labour climate is a function of wage rates, training requirements, attitude toward work, worker productivity, and union strength. Having a favourable climate applies not just to the workforce already on site, but in the case of relocation decisions, also to the employees that a firm hopes will transfer or will be attracted there.

PROXIMITY TO MARKETS. After determining where the demand for goods and services is greatest, management must select a location for the facility that will supply that demand. Locating near markets is particularly important when the final goods are bulky or heavy and *outbound* transportation rates are high. For example, manufacturers of products such as plastic pipe and heavy metals all emphasize proximity to their markets.

quality of life A factor that includes a diverse mix of lifestyle concerns such as good schools, climate, housing, recreational facilities, and cultural events.

QUALITY OF LIFE. Good schools, recreational facilities, cultural events, and an attractive lifestyle contribute to **quality of life** for employees. This factor is relatively unimportant on its own, but it can make the difference in location decisions. In Japan, the United States, and Europe, many new industrial jobs are shifting outside of urban centres. Reasons for this movement include high costs of living, high crime rates, and general decline in the quality of life in many large cities.

PROXIMITY TO SUPPLIERS AND RESOURCES. Firms dependent on inputs of bulky, perishable, or heavy raw materials emphasize proximity to suppliers and resources. In such cases, *inbound* transportation costs become a dominant factor, encouraging such firms to locate facilities near suppliers. For example, locating paper mills near forests and grain processing facilities near farms is practical. Another advantage of locating near suppliers is the ability to maintain lower inventories.

PROXIMITY TO THE FIRM'S OTHER FACILITIES. In many companies, plants supply parts to other facilities or rely on other facilities for management and staff support. These ties require frequent coordination and communication, which can become more difficult as distance increases. Also, close proximity can help a new facility start up more quickly through sharing personnel and other resources. For example, Toyota's new plant in Woodstock, Ontario, is less than 50 kilometres from a large well-established facility in Cambridge.

UTILITIES, TAXES, AND REAL ESTATE COSTS. Other important factors that may emerge include utility costs (telephone, energy, and water), local and provincial taxes, financing incentives offered by local or provincial governments, relocation costs, and land costs. Currently, there is increasing pressure on provincial and local governments in Canada to provide major tax and financial incentives to automobile manufacturers and parts suppliers, in order to compete with aggressive offers from states in the southern United States.

OTHER FACTORS. Still other factors may need to be considered, including room for expansion, construction costs, accessibility to multiple modes of transportation, the cost of shuffling people and materials between plants, insurance costs, competition from other firms for the workforce, local ordinances (such as pollution or noise control regulations), community attitudes, and many others. For global operations, firms are emphasizing local employee skills and education and the local infrastructure. Many firms are concluding that large, centralized manufacturing facilities in low-cost countries with poorly trained workers are not sustainable. Smaller, flexible facilities serving multiple markets allow the firm to deal with nontariff barriers such as sales volume limitations, regional trading blocs, political risks, and exchange rates.

DOMINANT FACTORS IN SERVICES

The factors mentioned for manufacturers also apply to service providers with one important addition: the impact that the location might have on sales and customer satisfaction. Customers usually care about how close a service facility is, particularly if the process requires considerable customer contact. However, even this is changing with the increasing adoption of Web-based technologies to simplify interaction with customers in many industries.

PROXIMITY TO CUSTOMERS. Location is a key factor in determining how conveniently customers can carry on business with a firm. For example, few people will patronize a remotely located dry cleaner or supermarket if another is more convenient. Thus, the influence of location on revenues tends to be the dominant factor. The key is proximity to customers who will patronize the facility and seek its services.

TRANSPORTATION COSTS AND PROXIMITY TO MARKETS. For warehousing and distribution operations, transportation costs and proximity to markets are extremely important. With a warehouse nearby, many firms can hold inventory closer to the customer, thus reducing delivery time and promoting sales. For example, Invacare Corporation gained a competitive edge in the distribution of home health-care products by decentralizing inventory from Ohio into 32 warehouses across the United States. With Invacare's new distribution network, the dealers get daily deliveries of products from one source. Invacare's location strategy shows how timely delivery can be a competitive advantage.

LOCATION OF COMPETITORS. One complication in estimating the sales potential at different locations is the impact of competitors. Management must not only consider the current location of competitors but also try to anticipate their reaction to the firm's new location. Avoiding areas where competitors are already well established often pays. However, in some industries, such as new-car sales showrooms and fast-food chains, locating near competitors is actually advantageous. The strategy is to create a **critical mass**, whereby several competing firms clustered in one location attract more customers than the total number who would shop at the same stores at scattered locations. Recognizing this effect, some firms use a follow-the-leader strategy when selecting new sites.

SITE-SPECIFIC FACTORS. Retailers also must consider the level of retail activity, residential density, traffic flow, and site visibility. Retail activity in the area is important, as shoppers often decide on impulse to go shopping or to eat in a restaurant. Traffic flows and visibility are important, because businesses' customers often arrive in cars. Management considers possible traffic tieups, traffic volume and direction by time of

critical mass A situation whereby several competing firms clustered in one location attract more customers than the total number who would shop at the same stores at scattered locations.

day, traffic signals, intersections, and the position of traffic medians. Visibility involves distance from the street and size of nearby buildings and signs. High residential density ensures evening and weekend business when the population in the area fits the firm's competitive priorities and target market segment.

GEOGRAPHICAL INFORMATION SYSTEMS AND LOCATION DECISIONS

geographical information system (GIS) A system of computer software, hardware, and data that the firm's personnel can use to manipulate, analyze, and present information relevant to a location decision.

A **geographical information system (GIS)** is a system of computer software, hardware, and data that the firm's personnel can use to manipulate, analyze, and present information relevant to a location decision. A GIS can also integrate different systems to create a visual representation of a firm's location choices. Among other things, it can be used to (1) store databases; (2) display maps; and (3) create models that can take information from existing datasets, apply analytic functions, and write results into new derived datasets. Together, these three functionalities of data storage, map displays, and modelling are critical parts of an intelligent GIS, and used to a varying extent in all GIS applications.

A GIS can be a really useful decision-making tool because many of the decisions made by businesses today have a geographical aspect. Information is stored in databases and can be naturally linked to places; for example, customer sales can be mapped to locations, or demographic information about that location, such as the percentage of residents in a neighbourhood with a particular income level. More generally, demographics include the number of people in the metropolitan statistical area, city, or postal code; average income; number of families with children; and so forth. These demographics may all be important variables in the decision of how best to reach the target market. Similarly, the road system, including bridges and highways, location of nearby airports and seaports, and the terrain (mountains, forests, lakes, and so forth) play an important role in facility location decisions. As such, a GIS can have a diverse set of location-related applications that can be used in different industries, such as retail, real estate, government, transportation, and logistics.

Governmental data can provide a wealth of statistical information used to make better GIS-based location decisions. For example, the federal government is working to develop the Canadian Geospatial Data Infrastructure (www.cgdi.ca), which provides access to a wide variety of location-based information through a network of data, service, and technology suppliers. Similarly, the U.S. Census Bureau has a minutely detailed computerized map of the entire United States—the so-called Tiger file. Its formal name is the Topologically Integrated Geographic Encoding and Reference file. It lists in digital form every highway, street, bridge, and tunnel in the 50 states. When combined with a database, such as the results of a Canadian census or a company's own customer files, managers have the ability to ask various "what-if" questions about location alternatives.

Internet sites on Yahoo!, Mapquest, and Expedia, among others, allow people to pull up maps, distances and travel times, and routes between locations, such as between Toronto, Ontario, and San Diego, California. In addition, search engines such as Google can be integrated with population demographics to create information of interest in social and business domains. Web sites are using Google maps to display crime sites, locations of inexpensive gas, and apartments for rent.

Many different types of GIS packages are available, and some have been tailored to a specific application such as locating retail stores, redistricting legislative districts, analyzing logistics and marketing data, environmental management, and so forth. In this chapter, we illustrate the use of one GIS program, Microsoft's MapPoint. One of the nice features of MapPoint is that the maps and much of the census data come with the software itself, while in many other systems, the maps and the data are purchased separately from the GIS software vendor. MapPoint is an easy-to-use and fairly inexpensive GIS that mainly focuses on everyday business use by nontechnical analysts. Its ability to display information on maps can be a powerful decision-making tool.

USING GIS TO IDENTIFY LOCATIONS AND DEMOGRAPHIC CUSTOMER SEGMENTS

GIS can be useful for identifying locations that relate well to a firm's target market based on customer demographics. When coupled with other location models, sales

MANAGERIAL PRACTICE
Location Challenges at Starbucks

An important aspect of the Starbucks service strategy is the location of its stores. In 2005 alone the chain opened almost 1700 stores, bringing the total to approximately 10 500 stores in 37 countries. This phenomenal growth is aided by new site selection technology. Starbucks relies on location analysis to evaluate where to place new stores.

In Starbucks' early days, a relatively small number of people participated in new store decisions, which was more of an experiential than a systematic process. As Starbucks grew, however, more planners became involved in the process and used a more standard, formal analysis. If a site's potential is not within a certain set of parameters, its planners do not waste their time giving it additional consideration.

Starbucks' original strategy was to expand in major urban areas, clustering in prime locations and placing outlets across from one another, sometimes even in the same block. This approach maximized the company's market share in areas with the highest volume potential—usually urban, affluent areas. Then rural areas began demanding Starbucks be located there too. Over the past few years, Starbucks' domestic expansion strategy definitely evolved. Smaller city markets and new store types, like those located in retail and airport locations, are being utilized.

Another change to the original strategy is the implementation of a geodemographic GIS as a productivity and process tool. It provides a description of different characteristics about people based upon the location where they live. The system determines the impact over the course of a year of opening an additional store one day sooner or one day later. Starbucks' site-acquisition process includes a number of elements that use spatial models, geodemographics, and sales-forecasting models. To identify potential locations, maps (such as those shown in Figures 7.1 and 7.2) are used by the company to show walk-time trade areas that pinpoint hotspots for gourmet coffee consumption.

In addition to North America, Starbucks also opened stores in Asia, the Middle East, Europe, and South America. When

TRADE AREA MAP - HAMILTON, ON

seeking potentially viable sites abroad, Starbucks encounters additional challenges, such as the lack of available and accurate data. In many regions of the world, important statistics are not available and the systems that use any available data vary. There is no central place to get information about data availability in certain countries, which translates into comparability issues and increases the risks of erring in expansion analyses.

Although Starbucks continues to grow rapidly, it has already taken the premium locations in many markets. The company is now forced to look for lower-volume locations that will still provide a good return. More than ever before, the use of location analysis limits Starbucks' risk, and has become paramount to the firm.

Source: "Location Analysis Tools Help Starbucks Brew Up New Ideas," *Business Geographics*, www.geoplace.com; Vijay Vishwanath and David Hardling, "The Starbucks Effect," *Harvard Business Review* (March/April 2000), pp. 17–18; Starbucks Corporate Information page, www.starbucks.com (June 2005).

forecasting models, and geodemographic systems, GIS can give a firm a formidable array of decision-making tools for its location decisions. The Managerial Practice feature illustrates how Starbucks makes one of its most important strategic decisions: the location of its stores (see the Managerial Practice feature). A GIS also can be used to estimate drive times from a central site to surrounding locations, which is critical when locating emergency services, such as fire stations and ambulance dispatch facilities.

To get more practical insights into the application of GIS and demographics for understanding location choices made by Starbucks, let us examine further the Hamilton, Ontario, area showcased in the trade area map in Figure 7.1. The Starbucks store addresses within 20 miles (32 kilometres) of Hamilton were obtained from the Starbucks Web site and imported into MapPoint. These store locations are denoted by yellow dots around a coffee cup pushpin. Then, demographics that come with MapPoint were overlaid on the map. The first map shows the population density per square kilometre for each census subdivision. Hamilton (the darkest area) has a population density of 2730 per square kilometre, while Oakville has a population density of 1024 per square kilometre. Yet Oakville has more stores than Hamilton. It suggests that store location is not being driven by population density alone. The most densely populated area around Hamilton has only one Starbucks store; further investigation reveals that it is on a road leading to the airport. In contrast, Ancaster, in the bottom left corner of the map has a Starbucks, even though its population density is only 141 per square kilometre.

FIGURE 7.1

Trade Area and Population Map for Hamilton, Ontario

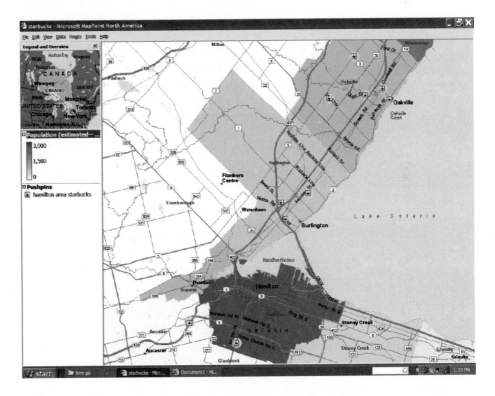

We then look to see whether per capita income could explain the locations of the Starbucks store. Figure 7.2 shows the demographics by average per capita household income. Applying these data to the map, we see that Oakville and Ancaster (the darkest cities in Figure 7.2) have a per capita income of $96 545 and $98 422, respectively. Burlington has a moderate population density and moderate per capita

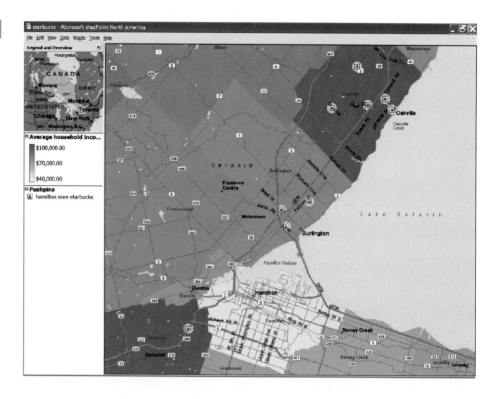

FIGURE 7.2

Per Capita Household Income Map of Hamilton

income. Oakville has five stores while Burlington has three stores, all of them located on well-trafficked roads. So, at least in this one particular case, it appears that Starbucks predominantly locates its stores in more affluent areas, and future expansion of stores in the area is likely to occur in and around Ancaster if population grows there further.

LOCATING A SINGLE FACILITY

Having examined trends and important factors in location, we now consider more specifically how a firm can make location decisions. In this section, we consider the case of locating only one new facility. When the facility is part of a firm's larger network of facilities, we assume that there is no interdependence; that is, a decision to open a restaurant in Calgary, Alberta, is independent of whether the chain has a restaurant in Halifax, Nova Scotia. Let's begin by considering how to decide whether a new location is needed and then examine a systematic selection process aided by the load-distance method to deal with proximity.

SELECTING ON-SITE EXPANSION, NEW LOCATION, OR RELOCATION

Management must first decide whether to expand on-site, build another facility, or relocate. A survey of Fortune 500 firms showed that 45 percent of expansions were on-site, 43 percent were in new plants at new locations, and only 12 percent were relocations of all facilities. On-site expansion has the advantage of keeping management together, reducing construction time and costs, and avoiding splitting up operations. However, a firm may expand a facility too much, at which point diseconomies of scale set in (see Chapter 4, "Capacity"). Poor materials handling, increasingly complex production control, and simple lack of space all are reasons for building a new plant or relocating the existing one.

The advantages of building a new plant or moving to a new retail or office space are that the firm does not have to rely on production from a single plant, it can hire new and possibly more productive labour, it can modernize with new technology, and it can reduce transportation costs. Most firms that choose to relocate are small (fewer than ten employees). They tend to be single-location companies cramped for space and needing to redesign their production processes and layouts. More than 80 percent of all relocations are within 35 kilometres of the first location, which enables the firm to retain its current workforce.

COMPARING SEVERAL SITES

A systematic selection process begins after there is a perception or evidence that opening a retail outlet, warehouse, office, or plant in a new location will increase profits. A team may be responsible for the selection decision in a large corporation, or an individual may make the decision in a small company. The process of selecting a new facility location involves a series of steps.

1. Identify the important location factors and categorize them as dominant or secondary.

2. Consider alternative regions; then narrow the choices to alternative communities and finally to specific sites.

3. Collect data on the alternatives from location consultants, provincial development agencies, city and county planning departments, chambers of commerce, land developers, electric power companies, banks, and on-site visits. Some of these data and information may also be contained inside the GIS.

4. Analyze the data collected, beginning with the *quantitative* factors—factors that can be measured in dollars, such as annual transportation costs or taxes. These dollar values may be broken into separate cost categories (e.g., inbound and outbound transportation, labour, construction, and utilities) and separate revenue sources (e.g., sales, stock or bond issues, and interest income). These financial factors can then be converted to a single measure of financial merit and used to compare two or more sites.

5. Bring the qualitative factors pertaining to each site into the evaluation. A *qualitative* factor is one that cannot be evaluated in dollar terms, such as community attitudes or quality of life. To merge quantitative and qualitative factors, some managers review the expected performance of each factor, while others assign each factor a weight of relative importance and calculate a weighted score for each site, using a preference matrix. What is important in one situation may be unimportant or less important in another. The site with the highest weighted score is best.

After thoroughly evaluating between 5 and 15 sites, those making the study prepare a final report containing site recommendations, along with a summary of the data and analyses on which they are based. A presentation of the key findings usually is delivered to top management in large firms.

| EXAMPLE 7.1 | *Calculating Weighted Scores in a Preference Matrix* |

A new medical facility, Health-Watch, is to be located in Edmonton, Alberta. The following table shows the location factors, weights, and scores (1 = poor, 5 = excellent) for one potential site. The weights in this case add up to 100 percent. A weighted score will be calculated for each site. What is the weighted score for this site?

LOCATION FACTOR	WEIGHT	SCORE
Total patient kilometres per month	25	4
Facility utilization	20	3
Average time per emergency trip	20	3
Expressway accessibility	15	4
Land and construction costs	10	1
Employee preferences	10	5

SOLUTION

The weighted score (WS) for this particular site is calculated by multiplying each factor's weight by its score and adding the results:

$$WS = (25 \times 4) + (20 \times 3) + (20 \times 3) + (15 \times 4) + (10 \times 1) + (10 \times 5)$$
$$= 100 + 60 + 60 + 60 + 10 + 50$$
$$= 340$$

The total weighted score of 340 can be compared with the total weighted scores for other sites being evaluated.

APPLYING THE LOAD-DISTANCE METHOD

In the systematic selection process, the analyst must identify attractive candidate locations and compare them on the basis of quantitative factors. The load-distance method can facilitate this step. Several location factors relate directly to distance: proximity to markets, average distance to target customers, proximity to suppliers and resources, and proximity to other company facilities. The **load-distance method** is a mathematical model used to evaluate locations on the basis of proximity factors. The objective is to select a location that minimizes the total weighted loads moving into and out of the facility. An alternative approach is to use time rather than distance.

load-distance method A mathematical model used to evaluate locations on the basis of proximity factors.

DISTANCE MEASURES. To calculate distance, we can use the driving distance between any two points estimated by a GIS system. Alternatively, a Euclidean or a rectilinear distance measure may be used. Euclidean distance is the straight-line distance, or shortest possible path, between two points. To calculate the **Euclidean distance**, we create a graph with grid coordinates. The distance between two points, say points A and B, is:

Euclidean distance The straight-line distance, or shortest possible path, between two points.

$$d_{AB} = \sqrt{(x_A - x_B)^2 + (y_A - y_B)^2}$$

where:

d_{AB} = Distance between points A and B
x_A = x-coordinate of point A
y_A = y-coordinate of point A
x_B = x-coordinate of point B
y_B = y-coordinate of point B

rectilinear distance The distance between two points with a series of 90° turns, as along city blocks.

Rectilinear distance measures distance between two points with a series of 90° turns, as along city blocks. The distance travelled in the x-direction is the absolute value of the difference in x-coordinates. Adding this result to the absolute value of the difference in the y-coordinates gives:

$$d_{AB} = |x_A - x_B| + |y_A - y_B|$$

CALCULATING A LOAD-DISTANCE SCORE. Suppose that a firm planning a new location wants to select a site that minimizes the distances that larger *loads* must travel to and from the site. Depending on the industry, loads may be expressed as the number of customers or workers that must travel to a facility. Loads may also be shipments from suppliers.

To calculate a load distance for any potential location, we multiply the loads flowing to and from the facility by their distances. The *ld score* is simply the sum of the load-distance products. By selecting a new location based on a low *ld score*, customer service is improved or transportation costs reduced.

$$ld = \sum_i l_i d_i$$

The goal is to find one acceptable facility location that minimizes the score, where the location is defined by its x-coordinate and y-coordinate. Practical considerations rarely allow managers to select the exact location with the lowest possible score. For example, land may not be available there at a reasonable price, or other location factors may make the site undesirable.

centre of gravity A good starting point in evaluating locations is with the load-distance model; the centre of gravity's x-coordinate is found by multiplying each point's x-coordinate by its load (l), summing these products, and then dividing by the sum of the loads.

CENTRE OF GRAVITY. Testing different locations with the load-distance model is relatively simple if some systematic search process is followed. A good starting point is the **centre of gravity** of the target area. The centre of gravity's x-coordinate, denoted x^*, is found by multiplying each point's x-coordinate (x_i) by its load (l_i), summing these products ($\sum l_i x_i$), and then dividing by the sum of the loads ($\sum l_i$). The y-coordinate, denoted y^*, is found the same way, with the y-coordinates used in the numerator. The formulas are:

$$x^* = \frac{\sum_i l_i x_i}{\sum_i l_i} \qquad \text{and} \qquad y^* = \frac{\sum_i l_i y_i}{\sum_i l_i}$$

This location usually is not the optimal one for the Euclidean or rectilinear distance measures, but it is still an excellent starting point. Calculate the load-distance scores for locations in its vicinity until you're satisfied that your solution is near-optimal.

EXAMPLE 7.2   *Finding the Centre of Gravity*

The new Health-Watch facility is targeted to serve seven areas, with customers travelling from these areas when they need health care. What is the centre of gravity for these target areas for the Health-Watch medical facility?

SOLUTION

To calculate the centre of gravity, we begin with the information in the following table in which population is given in thousands:

TARGET AREA GEOGRAPHIC LOCATION

	(x, y)	l	lx	ly
		POPULATION (thousands)		
A	(2.5, 4.5)	2	5	9
B	(2.5, 2.5)	5	12.5	12.5
C	(5.5, 4.5)	10	55	45
D	(5, 2)	7	35	14
E	(8, 5)	10	80	50
F	(7, 2)	20	140	40
G	(9, 2.5)	14	126	35
	Totals	68	453.5	205.5

Next we solve for x^* and y^*:

$$x^* = \frac{453.5}{68} = 6.67$$

$$y^* = \frac{205.5}{68} = 3.02$$

Decision Point The centre of gravity is (6.67, 3.02), which is not necessarily optimal. Using the centre of gravity as a starting point, managers can now search in its vicinity for the optimal location.

USING BREAK-EVEN ANALYSIS

Break-even analysis can help a manager compare location alternatives on the basis of quantitative factors that can be expressed in terms of total cost (see Chapter 2 "Process Management," for a similar analysis with process equipment). It is particularly useful when the manager wants to define the ranges over which each alternative is best. The basic steps for graphic and algebraic solutions are as follows:

1. Determine the variable costs and fixed costs for each site. Recall that *variable* costs are the portion of the total cost that varies directly with the volume of output. Recall that fixed costs are the portion of the total cost that remains constant regardless of output levels.

2. Plot the total cost lines—the sum of variable and fixed costs—for all the sites on a single graph.

3. Identify the approximate ranges for which each location has the lowest cost.

4. Solve algebraically for the break-even points over the relevant ranges.

EXAMPLE 7.3

Break-Even Analysis for Location

An operations manager has narrowed the search for a new facility location to four communities. The annual fixed costs (land, property taxes, insurance, equipment, and buildings) and the variable costs (labour, materials, transportation, and variable overhead) are:

COMMUNITY	FIXED COSTS PER YEAR	VARIABLE COSTS PER UNIT
A	$150 000	$62
B	$300 000	$38
C	$500 000	$24
D	$600 000	$30

a. Plot the total cost curves for all the communities on a single graph. Identify on the graph the approximate range over which each community provides the lowest cost.

b. Using break-even analysis, calculate the break-even quantities over the relevant ranges.

c. If the expected demand is 15 000 units per year, what is the best location?

SOLUTION

a. To plot a community's total cost line, let us first compute the total cost for two output levels: $Q = 0$ and $Q = 20\,000$ units per year. For the $Q = 0$ level, the total cost is simply the fixed costs. For the $Q = 20\,000$ level, the total cost (fixed plus variable costs) is:

COMMUNITY	FIXED COSTS	VARIABLE COSTS (COST PER UNIT)(NO. OF UNITS)	TOTAL COST (FIXED + VARIABLE)
A	$150 000	$62(20 000) = $1 240 000	$1 390 000
B	$300 000	$38(20 000) = $ 760 000	$1 060 000
C	$500 000	$24(20 000) = $ 480 000	$ 980 000
D	$600 000	$30(20 000) = $ 600 000	$1 200 000

Figure 7.3 shows the graph of the total cost lines. The line for community A goes from (0, 150) to (20, 1390). The graph indicates that community A is best for low volumes, B for intermediate volumes, and C for high volumes. We should no longer consider community D, as both its fixed *and* its variable costs are higher than community C's.

FIGURE 7.3

Break-Even Analysis of Four Candidate Locations

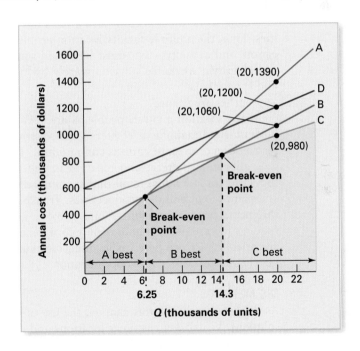

b. The break-even quantity between A and B lies at the end of the first range, where A is best, and the beginning of the second range, where B is best. We find it by setting their total cost equations equal to each other and solving:

$$\underset{\text{(A)}}{\$150\,000 + \$62Q} = \underset{\text{(B)}}{\$300\,000 + \$38Q}$$

$$Q = 6250 \text{ units}$$

The break-even quantity between B and C is at the end of the range over which B is best and the beginning of the final range where C is best. It is:

$$\text{(B)} \qquad\qquad \text{(C)}$$

$$\$300\ 000 + \$38Q = \$500\ 000 + \$24Q$$

$$Q = 14\ 286 \text{ units}$$

No other break-even quantities are needed. The break-even point between A and C does not mark either the start or the end of one of the three relevant ranges.

Decision Point Management located the new facility at Community C, because the 15 000-units-per-year demand forecast lies in the high-volume range.

LOCATING A FACILITY WITHIN A NETWORK OF FACILITIES

When a firm with a network of existing facilities plans a new facility, one of two conditions exists: either the facilities operate independently (e.g., a chain of restaurants, health clinics, banks, or retail establishments) or the facilities interact (e.g., component manufacturing plants, assembly plants, and warehouses). Independently operating units can be located by treating each as a separate single facility, as described in the preceding section. Locating interacting facilities introduces new issues, such as how to allocate work between the facilities and how to determine the best capacity for each. Changing work allocations in turn affects the size (or capacity utilization) of the facilities. Thus, the multiple-facility location problem has three dimensions—location, allocation, and capacity—that must be solved simultaneously. In many cases, the analyst can identify a workable solution merely by looking for patterns in the cost, demand, and capacity data and using trial-and-error calculations. In other cases, more formal approaches are needed.

Many location analysis problems are very complex. Consider the situation that a medium-sized manufacturer faces when distributing products through warehouse, or distribution centres, to various communities. The problem is to determine the number, size, allocation pattern, and location of the warehouses. The situation may involve thousands of individual retail outlets, hundreds of potential warehouse locations, several plants, and multiple product lines. Transportation rates depend on the direction of shipment, product, quantity, rate breaks, and geographic area. Such complexity requires the use of a computer for a comprehensive evaluation; four basic approaches are briefly described here for locating multiple facilities: (1) GIS methods, (2) heuristics, (3) simulation, and (4) optimization.

GIS METHODS

As discussed earlier in this chapter, the use of GIS tools often simplifies the search for solutions. Visualizing customer locations and data, as well as the transportation structure of roads and highways, allows the analyst to quickly arrive at a reasonable solution to the multiple facility location problems. Load-distance score and centre of gravity data can be merged with customer databases in Excel to arrive at trial locations for facilities, which can then be evaluated for annual driving time or distance using a GIS such as MapPoint and a Visual Basic Macro in Excel. Such an approach can have many applications, including the design of supply chain distribution networks. A five-step framework that captures the use of GIS for locating multiple facilities is outlined here.

1. Map the data for existing customers and facilities in the GIS.
2. Visually split the entire operating area into the number of parts or subregions that equal the number of facilities to be located.

3. Assign a facility location for each region based on the visual density of customer concentration or other factors. Alternately, determine the centre of gravity for each part or subregion identified in step 2 as the starting location point for the facility in that subregion.

4. Search for alternate sites around the centre of gravity to pick a feasible location that meets the firm's managerial criteria such as proximity to major metropolitan areas or highways.

5. Compute total load-distance scores and perform capacity checks before finalizing the locations for each region.

HEURISTICS

heuristics Solution guidelines, or rules of thumb, that find feasible—but not necessarily the best—solutions to problems.

Solution guidelines, or rules of thumb, that find feasible—but not necessarily the best—solutions to problems are called **heuristics**. Their advantages include efficiency and an ability to handle general views of a problem. The systematic search procedure utilizing a target area's centre of gravity, described earlier for single-facility location problems, is a typical heuristic procedure. One of the first heuristics to be computerized for location problems was proposed more than four decades ago to handle several hundred potential warehouse sites and several thousand demand centres (Kuehn and Hamburger, 1963). Many other heuristic models are available today for analyzing a variety of situations.

SIMULATION

simulation A modelling technique that reproduces the behaviour of a system.

A modelling technique that reproduces the behaviour of a system is called **simulation**. Simulation allows certain variables to be manipulated and shows what effect they have on select operating measures. Simulation models allow the analyst to evaluate different location alternatives by trial and error. It is up to the analyst to propose the most reasonable alternatives. A simulation model can handle more realistic views of a problem and involves the analyst in the solution process itself. For each run, the analyst inputs the facilities to be opened, and the simulator typically makes the allocation decisions based on some reasonable assumptions that have been written into the computer program. The Ralston-Purina Company used simulation to assist the company in locating warehouses to serve 137 demand centres, five warehouses, and four plants. Random demand at each demand centre by product type was simulated over a period of time. Demand was met by the closest warehouse that had available inventory. Data were produced by simulating inventory levels, transportation costs, warehouse operating costs, and backorders. Ralston-Purina implemented the result of the simulation, which showed that the least-cost alternative would be to consolidate the five warehouses down to three.

OPTIMIZATION

optimization A procedure used to determine the "best" solution; generally utilizes simplified and less realistic views of a problem.

In contrast to heuristics and simulation, **optimization** involves procedures to determine the *best* solution. The transportation method is one such optimization approach that can help solve multiple facility location problems, and it is based on linear programming (see Supplement I, "Linear Programming," on the Student CD-ROM). This method only finds the best shipping pattern between plants and warehouses for a particular set of plant locations, each with a given capacity. The analyst must try a variety of location-capacity combinations and find the optimal distribution for each. In the end, the payoffs can be substantial.

However, optimization procedures generally utilize simplified and less realistic views of a problem. For example, distribution costs (variable shipping and possibly variable production costs) captured with the transportation method are but one important input in evaluating a particular location-allocation combination. Investment costs and other fixed costs also must be considered, along with various qualitative factors. This complete analysis must be made for each reasonable location-capacity combination.

WHAT IS LAYOUT PLANNING?

After the location of a facility is determined, management attention can shift to develop the layout within that facility. In essence, layouts put other decisions on processes in tangible, physical form by converting process structures, flowcharts, technology choices, and capacity plans into bricks and mortar. Revising layouts also is a way to improve processes.

layout planning Planning that involves decisions about the physical arrangement of economic activity centres within a facility.

Layout planning involves decisions about the physical arrangement of economic activity centres within a facility. An **economic activity centre** can be anything that consumes space: a person or group of people, a teller window, a machine, a workstation, a department, an aisle, a storage room, and so on. Layout planning translates the broader decisions about a firm's competitive priorities, process, and capacity into actual physical arrangements of people, equipment, and space. The goal is to allow workers and equipment to operate most effectively. Before a manager can make decisions regarding physical arrangement, four questions must be addressed:

economic activity centre Anything that consumes space; for example, a person or a group of people, a teller window, a machine, a workstation, a department, an aisle, or a storage room.

1. *What centres should the layout include?* Centres should reflect process decisions and maximize productivity. For example, a central storage area for tools is most efficient for certain processes, but keeping tools at individual workstations makes more sense for other processes.

2. *How much space and capacity does each centre need?* Inadequate space can reduce productivity, deprive employees of privacy, and even create health and safety hazards. However, excessive space is wasteful, can reduce productivity, and can isolate employees unnecessarily.

3. *How should each centre's space be configured?* The amount of space, its shape, and the elements in a centre are interrelated. For example, the placement of a desk and chair relative to the other furniture is determined by the size and shape of the office, as well as the activities performed there. Providing a pleasing atmosphere also should be considered as part of the layout configuration decisions, especially in retail outlets and offices.

4. *Where should each centre be located?* Location can significantly affect productivity. For example, employees who must frequently interact with one another face to face should be placed in a central location rather than in separate, remote locations to reduce time lost travelling back and forth.

The location of a centre has two dimensions: (1) *relative location*, or the placement of a centre relative to other centres, and (2) *absolute location*, or the particular space that the centre occupies within the facility. Both affect a centre's performance. Look at the grocery store layout in Figure 7.4(a). It shows the location of five departments, with the dry groceries department allocated twice the space of each of the others. The location of frozen foods relative to bread is the same as the location of meats relative to vegetables, so the distance between the first pair of departments equals the distance between the second pair of departments. Relative location is normally the crucial issue when travel time, materials handling cost, and communication effectiveness are important.

FIGURE 7.4

Identical Relative Locations and Different Absolute Locations

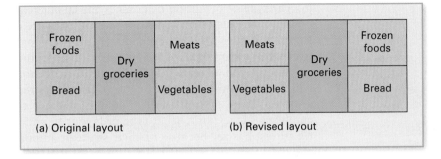

(a) Original layout (b) Revised layout

Now look at the plan in Figure 7.4(b). Although the relative locations are the same, the absolute locations have changed. This modified layout might prove unworkable. For example, the cost of moving the meats to the northwest corner could be excessive. Or customers might react negatively to the placement of vegetables in the southwest corner, preferring them to be near the entrance.

STRATEGIC ISSUES

Layout choices can help immensely in communicating an organization's product plans and competitive priorities. If a retailer plans to upgrade the quality of its merchandise, the store layout should convey more exclusiveness and luxury. The photo of a Limited Too store shows a much different atmosphere, because its target market is clothing for girls between 7 and 14 years old.

Layout has many practical and strategic implications. Altering a layout can affect an organization and how well it meets its competitive priorities by:

- Facilitating the flow of materials and information
- Increasing the efficient utilization of labour and equipment
- Increasing customer convenience and sales at a retail store
- Reducing hazards to workers
- Improving employee morale
- Improving communication

The new Limited Too stores, spun off by The Limited, Inc., in 1999, have layouts that are colourful and fun. The 3D banner is about 15 metres long and 1.5 metres high.

The type of operation determines the layout requirements. For example, in warehouses, materials flows and stock picking costs are dominant considerations. In retail stores, customer convenience and sales may dominate, whereas communication effectiveness and team building may be crucial in an office.

Among the several fundamental layout choices available to managers are whether to plan for current or future (and less predictable) needs, whether to select a single-storey or multi-storey design, whether to open the planning process to employee suggestions, what type of layout to choose, and what performance criteria to emphasize. Because of their strategic importance, we focus on the last two choices.

LAYOUT TYPES

The choice of layout type depends largely on process structure, described in Chapter 2, "Process Management." There are four basic types of layout: flexible-flow, line-flow, hybrid, and fixed-position.

flexible-flow layout A layout that groups workstations or departments according to function.

FLEXIBLE-FLOW LAYOUT. With a batch process, the demand levels are often too low or have high variability for management to set aside human and capital resources exclusively for a particular product line or type of customer. A **flexible-flow layout**, which groups workstations or departments according to function, accomplishes this purpose. For example, in the metalworking shop shown in Figure 7.5(a), all drills are located in one area of the machine shop and all milling machines are located in another. The flexible-flow layout is most common when the same operation must intermittently produce many different products or serve many different customers.

The flexible-flow layout has a number of advantages over the line-flow layout shown in Figure 7.5(b):

1. Resources are relatively general purpose and less capital intensive.

2. The process layout is less vulnerable to changes in product mix or new marketing strategies and is therefore more flexible.

FIGURE 7.5

Two Layout Types

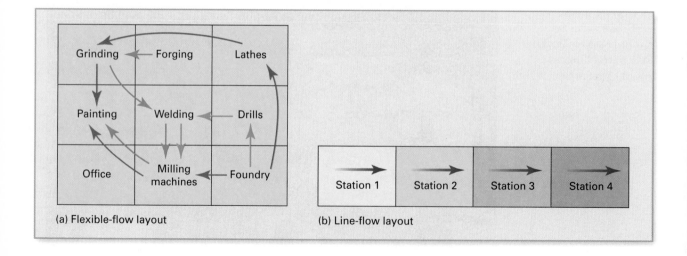

(a) Flexible-flow layout   (b) Line-flow layout

3. Equipment utilization can be higher with low-volume products or services. When volumes are low, dedicating resources to each product or service (as is done with a line-flow layout) would require more equipment than pooling the requirements for all products does.[1]

4. Employee supervision can be more specialized, an important factor when job content requires a good deal of technical knowledge.

However, the flexible-flow layout has its disadvantages:

1. Processing rates tend to be slower.

2. Productive time is lost in changing from one product or service to another.

3. More space and capital are tied up in inventory, which helps workstations to work independently despite their variable output rates.

4. The time lags between when customer orders start and end are relatively long.

5. Materials handling tends to be costly. Jumbled flows and changing routings usually require the use of less automated equipment to move orders through the process (e.g., carts rather than conveyors).

6. Production planning and control is more difficult.

A major challenge in designing a flexible-flow layout is to locate centres so that they bring some order to the apparent chaos of a wide variety of customer orders.

LINE-FLOW LAYOUT. Back offices, assembly lines, and continuous-flow processes typically have linear work flows and repetitive tasks. For such processes, the manager should dedicate resources to individual services, products, or tasks. This strategy is achieved by a **line-flow layout**, illustrated by Figure 7.5(b), in which workstations or departments are arranged in a linear path. As in an automated car wash, the product or customer moves along in a smooth, continuous path. Resources are arranged around the product's route rather than shared across many products. Although this layout often follows a straight line, an L, O, S, or U shape is also possible. A line-flow layout often is called a *production line* or an *assembly line*. The difference between the two is that an assembly line is limited to assembly processes, whereas a production line can be used to perform other processes such as machining.

Line-flow layouts often rely heavily on specialized, capital-intensive resources. When volumes are high, the advantages of line-flow over flexible-flow layouts include:

1. Faster processing rates

2. Lower inventories

3. Less unproductive time lost to changeovers and materials handling

Assuming that each operation is reliable (i.e., low variability), there is little need to decouple one operation from the next, without waiting in queues. This layout significantly improves throughput time and cuts inventories. The disadvantages of line-flow layouts include:

line-flow layout A layout in which workstations or departments are arranged in a linear path.

---

[1]However, management can't allow utilization to get too high. A larger capacity cushion with process layouts absorbs the more variable, less predictable demands of customized products and services.

1. Greater risk of layout redesign—added cost—for products or services with short or uncertain lives

2. Less flexibility

3. Low resource utilization for low-volume products or services

Deciding where to locate centres is easy, because operations must occur in a prescribed order. Centres can simply be placed to follow the customer's or product's routing, ensuring that all interacting pairs of centres are as close together as possible or have a common boundary. The challenge of line-flow layout is to group activities into workstations and achieve the desired output rate with the least resources. The composition and number of workstations are crucial decisions, which we explore later in the chapter.

hybrid layout A layout in which some portions of the facility are arranged in a flexible-flow layout and others are arranged in a line-flow layout.

HYBRID LAYOUT. A **hybrid layout** uses an intermediate strategy, in which some portions of the facility are arranged in a flexible-flow layout and others are arranged in a line-flow layout. Hybrid layouts are used in facilities having both fabrication and assembly operations, as would be the case if both types of layout shown in Figure 7.5 were in the same building. Fabrication operations—in which components are made from raw materials—have a flexible flow, whereas assembly operations—in which components are assembled into finished products—have a line flow. Operations managers also create hybrid layouts when introducing cells and flexible automation, such as a flexible manufacturing system (see Supplement E, "Computer-Integrated Manufacturing," on the Student CD-ROM). A *cell* is two or more dissimilar workstations located close together through which a limited number of parts or models are processed with line flows.

fixed-position layout An arrangement in which the product is fixed in place; workers, along with their tools and equipment, come to the product to work on it.

FIXED-POSITION LAYOUT. The fourth basic type of layout is the **fixed-position layout**. In this arrangement, the product is fixed in place; workers, along with their tools and equipment, come to the product to work on it. Many project processes have this arrangement. This type of layout makes sense when the product is particularly massive or difficult to move, as in shipbuilding, assembling locomotives, making huge pressure vessels, building dams, or repairing home furnaces. A fixed-position layout minimizes the number of times that the product must be moved and is often the only feasible solution. Resources, including workers and equipment, must be mobile to move between products or service sites.

PERFORMANCE CRITERIA

Other fundamental choices facing the layout planner concern *performance criteria*, which may include one or more of the following factors:

- Level of capital investment
- Requirements for materials handling
- Ease of stock picking
- Work environment and "atmosphere"
- Ease of equipment maintenance
- Employee attitudes
- Amount of flexibility needed
- Customer convenience and level of sales

Managers must decide early in the process which factors to emphasize in order to come up with a good layout solution. In most cases, multiple criteria are used. For example, a warehouse manager may emphasize ease in stock picking, flexibility, and amount of space needed (capital investment), whereas a retail store manager may emphasize flexibility, atmosphere, customer convenience, and sales. Sales are particularly important to retailers, who place items with high profitability per cubic metre of shelf space in the most prominent display areas and impulse-buy items near the entrance or checkout counter.

CAPITAL INVESTMENT. Floor space, equipment needs, and inventory levels are assets that the firm buys or leases. These expenditures are an important criterion in all settings. If an office layout is to have partitions to increase privacy, the cost rises. Even increasing space for filing cabinets can add up. A four-drawer lateral file occupies about 1.5 square metres, including the space needed to access it. At $200 per square metre, that translates into a floor space "rental" of $300 annually.

MATERIALS HANDLING. Relative locations of centres should restrict large flows to short distances. Centres between which frequent trips or interactions are required should be placed close to one another. In a manufacturing plant, this approach minimizes materials handling costs. In a warehouse, stock picking costs can be reduced with a good layout design. In a retail store, customer convenience improves if items are grouped predictably to minimize customer search and travel time. In an office, communication and cooperation often improve when people or departments that must interact frequently are located near one another, because telephone calls and memos can be poor substitutes for face-to-face communication. Spatial separation is one big reason why cross-functional coordination between departments can be challenging.

layout flexibility The property of a facility to be desirable after significant changes occur, or to be easily and inexpensively adapted in response to changes.

FLEXIBILITY. A flexible layout allows a firm to adapt quickly to changing customer needs and preferences and is best for many situations. **Layout flexibility** means either that the facility remains desirable after significant changes occur or that it can be easily and inexpensively adapted in response to changes. The changes can be in the mix of customers served by a store, goods made at a plant, space requirements in a warehouse, or organizational structure in an office. Using modular furniture and partitions, rather than permanent load-bearing walls, is one way to minimize the cost of office layout changes. Having wide bays (fewer columns), heavy-duty floors, and extra electrical connections in a plant can also minimize costs.

OTHER CRITERIA. Other criteria that may be important include labour productivity, machine maintenance, work environment, and organizational structure. For example, labour productivity can be affected if certain workstations can be operated by common personnel in some layouts but not in others. Downtime spent waiting for materials can be caused by materials handling difficulties resulting from poor layout.

CREATING HYBRID LAYOUTS

When volumes are not high enough to justify dedicating a single line of multiple workers to a single product, managers still may be able to derive the benefits of line-flow layout—straightforward routes, simpler materials handling, low setups, and reduced labour costs—by creating line-flow layouts in some portions of the facility. Two techniques for creating hybrid layouts are one-worker, multiple-machines (OWMM) cells and group technology (GT) cells. They are special types of cells that help to focus operations on serving particular customer segments very well. In addition, a flexible manufacturing system (FMS) can create a highly automated cell, consisting of computer-controlled, semi-independent workstations where materials are automatically handled and machine-loaded (see Supplement E, "Computer-Integrated Manufacturing," on the Student CD-ROM).

ONE WORKER, MULTIPLE MACHINES

one-worker, multiple-machines (OWMM) cell A one-person cell in which a worker operates several different machines simultaneously to achieve a line flow.

If volumes are not sufficient to keep several workers busy on one production line, the manager might set up a line small enough to keep one worker busy. A one-person cell is the theory behind the **one-worker, multiple-machines (OWMM) cell**, in which a worker operates several different machines simultaneously to achieve a line flow. Having one worker operate several identical machines is not unusual. However, with an OWMM cell, several different machines are in the line.

An OWMM arrangement reduces both inventory and labour requirements. Inventory is cut because, rather than piling up in queues, materials move directly into the next operation. Labour is cut because more work is automated. The addition of several low-cost automated devices can maximize the number of machines included in an OWMM arrangement: automatic tool changers, loaders and unloaders, start and stop devices, and failsafe devices that detect defective parts or products.

GROUP TECHNOLOGY

group technology (GT) An option for achieving product layouts with low-volume processes; creates cells not limited to just one worker and has a unique way of selecting work to be done by the cell.

A second option for achieving product layouts with low-volume processes is **group technology (GT)**. This manufacturing technique creates cells not limited to just one worker and has a unique way of selecting work to be done by the cell. The GT method groups parts or products with similar characteristics into *families* and sets aside groups of machines for their production. Families may be based on size, shape, manufacturing or routing requirements, or demand. The goal is to identify a set of products with similar processing requirements and minimize machine changeover or setup. For example, all bolts might be assigned to the same family because they all require the same basic processing steps regardless of size or shape.

Once parts have been grouped into families, the next step is to organize the machine tools needed to perform the basic processes on these parts into separate cells. The machines in each cell require only minor adjustments to accommodate product changeovers from one part to the next in the same family. By simplifying product routings, GT cells reduce the time a customer order is in the shop. Queues of materials waiting to be worked on are shortened or eliminated. Frequently, materials handling is automated so that, after loading raw materials into the cell, a worker does not handle machined parts until the customer order has been completed.

Figure 7.6 compares process flows before and after creation of GT cells. Figure 7.6(a) shows a facility where machines are grouped according to function: lathing, milling, drilling, grinding, and assembly. After lathing, a part is moved to one of the milling machines, where it waits in line until it has a higher priority than any other order competing for the machine's capacity. When the milling operation on the part has been finished, the part is moved to a drilling machine, and so on. The queues can be long, creating significant time delays. Flows of materials are jumbled because the parts being processed in any one area of the shop have so many different routings.

FIGURE 7.6

Process Flows Before and After the Use of GT Cells

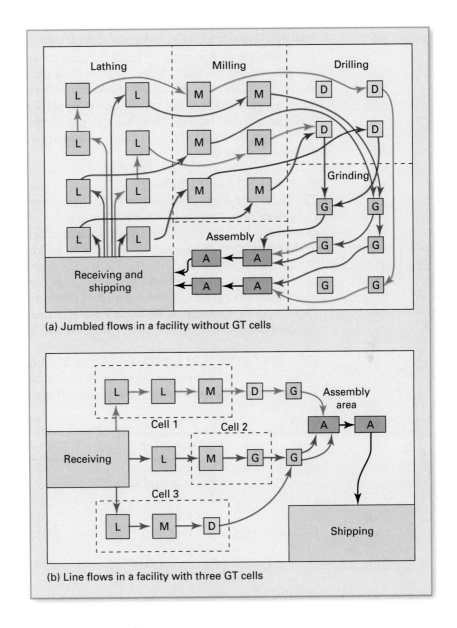

(a) Jumbled flows in a facility without GT cells

(b) Line flows in a facility with three GT cells

By contrast, the manager of the facility shown in Figure 7.6(b) has identified three product families that account for a majority of the firm's production. One family always requires two lathing operations followed by one operation at the milling machines. The second family always requires a milling operation followed by a grinding operation. The third family requires the use of a lathe, milling machine, and drill press. For simplicity, only the flows of parts assigned to these three families are shown. The remaining parts are produced at machines outside the cells and still have jumbled routings. Some equipment might have to be duplicated, as when a machine is required for one or more cells and for operations outside the cells. However, by creating three GT cells, the manager has definitely created simplified routings.

DESIGNING FLEXIBLE-FLOW LAYOUTS

The approach to designing a layout depends on whether a flexible-flow layout or a line-flow layout has been chosen. A fixed-position format basically eliminates the layout problem, whereas the design of the hybrid layout partially uses flexible-flow layout principles and partially uses line-flow layout principles.

Process layout involves three basic steps, whether the design is for a new layout or for revising an existing one: (1) gather information, (2) develop a block plan, and (3) design a detailed layout.

STEP 1: GATHER INFORMATION

The Office of Budget Management (OBM), which is a major division in a large provincial government, consists of 70 employees assigned to six different departments. It is one of several divisions occupying a relatively new office tower. Workloads have expanded to the extent that 30 new employees must be hired and somehow housed in the space allocated to OBM. While changing the layout, it also makes sense to review the layout to make sure that it is arranged as effectively as possible. The goal is to improve communication among people who must interact and to create a good work environment. Three types of information are needed to begin designing the revised layout for OBM: (1) space requirements by centre, (2) available space, and (3) closeness factors.

SPACE REQUIREMENTS BY CENTRE. OBM has grouped its processes into six different departments: administration, social services, institutions, accounting, education, and internal audit. The exact space requirements of each department, in square metres, are as follows:

Department	Area Needed (m²)
1. Administration	110
2. Social services	105
3. Institutions	85
4. Accounting	130
5. Education	90
6. Internal audit	80
Total	600

The layout designer must tie space requirements to capacity and staffing plans; calculate the specific equipment and space needs for each centre; and allow circulation space, such as aisles and the like. At OBM, a way must be found to include all 150 employees in its assigned area. Consulting with the managers and employees involved can help avoid excessive resistance to change and make the transition smooth.

block plan A plan that allocates space and indicates placement of each department.

AVAILABLE SPACE. A **block plan** allocates space and indicates placement of each department. To describe a new facility layout, the plan need only provide the facility's dimensions and space allocations. When an existing facility layout is being modified, the current block plan also is needed. OBM's available space is 30 metres by 20 metres, or 600 square metres. The designer could begin the design by dividing the total amount of space into six equal blocks (100 square metres each), even though Internal Audit needs on 80 square metres and Accounting needs 130 square metres. The equal-space approximation shown in Figure 7.7 is sufficient until the detailed layout stage, when larger departments (such as Accounting) are assigned more space than smaller departments.

FIGURE 7.7

Current Block Plan for Office of Budget Management

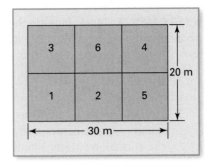

CLOSENESS FACTORS. The layout designer must also know which centres need to be located close to one another. The following table shows OBM's **closeness matrix,** which gives a measure of the relative importance of each pair of centres being located close together. The specific metric used to quantify "closeness" depends on the type of processes involved and the organizational setting. It can be a qualitative judgment on a scale from 0 to 10 that the manager uses to account for multiple performance criteria, as in the OBM's case. Only the upper right-hand portion of the matrix is used.

closeness matrix A matrix that gives the number of trips (or some other measure of materials movement) between each pair of departments per day.

Closeness Matrix

Department	Need for Interaction					
	1	**2**	**3**	**4**	**5**	**6**
1. Administration	—	3	6	5	6	10
2. Social services		—	8	1	1	
3. Institutions			—	3	9	—
4. Accounting				—	2	
5. Education					—	1
6. Internal audit						—

The closeness factors are indicators of the need for proximity based on an analysis of information flows and the need for face-to-face meetings. They give clues as to which departments should be located close together. For example, the most important interaction is between the administration and internal audit departments for OBM, with a score of 10 (first row and last column). Thus, the designer should locate departments 1 and 6 close together, which is not the arrangement in the current layout. Entries in both the columns and rows result in five factor scores for each department.

At a manufacturing plant, the closeness factor could be the number of trips (or some other measure of materials movement) between each pair of centres per day. This information can be gleaned by conducting a statistical sampling, polling supervisors and materials handlers, or using the routings and ordering frequencies for typical items made at the plant.

OTHER CONSIDERATIONS. Finally, the information gathered for OBM includes performance criteria that depend on the absolute location of a department. OBM has two criteria based on absolute location:

1. Education (department 5) should remain where it is because it is next to the office library.
2. Administration (department 1) should remain where it is because that location has the largest conference room, which administration uses often. Relocating the conference room would be costly.

Noise levels and management preference are other potential sources of performance criteria that depend on absolute location. The closeness matrix cannot reflect these criteria because it reflects only relative location considerations. The layout designer must list these criteria separately.

STEP 2: DEVELOP A BLOCK PLAN

The second step in layout design is to develop a block plan that best satisfies performance criteria and area requirements. The most elementary way to do so is by trial and error. Because success depends on the designer's ability to spot patterns in the data, this approach does not guarantee the selection of the best or even a nearly best solution. When supplemented by the use of a computer to evaluate solutions, however, such an approach often compares quite favourably with more sophisticated computerized techniques.

EXAMPLE 7.4   *Developing a Block Plan*

Develop an acceptable block plan for the Office of Budget Management, using trial and error. The goal is to locate the departments that have the greatest interaction between them (largest closeness factor) as close to each other as possible.

SOLUTION

A good place to start is with the largest closeness ratings (say, 8 and above). Beginning with the largest factor scores and working down the list, you might plan to locate departments as follows:

a. Departments 1 and 6 close together,
b. Departments 3 and 5 close together,
c. Departments 2 and 3 close together.

Departments 1 and 5 should remain at their current locations because of the "other considerations."

If after several attempts you cannot meet all three requirements, drop one or more and try again. If you can meet all three easily, add more (such as for interactions below 8). The block plan in Figure 7.8 shows a trial-and-error solution that satisfies all three requirements. We started by keeping departments 1 and 5 in their original locations. As the first requirement is to locate departments 1 and 6 close to each other, we put 6 in the upper-left corner of the layout. The second requirement is to have departments 3 and 5 close to each other, so we placed 3 in the space just above the 5, and so on.

Decision Point This solution fell into place easily for this particular problem, but it might not be the best layout. Management wants to consider several alternative layouts before making a final choice and needs some measure of effectiveness with which to compare them.

FIGURE 7.8

Proposed Block Plan

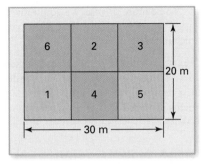

When *relative* locations are a primary concern, such as for effective materials handling, stock picking, and communication, the load-distance method can be used to compare alternative block plans. Just as with facility location decisions, we can use the total load-distance (*ld*) score by multiplying each load by the distance travelled and then summing over all of the loads. Here the loads are just the closeness factors (i.e., need for interaction) between each department in the closeness matrix. Each load goes between two centres (each represented by a row and a column in the matrix). The distance (actual, Euclidean, or rectilinear) between them is calculated from the block plan being evaluated.

EXAMPLE 7.5

Calculating the Total Desirability Score

How much better, in terms of the *ld* score, is the proposed block plan in Figure 7.8 than the current plan that was shown in Figure 7.7? Use the rectilinear distance measure.

SOLUTION

The accompanying table lists each pair of departments that has a nonzero closeness factor in the closeness matrix. For the third column, calculate the rectilinear distances between the departments in the current layout. For example, departments 3 and 5 in the current plan are in the upper-left corner and bottom-right corner of the building, respectively. The distance between the centres of these blocks is three units (two horizontally and one vertically). For the fourth column, we multiply the weights (closeness factors) by the distances, and then add the results for a total *ld* score of 112 for the current plan. Similar calculations for the proposed plan produce an *ld* score of only 82. For example, between departments 3 and 5 is just one unit of distance (one vertically and zero horizontally).

Department Pair	Closeness Factor, *I*	CURRENT PLAN		PROPOSED PLAN	
		Distance *d*	Load-Distance Score, *ld*	Distance *d*	Load-Distance Score, *ld*
1, 2	3	1	3	2	6
1, 3	6	1	6	3	18
1, 4	5	3	15	1	5
1. 5	6	2	12	2	12
1, 6	10	2	20	1	10
2, 3	8	2	16	1	8
2, 4	1	2	2	1	1
2, 5	1	1	1	2	2
3, 4	3	2	6	2	6
3, 4	9	3	27	1	9
4, 5	2	1	2	1	2
5, 6	1	2	2	3	3
			Total = 112		Total = 82

Current Plan

3	5	4
1	2	5

Proposed Plan

6	2	3
1	4	5

To be more precise, we could multiply the two *ld* total scores by 10 because each unit of distance represents 10 metres. However, the relative difference between the two totals remains unchanged.

Decision Point   Although the *ld* score in Example 7.5 for the proposed layout represents an almost 27 percent improvement, the designer may be able to do better. However, the designer must first determine whether the revised layout is worth the cost of relocating four of the six departments (all but 1 and 5). If relocation costs are too high, a less-expensive proposal must be found.

STEP 3: DESIGN A DETAILED LAYOUT

After finding a satisfactory block plan, the layout designer translates it into a detailed representation, showing the exact size and shape of each centre, the arrangement of elements (e.g., desks, machines, and storage areas), and the location of aisles, stairways, and other service space. These visual representations can be two-dimensional drawings, three-dimensional models, or computer-aided graphics. This step helps decision makers discuss the proposal and problems that might otherwise be overlooked.

DESIGNING LINE-FLOW LAYOUTS

Line-flow layouts raise management issues entirely different from those of process layouts. Often called a production or assembly line, a line-flow layout arranges workstations in sequence. The customer or product moves from one station to the next until its completion at the end of the line. Typically, one worker operates each station, performing repetitive tasks. Little inventory is built up between stations, so stations cannot operate independently. Thus, the line is only as fast as its slowest workstation or bottleneck. In other words, if the slowest station takes 45 seconds per unit, the line's fastest possible output is one product every 45 seconds.

LINE BALANCING

line balancing The assignment of work to stations in a line so as to achieve the desired output rate with the smallest number of workstations.

work elements The smallest units of work that can be performed independently.

immediate predecessors Work elements that must be done before the next element can begin.

precedence diagram A diagram that allows you to visualize immediate predecessors better; work elements are denoted by circles, with the time required to perform the work shown below each circle.

Line balancing is the assignment of work to stations in a line so as to achieve the desired output rate with the smallest number of workstations. Normally, one worker is assigned to a station. Thus, the line that produces at the desired pace with the fewest workers is the most efficient one. Line balancing must be performed when a line is set up initially, when a line is rebalanced to change its hourly output rate, or when product or process changes. The goal is to obtain workstations with well-balanced workloads (e.g., every station takes roughly 45 seconds per unit produced).

The analyst begins by separating the work into **work elements**, the smallest units of work that can be performed independently. The analyst then obtains the labour standard (see Supplement C, "Work Measurement," on the Student CD-ROM) for each element and identifies the work elements, called **immediate predecessors**, that must be done before the next can begin.

PRECEDENCE DIAGRAM.   Most lines must satisfy some technological precedence requirements—that is, certain work elements must be done before the next can begin. However, most lines also allow for some latitude and more than one sequence of operations. To help you visualize immediate predecessors better, let us run through the construction of a **precedence diagram**.[2] We denote the work elements by circles, with the time required to perform the work shown below each circle. Arrows lead from immediate predecessors to the next work element.

---

[2]Precedence relationships and precedence diagrams are also very important in the entirely different context of project scheduling (see Chapter 3, "Managing Projects").

| EXAMPLE 7.6 | *Constructing a Precedence Diagram* |

Green Grass, Inc., a manufacturer of lawn and garden equipment, is designing an assembly line to produce a new fertilizer spreader, the Big Broadcaster. Using the following information on the production process, construct a precedence diagram for the Big Broadcaster.

WORK ELEMENT	DESCRIPTION	TIME (sec)	IMMEDIATE PREDECESSOR(S)
A	Bolt leg frame to hopper	40	None
B	Insert impeller shaft	30	A
C	Attach axle	50	A
D	Attach agitator	40	B
E	Attach drive wheel	6	B
F	Attach free wheel	25	C
G	Mount lower post	15	C
H	Attach controls	20	D, E
I	Mount nameplate	18	F, G
		Total 244	

SOLUTION

Figure 7.9 shows the complete diagram. We begin with work element A, which has no immediate predecessors. Next, we add elements B and C, for which element A is the only immediate predecessor. After entering labour standards and arrows showing precedence, we add elements D and E, and so on. The diagram simplifies interpretation. Work element F, for example, can be done anywhere on the line after element C is completed. However, element I must await completion of elements F and G.

| FIGURE 7.9 |

Precedence Diagram for Assembling the Big Broadcaster

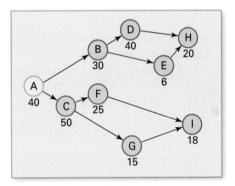

Decision Point Management now has enough information to develop a layout that clusters work elements to form workstations, with a goal being to balance the workloads and in the process minimize the number of workstations required.

DESIRED OUTPUT RATE. The goal of line balancing is to match the output rate to the production plan. For example, if the production plan calls for 4000 units per week and the line operates 80 hours per week, the desired output rate ideally would be 50 units (4000/80) per hour. Matching output to demand ensures on-time delivery and prevents buildup of unwanted inventory. However, managers should avoid rebalancing a line too frequently: every time a line is rebalanced many workers' jobs on the line have to be redesigned, temporarily hurting productivity and sometimes even requiring a new detailed layout for some stations.

Some automobile plants avoid frequent changes by eliminating a shift entirely when demand falls and inventory becomes excessive, rather than gradually scaling back the output rate. Managers can also add shifts to increase equipment utilization, which is crucial for capital-intensive facilities. However, higher pay rates or low demand may make multiple shifts undesirable or unnecessary.

cycle time The maximum time allowed for work on a unit at each station.

CYCLE TIME. After determining the desired output rate for a line, the analyst can calculate the line's cycle time. A line's **cycle time** is the maximum time allowed for work on a unit at each station.[3] If the time required for work elements at a station exceeds the line's cycle time, the station will be a bottleneck, preventing the line from reaching its desired output rate. The target cycle time is the reciprocal of the desired hourly output rate:

$$c = \frac{1}{r}$$

where:

c = Cycle time in hours per unit

r = Desired output rate in units per hour

For example, if the line's desired output rate is 60 units per hour, the cycle time is $c = 1/60$ hour per unit, or 1 minute.

THEORETICAL MINIMUM. To achieve the desired output rate, managers use line balancing to assign every work element to a station, making sure to satisfy all precedence requirements and to minimize the number of stations, n, formed. If each station is operated by a different worker, minimizing n also maximizes worker productivity. Perfect balance is achieved when the sum of the work-element times at each station equals the cycle time, c, and no station has any idle time. For example, if the sum of each station's work-element times is 1 minute, which is also the cycle time, there is perfect balance. Although perfect balance usually is unachievable in practice, owing to the unevenness of work-element times and the inflexibility of precedence requirements, it sets a benchmark, or goal, for the smallest number of stations possible. The **theoretical minimum** (**TM**) for the number of stations is:

theoretical minimum (TM) A benchmark or goal for the smallest number of stations possible, where the total time required to assemble each unit (the sum of all work-element standard times) is divided by the cycle time.

$$TM = \frac{\Sigma t}{c}$$

where:

Σt = Total time required to assemble each unit (the sum of all work-element standard times)

c = Cycle time

For example, if the sum of the work-element times is 15 minutes and the cycle time is 1 minute, TM = 15/1, or 15 stations. Any fractional values obtained for TM are rounded up because fractional stations are impossible.

IDLE TIME, EFFICIENCY, AND BALANCE DELAY. Minimizing n automatically ensures (1) minimal idle time, (2) maximal efficiency, and (3) minimal balance delay. Idle time is the total unproductive time for all stations in the assembly of each unit:

---

[3]The term *cycle time* can have multiple meanings. In addition to this definition for line balancing, cycle time can also mean the elapsed time between starting and finishing a component or product, or the time between successive units being completed for a process. You must be careful to clarify the use of the term in different settings.

$$\text{Idle time} = nc - \Sigma t$$

where:

n = Number of stations

c = Cycle time

Σt = Total standard time required to assemble each unit

Efficiency is the ratio of productive time to total time, expressed as a percent:

$$\text{Efficiency (percent)} = \frac{\Sigma t}{nc}(100)$$

balance delay The amount by which efficiency falls short of 100 percent.

Balance delay is the amount by which efficiency falls short of 100 percent:

$$\text{Balance delay (percent)} = 100 - \text{Efficiency}$$

As long as c is fixed, we can optimize all three goals by minimizing n.

EXAMPLE 7.7

Calculating the Cycle Time, Theoretical Minimum, and Efficiency

Green Grass's plant manager has just received marketing's latest forecasts of Big Broadcaster sales for the next year. She wants its production line to be designed to make 2400 spreaders per week for at least the next three months. The plant will operate 40 hours per week.

a. What should be the line's cycle time?

b. What is the smallest number of workstations that she could hope for in designing the line for this cycle time?

c. Suppose that she finds a solution that requires only five stations. What would be the line's efficiency?

SOLUTION

a. First, convert the desired output rate (2400 units per week) to an hourly rate by dividing the weekly output rate by 40 hours per week to get $r = 60$ units per hour. Then the cycle time is:

$$c = \frac{1}{r} = \frac{1}{60} \text{ hour/unit} = 1 \text{ minute/unit}$$

b. Now calculate the theoretical minimum for the number of stations by dividing the total time, Σt, by the cycle time, $c = 1$ minute = 60 seconds. Assuming perfect balance, we have:

$$\text{TM} = \frac{\Sigma t}{c} = \frac{244 \text{ seconds}}{60 \text{ seconds}} = 4.067, \quad \text{or} \quad 5 \text{ stations}$$

c. Now calculate the efficiency of a five-station solution, assuming for now that one can be found:

$$\text{Efficiency (percent)} = \frac{\Sigma t}{nc}(100) = \frac{244}{5(60)}(100) = 81.3\%$$

Decision Point Thus, if the manager finds a solution with five stations, that is the minimum number of stations possible. However, the efficiency (sometimes called the *theoretical maximum efficiency*) will be only 81.3 percent. Perhaps the line should be operated fewer than 40 hours per week and the employees transferred to other kinds of work when the line does not operate.

FINDING A SOLUTION. Often, many assembly-line solutions are possible, even for such simple problems as those of Green Grass. The goal is to cluster the work elements into workstations so that (1) the number of workstations required is minimized and (2) the precedence and cycle-time requirements are not violated. Here we use the trial-and-error method to find a solution, although commercial software packages are also available. Figure 7.10 shows a good solution that creates just five workstations, which we already calculated as the theoretical minimum. All of the precedence and cycle-time requirements are also satisfied. For example, workstation S5 consists of work elements E, H, and I, which one worker will perform on each unit that comes along the assembly line. The total processing time per unit is 44 seconds (or 6 + 20 + 18), which does not exceed the cycle time of 60 seconds (see Example 7.7). Furthermore, the immediate predecessors of these three work elements are assigned to this workstation or upstream workstations, so their precedence requirements are satisfied. For example, the worker at workstation S5 can do element I at any time but will not start element H until element E is finished.

FIGURE 7.10

Big Broadcaster Precedence Diagram Solution

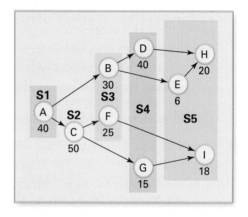

OTHER CONSIDERATIONS

In addition to balancing a line for a given cycle time, managers must also consider four other options: pacing, behavioural factors, number of models produced, and cycle times.

PACING. The movement of product from one station to the next as soon as the cycle time has elapsed is called **pacing**. Pacing allows materials handling to be automated and requires less inventory storage area. However, it is less flexible in handling unexpected delays that require either slowing down the entire line or pulling unfinished work off-line to be completed later.

pacing The movement of product from one station to the next after the cycle time has elapsed.

BEHAVIOURAL FACTORS. The most controversial aspect of product layouts is behavioural response. Studies have shown that installing production lines increases absenteeism, turnover, and grievances. Paced production and high specialization (e.g., cycle times of less than two minutes) lower job satisfaction. Workers generally favour inventory buffers as a means of avoiding mechanical pacing. One study even showed that productivity increased on unpaced lines.

mixed-model line A product line that produces several items belonging to the same family.

NUMBER OF MODELS PRODUCED. A **mixed-model line** produces several items belonging to the same family. In contrast, a single-model line produces one model with no variations. Mixed-model production enables a plant to achieve both high-volume production *and* product variety. However, it complicates scheduling and increases the need for good communication about the specific parts to be produced at each station.

CYCLE TIMES. A line's cycle time depends on the desired output rate (or sometimes on the maximum number of workstations allowed). In turn, the maximum line efficiency varies considerably with the cycle time selected. Thus, exploring a range of cycle times makes sense. A manager might go with a particularly efficient solution even if it does not match the output rate. The manager can compensate for the mismatch by varying the number of hours the line operates through overtime, extending shifts, or adding shifts. Multiple lines might even be the answer.

LOCATION AND LAYOUT PLANNING ACROSS THE ORGANIZATION

Location decisions affect processes and departments throughout the organization. When locating new retail facilities, marketing must carefully assess how the location will appeal to customers. Relocating all or part of an organization can significantly affect workforce attitudes and the ability to operate effectively across department lines. Operations management also has an important stake in location decisions. The choices can significantly affect supply chain effectiveness, workforce productivity, and the ability to provide quality products and services.

Similarly, layouts have a big impact throughout a business because every facility has a layout. Good layouts can improve coordination across departmental lines and functional area boundaries. Each process in a facility has a layout that should be carefully designed. The layouts of retail operations, such as RiverTown Crossings Mall, can affect customer attitudes and, therefore, sales. How a manufacturing or warehousing process is laid out affects materials handling costs, throughput times, and worker productivity. Redesigning layouts can require significant capital investments, which need to be analyzed from an accounting and financial perspective. Layouts also affect employee attitudes, whether on a production line or in an office.

EQUATION SUMMARY

1. Euclidean distance: $d_{AB} = \sqrt{(x_A - x_B)^2 + (y_A - y_B)^2}$

2. Rectilinear distance: $d_{AB} = |x_A - x_B| + |y_A - y_B|$

3. Load-distance score: $ld = \sum_i l_i d_i$

4. Centre of gravity: $x^* = \dfrac{\sum_i l_i x_i}{\sum_i l_i}$ and $y^* = \dfrac{\sum_i l_i y_i}{\sum_i l_i}$

5. Cycle time: $c = \dfrac{1}{r}$

6. Theoretical minimum number of workstations: $TM = \dfrac{\Sigma t}{c}$

7. Idle time (in seconds): $nc - \Sigma t$

8. Efficiency (percent): $\dfrac{\Sigma t}{nc}(100)$

9. Balance delay (percent): $100 - $ Efficiency

CHAPTER HIGHLIGHTS

● The globalization of operations affects both manufacturing and service industries. More facilities are being located in other countries, and offshore sales (and imports) are increasing. Offsetting the advantages of global operations are differences in language, regulations, and culture that create new management problems.

● Location decisions depend on many factors. For any situation some factors may be disregarded entirely; the remainder may be divided into dominant and secondary factors.

● Labour climate, proximity to markets, quality of life, proximity to suppliers and resources, and proximity to other company facilities are important factors in most manufacturing plant location decisions. Proximity to markets, clients, or customers usually is the most important factor in service industry location decisions. Competition is a complicating factor in estimating the sales potential of a location. Having competitors' facilities nearby may be an asset or a liability, depending on the type of business.

● One way of evaluating qualitative factors is to calculate a weighted score for each alternative location by using the preference matrix approach. The load-distance method brings together concerns of proximity (to markets, suppliers, resources, and other company facilities) during the early stages of location analysis. By making a full grid or patterned search of an area, an analyst identifies locations resulting in lower *ld* scores. The centre of gravity of an area is a good starting point for making a patterned search. Break-even analysis can help compare location alternatives when location factors can be expressed in terms of variable and fixed costs.

● Locating multiple facilities can be very complex. A variety of computerized heuristic, simulation, and optimization models have been developed over the last two decades to help analysts deal with this complexity.

● Layout decisions focus on placing economic activity centres within a service or manufacturing facility. This analysis must also identify which centres to include, how much space they need, and how to configure their space.

● There are four layout types: flexible-flow, line-flow, hybrid, and fixed position. Management's choice should reflect process structure. Flexible flows call for a process layout, whereas linear, high volume flows call for a line-flow layout. Hybrid layouts include one-worker multiple-machines (OWMM), group technology (GT) cells, and flexible manufacturing system (FMS).

● Capital investment, materials handling cost, and flexibility are important criteria in judging most layouts. Entirely different criteria, such as encouraging sales or communication, might be emphasized for stores or offices.

● If product volumes are too low to justify dedicating a production line to a single product, at least two options are possible. The one-worker, multiple-machines (OWMM) concept or group technology (GT) cells, where machines are arranged to produce families of parts, may be feasible.

● Designing a flexible-flow layout involves gathering the necessary information, developing an acceptable block plan, and translating the block plan into a detailed layout. Information needed includes space requirements by centre, available space, the block plan for existing layouts, closeness ratings, and performance criteria relating to absolute location concerns. A manual approach to finding a block plan begins with listing key requirements, which may be based on high closeness ratings or on other considerations. Trial and error is then used to find a block plan that satisfies most of the requirements. A load-distance score is helpful in evaluating the plan for relative location concerns.

● In line-flow layouts, workstations are arranged in a somewhat naturally occurring, commonsense sequence as required for high-volume production of only one product or a family of products. Because the physical arrangement is determined by the product's design, management concerns become line balance, pacing, behaviour, number of models, and cycle times.

● In line balancing, tasks are assigned to stations so as to satisfy all precedence and cycle-time constraints while minimizing the number of stations required. Balancing minimizes idle time, maximizes efficiency, and minimizes delay. The desired output rate from a line depends not only on demand forecasts but also on frequency of rebalancing, capacity utilization, and job specialization.

CD-ROM RESOURCES

The Student CD-ROM that accompanies this text contains the following resources, which allow you to further practise and apply the concepts presented in this chapter.

- **Equation Summary**: All the equations for this chapter can be found in one convenient location.

- **Discussion Questions**: Six questions will challenge your understanding of location factors, ethical obligations in location, layout criteria, office layout, and layout differences between a health system and a steel factory.

- **Cases**:

  - *Tyler Emergency Medical Services*. A growing community requires the addition of a new facility to shorten response times.

  - *Locating Multiple Facilities at Witherspoon Automotive*. An aging distribution centre is being closed and two new sites need to be chosen to better service customers based on multiple criteria.

  - *Imaginative Toys*. What are the dominant and secondary factors in this location decision?

  - *Hightec, Inc*. What block plan do you propose, and why is it effective?

  - *The Pizza Connection*. Prepare a revised layout and explain why it addresses the issues that Dave Collier identified.

  - *R.U. Reddie for Location*. To maximize the net present value of the investment in a new plant, should Rhonda Reddie build the plant in Denver or St. Louis?

- **Videos of MapPoint**: Three videos demonstrate the use of Microsoft MapPoint software.

  - *Starbucks*. Explore how customer demographics determine service location, as described earlier in the Managerial Practice feature.

  - *Tyler Emergency Medical Services*. A growing community requires the addition of a new facility to improve response times. (A description of the case is provided separately.)

  - *Witherspoon Automotive*. An aging distribution centre is being closed and two new sites need to be chosen to better service customers based on multiple criteria. (A description of the case is provided separately.)

- **Experiential Exercise**: Use the *Pizza Connection* case as an in-class team experience.

- **OM Explorer Tutors**: OM Explorer contains five tutor programs that will help you learn how to use the preference matrix, distance measures, centre of gravity, break-even analysis, and line balancing.

- **OM Explorer Solvers**: OM Explorer has seven programs that can be used to solve general problems involving the centre of gravity (either with or without MapPoint) and driving distance (with MapPoint). In addition, one program explores options for a flexible-flow process layout.

- **Supplement A:** *Decision Making*. See how to do break-even analysis that can be applied to location analysis.

- **Supplement C:** *Work Measurement*. See how to obtain the labour standards needed for the task times in line balancing.

- **Supplement I:** *Linear Programming*. Learn about linear programming, an important tool in solving multiple-facility location problems.

SOLVED PROBLEM 1

An electronics manufacturer must expand by building a second facility. The search has been narrowed to four locations, all acceptable to management in terms of dominant factors. Assessment of these sites in terms of seven location factors is shown in Table 7.1. For example, location A has a factor score of 5 (excellent) for labour climate; the weight for this factor (20) is the highest of any.

TABLE 7.1 *Factor Information for Electronics Manufacturer*

LOCATION FACTOR	FACTOR WEIGHT	FACTOR SCORE FOR EACH LOCATION			
		A	B	C	D
1. Labour climate	20	5	4	4	5
2. Quality of life	16	2	3	4	1
3. Transportation system	16	3	4	3	2
4. Proximity to markets	14	5	3	4	4
5. Proximity to materials	12	2	3	3	4
6. Taxes	12	2	5	5	4
7. Utilities	10	5	4	3	3

Calculate the weighted score for each location. Which location should be recommended?

SOLUTION

On the basis of the weighted scores in Table 7.2, location C is the preferred site, although location B is a close second.

TABLE 7.2 *Calculating Weighted Scores for Electronics Manufacturer*

LOCATION FACTOR	FACTOR WEIGHT	WEIGHTED SCORE FOR EACH LOCATION			
		A	B	C	D
1. Labour climate	20	100	80	80	100
2. Quality of life	16	32	48	64	16
3. Transportation system	16	48	64	48	32
4. Proximity to markets	14	70	42	56	56
5. Proximity to materials	12	24	36	36	48
6. Taxes	12	24	60	60	48
7. Utilities	10	50	40	30	30
Totals	100	348	370	374	330

SOLVED PROBLEM 2

The operations manager for Fizzy Beverage Company has narrowed the search for a new facility location to seven communities. Annual fixed costs (land, property taxes, insurance, equipment, and buildings) and variable costs (labour, materials, transportation, and variable overhead) are shown in Table 7.3.

a. Which of the communities can be eliminated from further consideration because they are dominated (both variable and fixed costs are higher) by another community?

b. Plot the total cost curves for all remaining communities on a single graph. Identify on the graph the approximate range over which each community provides the lowest cost.

c. Using break-even analysis, calculate the break-even quantities to determine the range over which each community provides the lowest cost.

TABLE 7.3 *Fixed and Variable Costs for Fizzy Beverage Company*

COMMUNITY	FIXED COSTS PER YEAR	VARIABLE COSTS PER CASE
Aurora	$1 600 000	$17
Boulder	$2 000 000	$12
Cranbrook	$1 500 000	$16
Deerfield	$3 000 000	$10
Essex	$1 800 000	$15
Farber	$1 200 000	$15
Grafton	$1 700 000	$14

SOLUTION

a. Aurora and Cranbrook are dominated by Farber, as both fixed and variable costs are higher for those communities than for Farber. Essex is dominated by Grafton.

b. Figure 7.11 shows that Farber is best for low volumes, Boulder for intermediate volumes, and Deerfield for high volumes. Although Grafton is not dominated by any community, it is the second or third choice over the entire range. Grafton does not become the lowest-cost choice at any volume.

FIGURE 7.11

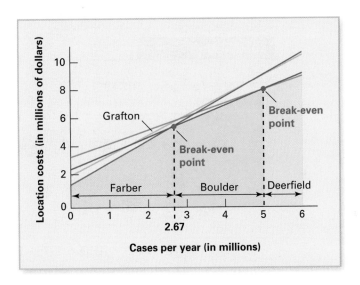

c. The break-even point between Farber and Boulder is:

$$\$1\ 200\ 000 + \$1.50Q = \$2\ 000\ 000 + \$1.20Q$$
$$Q = 2.67 \text{ million cases per year}$$

The break-even point between Deerfield and Boulder is:

$$\$3\ 000\ 000 + \$1Q = \$2\ 000\ 000 + \$1.20Q$$
$$Q = 5.0 \text{ million cases per year}$$

SOLVED PROBLEM 3

A supplier to the electric utility industry has a heavy product, and transportation costs are high. One market area includes the lower part of the Great Lakes region and the upper portion of the southeastern region. More than 600 000 tonnes are to be shipped to eight major customer locations, as shown in Table 7.4.

TABLE 7.4 *Markets for Electric Utilities Supplier*

CUSTOMER LOCATION	TONNES SHIPPED	XY-COORDINATES
Three Rivers, MI	5 000	(7,13)
Fort Wayne, IN	92 000	(8,12)
Columbus, OH	70 000	(11,10)
Ashland, KY	35 000	(11,7)
Kingsport, TN	9 000	(12,4)
Akron, OH	227 000	(13,11)
Wheeling, WV	16 000	(14,10)
Roanoke, VA	153 000	(15,5)

a. Calculate the centre of gravity, rounding distance to the nearest tenth.

b. Calculate the load-distance score for this location, using rectilinear distance.

SOLUTION

a. The centre of gravity is $(12.4, 9.2)$.

$$\sum_i l_i = 5 + 92 + 70 + 35 + 9 + 227 + 16 + 153 = 607$$

$$\sum_i l_i x_i = 5(7) + 92(8) + 70(11) + 35(11) + 9(12) + 227(13) + 16(14) + 153(15)$$

$$= 7504$$

$$x^* = \frac{\sum_i l_i y_i}{\sum_i l_i} = \frac{7504}{607} = 12.4$$

$$\sum_i l_i y_i = 5(13) + 92(12) + 70(10) + 35(7) + 9(4) + 227(11) + 16(10) + 153(5) = 5572$$

$$y^* = \frac{\sum_i l_i y_i}{\sum_i l_i} = \frac{5572}{607} = 9.2$$

b. The load-distance score is:

$$ld = \sum_i l_i d_i = 5(5.4 + 3.8) + 92(4.4 + 2.8) + 70(1.4 + 0.8) + 35(1.4 + 2.2)$$

$$+ 9(0.4 + 5.2) + 227(0.6 + 1.8) + 16(1.6 + 0.8) + 153(2.6 + 4.2)$$

$$= 2662.4$$

where:

$$d_i = |x_i - x^*| + |y_i - y^*|$$

SOLVED PROBLEM 4

A defence contractor is evaluating its machine shop's current process layout. Figure 7.12 shows the current layout, and the table shows the trip matrix for the facility. Safety and health regulations require departments E and F to remain at their current locations.

FIGURE 7.12

Current Layout

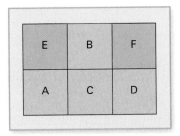

	TRIPS BETWEEN DEPARTMENTS					
DEPARTMENT	**A**	**B**	**C**	**D**	**E**	**F**
A	—	8	3		9	5
B		—		3		
C			—		8	9
D				—		3
E					—	3
F						—

a. Use trial and error to find a better layout.
b. How much better is your layout than the current one in terms of the *ld* score? Use rectilinear distance.

SOLUTION

a. In addition to keeping departments E and F at their current locations, a good plan would locate the following department pairs close to each other: A and E, C and F, A and B, and C and E. Figure 7.13 was worked out by trial and error and satisfies all these requirements. Start by placing E and F at their current locations. Then, because C must be as close as possible to both E and F, put C between them. Place A directly south of E, and B next to A. All of the heavy traffic concerns have now been accommodated. Department D is located in the remaining space.

FIGURE 7.13

Proposed Layout

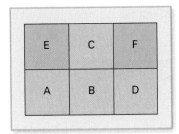

DEPARTMENT PAIR	NUMBER OF TRIPS (1)	CURRENT PLAN		PROPOSED PLAN	
		DISTANCE (2)	LOAD × DISTANCE (1) × (2)	DISTANCE (3)	LOAD × DISTANCE (1) × (3)
A, B	8	2	16	1	8
A, C	3	1	3	2	6
A, E	9	1	9	1	9
A, F	5	3	15	3	15
B, D	3	2	6	1	3
C, E	8	2	16	1	8
C, F	9	2	18	1	9
D, F	3	1	3	1	3
E, F	3	2	6	2	6
			ld = 92		*ld* = 67

b. The table reveals that the *ld* score drops from 92 for the current plan to 67 for the revised plan, a 27 percent reduction.

SOLVED PROBLEM 5

A company is setting up an assembly line to produce 192 units per eight-hour shift. The following table identifies the work elements, times, and immediate predecessors.

WORK ELEMENT	TIME (sec)	IMMEDIATE PREDECESSOR(S)
A	40	None
B	80	A
C	30	D, E, F
D	25	B
E	20	B
F	15	B
G	120	A
H	145	G
I	130	H
J	115	C, I
Total	720	

a. What is the desired cycle time?

b. What is the theoretical minimum number of stations?

c. Use trial and error to work out a solution, and show your solution on a precedence diagram.

d. What are the efficiency and balance delay of the solution found?

SOLUTION

a. Substituting in the cycle-time formula, we get:

$$c = \frac{1}{r} = \frac{8 \text{ hours}}{192 \text{ units}} (3600 \text{ seconds/hour}) = 150 \text{ seconds/unit}$$

b. The sum of the work-element times is 720 seconds, so:

$$TM = \frac{\Sigma t}{c}$$

$$= \frac{720 \text{ seconds/unit}}{150 \text{ seconds/unit-station}} = 4.8 \qquad \text{or} \qquad 5 \text{ stations}$$

which may not be achievable.

c. The precedence diagram is shown in Figure 7.14. Each row in the following table shows work elements assigned to each of the five workstations in the proposed solution.

FIGURE 7.14

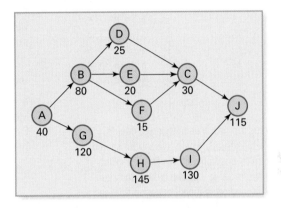

STATION	WORK ELEMENT	WORK-ELEMENT TIME (sec)	CUMULATIVE TIME TIME (sec)	IDLE TIME (C = 150 sec)
S1	A	40	40	110
	B	80	120	30
	D	25	145	5
S2	G	120	120	30
	E	20	140	10
S3	H	145	145	5
S4	I	130	130	20
	F	15	145	5
S5	C	30	30	120
	J	115	145	5

d. Calculating the efficiency, we get:

$$\text{Efficiency} = \frac{\Sigma t}{nc}(100)$$

$$= \frac{720 \text{ seconds/unit}}{5(150 \text{ seconds/unit})}(100)$$

$$= 96\%$$

Thus, the balance delay is only 4 percent (100 − 96).

PROBLEMS

1. Calculate the weighted score for each location (A, B, C, and D) shown in Table 7.5. Which location would you recommend?

TABLE 7.5 *Factors for Locations A–D*

LOCATION FACTOR	FACTOR WEIGHT	FACTOR SCORE FOR EACH LOCATION			
		A	B	C	D
1. Labour climate	5	5	4	3	5
2. Quality of life	30	2	3	5	1
3. Transportation system	5	3	4	3	5
4. Proximity to markets	25	5	3	4	4
5. Proximity to materials	5	3	2	3	5
6. Taxes	15	2	5	5	4
7. Utilities	15	5	4	2	1
Total	100				

2. John and Jane Darling are newlyweds trying to decide among several available rentals. Alternatives were scored on a scale of 1 to 5 (5 = best) against weighted performance criteria, as shown in Table 7.6. The criteria included rent, proximity to work and recreational opportunities, security, and other neighbourhood characteristics associated with the couple's values and lifestyle. Alternative A is an apartment, B is a bungalow, C is a condo, and D is a downstairs apartment in Jane's parents' home.

TABLE 7.6 *Factors for Newlyweds*

LOCATION FACTOR	FACTOR WEIGHT	FACTOR SCORE FOR EACH LOCATION			
		A	B	C	D
1. Rent	25	3	1	2	5
2. Quality of life	20	2	5	5	4
3. Schools	5	3	5	3	1
4. Proximity to work	10	5	3	4	3
5. Proximity to recreation	15	4	4	5	2
6. Neighbourhood security	15	2	4	4	4
7. Utilities	10	4	2	3	5
Total	100				

Which location is indicated by the preference matrix? What qualitative factors might cause this preference to change?

3. Two alternative locations are under consideration for a new plant: Winnipeg and Montreal. The Winnipeg location is superior in terms of costs. However, management believes that sales volume would decline if this location were chosen because it is farther from the market and the firm's customers prefer local suppliers. The selling price of the product is $250 per unit in either case. Use the following information to determine which location yields the higher total profit contribution per year.

LOCATION	ANNUAL FIXED COST	VARIABLE COST PER UNIT	FORECAST DEMAND PER YEAR
Winnipeg	$1 500 000	$50	30 000 units
Montreal	$2 800 000	$85	40 000 units

4. Fall-Line, Inc., is a Great Falls, Montana, manufacturer of a variety of downhill skis. Fall-Line is considering four locations for a new plant: Aspen, Colorado; Medicine Lodge, Kansas; Broken Bow, Nebraska; and Wounded Knee, South Dakota. Annual fixed costs and variable costs per pair of skis are shown in the following table:

LOCATION	ANNUAL FIXED COSTS	VARIABLE COSTS PER PAIR
Aspen	$8 000 000	$250
Medicine Lodge	$2 400 000	$130
Broken Bow	$3 400 000	$90
Wounded Knee	$4 500 000	$65

a. Plot the total cost curves for all the communities on a single graph (see Solved Problem 2 on page 270). Identify on the graph the range in volume over which each location would be best.

b. What break-even quantity defines each range?

Although Aspen's fixed and variable costs are dominated by those of the other communities, Fall-Line believes that both the demand and the price would be higher for skis made in Aspen than for skis made in the other locations. The following table shows those projections:

LOCATION	PRICE PER PAIR	FORECAST DEMAND PER YEAR
Aspen	$500	60 000 pairs
Medicine Lodge	$350	45 000 pairs
Broken Bow	$350	43 000 pairs
Wounded Knee	$350	40 000 pairs

c. Determine which location yields the highest total profit contribution per year.

d. Is this location decision sensitive to forecast accuracy? At what minimum sales volume does Aspen become the location of choice?

5. The operations manager for Hot House Roses has narrowed the search for a new facility location to seven communities. Annual fixed costs (land, property taxes, insurance, equipment, and buildings) and variable costs (labour, materials, transportation, and variable overhead) are shown in the following table:

COMMUNITY	FIXED COSTS PER YEAR	VARIABLE COSTS PER DOZEN
Aurora	$210 000	$7.20
Bedford	$200 000	$7.00
Garden City	$150 000	$9.00
Kentville	$280 000	$6.20
Roseland	$260 000	$6.00
Seaforth	$420 000	$5.00
Waterford	$370 000	$8.00

a. Which of the communities can be eliminated from further consideration because they are dominated (both variable and fixed costs are higher) by another community?

b. Plot the total cost curves for the remaining communities on a single graph. Identify on the graph the approximate range over which each community provides the lowest cost.

c. Using break-even analysis, calculate the break-even quantities to determine the range over which each community provides the lowest cost.

6. The following three points are the locations of important facilities in a transportation network: (20, 20), (30, 50), and (60, 0). The coordinates are in kilometres.

a. Calculate the Euclidean distances (in kilometres) between each of the three pairs of facilities.

b. Calculate these distances using rectilinear distances.

7. Centura High School is to be located at the population centre of gravity of three communities: Boelus, population 228; Cairo, population 737; and Dannebrog, population 356. The coordinates (on a grid of square kilometres) for the communities are provided in Figure 7.15. Where should Centura High School be located? (Round to the nearest 0.1 kilometres.) What factors may result in locating at the site indicated by this technique?

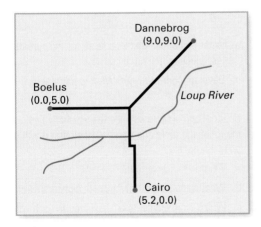

Dannebrog
(9.0, 9.0)

Boelus
(0.0, 5.0)

Loup River

Cairo
(5.2, 0.0)

FIGURE 7.15

8. A larger and more modern main post office is to be constructed at a new location. Growing suburbs have shifted the population density from where it was 40 years ago, when the current facility was built. Annette Werk, the postmaster, asked her assistants to draw a grid map of the seven points where mail is picked up and delivered in bulk. The coordinates and trips per day to and from the seven mail source points and the current main post office, M, are shown in the following table. M will continue to act as a mail source point after relocation.

MAIL SOURCE POINT	ROUND TRIPS PER DAY (l)	XY-COORDINATES (km)
1	6	(2, 8)
2	3	(6, 1)
3	3	(8, 5)
4	3	(13, 3)
5	2	(15, 10)
6	7	(6, 14)
7	5	(18, 1)
M	3	(10, 3)

a. Calculate the centre of gravity as a possible location for the new facility (round to the nearest whole number).

b. Compare the load-distance scores for the location in part (a) and the current location, using rectilinear distance.

9. Paramount Manufacturing is investigating which location would best position its new plant relative to two suppliers (located in cities A and B) and one market area (represented by city C). Management has limited the search for this plant to those three locations. The following information has been collected:

LOCATION	XY-COORDINATES (km)	TONNES PER YEAR	FREIGHT RATE ($/TONNE-km)
A	(100, 200)	4000	3
B	(400, 100)	3000	1
C	(100, 100)	4000	3

a. Which of the three locations gives the lowest total cost, based on Euclidean distances? *Hint:* The annual cost of inbound shipments from supplier A to the new plant is $12 000 per kilometre (4000 tonnes per year × $3 per tonne-kilometre).

b. Which location is best, based on rectilinear distances?

c. What are the coordinates of the centre of gravity?

10. Baker Machine Company specializes in manufacturing precision parts for firms in the aerospace industry. Figure 7.16 shows the current block plan for the key manufacturing centres of the 7500-square-metre facility. Referring to the trip matrix below the figure, use rectilinear distance (the current distance from inspection to shipping and receiving

is 3 units) to calculate the change in the load-distance, *ld*, score if Baker exchanges the locations of the tool crib and inspection.

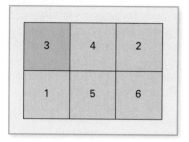

FIGURE 7.16

Trip Matrix

DEPARTMENT	TRIPS BETWEEN DEPARTMENTS					
	1	2	3	4	5	6
1. Burr and grind	—	8	3		9	5
2. NC equipment		—		3		
3. Shipping and receiving			—		8	9
4. Lathes and drills				—		3
5. Tool crib					—	3
6. Inspection						—

11. Use trial and error to find a particularly good block plan for Baker Machine (see Problem 10). Because of excessive relocation costs, shipping and receiving (department 3) must remain at its current location. Compare *ld* scores to evaluate your new layout, again assuming rectilinear distance.

12. Richard Garber is the head designer for Matthews and Novak Design Company. Garber has been called in to design the layout for a newly constructed office building. From statistical samplings over the past three months, Garber developed the trip matrix shown here for daily trips between the department's offices.

Trip Matrix

DEPARTMENT	TRIPS BETWEEN DEPARTMENTS					
	A	B	C	D	E	F
A	—	25	90			165
B		—			105	
C			—		125	125
D				—	25	
E					—	105
F						—

a. If other factors are equal, which two offices should be located closest together?

b. Figure 7.17 shows an alternative layout for the department. What is the total load-distance score for this plan,

using rectilinear distance and assuming that offices A and B are 3 units of distance apart?

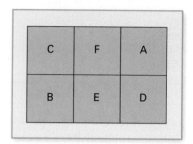

FIGURE 7.17

c. Switching which two departments will most improve the total load-distance score?

13. A firm with four departments has the following trip matrix and the current block plan shown in Figure 7.18.

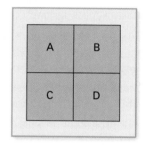

FIGURE 7.18 Current Block Plan

Closeness Matrix

DEPARTMENT	TRIPS BETWEEN DEPARTMENTS			
	A	B	C	D
A	—	12	10	8
B		—	20	6
C			—	0
D				—

a. What is the load-distance score for the current layout (assuming rectilinear distance)?

b. Develop a better layout. What is its total load-distance score?

14. Use trial and error to balance the assembly line described in the following table and Figure 7.19 so that it will produce 40 units per hour.

a. What is the cycle time?

b. What is the theoretical minimum number of workstations?

c. Which work elements are assigned to each workstation?

d. What are the resulting efficiency and balance delay percentages?

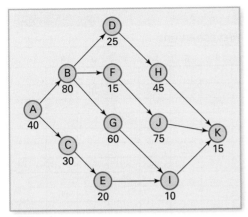

FIGURE 7.19

WORK ELEMENT	TIME (sec)	IMMEDIATE PREDECESSOR(S)
A	40	None
B	80	A
C	30	A
D	25	B
E	20	C
F	15	B
G	60	B
H	45	D
I	10	E, G
J	75	F
K	15	H, I, J
	Total 415	

15. Johnson Cogs wants to set up a line to produce 60 units per hour. The work elements and their precedence relationships are shown in the following table.

WORK ELEMENT	TIME (sec)	IMMEDIATE PREDECESSOR(S)
A	40	None
B	30	A
C	50	A
D	40	B
E	6	B
F	25	C
G	15	C
H	20	D, E
I	18	F, G
J	30	H, I
	Total 274	

a. What is the theoretical minimum number of stations?

b. How many stations are required, using trial and error to find a solution?

c. Suppose that a solution requiring five stations is obtained. What is its efficiency?

16. The *trim line* at PW is a small subassembly line that, along with other such lines, feeds into the final chassis line. The entire assembly line, which consists of more than 900 work-stations, is to make PW's new E cars. The trim line itself involves only 13 work elements and must handle 20 cars per hour. In addition to the usual precedence constraints, there are two *zoning constraints*. First, work elements 11 and 12 should be assigned to the same station; both use a common component, and assigning them to the same station con-serves storage space. Second, work elements 8 and 10 can-not be performed at the same station. Work-element data are as follows:

WORK ELEMENT	TIME (sec)	IMMEDIATE PREDECESSOR(S)
A	1.8	None
B	0.4	None
C	1.6	None
D	1.5	A
E	0.7	A
F	0.5	E
G	0.8	B
H	1.4	C
I	1.4	D
J	1.4	F, G
K	0.5	H
L	1.0	J
M	0.8	I, K, L

a. Draw a precedence diagram.

b. What cycle time (in minutes) results in the desired output rate?

c. What is the theoretical minimum number of stations?

d. Using trial and error, balance the line as best you can.

e. What is the efficiency of your solution?

17. CCI Electronics makes various products for the communica-tions industry. One of its manufacturing plants makes a device for sensing when telephone calls are placed. A from-to matrix is shown in Table 7.7; the current layout appears in Figure 7.21. Management is reasonably satisfied with the current layout, although it has heard some complaints about the placement of departments D, G, K, and L. Use informa-tion in the from-to matrix to create a trip matrix, and then find a revised block plan for moving only the four depart-ments about which complaints have been made. Show that the load-distance score is improved. Assume rectilinear distance.

TABLE 7.7 *From-To Matrix*

DEPARTMENT	A	B	C	D	E	F	G	H	I	J	K	L
A. Network lead forming	—											80
B. Wire forming and subassembly		—							50	70		
C. Final assembly			—			120						
D. Inventory storage				—	40							
E. Presoldering				80	—						90	
F. Final testing						—	120					
G. Inventory storage		30					—	40	50			
H. Coil winding								—	80			
I. Coil assembly			70		40				—		60	
J. Network preparation	90									—		
K. Soldering			80								—	
L. Network insertion			60									—

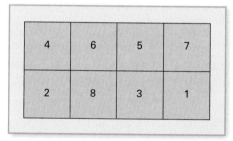

FIGURE 7.20 Current Block Plan

Block plan grid:
L	H	B	K
F	I	J	A
C	D	E	G

18. A paced assembly line has been devised to manufacture calculators, as the following data show:

STATION	WORK ELEMENT ASSIGNED	WORK ELEMENT TIME (min)
S1	A	2.7
S2	D, E	0.6, 0.9
S3	C	3.0
S4	B, F, G	0.7, 0.7, 0.9
S5	H, I, J	0.7, 0.3, 1.2
S6	K	2.4

a. What is the maximum hourly output rate from this line? *Hint:* The line can go only as fast as its slowest workstation.

b. What cycle time corresponds to this maximum output rate?

c. If a worker is at each station and the line operates at this maximum output rate, how much idle time is lost during each 10-hour shift?

d. What is the line's efficiency?

19. The associate administrator at Getwell Hospital wants to evaluate the layout of the outpatient clinic. Table 7.8 shows the interdepartmental flows (patients/day) between departments; Figure 7.21 shows the current layout.

TABLE 7.8 *Trip Matrix*

DEPARTMENT	1	2	3	4	5	6	7	8
1. Reception	—	25	35	5	10	15		20
2. Business office		—	5	10	15			15
3. Examining room			—	20	30	20		10
4. X-ray				—	25	15		25
5. Laboratory					—	20		25
6. Surgery						—	40	
7. Postsurgery							—	15
8. Doctor's office								—

FIGURE 7.21 Current Layout

Layout grid:
| 4 | 6 | 5 | 7 |
| 2 | 8 | 3 | 1 |

a. Determine the effectiveness of the current layout, as measured by the total *ld* score, using rectilinear distances.

b. Try to find the best possible layout on the basis of the same effectiveness measure.

c. What is the impact on your new solution if it must be revised to keep department 1 at its present location?

d. How should the layout developed in part (c) be revised if the interdepartmental flow between the examining room and the X-ray department is increased by 50 percent? decreased by 50 percent?

REFERENCES AND FURTHER READINGS

Andel, T. "Site Selection Tools Dig Data." *Transportation & Distribution,* vol. 37 (1996), no. 6, pp. 77–81.

Bartness, A. D. "The Plant Location Puzzle." *Harvard Business Review,* March/April, 1994, pp. 20–30.

Bitner, Mary Jo. "Servicescapes: The Impact of Physical Surroundings on Customers and Employees." *Journal of Marketing,* vol. 56 (April 1992), pp. 57–71.

"The Boom Belt." *Business Week,* September 27, 1993, pp. 98–104.

Bozer, Y. A., and R. D. Meller. "A Reexamination of the Distance-Based Layout Problem." *IIE Transactions,* vol. 29 (1997), no. 7, pp. 549–560.

Cook, Thomas M., and Robert A. Russell. *Introduction to Management Sciences.* Englewood Cliffs, NJ: Prentice-Hall, 1993.

"Cool Offices." *Fortune,* December 9, 1996, pp. 204–210.

"Cummins Engine Flexes Its Factory." *Harvard Business Review,* March/April 1990, pp. 120–127.

DeForest, M. E. "Thinking of a Plant in Mexico?" *The Academy of Management Executive,* vol. 8 (1994), no. 1, pp. 33–40.

Drezner, Z. *Facility Location: A Survey of Applications and Methods.* Secaucus, NJ: Springer-Verlag, 1995.

Ferdows, Kasra. "Making the Most of Foreign Factories." *Fortune,* March/April 1997, pp. 73–88.

Frazier, G. V., and M. T. Spriggs, "Achieving Competitive Advantage Through Group Technology," *Business Horizons,* vol. 39 (1996), no. 3, pp. 83–90.

Heragu, Sunderesh. *Facilities Design.* Boston, MA: PWS Publishing Company, 1997.

Hyer, N. L., and K. H. Brown. "The Discipline of Real Cells." *Journal of Operations Management,* vol. 17 (1999), no. 5, pp. 557–574.

Kanter, Rosabeth Moss. "Transcending Business Boundaries: 12,000 World Managers View Change." *Harvard Business Review,* May/June 1991, pp. 151–164.

Klassen, Robert D., and D. Clay Whybark. "Barriers to the Management of International Operations." *Journal of Operations Management,* vol. 11 (1994), no. 4, pp. 385–396.

Kuehn, Alfred A., and Michael J. Hamburger. "A Heuristic Program for Locating Warehouses." *Management Science,* vol. 9, (1963), no. 4, pp. 643–666.

"Long Distance: Innovative MCI Unit Finds Culture Shock in Colorado Springs." *Wall Street Journal,* June 25, 1996.

MacCormack, A. D., L. J. Newman III, and D. B. Rosenfield. "The New Dynamics of Global Manufacturing Site Location." *Sloan Management Review,* Summer 1994, pp. 69–77.

"Making Malls (Gasp!) Convenient." *Wall Street Journal,* February 8, 2000.

"Mexico: A Rough Road Back." *Business Week,* November 13, 1995, pp. 104–107.

"Retailing: Confronting the Challenges That Face Bricks-and-Mortar Stores." *Harvard Business Review,* July/August 1999, p. 159.

Sugiura, Hideo. "How Honda Localizes Its Global Strategy." *Sloan Management Review,* Fall 1990, pp. 77–82.

Sule, D. R. *Manufacturing Facilities: Location, Planning, and Design.* Boston, MA: PWS Publishing Company, 1994.

Suresh, N. C., and J. M. Kay, eds. *Group Technology and Cellular Manufacturing: A State-of-the-Art Synthesis of Research and Practice.* Boston, MA: Kluwer Academic Publishers, 1997.

"Tools of the Remote Trade." *Business Week,* March 27, 2000, p. F20.

Vargas, G. A., and T. W. Johnson. "An Analysis of Operational Experience in the U.S./Mexico Production Sharing (Maquiladora) Program." *Journal of Operations Management,* vol. 11 (1993), no. 1, pp. 17–34.

"Will This Open Space Work?" *Harvard Business Review,* May/June 1999, p. 28.

Across the Organization

Forecasting is important to:

- **finance,** which uses long-term forecasts to project needs for capital.
- **human resources,** which uses forecasts to estimate the need for workers.
- **management information systems,** which designs and implements forecasting systems.
- **marketing,** which develops sales forecasts that are used for medium and long-range plans.
- **operations,** which develops and uses forecasts for decisions such as scheduling workers, short-term inventory replenishment, and long-term planning for capacity.

Learning Goals

After reading this chapter, you will be able to:

1. explain collaborative planning, forecasting, and replenishment (CPFR).
2. describe the various judgmental forecasting approaches.
3. explain the use of regression to make forecasts.
4. show how to compute forecasts using the most common approaches for time-series analysis.
5. describe the various measures of forecast errors.
6. explain how forecast errors are used to monitor and control forecast performance.

One of the critical drivers in managing value chains is effective customer demand planning (CDP), which begins with accurate forecasts. CDP is a business-planning process that enables sales teams (and customers) to develop demand forecasts as input to service-planning processes, production and inventory planning, and revenue planning. Forecasting is generally seen as the process of developing the most probable view of what future demand will be, given a set of assumptions about technology, competitors, pricing, marketing, expenditures, and sales effort. Planning, on the other hand, is the process of making management decisions on how to deploy resources to best respond to the demand forecasts. Forecasts must generally precede plans: It is not possible to make decisions on staffing levels, purchasing commitments, and inventory levels until forecasts that give reasonably accurate views of demand over the forecasting time horizon are developed.

Unilever—the purveyor of fast-moving consumer products like Dove, Lipton, Hellmann's, and hundreds of other brands—has a state-of-the-art CDP system. Using computer software, historical shipment data is blended with promotional data, allowing information sharing and collaboration with important customers. The system begins with shipment history and current order information; reliable data is a critical requirement for constructing an initial baseline forecast. However, because data frequently are collected from disparate legacy systems, they may contain errors and may not necessarily lead to the best forecast. Moreover, historical statistical information is not useful in forecasting the outcomes of certain events, promotions, rollouts, and special packages, which are common in the industry.

Lipton Tea is one of the many Unilever products, and its demand must be forecast for around the world. For centuries, globalism's story travelled with merchants who shepherded spices along Eurasian trade routes. Now it travels over wires and radio waves, satellites, airplanes, and gigabytes.

To overcome these problems, planners must adjust initial forecasts with additional input from others. For each promotion, special sales teams predict the "lift," or projected increase in sales. These data are routed to the demand-planning system, where changes are applied weekly to specific stock-keeping units (SKUs) and distribution centres. In turn, these forecasts are reviewed and further adjusted if needed. Unilever also conducts external market research, which is analyzed and combined with the retail customer promotions, and fed into the demand-planning system.

To further improve the accuracy of its forecasts and reduce inventory lead times, Unilever compares point-of-sale (POS) data with its own forecasts. Unfortunately, not all customers provide POS data, and integrating the data from those that do is challenging given the many different formats. Because of this complexity, Unilever only collects POS data from its largest customers. Ultimately, planners must negotiate the final numbers each week and feed these forecasts into the demand-planning system.

Overall, the current CDP system has been a success. Unilever has reduced its inventory and improved its customer service. However, if collaboration and the usage of POS data were to increase, Unilever would likely reap even larger benefits. The next step for Unilever is to collaborate with its customers and suppliers, a process by which forecasts, promotion plans, and other data are shared among these firms to determine the final forecast. This process is known as collaborative planning, forecasting, and replenishment (CPFR).

Source: Robert L. Mitchell, "Case Study: Unilever Crosses the Data Streams," *Computerworld* (December 17, 2001); Robert L. Mitchell, "Tech Check: Getting Demand Planning Right," *Computerworld* (December 17, 2001); Chana R. Schoenberger, "The Weakest Link," *Forbes* (October 1, 2001), p. 114.

forecast A prediction of
future events used for
planning purposes.

Unilever's success to date demonstrates the value of forecasting. A **forecast** is a prediction of future events used for planning purposes. Changing business conditions resulting from global competition, rapid technological change, and increasing environmental concerns exert pressure on a firm's capability to generate accurate forecasts. Forecasts are needed to aid in determining what resources are needed, scheduling existing resources, and acquiring additional resources. Accurate forecasts allow schedulers to use capacity efficiently, reduce customer response times, and cut inventories.

Forecasting methods may be based on mathematical models using historical data available, qualitative methods drawing on managerial experience, or a combination of both. Variations of these methods are valuable in estimating future processing times and learning-curve effects (see Supplement C, "Measuring Output Rates," and Supplement D, "Learning Curve Analysis," on the Student CD-ROM). In this chapter, our focus is on demand forecasts. We will explore several forecasting methods commonly used today and their advantages and limitations. We also identify the decisions that managers should make in designing a forecasting system.

DEMAND PATTERNS

At the root of most business decisions is the challenge of forecasting customer demand. It is a difficult task, because the demand for goods and services can vary greatly. For example, demand for lawn fertilizer predictably increases in the spring and summer months; however, the particular weekends when demand is heaviest may depend on uncontrollable factors such as the weather. Sometimes patterns are more predictable. Thus, weekly demand for haircuts at a local barbershop may be quite stable from week to week, with daily demand being heaviest on Saturday mornings and lightest on Mondays and Tuesdays. Forecasting demand in such situations requires uncovering the underlying patterns from available information. In this section, we first discuss the basic patterns of demand.

time series The repeated
observations of demand
for a product or service in
their order of occurrence.

The repeated observations of demand for a product or service in their order of occurrence form a pattern known as a **time series**. The five basic patterns of most demand time series are:

1. *Horizontal,* or the fluctuation of data around a constant mean

2. *Trend,* or systematic increase or decrease in the mean of the series over time

3. *Seasonal,* or a repeatable pattern of increases or decreases in demand, depending on the time of day, week, month, or season

4. *Cyclical,* or less predictable gradual increases or decreases in demand over longer periods of time (years or decades)

5. *Random,* or unforecastable, variation in demand

Cyclical patterns arise from two influences. The first is the business cycle, which includes factors that cause the economy to go from recession to expansion over a number of years. The other influence is the product or service life cycle, which reflects the stages of demand from development through decline. Business cycle movement is difficult to predict because it is affected by national or international events, such as parliamentary elections or political turmoil in other countries. Predicting the rate of demand increase or decline in the life cycle also is difficult. Sometimes firms estimate demand for a new product by starting with the demand history for the product it is replacing.

Four of the patterns of demand—horizontal, trend, seasonal, and cyclical—combine in varying degrees to define the underlying time pattern of demand for a product or service. The fifth pattern, random variation, results from chance causes and, thus, cannot be predicted. Random variation is an aspect of demand that makes every forecast wrong. Figure 8.1 shows the first four patterns of a demand time series, all of which contain random variation. A time series may comprise any combination of these patterns.

FIGURE 8.1

Patterns of Demand

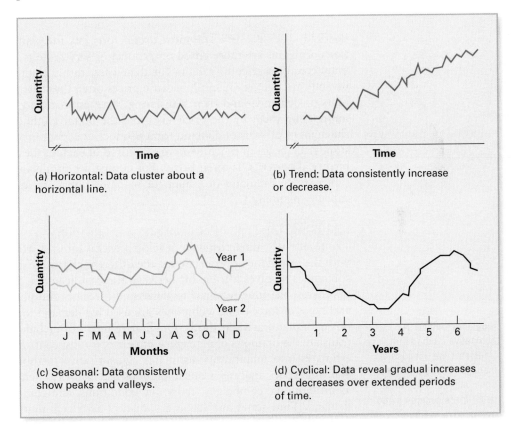

(a) Horizontal: Data cluster about a horizontal line.

(b) Trend: Data consistently increase or decrease.

(c) Seasonal: Data consistently show peaks and valleys.

(d) Cyclical: Data reveal gradual increases and decreases over extended periods of time.

DESIGNING THE FORECASTING SYSTEM

Before using forecasting techniques to analyze operations management problems, a manager must make three decisions: (1) what to forecast, (2) what type of forecasting technique to use, and (3) what type of computer hardware or software (or both) to use. We discuss each of these decisions before examining specific forecasting techniques.

DECIDING WHAT TO FORECAST

Although some sort of demand estimate is needed for the individual goods or services produced by a company, forecasting total demand for groups or clusters and then deriving individual product or service forecasts may be easiest. Also, selecting the correct unit of measurement (e.g., product or service units or machine-hours) for forecasting may be as important as choosing the best method.

LEVEL OF AGGREGATION. Few companies err by more than 5 percent when forecasting total demand for all their products. However, errors in forecasts for individual items

aggregation The act of clustering several similar products or services so that companies can obtain more accurate forecasts.

may be much higher. By clustering several similar products or services in a process called **aggregation**, companies can obtain more accurate forecasts. Many companies utilize a two-tier forecasting system, first making forecasts for families of goods or services that have similar demand requirements and common processing, labour, and materials requirements and then deriving forecasts for individual items. This approach maintains consistency between planning for the final stages of manufacturing (which requires the unit forecasts) and longer-term planning for sales, profit, and capacity (which requires the product family forecasts).

UNITS OF MEASUREMENT. The most useful forecasts for planning and analyzing operations problems are those based on product or service units, such as customers needing maintenance service or repairs for their cars, rather than dollars. Forecasts of sales revenue are not very helpful, because prices often fluctuate. Forecasting the number of units of demand—and then translating these estimates to sales revenue estimates by multiplying them by the price—is often the better method. If accurately forecasting the number of units of demand for a product or service is not possible, forecasting the standard labour- or machine-*hours* required of each of the critical resources, based on historical patterns, is often better. For companies producing goods or services to customer order, estimates of labour- or machine-hours are important to scheduling and capacity planning.

CHOOSING THE TYPE OF FORECASTING TECHNIQUE

The forecaster's objective is to develop a useful forecast from the information at hand with the technique appropriate for the different characteristics of demand. This choice sometimes involves a trade-off between forecast accuracy and costs, such as software purchases, the time required to develop a forecast, and personnel training. Two general types of forecasting techniques are used for demand forecasting: qualitative methods and quantitative methods. Qualitative methods include **judgment methods**, which translate the opinions of managers, expert opinions, consumer surveys, and sales-force estimates into quantitative estimates. Quantitative methods include causal methods and time-series analysis. **Causal methods** use historical data on related variables, such as promotional campaigns, economic conditions, and competitors' actions, to predict demand. **Time-series analysis** is a statistical approach that relies heavily on historical demand data to project the future size of demand and recognizes trends and seasonal patterns.

A key factor in choosing the proper forecasting approach is the time horizon for the decision requiring forecasts. Forecasts can be made for the short term, medium term, and long term. Table 8.1 contains examples of demand forecast applications and the typical planning horizon for each.

judgment method A qualitative method that translates the opinions of managers, expert opinions, consumer surveys, and sales-force estimates into quantitative estimates.

causal method A quantitative method that uses historical data on related variables, such as promotional campaigns, economic conditions, and competitors' actions to predict demand.

time-series analysis A statistical approach that relies heavily on historical demand data to project the future size of demand and recognizes trends and seasonal patterns.

FORECASTING WITH COMPUTERS

In many short-term forecasting applications, computers are a necessity. Often companies must prepare forecasts for hundreds or even thousands of services or products repeatedly. For example, a large network of health-care facilities must calculate demand forecasts for each of its services for every department. This undertaking involves voluminous data that must be manipulated frequently. Analysts must examine the time series for each service or product and arrive at a forecast (see the Managerial Practice box on page 288). Both off-the-shelf and custom software are widely used to ease the burden of tracking and coordinating forecasts.

An important development in forecasting is a general approach whereby a firm uses software to share information and work together with its customers to make and refine

TABLE 8.1

Demand Forecast Applications

Application	Time Horizon		
	Short Term (0–3 months)	**Medium Term (3 months–2 years)**	**Long Term (more than 2 years)**
Forecast quantity	Individual products or services	Total sales Groups of families of products or services	Total sales
Decision area	Inventory management Final assembly scheduling Workforce scheduling Master production scheduling	Staff planning Production planning Master production sheduling Purchasing Distribution	Facility location Capacity planning Process management
Forecasting technique	Time series Causal Judgment	Causal Judgment	Causal Judgment

collaborative planning, forecasting, and replenishment (CPFR) An approach to forecasting that allows a manufacturer and its customers to work together to make and refine a forecast over the Internet.

forecasts over the Internet. **The collaborative planning, forecasting, and replenishment (CPFR)** model calls for the comparison of two forecasts, one from each partner in a supply chain (e.g., manufacturer and retailer). If the forecasts differ by more than a predetermined percentage, the partners share comments and supporting data until an acceptable forecast is achieved.

Benefits of CPFR can be significant for both firms. Experience reported by companies such as Wal-Mart and Warner-Lambert show that the retailer has products in stock with greater reliability, thus increasing sales. The manufacturer benefits from smoother production plans and lower overall costs. However, factors such as legacy systems, mutual trust, and geography have limited adoption of CPFR to date.

JUDGMENT METHODS

When adequate historical data are lacking, as when a new product is introduced or technology is expected to change, firms rely on managerial judgment and experience to generate forecasts. Judgment methods can also be used to modify forecasts generated by quantitative methods. In this section, we discuss four of the more successful methods currently in use: sales-force estimates, executive opinion, market research, and the Delphi method. As noted in the Managerial Practice, the first two are among the most popular in use in Canada.

SALES FORCE ESTIMATES

sales force estimates The forecasts that are compiled from estimates of future demands made periodically by members of a company's sales force.

Sometimes the best information about future demand comes from the people closest to the customer. **Sales force estimates** are forecasts compiled from estimates of future demands made periodically by members of a company's sales force. This approach has several advantages:

- The sales force is the group most likely to know which products or services customers will be buying in the near future and in what quantities.
- Sales territories often are divided by district or region. Information broken down in this manner can be useful for inventory management, distribution, and sales-force staffing purposes.
- The forecasts of individual sales-force members can be combined easily to get regional or national sales.

MANAGERIAL PRACTICE
Canadian Forecasting Practices

As senior managers develop strategy and plan execution, forecasting is a critical element. Accurate and timely forecasts allow managers to improve customer responsiveness, to reduce inventory holding costs, to adjust capacity expansion, to better schedule supplier deliveries, and, ultimately, to contribute to the bottom line. A recent study of Canadian forecasting practices assessed the methods and results for a broad cross-section of large and small manufacturing and service firms. The 118 survey respondents had an average revenue of approximately $800 million.

Managers reported that forecasting is both time-consuming and costly. One-third of companies spend over $50 000 annually on forecasting systems. Very similar methods were used by service and manufacturing firms. The three most commonly used forecasting methods were:

- Naive forecast (most recent period's sales)

- Sales-force composite

- Jury of executive opinion

Short-term forecasts tend to rely on the first two methods, while the last one is used for longer-term projections of one to two years. For the most part, these methods are qualitative in nature, as even last-period sales is often modified on the basis of the judgment of senior management or the marketing group. More complex quantitative approaches, such as econometric models or regression analysis, have made relatively few inroads into Canadian practice, even in larger firms.

A significant percentage of managers, 40 percent, reported using several forecasting methods, and generally combined these using either judgment or a weighted average. Managers who rely on more than one method indicated that their forecast accuracy improved by almost 10 percent. Given the data requirements of various methods, it is not surprising that most managers reported using computer software to assist with forecasting. With almost half the firms, this software takes the form of custom, in-house programs; the balance rely on commercial applications and typically use a spreadsheet.

Monitoring forecast accuracy is an important first step in assessing the overall effectiveness of alternative methods. Without such efforts, there is little hope for systematic improvement in practice over time. Yet, managers in only about 60 percent of firms reported that forecast accuracy was formally monitored; for these, the average error ranged from 5.9 percent for annual forecasts to 7.1 percent for monthly forecasts. Clearly, monitoring remains an area that needs greater attention from senior management. As described in Chapter 6, "Inventory Management," improved forecasting proved to be a critical element in reducing inventory levels reported by Xerox Canada.

Source: R. D. Klassen, *Global Manufacturing Practices Project: Canadian Forecasting Practices* (London, ON: Ivey Publishing, 1998).

But it also has several disadvantages:

- Individual biases of the salespeople may taint the forecast; moreover, some people are naturally optimistic, whereas others are more cautious.

- Salespeople may not always be able to detect the difference between what a customer "wants" (a wish list) and what a customer "needs" (a necessary purchase).

- If the firm uses individual sales as a performance measure, salespeople may underestimate their forecasts so that their performance will look good when they exceed their projections or may work hard only until they reach their required minimum sales.

EXECUTIVE OPINION

executive opinion A forecasting method in which the opinions, experience, and technical knowledge of one or more managers are summarized to arrive at a single forecast.

When a new product or service is contemplated, the sales force may not be able to make accurate demand estimates. **Executive opinion** is a forecasting method in which the opinions, experience, and technical knowledge of one or more managers are summarized to arrive at a single forecast. As we discuss later, executive opinion can be used to modify an existing sales forecast to account for unusual circumstances, such as a new sales promotion or unexpected international events. Executive opinion can also be used for **technological forecasting**, as the quick pace of technological change makes keeping abreast of the latest advances difficult. The key to effective use of executive opinion is to ensure that the forecast reflects not a series of independent modifications but consensus among executives on a single forecast.

technological forecasting An application of executive opinion to account for the difficulties of keeping abreast of the latest advances in technology.

MARKET RESEARCH

market research A systematic approach to gathering market information to determine customer interest in a product or service, including surveys of potential customers.

Market research is a systematic approach to gathering market information to determine customer interest in purchasing a product or service. A variety of techniques are possible, including assessing the demand for a related product, using focus groups, and administering data-gathering surveys. Although market research yields important information, one shortcoming is the numerous qualifications and hedges typically included in the findings. Another is that the typical response rate for survey questionnaires, either postal or e-mail, is very low, which can add to cost and reduce confidence in the forecast. Finally, the survey might be based on imitative, rather than innovative, ideas and behaviour, because the customer's reference point is often limited.

DELPHI METHOD

Delphi method A process of gaining consensus from a group of experts while maintaining their anonymity.

The **Delphi method** is a process of gaining consensus from a group of experts while maintaining their anonymity. This form of forecasting is useful when there are no historical data from which to develop statistical models and when managers inside the firm have no experience on which to base informed projections. A coordinator sends questions to each member of the group of outside experts, who may not even know who else is participating. Anonymity is important when some members of the group tend to dominate discussion or command a high degree of respect in their fields. In an anonymous group, the members tend to respond to the questions and support their responses freely. The coordinator prepares a statistical summary of the responses along with a summary of arguments for particular responses. The report is sent to the same group for another round, and the participants may choose to modify their previous responses. These rounds continue until consensus is obtained.

The Delphi method can be used to develop long-range forecasts of product demand and new-product sales projections or to make technological forecasts. It can also be used to obtain a consensus from a panel of experts who devote their attention to following scientific advances, changes in society, governmental regulations, and the competitive environment. The results can provide direction for a firm's research and development staff.

GUIDELINES FOR USING JUDGMENT FORECASTS

Judgment forecasting is clearly needed when no quantitative data are available to use in quantitative forecasting approaches. However, judgment approaches can be used in concert with quantitative approaches to improve forecast quality. Among the guidelines for the use of judgment to adjust the results of quantitative forecasts are the following:

● *Adjust quantitative forecasts when they tend to be inaccurate and the decision maker has important contextual knowledge.* Contextual knowledge is knowledge that practitioners gain through experience, such as cause-and-effect relationships, environmental cues, and organizational information, that may have an effect on the variable being forecast. Often these factors cannot be incorporated into quantitative forecasting approaches. The quality of forecasts generated by quantitative approaches also deteriorates as the variability of the data increases, particularly for time series. The more variable the data, the more likely it is that judgment forecasting will improve the forecasts.

● *Make adjustments to quantitative forecasts to compensate for specific events.* Specific events such as advertising campaigns, the actions of competitors, or international developments are often not recognized in quantitative forecasting and should be acknowledged when a final forecast is being made.

In the remainder of this chapter, we focus on the commonly used quantitative forecasting approaches.

CAUSAL METHODS: LINEAR REGRESSION

linear regression A causal method in which one variable (the dependent variable) is related to one or more independent variables by a linear equation.

dependent variable The measure or quantity that is being forecast.

independent variables Variables assumed to be related to the dependent variable and therefore predict or "cause" the results observed in the past.

Causal methods are used when historical data are available and the relationship between the factor to be forecasted and other external or internal factors (e.g., government actions or advertising promotions) can be identified. These relationships are expressed in mathematical terms and can be very complex. Causal methods provide the most sophisticated forecasting tools and are very good for predicting turning points in demand and preparing long-range forecasts. Although many causal methods are available, we focus here on linear regression, one of the best-known and most commonly used causal methods.

In **linear regression**, one variable, called a **dependent variable**, is related to one or more **independent variables** by a linear equation. The dependent variable, such as demand for doorknobs, is the one the manager wants to forecast. The independent variables, such as advertising expenditures and new housing starts, are assumed to affect the dependent variable and thereby "cause" the results observed in the past. Figure 8.2 shows how a linear regression line relates to the data. In technical terms, the regression line minimizes the squared deviations from the actual data.

FIGURE 8.2

Linear Regression Line Relative to Actual Data

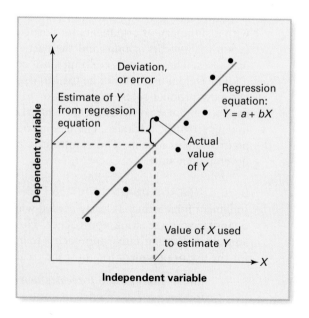

In the simplest linear regression models, the dependent variable is a function of only one independent variable, and therefore the theoretical relationship is a straight line:

$$Y = a + bX$$

where:

$Y =$ Dependent variable
$X =$ Independent variable
$a =$ Y-intercept of the line
$b =$ Slope of the line

The objective of linear regression analysis is to find values of a and b that minimize the sum of the squared deviations of the actual data points from the graphed line. Computer programs are used for this purpose. For any set of matched observations for Y and X, the program computes the values of a and b and provides measures of forecast accuracy. Three measures commonly reported are the sample correlation coefficient, the sample coefficient of determination, and the standard error of the estimate.

The *sample correlation coefficient*, r, measures the direction and strength of the relationship between the independent variable and the dependent variable. The value of r can range from -1 to $+1$. A correlation coefficient of 1 implies that period-by-period changes in direction (increases or decreases) of the independent variable are always accompanied by changes in the same direction by the dependent variable. An r of -1 means that decreases in the independent variable are always accompanied by increases in the dependent variable, and vice versa. A zero value of r means that there is no relationship between the variables. The closer the value of r is to ± 1, the better the regression line fits the points.

The *sample coefficient of determination* measures the amount of variation in the dependent variable about its mean that is explained by the regression line. The coefficient of determination is the square of the correlation coefficient, or r^2, and its value ranges from 0 to 1. Higher values of r^2 indicate that more variance is explained, which indicates that the forecasts generated by the regression equation are closely related to the dependent variable.

The *standard error of the estimate*, s_{yx}, measures how closely the data on the dependent variable cluster around the regression line. Although it is similar to the sample standard deviation, it measures the error from the dependent variable, Y, to the regression line, rather than to the mean. More specifically, it is the standard deviation of the difference between the actual demand and the estimate provided by the regression equation. When determining which independent variable to include in the regression equation, you should choose the one with the smallest standard error of the estimate.

| EXAMPLE 8.1 | *Using Linear Regression to Forecast Product Demand* |

The person in charge of production scheduling for a company must prepare forecasts of product demand in order to plan for appropriate production quantities. During a luncheon meeting, the marketing manager gives her information about the advertising budget for a brass door hinge. The following are sales and advertising data for the past five months:

MONTH	SALES (thousands of units)	ADVERTISING (thousands of $)
1	264	2.5
2	116	1.3
3	165	1.4
4	101	1.0
5	209	2.0

The marketing manager says that next month the company will spend $1750 on advertising for the product. Use linear regression to develop an equation and a forecast for this product.

SOLUTION

We assume that sales are linearly related to advertising expenditures. In other words, sales are the dependent variable, Y, and advertising expenditures are the independent variable, X. Using the paired monthly observations of sales and advertising expenditures supplied by the marketing manager, we use the Regression Solver (see OM Explorer on the Student CD-ROM) to determine the best values of a, b, the correlation coefficient, the coefficient of determination, and the standard error of the estimate.

$$a = -8.137$$
$$b = 109.230$$
$$r = 0.980$$
$$r^2 = 0.960$$
$$s_{yx} = 15.603$$

The regression equation is:

$$Y = -8.137 + 109.230X$$

and the regression line is shown in Figure 8.3.

FIGURE 8.3

Linear Regression Line for the Sales Data

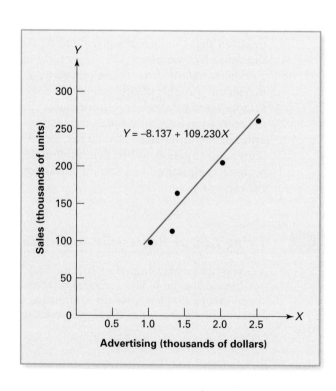

Are advertising expenditures a good choice to use in forecasting sales? Note that the sample correlation coefficient, r, is 0.98. Because the value of r is very close to 1, we conclude that there is a strong positive relationship between sales and advertising expenditures and that the choice was a good one.

Next, we examine the sample coefficient of determination, r^2, or 0.96. This value of r^2 implies that 96 percent of the variation in sales is explained by advertising expenditures. Most relationships between advertising and sales in practice are not this strong, because other variables such as general economic conditions and the strategies of competitors often combine to affect sales.

As the advertising expenditure will be $1750, the forecast for month 6 is:

$$Y = -8.137 + 109.230(1.75)$$
$$= 183.016 \text{ or } 183\ 016 \text{ units}$$

Decision Point The production scheduler can use this forecast to determine the quantity of brass door hinges needed for month 6. Suppose that she has 62 500 units in stock. The requirement to be filled from production is 183 015 − 62 500 = 120 015 units, assuming that she does not want to lose any sales.

Often several independent variables may affect the dependent variable. For example, advertising expenditures, new corporation startups, and residential building contracts may be important for estimating the demand for door hinges. In such cases, *multiple regression analysis* is helpful in determining a forecasting equation for the dependent variable as a function of several independent variables. Such models can be analyzed with OM Explorer, and they can be quite useful for predicting turning points and solving many planning problems.

TIME-SERIES METHODS

Rather than using independent variables for the forecast as regression models do, time-series methods use historical information regarding only the dependent variable. These methods are based on the assumption that the dependent variable's past pattern will continue in the future. Time-series analysis identifies the underlying patterns of demand that combine to produce an observed historical pattern of the dependent variable and then develops a model to replicate it. In this section, we focus on time-series methods that address the horizontal, trend, and seasonal patterns of demand. Before we discuss statistical methods, let us take a look at the simplest time-series method for addressing all patterns of demand—the naive forecast.

NAIVE FORECAST

naive forecast A time-series method whereby the forecast for the next period equals the demand for the current period.

A method often used in practice is the **naive forecast**, whereby the forecast for the next period equals the demand for the current period. So, if the actual demand for Wednesday is 35 customers, the forecasted demand for Thursday is 35 customers. If the actual demand on Thursday is 42 customers, the forecasted demand for Friday is 42 customers.

The naive-forecast method may take into account a demand trend. The increase (or decrease) in demand observed between the last two periods is used to adjust the current demand to arrive at a forecast. Suppose that last week the demand was 120 units and the week before it was 108 units. Demand increased 12 units in one week, so the forecast for next week would be 120 + 12 = 132 units. If the actual demand next week turned out to be 127 units, the next forecast would be 127 + 7 = 134 units. The naive-forecast method also may be used to account for seasonal patterns. If the demand last July was 50 000 units, the forecast for this July is 50 000 units. Similarly, forecasts of demand for each month of the coming year may simply reflect actual demand in the same month last year.

The advantages of the naive-forecast method are its simplicity and low cost. The method works best when the horizontal, trend, or seasonal patterns are stable and random variation is small. If random variation is large, using last period's demand to estimate next period's demand can result in highly variable forecasts that are not useful for planning purposes. Nonetheless, if its level of accuracy is acceptable, the naive forecast is an attractive approach for time-series forecasting.

ESTIMATING THE AVERAGE

Every demand time series has at least two of the five patterns of demand: horizontal and random. It *may* have trend, seasonal, or cyclical patterns. We begin our discussion of statistical methods of time-series forecasting with demand that has no trend, seasonal, or cyclical patterns. The horizontal pattern in a time series is based on the mean of the demands, so we focus on forecasting methods that estimate the average of a time series of data. Consequently, for all the methods of forecasting we discuss in this section, the forecast of demand for *any* period in the future is the average of the time series computed in the current period. For example, if the average of past demand calculated on Tuesday is 65 customers, the forecasts for Wednesday, Thursday, and Friday are 65 customers each day.

Consider Figure 8.4, which shows patient arrivals at a medical clinic over the past 28 weeks. Assume that the demand pattern for patient arrivals has no trend, seasonal, or cyclical pattern. The time series has only a horizontal and random pattern. As no one can predict random error, we focus on estimating the average. The statistical techniques useful for forecasting such a time series are (1) simple moving averages, (2) weighted moving averages, and (3) exponential smoothing.

FIGURE 8.4

Weekly Patient Arrivals at a Medical Clinic

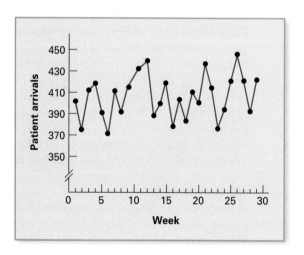

simple moving average method A time-series method used to estimate the average of a demand time series by averaging the demand for the *n* most recent time periods.

SIMPLE MOVING AVERAGES. The **simple moving average method** is used to estimate the average of a demand time series and thereby remove the effects of random fluctuation. It is most useful when demand has no pronounced trend or seasonal influences. Applying a moving average model simply involves calculating the average demand for the *n* most recent time periods and using it as the forecast for the next time period. For the next period, after the demand is known, the oldest demand from the previous average is replaced with the most recent demand and the average is recalculated. In this way, the *n* most recent demands are used, and the average "moves" from period to period.

Specifically, the forecast for period $t + 1$ can be calculated as:

$$F_{t+1} = \frac{\text{Sum of last } n \text{ demands}}{n} = \frac{D_t + D_{t-1} + D_{t-2} + \cdots + D_{t-n+1}}{n}$$

where:

D_t = Actual demand in period t

n = Number of most recent periods in the average

F_{t+1} = Forecast for period $t + 1$

With the moving average method, the forecast of next period's demand equals the average calculated at the end of this period.

| EXAMPLE 8.2 | *Using the Moving Average Method to Estimate Average Demand* |

a. Compute a *three-week* moving average forecast for the arrival of medical clinic patients in week 4. The numbers of arrivals for the past three weeks were:

WEEK	PATIENT ARRIVALS
1	400
2	380
3	411

b. If the actual number of patient arrivals in week 4 is 415, what is the forecast for week 5?

SOLUTION

a. The moving average forecast at the end of week 3 is:

$$F_4 = \frac{411 + 380 + 400}{3} = 397.0$$

b. The forecast for week 5 requires the actual arrivals from weeks 2–4, the three most recent weeks of data.

$$F_5 = \frac{415 + 411 + 380}{3} = 402.0$$

Decision Point Thus, the forecast at the end of week 3 would have been 397 patients for week 4. The forecast for week 5, made at the end of week 4, would have been 402 patients. In addition, at the end of week 4 the forecast for week 6 and beyond is also 402 patients.

The moving average method may involve the use of as many periods of past demand as desired. The stability of the demand series generally determines how many periods to include (i.e., the value of n). Stable demand series are those for which the average (to be estimated by the forecasting method) only infrequently experiences changes. Large values of n should be used for demand series that are stable and small values of n for those that are susceptible to changes in the underlying average.

Including more historical data in the average by increasing the number of periods results in a forecast that is less susceptible to random variations. If the underlying average in the series is changing, however, the forecasts will tend to lag behind the changes for a longer time interval, because of the additional time required to remove the old data from the forecast. We address other considerations in the choice of n when we discuss choosing a time-series method.

weighted moving average method A time-series method in which each historical demand in the average can have its own weight; the sum of the weights is equal to 1.

WEIGHTED MOVING AVERAGES. In the simple moving average method, each demand has the same weight in the average—namely, $1/n$. In the **weighted moving average method**, each historical demand in the average can have its own weight, with the sum of the weights equalling 1. For example, in a *three-period* weighted moving average model, the most recent period might be assigned a weight of 0.50, the second most recent might be weighted 0.30, and the third most recent might be weighted 0.20. The average is obtained by multiplying the weight of each period by the value for that period and adding the products together (see Solved Problem 2 on page 307 for a numerical example). The advantage of a weighted moving average method is that it allows you to emphasize recent demand over earlier demand.

exponential smoothing method A weighted moving average method that calculates the average of a time series by giving recent demands more weight than earlier demands.

EXPONENTIAL SMOOTHING. The **exponential smoothing method** is a sophisticated weighted moving average method that calculates the average of a time series by giving recent demands more weight than earlier demands. It is the most frequently used formal forecasting method because of its simplicity and the small amount of data needed to support it. Unlike the weighted moving average method, which requires n periods of past demand and n weights, exponential smoothing requires only three items of data: the last period's forecast; the demand for this period; and a smoothing parameter, alpha (α), which has a value between 0 and 1. To obtain an exponentially smoothed forecast, calculate a weighted average of the most recent demand and the forecast calculated last period. The equation for the forecast is:

$$F_{t+1} = \alpha(\text{Demand this period}) + (1 - \alpha)(\text{Forecast calculated last period})$$
$$= \alpha D_t + (1 - \alpha)F_t$$

An equivalent equation is:

$$F_{t+1} = F_t + \alpha(D_t - F_t)$$

This form of the equation shows that the forecast for the next period equals the forecast for the current period plus a proportion of the forecast error for the current period.

The emphasis given to the most recent demand levels can be adjusted by changing the smoothing parameter. Larger α values emphasize recent levels of demand and result in forecasts more responsive to changes in the underlying average. Smaller α values treat past demand more uniformly and result in more stable forecasts. This approach is analogous to adjusting the value of n in the moving average methods, except there smaller values of n emphasize recent demand and larger values give greater weight to past demand. In practice, various values of α are tried and the one producing the best forecasts is chosen.

Exponential smoothing requires an initial forecast to get started. There are two ways to get this initial forecast: either use last period's demand or, if some historical data are available, calculate the average of several recent periods of demand. The effect of the initial estimate of the average on successive estimates of the average diminishes over time, because the weights given to successive historical demands used to calculate the average decay exponentially.

EXAMPLE 8.3   *Using Exponential Smoothing to Estimate Average Demand*

Again consider the patient arrival data in Example 8.2. It is now the end of week 3. Using $\alpha = 0.10$, calculate the exponential smoothing forecast for week 4.

SOLUTION

The exponential smoothing method requires an initial forecast. Suppose that we take the demand data for the past two weeks and average them, obtaining $(400 + 380)/2 = 390$ as an initial forecast. To obtain the forecast for week 4, using exponential smoothing with $\alpha = 0.10$, we calculate the average at the end of week 3 as:

$$F_4 = 0.10(411) + 0.90(390) = 392.1$$

Thus, the forecast for week 4 would be 392 patients. If the actual demand for week 4 proved to be 415, the new forecast for week 5 would be:

$$F_5 = 0.10(415) + 0.90(392.1) = 394.4$$

or 394 patients. Note that we used F_4, not the integer-value forecast for week 4, in the computation for F_5. In general, we round off (when it is appropriate) only the final result to maintain as much accuracy as possible in the calculations.

Decision Point Using this exponential smoothing model, the analyst's forecasts would have been 392 patients for week 4 and then 394 patients for week 5 and beyond. As soon as the actual demand for week 5 is known, then the forecast for week 6 will be updated.

Exponential smoothing has the advantages of simplicity and minimal data requirements. It is inexpensive to use and, therefore, very attractive to firms that make thousands of forecasts for each time period. However, its simplicity is also a disadvantage when the underlying average is changing, as in the case of a demand series with a trend. Like any method geared solely to the assumption of a stable average, exponential smoothing results will lag behind changes in the underlying average of demand. Higher α values may help reduce forecast errors when there is a change in the average of the time series; however, the lags will still be there if the average is changing systematically. Typically, if large α values (e.g., greater than 0.5) are required for an exponential smoothing application, chances are good that a more sophisticated model is needed because of a significant trend or seasonal influence in the demand series.

INCLUDING A TREND

Let's now consider a demand time series that has a trend. A trend in a time series is a systematic increase or decrease in the average of the series over time. Where a trend is present, exponential smoothing approaches must be modified; otherwise, the forecasts always will be below or above the actual demand.

To improve the forecast we need to calculate an estimate of the trend. We start by calculating the *current* estimate of the trend, which is the difference between the average of the series computed in the current period and the average computed last period. To obtain an estimate of the long-term trend, you can average the current estimates. The method for estimating a trend is similar to that used for estimating the demand average with exponential smoothing.

trend-adjusted exponential smoothing method
The method for incorporating a trend in an exponentially smoothed forecast.

The method for incorporating a trend in an exponentially smoothed forecast is called the **trend-adjusted exponential smoothing method**. With this approach the estimates for both the average and the trend are smoothed, requiring two smoothing constants. For each period, we calculate the average and the trend:

$$A_t = \alpha(\text{Demand this period}) + (1 - \alpha)(\text{Average} + \text{Trend estimate last period})$$

$$= \alpha D_t + (1 - \alpha)(A_{t-1} + T_{t-1})$$

$$T_t = \beta(\text{Average this period} - \text{Average last period})$$
$$+ (1 - \beta)(\text{Trend estimate last period})$$

$$= \beta(A_t - A_{t-1}) + (1 - \beta)T_{t-1}$$

$$F_{t+1} = A_t + T_t$$

where:

A_t = Exponentially smoothed average of the *series* in period t

T_t = Exponentially smoothed average of the *trend* in period t

α = Smoothing parameter for the average, with a value between 0 and 1

β = Smoothing parameter for the trend, with a value between 0 and 1

F_{t+1} = Forecast for period $t + 1$

To make forecasts for periods beyond the next period, we multiply the trend estimate (T_t) by the number of additional periods that we want in the forecast and add the results to the current average (A_t).

Estimates for last period's average and trend needed for the first forecast can be derived from past data or based on an educated guess if no historical data exist. To find values for α and β, often an analyst systematically adjusts α and β until the forecast errors are lowest. This process can be carried out in an experimental setting with the model used to forecast historical demands.

For a numerical example of the trend-adjusted exponential smoothing method, see Solved Problem 4 on page 309.

SEASONAL PATTERNS

Many organizations experience seasonal demand for their goods or services. Seasonal patterns are regularly repeating upward or downward movements in demand measured in periods of less than one year (hours, days, weeks, months, or quarters). In this context, the time periods are called *seasons*. For example, customer arrivals at a fast-food shop on any day may peak between 11 a.m. and 1 p.m. and again from 5 to 7 p.m. Here the seasonal pattern lasts a day, and each hour of the day is a season. Similarly, the demand for haircuts may peak on Saturday, week to week. In this case, the seasonal pattern lasts a week, and the seasons are the days of the week. Seasonal patterns may last a month, as in the weekly applications for driver's licence renewals, or a year, as in the monthly volumes of mail processed and the monthly demand for automobile tires.

An easy way to account for seasonal effects is to use one of the techniques already described but to limit the data in the time series to those time periods in the same season. For example, if there is day-of-the-week seasonal effect, then one time series would be for Mondays, one for Tuesdays, and so on. If the naive forecast is used, then the forecast for this Tuesday is the actual demand seven days ago (last Tuesday), rather than the actual demand one day ago (Monday). This method accounts for seasonal effects but has the disadvantage of discarding considerable information on past demand.

multiplicative seasonal method A method whereby seasonal factors are multiplied by an estimate of average demand to arrive at a seasonal forecast.

Other methods are available that analyze all past data, using one model to forecast demand for all of the seasons. We describe only the **multiplicative seasonal method**, whereby seasonal factors are multiplied by an estimate of average demand to arrive at a seasonal forecast. The four-step procedure presented here involves the use of simple averages of past demand, although more sophisticated methods for calculating aver-

Greeting cards have a strong seasonal demand pattern, requiring careful forecasting and management of inventory.

ages, such as a moving average or exponential smoothing approach, could be used. The following description is based on a seasonal pattern lasting one year and seasons of one month, although the procedure can be used for any seasonal pattern and seasons of any length.

1. For each year, calculate the average demand per season by dividing annual demand by the number of seasons per year. For example, if the total demand for a year is 6000 units and each month is a season, the average demand per season is 6000/12 = 500 units.

2. For each year, divide the actual demand for a season by the average demand per season. The result is a *seasonal index* for each season in the year, which indicates the level of demand relative to the average demand. For example, suppose that the demand for March was 400 units. The seasonal index for March then is 400/500 = 0.80, which indicates that March's demand is 20 percent below the average demand per month. Similarly, a seasonal index of 1.14 for April implies that April's demand is 14 percent greater than the average demand per month.

3. Calculate the average seasonal index for each season, using the results from step 2. Add the seasonal indices for a season and divide by the number of years of data. For example, suppose that we have calculated seasonal indices for April based on the last three years: 1.14, 1.18, and 1.04. The three-year average seasonal index for April is (1.14 + 1.18 + 1.04)/3 = 1.12. This is the index we will use for forecasting April's demand.

4. Calculate each season's forecast for next year. Begin by estimating the average demand per season for next year. Use the naive method, moving averages, exponential smoothing, trend-adjusted exponential smoothing, or linear regression to forecast annual demand. Divide annual demand by the number of seasons per year. Then obtain the seasonal forecast by multiplying the seasonal index by the average demand per season.

For a detailed numerical example of the multiplicative seasonal method, see Solved Problem 5 on page 310.

CHOOSING A TIME-SERIES METHOD

We now turn to factors that managers must consider in selecting a method for time-series forecasting. One important consideration is forecast performance, as determined by forecast errors. Managers need to know how to measure forecast errors and how to detect when something is going wrong with the forecasting system. After examining forecast errors and their detection, we discuss criteria that managers can use to choose an appropriate time-series forecasting method.

FORECAST ERROR

Forecasts almost always contain errors. Forecast errors can be classified as either *bias errors* or *random errors*. Bias errors are the result of consistent mistakes—the forecast is always too high or too low. These errors often are the result of neglecting or not accurately estimating patterns of demand, such as a trend, seasonal, or cyclical pattern.

The other type of forecast error, random error, results from unpredictable factors that cause the forecast to deviate from the actual demand. Forecasting analysts try to minimize the effects of bias and random errors by selecting appropriate forecasting models, but eliminating all forms of errors is impossible.

forecast error The difference found by subtracting the forecast from actual demand for a given period.

MEASURES OF FORECAST ERROR. Before they can think about minimizing forecast error, managers must have some way to measure it. **Forecast error** is simply the difference between the forecast and actual demand for a given period, or:

$$E_t = D_t - F_t$$

where:

E_t = Forecast error for period t

D_t = Actual demand for period t

F_t = Forecast for period t

However, managers are usually more interested in measuring forecast error over a relatively long period of time.

The **cumulative sum of forecast errors (CFE)** measures the total forecast error:

$$\text{CFE} = \Sigma E_t$$

cumulative sum of forecast errors (CFE) A measurement of the total forecast error that assesses the bias in a forecast.

Large positive errors tend to be offset by large negative errors in the CFE measure. Nonetheless, CFE is useful in assessing bias in a forecast. For example, if a forecast is always lower than actual demand, the value of CFE will gradually get larger and larger. This increasingly large error indicates some systematic deficiency in the forecasting approach. Perhaps the analyst omitted a trend element or a cyclical pattern, or perhaps seasonal influences changed from their historical pattern. Note that the average forecast error is simply:

$$\overline{E} = \frac{\text{CFE}}{n}$$

mean squared error (MSE) A measurement of the dispersion of forecast errors.

standard deviation (σ) A measurement of the dispersion of forecast errors.

mean absolute deviation (MAD) A measurement of the dispersion of forecast errors.

The **mean squared error (MSE)**, **standard deviation (σ)**, and **mean absolute deviation (MAD)** measure the dispersion of forecast errors:

$$\text{MSE} = \frac{\Sigma E_t^2}{n}$$

$$\sigma = \sqrt{\frac{\Sigma(E_t - \overline{E})^2}{n - 1}}$$

$$MAD = \frac{\Sigma |E_t|}{n}$$

The mathematical symbol | | is used to indicate the absolute value—that is, it tells you to disregard positive or negative signs. If MSE, σ, or MAD is small, the forecast is typically close to actual demand; a large value indicates the possibility of large forecast errors. The measures differ in the way they emphasize errors. Large errors get far more weight in MSE and σ, because the errors are squared. MAD is a widely used measure of forecast error because managers can easily understand it; it is merely the mean of the forecast errors over a series of time periods, without regard to whether the error was an overestimate or an underestimate. MAD also is used in tracking signals and inventory control. Earlier, we discussed how MAD or σ can be used to determine safety stocks for inventory items (see Chapter 6, "Inventory Management").

mean absolute percent error (MAPE) A measurement that relates the forecast error to the level of demand.

The **mean absolute percent error (MAPE)** relates the forecast error to the level of demand and is useful for putting forecast performance in the proper perspective:

$$MAPE = \frac{\sum \frac{|E_t|}{D_+}}{n} (100) \quad \text{(expressed as a percent)}$$

For example, an absolute forecast error of 100 results in a larger percentage error when the demand is 200 units than when the demand is 10 000 units.

EXAMPLE 8.4   *Calculating Forecast Error Measures*

The following table shows the actual sales of upholstered chairs for a furniture manufacturer and the forecasts made for each of the last eight months. Calculate CFE, MSE, σ, MAD, and MAPE for this product.

MONTH, t	DEMAND, D_t	FORECAST, F_t	ERROR, E_t	ERROR SQUARED, E_t^2	ABSOLUTE ERROR, $|E_t|$	ABSOLUTE PERCENT ERROR, $(|E_t|/D_t)(100)$
1	200	225	−25	625	25	12.5%
2	240	220	20	400	20	8.3
3	300	285	15	225	15	5.0
4	270	290	−20	400	20	7.4
5	230	250	−20	400	20	8.7
6	260	240	20	400	20	7.7
7	210	250	−40	1600	40	19.0
8	275	240	35	1225	35	12.7
		Total	−15	5275	195	81.3%

SOLUTION

Using the formulas for the measures, we get:

Cumulative forecast error: CFE = −15

Average forecast error: $\bar{E} = \dfrac{CFE}{8} = -1.875$

Mean squared error: $MSE = \dfrac{\Sigma E_t^2}{n} = \dfrac{5275}{8} = 659.4$

Standard deviation:
$$\sigma = \sqrt{\frac{\Sigma\,[E_t - (-1.875)]^2}{7}} = 27.4$$

Mean absolute deviation:
$$\mathrm{MAD} = \frac{\Sigma\,|E_t|}{n} = \frac{195}{8} = 24.4$$

Mean absolute percent error:
$$\mathrm{MAPE} = \frac{[\Sigma\,|E_t|/D_t]\,100}{n} = \frac{81.3\%}{8} = 10.2\%$$

A CFE of −15 indicates that the forecast has a tendency to overestimate demand. The MSE, σ, and MAD statistics provide measures of forecast error variability. A MAD of 24.4 means that the average forecast error was 24.4 units in absolute value. The value of σ, 27.4, indicates that the sample distribution of forecast errors has a standard deviation of 27.4 units. A MAPE of 10.2 percent implies that, on average, the forecast error was about 10 percent of actual demand. These measures become more reliable as the number of periods of data increases.

Decision Point   Although reasonably satisfied with these forecast performance results, the analyst decided to test out a few more forecasting methods before reaching a final forecasting method to use for the future.

---

tracking signal A measure that indicates whether a method of forecasting is accurately predicting actual changes in demand.

TRACKING SIGNALS. A **tracking signal** is a measure that indicates whether a method of forecasting is accurately predicting actual changes in demand. The tracking signal measures the number of MADs represented by the cumulative sum of forecast errors, the CFE. The CFE tends to be zero when a correct forecasting system is being used. At any time, however, random errors can cause the CFE to be a nonzero number. The tracking signal formula is:

$$\text{Tracking signal} = \frac{\text{CFE}}{\text{MAD}}$$

Each period, the CFE and MAD are updated to reflect current error, and the tracking signal is compared to some predetermined limits. The MAD can be calculated in one of two ways: (1) as the simple average of all absolute errors (as demonstrated in Example 8.4) or (2) as a weighted average determined by the exponential smoothing method:

$$\mathrm{MAD}_t = \alpha|E_t| + (1 - \alpha)\mathrm{MAD}_{t-1}$$

If forecast errors are normally distributed with a mean of 0, there is a simple relationship between σ and MAD:

$$\sigma = (\sqrt{\pi/2})(\mathrm{MAD}) \cong 1.25(\mathrm{MAD})$$

$$\mathrm{MAD} = 0.7978\sigma \cong 0.8\sigma$$

(Recall that: $\pi \cong 3.1416$.)

This relationship allows use of the normal probability tables to specify limits for the tracking signal. If the tracking signal falls outside those limits, the forecasting model no longer is tracking demand adequately. A tracking system is useful when forecasting systems are computerized because it alerts analysts when forecasts are getting far from desirable limits.

Figure 8.5 shows tracking signal results for 23 periods plotted on a *control chart*. The control chart is useful for determining whether any action needs to be taken to improve the forecasting model. In the example, the first 20 points cluster around zero, as we would expect if the forecasts are not biased. The CFE will tend toward zero.

When the underlying characteristics of demand change but the forecasting model does not, the tracking signal eventually goes out of control. The steady increase after the 20th point in Figure 8.5 indicates that the process is going out of control. The 21st and 22nd points are acceptable, but the 23rd point is not.

FIGURE 8.5

Tracking Signal

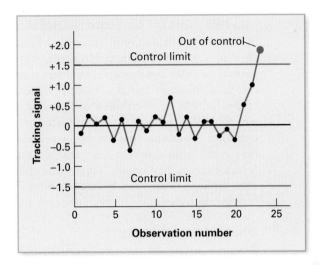

FORECAST ERROR RANGES. Calculating MAD can also provide additional information. Forecasts that are stated as a single value, such as 1200 units or 26 customers, can be less useful because they do not indicate the range of likely errors that the forecast typically generates. A better approach can be to provide the manager with a forecasted value and an error range. For example, suppose that the forecasted value for a product is 1000 units, with a MAD of 20 units. This MAD is equivalent to $\sigma = 25$ units, which means that we can say with a 95 percent confidence level (i.e., $\pm 2\sigma$) that actual demand will fall in the range of 950 to 1050 units.

CRITERIA FOR SELECTING TIME-SERIES METHODS

Forecast error measures provide important information for choosing the best forecasting method for a product or service. They also guide managers in selecting the best values for the parameters needed for a particular time-series method. For example, measures of error can assist in selecting n for the moving average method. Two guidelines that help when searching for the best time-series models are:

1. For projections of more stable demand patterns, use lower α and β values for the exponential smoothing method or larger n values for the moving average method to emphasize historical experience.

2. For projections of more dynamic demand patterns, try higher α and β values or smaller n values. When historical demand patterns are changing, recent history should be emphasized.

holdout set Actual demands from the more recent time periods in the time series, which are set aside to test different models developed from the earlier time periods.

Often the forecaster must make trade-offs between bias (CFE) and the measures of forecast error dispersion (MAD, MSE, and MAPE). Managers also must recognize that the best technique in explaining the past data is not necessarily the best to predict the future. For this reason, some analysts prefer to use a **holdout set** as a final test. To do so, they set aside some of the more recent periods from the time series and use only the earlier time periods to develop and test different models. Once the final models have been selected in the first phase, then they are tested again with the holdout set. Whether or not this idea is used, managers should monitor future forecast errors, perhaps with tracking signals, and modify their forecasting approaches as needed. Maintaining data on forecast performance is the ultimate test of forecasting power—rather than how well a model fits past data or holdout samples.

USING MULTIPLE TECHNIQUES

We have described several individual forecasting methods and shown how to assess their forecast performance. However, there is no need to rely on only a single forecasting method. For example, Unilever combines several different forecasts to arrive at the final forecast. Initial statistical forecasts using several time-series methods and regression can be distributed to knowledgeable individuals, such as marketing directors and sales teams, for their adjustments. They can account for current market and customer conditions that are not necessarily reflected in past data. Multiple forecasts may come from different sales teams, and some teams may have a better record on forecast errors than others. Finally, the collaborative process of CPFR introduces forecasts from suppliers and even customers. There are two approaches to using several forecasting techniques in unison—combination forecasts and focus forecasting.

COMBINATION FORECASTS

combination forecasts
Forecasts produced by averaging independent forecasts based on different methods or different data, or both.

Research during the last two decades suggests that combining forecasts from multiple sources often produces more accurate forecasts. **Combination forecasts** are forecasts that are produced by averaging independent forecasts based on different methods or different data, or both. It is intriguing that combination forecasts often perform better over time than do even the *best* single forecasting method.

For example, suppose that the forecast for next period is 100 units from method #1 and 120 units from method #2, and that method #1 has been the single best method to date. The combination forecast for next period, giving equal weight to each technique, is 110 units (or $0.5 \times 100 + 0.5 \times 120$). When this averaging technique is used consistently into the future, its combination forecasts often will be much more accurate than either method on its own. Combining methods is most effective when the individual forecasts bring different kinds of information into the forecasting process. Forecasters have achieved excellent results by weighting forecasts equally, and this is a good starting point. However, unequal weights may provide better results under some conditions.

FOCUS FORECASTING

focus forecasting A method of forecasting that selects the best forecast from a set of forecasts generated by simple techniques.

Another way to take advantage of multiple techniques is **focus forecasting**, which selects the best forecast from a set of several, often simpler, forecast methods. Using historical data as a starting point, a set of forecasts is prepared using each method for each item and then compared to actual demand for each item. On the basis of this exhaustive analysis, the method that produces the forecast with the least error is used to make the forecast for the next period, again on an item-by-item basis. Thus, many different methods might be used in the same period (for different items) and the method used for a particular item may change from period to period. This analysis must be conducted on a computer, because forecasts for tens of thousands of different items are made using a half a dozen or more different methods.

FORECASTING ACROSS THE ORGANIZATION

The process of developing and monitoring forecasts cuts across functional areas. Forecasting overall demand typically originates with marketing, but internal customers throughout the organization depend on forecasts to formulate and execute their plans. Forecasts are critical inputs to business plans, annual plans, and budgets. Finance needs forecasts to project cash flows and capital requirements. Human resources needs forecasts to anticipate hiring and training needs. Marketing is a primary source for sales forecast information, because they are closest to external customers. Operations needs forecasts to plan output levels, purchases of materials and services, workforce and output schedules, inventories, and long-term capacities.

Managers throughout the organization make forecasts on many variables other than future demand, such as competitor strategies, regulatory changes, technological change, processing times, supplier lead times, and quality losses. Tools for making these forecasts are basically the same ones covered here for demand: judgment, opinions of knowledgeable people, averages of past experience, regression, and time-series techniques. Using them, forecasting performance can be improved, but forecasts are rarely perfect. As Mark Twain said in *Following the Equator*, "Prophecy is a good line of business, but it is full of risks." Smart managers recognize this reality and find ways to update their plans when the inevitable forecast error or unexpected event occurs.

EQUATION SUMMARY

1. Naive forecasting: Forecast $= D_t$

2. Simple moving average: $F_{t+1} = \dfrac{D_t + D_{t-1} + D_{t-2} + \ldots + D_{t-n+1}}{n}$

3. Weighted moving average:

$$F_{t+1} = \text{Weight}_1(D_t) + \text{Weight}_2(D_{t-1}) + \text{Weight}_3(D_{t-2}) + \ldots + \text{Weight}_n(D_{t-n+1})$$

4. Exponential smoothing: $F_{t+1} = \alpha D_t + (1 - \alpha)F_t$

5. Trend-adjusted exponential smoothing:

$$A_t = \alpha D_t + (1 - \alpha)(A_{t-1} + T_{t-1})$$

$$T_t = \beta(A_t - A_{t-1}) + (1 - \beta)T_{t-1}$$

$$F_{t+1} = A_t + T_t$$

6. Forecast error: $E_t = D_t - F_t$

$$CFE = \Sigma E_t$$

$$\bar{E} = CFE/n$$

$$MSE = \frac{\Sigma E_t^2}{n}$$

$$\sigma = \sqrt{\frac{\Sigma(E_t - \bar{E})^2}{n - 1}}$$

$$MAD = \frac{\Sigma |E_t|}{n}$$

$$MAPE = \frac{\Sigma \dfrac{|E_t|}{D_t}}{n}(100)$$

7. Exponentially smoothed error: $MAD_t = \alpha|E_t| + (1 - \alpha)MAD_{t-1}$

8. Tracking signal: $\dfrac{CFE}{MAD}$

CHAPTER HIGHLIGHTS

- The five basic patterns of demand are the horizontal, trend, seasonal, cyclical, and random variation.

- Designing a forecasting system involves determining what to forecast, which forecasting technique to use, and how computerized forecasting systems can assist managerial decision making.

- Level of data aggregation and units of measure are important considerations in managerial decisions about what to forecast. Two general types of demand forecasting are used: qualitative methods and quantitative methods. Qualitative methods include judgment methods, and quantitative methods include causal methods and time-series analysis.

- Collaborative planning, forecasting, and replenishment (CPFR) uses software to enable a supplier and customer to work together over the Internet to develop a better forecast. If the forecasts from each firm differ by more than a predetermined percentage, they share comments and supporting data until an acceptable forecast is achieved.

- Judgment methods of forecasting are useful in situations where relevant historical data are lacking. Sales-force estimates, executive opinion, market research, and the Delphi method are judgment methods. Judgment methods require the most human interaction and so are the most costly of these methods. Facility location and capacity planning are examples of long-term decisions that justify the expense of generating a judgment forecast.

- Causal forecasting methods hypothesize a functional relationship between the factor to be forecasted and other internal or external factors. Causal methods identify turning points in demand patterns but require more extensive analysis to determine the appropriate relationships between the item to be forecast and the external and internal factors. Causal methods tend to be used in medium-term production planning for product families. Linear regression is one of the more popular causal forecasting methods.

- Time-series analysis is often used with computer systems to generate quickly the large number of short-term forecasts required for scheduling products or services. Simple moving averages, weighted moving averages, and exponential smoothing are used to estimate the average of a time series. The exponential smoothing technique has the advantage of requiring that only a minimal amount of data be kept for use in updating the forecast. Trend-adjusted exponential smoothing is a method for including a trend estimate in exponentially smoothed forecasts. Estimates for the series average and the trend are smoothed to provide the forecast.

- Although many techniques allow for seasonal influences, a simple approach is the multiplicative seasonal method, which is based on the assumption that the seasonal influence is proportional to the level of average demand.

- The cumulative sum of forecast errors (CFE), mean squared error (MSE), standard deviation of forecast errors (σ), mean absolute deviation (MAD), and mean absolute percent error (MAPE) are all measures of forecast error used in practice. The CFE and MAD are used to develop a tracking signal that determines when a forecasting method no longer is yielding acceptable forecasts. Forecast error measures also are used to select the best forecast methods from available alternatives.

- Combination forecasts produced by averaging two or more independent forecasts often provide more accurate forecasts.

SOLVED PROBLEM 1

Chicken Palace periodically offers carryout five-piece chicken dinners at special prices. Let Y be the number of dinners sold and X be the price. On the basis of the historical observations and calculations in the following table, determine the regression equation, correlation coefficient, and coefficient of determination. How many dinners can Chicken Palace expect to sell at $3 each?

OBSERVATION	PRICE, X	DINNERS SOLD, Y
1	$ 2.70	760
2	$ 3.50	510
3	$ 2.00	980
4	$ 4.20	250
5	$ 3.10	320
6	$ 4.05	480
Total	$19.55	3300
Average	$ 3.26	550

SOLUTION

We use the computer to calculate the best values of a, b, the correlation coefficient, and the coefficient of determination.

$$a = 1450.12$$
$$b = -276.28$$
$$r = -0.84$$
$$r^2 = 0.71$$

The regression line is:

$$Y = a + bX = 1450.12 - 276.28X$$

The correlation coefficient ($r = -0.84$) shows a negative correlation between the variables. The coefficient of determination ($r^2 = 0.71$) indicates that other variables (in addition to price) appreciably affect sales.

If the regression equation is satisfactory to the manager, estimated sales at a price of $3 per dinner may be calculated as follows:

$$Y = a + bX = 1450.12 - 276.28(3)$$
$$= 621.27 \quad \text{or} \quad 621 \text{ dinners}$$

SOLVED PROBLEM 2

The Polish General's Pizza Parlour is a small restaurant catering to patrons with a taste for European pizza. One of its specialties is Polish Prize pizza. The manager must forecast weekly demand for these special pizzas so that he can order pizza shells weekly. Recently demand has been as follows:

WEEK OF:	PIZZAS	WEEK OF:	PIZZAS
June 2	50	June 23	56
June 9	65	June 30	55
June 16	52	July 7	60

a. Forecast the demand for pizza for June 23 to July 14 by using the simple moving average method with $n = 3$. Then repeat the forecast by using the weighted moving average method with $n = 3$ and weights of 0.50, 0.30, and 0.20, with 0.50 applying to the most recent demand.

b. Calculate the MAD for each method.

SOLUTION

a. The simple moving average method and the weighted moving average method give the following results.

CURRENT WEEK	SIMPLE MOVING AVERAGE FORECAST FOR NEXT WEEK	WEIGHTED MOVING AVERAGE FORECAST FOR NEXT WEEK
June 16	$\dfrac{52 + 65 + 50}{3} = 55.7$ or 56	$[(0.5 \times 52) + (0.3 \times 65) + (0.2 \times 50)] = 55.5$, or 56
June 23	$\dfrac{56 + 52 + 65}{3} = 57.7$ or 58	$[(0.5 \times 56) + (0.3 \times 52) + (0.2 \times 65)] = 56.6$, or 57
June 30	$\dfrac{55 + 56 + 52}{3} = 54.3$ or 54	$[(0.5 \times 55) + (0.3 \times 56) + (0.2 \times 52)] = 54.7$, or 55
July 7	$\dfrac{60 + 55 + 56}{3} = 57$	$[(0.5 \times 60) + (0.3 \times 55) + (0.2 \times 56)] = 57.7$, or 58

b. The mean absolute deviation is calculated as follows:

WEEK	ACTUAL DEMAND	SIMPLE MOVING AVERAGE		WEIGHTED MOVING AVERAGE	
		Forecast	Absolute Errors $|E_t|$	Forecast	Absolute Errors, $|E_t|$
June 23	56	56	$|56 - 56| = 0$	56	$|56 - 56| = 0$
June 30	55	58	$|55 - 58| = 3$	56	$|55 - 57| = 2$
July 7	60	54	$|60 - 54| = 6$	56	$|60 - 55| = 5$
			$MAD = \dfrac{0 + 3 + 6}{3} = 3$		$MAD = \dfrac{0 + 2 + 5}{3} = 2.3$

For this limited set of data, the weighted moving average method resulted in a slightly lower mean absolute deviation. However, final conclusions can be made only after analyzing much more data.

SOLVED PROBLEM 3

The monthly demand for units manufactured by the Acme Rocket Company has been as follows:

MONTH	UNITS	MONTH	UNITS
May	100	September	105
June	80	October	110
July	110	November	125
August	115	December	120

a. Use the exponential smoothing method to forecast the number of units for June to January. The initial forecast for May was 105 units; $\alpha = 0.2$.

b. Calculate the absolute percentage error for each month from June through December and the MAD and MAPE of forecast error as of the end of December.

c. Calculate the tracking signal as of the end of December. What can you say about the performance of your forecasting method?

SOLUTION

a.

CURRENT MONTH, t	$F_{t+1} = \alpha D_t + (1 - \alpha)F_t$	FORECAST, MONTH $t+1$
May	$0.2(100) + 0.8(105) = 104.0$, or 104	June
June	$0.2(80) + 0.8(104.0) = 99.2$, or 99	July
July	$0.2(110) + 0.8(99.2) = 101.4$, or 101	August
August	$0.2(115) + 0.8(101.4) = 104.1$, or 104	September
September	$0.2(105) + 0.8(104.1) = 104.3$, or 104	October
October	$0.2(110) + 0.8(104.3) = 105.4$, or 105	November
November	$0.2(125) + 0.8(105.4) = 109.3$, or 109	December
December	$0.2(120) + 0.8(109.3) = 111.4$, or 111	January

b.

MONTH, t	ACTUAL DEMAND D_t	FORECAST F_t	ERRORS, $E_t = D_t - F_t$	ABSOLUTE ERRORS $\|E_t\|$	ABSOLUTE PERCENTAGE ERROR, $(\|E_t\|/D_t)(100\%)$
June	80	104	−24	24	30.0%
July	110	99	11	11	10.0
August	115	101	14	14	12.2
September	105	104	1	1	0.9
October	110	104	6	6	5.4
November	125	105	20	20	16.0
December	120	109	11	11	9.2
Total	765		39	87	83.7%

$$\text{MAD} = \frac{\Sigma \|E_t\|}{n} = \frac{87}{7} = 12.4 \quad \text{and} \quad \text{MAPE} = \frac{\Sigma[\|E_t\|(100)]/D_t}{n} = \frac{83.7\%}{7} = 11.9$$

c. As of the end of December, the cumulative sum of forecast errors (CFE) is 39. Using the mean absolute deviation calculated in part (b), we calculate the tracking signal:

$$\text{Tracking signal} = \frac{\text{CFE}}{\text{MAD}} = \frac{39}{12.4} = 3.14$$

The probability that a tracking signal value of 3.14 could be generated completely by chance is very small. Consequently, we should revise our approach. The long string of forecasts lower than actual demand suggests use of a trend method.

SOLVED PROBLEM 4

The demand for Krispee Crunchies, a favourite breakfast cereal of people born in the 1940s, is experiencing a decline. The company wants to monitor demand for this product closely as it nears the end of its life cycle. The trend-adjusted exponential smoothing method is used with $\alpha = 0.1$ and $\beta = 0.2$. At the end of December, the January estimate for the average number of cases sold per month, A_t, was 900 000 and the trend, T_t, was −50 000 per month. The following table shows the actual sales history for January, February, and March. Generate forecasts for February, March, and April.

MONTH	SALES
January	890 000
February	800 000
March	825 000

SOLUTION

We know the initial condition at the end of December and actual demand for January, February, and March. We must now update the forecast method and prepare a forecast for April. All data are expressed in thousands of cases. Our equations for use with trend-adjusted exponential smoothing are:

$$A_t = \alpha D_t + (1 - \alpha)(A_{t-1} + T_{t-1})$$
$$T_t = \beta(A_t - A_{t-1}) + (1 - \beta)T_{t-1}$$
$$F_{t+1} = A_t + T_t$$

For January, we have:

$$A_{Jan} = 0.1(890\,000) + 0.9(900\,000 - 50\,000)$$
$$= 854\,000 \text{ cases}$$

$$T_{Jan} = 0.2(854\,000 - 900\,000) + 0.8(-50\,000)$$
$$= -49\,200 \text{ cases}$$

$$F_{Feb} = A_{Jan} + T_{Jan} = 854\,000 - 49\,200 = 804\,800 \text{ cases}$$

For February, we have:

$$A_{Feb} = 0.1(800\,000) + 0.9(854\,000 - 49\,200)$$
$$= 804\,320 \text{ cases}$$

$$T_{Feb} = 0.2(804\,320 - 854\,000) + 0.8(-49\,200)$$
$$= -49\,296 \text{ cases}$$

$$F_{Mar} = A_{Feb} + T_{Feb} = 804\,320 - 49\,296 = 755\,024 \text{ cases}$$

For March, we have:

$$A_{Mar} = 0.1(825\,000) + 0.9(804\,320 - 49\,296)$$
$$= 762\,022 \text{ cases}$$

$$T_{Mar} = 0.2(762\,022 - 804\,320) + 0.8(-49\,296)$$
$$= -47\,897 \text{ cases}$$

$$F_{Apr} = A_{Mar} + T_{Mar} = 762\,022 - 47\,897 = 714\,125 \text{ cases}$$

SOLVED PROBLEM 5

The Northville Post Office experiences a seasonal pattern of daily mail volume every week. The following data for two representative weeks are expressed in thousands of pieces of mail:

DAY	WEEK 1	WEEK 2
Sunday	5	8
Monday	20	15
Tuesday	30	32
Wednesday	35	30
Thursday	49	45
Friday	70	70
Saturday	15	10
Total	224	210

a. Calculate a seasonal factor for each day of the week.

b. If the postmaster estimates that there will be 230 000 pieces of mail to sort next week, forecast the volume for each day of the week.

SOLUTION

a. Calculate the average daily mail volume for each week. Then for each day divide the mail volume by the week's average to get the seasonal factor. Finally, for each day, add the two seasonal factors and divide by 2 to obtain the average seasonal factor to use in the forecast (see part (b)).

DAY	WEEK 1		WEEK 2		AVERAGE SEASONAL FACTOR [(1) + (2)]/2
	Mail Volume	Seasonal Factor (1)	Mail Volume	Seasonal Factor (2)	
Sunday	5	5/32 = 0.15625	8	8/30 = 0.26667	0.21146
Monday	20	20/32 = 0.62500	15	15/30 = 0.50000	0.56250
Tuesday	30	30/32 = 0.93750	32	32/30 = 1.06667	1.00209
Wednesday	35	35/32 = 1.09375	30	30/30 = 1.00000	1.04688
Thursday	49	49/32 = 1.53125	45	45/30 = 1.50000	1.51563
Friday	70	70/32 = 2.18750	70	70/30 = 2.33333	2.26042
Saturday	15	15/32 = 0.46875	10	10/30 = 0.33333	0.40104
Total	224		210		
Average	224/7 = 32		210/7 = 30		

b. The average daily mail volume is expected to be 230 000/7 = 32 857 pieces of mail. Using the average seasonal factors calculated in part (a), we obtain the following forecasts:

DAY	CALCULATION	FORECAST
Sunday	0.21146(32 857) =	6 948
Monday	0.56250(32 857) =	18 482
Tuesday	1.00209(32 857) =	32 926
Wednesday	1.04688(32 857) =	34 397
Thursday	1.51563(32 857) =	49 799
Friday	2.26042(32 857) =	74 271
Saturday	0.40104(32 857) =	13 177
	Total	230 000

CD-ROM RESOURCES

The Student CD-ROM that accompanies this text contains the following resources, which allow you to further practise and apply the concepts presented in this chapter.

- **Equation Summary**: All the equations for this chapter can be found in one convenient location.

- **Discussion Questions**: Two questions will challenge your understanding of forecasting, applied to air visibility data subscriptions for a biweekly newspaper.

- **Case**: *Yankee Fork and Hoe Company*. What are your forecasts for bow rakes in year 5?

- **Experiential Exercise**: Use the *Yankee Fork and Hoe Company* case as an in-class team experience.

- **OM Explorer Tutors**: OM Explorer contains four tutor programs that will help you learn how to use the moving average, weighted moving average, exponential smoothing, and trend-adjusting exponential smoothing techniques.

- **OM Explorer Solvers**: OM Explorer has three programs that can be used to solve general problems involving regression analysis, seasonal forecasting, and time-series models.

PROBLEMS

1. Sales for the past 12 months at Dalworth Company are given here.

MONTH	SALES ($ Millions)	MONTH	SALES ($ Millions)
January	20	July	53
February	24	August	62
March	27	September	54
April	31	October	36
May	37	November	32
June	47	December	29

a. Use a three-month moving average to forecast the sales for the months April through December.

b. Use a four-month moving average to forecast the sales for the months May through December.

c. Compare the performance of the two methods by using the mean absolute deviation as the performance criterion. Which method would you recommend?

d. Compare the performance of the two methods by using the mean absolute percent error as the performance criterion. Which method would you recommend?

e. Compare the performance of the two methods by using the mean squared error as the performance criterion. Which method would you recommend?

2. Karl's Copiers sells and repairs photocopy machines. The manager needs weekly forecasts of service calls so that he can schedule service personnel. The forecast for the week of July 3 was 24 calls. The manager uses exponential smoothing with $\alpha = 0.20$. Forecast the number of calls for the week of August 7, which is next week.

WEEK OF:	ACTUAL SERVICE CALLS
July 3	24
July 10	32
July 17	36
July 24	23
July 31	25

3. Consider the sales data for Dalworth Company given in Problem 1.

a. Use a three-month weighted moving average to forecast the sales for the months April through December. Use weights of (3/6), (2/6), and (1/6), giving more weight to more recent data.

b. Use exponential smoothing with $\alpha = 0.6$ to forecast the sales for the months April through December. Assume that the initial forecast for January was $22 million.

c. Compare the performance of the two methods by using the mean absolute deviation as the performance criterion. Which method would you recommend?

d. Compare the performance of the two methods by using the mean absolute percent error as the performance criterion. Which method would you recommend?

e. Compare the performance of the two methods by using the mean squared error as the performance criterion. Which method would you recommend?

4. A convenience store recently started to carry a new brand of soft drink in its territory. Management is interested in estimating future sales volume to determine whether it should continue to carry the new brand or replace it with another brand. At the end of April, the average monthly sales volume of the new soft drink was 700 cans and the trend was +50 cans per month. The actual sales volume figures for May, June, and July are 760, 800, and 820, respectively. Use trend-adjusted exponential smoothing with $\alpha = 0.2$ and $\beta = 0.1$ to forecast usage for June, July, and August.

5. The following data are for calculator sales in units at an electronics store over the past five weeks:

WEEK	SALES
1	46
2	49
3	43
4	50
5	53

Use trend-adjusted exponential smoothing with $\alpha = 0.2$ and $\beta = 0.2$ to forecast sales for weeks 3–6. Assume that the average of the time series was 45 units and that the average trend was +2 units per week just before week 1.

6. The manager of Snyder's Garden Centre must make her annual purchasing plans for rakes, gloves, and other gardening items. One of the items she stocks is Fast-Grow, a liquid fertilizer. The sales of this item are seasonal, with peaks in the spring, summer, and fall months. Quarterly demand (in cases) for the past two years follows:

QUARTER	YEAR 1	YEAR 2
1	40	60
2	350	440
3	290	320
4	210	280
Total	890	1100

If the expected sales for Fast-Grow are 1150 cases for year 3, use the multiplicative seasonal method to prepare a forecast for each quarter of the year.

7. The manager of a utility company in the Texas panhandle wants to develop quarterly forecasts of power loads for the next year. The power loads are seasonal, and the data on the quarterly loads in megawatts (MW) for the last four years are as follows:

YEAR	QUARTER 1	QUARTER 2	QUARTER 3	QUARTER 4
1	103.5	94.7	118.6	109.3
2	126.1	116.0	141.2	131.6
3	144.5	137.1	159.0	149.5
4	166.1	152.5	178.2	169.0

The manager has estimated the total demand for the next year at 780 MW. Use the multiplicative seasonal method to develop the forecast for each quarter.

8. Demand for oil changes at Garcia's Garage has been as follows:

MONTH	NUMBER OF OIL CHANGES
January	41
February	46
March	57
April	52
May	59
June	51
July	60
August	62

a. Use simple linear regression analysis to develop a forecasting model for monthly demand. In this application, the dependent variable, Y, is monthly demand and the independent variable, X, is the month. For January, let $X = 1$; for February, let $X = 2$; and so on.

b. Use the model to forecast demand for September, October, and November. Here, $X = 9$, 10, and 11, respectively.

9. The director of a large public library must schedule employees to service customers, as well as reshelve books and periodicals checked out of the library. The number of items checked out will determine the labour requirements. The following data reflect the numbers of items checked out of the library for the past three years. The director needs a time-series method for forecasting the number of items to be checked out during the next month. Find the best simple moving average forecast you can. Decide what is meant by "best" and justify your decision.

MONTH	YEAR 1	YEAR 2	YEAR 3
January	1847	2045	1986
February	2669	2321	2564
March	2467	2419	2635
April	2432	2088	2150
May	2464	2667	2201
June	2378	2122	2663
July	2217	2206	2055
August	2445	1869	1678
September	1894	2441	1845
October	1922	2291	2065
November	2431	2364	2147
December	2274	2189	2451

10. Using the data in Problem 9, find the best exponential smoothing solution you can. Justify your choice.

11. Using the data in Problem 9, find the best trend-adjusted exponential smoothing solution you can. Compare the performance of this method with those of the best moving average method and the exponential smoothing method. Which of the three would you choose?

12. Canister, Inc., specializes in the manufacture of plastic containers. The data on the monthly sales of 300 millilitre shampoo bottles for the last five years are as follows:

YEAR	1	2	3	4	5
January	742	741	896	951	1030
February	697	700	793	861	1032
March	776	774	885	938	1126
April	898	932	1055	1109	1285
May	1030	1099	1204	1274	1468
June	1107	1223	1326	1422	1637
July	1165	1290	1303	1486	1611
August	1216	1349	1436	1555	1608
September	1208	1341	1473	1604	1528
October	1131	1296	1453	1600	1420
November	971	1066	1170	1403	1119
December	783	901	1023	1209	1013

a. Using the multiplicative seasonal method, calculate the monthly seasonal indices.

b. Develop a simple linear regression equation to forecast annual sales. For this regression, the dependent variable, Y, is the demand in each year and the independent variable, X, is the index for the year (i.e., $X = 1$ for year 1, $X = 2$ for year 2, and so on until $X = 5$ for year 5).

c. Forecast the annual sales for year 6 by using the regression model you developed in part (b).

d. Prepare the seasonal forecast for each month by using the monthly seasonal indices calculated in part (a).

13. A certain food item at P&Q Supermarkets has the demand pattern shown in the following table. Find the "best" forecast you can for month 25 and justify your methodology. You may use some of the data to find the best parameter value(s) for your method and the rest to test the forecast model. Your justification should include both quantitative and qualitative considerations.

MONTH	DEMAND	MONTH	DEMAND
1	33	13	37
2	37	14	43
3	31	15	56
4	39	16	41
5	54	17	36
6	38	18	39
7	42	19	41
8	40	20	58
9	41	21	42
10	54	22	45
11	43	23	41
12	39	24	38

REFERENCES AND FURTHER READINGS

Armstrong, J. S. *Long-Range Forecasting: From Crystal Ball to Computer.* New York: John Wiley & Sons, 1995.

Armstrong, J. Scott (ed.). *Principles of Forecasting: A Handbook for Researchers and Practitioners.* Norwell, MA: Kluwer Academic Publishers, 2001. Also visit Wharton School of the University of Pennsylvania, "Forecasting Principles," <morris.wharton.upenn.edu/forecast>, accessed April 29, 2003, for valuable information on forecasting, including frequently asked questions, forecasting methodology tree, and dictionary.

Bowerman, Bruce L., and Richard T. O'Connell. *Forecasting and Time Series: An Applied Approach*, 3rd ed. Belmont, CA: Duxbury Press, 1993.

Clemen, R. T. "Combining Forecasts: A Review and Annotated Bibliography." *International Journal of Forecasting*, vol. 5 (1989), pp. 559–583.

Hudson, William J. *Executive Economics: Forecasting and Planning for the Real World of Business.* New York: John Wiley & Sons, 1993.

Klassen, Robert D., and Benito E. Flores. "Forecasting Practices of Canadian Firms: Survey Results and Comparisons." *International Journal of Production Economics*, vol. 70 (2001), no. 2, pp. 163–174.

Li, X. "An Intelligent Business Forecaster for Strategic Business Planning." *Journal of Forecasting*, vol. 18 (1999), no. 3, pp. 181–205.

Lim, J. S., and M. O'Connor. "Judgmental Forecasting with Time Series and Causal Information." *International Journal of Forecasting*, vol. 12 (1996), pp. 139–153.

Sanders, Nada R., and Larry P. Ritzman. "Bringing Judgment into Combination Forecasts." *Journal of Operations Management*, vol. 13 (1995), pp. 311–321.

Sanders, Nada R., and K. B. Manrodt. "Forecasting Practices in U.S. Corporations: Survey Results." *Interfaces*, vol. 24 (1994), pp. 91–100.

Sanders, Nada R., and Larry P. Ritzman. "The Need for Contextual and Technical Knowledge in Judgmental Forecasting." *Journal of Behavioral Decision Making*, vol. 5 (1992), no. 1, pp. 39–52.

Smith, Bernard. *Focus Forecasting: Computer Techniques for Inventory Control.* Boston: CBI Publishing, 1984.

Yurkiewicz, Jack. "Forecasting 2000." *OR/MS Today*, vol. 27 (2000), no. 1, pp. 58–65.

Supply Chain Management

Across the Organization

Supply chain management is important to:

- **distribution**, which determines the best placement of finished goods inventories and selects the appropriate modes of transportation for serving the external supply chain.
- **finance and accounting**, which must understand how the performance of the supply chain affects key financial measures and how information flows into the billing process.
- **information systems**, which design the information flows that are essential to effective supply chain performance.
- **marketing**, which involves contact with the firm's customers and needs a supply chain that ensures responsive customer service.
- **operations**, which is responsible for managing effective supply chains.
- **purchasing**, which selects the suppliers for the supply chain.

Learning Goals

After reading this chapter, you will be able to:

1. define the nature of supply chain management for service providers and manufacturing firms.
2. describe the strategic importance of supply chain management and give real examples of its application in manufacturing and service industries.
3. explain how the Internet has changed the ways companies used to manage customer and supplier interfaces and has enabled the development of virtual supply chains.
4. discuss how critical operating measures of supply chain performance are linked to key financial measures.
5. describe the causes of supply chain dynamics and their effects.
6. distinguish between efficient supply chains and responsive supply chains, and understand why firms choose different strategies.
7. describe the competitive implications of strategies that leverage outsourcing, offshoring, and virtual supply chains.

Bombardier (www.bombardier.com) has taken dramatic measures to redesign its supply chain in its Learjet subsidiary. The Montreal-based company has drawn on both in-house capabilities and supplier expertise from around the world to reduce production times, improve quality, and lower cost for its new "Continental" aircraft. Final assembly occurs in the United States, with each new corporate jet taking shape as it moves through five production stations in which large modules of the plane are rolled in and joined together. The nose and cockpit come from Montreal, the engines from Phoenix, the mid-fuselage from Belfast, the tail from Taichung, the wings from Nagoya, and lesser parts from cities in four other countries.

Bombardier hasn't arrived at this supply chain without significant pain. (In contrast, Cessna, the executive-jet volume leader, relies on a much greater degree of vertical integration.) Construction of an earlier generation aircraft, the Model 45, was greatly delayed as components were divided across three Bombardier subsidiaries. For example, as engineering teams identified and dealt with typical startup problems, the two plants in Toronto and Belfast could not easily implement the necessary changes because of different specifications, different materials, and different fasteners. Wings that arrived ready-to-mount had to be taken apart and rebuilt. At one point, 27 aircraft were scattered about the factory in various stages of completion while customers waited.

Undeterred, Bombardier fixed the problems and, on its next-generation executive jet, the Global Express, management enlisted outside supplier Mitsubishi to build the wings. With that crucial part covered, the other major components were parcelled out internally on the understanding that, this time, if there was a problem with a part, those who built it would resolve it. Bombardier also learned to look to suppliers for solutions rather than just parts. Now, landing gear is bought

Bombardier's supply chain brings together basic parts for the Continental aircraft from internal and external sources located around the globe.

Challenger 300 Partnerships: From Avionics to Interiors

Main System Suppliers

Powerplant - **Honeywell**
APU - **Honeywell**
Avionics - **Rockwell Collins**
Landing Gear - **Messier Dowty**
Electrical System, Cockpit Lighting -
    ECE/Groupe Intertechnique
Pressurization - **Liebherr (Toulouse)**
Hydraulics - **Parker Abex**
Fuel - **Intertechnique**
Flaps - **Liebher (Lindenberg)**
Flight Controls - **Moog**
Lighting - **Hella**
Firex - **Kidde Aerospace**
Windshields/Cabin Windows - **PPG**
Wheels/Brakes/Rolling Stock -
    Goodrich
Oxygen - **Intertechnique**
Completions Integrator - **DeCrane**
Simulator - **NLX**

Structural Suppliers

(Wings) **MHI**

(Centre Fuse) **Bombardier - Belfast**

(Rear Fuse) **AIDC**

(Vert. Stab.) **AIDC**

(Horiz. Stab.) **AIDC**

(Forward Fuse & Flight Controls)

    Bombardier - Montreal

(Tailcone/APU Install. Kit) **Hawker de Havilland**

(Wing to Body Fairings) **Fischer**

as a system rather than as separate pieces.

As this extensive supplier involvement indicates, Bombardier has evolved to focus on design, while developing capabilities for process integration. Scheduling and assembly still remain critical elements; however, managers and teams must now coordinate a multinational, multicompany endeavour. The Continental, the third generation in this ongoing evolution of Bombardier's supply chain, represented the most ambitious project so far. While Bombardier invested about $250 million in the design and roll-out of this plane, its partners have needed to make similar investments. The director of operations on the Continental line observed, "We looked at every part of the aircraft and got agreement on whether it was going to be manufacturable and whether the design was as good for, say Mitsubishi, as for us as the integrator."

Canadian cockpit meets Irish-made fuselage in final assembly in the United States.

The results have been impressive. The time for new product introduction has fallen significantly. The Model 45 took 71 months from program launch to first delivery; the Global Express took 67 months. The Continental was expected to take 41 months. Productivity has also risen dramatically.

Despite the increased reliance on supply chain partners, Bombardier still keeps a hand in basic production. While a great deal of know-how is shifting to the partners, it continues to build wings for its regional jets and has a core competency in cockpit design and production. Increasingly, it appears that the best solution to Bombardier's supply chain is to make the relationships so seamless that each partner is, in some way, dependent on the others.

Source: P. Siekman, "The Snap-Together Business Jet," *Fortune*, vol. 145, no. 2 (July 21, 2002), p. 104A. © 2002 Time Inc. All rights reserved.

supply chain management
The synchronization of a firm's processes and those of its suppliers to match the flow of materials, services, and information with customer demand.

Supply chain management seeks to synchronize a firm's processes and those of its suppliers and customers to match the flow of materials, services, and information with customer demand. Supply chain management has strategic implications, because the supply system can be used to achieve important competitive priorities, as with Bombardier's Learjet. It also involves the coordination of key processes in the firm such as order placement, order fulfillment, and purchasing, which are supported by marketing, finance, engineering, information systems, operations, and logistics. We begin by taking a bird's-eye view of supply chain management, focusing on its implications for service providers and manufacturers. We then describe how companies manage their customer and supplier interfaces. Next, we discuss the important operating and financial measures of supply chain performance, followed by a discussion of the dynamics of supply chains. We conclude with a comparison of basic supply chain designs, their competitive implications, and options for structuring supply chains.

OVERVIEW OF SUPPLY CHAIN MANAGEMENT

Supply chain design for a service provider is driven by the need to provide support for the essential elements of the various service packages it delivers. Recall that a customer benefit bundle consists of a core service along with a set of peripheral products and services. Management must design and leverage the firm's supply chain both to acquire supporting goods and services and to reach the customer.

To see the connection between supply chains and customer benefit bundle, consider the example of atWork Office Furniture (www.atwork.ca), a service provider that offers customized office design and a wide variety of business furnishings, from a single workstation to an entire office. Customers can view new and used furniture online, consult with staff using a 1-800 number, or visit one of seven retail locations across Ontario. The new furnishings are sourced globally, and used products are acquired from many local businesses (essentially suppliers, who, in turn, are likely to be customers).

A simplified supply chain for this firm is illustrated in Figure 9.1, which shows how the suppliers support various elements of the service. Each of the suppliers, of course, has its own supply chain (not shown). For example, the supplier of desks may get steel tubes from one supplier and wood panels from another. All of the suppliers in this firm's supply chain play an integral role in its ability to meet its competitive priorities for the customer benefit bundle, such as top quality, delivery speed, and customization.

FIGURE 9.1

Supply Chain for an Office Furniture Retailer

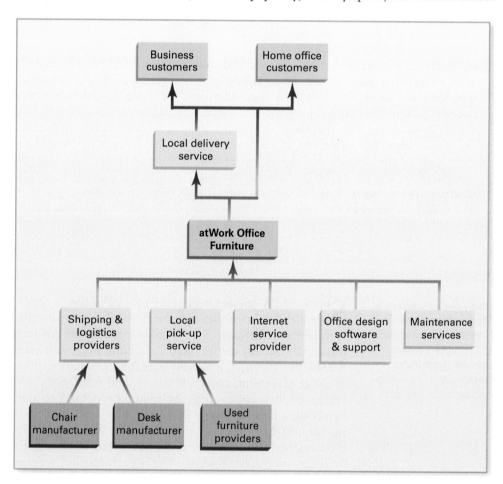

As the degree of customer interaction increases in the service process, the complexity and challenges also tend to increase. For example, an airline's supply chain provides soft drinks, peanuts, in-flight meals, and airsickness bags, as well as maintenance and repair items such as engine parts and motor lubricants. Timing and coordination in this supply chain are often very visible to customers, and any miscues are immediately evident and often interpreted as poor service.

FIGURE 9.2

Supply Chain for a Manufacturing Firm

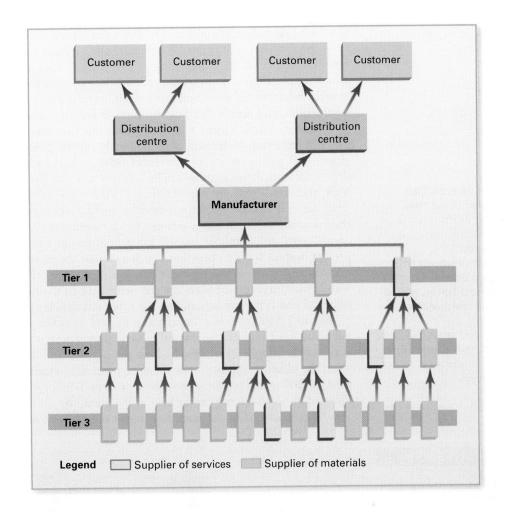

The supply chain for manufacturing firms, such as the chair manufacturer shown at the bottom of Figure 9.1, can also be very complicated because many companies have hundreds, if not thousands, of suppliers (Figure 9.2 is a generalization). Suppliers are often identified by their position in the supply chain. Here, tier 1 suppliers provide materials or services that are used directly by the firm, tier 2 suppliers supply tier 1 suppliers, and so on. In this diagram, the firm owns its own distribution and transportation services. However, companies that engineer products to customer specifications normally do not have distribution centres as part of their supply chains. Such companies often ship products directly to their customers.

The value of careful design and consistent execution for supply chain management becomes apparent when the complexity of the supply chain is recognized. However, the challenges don't stop here. As we showed in Chapter 4, "Capacity," inventory levels combine with variability and capacity utilization to affect the flow of materials.

inventory A stock of items, including materials, orders, information, and people, that flow through or are used in a process to satisfy customer demand.

FORMS OF INVENTORY

One of several basic objectives of supply chain management is to control inventory by managing the flows of materials. As noted earlier, **inventory** is a stock of items used to satisfy customer demand or support the production of goods or services. A traditional accounting definition limits inventory to materials, components, and products. The typical manufacturer spends more than 60 percent of its total income from sales on purchased services and materials, whereas the typical service provider spends only 30 to 40 percent. Because materials comprise such a large component of the sales dollar, manufacturers can reap large profits with a small reduction in the cost of materials, which makes supply chain management a key competitive weapon. However, a more general definition for managing processes must be expanded to include materials, orders, information, and people that flow through or are used in a process.

Inventory exists in three aggregate forms: raw materials, work-in-process, or finished goods. Identifying each form is based partly on the process (Where does it start and stop?) and partly on the organization (Where do hand-offs occur and what is the degree of vertical integration?). These forms are also useful for accounting purposes. **Raw materials (RM)** are inventories needed for the production of goods or services. They are considered to be inputs to the transformation processes of the firm, whether they produce a product or a service. **Work-in-process (WIP)** consists of items such as components or assemblies needed for a final product in manufacturing. WIP is also present in some service operations, such as repair shops, restaurants, cheque-processing centres, and package delivery services. **Finished goods (FG)** in manufacturing plants, warehouses, and retail outlets are the items sold to the firm's customers. The finished goods of one firm may actually be the raw materials for another.

Figure 9.3 shows how inventory can be held in different forms and at various stocking points for a typical manufacturing firm. In this example, raw materials—the finished goods of the supplier—are held by both the supplier and the manufacturer. Raw materials at the plant pass through one or more processes, which transform them into various levels of WIP inventory. Final processing of this inventory yields finished goods inventory. Finished goods inventory can be held at the plant, the distribution centre (which may be a warehouse owned by the manufacturer or the retailer), and retail locations.

raw materials (RM) Materials and items used as inputs for the production of goods and services.

work-in-process (WIP) Items partway through a process that are needed for a final product or service.

finished goods (FG) Items that have completed the manufacturing or service process.

FIGURE 9.3

Inventory at Successive Stocking Points

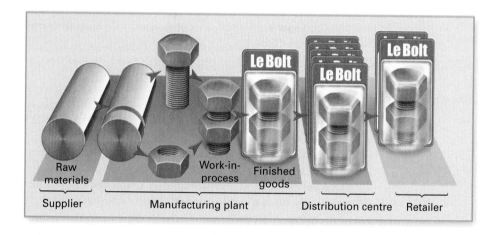

DEVELOPING INTEGRATED SUPPLY CHAINS

Imagine the chaos if all the firm's suppliers acted independently and never adjusted to changes in the firm's schedules. Hence, management of the flow of materials is crucial. But how much control does a firm have over its suppliers? One way to gain control is to buy controlling interest in the firm's major suppliers, which is called *backward integration*. The firm can then ensure its priority with the supplier and more forcefully lead efforts to improve efficiency and productivity. However, acquiring other companies can require significant capital investment and can reduce flexibility as products and customer demands change.

Another approach is to write contracts with the first-tier suppliers that hold them accountable for the performance of their own suppliers. For example, customers can provide a uniform set of guidelines to be followed throughout the supply chain. First-tier suppliers then incorporate these guidelines in agreements with their own suppliers. A third approach is to develop strategic partnerships, where major suppliers are responsible for large components or modules, as Bombardier has done to an increasing degree with each successive generation of its Learjet. The challenges in managing the supply chain then shift from writing contracts to identifying strong partners. Managers in the firm must work to build solid processes to integrate the components and systems of suppliers—first for design, and later for manufacturing and customer service. Moreover, each of these options also are available to the firm's customers, creating a complex network of contracts and partnerships.

Such integration does not happen overnight. Traditionally, organizations have divided the responsibility for managing the flow of materials and services among three departments: purchasing, production, and distribution. **Purchasing** is the management of the acquisition process, which includes deciding which suppliers to use, negotiating contracts, and deciding whether to buy locally. Purchasing is usually responsible for working with suppliers to ensure the desired flow of materials and services for both short and long terms. Purchasing may also be responsible for the levels of raw materials and maintenance and repair inventories.

Production is the management of the transformation processes devoted to producing the product or service. It is responsible for determining production quantities and scheduling the machines and employees directly responsible for the production of the good or service. **Distribution** is the management of the flow of materials from manufacturers to customers and from warehouses to retailers, involving the storage and transportation of products. It may also be responsible for finished goods inventories and the selection of transportation service providers.

Typically, firms willing to undergo the development of a well-integrated supply chain progress through a series of phases, as shown in Figure 9.4. In phase 1, a starting point for most firms, external suppliers and customers are considered to be independent of the firm. Relations with these entities are formal, and there is little sharing of operating

purchasing The management of the buying and acquisition process, which includes sourcing inputs, deciding which suppliers to use, and negotiating contracts.

production The management of the transformation process devoted to producing the good or service.

distribution The management of the flow of finished goods from manufacturers to customers and from warehouses to retailers, involving the storage and transportation of products.

FIGURE 9.4

Developing an Integrated Supply Chain

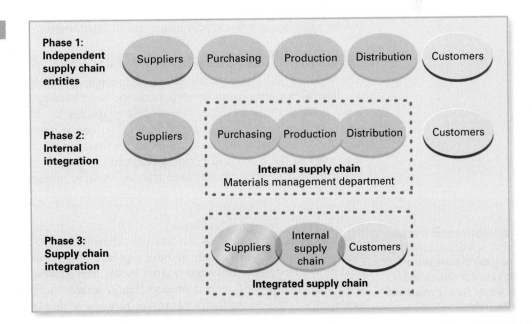

information and costs. Internally, purchasing, production, and distribution act independently, each optimizing its own activities and inventories without considering the other entities. Because of organizational and functional boundaries, large amounts of inventory exist in the supply chain and the overall flow of materials and services is ineffective.

In phase 2, the firm initiates internal integration by creating a materials management department. **Materials management** is concerned with decisions about purchasing materials and services, inventories, production levels, staffing patterns, schedules, and distribution. The focus is on the integration of those aspects of the supply chain directly under the firm's control to create an *internal supply chain*. Firms in this phase utilize a seamless information and materials control system from distribution to purchasing, integrating marketing, finance, accounting, and operations. Efficiency and electronic linkages to customers and suppliers are emphasized. Nonetheless, the firm still considers its suppliers and customers to be independent entities and focuses on tactical, rather than strategic, issues.

Further development of external linkages forms the basis for phase 3, supply chain integration. The internal supply chain is extended to embrace suppliers and customers, thereby linking it to the *external supply chain*, which is not under the direct control of the firm. The firm must change its focus from a product or service orientation to a customer orientation. This new focus means that the firm must identify the appropriate competitive priorities for each of its market segments. For its industrial customers, the firm must develop a better understanding of their products, culture, markets, and organization. Rather than merely reacting to customer demand, the firm strives to work with its customers so that both benefit from improved flows of materials and services. Similarly, the firm must develop better understanding of its suppliers' organizations, capacities, and strengths and weaknesses—and include its suppliers earlier in the design process for new products or services. Phase 3 embodies what we call supply chain management and seeks to integrate the internal and external supply chains.

The integrated supply chain provides a framework for the operating decisions in a firm. Managing the internal supply chain involves issues of inventory management, forecasting, aggregate planning and scheduling, and resource planning, all topics in other chapters of this text. In this chapter, we focus on the interfaces shown in Figure 9.4 between the internal supply chain and the customers and suppliers.

MANAGING THE CUSTOMER INTERFACE

The Internet has dramatically changed the way companies serve their customers. Traditional supply chains involve factories, warehouses, distributors, and retailers. Some companies, however, have been able to use the Internet to eliminate certain elements of their supply chains by substituting information for inventories. Other firms have used it to reduce the transaction costs in their supply chains. Still others have used it to expand the reach and responsiveness of the supply chain. We use the term *customer* to refer to an entity the firm is trying to serve, which could be a consumer or a business.

ORDER-PLACEMENT PROCESS

The **order-placement process** involves the activities required to register the need for a product or service and to confirm the acceptance of the order. These activities are initiated by the customer but consummated by the firm producing the product or service. Since it is the order-placement process that generates demand backward through the supply chain, it is to the firm's advantage to make it simple and fast. The Internet has

materials management
Supply chain decisions about the purchase of materials and services, including placement and size of inventories.

order-placement process
The activities required to register the need for a product or service and to confirm the acceptance of the order.

enabled firms to re-engineer their order-placement process to benefit both the customer and the firm. The Internet provides the following advantages for a firm's order-placement process.

COST REDUCTION. Using the Internet can reduce the costs of processing orders because it allows for greater participation by the customer. Customers can select the products or services they want and place an order with the firm without actually talking to anyone. This approach reduces the need for call centres, which are labour intensive and often take the customer longer to place orders.

REVENUE FLOW INCREASE. A firm's Web page can allow customers to enter credit card information or purchase order numbers as part of the order-placement process. This approach reduces the time lags often associated with billing the customer or waiting for cheques sent in the mail.

GLOBAL ACCESS. The Internet also allows firms to accept orders 24 hours a day from virtually any location. Traditional bricks-and-mortar firms take standard orders during their normal business hours. Firms with Internet access can reduce the time it takes to satisfy a customer, thereby gaining a competitive advantage over bricks-and-mortar firms.

PRICING FLEXIBILITY. Firms with their products and services posted on the Web can easily change prices as the need arises, thereby avoiding the cost and delay of publishing new catalogues. Customers placing orders have current prices to consider when making their choices. From the perspective of supply chains, Dell Computer uses this capability to control for component shortages. Because of its direct sales approach and promotional pricing, Dell can steer customers to certain configurations of computers for which ample supplies exist.

ORDER-FULFILLMENT PROCESS

order-fulfillment process
The activities required to deliver a product or service to a customer.

The **order-fulfillment process** involves the activities required to deliver a product or service to a customer. This process might be called upon to address any of the competitive priorities falling under the categories of cost, quality, time, or flexibility. We have separated the order-placement process from the order-fulfillment process in our discussion; however, in many instances, they occur simultaneously.

For example, a customer at a Loblaws grocery store in Canada has in effect ordered groceries, performed the work to actually find it in the inventory, and taken delivery when the groceries were paid for at the checkout cashier. However, Grocery Gateway in Toronto (www.grocerygateway.com) uses a Web page, which essentially separates the order-placement and order-fulfillment processes. Customers doing business on its Web page must accept a delay in receiving their groceries, a delay that Grocery Gateway seeks to minimize through effective management of its supply chain. Adding a new order-fulfillment process can have significant competitive implications, particularly in terms of changing the value offered to customers.

As we mentioned earlier, many activities of the order-fulfillment process associated with the internal supply chain are covered in the chapters to follow. In this section, we will focus on information sharing, the placement of inventories, and postponement.

INFORMATION SHARING. The Internet provides a quick and efficient means to share information along the supply chain. Within a firm, enterprise resource planning (ERP) systems facilitate the flow of information across functional areas, business units, geographic regions, and product lines (see Chapter 11, "Managing Technology"). For a manufacturing firm, accurate information about its customers' operations, such as current inventory positions, future demands and production schedules, or expected orders for the firm's products, enables the firm's order-fulfillment process to better anticipate the future needs of its customers. The supply chain can better match supply with demand, thereby reducing inventory costs and decreasing the time to fulfill orders. For a service provider, accurate forecasts of its customers' demands enable the firm to derive its own forecasts of demand for its services. For example, Purolator Courier can better plan its delivery services when it has information about the demands faced by its major corporate customers. Although electronic sharing of information can improve supply chain operations, those firms that have successfully integrated the internal and external supply chains can only enjoy the advantage. Going online may require a significant investment in information systems and support.

INVENTORY PLACEMENT. A fundamental supply chain decision is where to locate inventories of raw materials, work-in-process, or finished goods. At one extreme, the firm could keep the entire finished goods inventory at the manufacturing plant and ship directly to each of its customers. The advantage would come from what is referred to as **inventory pooling**, which is a reduction in inventory and safety stock because of the merging of variable demands from the customers. A higher-than-expected demand from one customer can be offset by a lower-than-expected demand from another. However, a disadvantage of placing the entire inventory in one location is the added cost of shipping smaller, uneconomical quantities directly to the customers, typically over long distances.

Another approach is to use **forward placement**, which means locating stock closer to customers at a warehouse, distribution centre (DC), wholesaler, or retailer. Forward placement can have two advantages for the order-fulfillment process—faster delivery times and reduced transportation costs—that can stimulate sales. As inventory is placed closer to the customer, such as at a DC, the pooling effect of the inventories is reduced because safety stocks for the item must increase to take care of uncertain demands at each DC, rather than just a single location. However, the time to get the product to the customer is reduced. Consequently, service to the customer is quicker, and the firm can take advantage of larger, less costly shipments to the DCs from the manufacturing plant, at the expense of larger overall inventories.

VENDOR-MANAGED INVENTORIES. A tactic that employs an extreme case of forward placement is **vendor-managed inventories (VMI)**, a system in which the supplier has access to the customer's inventory data and is responsible for maintaining the inventory level required by the customer. Service providers and manufacturers use VMI, including such firms as AT&T, Roadway Express, Wal-Mart, Dell, Westinghouse, and Bose. In some cases, although the inventory is on the customer's site, the supplier retains possession of the inventory until it is used. For example, Dell Computer has inventories of materials on consignment from its suppliers, and pays for them only when they are assembled into a product.

Vendor-managed inventories have several key elements.

- *Collaborative effort.* For VMI to succeed, the customers must be willing to allow the supplier access to their inventory. The implication is that the supplier assumes an important administrative role in the management of the inventory. Thus, an atmosphere of trust and accountability is required.

inventory pooling A reduction in inventory and safety stock because of the merging of variable demands from customers.

forward placement Locating stock closer to customers at a warehouse, distribution centre, wholesaler, or retailer.

vendor-managed inventories (VMI) An extreme application of the forward placement tactic that involves locating the inventories at the customer.

- *Cost savings*. Suppliers and customers eliminate the need for excess inventory through better operational planning. VMI reduces costs by removing administrative and inventory costs. Order placement costs are also reduced.

- *Customer service*. The supplier is frequently on site and better understands the operations of the customer, improving response times and reducing stockouts.

- *Written agreement*. It is important that both parties fully understand the responsibilities of each partner. Areas such as billing procedures, forecast methods, and replenishment schedules should be clearly specified. Further, the responsibility for obsolete inventory resulting from forecast revisions and changes in contract lengths should be included.

continuous replenishment A VMI method in which the supplier monitors inventory levels at the customer and replenishes the stock as needed to avoid shortages.

If stock is replenished only as needed to avoid shortages, called **continuous replenishment**, inventories can be reduced while achieving greater efficiencies in warehousing and transportation.

postponement A tactic used by assemble-to-order and mass-customization firms that refers to delaying the customizing of a product or service until the last possible moment.

POSTPONEMENT. Assemble-to-order and mass-customization firms use a tactic called **postponement**, which refers to delaying the customizing of a product or service until the last possible moment. Mass-customized products are assembled from a variety of standard components according to the specifications from a customer. When the order-placement process is separated from the order-fulfillment process, manufacturing and order fulfillment can take place after the customer has placed the order. The manufacturing process must be flexible to quickly respond to the customer's order. By forcing customization to the last possible moment, the manufacturing process spends more of its time on standardized components and assemblies, which are less costly to produce.

channel assembly The process of using members of the distribution channel to put together components as if they were assembly stations in the factory.

Postponement can be extended to the distribution channel. **Channel assembly** is the process of using members of the distribution channel as if they were assembly stations in the factory. Distributors might perform the final, customized assembly of a product for delivery to a particular customer. A special case of channel assembly is the organization and shipment of many disparate items for assembly at the customer's site. For example, FedEx is devising a system for Cisco that will transport as many as 100 different boxes destined for one of Cisco's customers from factories around the world and deliver them to the customer's door within hours of each other for final assembly. Such a system bypasses warehouses in the supply chain and reduces the cost and time required to fulfill an order.

radio frequency identification (RFID) A method for identifying items through the use of radio signals from a tag attached to an item.

RADIO FREQUENCY IDENTIFICATION. An important requirement for the execution of order-fulfillment processes is accurate information regarding the quantity and location of inventories. A new application of an old technology presents some tantalizing benefits. **Radio frequency identification (RFID)** is a method for identifying items through the use of radio signals from a tag attached to an item. The tag has information about the item and sends signals to a device that can read the information and even write new information on the tag. Data from the tags can be transmitted wirelessly from one place to another through electronic product code (EPC) networks and the Internet, making it theoretically possible to uniquely identify every item a company produces and track it until the tag is destroyed.

Wal-Mart and Gillette, among a number of large retailers, manufacturers, government agencies, and suppliers, are in the process of implementing RFID in their supply chains. In Wal-Mart's case, RFID tags on cases and pallets will be read when inventory enters a stockroom and when those cases and pallets go to the retail floor. Wal-Mart will use the data to draw conclusions about when to bring additional stock to the floor and to figure out if too much of a product has been ordered by a store and is sitting in the stockroom or in the distribution centre. The data could also help some 30 000 suppliers check inventory levels and sales. The use of RFID data can increase a supplier's service level to Wal-Mart. Pilferage reduction is another major advantage of the RFID technology. Gillette hopes to use RFID to reduce the amount of razor-blade theft, which amounts to as much as 30 percent.

Whether RFID will be universally accepted is still unknown. Global data synchronization using industry standards is critical to ensure that accurate and consistent product information is exchanged between trading partners. Much work is still to be done. According to Wal-Mart managers, the best way to make RFID happen is if retail stores work collaboratively on the project.

cross-docking The packing of products on incoming shipments so that they can be easily sorted at intermediate warehouses and immediately transferred for outgoing shipment based on their final destinations.

CROSS-DOCKING. Low-cost operations and delivery speed can be enhanced with a technique called **cross-docking**, which is the packing of products on incoming shipments so that they can be easily sorted at intermediate warehouses for outgoing shipments based on their final destinations; the items are carried from the incoming-vehicle docking point to the outgoing-vehicle docking point without being stored in inventory at the warehouse. For example, a truck from Montreal carrying shipments to customers in Ontario might arrive at a warehouse in Mississauga, where warehouse personnel unload its contents and reload them on trucks headed for destinations in neighbouring cities, such as Toronto, Hamilton, and London. Inbound shipments must be tightly coordinated with outbound shipments for cross-docking to work. The warehouse becomes a short-term staging area for organizing efficient shipments to customers. The benefits of cross-docking include reductions in inventory investment, storage space requirements, handling costs, and lead times, as well as increased inventory turnover and accelerated cash flow.

MANAGING THE SUPPLIER INTERFACE

The supplier relationship process focuses on the interaction of the firm and upstream suppliers. In this section we focus on several important decision areas that affect the design of the supplier relationship process. We begin our discussion with the considerations firms make in selecting and certifying suppliers, both important activities in the sourcing process. Next, we discuss the nature of supplier relations, which affects negotiations and collaboration on new product and service design. The next decision area is electronic purchasing. We then discuss the implications of centralized versus localized buying, and a technique called value analysis, which helps to drive improvements in supplier management.

SUPPLIER SELECTION AND CERTIFICATION

The purchasing function is the eyes and ears of the organization in the supplier marketplace, continuously seeking better buys and new materials from suppliers. Consequently, purchasing is in a good position to select suppliers for the supply chain and to conduct certification programs.

SUPPLIER SELECTION. Three criteria most often considered by firms selecting new suppliers are price, quality, and delivery. Because firms spend a large percentage of their total income on purchased items, finding suppliers that charge *low prices* is a key objective. However, as noted by Deming (see Chapter 5, "Quality"), lowest price should not be the only purchasing criterion. The *quality* of a supplier's materials can dramatically affect the *total* cost of using that supplier. The hidden costs of poor quality can be high, particularly if defects are not detected until after considerable value has been added by subsequent operations. For a retailer, poor merchandise quality can mean loss of customer goodwill and future sales. Finally, shorter lead times and on-time *delivery* help the buying firm maintain acceptable customer service with less inventory.

Another criterion is becoming increasingly important in the selection of suppliers—environmental performance. Many firms are engaging in **green purchasing**, which involves buying from firms with strong environmental management systems. These typically include identifying, assessing, and managing the flow of environmental waste and finding ways to reduce it and minimize its impact on the environment. Suppliers are being asked to be environmentally conscious when designing and manufacturing their products, and claims such as *green, biodegradable, natural,* and *recycled* must be substantiated when bidding on a contract. In the not-too-distant future, this criterion could be one of the most important in the selection of suppliers, particularly for consumer-oriented markets.

green purchasing Using environmental criteria in purchasing decisions to favour suppliers (and inputs) with strong environmental management systems, performance, or certification.

SUPPLIER CERTIFICATION. Supplier certification programs verify that potential suppliers have the capability to provide the materials or services the buying firm requires. Certification typically involves site visits by a cross-functional team from the buying firm who do an in-depth evaluation of the supplier's capability to meet cost, quality, delivery, and flexibility targets from process and information system perspectives. The team may consist of members from operations, purchasing, engineering, information systems, and accounting. Every aspect of producing the materials or services is explored through observation of the processes in action and review of documentation for completeness and accuracy. Once certified, the supplier can be used by purchasing without its having to make background checks. Performance is monitored and performance records are kept. After a certain period of time or if performance declines, the supplier may need recertification.

SUPPLIER RELATIONS
The nature of the relationship between a supplier and its customers can affect the quality, timeliness, and price of a firm's products and services. The firm's orientation toward supplier relations affects negotiation and collaboration on new service and product design.

COMPETITIVE ORIENTATION. The **competitive orientation** to supplier relations views negotiations between buyer and seller as a zero-sum game: whatever one side loses, the other side gains. Short-term advantages are prized over long-term commitments. The buyer may try to beat the supplier's price down to the lowest survival level or to push demand to high levels during boom times and order almost nothing during recessions. In contrast, the supplier presses for higher prices for specific levels of quality, customer service, and volume flexibility. Which party wins depends largely on who has the most clout.

competitive orientation A supplier relation that views negotiations between buyer and seller as a zero-sum game: whatever one side loses, the other side gains; short-term advantages are prized over long-term commitments.

Purchasing power determines the clout that a firm has. A firm has purchasing power when its purchasing volume represents a significant share of the supplier's sales or the purchased item or service is standardized and many substitutes are available. For example, by 2002 Staples had created a chain of almost 1300 office supply stores in Canada and the United States. The buying power of this growing company has become enormous. Home Hardware, a lumber and home improvement cooperative with almost 1000 stores across Canada, aggregates the purchases of independent dealers to reduce the costs for materials and services for its members. Suppliers are willing to give Home Hardware lower prices because of the large-scale purchasing power.

cooperative orientation A supplier relation in which the buyer and seller are partners, each helping the other to achieve mutually beneficial objectives.

COOPERATIVE ORIENTATION. With the **cooperative orientation** to supplier relations, the buyer and seller are partners, each helping the other as much as possible. A cooperative orientation translates into a longer-term commitment, joint work on quality, and support by the buyer of the supplier's managerial, technological, and capacity development. A cooperative orientation favours few suppliers of a particular item or service, with just one or two suppliers being the ideal number. As order volumes increase, the supplier gains repeatability, which helps movement toward high-volume operations at a low cost. When contracts are large and a long-term relationship is ensured, the supplier might even build a new facility and hire a new workforce, perhaps relocating close to the buyer's plant. Reducing the number of suppliers also can help the buyer, as suppliers become almost an extension of the buyer.

A cooperative orientation means that the buyer shares more information with the supplier on its future buying intentions. This forward visibility allows suppliers to make better, more reliable forecasts of future demand. The buyer visits suppliers' plants and cultivates cooperative attitudes. The buyer may even suggest ways to improve the suppliers' operations. Similarly, the supplier may offer suggestions to the buyer to improve quality and reliability, or reduce costs. This close cooperation with suppliers could even mean that the buyer does not need to inspect incoming materials. It also could mean giving the supplier more latitude in specifications, involving the supplier more in designing parts, implementing cost-reduction ideas, and sharing in savings.

A cooperative orientation has opened the door for innovative arrangements with suppliers. One extreme example of such an arrangement is the Volkswagen (VW) factory in Brazil. There, seven major suppliers make components on their own equipment. Then, their own workers actually assemble the components into finished trucks and buses. Of 1000 workers at the plant, only 200 are VW employees. This arrangement has several advantages. First, VW's capital investment is less: VW provides the building and the assembly-line conveyors, but suppliers install their own tools and fixtures. Second, if sales of trucks and buses go below the projected 30 000 annual capacity, all the partners take a hit, not just VW. Third, parts will arrive just before they are needed, so everyone's inventory costs will be low. Finally, improvements by suppliers in the assembly process will benefit all parties.

One advantage of reducing the number of suppliers in the supply chain is a reduction in the complexity of the procedures needed to support and manage them. However, reducing the number of suppliers for an item or service may have the disadvantage of increased risk of an interruption in supply. Also, there is less opportunity to drive a good bargain in prices unless the buyer has considerable clout. The extreme situation, **sole sourcing**, is the awarding of a contract for an item or service to only one supplier. Doing so is particularly attractive if development and market risks are shared, as with key suppliers for Bombardier's new Learjet; however, such an arrangement can amplify any supply problems that may arise over the life of the product.

sole sourcing The awarding of a contract for an item or service to only one supplier.

Both the competitive and the cooperative orientation have advantages and disadvantages. The key is to use the approach that best serves the firm's competitive priorities. Some companies utilize a mixed strategy. Managers can use a competitive approach for a firm's commodity-like supplies and a cooperative approach for its complex, high-valued, or high-volume services and materials. However, even cooperation does not preclude the obligation to reduce costs.

E-PURCHASING

The emergence of virtual marketplaces, enabled by Internet technologies, has provided firms with many opportunities to improve their purchasing processes. Not all e-purchasing opportunities, however, involve the Internet. In this section, we will discuss four approaches to e-purchasing: electronic data interchange, catalogue hubs, exchanges, and auctions.

electronic data interchange (EDI) A technology that enables the transmission of routine business documents having a standard format from computer to computer over telephone or direct leased lines.

ELECTRONIC DATA INTERCHANGE. The most used form of e-purchasing today is **electronic data interchange (EDI)**, a technology that enables the transmission of routine business documents having a standard format from computer to computer over telephone or direct leased lines. Special communications software translates documents into and out of a generic form, allowing organizations to exchange information even if they have different hardware and software components. Invoices, purchase orders, and payments are some of the routine documents that EDI can handle—it replaces the phone call or mailed document. An electronic purchasing system with EDI might work as follows. Buyers browse an electronic catalogue and click on items to purchase from a supplier. A computer sends the order directly to the supplier. The supplier's computer checks the buyer's credit and determines whether the items are available. The supplier's warehouse and shipping departments are notified electronically, and the items are readied for shipment. Finally, the supplier's accounting department bills the buyer electronically. EDI saves the cost of opening mail, directing it to the right department, checking the document for accuracy, and re-entering the information in a computer system. It also improves accuracy, shortens response times, and can even reduce inventory. Savings (ranging from $5 to $125 per document) are considerable in the light of the hundreds to thousands of documents many firms typically handle daily.

catalogue hubs Posting of a centralized electronic catalogue online that enables employees to place orders for pre-approved items.

CATALOGUE HUBS. The costs of placing orders to suppliers, as well as the goods and services themselves, can be reduced through the use of **catalogue hubs**. Suppliers post their catalogue of items on the hub, and buyers select what they need and purchase them electronically. Moreover, a buying firm can negotiate prices with specific suppliers for items such as office supplies, technical equipment, specialized items, services, or furniture. The catalogue that the buying firm's employees see consists only of the approved items and their negotiated prices. The hub connects the firm to potentially hundreds of suppliers through the Internet, saving the costs of EDI, which requires one-to-one connections to individual suppliers.

exchange An electronic marketplace where buying firms and selling firms come together to do business.

EXCHANGES. An **exchange** is an electronic marketplace where buying and selling firms come together to do business. The exchange maintains relationships with buyers and sellers, making it easy to do business without the aspect of contract negotiations or other sorts of long-term conditions. Exchanges are often used for "spot" purchases, which are needed to satisfy an immediate need at the lowest possible cost. Commodity items such as oil, steel, or energy fit this category. However, exchanges can also be used for almost any item. For example, Marriott International, Hyatt Hotels, Fairmont Hotels, and others formed an exchange for hotels (www.avendra.com). Hotels traditionally have bought supplies from thousands of firms, each focusing on selected items such as soap, food, and equipment, using faxes, telephones, and forms that were made in quadruplicate. The new exchange aimed to create one-stop shopping for hotels using the service.

auction An extension of the exchange in which firms place competitive bids to buy something.

AUCTIONS. An extension of the exchange is the **auction**, where firms place competitive bids to buy something. For example, a site may be formed for a particular industry at which firms with excess capacity or materials can offer them for sale to the highest bidder. Bids can either be closed or open to the competition. Industries where auctions have value include steel, chemicals, and the home mortgage industry, where financial institutions can bid for mortgages.

An approach that has received considerable attention is the so-called *reverse auction*, in which suppliers bid for contracts with buyers. One such site is FreeMarkets (www.freemarkets.com). With market operation centres in Europe, the United States, and Asia, the firm offers a Web site where large companies offer supply contracts for open bidding. Each bid is posted, so suppliers can see how much lower their next bid must be to remain in the running for the contract. Each contract has an electronic prospectus that provides all the specifications, conditions, and other requirements that are non-negotiable. The only thing left to determine is the cost to the buyer. Savings can be dramatic.

Our discussion of these electronic approaches in purchasing should not leave the impression that cost is the only consideration in selecting a supplier. Exchanges and auctions are more useful for commodities, near-commodities, or infrequently needed items that require only short-term relationships with suppliers. The past two decades have taught us the lesson that suppliers should be thought of as partners when the needed supply is significant and steady over extended periods of time. Supplier involvement in product or service design and supply chain performance improvement requires long-term relationships not found by competitive pricing on the Internet.

CENTRALIZED VERSUS LOCALIZED BUYING

When an organization has several facilities (e.g., stores, hospitals, or plants), management must decide whether to buy locally or centrally. This decision has implications for the control of supply chain flows.

Centralized buying has the advantage of increasing purchasing clout. Savings can be significant, often on the order of 10 percent or more. Increased buying power can mean getting better service, ensuring long-term supply availability, or developing new supplier capability. Companies with overseas suppliers favour centralization because of the specialized skills (e.g., understanding of foreign languages and cultures) needed to buy from foreign sources. Buyers also need to understand international commercial and contract law regarding the transfer of goods and services. Another trend that favours centralization is the growth of computer-based information systems and the Internet, which give specialists at headquarters access to data previously available only at the local level.

Probably the biggest disadvantage of centralized buying is loss of control at the local level. When plants or divisions are evaluated as profit or cost centres, centralized buying is undesirable for items unique to a particular facility. These items should be purchased locally whenever possible. The same holds for purchases that must be closely meshed with production schedules. Further, localized buying is an advantage when the firm has major facilities in foreign countries, because the managers there, often foreign nationals, have a much better understanding of the culture than a staff would at the home office. Also, centralized purchasing often contributes to longer lead times and another hierarchical level in the organization, which can slow decision making and hurt responsiveness.

As with supplier relations, management usually must develop a mixed approach and leverage both centralized buying and local autonomy. For example, the corporate purchasing group at IBM negotiates contracts on a centralized basis only at the request of local plants. Then management at one of the facilities monitors the contract for all the participating plants. Alternatively, commodity-based purchases might be made by a centralized group, while specialized parts and services are bought at the local level in a decentralized fashion.

VALUE ANALYSIS

A systematic effort to reduce the cost or improve the performance of products or services, either purchased or produced, is referred to as **value analysis**. It is an intensive examination of the materials, processes, information systems, and flows of material involved in the production of an item. Benefits include reduced production, materials, and distribution costs; improved profit margins; and increased customer satisfaction. Because teams involving purchasing, production, and engineering personnel from both the firm and its major suppliers play a key role in value analysis, another potential benefit is increased employee morale.

Value analysis encourages employees of the firm and its suppliers to address questions such as the following: What is the function of the item? Is the function necessary? Can a lower-cost standard part that serves the purpose be identified? Can similar parts be substituted with a common part? Can the item be simplified, or its specifications relaxed, to achieve a lower price? Can the item be designed so that it can be produced more efficiently or more quickly? Can features that the customer values highly be added to the item? Value analysis should be part of a continual effort to improve the performance of the supply chain and increase the value of the item to the customer.

Value analysis can focus solely on the *internal* supply chain with some success, but its true potential lies in applying it to the *external* supply chain as well. An approach that many firms are using is called **early supplier involvement**, which is a program that includes suppliers in the design phase of a product or service.

Suppliers provide suggestions for design changes and materials choices that will result in more efficient operations and higher quality. In the automotive industry, an even higher level of early supplier involvement is known as **presourcing**, whereby suppliers are selected early in a vehicle's concept development stage and are given significant, if not total, responsibility for the design of certain components or systems. Presourced suppliers also take responsibility for the cost, quality, and on-time delivery of the items they produce.

MEASURES OF SUPPLY CHAIN PERFORMANCE

As we have shown, supply chain management involves managing the flow of materials that create inventories in the supply chain. For this reason, managers closely monitor inventories to keep them at acceptable levels. Inventory levels also have implications for the responsiveness of the supply chain and, ultimately, the level of customer service. In this section, we first define the typical inventory measures used to monitor supply chain performance and then discuss some process measures. Finally, we relate some commonly used supply chain performance measures to several important financial measures.

INVENTORY MEASURES

All methods of measuring inventory begin with a physical count of units, volume, or weight. However, measures of inventories are reported in three basic ways: average aggregate inventory value, weeks of supply, and inventory turnover.

The **average aggregate inventory value** is the total value of all items held in inventory for a firm. Consistent with accounting conventions, valuation is at cost, summing the value of individual items in raw materials, work-in-process, and finished goods. Because this measure is taken at a particular point in time, it is usually more meaningful to estimate the average inventory investment over some period of time.

The raw materials typically cost much less than a finished product, which may be valued in the hundreds of dollars because of the labour, technology, and other value-added operations performed in manufacturing the product. For example, the value of raw materials, such as iron ore, must be added to that of finished products, such as steel coils, for a steel manufacturer. To estimate the approximate average aggregate inventory value, sum the values of individual inventory items:

$$\text{Average aggregate inventory value} = (N_a c_a) + (N_b c_b) + \dots + (N_n c_n)$$

where:

N_a = Average quantity of materials, part, component, or product a

c_a = Average cost per unit of materials, part, component, or product a

n = Total number of materials, parts, components, and products

Summed over all items in an inventory, this total value tells managers how much of a firm's assets are tied up in inventory. Manufacturing firms typically have about 25 percent of their total assets in inventory, whereas wholesalers and retailers average about 75 percent.

To some extent, managers can decide whether the aggregate inventory value is too low or too high by historical or industry comparison or by managerial judgment. However, a better performance measure would take demand into account. **Weeks of supply** is an inventory measure obtained by dividing the average aggregate inventory value by sales per week, again at cost. (In some low-inventory operations, days or even hours of supply are a better unit of time for measuring inventory.) The formula expressed using weeks is:

weeks of supply An inventory measure obtained by dividing the average aggregate inventory value by sales per week at cost.

$$\text{Weeks of supply} = \frac{\text{Average aggregate inventory value}}{\text{Weekly sales (at cost)}}$$

Although the numerator includes the value of all items (raw materials, WIP, and finished goods), the denominator represents only the finished goods sold—at cost rather than the sale price after markups or discounts. This cost is referred to as the *cost of goods sold*. (Within the supply chain, the weeks of supply can be calculated for specific items in a similar way, using the average inventory value for that item and the demand for that item.)

Third, **inventory turnover** (or *turns*) is an inventory measure obtained by dividing annual sales at cost by the average aggregate inventory value maintained during the year, or:

inventory turnover A measure of the rate at which inventory is consumed, obtained by dividing annual sales at cost by the average aggregate inventory value maintained during the year.

$$\text{Inventory turnover} = \frac{\text{Annual sales (at cost)}}{\text{Average aggregate inventory value}}$$

The "best" inventory level, even when expressed as turnover, cannot be determined easily. Although six or seven turns per year is typical, the average high-tech firm settles for only about three turns. At the other extreme, some automobile firms report 40 turns per year for selected products. See the Solved Problem at the end of this chapter for a detailed example of the three inventory measures.

PROCESS MEASURES

We have discussed three major processes related to supply chain management: order placement, order fulfillment, and purchasing. Supply chain managers monitor performance by measuring cost, time, and quality. Table 9.1 contains examples of operating measures for the three processes.

TABLE 9.1	Order Placement	Order Fulfillment	Purchasing
Supply Chain Process Measures	• Percentage of orders taken accurately • Time to complete the order-placement process • Customer satisfaction with the order-placement process	• Percentage of incomplete orders shipped • Percentage of orders shipped on time • Time to fulfill the orders • Percentage of returned items or botched services • Cost to produce the item or service • Customer satisfaction with the order-fulfillment process	• Percentage of suppliers' deliveries on time • Suppliers' lead times • Percentage of defects in purchased materials and services • Cost of purchased materials and services

Managers also can collect data on measures such as these and track them to note changes in level or direction. Statistical process control charts can be used to determine whether the changes are statistically significant, thereby prompting management's attention (see Chapter 5, "Quality"). The impact of improvements to the three processes also can be monitored using control charts.

LINKS TO FINANCIAL MEASURES

Effective management of the supply chain has a fundamental impact on the financial status of a firm. Inventory should be considered an investment, because it is created for future use. However, inventory is also a liability, in that it ties up funds that might be used more profitably elsewhere or can hide operational problems. Managing the supply chain so as to reduce the aggregate inventory investment will reduce the *total assets* portion of the firm's balance sheet. An important financial measure is *return on assets* (ROA), which is net income divided by total assets. Consequently, reducing aggregate inventory investment will increase ROA. Nonetheless, given that inventory can serve several important functions, as discussed in Chapter 6, "Inventory Management," the objective is to have the *proper* amount of inventory, not the least amount of inventory.

Weeks of inventory and inventory turns have an impact on another financial measure, *working capital*, which is money used to finance ongoing operations. Increases in inventory require greater investment, which increases the need for working capital. Depending on the function of the inventory, greater inventory turnover can be accomplished by improving supply chain processes. For example, reducing supplier lead times has the effect of allowing a reduction in pipeline and buffer inventory, as the flows of materials are easier to manage because shorter-range, more reliable forecasts of demand are possible. As a result, the weeks of supply decrease and inventory turnover increases, thereby reducing overall working capital. Similarly, improvements in the other measures in Table 9.1 can contribute to a reduction in working capital.

Managers can also reduce production and material costs through effective supply chain management. Costs of materials are determined through the financial arrangements with suppliers, and production costs are a result of the design and execution of the internal supply chain. In addition, the percent of defects, experienced in the external as well as internal supply chains, also affects the costs of operation. Improvements in these measures are reflected in the *cost of goods sold* and ultimately in the *net income* of the firm. They also have an effect on *contribution margin*, which is the difference between price and variable costs to produce a good or service.

Supply chain performance measures related to time also have financial implications. Many manufacturers and service providers measure the percent of on-time deliveries of their product or services to their customers, as well as materials and services from their suppliers. Increasing the percent of on-time deliveries to customers will increase *total revenue*, because satisfied customers will buy more products and services from the firm. Increasing the percent of on-time deliveries from suppliers has the effect of reducing uncertainty, which allows reductions in inventory levels and, thus, a reduction in working capital.

The Internet has brought to the forefront another financial measure related to time: *cash-to-cash*, which is the time lag between paying for the materials and services needed to produce a product or service and receiving payment for it. The shorter the time lag, the less working capital that is needed to finance operations. Re-engineering the customer's order-placement process so that payment for the product or service is made at the time the order is placed can reduce the time lag. Pushed one step further, a firm can create a negative cash-to-cash situation, where the customer pays for the product before the firm is required to pay for the materials used to make it. Dell Computer is a prime example of a negative cash-to-cash situation. In such a case, the firm must be using an assemble-to-order strategy and have supplier inventories on consignment, which allows payment for materials only after they are used.

SUPPLY CHAIN DYNAMICS

Supply chains often involve linkages among many firms, and supply chain dynamics can wreak havoc on performance. Each firm in a supply chain depends on other firms for services, materials, or the information needed to supply its immediate external customer in the chain. Yet, the actions of downstream supply chain members (positioned nearer the ultimate consumer of the service or product) can indirectly affect the operations of upstream members, even several tiers away. The reason is that upstream members of a supply chain must react to the demands placed on them by downstream members of the chain. These demands are partly driven by policies for replenishing inventories, the actual levels of those inventories, the demands of their customers, and the accuracy of the information.

As you examine the order patterns of firms in a supply chain, you will frequently see the variability in order quantities increase as you proceed upstream. This increase in variability is referred to as the **bullwhip effect**, which gets its name from the action of a bullwhip—the handle of the whip initiates the action; however, the tip of the whip experiences the wildest action. The slightest change in customer demands can ripple through the entire chain, with each member receiving more variability in demands from the member immediately downstream.

The bullwhip effect in a supply chain for facial tissue is depicted in Figure 9.5. The retailer's orders to the manufacturer exhibit more variability than the actual demands from the consumers of the facial tissue because shipments to a retailer occur much less frequently than a customer buying individual packages. The manufacturer's orders to the package supplier have more variability than the retailer's orders. Finally, the package supplier's orders to the cardboard supplier have the most variability. Because supply patterns do not match demand patterns, inventories accumulate in some firms and shortages occur in others. The firms with too much inventory stop ordering, and those that have shortages place expedite orders. The culprits are unexpected changes in demands or supplies that are based on a number of causes.

EXTERNAL CAUSES

A firm has the least amount of control over its external customers and suppliers, who can periodically cause disruptions. Typical disruptions include:

bullwhip effect The phenomenon in supply chains whereby ordering patterns show increasing variance as you move upstream in the chain.

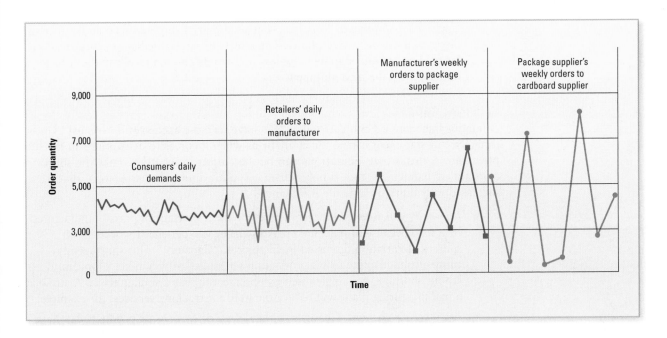

FIGURE 9.5

Supply Chain Dynamics for Facial Tissue

The bullwhip effect can cause costly disruptions to upstream facilities of a supply chain, such as a paperboard manufacturing process at this Weyerhauser Co. plant.

● *Volume changes.* Customers may change the quantity of the service or product they had ordered for a specific date or unexpectedly demand more of a standard service or product. If the market demands short lead times, the firm needs a quick reaction from its suppliers. For example, an electric company experiencing an unusually warm day may require immediate power backup from another electric company to avoid a brownout.

● *Service and product mix changes.* Customers may change the mix of items in an order and cause a ripple effect throughout the supply chain. For example, a major-appliance store chain may change the mix of washing machines in its orders from 60 percent Whirlpool brand and 40 percent Kitchen Aid brand to 30 percent Whirlpool and 70 percent Kitchen Aid. This decision changes the production schedule of the Whirlpool plant that makes both brands, causing imbalances in its inventories. In addition, the company that makes the faceplates for the washing machines must change its schedules, thereby affecting its suppliers.

● *Late deliveries.* Late deliveries of materials or delays in essential services can

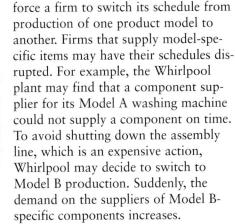

force a firm to switch its schedule from production of one product model to another. Firms that supply model-specific items may have their schedules disrupted. For example, the Whirlpool plant may find that a component supplier for its Model A washing machine could not supply a component on time. To avoid shutting down the assembly line, which is an expensive action, Whirlpool may decide to switch to Model B production. Suddenly, the demand on the suppliers of Model B-specific components increases.

● *Underfilled shipments*. Suppliers that send partial shipments do so because of disruptions at their own plants. The effects of underfilled shipments are similar to those of late shipments unless it contains enough to allow the firm to operate until the next shipment.

INTERNAL CAUSES

A famous line from a Pogo cartoon is "We have seen the enemy, and he is us!" Unfortunately, this statement is true for many firms when it comes to disruptions in the supply chain. A firm's own operations can be the culprit in what becomes the source of constant dynamics in the supply chain. Typical internal disruptions that cause increased variability include the following:

● *Internally generated shortages*. There may be a shortage of parts manufactured by a firm because of machine breakdowns or inexperienced workers—all sources of variation discussed in Chapter 4, "Capacity." This shortage may cause a change in the firm's production schedule that will affect suppliers. A labour shortage, possibly caused by absenteeism, has a similar effect. A strike at a manufacturing plant will reduce the need for trucking services, for example.

● *Engineering changes*. Changes to the design of services or products can have a direct impact on suppliers. For example, changing cable TV feed lines to fibre-optic technology increases the benefits to the cable company's customers but affects the demand for cable. Similarly, reducing the complexity of a dashboard assembly may not be noticeable (functionally) to the buyers of an automobile, but it will change demand for the outsourced parts that go into the dashboard.

● *New service or product introductions*. New services or products always affect the supply chain. A firm decides on the number of introductions, as well as their timing, and hence introduces a dynamic in the supply chain. New services or products may even require a new supply chain or the addition of new members to an existing supply chain. For example, the introduction of a new refrigerated trucking service will affect the suppliers of refrigerated trucks and the maintenance items for the new service.

● *Service or product promotions*. A common practice of firms producing standardized products or services is to use occasional price discounts to promote sales. This practice has the effect of creating a spike in demand that is felt throughout the supply chain. That is what the Campbell Soup Company found out when its annual deep-discount pricing program in January caused retailers and customers to stock up with large quantities of chicken soup, which in turn created the need for overtime production at its plants as early as October. Moving to "everyday" low pricing, coupled with daily replenishment to distribution warehouses, smoothed the demand pattern from grocers, and allowed Campbell's to reduce overtime costs and expand sales.

● *Information errors*. Demand forecast errors could cause a firm to order too many, or too few, services and materials. Also, forecast errors can result in expedited orders that force suppliers to react more quickly to avoid shortages in the supply chain. In addition, errors in the physical count of items in stock can cause shortages (leading to panic purchases) or too much inventory (leading to a slowdown in purchases). Finally, communication links between buyers and suppliers can be faulty. For example, inaccurate order quantities and delays in information flows will affect supply chain dynamics.

Many disruptions are simply caused by ineffective coordination in the supply chain because so many firms and separate operations are involved. It is therefore unrealistic to think that all disruptions can be eliminated. As firms move toward more integrated supply chains, described earlier in this chapter, it is possible to reduce the number of disruptions and minimize the impact of those that cannot be eliminated.

SUPPLY CHAIN STRATEGIES

Operations strategy seeks to link the design and use of a firm's infrastructure and processes, including suppliers, to the competitive priorities of each of its products or services so as to maximize its potential in the marketplace. Yet a supply chain is a network of firms, each with its own operations strategy. So each firm in the chain must build its own supply chain with a consistent understanding and support for the competitive priorities of the overall supply chain.

This challenge helps to explain why the performance of many supply chains has been dismal, with high costs and slow response times, despite great investment in advanced technologies such as the Internet, flexible manufacturing, and automated warehousing across the supply chain. One cause of these failures is that managers do not link the design of the supply chain to the operations strategy of the firm. The supply chain for a firm with a strategy to offer innovative, customized high-margin products should be very different from that with a strategy for basic, functional products with small contribution margins. Thus, the design of the supply chain must be aligned with operations strategy and the characteristics of the service or product. In this section, we highlight two distinct supply chain designs and demonstrate how they can support the operations strategies of firms. We also discuss how a firm can leverage opportunities for greater vertical integration and outsourcing.

EFFICIENT VERSUS RESPONSIVE SUPPLY CHAINS

Depending on the characteristics of the product or service, two distinct supply chain designs can be used for competitive advantage: *efficient* or *responsive* supply chains (Fisher, 1997). The purpose of efficient supply chains is to coordinate the flow of materials and services so as to minimize inventories and maximize the efficiency of the manufacturers and service providers in the chain. Responsive supply chains are designed to react quickly to market demands by positioning inventories and capacities in order to hedge against variation and uncertainties in demand. Table 9.2 shows the environments that best suit each design.

TABLE 9.2	Factor	Efficient Supply Chains	Responsive Supply Chains
Environments Best Suited for Efficient and Responsive Supply Chains	**Demand**	Predictable; low forecast errors	Unpredictable; high forecast errors
	Competitive priorities	Low cost; consistent quality; on-time delivery	Development speed; fast delivery times; customization; volume flexibility; high-performance design quality
	New-product introduction	Infrequent	Frequent
	Contribution margins	Low	High
	Product variety	Low	High

EFFICIENT SUPPLY CHAINS. The pattern of demand for the firm's products or services is a key factor in the best choice of supply chain design. Efficient supply chains work best in environments where demand is highly predictable, such as demand for staple items purchased at grocery stores or demand for a package delivery service. The focus of the supply chain is on the efficient flows of materials and services, that is, keeping inventories to a minimum. Product or service designs last a long time, new introductions are infrequent, and variety is small. Such firms typically produce for markets in which price is crucial to winning an order; therefore, contribution margins are low and efficiency is important. Consequently, the firm's competitive priorities are low-cost operations, consistent quality, and on-time delivery.

RESPONSIVE SUPPLY CHAINS. Responsive supply chains work best when firms offer a great variety of products or services and demand predictability is low. Demand may also be short-lived, as in the case of fashion goods. The focus of responsive supply chains is reaction time to meet rapidly changing demand, with judiciously placed inventories along the supply chain to meet peak demand. In other markets, firms may not know what products or services they need to provide until customers place orders. This is the situation facing firms that compete using an operations strategy of mass customization or assemble-to-order (see Chapter 1, "Competing with Operations"). To be competitive, such firms must frequently introduce new products or services to generate high contribution margins. Typical competitive priorities are development speed, fast delivery times, customization, volume flexibility, and high-performance design quality.

IMPLEMENTING THE RIGHT DESIGN

The alignment with operations strategy and implementation for efficient and responsive supply chains are summarized in Table 9.3. The further upstream in an efficient supply chain that a firm is positioned, the more likely it is to have a continuous or line flow process that supports high volumes of standardized products or services. Consequently, suppliers in efficient supply chains tend to have low capacity cushions because high utilization helps to keep the cost per unit low. Higher inventory turnover is desired to keep inventory investment low, and thus reduce costs. Firms should work with their suppliers to shorten lead times, but care must be taken to use tactics that do not appreciably increase costs. For example, lead times for a supplier could be shortened by switching from rail to air transportation; however, the added cost may offset the savings obtained from the shorter lead times. Suppliers should be selected with emphasis on low prices, consistent quality, and on-time delivery. Because of low capacity cushions, disruptions in an efficient supply chain can be costly and must be avoided.

TABLE 9.3			
Design Features for Efficient and Responsive Supply Chains	**Factor**	**Efficient Supply Chains**	**Responsive Supply Chains**
	Operations strategy	Emphasize high-volume, standardized products or services, such as make-to-stock	Emphasize product or service variety, including assemble-to-order, make-to-order, or customization
	Capacity cushion	Low	High
	Inventory investment	Low; focus on high inventory turnover	Higher at critical points in supply chain to enable fast delivery time; use modular components.
	Lead time	Shorten, if possible without driving up cost	Shorten aggressively
	Supplier selection	Emphasize low prices, consistent quality, on-time delivery	Emphasize fast delivery time, customization, volume flexibility, high-performance design quality

Because of the need for quick reactions and the high levels of product or service variety, firms in a responsive supply chain must have a more flexible process, such as a project or batch process. Consequently, suppliers tend to have high capacity cushions or very flexible operations. Inventories should be positioned in the chain to support delivery speed, but inventories of expensive finished goods should be avoided. Firms should aggressively work with their suppliers to shorten lead times because that allows firms to wait longer before committing to customer orders. Firms should select suppliers to support the competitive priorities of the products or services provided, which in this case would include the ability to provide quick deliveries, customize parts or components, adjust volumes quickly to match demand cycles in the market, and provide high-performance quality.

Poor supply chain performance is often the result of using the wrong supply chain design for the products or services provided. A common mistake is to use an efficient supply chain in an environment that calls for a responsive supply chain. Or alternatively, a single design across all market segments. Instead, a firm may need to utilize more than one supply chain design when its operations compete in multiple market segments. For example, the supply chain for a standard product such as an oil tanker has different requirements than that for a customized product such as a luxury liner, even though both are ocean-going vessels and both may be manufactured by the same company.

Finally, the design of supply chains becomes more complex as markets evolve and firms move to reposition products over time. Over time, a firm may add options to its basic product, or introduce variations of that product, so that the variety of products and options increases dramatically. Yet, all too often, the design of the supply chain changes little, and the firm continues to measure the supply chain's performance as it always has, emphasizing efficiency, even when characteristics of the product and market require a more responsive supply chain design. For some firms, an intermediate design step is to identify modular subassemblies or service elements that can be combined using postponement. For example, Gillette uses an efficient supply chain to manufacture some products so that it can more fully utilize a capital-intensive manufacturing process. However, in response to increasingly uncertain and fragmented retail markets, managers have developed a supply chain that postpones the packaging of the products until the very last moment. The packaging operation involves customization in the form of printing different graphics and languages. Clearly, effective alignment of operations and its competitive priorities with supply chain design has strategic implications for a firm.

OUTSOURCING AND OFFSHORING

All businesses buy at least some inputs to their processes, such as professional services, raw materials, or manufactured parts, from other producers. Vertical integration is the degree to which a firm's own production system or service facility handles the entire supply chain. The more processes that are performed in-house rather than by suppliers or customers, the greater the degree of vertical integration. Management decides the level of vertical integration by looking at all the processes performed between the acquisition of raw materials or outside services and the delivery of finished goods or services.

If a company doesn't perform some processes itself, it must rely on **outsourcing**, or paying suppliers and distributors to perform those processes and provide needed services and materials. When managers opt for more vertical integration, there is by definition less outsourcing. These decisions are sometimes called **make-or-buy decisions**, with a make decision meaning more integration and a buy decision meaning more outsourcing. After deciding what to outsource and what to do in-house, management must find ways to coordinate and integrate the various processes and suppliers involved.

outsourcing Allotting payment to suppliers and distributors to provide needed services and materials and to perform those processes that the organization does not perform itself.

make-or-buy decisions Decisions that either involve more integration (a *make* decision) or more outsourcing (a *buy* decision).

backward integration
A firm's movement upstream toward the sources of raw materials and parts.

forward integration
A firm's movement downstream by acquiring channels of distribution, finished goods manufacturing, or supplemental service.

VERTICAL INTEGRATION. Vertical integration can be in two directions. **Backward integration** represents movement upstream toward the sources of raw materials and parts, such as a major grocery chain having its own plants to produce house brands of ice cream, frozen pizza dough, and peanut butter. Alternatively, **forward integration** represents movement downstream, such as acquiring new channels of distribution, warehouses, and retail stores. It can also mean that a firm begins to acquire or compete against its customers. For example, a commodity-based raw material supplier can expand to manufacture finished goods, such as a sugar refinery forward-integrating into candy production.

ADVANTAGES OF VERTICAL INTEGRATION. A firm tends to choose vertical integration when it has the skills, volume, and resources to perform processes at lower cost and produce higher-quality goods and services than outsiders can. Doing the work in-house may mean better quality and more timely delivery—and taking better advantage of the firm's human resources, equipment, and space. Extensive vertical integration is generally attractive when input volumes are high because high volumes allow for task specialization and greater efficiency. It is also attractive if the firm has the relevant skills and views the processes that it is integrating as particularly important to its future success.

Management must identify, cultivate, and exploit its core competencies to prevail in global competition. Recall that core competencies are the collective learning and skills of the firm, especially its ability to coordinate diverse processes and integrate multiple technologies. Management must look upstream toward its suppliers and downstream toward its customers and bring in-house those processes that give it the right core competencies—those that allow the firm to organize work and deliver value better than its competitors. Management should also realize that if the firm outsources a critical process, it might lose control over that area of its business—and perhaps foster future competition.

ADVANTAGES OF OUTSOURCING. Outsourcing, in contrast to vertical integration, offers several advantages to firms. It is particularly attractive to those that have low volumes or need specialized expertise. Outsourcing can also provide better quality and cost savings. For example, foreign locations managed by a supplier can offer lower wages and yield higher productivity. Firms are doing more outsourcing than ever before. Two factors contributing to this trend are global competition and information technology. Globalization creates more supplier options, and advances in information technology make coordination with suppliers easier. IKEA, the largest retailer of home furnishings, has 30 buying offices around the world to seek out suppliers. Its Vienna-based business service department runs a computer database that helps suppliers locate raw materials and new business partners. Cash registers at its stores around the world relay sales data to the nearest warehouse and its operational headquarters in Älmhult, Sweden, where its information systems provide the data needed to control its shipping patterns worldwide.

offshoring A supply chain strategy that involves moving processes to another country.

OFFSHORING. The strategy of globalizing a firm adds a new dimension to the development of supply chains. **Offshoring** is a supply chain strategy that involves moving processes to another country. As such, offshoring is more encompassing than outsourcing because it also includes vertical integration by locating internal processes in other countries. Firms are motivated to initiate operations offshore by the market potential and the cost advantages it provides. The firm may be able to create new markets because of its presence in other countries and its ability to offer competitive prices due to its cost efficiencies. Competitive priorities other than low costs, such as delivery speed to distant customers, can drive the decision, too.

As for costs, several factors drive the offshoring strategy. Labour costs can be lower, and logistics costs to distant international markets can be reduced. In addition, tax incentives might be offered for locating service or manufacturing operations within particular countries. Tariffs can also be a stumbling block, sometimes pushing a firm to assemble, rather than import, products in that country. For example, Hewlett-Packard sourced the final assembly of a computer server to Singapore and Australia to get closer to targeted customers in Southeast Asia. Hewlett-Packard decided to assemble a product for sale to customers in India with imported parts to reduce the costs of tariffs. While distance generally adds to the complexity of managing operations, the Internet has reduced many of the communication and monitoring costs of dealing with distant facilities.

Even though offshoring appears to offer some big advantages, it also has some pitfalls that firms should carefully explore before using this strategy:

- *Moving too quickly.* A critical mistake is to decide to move a process offshore before making a major effort to fix the existing one. As we discussed in earlier chapters, there are many ways to improve processes in the areas of quality, efficiency, and customer responsiveness. These methods should be explored first. It is not always the case that offshoring or outsourcing is the answer, even if local labour wages far exceed those of other countries. Canon, for example, decided to keep its manufacturing in Japan rather than shift it to lower-cost countries in Southeast Asia. The strategy is to compete on technology innovations in its line of high-end cameras. To achieve that strategy, Canon kept its new product development process and its manufacturing process close to each other to support speedy new product introductions and communication between engineers and manufacturing managers. Assembly lines were replaced with manufacturing cells, thereby improving teamwork, reducing its inventory and factory costs, and increasing its ability to make innovative products faster. The message: Make sure you really need to offshore in order to accomplish your operations strategy.

- *Technology transfer.* Often an offshoring strategy involves creating a joint venture with a company in another country. With a joint venture, two firms agree to jointly produce a service or product together. Typically, a transfer of technology takes place to bring one partner up to speed regarding the service or product. The danger is that the firm with the technology advantage will set up the other firm to be a future competitor. For example, GM set up a joint venture with the Shanghai Auto Industry Corporation (SAIC) to produce Buicks. SAIC got a licence to use GM's technical know-how in the form of drawings, blueprints, math data, and computer files. As GM develops local engineering design capability, it transfers technical knowledge to the Chinese staff. Because SAIC is planning to develop and produce its own cars, it is possible that GM and other joint venture partners with SAIC are creating a new competitor in China.

- *Process integration.* Despite the power of the Internet, it is difficult to fully integrate offshore processes with the firm's other processes. Time, distance, and communication can be formidable hurdles. Managing offshore processes won't be the same as managing processes located next door. Often considerable managerial time must be expended to coordinate offshore processes.

Thus, offshoring carries opportunities, challenges, and threats. As with any critical decision affecting operations strategy, trade-offs must be carefully assessed and risks actively managed.

VIRTUAL SUPPLY CHAINS

The advent of the Internet opened an entirely new set of opportunities for supply chain design. Many companies redesign their supply chains to outsource some part of their order-fulfillment process with the help of sophisticated, Web-based information technology support packages. In effect, these companies manage the order-fulfillment aspects of their business as if the process was actually in-house. For example, Li & Fung coordinates the manufacture and distribution of apparel worldwide while maintaining only a few high-value processes in Hong Kong (see the Managerial Practice Feature). This approach allows Li & Fung to focus on its core processes of designing products, scheduling and coordination, and managing customer relationships.

About 30 percent of all Internet retailers embrace the idea of virtual supply chains by using a technique called drop shipping, whereby a retailer passes customer orders directly to a wholesaler or manufacturer, which then ships the order directly to the customer with the retailer's label on it. These retailers outsource their warehouse operations to avoid the costs of holding their own inventories. Developing a virtual supply chain also provides the firm with a great deal of flexibility to change the design of its customer benefit bundle, whether a product or service.

The virtual supply chain offers a number of advantages, and is favoured by managers in the following situations:

- *When demand is highly volatile.* Volatile demand, particularly if overall volumes are low, presents risks for holding inventories, which can prove costly for a firm. In addition, investments in inventory, equipment, warehouses, and personnel to operate an order-fulfillment process may be prohibitively high. A more cost-effective approach may be to find a supplier that is supplying the same stock item for other firms with similar demand uncertainties. The suppliers can smooth the random fluctuations in demands from multiple customers and provide the item at a cost-effective price, with less risk of stockouts.

- *When high service or product variety is important.* Partnering with a supplier can broaden the provision of services or products dramatically. In addition, the firm can have the freedom to select from a wide variety of wholesalers, service providers, and manufacturers, thereby providing the firm with the flexibility to match dynamic competitive priorities. For example, a typical Circuit City store in the U.S. carries 500 to 3000 movie titles. When designing the Internet presence for the company, management discovered that Internet shoppers expected to have about 55 000 titles to choose from. The solution was to partner with another company to provide the necessary product variety. Shoppers using CircuitCity.com can now place orders for movie titles, which will be fulfilled through virtual inventories.

- *When there are lower costs due to economies of scale at suppliers.* A supplier may handle much higher volumes than the firm doing the outsourcing because the supplier may have a number of customers for the same service or product. This added volume opens the possibility that the costs of the outsourcing firm will be much lower than if the order fulfillment process were done in-house.

- *When there are lower transportation costs.* Retailers realize the advantage of lower transportation costs. Traditionally, retailers pay transportation costs to acquire the goods from a wholesaler and then pay to have the goods shipped to the customer. With drop shipping in a virtual supply chain, the only transportation cost is shipping the goods from the wholesaler to the customer.

MANAGERIAL PRACTICE
Choosing the Right Amount of Vertical Integration

More Integration (Less Outsourcing)

Vincor International, Canada's largest producer of wine, is a model of vertical integration. Vincor's 270 brands run the gamut from basic to premium wines. Upstream, it owns or leases thousands of hectares of vineyards in Ontario, British Columbia, and California. Downstream, it sells its products through its own chain of 165 Wine Rack stores. It also caters to untrained palates with alcoholic lemonade and the do-it-yourself crowd with wine kits. Recent acquisitions of prestigious U.S. wineries have laid the foundation for building critical new distribution channels for Canadian wines in the U.S. market. Finally, winery tours through new state-of-the-art operations and a 500-seat amphitheatre have been developed and built to lure wine lovers and concertgoers to increase cellar-door sales in the Niagara region of Ontario.

In a similar way, a merger of Canada's two largest sugar refiners, Rogers and Lantic Sugar, opened up a number of strategic options, including greater efficiencies and forward integration into food products that use sugar. According to CEO Pierre Côté, the food industry is fragmented, and this expansion could involve retail products from jellybeans to iced tea. These products might capture higher margins and the streamlined operations could reduce costs. However, such a move can create friction with existing food industry customers, as they compete for the same end consumers.

C-MAC Industries, a Montreal-based manufacturer of electronic systems, had made a series of acquisitions as part of a vertical integration strategy, which in turn helped the company boost its margins. Although competitors such as Celestica typically assembled components that were produced by subcontractors, C-MAC backward-integrated to include both the design and the manufacture of sensors, circuit boards, and other components. Ultimately, this vertical integration proved attractive to Solectron Corp., Celestica's competitor, which acquired CMAC in 2001.

Less Integration (More Outsourcing)

Li & Fung (www.lifung.com), Hong Kong's largest export trading company, has a predominantly North American and European customer base. This multinational firm outsources most of its manufacturing, using what is called "dispersed manufacturing" or "borderless manufacturing." It still performs the higher-value-added processes in Hong Kong but outsources lower-value-added processes to the best possible locations around the

Forward integration from sugar refinery to food products can allow for higher margins and streamlined operations.

world. Thus, it retains processes for designing products, buying and inspecting raw materials, managing factories and developing production schedules, and controlling quality. But it does not manage the workers, and it does not own the factories.

Li & Fung's approach goes beyond outsourcing to suppliers and letting them worry about contracting for raw materials. Any single factory is small and does not have the buying power to demand fast deliveries and good prices. Li & Fung may know, for instance, that a retailer is going to order 100 000 garments, but it does not yet know the style or colours. The firm reserves undyed yarn from its yarn supplier and locks up capacity at supplier mills for weaving.

Because this approach is more complicated, Li & Fung was forced to get smart about logistics and dissecting the value chain. It is an innovator in supply chain management techniques, using a host of information-intensive service processes for product development, sourcing, shipping, handling, and logistics. For its enterprise process of executing and tracking orders, it has its own standardized, fully computerized operating system, and everybody in the company uses it. Essentially, therefore, Li & Fung manages information and the relationships among 350 customers and 7500 suppliers and does so with a lot of phone calls, faxes, and on-site visits. In time, the firm will need a sophisticated information system with an open architecture that can handle work in Hong Kong and New York, as well as in places like Bangladesh, where you cannot always count on a good phone line.

The competitive priorities of customization and fast delivery usually do not match up well, but Li & Fung achieves both by organizing around small, customer-focused units. One unit might be a theme-store division that serves a handful of customers such as Warner Brothers stores and Rainforest Café. Its retailing customers are in consumer-driven, fast-moving markets and face the problem of inventory that is quickly obsolete. If a retailer shortens its buying cycle from three months to five weeks, it gains eight weeks to develop a better sense of where the market is heading. Forecasting accuracy improves, and there is less need for markdowns of obsolete inventory at the end of

the selling season. Such payoffs to Li & Fung's customers make it a valued supplier. During the last decade, the focus was on supplier partnerships to improve cost and quality. In today's faster-paced markets, the focus has shifted to innovation, flexibility, and speed.

Source: D. Olive, "Vintner's Heaven, and It's Made in Canada: Vincor's Bit of Hollywood," *National Post*, July 28, 2001, pp. C1, C4; A. Swift, "Rogers and Lantic Sugar Makers Merge to Become the Dominant Player in Canada," *Canadian Press Newswire*, January 8, 2002; J. Gray, "A Profitable Tech: C-MAC Swims Against the Tide," *Canadian Business*, vol. 74 (2001), no. 15, p. 24; "Fast, Global, and Entrepreneurial: Supply Chain Management, Hong Kong Style: An Interview with Victor Fung," *Harvard Business Review*, September/October 1998, pp. 103–115.

Virtual supply chains are not a panacea for all the problems service providers or manufacturers face in their supply chains. First, virtual supply chains relinquish direct control of the order fulfillment process to other firms. Consequently, it is important to have the appropriate contractual relationship with members of the virtual supply chain. Strategic alliances, partnerships, and long-term contracts provide much more control than do short-term contracts. The more important an activity is for the achievement of the firm's competitive priorities, the greater the degree of control the firm will want.

Second, if information is not clearly and immediately available to the firm and its virtual supply chain partner, customer service problems are likely to result. For example, the firm needs to know whether the partner has the inventory to transact a sale or enough capacity to provide a critical service. The firm is also vulnerable to rationing if supplies are limited or oversubscribed. Finally, the flow of information between the firm and its partners poses the risk that one or more partners could use the information to bypass the firm and directly service its customers.

Overall, firms leveraging virtual supply chains can move in and out of markets, riding the waves of fashion and technology. However, these companies are vulnerable to new competition, because the investment barriers to enter their businesses are low and because they lose business if their suppliers integrate forward or their customers integrate backward. Managers need to balance the need for control of specific processes and close relationships with customers against the need for flexibility in choosing a supply chain design.

SUPPLY CHAIN MANAGEMENT ACROSS THE ORGANIZATION

Supply chains permeate the entire organization. It is hard to envision a process in a firm that is not in some way affected by a supply chain. Supply chains must be managed to coordinate the inputs with the outputs in a firm so as to achieve the appropriate competitive priorities of the firm's enterprise processes. The Internet has offered firms an alternative to traditional methods for managing the supply chain. However, the firm must be committed to re-engineering its information flows throughout the organization. The supply chain processes most affected are the order-placement, order-fulfillment (including the internal supply chain), and purchasing processes. These processes intersect all of the traditional functional areas of the firm.

Supply chain management is essential for manufacturing as well as service firms. In fact, service providers are beginning to realize the potential for organizational benefits through the re-engineering of supply chain processes. For example, hospitals have notoriously held to old-fashioned approaches for purchasing and materials management. Even with the advent of group purchasing organizations and centralized buying groups, the materials management department in a typical hospital collects orders from throughout the hospital for medical supplies and equipment ranging from latex gloves to operating tables from a stack of often-outdated catalogues. Prices must be checked and the orders sent by phone or fax to literally thousands of distributors and suppliers.

Can this process be improved? A number of Canadian hospitals think so. They are beginning to develop and join a number of separate ventures that are creating electronic marketplaces for placing and tracking orders online. The systems will include catalogue hubs, which will contain several hundred thousand medical and surgical supplies. Healthcare Materials Management Services, based in London, Ontario, supplies about 26 hospitals using EDI technology to improve timeliness and reduce costs. Efforts to improve the system have evolved to integrate a business-to-business (B2B) portal developed by a nonprofit exchange, Global Healthcare Exchange (Canada). This exchange is vendor-managed by several health-care industry leaders (including Johnson & Johnson, GE Medical Systems, and Baxter International) and brings together inventories for about 80 suppliers.

Of course, to take full advantage of the marketplace, the hospitals will have to re-engineer their supply chain processes to enable electronic ordering. The potential benefits to the health-care industry of improved supply chain practices are enormous. Canadian hospitals spend about $4 billion annually on supplies, plus an estimated $750 million on procuring and managing those supplies. A study undertaken by the Ontario Hospital Association estimates that hospitals in Ontario could save roughly $120 million by adopting best-practices to reduce transaction costs and the costs of the supplies. Additional benefits of an improved health-care supply chain include fewer medical errors and more time available to medical staff to spend on patient care.

EQUATION SUMMARY

1. Weeks of supply $= \dfrac{\text{Average aggregate inventory value}}{\text{Weekly sales (at cost)}}$

2. Inventory turnover $= \dfrac{\text{Annual sales (at cost)}}{\text{Average aggregate inventory value}}$

CHAPTER HIGHLIGHTS

● A basic purpose of supply chain management is to control inventory by managing the flows of materials that create it. Three aggregate categories of inventories are raw materials, work-in-process, and finished goods. An important aspect of supply chain management is materials management, which coordinates the firm's purchasing, production control, and distribution functions.

● A supply chain is a set of linkages among suppliers of materials and services that spans the transformation of raw materials into products and services and delivers them to a firm's customers. Supply chains can be very complicated, involving thousands of firms at various tiers in the chain. Both service providers and manufacturers have supply chains to manage.

- Firms that develop an integrated supply chain first link purchasing, production, and distribution to create an internal supply chain that is the responsibility of a materials management department. Then they link suppliers and customers, an external supply chain, to the internal supply chain to form an integrated supply chain.

- The Internet has dramatically changed the way companies can manage their supply chains. The order-placement process can be re-engineered to allow for more customer involvement and less employee involvement, to remain open for business 24 hours a day, and to enable the firm to use pricing as a means to control for material or product shortages. Designing the order-fulfillment process involves decisions regarding the postponement of customization until the last possible moment, forward placement of inventories, and final assembly of orders in the distribution channel.

- Electronic purchasing is changing the way that many firms are handling the purchasing function. Electronic data interchange (EDI) has been used since the 1970s. It is now more accessible through the Internet, and it will enable firms to include more suppliers in their supply chains. Catalogue hubs, exchanges, and auctions are among the latest innovations made possible by the Internet.

- Buyers can take two approaches in dealing with their suppliers. The competitive orientation pits supplier against supplier in an effort to get the buyer's business. Price concessions are a major bargaining point, and the amount of clout that a buyer or supplier has often determines the outcome of the negotiations. The cooperative orientation seeks to make long-term commitments to a small number of suppliers, with advantages accruing to both parties. The ultimate form of a cooperative orientation is sole sourcing, whereby only one supplier is responsible for providing an item or service. The orientation utilized should be chosen so as to achieve the firm's competitive priorities.

- It is becoming more and more popular to award the supply of an item or service previously produced by the firm to another firm under a long-term arrangement. It is important for supply chain management because it shifts an activity from direct control in an internal supply chain to less control in an external supply chain.

- Value analysis is used to reduce the cost or improve the performance of products or services either purchased or produced. It is an intensive examination of the materials, process, and information flows involved in the production of an item. Programs such as early supplier involvement and presourcing involve suppliers in the value analysis.

- Supply chain performance is tracked with inventory measures such as aggregate inventory level, weeks of supply, and inventory turnover. Supply chain process measures include production and materials costs, percent defects, percent on-time delivery, and supplier lead times. These measures are related to financial measures such as total assets, return on assets, working capital, contribution margin, total revenue, and cash-to-cash.

- Because supply chains consist of many independent firms linked to other firms, disruptions at the top end can spread through the entire supply chain, causing firms lower in the supply chain to experience significant swings in demand. Such disruptions are caused by the dynamics of both external and internal supply chains.

- Efficient supply chains are designed to coordinate the flows of materials and services so as to minimize inventories and maximize the efficiency of the firms in the supply chain. Responsive supply chains are designed to react quickly to market demand through judicious use of inventories and capacities. A common error that firms make is to use an efficient supply chain design when product variety is high and product demand is unpredictable.

CD-ROM RESOURCES

The Student CD-ROM that accompanies this text contains the following resources, which allow you to further practise and apply the concepts presented in this chapter.

- **Equation Summary**: All the equations for this chapter can be found in one convenient location.

- **Discussion Questions**: Four questions will challenge your understanding of supply chain management and how to work with suppliers.

- **Cases**:

  - *Wolf Motors.* How should John Wolf restructure the purchasing process at his newly acquired automotive dealership?

  - *Brunswick Distribution Inc.* Use the DuPont Analysis spreadsheet to determine the effects of purchasing additional warehouse facilities or investing in an improved distribution system on key business measures.

- **Experiential Exercise**: *Sonic Distributors.* You will experience the challenges of managing a distribution chain in this exciting in-class simulation.

- **OM Explorer Tutor**: OM Explorer contains a tutor program that will help you learn how to calculate inventory measures.

- **OM Explorer Solver**: The Inventory Estimator and Financial Measures in OM Explorer can be used to solve general problems involving the common inventory measures.

- **Extend LT**: *Managing the Supply Chain at Compware Peripherals.* Options to improve the cost and timely delivery of components along Compware's supply chain were being assessed.

SOLVED PROBLEM

A firm's cost of goods sold last year was $3 410 000, and the firm operates 52 weeks per year. It carries seven items in inventory: three raw materials, two work-in-process items, and two finished goods. The following table contains last year's average inventory level for each item, along with its value.

CATEGORY	PART NUMBER	AVERAGE LEVEL	UNIT VALUE
Raw materials	1	15 000	$ 3
	2	2 500	5
	3	3 000	1
Work-in-process	4	5 000	14
	5	4 000	18
Finished goods	6	2 000	48
	7	1 000	62

a. What is the average aggregate inventory value?

b. How many weeks of supply does the firm maintain?

c. What was the inventory turnover last year?

SOLUTION

a.

PART NUMBER	AVERAGE LEVEL		UNIT VALUE		TOTAL VALUE
1	15 000	×	$ 3	=	$ 45 000
2	2 500	×	$ 5	=	$ 12 500
3	3 000	×	$ 1	=	$ 3 000
4	5 000	×	$14	=	$ 70 000
5	4 000	×	$18	=	$ 72 000
6	2 000	×	$48	=	$ 96 000
7	1 000	×	$62	=	$ 62 000
	Average aggregate inventory value			=	$360 500

b. Average weekly sales at cost = $3 410 000/52 weeks = $65 577/week

$$\text{Weeks of supply} = \frac{\text{Average aggregate inventory value}}{\text{Weekly sales (at cost)}} = \frac{\$360\ 500}{\$65\ 577} = 5.5 \text{ weeks}$$

c. $$\text{Inventory turnover} = \frac{\text{Annual sales (at cost)}}{\text{Average aggregate inventory value}} = \frac{\$3\ 410\ 000}{\$360\ 500} = 9.5 \text{ turns}$$

PROBLEMS

1. Buzzrite ended the current year with annual sales (at cost) of $48 million. During the year, the inventory turnover was six turns. For the next year, Buzzrite plans to increase annual sales (at cost) by 25 percent.

    a. What is the increase in the average aggregate inventory value required if Buzzrite maintains the same inventory turnover during the next year?

    b. What change in inventory turnover must Buzzrite achieve if, through better supply chain management, it wants to support next year's sales with no increase in the average aggregate inventory value?

2. Jack Jones, the materials manager at Precision Enterprises, is beginning to look for ways to reduce inventories. A recent accounting statement shows the following inventory investment by category: raw materials $3 129 500; work-in-process $6 237 000; and finished goods $2 686 500. This year's cost of goods sold will be about $32.5 million. Assuming 52 business weeks per year, express total inventory as:

    a. Weeks of supply

    b. Inventory turnover

3. Beagle Company uses a weighted score for the evaluation and selection of its suppliers. Each supplier is rated on a 10-point scale (10 = highest) for four different criteria: price, quality, delivery, and flexibility (to accommodate changes in quantity and timing). Because of the volatility of the business in which Beagle Company operates, flexibility is given twice the weight of each of the other three criteria, which are equally weighted. Table 9.4 shows the scores for three potential suppliers for the four performance criteria. On the basis of the highest weighted score, which supplier should be selected?

TABLE 9.4 *Supplier Performance Scores*

CRITERIA	SUPPLIER A	SUPPLIER B	SUPPLIER C
Price	8	6	6
Quality	9	7	7
Delivery	7	9	6
Flexibility	5	8	9

4. Sterling, Inc., operates 52 weeks per year, and its cost of goods sold last year was $6 500 000. The firm carries eight items in inventory: four raw materials, two work-in-process items, and two finished goods. Table 9.5 shows last year's average inventory levels for these items, along with their unit values.

TABLE 9.5 *Inventory Items*			
CATEGORY	PART NUMBER	AVERAGE INVENTORY UNITS	VALUE PER UNIT
Raw materials	RM-1	20 000	$ 1
	RM-2	5 000	5
	RM-3	3 000	6
	RM-4	1 000	8
Work-in-process	WIP-1	6 000	10
	WIP-2	8 000	12
Finished goods	FG-1	1 000	65
	FG-2	500	88

a. What is the average aggregate inventory value?

b. How many weeks of supply does the firm have?

c. What was the inventory turnover last year?

REFERENCES AND FURTHER READINGS

Bowersox, D. J., and D. J. Closs. *Logistical Management: The Integrated Supply Chain Process.* New York: McGraw-Hill, 1996.

Bridleman, Dan, and Jeff Herrmann. "Supply Chain Management in a Make-to-Order World." *APICS—The Performance Advantage*, March 1997, pp. 32–38.

Dyer, Jeffrey H. "How Chrysler Created an American Keiretsu." *Harvard Business Review*, July/August 1996, pp. 42–56.

Fisher, Marshall L. "What Is the Right Supply Chain for Your Product?" *Harvard Business Review*, March/April 1997, pp. 105–116.

Gurusami, Senthil A. "Ford's Wrenching Decision." *OR/MS Today*, December 1998, pp. 36–39.

Harwick, Tom. "Optimal Decision Making for the Supply Chain." *APICS—The Performance Advantage*, January 1997, pp. 42–44.

Kaplan, Steven, and Mohanbir Sawhney. "E-Hubs: The New B2B Marketplaces." *Harvard Business Review*, May/June 2000, pp. 97–103.

Latamore, G. Benton. "Supply Chain Optimization at Internet Speed." *APICS—The Performance Advantage*, May 2000, pp. 37–40.

Lee, Hau L., and Corey Billington. "Managing Supply Chain Inventory: Pitfalls and Opportunities." *Sloan Management Review*, Spring 1992, pp. 65–73.

Maloni, M., and W. C. Benton. "Power Influences in the Supply Chain." *Journal of Business Logistics*, vol. 21 (2000), pp. 49–73.

Tully, Shawn. "The B2B Tool That Really Is Changing the World." *Fortune*, March 20, 2000, pp. 132–145.

Vachon, Stephan, Robert D. Klassen, and P. Fraser Johnson. "Customers as Green Suppliers: Managing the Complexity of the Reverse Supply Chain." In J. Sarkis (ed.), *Green Manufacturing and Operations: From Design to Delivery and Back*, Sheffield, UK: Greenleaf Publishing, 2001, pp. 136–149.

van Hoek, Remko I. "From Reversed Logistics to Green Supply Chains," *Supply Chain Management*, vol. 4 (1999), no. 3, pp. 129–134.

10 Lean Systems

Across the Organization

Lean systems are important to:

- **accounting,** which must often adjust its billing and cost accounting practices to take advantage of lean systems.
- **engineering,** which must design products that use more common parts so that fewer setups are required and focused factories and group technology can be used.
- **finance,** which must secure the working capital needed for a lean system.
- **human resources,** which must recruit, train, and evaluate the employees needed to successfully operate a lean system.
- **management information systems,** which must integrate the lean system with other information systems in the firm.
- **marketing,** which relies on lean systems to deliver high-quality products or services on time, at reasonable prices.
- **operations,** which is responsible for using the lean system in the production of goods or services.

Learning Goals

After reading this chapter, you will be able to:

1. identify the characteristics of lean systems that enable the realization of the lean system philosophy.
2. describe how lean systems can facilitate the continuous improvement of operations.
3. understand kanban systems for creating a production schedule in a lean system.
4. use value stream mapping to identify and reduce waste.
5. discuss the strategic advantages of lean systems and the implementation issues associated with the application of these systems.

For some companies, the drive for leaner operations is prompted by a customer-related crisis. For others, it is the accumulation of many small changes in the marketplace over time that significantly erodes competitiveness. Still others see it as a path to growth and expansion.

For CGL Manufacturing, located in Guelph, Ontario, it was a combination of these factors that persuaded management to reshape operations into a leaner system. This manufacturer of machined and fabricated parts for off-road equipment, with revenues of $25 million, had established a strong reputation for quality and service over the previous two decades. Growth in the 1990s had been solid but was slowing. Also, global competition had recently pushed key customers, including Volvo Construction Equipment, Komatsu, and GE Locomotive, to demand significant cost reductions, in some cases reaching as high as 20 percent.

CGL Manufacturing's lean operations have cut costs, smoothed product flows, and improved customer responsiveness.

Lean manufacturing was to form the foundation for better integration and improved competitiveness. Yet David Deskur, the general manager, didn't see this as a short-term project that would quickly fix problems. Instead, a three-year plan was developed to educate management and the workforce, diagnose areas of high impact, build new skills and capabilities, and implement critical process changes. Ultimately, lean systems were to extend upstream from CGL's operations using a lean supplier certification program.

At the outset, team building for all 140 managers and employees was essential. Consultants initially helped with education, simulation exercises, and skill development. However, much of the responsibility soon shifted to Deskur, who became the "lean champion."

Next, managers and employees undertook value stream mapping, whereby the current state of a process was compared to an idealized future state, with the objective of eliminating non-value-added steps and waste. Initial efforts focused on processes that directly linked customers and managers, such as requests for quotes and order entry. Doing so reinforced a strong customer orientation, and opened the eyes of senior people in other functional areas such as marketing to the potential impact of lean systems.

Given the historical high quality levels at CGL, early emphasis on the factory floor targeted faster customer responsiveness. Production processes for higher-volume parts were reorganized into five cells (low-volume orders continued with a job shop layout). These cells relied heavily on visual controls, preventive maintenance, and pull production using kanbans to achieve dramatic reductions in lead times, dropping from ten days down to two days or less. Other lean tools, including continuous improvement, "5S Fridays" (sort, set in order, shine, standardize, sustain), setup time reduction, and small lot sizes improved efficiency and safety. By 2003, inventory levels across the firm had fallen by 40 percent, freeing up space to create a pre-production prototype area.

Deskur observed, "People are really key to making lean systems work." In addition to training, employee suggestions were encouraged and rewarded. The response has been almost overwhelming—three years later, about three-quarters of employees have proposed improvements, many of which have been adopted.

In retrospect, regular communication throughout CGL and measuring performance improvement have proven critical to both learning and motivating further effort. And both customers and others, such as the Association for Manufacturing Excellence and Industry Canada, have recognized the dramatic improvements at CGL. As Deskur concludes, "Lean thinking is the means by which we have become world-class."

Source: Company interview and Web site. Copyright Robert D. Klassen.

lean systems Operations systems that maximize the value added by each of a firm's activities by paring unnecessary operations and delays.

just-in-time (JIT) philosophy The belief that waste can be eliminated by cutting unnecessary inventory and removing non-value-added activities in operations.

JIT systems The organization of resources, information flows, and decision rules that enable an organization to realize the benefits of a JIT philosophy.

CGL Manufacturing is an excellent example of a company that has adopted an approach for designing value chains known as lean systems. **Lean systems** are operations systems that maximize the value added by each of a company's activities by paring unnecessary resources and delays. This concept brings together much of what we have already covered in this textbook, and integrates operations strategy, technology, capacity, quality, inventory, layout, supply chains, and resource planning to create efficient processes.

Lean systems can be leveraged by both service and manufacturing firms. For example, a service business might take an order from a customer, complete a process and then collect revenue. This firm purchases items or other services, receives and pays for them, and hires and pays employees. Each of these activities is very similar to those in manufacturing firms, and each often has huge amounts of waste. Also, while customer involvement may vary considerably between different service processes, lean systems always emphasize reducing non-value-added time, whether by employees or customers.

One of the most popular systems to incorporate the generic elements of lean systems is the just-in-time (JIT) system. The **just-in-time (JIT) philosophy** is simple but powerful—eliminate waste by cutting excess capacity or inventory and removing non-value-added activities. The goals are to produce services and products as needed and to continuously improve the value-added benefits of operations. A **JIT system** organizes the resources, information flows, and decision rules that enable a firm to minimize wasted resources and improve customer responsiveness.

We begin this chapter by identifying the characteristics of lean systems for service and manufacturing processes. We then discuss how lean systems can be used to continuously improve operations. We also address some of the implementation issues that companies face.

CHARACTERISTICS OF LEAN SYSTEMS

As overviewed above, lean systems focus on reducing inefficiency and unproductive time in processes to continuously improve the quality and value of the products or services produced. Managing variability is a critical aspect, as depicted in the process management triangle (see Figure 4.1 on page 92). Several characteristics of lean systems reduce process variability: consistent quality at the source, small lot sizes, uniform workstation loads, standardized components and work methods, close supplier ties, automation, Five S (5S) practices, and preventive maintenance. The reduction of variability makes the process more predictable for managers, reduces investment in equipment and inventories, and offers customers more dependable deliveries and services. In addition, several characteristics help accommodate variability from either external demands or internal operations: the pull method of materials flow, close supplier ties, and a flexible workforce.

PULL METHOD OF WORK FLOW

Lean systems utilize the pull method of work flow. In contrast, another popular method is the push method. To differentiate between these two systems, let's first consider the production system used by McDonald's Restaurants in Canada (and the rest of the world) in the 1990s. There were four basic operations for producing a hamburger: cooking, preparation, assembly, and packaging. For the cooking operation, a batch of hamburger patties was fried. For the preparation operation, the same-sized batch of buns was toasted on a tray and then dressed with condiments such as mustard, ketchup, pickles, and cheese. The assembly operation placed the cooked patties into prepared buns. Finally, the packaging operation took the tray, wrapped the burgers in paper, and restocked the inventory bins in front of customers. Efforts were made to minimize inventories, because any hamburgers left unsold after ten minutes had to be discarded.

The flow of materials was from cooking and preparation to assembly to packaging to the customer. Historically, this flow has been managed using the **push method**, in which the production of the item begins in anticipation of customer needs. With this method, management schedules the receipt of all raw materials (e.g., meat patties, buns, and condiments) and authorizes the start of production, all before customers arrive to purchase hamburgers. The cooking starts production of a batch of hamburgers (often a dozen patties based on the size of the tray) and, when they are completed, pushes them along to assembly and then packaging, where they might have to wait until someone at packaging is ready for them. The packaged hamburgers then wait in a warming bin until a customer purchases one.

The other way to manage the flow between cooking, preparation, assembly, packaging, and the customer is to use the **pull method**, in which customer demand activates production or assembly of the final product. Since 2000, McDonald's in Canada and the United States has implemented a system that more closely matches the pull method called "Made for You." Now, as customers purchase hamburgers, the preparation operation is informed of each specific order, and begins toasting and dressing the bun. After completion, the assembly operation removes a cooked patty from a warming oven, places it in the bun, and packages the final product for the customer.

push method A method in which the production of the item begins in advance of customer needs.

pull method A method in which customer demand activates production of the item.

Fast-food workers using the pull system to serve their customers at a McDonald's store in Taipei, Taiwan. Using the older push method, the cooking, assembly, and packaging operations are behind the holding bin, which are available to the workers serving customers at the counter.

As cooked patties are taken from the warming oven, the assembly operation checks the inventory level of patties. If the level falls below a target range, which varies by time of day, the assembly person calls or signals for the cooking operation to grill more patties. After grilling, the patties are placed in the warming oven. In general, the pull method is better for the production of hamburgers: operations can be visually coordinated to reduce inventories based on customer demand; hot and cold materials are kept separate until just before purchase; and individual customer preferences are quickly accommodated. The production of hamburgers is a highly repetitive process, setup times and process times are low, and the flow of materials is well-defined.

The choice between the push and pull methods is often situational. Service and manufacturing firms with highly repetitive processes, well-defined work flows, and standardized outputs (either involving customers or physical goods) often use the pull method because it allows better control. After significant process changes, CGL Manufacturing used the pull method to dramatically reduce inventory and improve responsiveness. However, there are circumstances where a push system is better. As more of the following conditions are met, the attractiveness of a push system increases:

- Processes that involve long lead times
- Reasonably accurate forecasts of demand
- Variety of products created on common processes with long setup times
- Customers who will not wait long for the product

In many processes, the push and pull methods should be thoughtfully combined, for example, in the form of an assemble-to-order process. The push method is used to produce standardized components in high volumes, and the pull method to fulfill the customer's request for a particular combination of goods or services. So in the case of McDonald's, the push method is used to order food supplies in advance, and cook some ingredients in anticipation of orders, such as grilled patties. However, the customer order, including one or more grilled products, is assembled only after it is received, based on a pull method. Thus, pull systems must be applied widely, not universally.

QUALITY AT THE SOURCE

Consistently meeting the customer's expectations is an important characteristic of lean systems. One way to achieve this goal is by adhering to a practice called *quality at the source*, which is an organization-wide effort to improve the quality of a firm's products by having employees act as their own quality inspectors. For workers, the goal is to pass along only high-quality units to the next process. For example, a soldering operation at the Texas Instruments antenna department had a defect rate that varied from zero to 50 percent on a daily basis, averaging about 20 percent. To compensate, production planners increased the lot sizes, which only increased inventory levels and did nothing to reduce the number of defective items. The company's engineers then discovered through experimentation that gas temperature was a critical variable in producing defect-free items. They subsequently devised statistical control charts for the firm's equipment operators to use to monitor the temperature and adjust it themselves. Process yields immediately improved and stabilized at 95 percent, and Texas Instruments was eventually able to implement a lean system.

poka-yoke Mistake-proofing methods aimed at designing fail-safe systems that minimize human and equipment error.

One approach for implementing quality at the source is to use **poka-yoke**, or mistake-proofing. This method aims to design fail-safe systems that attack and minimize human error. Consider, for instance, a company that makes modular products. The company could use the poka-yoke method by making different parts of the modular product in such a way that allows them to be assembled in only one way—the correct way. Similarly, a company's shipping boxes could be designed to be packed only in a particular way that minimizes damage and eliminates chances of missed components and other mistakes.

Another approach for implementing quality at the source is a practice the Japanese call *jidoka*, or making mistakes or problems evident. Workers and machines must have the means to quickly and accurately detect the occurrence of any abnormal condition. In response, employees are then authorized to signal for help and resolve the problem, termed *andon*, which may require stopping the production line. Of course, stopping a production line can cost a company thousands of dollars each minute production is halted. However, this additional attention pushes managers, quality experts, engineers, and workers to jointly identify opportunities to prevent defects, and to recover quickly when they occasionally occur. Management must realize the enormous responsibility this method puts on employees, must prepare them properly with training, and must implement systems that build high quality.

SMALL LOT SIZES

lot A quantity of items that are processed together.

Rather than build up a cushion of inventory, queue of orders, or waiting line of customers, lean systems use lot or batch sizes that are as small as possible. A **lot** is a quantity of items that are processed together. Small lot sizes reduce process variability and overall inventory levels by four mechanisms. First, small lot sizes reduce *cycle* inventory (see Chapter 6, "Inventory Management"). The average cycle inventory equals one-half the lot size: As the lot size gets smaller, so does cycle inventory. Reducing cycle inventory reduces the time and space involved in manufacturing and holding inventory. Figure 10.1 shows the effect on cycle inventory of reducing the lot size from 100 to 50 for a uniform demand of 10 units per hour: cycle inventory is cut in half.

FIGURE 10.1

Implications of Small and Large Lot Sizes for Cycle Inventory

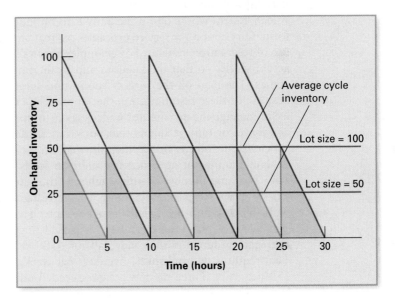

Second, small lot sizes help cut lead times. A decline in lead time in turn reduces WIP inventory because the total processing time at each workstation is greater for large lots than for small lots. Also, a large lot often has to wait longer to be processed at the next workstation while that workstation finishes working on another large lot. In addition, if any defective items are discovered, large lots cause longer delays, because the entire lot must be inspected to find all the items that need rework.

Finally, small lots help achieve a uniform operating system workload. Large lots consume large chunks of processing time on workstations and, therefore, complicate scheduling. Small lots can be juggled more effectively, enabling schedulers to utilize capacities more efficiently. In addition, small lots allow workstations to accommodate mixed-model production (more than one item) by reducing waiting-line times for production. We return to this point when we discuss uniform workstation loads.

setup The group of activites needed to change or readjust a process between different lots.

Although small lot sizes are beneficial to operations, they have the disadvantage of increased **setup** frequency. In operations where the setup times are normally low, as in the McDonald's example, small lots are feasible. However, in fabrication operations with sizable setup times, increasing the frequency of setups may result in wasting employee and equipment time.

The key issue is that managers cannot view setup times as fixed; instead improvements must be developed to reduce setup times to achieve the benefits of small-lot production. Achieving low setup times often requires close cooperation among engineering, management, and labour. For example, changing dies on large presses to form automobile parts from sheet metal can take three to four hours. At one of Honda's plants that produced the Accord, teams worked to identify and implement improvements to reduce the changeover time for these massive dies. As a result, a complete change of dies for a giant 2400-ton press now takes less than eight minutes. The goal of **single-digit setup** means having setup times shorter than 10 minutes. Some techniques to reduce setup times include using conveyors for die storage, moving large dies with cranes, simplifying dies, enacting machine controls, using microcomputers to automatically feed and position work, and preparing for changeovers while the current job is being processed.

single-digit setup The goal of having a setup time shorter than 10 minutes.

UNIFORM WORKSTATION LOADS

A lean system works best if the daily load on individual workstations is relatively uniform. One option for service processes to create more uniform workstation loads is the use of reservation systems. For example, hospitals schedule surgeries in advance of the actual service so that the facilities and facilitating goods can be ready when the time comes. The load on the surgery rooms and surgeons can be evened out to make the best use of these resources. Another approach is to use differential pricing of the service to manage the demand for it. This is one of the reasons that airlines promote weekend travel or red-eye flights that begin late in the day and end in the early morning. Efficiencies can be realized when the load on the firm's resources can be managed.

For manufacturing processes, uniform loads can be achieved by assembling the same type and number of units each day, thus creating a uniform daily demand at all workstations. Capacity planning, which recognizes capacity constraints at critical workstations, and line balancing are used to develop the monthly master production schedule. For example, at Toyota, discussed in greater detail later in the chapter, the aggregate production plan may call for 4500 vehicles per week for the next month. That requires two full shifts, five days per week, producing 900 vehicles each day, or 450 per shift. Three models are produced: Camry (C), Avalon (A), and Sienna (S). Suppose that Toyota needs 200 Camrys, 150 Avalons, and 100 Siennas per shift to satisfy market demand. To produce 450 units in one shift of 480 minutes, the line must roll out a vehicle every $480/450 = 1.067$ minutes.

Three ways of devising a master production schedule for the vehicles are of interest here. First, with big-lot production, all daily requirements of a model are produced in one batch before another model is started. The sequence of 200 C's, 150 A's, and 100 S's would be repeated once per shift. Not only would these big lots increase the average cycle-inventory level, but they also would cause lumpy requirements on all the workstations feeding the assembly line, as well as outside suppliers.

mixed-model assembly A type of assembly that produces a mix of models in smaller lots.

The second option uses **mixed-model assembly**, producing a mix of models in smaller lots. Note that the production requirements are in the ratio of 4 C's to 3 A's to 2 S's (i.e., divide by 50). Thus, the Toyota planner could develop a production cycle consisting of 9 units: 4 C's, 3 A's, and 2 S's. The cycle would repeat in $9(1.067) = 9.60$ minutes, for a total of 50 times per shift (480 minutes/9.60 minutes = 50). A lot could now consist of 4 C's, followed by a lot of 3 A's, and then 2 C's. Ideally, taken to its extreme, mixed-model assembly uses a sequence of C–S–C–A–C–A–C–S–A, repeated 50 times per shift. As demand shifts between the three models of cars, the sequence of models is adjusted accordingly, either adding or dropping a few vehicles from the sequence.

This mixed-model option is feasible only if the setup times are very short. The sequence generates a steady rate of component requirements for the various models and allows the use of small lot sizes at the feeder workstations. Consequently, the capacity requirements at those stations are greatly smoothed. These requirements can be compared to actual capacities during the planning phase, and modifications to the production cycle, production requirements, or capacities can be made as necessary.

STANDARDIZED COMPONENTS AND WORK METHODS

In highly repetitive service operations, great efficiencies can be gained by analyzing work methods and documenting the improvements for all employees to use. For example, courier companies, such as Purolator, must monitor their work methods and revise them as necessary to improve service. In manufacturing, the standardization of components, called *part commonality* or *modularity*, increases repeatability. For example, a firm producing 10 products from 1000 different components might redesign its products so that they would draw from a common pool of only 100 different components or modules. Because the requirements per component increase, so does repeatability; that is, each worker performs a standardized task or work method more often every day. Productivity tends to increase because, with increased repetition, workers learn to do the task more efficiently. Standardization of components and work methods aids in achieving the high-productivity, low-inventory objectives of lean systems.

CLOSE SUPPLIER TIES

Because lean systems operate with low levels of inventory or excess capacity, close relationships with suppliers are necessary. Supplies must be shipped frequently, have short lead times, arrive on schedule, and be of high quality. A contract might require a supplier to deliver goods to a factory as often as several times per day. Purchasing managers focus on three areas to tighten ties with suppliers: reducing the number of suppliers, using local suppliers, and improving supplier relations.

Typically, one of the first actions undertaken when a lean system is implemented is to pare the number of suppliers. Xerox, for example, reduced the number of its suppliers from 5000 to just 300. This approach puts a lot of pressure on these suppliers to deliver high-quality components on time. To compensate, contracts with these suppliers are extended to give them fixed advance-order information. In addition, they include their suppliers in the early phases of product design to avoid problems after production has begun. They also work with their suppliers' vendors, trying to achieve timely inventory flows throughout the entire supply chain.

Manufacturers using lean systems generally utilize local suppliers. For instance, when GM located its Saturn complex in Tennessee, many suppliers clustered nearby. Harley-Davidson reduced the number of its suppliers and gave preference to those close to its plants—for example, three-fourths of the suppliers for the Milwaukee engine plant are located within a 300-kilometre radius. Geographic proximity means that the company can reduce the need for safety stocks. Companies that have no suppliers close by must rely on a finely tuned supplier delivery system. For example, New United Motor Manufacturing, Incorporated (NUMMI), the joint venture between GM and Toyota in California, has suppliers in Indiana, Ohio, and Michigan. Through a carefully coordinated system involving trains and piggyback truck trailers, suppliers deliver enough parts for exactly one day's production each day.

Users of lean systems also find that a cooperative orientation with suppliers is essential. Close cooperation between companies and their suppliers can be a win-win situation for everyone. Better communication of component requirements, for example, enables more efficient inventory planning and delivery scheduling by suppliers, thereby improving supplier profit margins. Customers can then negotiate lower component prices. Suppliers also should be included in the design of new products so that inefficient component designs can be avoided before production begins. Close supplier relations cannot be established and maintained if companies view their suppliers as adversaries whenever contracts are negotiated. Rather, they should consider suppliers to be partners in a venture wherein both parties have an interest in maintaining a long-term, profitable relationship.

FLEXIBLE WORKFORCE

Employees in flexible workforces can be trained to perform more than one job. A benefit of flexibility is the ability to shift workers among workstations to help relieve bottlenecks as they arise without the need for long waiting lines of customers or inventory buffers of parts—an important aspect of the uniform flow of lean systems. Also, workers can step in and do the job for those who are on vacation or who are out sick. Although assigning workers to tasks they do not usually perform can temporarily reduce their efficiency, some job rotation tends to relieve boredom, encourages new ideas, and refreshes workers.

The more customized the service or product is, the greater the firm's need for a multi-skilled workforce. For example, a household appliance repair service requires broadly trained personnel who can identify a wide variety of component problems when the customer brings the defective unit into the shop, or a service technician must repair an appliance in the field. Alternatively, back-office operations, such as the mail-processing operations at a large post office, have employees with more narrowly defined jobs because of the repetitive nature of the tasks they must perform. These employees do not have to acquire as many alternative skills. In situations such as at the Texas Instruments antenna department mentioned earlier, shifting workers to other jobs may require them to undergo extensive, costly training.

AUTOMATION

Automation plays a big role in lean systems and is often a key to low-cost operations and high quality in repetitive assembly tasks. Automation also can play a big role when developing and providing lean services, while simultaneously expanding customer service. For example, banks offer Web banking and ATMs that provide various financial services on demand, 24 hours a day, 7 days per week. Automation should be planned carefully, however. Many managers believe that if some automation is good, more is better, which is not always the case. When GM greatly expanded automation in one plant, Buick City, it installed 250 robots, some with vision systems for mounting windshields. Unfortunately, the robots skipped black cars because they could not "see" them. New software eventually solved the problem. Nonetheless, 30 robots were replaced with humans because GM found that humans do some jobs better.

FIVE S

five S (5S) A methodology consisting of five work-place practices—sort, set in order, shine, standardize, and sustain—that are conducive to visual controls and lean production.

As we saw in the CGL Manufacturing case at the beginning of the chapter, **five S (5S)** practices focus on organizing, cleaning, developing, and sustaining a productive work environment. It represents five related terms, each beginning with an *S*, that describe workplace practices conducive to visual controls and lean production. These five practices of sorting, straightening, shining, standardizing, and sustaining are done systematically to achieve lean systems (see Table 10.1). They are not something that can be done as a stand-alone program. As such, they represent an essential foundation of lean systems.

	5S Term	Definition
TABLE 10.1 *5S Defined*	Sort	Separate needed from unneeded items (including tools, parts, materials, and paperwork), and discard the unneeded.
	Set in order	Neatly arrange what is left, with a place for everything and everything in its place. Organize the work area so that it is easy to find what is needed.
	Shine	Clean and wash the work area and make it shine.
	Standardize	Establish schedules and methods of performing the cleaning and sorting. Formalize the cleanliness that results from regularly doing the first three S practices so that perpetual cleanliness and a state of readiness is maintained.
	Sustain	Create discipline to perform the first four S practices, whereby everyone understands, obeys, and practises the rules when in the plant. Implement mechanisms to sustain the gains by involving people and recognizing them via a performance measurement system.

Note: The Japanese words for these 5S terms are *seiri*, *seiton*, *seiso*, *seiketsu*, and *shitsuke*, respectively.

It is commonly accepted that the 5S practices, when done together, form an important cornerstone of waste reduction and removal of unneeded tasks, activities, and materials. Implementation of 5S practices can lead to lowered costs, improved on-time delivery and productivity, higher product quality, and a safer working environment.

PREVENTIVE MAINTENANCE

Because lean systems emphasize finely tuned work flows and little slack capacity or buffer inventory between workstations, unplanned machine downtime—one form of process variability—can be very disruptive. Preventive maintenance is designed to reduce the frequency and duration of machine downtime. After performing routine maintenance activities, the technician can test other parts that might need to be replaced. Replacement during regularly scheduled maintenance periods is easier and quicker than dealing with machine failures during production. Maintenance is done on a schedule that balances the cost of the preventive maintenance program against the risks and costs of machine failure. Routine preventive maintenance is particularly important for capital-intensive service or manufacturing processes, such as airlines, telecommunications, and financial services.

A related approach is to make workers responsible for routinely maintaining their own equipment and develop employee pride in keeping their machines in top condition. This practice, however, typically is limited to general housekeeping chores, minor lubrication, and adjustments. Maintenance of high-tech machines needs trained specialists. Doing even simple maintenance tasks goes a long way toward improving machine performance.

EOQ AND LEAN SYSTEMS

In Chapter 6, "Inventory Management," the economic order quantity (EOQ) was presented as a way of balancing holding and setup (or ordering) costs. On the surface it may appear that the EOQ is diametrically opposed to the principles of lean systems, because EOQ gives an optimal order size that might require very large levels of inventory. In contrast, lean systems rely on the philosophy of very low inventory levels.

However, the same process improvements that lead to a lean system create the basis for a very small EOQ with a very small order or lot size; for example, monthly, daily, or hourly demand rates are known with reasonable certainty in lean systems, and the rate of demand is relatively uniform. In addition, lean systems strive to reduce variability, either through improved quality or reliable delivery lead times from suppliers. Finally, the very short setup times, frequent information exchange with suppliers, and frequent deliveries translate to small setup costs and little need to hold inventory. Consequently, the EOQ as a lot-sizing tool is quite compatible with the principles of lean systems.

CONTINUOUS IMPROVEMENT

By spotlighting areas that need improvement, lean systems lead to continuous improvement in quality and productivity. The Japanese term for this approach to process improvement is *kaizen*. The key to kaizen is the understanding that excess capacity or inventory hides underlying problems with the processes that produce a service or product. Lean systems provide the mechanism for management to reveal the problems by systematically lowering capacities or inventories until the problems are exposed.

The principles behind continuous improvement with lean systems are illustrated in Figure 10.2. The water surface represents service system capacity, such as staff levels in services. In manufacturing, the water surface may also represent product and component inventory levels. The rocks represent problems encountered in the provision of services or products. When the water surface is high enough, the boat passes over the rocks because the high level of capacity or inventory covers up problems. As capacity or inventory shrinks, rocks are exposed. Ultimately, the boat will hit a rock if the water surface falls far enough. Through lean systems, workers, managers, engineers, and analysts apply methods for continuous improvement to demolish the exposed rock (see Chapter 2, "Process Management," and Chapter 5, "Quality"). The coordination required for the pull system of material flows in lean systems identifies problems in time for corrective action to be taken.

Maintaining low inventories, periodically stressing the system to identify problems, and focusing on the elements of the lean system lie at the heart of continuous improvement. For example, a Kawasaki plant periodically cuts its safety stocks almost to zero.

FIGURE 10.2

Continuous Improvement with Lean Systems

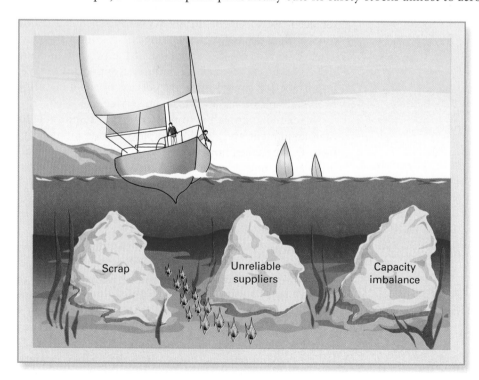

The problems at the plant are exposed, recorded, and later assigned to employees as improvement projects. After improvements are made, inventories are permanently cut to the new level. Many firms use this trial-and-error process to develop more efficient manufacturing operations.

Service processes, such as scheduling, billing, order taking, accounting, and financial planning, can be dramatically improved with lean systems, too. Here managers can place stress on the system by setting new short-term performance targets or temporarily reducing the number of employees working until problems become apparent. Of course, a means for quick recovery is needed, after which problems can be diagnosed, and ways for overcoming them explored. Other kaizen tactics can be used as well. Eliminating the problem of poor quality, scrap materials, and customer complaints might require improving the firm's work processes, providing employees with additional training, or finding higher-quality suppliers. Eliminating capacity imbalances might involve improving the flexibility of the firm's workforce.

THE KANBAN SYSTEM

kanban A word meaning "card" or "visible record" in Japanese; refers to cards used to control the flow of production through a factory.

One of the most publicized aspects of lean systems, and the Toyota production system in particular, is the kanban system developed by Toyota. **Kanban**, meaning "card" or "visible record" in Japanese, refers to cards used to control the flow of production through a factory. In the most basic kanban system, a card is attached to each container of items that have been produced. The container holds a given percent of the daily requirements for an item. When the user of the parts empties a container, the card is removed from the container and put on a receiving post. The empty container is taken to the storage area. The card signals the need to produce another container of the part. When a container has been refilled, the card is put on the container, which is then returned to a storage area. The cycle begins again when the user of the parts retrieves the container with the card attached.

Figure 10.3 shows how a single-card kanban system works when a fabrication cell feeds two assembly lines. As an assembly line needs more parts, the kanban card for

FIGURE 10.3

Single-Card Kanban System

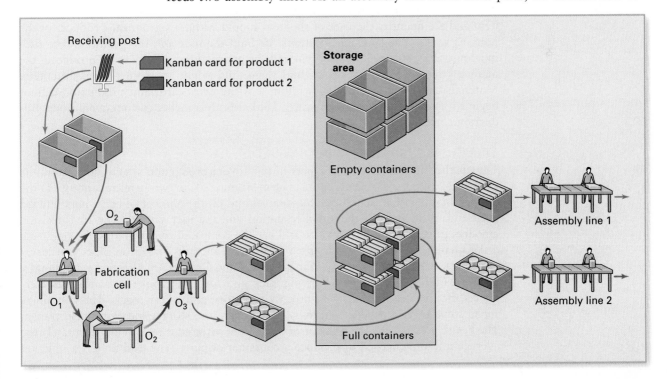

those parts is taken to the receiving post and a full container of parts is removed from the storage area. The receiving post accumulates cards for both assembly lines and sequences the production of replenishment parts. In this example, the fabrication cell will produce product 2 before it produces product 1. The cell consists of three different operations, but operation 2 has two workstations. Once production has been initiated in the cell, the product begins at operation 1 but could be routed to either of the workstations performing operation 2, depending on the workload at the time. Finally, the product is processed in operation 3 before being taken to the storage area.

GENERAL OPERATING RULES

The operating rules for the single-card system are simple and are designed to facilitate the flow of materials while maintaining control of inventory levels:

1. Each container must have a card.

2. The assembly line always withdraws materials from the fabrication cell. The fabrication cell never pushes parts to the assembly line because, sooner or later, parts will be supplied that are not yet needed for production.

3. Containers of parts must never be removed from a storage area without a kanban first being posted on the receiving post.

4. The containers should always contain the same number of good parts. The use of nonstandard containers or irregularly filled containers disrupts the production flow of the assembly line.

5. Only nondefective parts should be passed along to the assembly line to make the best use of materials and workers' time.

6. Total production should not exceed the total amount authorized on the kanbans in the system.

Toyota uses a two-card system, based on a withdrawal card and a production-order card, to control withdrawal quantities more closely. The withdrawal card specifies the item and the quantity the user of the item should withdraw from the producer of the item, as well as the stocking locations for both the user and the producer. The production-order card specifies the item and the production quantity to be produced, the materials required and where to find them, and where to store the finished item. Materials cannot be withdrawn without a withdrawal card, and production cannot begin without a production-order card. The cards are attached to containers when production commences.

DETERMINING THE NUMBER OF CONTAINERS

The number of authorized containers in the Toyota production system determines the amount of authorized inventory. Management must make two determinations: (1) the number of units to be held by each container and (2) the number of containers flowing back and forth between the supplier station and the user station. The first decision amounts to determining the lot size and may be compared to calculating the economic order quantity (EOQ) or specifying a fixed order quantity based on other considerations (see Chapter 6, "Inventory Management," and Chapter 13, "Resource Planning").

The number of containers flowing back and forth between two stations directly affects the quantities of work-in-process inventory and safety stock. The containers spend some time in production, in a line waiting, in a storage location, or in transit. The key to determining the number of containers required is to estimate accurately the average lead time needed to produce a container of parts. The lead time is a function of the processing time per container at the supplier station, the waiting time during the production process, and the time required for materials handling. The number of containers needed to support the user station equals the average demand during the lead time plus some safety stock to account for unexpected circumstances, divided by the number of units in one container. Therefore, the number of containers is:

$$k = \frac{\text{Average demand during lead time } plus \text{ safety stock}}{\text{Number of units per container}}$$

$$= \frac{d(\overline{w} + \overline{p})(1 + \alpha)}{c}$$

where:

k = Number of containers for a part

d = Expected daily demand for the part, in units

$\overline{w}$ = Average waiting time during the production process plus materials handling time per container, in fractions of a day

$\overline{p}$ = Average processing time per container, in fractions of a day

c = Quantity in a standard container of the part

α = Policy variable that reflects the efficiency of the workstations producing and using the part (Toyota uses a value of no more than 10 percent)

The number of containers must, of course, be an integer. Rounding k up provides more inventory than desired, whereas rounding k down provides less.

The kanban system allows management to fine-tune the flow of materials in the system in a straightforward way. For example, removing cards from the system reduces the number of authorized containers of the part, thus reducing the inventory of the part.

The container quantity, c, and the efficiency factor, α, are variables that management can use to control inventory. Adjusting c changes the lot sizes, and adjusting α changes the amount of safety stock. The kanban system actually is a special form of the base-stock system (see Chapter 6, "Inventory Management"). In this case, the stocking level is $(\overline{w} + \overline{p})(1 + \alpha)$, and the order quantity is fixed at c units. Each time a container of parts is removed from the base stock, authorization is given to replace it. See the Solved Problem on page 372 for a detailed example of how to apply the equation for the number of containers in a kanban system.

OTHER KANBAN SIGNALS

Cards are not the only way to signal the need for more production of a part. Other, less formal methods are possible, including container and containerless systems.

CONTAINER SYSTEM. Sometimes the container itself can be used as a signal device: an empty container signals the need to fill it. Unisys took this approach for low-value items. The amount of inventory of the part is adjusted by adding or removing containers. This system works well when the container is specially designed for a part and no other parts could accidentally be put in it. Such is the case when the container is actually a pallet or fixture used to position the part during precision processing.

CONTAINERLESS SYSTEM. Systems that require no containers have been devised. In assembly-line operations, operators having their own workbench areas put completed units on painted squares, one unit per square. Each painted square represents a container, and the number of painted squares on each operator's bench is calculated to balance the line flow.

When the subsequent user removes a unit from one of the producer's squares, the empty square signals the need to produce another unit.

McDonald's uses a containerless system. An order from a customer flows back to the preparation and assembly operations, and finally to the cooking operation. As a result, the customer, and then the number of patties in the heating oven, signal the need for production.

VALUE STREAM MAPPING

value stream mapping (VSM) A qualitative lean tool for eliminating waste that involves a current state drawing, a future state drawing, and an implementation plan.

Value stream mapping (VSM) is a widely used qualitative lean tool aimed at eliminating waste (or *muda*), as described in the opening vignette about CGL Manufacturing. Waste in many processes can be as high as 60 percent. Value stream mapping is helpful because it creates a visual "map" of every process involved in the flow of materials and information in a product's value chain. These maps consist of a current state drawing, a future state drawing, and an implementation plan. Value stream mapping spans the entire value chain, from the firm's receipt of raw materials to the delivery of the finished good to the customer. Thus, it tends to be broader in scope, displaying far more information than a typical process map or a flowchart used with Six Sigma process improvement efforts. Creating such a big picture representation helps managers identify the source of wasteful non-value-added activities.

Value stream mapping follows the steps shown in Figure 10.4. The first step is to focus on one product family for which mapping can be done. It is then followed by drawing a current state map of the existing process: Analysts start from the customer and work upstream. The process map is often drawn manually, and actual process times, not "idealized" times, are recorded based on firsthand observation. Information for drawing the material and information flows is gathered from the front lines, including the data related to each process: cycle time (C/T), setup or changeover time (C/O), uptime (on-demand available machine time expressed as a percentage), production batch sizes, number of people required to operate the process, number of product variations, pack size (for moving the product to the next stage), working time (minus breaks), and scrap rate.

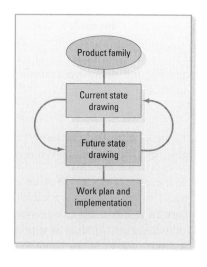

FIGURE 10.4

Value Stream Mapping Steps

Source: Mike Rother and John Shook, *Learning to See* (Brookline, MA: The Lean Enterprise Institute, 2003), p. 9.

Value stream mapping uses a standard set of icons for material flow, information flow, and general information (to denote workers, safety stock buffers, and so on). Even though the complete glossary is extensive, a representative set of these icons is shown in Figure 10.5. These icons provide a common language for describing in detail how a facility should operate to create a better flow.

We use the VSM icons to illustrate in Figure 10.6 what a current state map could look like for a hypothetical bearing manufacturing company, which receives raw material sheets from Kline Steel Company every Monday for a product family of retainers (casings in which ball bearings are held), and then ships its finished product on a daily basis to a second-tier automotive manufacturing customer named GNK Enterprises. The product family of the bearing manufacturing company under consideration consists of two types of retainers—large (L) and small (S)—that are packaged for shipping in returnable trays with 60 retainers in each tray. The manufacturing process consists of a pressing operation, a piercing and forming cell, and a finish grind operation, after which the two types of retainers are staged for shipping. The process characteristics and inventory buffers in

FIGURE 10.5

Selected Set of Value Stream Mapping Icons

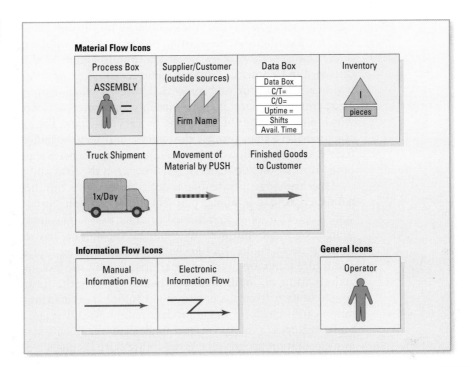

FIGURE 10.5

Selected Set of Value Stream Mapping Icons

FIGURE 10.6

A Representative Current State Map for a Family of Retainers at a Bearings Manufacturing Company

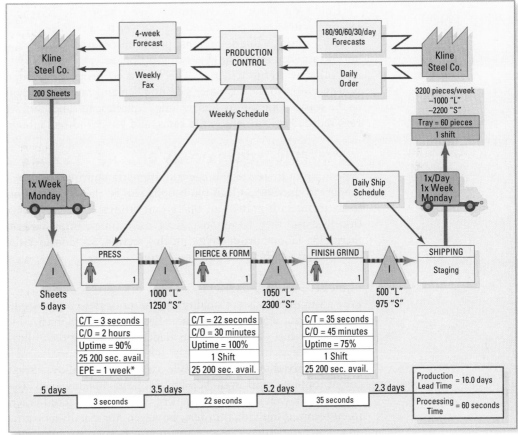

front of each process are shown in the current state map of Figure 10.6. One worker occupies each station. Although the total processing time for each retainer is only 1 minute, it takes 16 days for the cumulative production lead time. Clearly, opportunities exist for reconfiguring the existing processes and eliminating inventories.

The process flows shown at the bottom of Figure 10.6 are similar to the flowcharts discussed in Chapter 2, "Process Management," except that more detailed information is presented here for each process. However, what really sets the value stream maps apart from flowcharts is the inclusion of information flows at the top of Figure 10.6, which plan and coordinate all the process activities. The value stream maps are more comprehensive than process flowcharts, and meld together planning and control systems with detailed flowcharts to create a comprehensive supply chain view that includes both information and material flows between the firm and its suppliers and customers.

Once the current state map is done, the analysts can then use principles of lean systems such as load levelling, pull scheduling, kanban cards, and such to create a future state map with more streamlined product flows. The future state drawing highlights sources of waste and how to eliminate them. The arrows between the current and future state in Figure 10.4 go both ways, indicating that development of the current and future states are overlapping efforts. Finally, the last step is aimed at preparing and actively using an implementation plan to achieve the future state. It may take only a couple of days from the creation of a future state map to the point where implementation can begin for a single product family. At this stage, the future state map essentially becomes a blueprint for implementing a lean system, and is fine-tuned as implementation progresses. As the future state becomes reality, a new future state map is drawn, thus denoting continuous improvement at the value stream level.

Unlike the theory of constraints (see Chapter 4, "Capacity"), which accepts the existing system bottlenecks and then strives to maximize the throughput given that set of constraint(s), value stream mapping endeavours to understand through current state and future state maps how existing processes can be altered to eliminate bottlenecks and other wasteful activities. The goal is to bring the production rate of the entire process closer to the customer's desired demand rate. The benefits of applying this tool to the waste-removal process include reduced lead times and work-in-process inventories, reduced rework and scrap rates, and lower indirect labour costs.

STRATEGIC IMPLICATIONS OF LEAN SYSTEMS

When corporate strategy hinges on dramatic improvements in inventory turnover and labour productivity, a lean philosophy can be the solution. For example, lean systems form an integral part of an operations strategy that emphasizes time-based competition, because they focus on cutting cycle times, improving inventory turnover, and increasing labour productivity. In this section, we consider the competitive priorities and operational benefits of lean systems.

COMPETITIVE PRIORITIES

Low cost and consistent quality are the priorities emphasized most often in lean systems. Superior features and volume flexibility are emphasized less often. The ability to provide product or service variety depends on the degree of flexibility designed into the production system. Such is the case with firms using an assemble-to-order strategy. For example, mixed-model automobile assembly lines allow variety in output in terms of colour, options, and even body style. Lean systems such as the Toyota Production System work well in this environment (see the Managerial Practice feature). Production to customized individual orders, however, are usually not attempted with a lean system. The erratic demand and last-minute rush jobs of customized orders in make-to-order or customized service environments do not link well with a system designed to produce at a constant daily rate utilizing low inventory or capacity buffers.

MANAGERIAL PRACTICE
Toyota's Lean Manufacturing Leads the Way

One company often viewed as exemplary of excellence in automobile manufacturing is Toyota (www.toyota.com). Worldwide in its presence, it has a total investment of US$12 billion in ten manufacturing plants that employ 30 500 associates in North America alone. Toyota was at the forefront of firms developing lean systems for manufacturing, and today the Toyota Production System (TPS) is one of the most admired lean manufacturing systems in existence. Replicating the system, however, is fraught with difficulties. What makes the system tick, and why could Toyota employ the system in so many different plants when others have difficulty?

Most outsiders see the Toyota production system as a set of tools and procedures that are readily visible during a plant tour. While they are important for the success of the TPS, they are not the keys to the heart of the system. What most people overlook is that Toyota has built a learning organization over the course of 50 years. Lean systems require constant improvements to increase efficiency and reduce waste. Toyota has created a system that stimulates employees to experiment with their environment by seeking better ways whenever things go wrong. Toyota sets up all operations as experiments and teaches employees at all levels how to use the scientific method of problem solving.

There are four underlying principles of the Toyota production system. First, all work must be completely specified as to content, sequence, timing, and outcome. Detail is important, otherwise there is no foundation for improvements. Second, every customer-supplier connection must be direct, unambiguously specifying the people involved, the form and quantity of the goods or services to be provided, the way the requests are made by each customer, and the expected time in which the requests will be met. Customer-supplier connections can be internal—employee-to-employee—or external—company-to-company.

Third, the pathway for every product and service must be simple and direct. That is, goods and services do not flow to the next available person or machine, but to a specific person or machine. With this principle, employees can determine, for example, that there is a capacity problem at a particular workstation and then analyze ways to resolve it.

The first three principles define the system in detail by specifying how employees do work, interact with each other, and design work flows. These specifications actually are "hypotheses" about the way the system should work. For example, if something goes wrong at a workstation enough

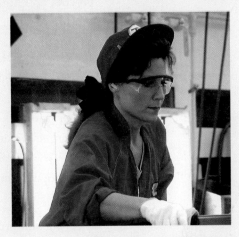

A team member is preparing a vehicle for paint application, which involves careful examination for imperfections before the first coat of paint is applied. Note the clothing and gloves that the employee wears, designed to keep the vehicles from being accidentally marred in the painting process.

times, the hypothesis about the methods the employee uses to do work is rejected. The fourth principle, then, is that any improvement to the system must be made in accordance with the scientific method, under the guidance of a teacher, at the lowest possible organizational level. The scientific method involves clearly stating a verifiable hypothesis of the form, "If we make the following specific changes, we expect to achieve this specific outcome." The hypothesis must then be tested under a variety of conditions. Working with a teacher, who is often the employees' supervisor, is a key to becoming a learning organization. Employees learn the scientific method and eventually become teachers of others. Finally, making improvements at the lowest level of the organization means that the employees who are actually doing the work are actively involved in making improvements.

These four principles are deceptively simple; they are difficult to replicate. Nonetheless, those organizations that have successfully implemented them have enjoyed the benefits of a lean system that adapts to change.

Source: Steven Spear and H. Kent Bowen, "Decoding the DNA of the Toyota Production System," *Harvard Business Review*, September/October 1999, pp. 97–106.

OPERATIONAL BENEFITS

Lean systems are linked with many operational benefits. As a company implements and refines leaner systems, processes have:

- lower space requirements.
- lower inventory investment in purchased parts, raw materials, work-in-process, and finished goods.
- shorter lead times.
- greater productivity of direct-labour employees, indirect-support employees, and clerical staff.
- greater equipment utilization.
- less paperwork, often requiring only simple planning systems.
- clearer priorities for scheduling.
- greater participation by the workforce.
- greater product or service quality.

A primary operational benefit is the simplicity of the system. For example, product mix or volume changes can be accomplished by adjusting the number of kanbans in the system. The priority of each order is reflected in the sequence of the kanbans on the post. Production orders for parts that are running low are placed before those for parts that have more supply.

Ideally, one objective is to produce a single product or part when ordered—economically. This requires a very responsive process, with short order lead times, rapid processing times, and almost no setup times. In addition, constant attention must be given to removing non-value-added activities in processes. The result is less need for storage space, inventory investment, or capacity. Smaller lot sizes and smoothed flows of materials also help to increase employee productivity, and improve equipment utilization, which reduces cost.

Lean systems also involve a considerable amount of employee participation through small-group interaction sessions, which have resulted in improvements in many aspects of operations, not the least of which is product or service quality. Overall, the advantages of lean systems have caused many managers to re-evaluate their own systems and consider adapting operations to the lean philosophy.

IMPLEMENTATION ISSUES

The benefits of lean systems seem to be outstanding, yet problems can arise even after a lean system has long been in place. In this section, we address some of the issues managers should be aware of when implementing a lean system.

ORGANIZATIONAL CONSIDERATIONS

Implementing a lean system requires management to consider issues of worker stress, cooperation and trust among workers and management, and reward systems and labour classifications.

HUMAN COSTS. Lean systems can be coupled with statistical process control (SPC) to reduce variations in outputs. However, this combination requires training and a high degree of regimentation, which can create stress in the workforce. For example, workers must meet specified cycle times, and, with SPC, they must follow prescribed problem-solving methods to improve quality. Such systems might make workers feel pushed, causing productivity losses or quality reductions. In addition, workers might feel that they have lost some autonomy because of the close linkages in materials flows between stations with little or no safety stocks. Managers can mitigate some of these effects by emphasizing materials flows instead of worker pace, and judiciously allowing some slack in the system through small safety stock inventories or slack capacity. Managers also can promote the use of work teams and allow them to determine their task assignments or rotations within the team's domain of responsibility.

COOPERATION AND TRUST. Workers and first-line supervisors must take on responsibilities formerly assigned to middle managers and support staff. Activities such as scheduling, expediting, and improving productivity become part of the duties of lower-level personnel. Consequently, organizational relationships must be reoriented to build close cooperation and mutual trust between the workforce and management. Such cooperation and trust may be difficult to achieve, particularly in the light of the typical adversarial positions taken by labour and management in the past.

REWARD SYSTEMS AND LABOUR CLASSIFICATIONS. In some instances, the reward system must be revamped as lean systems are developed and implemented. At General Motors, for example, a plan to reduce stock at one plant ran into trouble because the production superintendent refused to cut back production of unneeded parts. Why? Because his salary was based on his plant's production volume.

The realignment of reward systems is not the only hurdle. Labour contracts traditionally have reduced management's flexibility in reassigning workers as the need arises. A large manufacturer in Canada, such as an automobile plant, might have several unions and dozens of labour classifications. To gain more flexibility, management in some cases has obtained union concessions by granting other types of benefits. In other cases, management has relocated plants to take advantage of nonunion or foreign labour. In contrast, at Toyota, management may deal with only one employee association or union, and there are a much smaller number of labour classifications in a typical plant.

PROCESS CONSIDERATIONS

Firms using lean systems typically have some dominant work flows. During implementation, managers often have to change the layouts of their existing processes. Certain workstations might have to be moved closer together, and cells of machines devoted to particular families of components may have to be established. Moving toward focused cells, as done by CGL Manufacturing, is often a very effective layout. However, rearranging a plant can be costly. For example, whereas many plants now receive raw materials and purchased parts by rail, to facilitate smaller, more frequent shipments, truck deliveries would be preferable. Loading docks might have to be reconstructed or expanded and certain operations relocated to accommodate the change in transportation mode and quantities of arriving materials.

INVENTORY AND SCHEDULING

Firms need to have stable production schedules, short setups, and frequent, reliable supplies of materials and components to achieve the full potential of the lean systems concept.

PRODUCTION SCHEDULE STABILITY. Daily production schedules in high-volume, make-to-stock environments must be stable for extended periods. At Toyota, the master production schedule is stated in fractions of days over a three-month period and is revised only once a month. The first month of the schedule is frozen to avoid disruptive changes in the daily production schedule for each workstation; that is, the workstations execute the same work schedule each day of the month. At the beginning of each month, kanbans are reissued for the new daily production rate. Stable schedules are needed so that production lines can be balanced and new assignments found for employees who otherwise would be underutilized. Lean systems used in high-volume, make-to-stock environments cannot respond quickly to scheduling changes, because little slack inventory or capacity is available to absorb these changes.

SETUPS. As noted earlier, adopting small lot sizes can yield big reductions in inventory. However, because small lots require a large number of setups, companies must significantly reduce setup times. Some companies have not been able to achieve short setup times and, therefore, have been compelled to use large-lot production, negating some of the advantages of just-in-time. Also, lean systems are vulnerable to lengthy changeovers to new products because the low levels of finished goods inventory will be insufficient to cover demand while the system is down. If changeover times cannot be reduced, large finished goods inventories of the old product must be accumulated to compensate.

PURCHASING AND LOGISTICS. If frequent, small shipments of purchased items cannot be arranged with suppliers, large inventory savings for these items cannot be realized. The shipments of raw materials and components must be reliable because of the low inventory levels in lean systems. A plant can be shut down because of a lack of materials. In Canada, such arrangements can prove to be challenging, because of the geographic dispersion of suppliers. Improvements in the reliability of road and rail transportation have generally contributed to significant inventory reductions (Chapter 9, "Supply Chain Management").

LEAN SYSTEMS ACROSS THE ORGANIZATION

The philosophy of lean systems has application throughout the organization. A theme of this textbook is that organizations create products or services with processes, which cut across functional boundaries to create value for customers—who can be internal or external. Lean systems focus on efficient value creation, which applies to any process in the organization.

To take advantage of lean systems, managers must clearly define the value of their products or services, as perceived by their customers. Every product or service category must be carefully scrutinized for excessive complexity or unnecessary features and options. The goal should be to deliver products or services that precisely match the customer's needs without waste. Then the company must identify the sequence of activities and the processes involved that are *essential* to the creation of the product or service by drawing flow charts and developing process charts. Activities that are value-added (those tasks that transform the product or service in some measurable way) should be clearly differentiated from those that are non-value-added, where wasted effort could be eliminated without any impact on the customer.

Once the activities are identified and the flows are charted, the barriers to the flow of value must be eliminated. For example, barriers can be found in operations in the form of large batches and excessive inventory; in the product development process in the form of excessive documentation, approvals, and meetings; or in the order-entry process in the form of incomplete product or service information or poorly designed Web pages. These barriers are examples of the rocks in Figure 10.2 (on page 360). Once these rocks are removed, the firm is free to allow its customers to "pull" value, which is the real market demand that becomes the trigger for all activities to follow. Moving toward leaner processes and systems is critical to the competitiveness of every organization.

EQUATION SUMMARY

1. Number of containers:

$$k = \frac{\text{Average demand during lead time} \; + \; \text{Safety stock}}{\text{Number of units per container}}$$

$$= \frac{d(\overline{w} + \overline{p})(1 + \alpha)}{c}$$

CHAPTER HIGHLIGHTS

- Lean systems focus on the efficient delivery of products and services. Just-in-time (JIT) systems, a popular type of lean system, are designed to produce or deliver just the right products or services in just the right quantities just in time to serve subsequent processes or customers.

- Some of the key elements of a lean system are a pull method to manage work flow, quality at the source, small lot sizes, uniform workstation loads, standardized components and work methods, close supplier ties, flexible workforce, automation, five S practices, preventive maintenance, and continuous improvement.

- A single-card lean system uses a kanban to control production flow. The authorized inventory of a part is a function of the number of authorized cards for that item. The number of cards depends on average demand during manufacturing lead time, the container size, and a policy variable to adjust for unexpected occurrences. Many other methods may be used to signal the need for material replenishment and production.

- For operations competing on the basis of low cost and consistent quality, lean system advantages include reductions in inventory, space requirements, and paperwork, and increases in productivity, employee participation, and quality. Lean systems require fundamental changes in the way *all* of the firm's business functions are performed. Increasing cooperation and trust between management and labour, basing rewards on team rather than individual performance, and replacing adversarial supplier relationships with partnerships are some of the basic cultural changes involved in lean system implementation.

CD-ROM RESOURCES

The Student CD-ROM that accompanies this text contains the following resources, which allow you to further practise and apply the concepts presented in this chapter.

- **Equation Summary**: All the equations for this chapter can be found in one convenient location.

- **Discussion Questions**: Two questions will challenge your understanding of the philosophy of lean systems and the human considerations in implementing these systems.

- **Case**: *Copper Kettle Catering*. What would you recommend the owners of Copper Kettle Catering do to take advantage of lean concepts in operating their business?

- **OM Explorer Tutor**: OM Explorer contains a tutor program that will help you learn how to apply the equation for determining the number of containers in a kanban system.

- **OM Explorer Solver**: OM Explorer has a program that can be used to solve general problems involving the determination of the correct number of containers for a kanban system.

- **Extend LT**: *Lean Systems at Heritage Furniture*. Management is exploring reducing the batch size and changing the number of kanbans between operations.

SOLVED PROBLEM

A company using a kanban system has an inefficient machine group. For example, the daily demand for part L105A is 3000 units. The average waiting time for a container of parts is 0.8 days. The processing time for a container of L105A is 0.2 days, and a container holds 270 units. Currently, there are 20 containers for this item.

a. What is the value of the policy variable, α?

b. What is the total planned inventory (work in process and finished goods) for item L105A?

c. Suppose that the policy variable α were 0. How many containers would be needed now? What is the effect of the policy variable in this example?

SOLUTION

a. We use the equation for the number of containers and then solve for α:

$$k = \frac{d(\overline{w} + \overline{p})(1 + \alpha)}{c}$$

$$= \frac{3000(0.8 + 0.2)(1 + \alpha)}{270} = 20$$

and:

$$(1 + \alpha) = \frac{20(270)}{3000(0.8 + 0.2)} = 1.8$$

$$\alpha = 1.8 - 1 = 0.8$$

b. With 20 containers in the system and each container holding 270 units, the total planned inventory is $20(270) = 5400$ units.

c. If $\alpha = 0$:

$$k = \frac{3000(0.8 + 0.2)(1 + 0)}{270} = 11.11 \quad \text{or} \quad 12 \text{ containers}$$

The policy variable adjusts the number of containers. In this case, the difference is quite dramatic because $\overline{w} + \overline{p}$ is fairly large and the number of units per container is small relative to daily demand.

PROBLEMS

1. Wilson Motorcycle Company produces three models: the Tiger, a sure-footed dirt bike; the LX2000, a nimble racer; and the Golden, a large touring model. This month's production schedule calls for the production of 54 Goldens, 42 LX2000s, and 30 Tigers per seven-hour shift.

a. What average cycle time is required for the assembly line to achieve the production quota in seven hours?

b. If mixed-model scheduling is used, how many of each model will be produced before the production cycle is repeated?

c. Determine a satisfactory production sequence for the ultimate in small-lot production: one unit.

d. The design of a new model, the Cheetah, includes features from the Tiger, LX2000, and Golden models. The resulting blended design has an indecisive character and is expected to attract some sales from the other models. Determine a mixed-model schedule resulting in 52 Goldens, 39 LX2000s, 26 Tigers, and 13 Cheetahs per seven-hour shift. Although the total number of motorcycles produced per day will increase only slightly, what problem might be anticipated in implementing this change from the production schedule indicated in part (b)?

2. A fabrication cell at Spradley's Sprockets uses the pull method to supply gears to an assembly line. George Jitson

is in charge of the assembly line, which requires 500 gears per day. Containers typically wait 0.20 days in the fabrication cell. Each container holds 20 gears, and one container requires 1.8 days in machine time. Setup times are negligible. If the policy variable for unforeseen contingencies is set at 5 percent, how many containers should Jitson authorize for the gear replenishment system?

3. An assembly line requires two components: gadjits (G) and widjits (W). G is produced by centre 1 and W by centre 2. Each unit of the end item, called a jit-together (J), requires 3 G's and 2 W's, as shown in Figure 10.7. The daily production quota on the assembly line is 800 J's.

    The container for G holds 80 units. The policy variable for centre 1 is set at 0.09. The average waiting time for a container of G is 0.09 days, and 0.06 days are needed to produce a container. The container for W holds 50 units, and the policy variable for centre 2 is 0.08. The average waiting time per container of W is 0.14 days, and the time required to process a container is 0.20 days.

    a. How many containers are needed for gadjits (G)?

    b. How many containers are needed for widjits (W)?

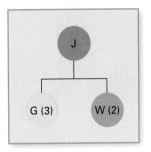

FIGURE 10.7

4. The production schedule at Mazda calls for 1200 Mazdas to be produced during each of 22 production days in January and 900 Mazdas to be produced during each of 20 production days in February. Mazda uses a kanban system to communicate with a nearby supplier of tires. Mazda purchases four tires per vehicle. The safety stock policy variable, α, is 0.15. The container (a delivery truck) holds 200 tires. The average waiting time plus materials handling time is 0.16 days per container. Assembly lines are rebalanced at the beginning of each month. The average processing time per container in January is 0.10 days. February processing time will average 0.125 days per container. How many containers should be authorized for January? How many for February?

REFERENCES AND FURTHER READINGS

Beckett, W. K., and K. Dang. "Synchronous Manufacturing, New Methods, New Mind Set." *Journal of Business Strategy*, vol. 12 (1992), pp. 53–56.

Billesbach, Thomas J. "A Study of the Implementation of Just-in-Time in the United States." *Production and Inventory Management Journal*, Third Quarter 1991, pp. 1–4.

Golhar, D. Y., and C. L. Stam. "The Just-in-Time Philosophy: A Literature Review." *International Journal of Production Research*, vol. 29 (1991), pp. 657–676.

Hall, Robert W. "The Americanization of the Toyota System." *Target*, vol. 15, no. 1 (First Quarter 1999), pp. 52–54.

Hall, R. W. *Driving the Productivity Machine*. Falls Church, VA: The American Production and Inventory Control Society, 1981.

Karmarkar, U. "Getting Control of Just-in-Time." *Harvard Business Review*, September/October 1989, pp. 123–131.

Klein, J. A. "The Human Costs of Manufacturing Reform." *Harvard Business Review*, March/April 1989, pp. 60–66.

Mascitelli, Ron. "Lean Thinking: It's About Efficient Value Creation." *Target*, vol. 16, no. 2 (Second Quarter 2000), pp. 22–26.

Millstein, Mitchell. "How to Make Your MRP System Flow." *APICS— The Performance Advantage*, July 2000, pp. 47–49.

Syberg, Keith. "Best Practices (BP) Program: Honda of America Manufacturing." *Target*, vol. 15, no. 2 (Second Quarter 1999), pp. 46–48.

Across the Organization

Management of technology is important to:

- **accounting,** which can use new technologies to perform its work better and provide important information on new product and process proposals.
- **engineering,** which designs products and processes that use new technologies.
- **finance,** which seeks better ways to perform its work, provides input to top management on the financial advisability of new products and process changes, and looks for ways to finance technological change.
- **human resources,** which needs to anticipate and manage the impact that technological change has on the workforce.
- **management information systems,** which help to identify and implement new information technologies.
- **marketing,** which seeks better technologies for new product and services, along with processes to meet customer needs.
- **operations,** which needs new technologies to produce products and services more effectively and provide better value to customers.

Learning Goals

After reading this chapter, you will be able to:

1. define the meaning of technology and describe how best to manage it.
2. identify and discuss how the three primary areas of technology affect the competitiveness of operations.
3. list the steps in the new service/product development process.
4. demonstrate the importance of technology to the firm's supply chain and within each functional area, and discuss real examples of its impact in manufacturing and service industries.
5. identify the factors that managers must consider when making technological choices.

Technology needs to be actively managed and leveraged, like any other aspect of processes. Nestlé, the world's largest food producer, is overhauling everything from buying raw materials to producing, marketing, and selling products such as KitKat chocolate bars and Nescafé instant coffee. The 134-year-old company employs 230 000 people and runs over 500 factories in 83 countries, producing an astounding 8000-plus different products, ranging from Friskies cat food to Perrier bottled water.

Electronic links between retail partners and Nestlé give accurate and timely buying information that have allowed inventory cuts of 15 percent.

Technology in general, including the Internet, promises to make this lumbering behemoth more agile and cut costs. Yet you will not see a Nestlé.com selling direct, as most of the changes will be invisible to diners guzzling Perrier or kids munching Nestlé Crunch bars. Instead, Nestlé wants to tie together its disparate operations, partner with suppliers and customers to cut waste, and move its food products more quickly from farm to factory to the family dinner table. "This isn't about squeezing suppliers as much as about increasing our own internal productivity," says Peter Brabeck, Nestlé's chief executive officer.

The first order of business has been to make it easier for retailers to stay in touch with Nestlé. Store owners in some countries are now able to order chocolates and other products online. The benefit: the new system cuts out expensive manual data entry and slashes processing costs for each order from US$2.35 to 21 cents. Overall, similar initiatives under way worldwide could trim as much as US$600 million from worldwide logistics and administrative costs.

The Internet also helps cut inventories. In the past, executing marketing promotions required management to guess at demand. Now, electronic links with supermarkets and other retail partners give Nestlé accurate and timely information on buying patterns, which in turn allows quick adjustment of production rates.

Similar benefits result from sharing information online internally too. For example, a buyer in Switzerland was having trouble getting kosher meat. He posted a message on an internal Web message board, and a colleague in the United States found him just the right supplier—in Uruguay. In addition, when the Swiss buyer saw that a buyer in Italy needed to get some mustard, he put her in contact with a Nestlé factory in Basel that could deliver.

Technology also allows Nestlé to take greater advantage of its size. Until recently, Nestlé had 12 buyers throughout Europe, dealing with 14 suppliers of lactose, a key ingredient in infant formula and chocolate bars. Although the 12 buyers remain—their knowledge of local demand is essential—the company now uses only four suppliers on the Continent. Lactose costs have come down by as much as 20 percent.

Several lessons can be learned from this experience. Nestlé's managers see this investment as just one competitive lever among many and, as such, a way to improve processes. They choose technology that helps to achieve process performance goals, and helps to respond to their customers better. Rather than seeking "technology for technology's sake," the key is to find appropriate, user-friendly technology that enables people to perform their jobs more effectively. Taken together, Nestlé's ongoing development and application of technology offers many opportunities that collectively build competitive advantage.

Source: William Echikson, "Nestlé: An Elephant Dances," *Business Week*, December 11, 2000, pp. EB 44–48. Reprinted from the December 11, 2000, issue of *Business Week* by special permission, copyright © 2000 by The McGraw-Hill Companies, Inc.

Technological change is a major factor in gaining competitive advantage. It can create whole new industries and dramatically alter the landscape in existing industries. The development and innovative use of technology can give a firm a distinctive competence that is difficult to match, or transform an existing organization, such as Nestlé. Competitive advantage comes not just from creating new technology but also from applying and integrating existing technologies. Advances in technology spawn new products and services and reshape processes. Thus, technology takes many elements, beginning with ideas, knowledge, and experience, and then uses them to create new and better ways of doing things.

In this chapter, we explore how technology can create a competitive advantage. We begin with a general definition of technology and then apply it specifically to products, processes, and information. Two areas receive particular attention: service and product development, and enterprise resource planning. Finally, we examine the management of technology strategy, offering guidelines on choosing new technologies.

THE MEANING AND ROLE OF TECHNOLOGY

technology The know-how, physical equipment and components, and procedures used to produce products and services.

We define **technology** as the know-how, physical equipment and components, and procedures used to produce products and services. Know-how is the knowledge and judgment of how, when, and why to employ equipment and procedures. Craftsmanship and experience are embodied in this knowledge and often cannot be written into manuals or routines. Equipment consists of such tools as computers, scanners, ATMs, or robots. Procedures are the rules and techniques for operating equipment and performing the work. All three components work together, as illustrated by air-travel technology. Knowledge is reflected in scheduling, routing, and pricing decisions. Equipment includes aircraft, as well as ground facilities, to name just two. The procedures are rules and manuals on aircraft maintenance and how to operate the airplane under many different conditions. Technologies do not occur in a vacuum but are embedded in support networks. A **support network** comprises the physical, informational, and organizational relationships that make a technology complete and allow it to function as intended. Thus, the support network for air-travel technology includes the infrastructure of airports, baggage-handling facilities, travel agencies, air traffic control operations, and the communication systems connecting them.

support network A network made up of the physical, informational, and organizational relationships that make a technology complete and allow it to function as intended.

THREE PRIMARY AREAS OF TECHNOLOGY

Within an organization, technologies reflect what people are working on and what they are using to do that work. The most widespread view of technology is that of *product technology*, which a firm's engineering and research groups develop when creating new products and services. Another view is that of *process technology*, which a firm's employees use to do their work. A third area, which is becoming increasingly important, is *information technology*, which a firm's employees, suppliers, and customers use to acquire, process, and communicate information. The way in which a specific technology is classified depends on its application. A product technology to one firm may be part of the process technology of another.

Operations managers are interested in all three aspects of technology. Technological advances often provide opportunities for new service and product offerings. These offerings can be leveraged to capture new markets, expand the customer benefit bundle, or simply maintain competitiveness. Process technology is important because it can improve methods currently used in operations. Information technology is important because it can improve decision making and responsiveness to customer needs.

NEW SERVICE AND PRODUCT DEVELOPMENT

New services or products are essential to the startup of many entrepreneurial firms and the long-term survival of established firms. Times change, people change, technologies change, and so services or products change. "New" refers to novel, new-to-the-world products and services, as well as significant changes to existing ones. For the customer, technology can increase service customization, expand product variety, add new features, dramatically reduce cost, or improve consistency of the benefit bundle. For the firm, this means better profitability for existing offerings, new customers, stronger loyalty from existing customers, and opening new markets. As we discuss the nature and importance of the new service and product development process, we will frequently refer to a firm's services or products as its "offerings."

The new service and product development process is often a core activity in a firm. Engineers, researchers and other specialists develop new knowledge and ways of doing things, merge them with and extend conventional capabilities, and translate them into specific offerings that customers value. Lasik eye surgery, CAT scans, handheld computers, cell phones, global positioning systems, and digital cameras are examples of innovative offerings that have opened new markets. Developing new technologies requires close cooperation with marketing to find out what customers really want, and with operations to determine how goods or services can be produced effectively.

Firms must also define the pace of their technology development and adoption relative to competitors. A firm can emphasize being a *market leader* (also known as first mover, who is first to introduce an innovative service or product), a *fast-follower* (who allows a leader to incur innovation costs and then introduces a very similar offering after the market has started to develop), or a *laggard* (who waits to see whether the service or product idea catches on in the market). This overall pace of development determines when the firm will initiate the new service or product development process.

DEVELOPMENT PROCESS

Whether a firm is a market leader or a laggard, the new service/product development process begins with design and ends with the launch of the new offering. Figure 11.1

FIGURE 11.1

New Service and Product Development Process

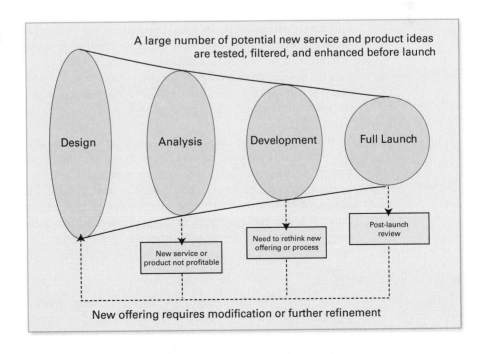

A large number of potential new service and product ideas are tested, filtered, and enhanced before launch

Design — Analysis — Development — Full Launch

New service or product not profitable

Need to rethink new offering or process

Post-launch review

New offering requires modification or further refinement

shows the four stages of the development process. For the market leader, many ideas might be put forward, relative to the few new offerings that are finally launched into the market. A quote attributed to Linus Pauling, winner of two Nobel Prizes, sums up product and service development in these firms: "The best way to have a good idea is to have lots of ideas ... then throw away the bad ones!" At the other end of the spectrum, the laggard may also be very successful by learning from the trials, miscues, and mistakes that frequently come with being the first to market with a new product or service.

DESIGN. The *design* stage is critical because it links the creation of new services or products to the corporate strategy of the firm. Ideas for new offerings are generated and screened for feasibility and market worthiness. Initially, the proposed designs emphasize the basic concept. Particular attention must be paid to customer needs that are largely unmet or novel attributes that might offer significant differentiation relative to those of competitors. As the basic concept starts to take specific shape, for services, these ideas specify which technologies are being considered, what role they play, how the customer connects with the service provider, how the service is delivered, and the benefits and value for the customer. A number of service offerings are considered and their feasibility is checked.

For manufactured products, new ideas include important decisions about a product's architecture, which can range from very *modular* to highly *integrated*. With a modular architecture, the product is an assembly of discrete, easily identifiable components. Several varieties of products can be made quickly using the same standardized components. This approach supports competitive priorities of product variety and delivery speed; however, it may cause lower product performance because of the pressure to use existing, off-the-shelf components in new products. In addition, such designs may be easier for competitors to copy. In contrast, with an integrated product architecture, the product's functions are performed by only a few components that are specifically designed for it. Integrated product structures often lead to better product performance and are more difficult to imitate; however, the design lead time is high and the ability to produce a variety of products might be limited.

The most promising new ideas are selected for more detailed attention, which includes diagramming processes, providing specifications for performance dimensions, and investigating costs. In this stage, firms need to engage a variety of individuals, including engineering, operations, and marketing personnel, to ensure that any new offering can be reasonably delivered to the market. For products, this consultation process is referred to as *design for manufacturing*. Even though the detailed specifications of the product and process have not yet been developed, this interaction of designers and manufacturing engineers can avoid costly mistakes.

ANALYSIS. The second stage, *analysis*, involves a critical review of the new offering and how it will be produced to make sure that it fits the corporate strategy, is compatible with regulatory standards, presents an acceptable market risk, and satisfies the needs of the intended customers. The resource requirements for the new offering must be examined from the perspective of the core capabilities of the firm and the need to acquire additional resources or form strategic partnerships with other firms. If the analysis reveals that the new offering has good market potential and that the firm has the capability (or can acquire it), the authorization is given to proceed to the next stage.

DEVELOPMENT. The third stage, *development*, brings more specificity to the new offering. The required competitive priorities are used as inputs to the design (or redesign) of the processes that will be involved in delivering the new offering. The processes are analyzed; each activity is designed to meet its required competitive priorities and to add value to the service or product. Pilot testing in limited markets might occur in this stage as product or service mock-ups are developed. Such testing allows for further refinement of the design. Once the new offering is specified and the processes have been designed, the market program can be developed. Finally, personnel are trained and some test runs can be conducted to iron out the kinks in production. At this stage in the development process, it is possible that some unforeseen problems may arise, forcing a reconsideration of the service or product or the processes required to produce it.

To avoid costly mismatches between the design of a new offering and the capability of the processes required to produce it, many manufacturing firms engage in a concept called **concurrent engineering**, which brings product engineers, process engineers, marketers, buyers, information specialists, quality specialists, and suppliers together to design a product and the processes that will meet customer expectations. For example, Ford Motor Company gives full responsibility for each new product to a program manager who forms a product team representing every relevant part of the organization. Each department can raise concerns or anticipate problems in time to alter the product or the manufacturing processes. Changes are much simpler and less costly at this stage. However, if major problems with the product design or the capability to deliver the product are uncovered, the product proposal may have to be scrapped or completely rethought.

FULL LAUNCH. The final stage, *full launch*, involves the coordination of many processes. Promotions for the new offering must be initiated, sales personnel briefed, distribution processes activated, and old services or products that the new offering is to replace withdrawn. A particular strain is placed on the processes needed to produce the offering during a period referred to as *ramp-up*, when the facilities and suppliers must increase volume to meet customer demand while coping with quality problems and last-minute design changes.

Competitive priorities may change over time. For example, consider what we now see as a high-volume standardized product, such as colour ink-jet desktop printers. Initially after market launch, when the printers were just beginning to appeal to the mass market, manufacturing processes required flexibility to adapt to changing volumes, features, and engineering specifications. Later, after the product was widely adopted and demand was high, the competitive priorities became low-cost operations, consistent quality, and on-time delivery. A post-launch review will compare the competitive priorities of the processes with their competitive capabilities and may signal a need to rethink the original product idea. The review also obtains additional input from customers, who will report on their experiences, critique the firm's product or service against competitors, and may share ideas for new offerings.

concurrent engineering A concept that brings product engineers, process engineers, marketers, buyers, information specialists, quality specialists, and suppliers together to work jointly to design a service or product and the required processes that will meet customer expectations.

Apple CEO Steve Jobs emphasizes Apple Computer's innovation during the launch of its online music store and iPod. Downloadable songs on the site cost 99 cents (US) apiece.

PROCESS TECHNOLOGY

process technology The methods by which an organization does things.

The methods by which an organization does things rely on the application of **process technology**. Some of the large number of process technologies used by an organization are unique to a functional area; others are used more universally. Figure 11.2 shows how technologies support the processes in the supply chain for both service providers and manufacturers. Each technology can be broken further into still more technologies, resulting in a diverse range of advanced technologies being used. However, some have been adopted to a much greater extent in manufacturing in Canada than others (see Figure 11.3). Technology use is influenced by the flexibility, cost, and sophistication of the technology. Just as important, internal research and development capabilities increase the rate of adoption.

For example, computer-integrated manufacturing (CIM) is an umbrella term for the integration of individual design, planning, and manufacturing technologies using complex computer systems. The individual technologies can include computer-aided design (CAD), industrial robots, and automated materials handling. (Supplement E, "Computer-Integrated Manufacturing," on the Student CD-ROM, further describes this family of manufacturing technologies.) These systems require internal expertise for both the initial implementation, and the subsequent maintenance and use for competitive advantage.

All functional areas, not just those areas directly involved with the supply chain, rely on technologies linked to operations. Figure 11.4 identifies the process technologies commonly used in these other functional areas. Consider sales processes that use vending machines to distribute products. This process technology is shedding its low-

FIGURE 11.2

Process Technologies Along the Supply Chain

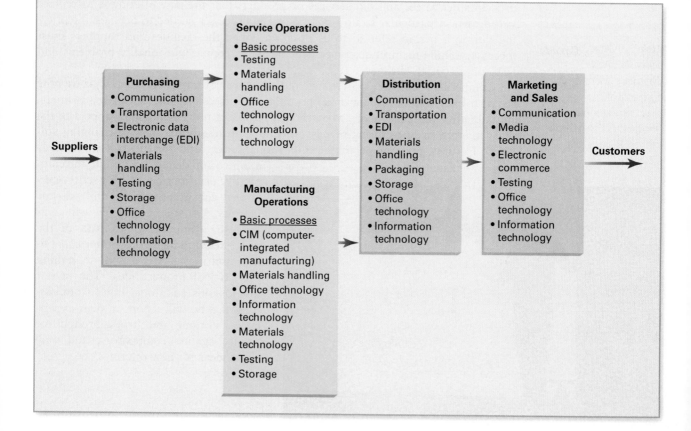

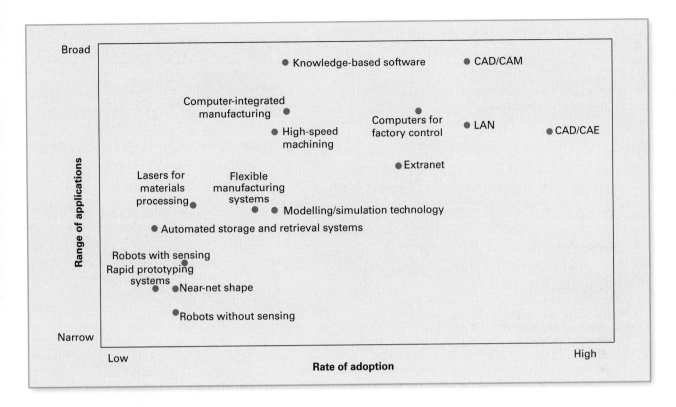

FIGURE 11.3

Adoption of Advanced Manufacturing Technologies in Canada

Source: Adapted from the Statistics Canada publication, *Patterns of Advanced Manufacturing Technology (AMT) Use in Canadian Manufacturing: 1998 AMT Survey Results*, Catalogue 88F0017MIE, released November 29, 2001, page11.

tech image. New electronic vending machines are loaded with circuit boards and microprocessors rather than gears and chains. They determine how much product is left, audit coin boxes, and make sure that the mechanisms work properly. These capabilities simplify product ordering and inventory control processes.

With more sophisticated versions, vending machine communication may even allow companies at distant locations to change product prices, reset thermostats, and verify credit cards. Handheld computers have also caught on, and some drivers tending vending machines use them to "read" the status of certain machines in just seconds. When the data are processed, the computers prepare restocking lists for route drivers. Now that replenishments can be made more quickly and accurately, some customers are reporting inventory reductions of 20 percent with no loss in service—a reduction that amounts to a significant savings in addition to the time savings for the drivers.

INFORMATION TECHNOLOGY

information technology
Technology used to acquire, process, and transmit information with which to make more effective decisions.

Managers use **information technology** to acquire, process, and transmit information with the intent of making more effective decisions. Information technology pervades every functional area in the workplace (see Figure 11.4). Computer-based information technology, in particular, has greatly influenced how offices work and how operations are managed, and has directly or indirectly spawned many other technological changes and innovations. Office workers now routinely access information simultaneously from several locations and diverse functional areas. In a manufacturing plant, information technologies can link people with the work centres, databases, and computers. Information technology makes cross-functional coordination easier and links a firm's basic processes. Moreover, information technology is crucial to coordinating and integrating the external supply chains, including customers. The following section explores

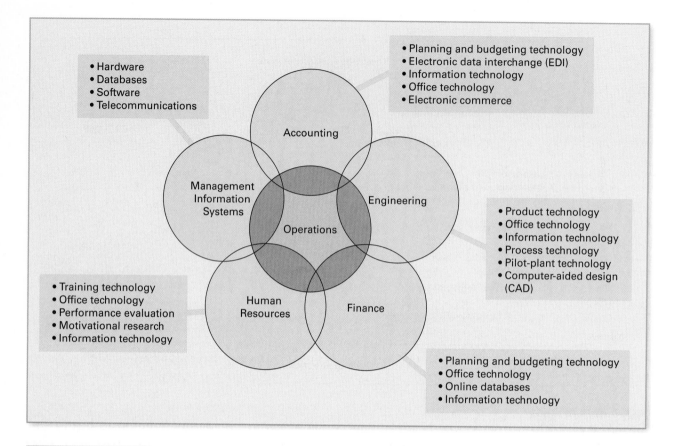

*Technologies for Other
Functional Areas*

how one form of information technology, *enterprise resource planning*, is increasingly being used to speed the exchange of critical data across the supply chain, support decision making, and improve customer responsiveness.

ENTERPRISE RESOURCE PLANNING

**enterprise resource
planning (ERP)** A large,
integrated information
system that supports
many enterprise
processes and data
storage needs.

Enterprise resource planning (ERP) refers to a large, integrated information system that supports many enterprise processes and data storage needs. An **enterprise process** is a companywide process that cuts across functional areas, business units, geographic regions, and product lines. Also known as an enterprise system, ERP is essentially a collection of compatible software modules, possibly interfacing to existing (sometimes called "legacy") information systems, that allow a company to have one comprehensive, fully integrated system. Designing an ERP system requires that a company carefully define its major processes so that appropriate decisions about the coordination of legacy systems and new software modules can be made. In many cases, a company's processes must be re-engineered before the company can enjoy the benefits of an integrated information system. Overall, ERP systems are designed to help coordinate relations among customers, internal operations, and suppliers.

enterprise process A
companywide process
that cuts across functional
areas, business units,
geographic regions, and
product lines.

WHAT ERP DOES

By integrating functional areas, ERP systems allow a firm to concentrate on enterprise processes rather than functional boundaries. For example, suppose that a Canadian manufacturer of telecommunication products has an ERP system and that an Athens-based sales representative wants to prepare a customer quote. When the salesperson enters

MANAGERIAL PRACTICE
Flexible Automation at R. R. Donnelley

R. R. Donnelley is the largest commercial printer in the United States and the number one printer of books. The industry makes huge capital investments in its printing presses to help drive down the variable unit cost of a book. It uses a make-to-order strategy, with customers such as book publishers placing new orders as their inventories became too low. However, the "make-ready" time to prepare for the new order and change over the presses for the next customer was time consuming. Keeping such expensive equipment idle for changeovers is costly. These high costs force customers such as book publishers to make large, infrequent orders for their books. They often ordered 100 000 copies of a new work—and sometimes wound up with 50 000 unsold books in their warehouses. All too often, they ended up being out of stock or having too much stock. They also placed orders well in advance of their desired delivery dates, because lead times were so long. R. R. Donnelley carefully allocated its production schedule well into the future, and the total time to run large batches (including preparation time) was large.

Flexible automation at its Roanoke, Virginia, plant allows R. R. Donnelley to take a different course, and it is reaping big rewards. The new process begins when the contents of a book arrive via the Internet as a PDF (portable document format) and go to the plant's prepress department. The intricate manual operations required to prepare text and pictures for printing traditionally caused the biggest bottlenecks. Roanoke now makes its plates digitally instead of from photographic film. With the elimination of steps such as duplicating and cleaning the file, a job that once took hours can now be completed in 12 minutes. The all-digital workflow also makes possible the creation of electronic instructions, known as ink presets, that improve productivity and quality. Cleaner and sharper plates are created for the presses because, unlike film, electronic type does not have to be repeatedly handled.

Quick, efficient press changeovers along with new types of automation make it possible to profitably print 50 copies of a single-colour book or 2,500 copies of a four-colour book. The publisher can then gradually increase the batch size after testing the market. The rise of book sales through

R. R. Donnelley has been able to achieve flexible automation by receiving books digitally and preparing them to go on press electronically. This allows the company to put books on press more quickly and print smaller, more manageable quantities in a single print run.

Amazon.com also boosted demand for small editions, and the new flexibility allows publishers to reprint classics and other books in manageable quantities. At the other extreme, Donnelley can still manufacture millions of copies of a single book, as it did when it turned out most of the 8 million copies of the latest Harry Potter book.

With more flexible automation, the Roanoke plant produces 75 percent of its titles in two weeks or less, compared with four to six weeks for a four-colour book using traditional technology. Management created a culture of continuous improvement at the plant, home of some 300 workers. Overall, Roanoke increased throughput 20 percent without having to buy an additional press and binding line, a savings of $15 million. Its presses run around the clock producing 3.5 million books a month; productivity has risen 20 percent, and service has improved. Book publishers now enjoy a just-in-time product when they want it.

Source: Gene Bylinsky, "Two of America's Best Have Found New Life Using Digital Tech," *Fortune*, vol. 148, no. 4 (2003), pp. 54–55. © 2004 Time Inc. All rights reserved.

information about the customer's needs into a laptop computer, the ERP system automatically generates a formal contract in Greek, giving the product's specifications, delivery date, and price. After the customer accepts it, the salesperson makes an entry, whereupon ERP verifies the customer's credit limit and records the order. The next application takes over to schedule shipment using the best routing. Backing up from the delivery date, it reserves the necessary materials from inventory and determines when to release production orders to its factories and purchase orders to its suppliers. Another application updates the sales and production forecasts, while still another credits the sales representative's payroll account the appropriate commission in drachmas. The accounting application calculates the actual product cost and profitability, in Canadian dollars, and reflects the transaction in the accounts payable and accounts receivable ledgers. Divisional and corporate balance sheets are updated, as are cash levels. In short, the system supports all of the enterprise processes that are activated as a result of the sale.

ERP APPLICATIONS

ERP revolves around a single comprehensive database that can be made available across the organization (or enterprise). Of course, security locks are possible and highly recommended in order to protect sensitive data from accidental or malicious damage. ERP provides visibility to relevant data enterprise-wide, for all products, at all locations, and at all times. The database collects data and feeds it into the various modular applications (or "suites") of the software system. As new information is entered as a *transaction* in one application, related information is automatically updated in the other applications, including (but not limited to) financial and accounting information, human resources and payroll information, supply chain information, and customer information. ERP streamlines data flows throughout the organization and allows management direct access to a wealth of real-time operating information. It seamlessly connects information among different enterprise processes and can eliminate many of the cross-functional coordination problems that existed under prior poorly integrated and noninterfaced legacy systems. Figure 11.5 shows some of the typical applications, with

FIGURE 11.5

ERP Application Modules

Source: Cedric X. Scalle and Mark J. Cotteleer, *Enterprise Resource Planning (ERP)*. Boston, MA: Harvard Business School Publishing, No. 9-699-020, 1999.

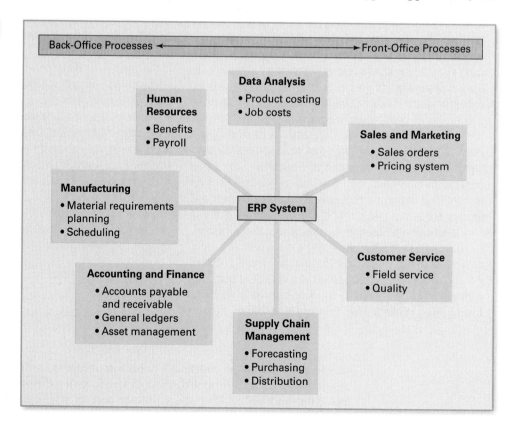

a few subprocesses nested within each. Some of the applications are for back-office operations such as manufacturing and payroll, while others are for front-office operations such as customer service and employee self-service.

ERP is used by both service providers and manufacturers. Amazon.ca is a value-added reseller that uses ERP. The supply chain application is of particular importance because it allows Amazon.ca to link customer orders to warehouse shipments and, ultimately, to supplier-replenishment orders. Services might put particular emphasis on the human resources and accounting and finance applications, and manufacturers have an interest in almost every application suite. Not all applications in Figure 11.5 need to be integrated into an ERP system, but those left out will not share their information in the corporate database.

HOW TO USE ERP

Most ERP systems today use a graphical user interface, although the older keyboard-driven, text-based systems are still very popular because of their dependability and technical simplicity. Users navigate through various screens and menus. When users are trained, such as during ERP implementation, the focus is on these screens and how to use them to get their jobs done. There has been much consolidation in this sector over the last few years as software providers work to provide the broadest range of integration possible. The largest suppliers of off-the-shelf commercial ERP packages include Germany's SAP AG (www.sap.com), Oracle (www.oracle.com), and SSA Global (www.ssaglobal.com). Figure 11.6 shows screen shots of SAP's software, and illustrates the strong integration between operations and sales.

interoperability The ability of one piece of software to interact with others.

ERP has changed a good deal over the last several years. One important direction is **interoperability**—the ability of one piece of software to interact with others. Electronic data interchange, a system that allows data interchange between companies on a batch basis, has been a major workhorse over the years. However, there is increasing interest in moving to more modular, Web-based approaches that let companies structure and exchange information without rewriting existing systems or adding large amounts of heavyweight middleware. These enablers of collaborative commerce are shaping the ways in which previously disparate and possibly competing pieces of software are working together to add value and reduce costs. The goal of all such methods is to automate, almost in real time, the sharing of information across enterprise boundaries.

TECHNOLOGY STRATEGY

Technology is probably the most important force driving the increase in global competition. As various studies show, companies that invest in and apply new technologies tend to have stronger financial positions than those that do not. One study of more than 1300 manufacturers in Europe, Japan, and North America focused on process technologies and revealed a strong link between financial performance and technological innovation. Companies with stellar performance in annual sales, inventory turnover, and profits had more experience with multiple advanced manufacturing technologies and demonstrated more leadership in technological change than their underperforming counterparts (Roth, 1996). Even small firms that have greater technological know-how and more intensively use computer-based information and manufacturing technologies enjoy stronger competitive positions (Lefebvre et al., 1992).

Because technology is changing so rapidly and because of the many technologies available, operations managers must more than ever make intelligent, informed decisions about new product and process technologies. The stakes are high, because such choices affect the human as well as the technical aspects of operations. Here we examine how technologies should be chosen and how these choices link with strategy to create a

FIGURE 11.6

*SAP ERP Software—
Linkages Between
Operations and Sales*

Source: SAP AG.
Permission granted by
SAP AG.

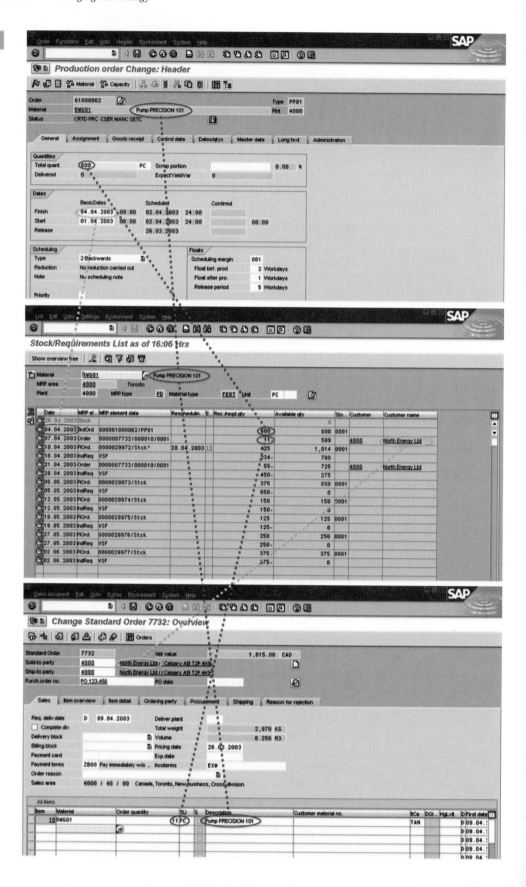

competitive advantage. An appropriate technology is one that fits corporate and operations strategies and gives the firm a sustainable advantage. Several tests of a potential technological change should be made. If the change being considered fails these tests, it shouldn't be pursued even if it represents an impressive technological accomplishment. For some jobs, a simple handsaw is a better choice than a computer-controlled laser.

Technology strategy deals with more than just choices about which specific technology to use. It also determines whether an organization should be a leader or follower in technological change and aids in evaluating radically new technologies when conventional financial analyses overlook important considerations.

TECHNOLOGY AS A COMPETITIVE ADVANTAGE

The relationship between technology and competitive advantage is often misunderstood. High technology and technological change for its own sake are not always best. A new technology should create some kind of competitive advantage. Competitive advantage is created by increasing the value of a product to a customer or reducing the costs of bringing the product to market. The potential for increasing value and reducing costs from a new technology is vast. The most obvious cost-reduction strategy is that of reducing the *direct costs* of labour and materials. Labour savings are still used to justify most automation projects, but labour is a shrinking component—only 10 percent to 15 percent—of total costs. Therefore, to understand a new technology's true value, a manager should assess factors other than cost savings.

For example, *sales can increase*, as Bell Mobility expected when it invested hundreds of millions of dollars to roll out new wireless third-generation (3G) networks to deliver additional Web services. *Quality can improve*, as illustrated by the new magnetic resonance imaging (MRI) machines that can diagnose heart and liver diseases without using X-rays and radioactive materials. With MRIs, scanning times are reduced from about 45 to 20 minutes, thus increasing the number of patients who can be served, *reducing costs* per patient, and increasing *patient comfort*.

In manufacturing, ATS Automation, headquartered in Cambridge, Ontario, designs and manufactures integrated systems that include automated materials handling equipment, sensors, controls, and software. With customers ranging from health care laboratories to silicon wafer manufacturers, these systems reduce human error and thus *improve product and service quality*. In addition, they yield *quicker delivery times* by reducing processing times. These reductions in turn allow for *lower inventories* in the process. Finally, *safety and environment* can benefit through less human contact and reduced waste.

Of course, new technology can also have its downside. Investment in new technology can be risky, particularly for complex and expensive projects that require new facilities or an extensive process overhaul. Uncertainties in demand and in per-unit benefits also create risks. Finally, technology may have hidden costs, requiring different employee knowledge and skills to maintain and operate the new equipment. Such requirements may generate employee resistance, lower morale, and increase turnover. Thus, the operations manager must sort out the many benefits and costs of different technological choices.

FIT WITH COMPETITIVE PRIORITIES

Another important test is how technological change will help a firm achieve the competitive priorities of cost, quality, time, and flexibility. Such a change should have a positive impact on one or more of these priorities, particularly on those that are emphasized for the product or service in question, and on determining whether this advantage can be protected from imitation. For example, FedEx promises fast delivery time (overnight delivery) and that parcels will be "absolutely, positively" delivered on time. FedEx chose bar-code technology to give it an early ability to track packages throughout the handling cycle—a capability possessed by none of its competitors at the time. Combining this technology with its own fleet of airplanes allowed its operations to support its strategic orientation and expand internationally. Its competitors could not easily match FedEx's differentiation strategy on the basis of time and global coverage.

FIRST-MOVER CONSIDERATIONS

This strategic consideration deals with *when* to adopt a new technology rather than which technology to choose. Being the first to market or a market leader with a new technology offers a firm numerous advantages that can outweigh the financial investment needed. Technological leaders lay down the competitive rules that others will follow with regard to a new product or process. A "first mover" may be able to gain an early large market share that creates an entry barrier for other firms. In addition, innovative new designs may be patented as intellectual property. Even if competitors are able to match the new technology, the first mover's initial advantage in the market can endure. Being first can give a firm the reputation that emulators will find difficult to overcome.

Of course, a company that pursues a first-mover strategy faces risks that can jeopardize its financial and market position. First, pioneering costs can be high, with R&D costs exceeding the firm's financial capabilities. Second, market demand for a new technology is speculative, and estimates of future financial gains may be overstated. Third, a new service, product, or process technology may well become outdated quickly because of new technological breakthroughs. Thus, managers must carefully analyze these risks and benefits before deciding which technologies to pursue.

ECONOMIC JUSTIFICATION

Managers should make every effort to translate considerations of sources of competitive advantages, fit with competitive priorities, existence of core competencies, and first-mover strategy into a financial analysis to estimate whether investment in a new technology is economically justified. Operations managers should state precisely what they expect from a new technology and then quantify costs and performance goals. They should determine whether the expected after-tax cash flows resulting from the investment are likely to outweigh the costs, after accounting for the time value of money. Traditional techniques such as the net present value method, internal rate of return method, and the payback method can be used to estimate financial impact (see Supplement B, "Financial Analysis," on the Student CD-ROM).

However, uncertainties and intangibles must also be considered, even though they cannot be easily measured. For example, there may be uncertainty about whether a new technology can be successfully developed. If it is a known technology, uncertainty may exist about how well it can be adapted to current processes or vice versa. Certain downstream benefits may be hard to quantify. For example, flexible automation might be of value for products that will be introduced well into the future, long after the life of the product for which it was first implemented. For these reasons, financial analyses should be augmented by qualitative judgments.

Operations managers must look beyond the direct costs of a new technology to its impact on customer service, delivery times, inventories, and resource flexibility. These are often the most important considerations. Quantifying such intangible goals as the ability to move quickly into a new market may be difficult. However, a firm that fails to make technological changes along with its competitors can quickly lose its competitive advantage and face declining revenues and layoffs. Justification should begin with financial analyses recognizing all quantifiable factors that can be translated into dollar values. The resulting financial measures should then be merged with an evaluation of the qualitative factors and intangibles involved. The manager can then estimate the risks associated with uncertain cost and revenue estimates. Decision-making tools such as the preference matrix approach, decision theory, and decision trees can help the manager make a final decision (see Supplement A, "Decision Making" on the Student CD-ROM).

DISRUPTIVE TECHNOLOGIES

Many companies have invested aggressively and successfully in technologies to retain current customers and to improve current processes. They have done all the right things in terms of seeking a competitive advantage and funding the technology projects that should lead to the highest profit margins and largest market share, relative to their *current* customers. They have pursued new process technologies that address the next-generation performance requirements of their customers. And yet, paradoxically, what seems like good business practice may be devastating and prevent many firms from investing in the technologies that *future* customers will want and need.

disruptive technology A technology that has performance attributes that are not valued yet by existing customers, or that performs much worse on some performance attributes but will quickly surpass existing technologies on such attributes when it is refined.

This paradox is likely to occur because of disruptive technologies, which occur infrequently and are nearly impossible to justify on the basis of rational, analytical investment techniques (Bower and Christensen, 1995). A **disruptive technology** is one that:

1. Has performance attributes that are not valued yet by *existing* customers or for current products, or

2. Performs much worse on some performance attributes that existing or future customers value but will quickly surpass existing technologies on such attributes when it is refined.

COUNTERING DISRUPTIVE TECHNOLOGIES. How can a company deal with the paradox of disruptive technology? The first step is to recognize when a technology is potentially disruptive rather than sustaining. One indicator could be internal disagreement over the advisability of producing the new technology. Marketing and financial managers will rarely support a disruptive technology, but technical personnel may argue forcibly that a new technology market can be achieved. A second indicator is to compare the likely slope of performance improvement of the technology with market demand. If its performance trajectory, as judged by knowledgeable analysts, is much faster than market expectations, it might be a disruptive technology that could become strategically crucial. It might best meet future market needs even though it is currently an inferior product.

Managers must be willing to undertake major and rapid change with disruptive technologies that are strategically crucial, even if doing so means initially serving emerging markets and realizing low profit margins. When both technology and customers change rapidly, as at many high-tech firms, one of two conflicting methods can be used to manage disruptive technologies. One method is to develop these technologies in a different part of the organization, with one part of the firm pursuing innovation and the other parts pursuing efficiency and continual improvement of technologies for existing customer bases. A team, sometimes referred to as a *skunk works*, can be formed to develop the new technology without upsetting normal operations. Such teams often work in close quarters, without many amenities, but band together in almost missionary zeal.

The other method is to use different methods of management at different times in the course of technological development. Firms can alternate periods of consolidation and continuity with sharp reorientation, interspersing periods of action and change with periods of evaluation and efficiency. With either method, the operations manager must seek ways to improve continually the existing technologies driving the production system, while being alert for radical innovations and discontinuities that can make technologies obsolete.

MANAGING TECHNOLOGY ACROSS THE ORGANIZATION

Technologies are embedded in processes throughout an organization (see Figure 11.4 on page 382). In each of their functional areas and business units, both service providers and manufacturers use many technologies. For example, Nestlé uses point-of-sale technology to assess customers' needs (*marketing*) and to control inventory in its supply chain (*operations*). Technology also creates special needs for training and supporting employees (*human resources*). The Toronto Stock Exchange uses computer equipment and software (*management information systems*) to streamline trading processes (*finance*). *Engineering* is heavily involved in R&D, creating new products and services and applying them to the organization's processes. Grocery Gateway's new Web services show how e-commerce has an increasingly important role in retail services. The very essence of enterprise resource planning illustrates many of the ways in which this chapter's topic, management of technology, is important to all business areas. ERP makes connections among applications in sales and marketing, customer service, supply chain management, accounting and finance, manufacturing, and human resources.

CHAPTER HIGHLIGHTS

- Technology consists of physical equipment, procedures, know-how, and the support network used in operations to produce products and services. Managers must make informed decisions about which technological possibilities to pursue and how best to implement those chosen.

- Innovation and technological change are primary sources of productivity improvement and drivers of global competition. Organizations more experienced at adapting to changing technologies tend to enjoy stronger competitive positions worldwide.

- New service and product development processes have four major steps: design, analysis, development, and full launch. Many ideas with multiple iterations of redesign and refinement are needed to realize a successful new service or product offering.

- Technologies are involved in all the processes along a firm's supply chain and in each of the firm's functional areas. Office and information technologies are pervasive. Managers need to invest the time to learn about the technologies that are used or could be used at their organizations.

- Enterprise resource planning is a large, integrated information system. Its applications cut across many processes, functional areas, business units, regions, and products.

- High-tech options are not necessarily appropriate solutions to operations problems. Tests of the advisability of technological change include competitive advantages measured in terms of costs, sales, quality, delivery times, inventory, and the environment; financial analyses; first-mover or follower considerations; identifying disruptive technologies; fit with competitive priorities; and core competencies.

CD-ROM RESOURCES

The Student CD-ROM that accompanies this text contains the following resources, which allow you to apply the concepts presented in this chapter.

- **Discussion Questions**: Five questions expand your thinking on evaluating new technologies, including their potential payoffs and costs.

- **Case**: *Bill's Hardware*. Should Bill Murton adopt the POS system, and how should he vote?

- **Supplement A:** *Decision Making*. Learn about the preference matrix approach, decision theory, and decision trees for evaluating new technologies for possible adoption.

- **Supplement E:** *Computer-Integrated Manufacturing*. See how to integrate product design and engineering, process planning, and manufacturing by means of complex computer systems.

PROBLEMS

Problems 3–5 require reading Supplement A, "Decision Making," and Problem 6 requires reading Supplement B, "Financial Analysis," on the Student CD-ROM. Problem 7 should be solved as a team exercise.

1. Why are traditional financial analysis techniques criticized when they are used to justify new technologies? Must such projects just be accepted as a leap of faith and an act of hope? Explain.

2. How might increased Internet use of business-to-business interactions affect customer–supplier relationships? Be specific for an organization of your choice, such as where you have previously worked.

3. You have been asked to analyze four new advanced manufacturing technologies and recommend the best one for adoption by your company. Management has rated these technologies with respect to seven criteria, using a 0–100 scale (0 = worst; 100 = best). Management has given the performance criteria different weights. Table 11.1 summarizes the relevant information. Which technology would you recommend?

TABLE 11.1 *Analysis of New Technologies*

CRITERION	WEIGHT	TECHNOLOGY RATING			
		A	B	C	D
Financial measures	25	60	70	10	100
Volume flexibility	15	90	25	60	80
Quality of output	20	70	90	75	90
Required facility space	5	60	20	40	50
Market share	10	60	70	90	90
Product mix flexibility	20	90	80	30	90
Required labour skills	5	80	40	20	10

4. Hitech Manufacturing Company must select a process technology for one of its new products from among three different alternatives. The following cost data have been obtained for the three process technologies:

COST	PROCESS A	PROCESS B	PROCESS C
Fixed costs per year	$20 000	$40 000	$100 000
Variable costs per unit	$15	$10	$6

a. Find the range for the annual production volume in which each process will be preferred.

b. If the expected annual production volume is 12 000 units, which process should be selected?

5. Super Innovators, Inc., is faced with the decision of switching its production facilities to new (promising but not yet completely tried) processing technology. The technology may be implemented in one or two steps, with the option to stop after the initial step. Because the benefits from the new technology (cost savings and productivity improvements) are subject to uncertainty, the firm is considering two options.

The first option is to make the full switchover in one step to take advantage of economies of scale in investment and opportunities to gain a larger market share.

For this choice the investment cost is $5 million. The expected present value of the cash flows is $20 million if the new processing technology works as well as expected, and $6 million if it does not work as well as expected.

The second option is to implement part of the system as a first step and then extend the system to full capability. The investment cost for the initial step is $2 million, and the present value of the combined investment in two steps will be $6 million. If both steps are implemented, the expected present value of the cash flows is $15 million if the new processing technology works as well as expected and $8 million otherwise. If only the first step is implemented, the expected present value of the cash flows is $4 million if the new processing technology works as well as expected and $2 million otherwise. The firm estimates that there is a 40 percent chance that the new technology will work as well as expected.

a. Draw a decision tree to solve this problem.

b. What should the firm do to achieve the highest expected payoff?

6. Riverbend Hospital is considering two different computerized information systems to improve pharmacy productivity. The first alternative is a portable computer system that will require a one-time investment of $80 000 for the computer hardware, software, and necessary employee training. After-tax cash flows attributable to the investment are expected to be $20 000 per year for the next eight years. Savings would accrue from increased pharmacist productivity and the value of having timely and accurate information. The second alternative is to install a mainframe computer linked to bedside terminals that would allow doctors to prescribe treatments directly to the pharmacy from patients' rooms. This system would require an investment of $170 000, but is expected to generate after-tax cash flows of $40 000 per year for eight years. The hospital seeks to earn 16 percent on its investments. Assume that both systems will have no salvage value at the end of eight years.

a. Calculate the net present value, internal rate of return (IRR), and payback period for each alternative.

b. On the basis of your financial analysis, what do you recommend?

c. Are there any valid considerations other than financial? If so, what are they?

7. Imagine that you are a member of the operations management team in a firm that manufactures flashlights. Your firm is faced with the problem of choosing the equipment and process technology for manufacturing the casings for the flashlights. After an evaluation of several alternative technologies, the choice has been narrowed to two technologies: (i) deep drawing of metal bars on a press using a die and (ii) injection moulding of a variety of plastic materials.

Compare the two technologies in terms of how each will influence various elements of the operating system.

a. First, make a list of the various elements (e.g., equipment, raw materials, building, operators, safety) and then indicate how the two technologies influence each element.

b. For which of these elements is the contrast between the influences of the two technologies most striking?

REFERENCES AND FURTHER READINGS

Arundel, Anthony, and Viki Sonntag. *Patterns of Advanced Manufacturing Technology Use in Canadian Manufacturing.* Ottawa: Statistics Canada, 88F0017MIE No. 12, 1999.

Bower, Joseph L., and Clayton M. Christensen. "Disruptive Technologies: Catching the Wave." *Harvard Business Review*, January/February 1995, pp. 43–53.

Burgelman, Robert A., Modesto A. Maidique, and Steven C. Wheelwright. *Strategic Management of Technology and Innovation.* Chicago: Irwin, 1996.

Cohen, Morris A., and Uday M. Apte. *Manufacturing Automation.* Chicago: Irwin, 1997.

Collier, David A. *Service Management: The Automation of Services.* Reston, VA: Reston, 1985.

Davenport, Thomas H. "Putting the Enterprise into the Enterprise System." *Harvard Business Review*, July/August 1998, pp. 121–131.

Earl, Michael, and M. M. Bensaou. "The Right Mind-Set for Managing Information Technology." *Harvard Business Review*, September/October 1998, pp. 119–129.

Iansiti, Marco, and Jonathan West. "Technology Integration: Turning Great Research into Great Products." *Harvard Business Review*, May/June 1997, pp. 69–79.

Industry Canada, 2001. *Key Statistics on ICT Infrastructure, Use and Content*, Catalogue No. C2-520/2001. Ottawa: Industry Canada, Spectrum, Information Technologies and Telecommunications Sector.

Jacobs, F. Robert, and D. Clay Whybark. *Why ERP?* New York: Irwin McGraw-Hill, 2000.

Lefebvre, Louis A., Ann Langley, Jean Harvey, and Elisabeth Lefebvre. "Exploring the Strategy-Technology Connection in Small Manufacturing Firms." *Production and Operations Management*, vol. 1 (1992), no. 3, pp. 269–285.

Noori, Hamid. *Managing the Dynamics of New Technology.* Englewood Cliffs, NJ: Prentice-Hall, 1990.

Pisano, Gary P., and Steven C. Wheelwright. "High-Tech R&D." *Harvard Business Review*, September/October 1995, pp. 93–105.

Quinn, James B., and Penny C. Paquette. "Technology in Services: Creating Organizational Revolutions." *Sloan Management Review*, Winter 1990, pp. 67–78.

Roth, Aleda V. "Neo-Operations Strategy: Linking Capabilities-Based Competition to Technology." In *Handbook of Technology Management*, G. H. Gaynor (ed.). New York: McGraw-Hill, 1996, pp. 38.1–38.44.

Scalle, Cedric X., and Mark J. Cotteleer. *Enterprise Resource Planning (ERP).* Boston, MA: Harvard Business School Publishing, No. 9-699-020, 1999.

Skinner, Wickham. "Operations Technology: Blind Spot in Strategic Management." *Interfaces*, vol. 14, January/February 1984, pp. 116–125.

Across the Organization

Aggregate planning is important to:

- **accounting,** which prepares cost accounting information needed to evaluate aggregate plans and which administers the billing process that is driven by schedules.

- **distribution,** which coordinates the outbound flow of materials in the supply chain with the aggregate plan and schedules.

- **finance,** which knows the financial condition of the firm, seeks ways to contain expensive inventory accumulations, and develops plans to finance the cash flows created by the aggregate plan and schedules.

- **human resources,** which is aware of how labour market conditions and training capacities constrain aggregate plans and schedules.

- **management information systems,** which develop information systems and decision support systems for creating aggregate plans and schedules.

- **marketing,** which provides demand forecasts and information on competition and customer preferences.

- **operations,** which develops plans and schedules that are the best compromise among cost, customer service, inventory investment, stable workforce levels, and facility utilization.

- **purchasing,** which provides information on supplier capabilities and coordinates the inbound flow of materials and services in the supply chain with the aggregate plan and schedules.

Learning Goals

After reading this chapter, you will be able to:

1. identify the dimensions on which aggregation is done and explain why aggregation helps in the planning process.

2. list the different types of capacity and demand alternatives and discuss the advantages and limitations of each.

3. use a spreadsheet approach to evaluate different level, chase, and mixed strategies for both service and manufacturing firms.

4. distinguish among the ways that service managers schedule customers to provide timely service and utilize fixed capacity.

5. schedule a workforce to allow each employee to have two consecutive days off.

The MacMillan Yard, a 400 hectare marshalling yard just north of Toronto, is critical to transferring much of Canadian National Railways' freight that crosses the continent. This freight-classification yard breaks trains apart and reassembles them for local deliveries or onward carriage. Everything is running well here, and trains are on time. The reason things are going so smoothly is because of a rigorous new approach known as the "scheduled railroad." In less than four years, the concept is making one of the most dramatic changes in railways since the introduction of diesel power.

It may come as a surprise that freight railways haven't run on schedules like those that discipline airlines, bus lines, and couriers. But within the capital-intensive and traditional world of freight railways, the notion of scheduling is a splendid and fearsome revolution. Most rail companies tell customers their products will get to market in a vague number of days—a real problem in the era of just-in-time deliveries.

Before CN began scheduling, service from Edmonton to Chicago would be quoted as taking six to eight days—give or take another day. So how did the customer respond? Plan for the worst: increase safety stock inventory, as well as order extra box cars in case the train didn't arrive. Costs for both the customer and CN were higher. The result: railways lost market share for the past 40 years as trucking snatched high-value, time-sensitive goods and left the railways with high-volume, low-margin commodities.

The chief architect of scheduling trains was CN's executive vice-president and chief operating officer E. Hunter Harrison. Scheduled service sounds simple, but its execution is symphonic in complexity. And like a symphony, it comprises three principal parts. First, service is enshrined at the front line, not just in upper management. Second, costs must be controlled, and third, asset utilization must be maximized.

Canadian National Railways' commitment to deliver freight on time across a vast North American network has dramatically transformed the railroad.

CN's commitment to deliver freight in hours—not days—and its ability to deliver on the promise have transformed it into the best railroad in North America. In 1998–99, the MacMillan Yard handled between 1800 and 2400 cars per day. Four years later, it has done up to 3300 per day. The goal is to do 4000, making it as busy as the mighty (and far larger) yards in Chicago. And those 4000 cars will all have individual "trip plans," unique and sacrosanct timetables that the railway must honour so customers can expect to receive their delivery when CN says they will.

Today, CN says, more than 90 percent of its trains arrive on time and customers can track their shipments over the Internet. The company is now so confident that it negotiates bonuses and penalties with customers such as Imperial Oil. If CN's on-time percentage is higher than promised, the customer pays it a bonus; if it's below, CN pays a penalty. Benefits come from better fleet productivity and smaller inventories. For Imperial Oil, a 10 percent improvement in turnaround times translates in a savings of $2 million to $3 million.

Even though its business is up since 1998, thanks to accurate scheduling CN has reduced its locomotive fleet to 1180, from 1965, boosted locomotive productivity by 25% to 30%, and eliminated 22 000 cars through better fleet utilization. Not that the efficiency is immediately evident. These days MacMillan Yard looks emptier, quieter than ever. But to the trained eye that is good, because it means cars are passing through more efficiently, which translates into lower costs for CN and better service for customers.

Source: Used with permission: Copyright 2002, Jared Mitchell. Condensed and adapted from "This Train Runs on Time," originally published in *National Post Business,* April 2002, pp. 50–58.

Planning for operations at companies such as CN must cover both the long-term planning horizon for resources and detailed schedules for facilities, equipment, and personnel. While long-term plans can stretch out five years or more, much management attention is often focused on some form of annual plan. The annual plan is then further broken down into detailed, short-term schedules for specific jobs, customers, and employees. In this chapter, we examine planning and scheduling that falls within this annual planning time frame.

The starting point is usually a financial assessment of the organization's near future—that is, for one or two years ahead. Service firms, such as a retail store or firm of lawyers, and manufacturing firms prepare business plans. A business plan is a projected statement of income, costs, and profits. It usually is accompanied by budgets, a projected (pro forma) balance sheet, and a projected cash flow statement, showing sources and allocations of funds. The business plan unifies the plans and expectations of a firm's operations, finance, sales, and marketing managers. In particular, it reflects plans for market penetration, new product introduction, and capital investment. Not-for-profit or government organizations, such as the United Way or a regional hospital, prepare a similar type of plan, often termed an annual plan. These business and annual plans are usually presented to and approved by a board of directors.

Given the business or annual plan, management develops an **aggregate plan** for its processes, which is a statement of its future production rates, workforce levels, and inventory holdings based on estimates of customer demand and capacity limitations. This statement is time-phased, meaning that the plan is projected for several time periods (such as months) into the future. A manufacturing firm's aggregate plan, called a **production plan**, generally focuses on production rates and inventory holdings, whereas a service firm's aggregate plan, called a **staffing plan**, centres on staffing and other labour-related factors. For both, the plan must balance conflicting objectives involving customer service, workforce stability, cost, and profit.

From aggregate plans, managers and analysts prepare detailed plans and then **schedules**. For manufacturing companies, they translate production plans into operations schedules for equipment, specific products and the components that go into them. For service firms, they translate the staffing plan into detailed workforce schedules. The staffing plan presents the number and types of employees needed, whereas the workforce schedule details the specific timetable for each category of employee. For example, a staffing plan might allocate ten police officers for the day shift in a particular district; the workforce schedule might assign five of them to work Monday through Friday and the other five to work Wednesday through Sunday to meet the varying daily needs for police protection in that district.

An analogy for the different planning levels is a student's calendar. Basing the choice of a school on career goals—a plan covering four or five years—corresponds to the highest planning level. Basing the choice of classes on that school's requirements—a plan for the next school year—corresponds to the middle planning level (or aggregate plan). Finally, scheduling group meetings and study times around work requirements in current classes—a plan for the next few weeks—corresponds to the most detailed planning level.

aggregate plan A statement of a company's production rates, workforce levels, and inventory holdings based on estimates of customer requirements and capacity limitations.

production plan A manufacturing firm's aggregate plan, which generally focuses on production rates and inventory holdings.

staffing plan A service firm's aggregate plan, which centres on staffing and other labour-related factors.

schedule A timetable that allocates and assigns resources such as equipment and people to accomplish specific tasks.

THE PURPOSE OF AGGREGATE PLANS

In this section, we explain why companies need aggregate plans and how they use them to take a macro, or big-picture, view of their business. The aggregate plan is useful because it focuses on a general course of action, consistent with the company's strategic goals and objectives, without getting bogged down in details. For this reason, production and staffing plans are prepared by grouping, or aggregating, similar products, services, units of labour, or units of time. For instance, a manufacturer of bicycles that produces 12 different models of bikes might divide them into two groups, mountain bikes and road bikes, for the purpose of preparing the aggregate plan. It might also consider its workforce needs in terms of units of labour needed per month. In general, companies aggregate products or services, labour, and time.

PRODUCT FAMILIES

Recall that a group of products or services that have similar demand requirements and common processing, labour, and materials requirements is called a *product family* (see Chapter 8, "Forecasting"). Sometimes product families relate to market groupings or, in the case of production plans, to specific manufacturing processes. A firm can aggregate its products or services into a set of relatively broad families, avoiding too much detail at this stage of the planning process. Common and relevant measurements, such as units, dollars, standard hours, litres, or kilograms, should be used. For example, consider the bicycle manufacturer that has aggregated all products into two families: mountain bikes and road bikes.

LABOUR

A company can aggregate labour in various ways, depending on workforce flexibility. For example, if workers at the bicycle manufacturer are trained to work on either mountain bikes or road bikes, for planning purposes management can consider its workforce to be a single aggregate group, even though the skills of individual workers may differ. Alternatively, management can aggregate labour along product family lines by splitting the workforce into subgroups and assigning a different group to the production of each product family. In service operations, such as a city government, workers are aggregated by the type of service they provide: firefighters, police officers, sanitation workers, and administrators.

TIME

planning horizon The length of time covered by an aggregate plan.

A **planning horizon** is the length of time covered by an aggregate plan. Typically, the planning horizon is one year, although it can differ in various situations. To avoid the expense and disruptive effect of frequent changes in output rates and the workforce, adjustments usually are made monthly or quarterly. In other words, the company looks at time in the aggregate—months, quarters, or seasons, rather than days or hours. In practice, planning periods reflect a balance between the needs for (1) a limited number of decision points to reduce planning complexity and (2) flexibility to adjust output rates and workforce levels when demand forecasts exhibit seasonal variations.

MANAGERIAL IMPORTANCE OF AGGREGATE PLANS

In this section, we concentrate on the managerial inputs, objectives, alternatives, and strategies associated with aggregate plans.

MANAGERIAL INPUTS

Figure 12.1 shows the types of information that managers from various functional areas supply to aggregate plans. One way of ensuring the necessary cross-functional coordination and supply of information is to create a committee of functional-area representatives. The committee, chaired by a general manager, has the overall responsibility of making sure that company policies are followed, conflicts are resolved, and a final plan is approved. Coordinating the firm's functions, with either formal or informal structures, helps to synchronize the flow of materials, services, and information through the supply chain and to better meet customer demand.

FIGURE 12.1

*Managerial Inputs
from Functional Areas
to Aggregate Plans*

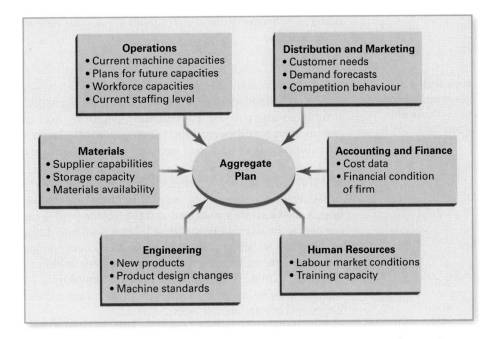

TYPICAL OBJECTIVES

The many functional areas in an organization that give input to the aggregate plan typically have conflicting objectives for the use of the organization's resources. Six objectives usually are considered during development of a production or staffing plan, and conflicts among them may have to be resolved:

1. *Minimize costs/maximize profits.* If customer demand is not affected by the plan, minimizing costs will also maximize profits.

2. *Maximize customer service.* Improving delivery time and on-time delivery may require additional workforce, machine capacity, or inventory resources.

3. *Minimize inventory investment.* Inventory accumulations are expensive, and the money could be used for more productive investments.

4. *Minimize changes in production rates.* Frequent changes in production rates can cause difficulties in coordinating the supplying of materials and require production line rebalancing.

5. *Minimize changes in workforce levels.* Fluctuating workforce levels may cause lower productivity because new employees typically need time to become fully productive.

6. *Maximize utilization of expensive assets.* For example, line processes require uniformly high utilization of plant and equipment.

The weight given to each one in the plan involves cost trade-offs and consideration of factors that are difficult to quantify. For example, maximizing customer service with fast, on-time delivery can be improved by increasing—not minimizing—the stock of finished goods in a production plan. Or, for example, a staffing plan that minimizes costs may not minimize changes in workforce levels or maximize customer service.

Balancing these various objectives to arrive at an acceptable aggregate plan involves consideration of various alternatives. The two basic types of alternatives are capacity and demand. Capacity alternatives are actions that respond to given demand patterns, whereas demand alternatives are actions that adjust the patterns of customer requirements.

CAPACITY ALTERNATIVES

capacity alternatives
Actions that can be taken to cope with demand requirements.

Capacity alternatives are actions that can be taken to adjust production and supply in order to accommodate demand requirements. Typically, an operations manager controls these alternatives. That is, the operations manager simply accepts forecasted demand and modifies workforce levels, inventory levels, overtime, vacation schedules, subcontracting, and planned backlogs to meet that demand.

WORKFORCE ADJUSTMENT. Management can adjust workforce levels through the hiring or layoff of employees. The use of this alternative can be attractive if the workforce is largely unskilled or semiskilled and the labour pool is large. However, for a particular company, the size of the qualified labour pool may limit the number of new employees that can be hired at any one time. Also, new employees must be trained, and the capacity of the training facilities themselves might limit the number of new hires at any one time. In some industries, the layoff of employees is difficult or unusual for contractual reasons (unions); in other industries, such as tourism and agriculture, seasonal hiring and layoffs are the norm.

ANTICIPATION INVENTORY. A plant facing seasonal demand can stock *anticipation inventory* (see Chapter 6, "Inventory Management") during light demand periods and use it during heavy demand periods. Although this approach stabilizes output rates and workforce levels, it can be costly because the value of the product is greatest in its finished state. Stocking components and subassemblies that can be assembled quickly when customer orders come in might be preferable to stocking finished goods.

Service providers generally cannot use anticipation inventory because services can't be stocked. In some instances, however, services can be performed prior to actual need. For example, telephone company workers usually lay cables for service to a new subdivision before housing construction begins. They can do this work during a period when the workload for scheduled services is low.

overtime The time that employees work that is longer than the regular workday or workweek, for which they receive premium pay for the extra hours.

undertime The situation that occurs when employees do not work *productively* for the regular-time workday or workweek.

WORKFORCE UTILIZATION. An alternative to workforce adjustment is workforce utilization, which might involve overtime and undertime. **Overtime** means that employees work longer than the regular workday or workweek and receive additional pay for the extra hours. It can be used to satisfy output requirements that cannot be completed on regular time. However, overtime is expensive (typically 50 percent premium over the regular-time pay rate). Moreover, workers often do not want to work a lot of overtime for an extended period of time, and excessive overtime may result in declining quality and productivity.

Undertime means that employees do not work *productively* for the regular-time workday or workweek. For example, they do not work productively for eight hours per day or for five days per week. Undertime occurs when labour capacity exceeds a period's demand requirements (net of anticipation inventory) and this excess capacity cannot or should not be used to build up inventory or to satisfy customer orders earlier than the delivery dates already promised. When products or services are customized, anticipation inventory isn't usually an option. A product cannot be produced to inventory if its specifications are unknown or if customers are unlikely to want what has been produced in advance because it doesn't meet their exact requirements.

Undertime can either be paid or unpaid. An example of *unpaid undertime* is when part-time employees are paid only for the hours or days worked. Perhaps they only work during the peak times of the day or peak days of the week. Sometimes part-time arrangements provide predictable work schedules, such as the same hours each day for five consecutive days each week. At other times, such as with stock pickers at some warehouse operations, worker schedules are unpredictable and depend on customer shipments expected for the next day. If the workload is light, some workers are not called in to work. Such arrangements are more common in low-skill positions or when the supply of workers seeking such an arrangement is sufficient. Although unpaid undertime may minimize costs, the firm must balance cost considerations against the ethical issues of being a good employer.

An example of *paid undertime* is when employees are kept on the payroll rather than being laid off. In this scenario, employees work a full day and receive their full salary but are not as productive because of the light workload. Some companies use paid undertime (though they do not call it that) during slack periods, particularly with highly skilled, hard-to-replace employees or when there are obstacles to laying off workers. The disadvantages of paid undertime include the cost of paying for work not performed and lowered productivity.

VACATION SCHEDULES. A firm can shut down during an annual lull in sales, leaving a skeleton crew to cover operations and perform maintenance. Employees might be required to take all or part of their allowed vacation time during this period. Use of this alternative depends on whether the employer can mandate the vacation schedules of its employees. In any case, employees may be strongly discouraged from taking vacations during peak periods or encouraged to take vacations during periods when replacement part-time labour is most abundant.

SUBCONTRACTORS. Subcontractors can be used to overcome short-term capacity short-ages, such as during peaks of the season or business cycle. Subcontractors can supply services, make components and subassemblies, or even assemble an entire product. If the subcontractor can supply components or subassemblies of equal or better quality less expensively than the company can produce them itself, these arrangements may become permanent.

BACKLOGS, BACKORDERS, AND STOCKOUTS. Firms that maintain a backlog of orders as a normal business practice can allow the backlog to grow during periods of high demand and then reduce it during periods of low demand. A **backlog** is an accumulation of customer orders that have been promised for delivery at some future date. Firms that use backlogs do not promise instantaneous delivery, as do wholesalers or retailers farther forward in the supply chain. Instead, they impose a lead time between when the order is placed and when it is delivered. Firms that are most likely to use backlogs—and increase the size of them during periods of heavy demand—make customized products and provide customized services. They tend to have a make-to-order or customized services strategy and include job shops, TV repair shops, automobile repair shops, and dental offices. Backlogs reduce the uncertainty of future production requirements and also can be used to level these requirements. However, they become a competitive disadvantage if they get too big. Fast delivery time often is an important competitive priority (see Chapter 1, "Competing with Operations"), but large backlogs mean long delivery times.

Manufacturers with a make-to-stock strategy and service providers with a standardized services strategy (see Chapter 1, "Competing with Operations") are expected to provide immediate delivery. For them, poor customer service during peak demand periods takes the form of backorders and stockouts rather than large backlogs. A

backlog An accumulation of customer orders that have been promised for delivery at some future date.

backorder An order that the customer expected to be filled immediately but reluctantly asks that it be delivered as soon as possible.

stockout An order that is lost and causes the customer to go elsewhere.

demand alternatives Actions that attempt to modify or shift customer demand and, consequently, resource requirements.

complementary products Products or services having similar resource requirements but different demand cycles.

revenue management The adjustment of price to maximize the revenue obtained for available capacity that is lost if not used.

backorder is an order that the customer expected to be filled immediately but reluctantly asks that it be delivered as soon as possible. Although the customer isn't pleased with the delay, the customer order is not lost and is filled at a later date.

In practical terms, backlogs for service firms are waiting lines of customers or orders; examples include TV repair shops, restaurants, banks, grocery stores, and barbershops. Various priority rules can be used to determine which order to process next. The usual rule is first come, first served, but if the order involves rework on a previous order, it may get a higher priority.

In contrast, a **stockout** is a lost order, and the customer goes elsewhere. Whereas a backorder adds to the next period's requirement, a stockout doesn't increase future requirements. Both backorders and stockouts can lead dissatisfied customers to do their future business with another firm, so generally backorders and stockouts are to be avoided. Planned stockouts may be used, but only when the expected loss in sales and customer goodwill is less than the cost of using other operations-based alternatives or marketplace alternatives, or adding the capacity needed to satisfy demand.

In conclusion, decisions about the use of each alternative for each period of the planning horizon specify the output rate for each period. In other words, the output rate is a function of the choices among these alternatives.

DEMAND ALTERNATIVES

Coping with seasonal or volatile demand by using capacity alternatives can be costly. Another approach is to attempt to change demand patterns to achieve efficiency and reduce costs. **Demand alternatives** are actions that attempt to modify demand and, consequently, resource requirements. Typically, marketing managers are responsible for specifying these actions in the marketing plan.

COMPLEMENTARY PRODUCTS. One way a company can even out the load on resources is to produce **complementary products** and services having similar resource requirements but different demand cycles. For example, in the service sector, city parks and recreation departments can counterbalance seasonal staffing requirements for summer activities by offering ice skating, tobogganing, or indoor activities during the winter months. The key is to find products and services that can be produced with existing resources and can level off the need for resources over the year.

PRICING. Promotional campaigns are designed to increase or adjust sales with creative pricing. Examples include automobile rebate programs, price reductions for winter clothing in the late summer months, and "two for the price of one" automobile tire sales. In services such as airlines and the hotel industry, where capacity is lost if not used (sometimes termed *perishable capacity*), **revenue management** (sometimes termed *yield management*), whereby prices are often adjusted in order to use all of the available capacity while maximizing revenue, has become commonplace. For example, if Air Canada finds that a particular flight from Calgary to Toronto is not selling as fast as expected, prices might be lowered until more seats are booked. Alternatively, if larger than expected demand is developing, prices for the remaining seats may be increased.

APPOINTMENTS AND RESERVATIONS. An appointment system assigns specific times for service to customers. The advantages of this method are timely customer service and high utilization of servers. Doctors, dentists, lawyers, and automobile repair shops are examples of service firms that use appointment systems. Doctors can use the system to schedule parts of their day to visit hospital patients, and lawyers can set aside time to prepare cases. If timely service is to be provided, however, care must be taken to tailor the length of appointments to individual customer needs rather than merely scheduling customers at equal time intervals.

Reservation systems, although quite similar to appointment systems, are used when the customer actually occupies or uses facilities associated with the service. For example, customers reserve hotel rooms, automobiles, airline seats, and concert seats. The major advantage of reservation systems is the lead time they give service managers to plan the efficient use of facilities. Often reservations require some form of down payment to reduce the problem of no-shows.

PLANNING STRATEGIES

Managers often combine operations- and demand-planning alternatives to arrive at an acceptable aggregate plan. For the remainder of this chapter, let us assume that the expected results of the demand alternatives have already been incorporated into the demand forecasts of product families or services. This assumption allows us to focus on the capacity alternatives that define output rates and workforce levels. Countless aggregate plans are possible even when just a few capacity alternatives are allowed. Four very different strategies, two chase strategies and two level strategies, are useful starting points in searching for the best plan. These strategies can be implemented with a limited or expanded set of capacity alternatives, as shown in Table 12.1. The specific capacity alternatives allowed, and how they are mixed, must be stated before a chase or level strategy can be translated into a unique aggregate plan.

TABLE 12.1 *Linking Reactive Alternatives with Planning Strategies*	Strategy	Possible Alternative During Slack Season	Possible Alternatives During Peak Season
	1. **Chase 1:** Vary *workforce level* to match demand	Layoffs	Hiring
	2. **Chase 2:** Vary *output rate* to match demand	Layoffs, undertime, vacations	Hiring, overtime, subcontracting
	3. **Level 1:** Constant *workforce level*	No layoffs, building anticipation inventory, undertime, vacations	No hiring, depleting anticipation inventory, overtime, subcontracting, backorders, stockouts
	4. **Level 2:** Constant *output rate*	Layoffs, building anticipation inventory, undertime, vacations	Hiring, depleting anticipation inventory, overtime, subcontracting, backorders, stockouts

chase strategy A strategy that matches demand during the planning horizon by varying either the workforce level or the output rate.

CHASE STRATEGIES. A **chase strategy** *matches* demand during the planning horizon by varying either (1) the workforce level or (2) the output rate. When a chase strategy uses the first method, varying the *workforce level* to match demand, it relies on just one capacity alternative—workforce variation. It uses hiring and layoffs to keep the workforce's regular-time capacity equal to demand. This chase strategy has the advantages of no inventory investment, overtime, or undertime. However, it has some drawbacks, including the expense of continually adjusting workforce levels, the potential alienation of the workforce, and the loss of productivity and quality because of constant changes in the workforce.

The second chase strategy, varying the *output rate* to match demand, opens up additional capacity alternatives beyond changing the workforce level. The extent and timing of the workforce's utilization are changed through overtime, undertime, and when vacations are taken. Subcontracting, including temporary help during the peak season, is another way of matching demand.

level strategy A strategy that maintains a constant workforce level or constant output rate during the planning horizon.

LEVEL STRATEGIES. A **level strategy** maintains a (1) constant workforce level or (2) constant output rate during the planning horizon. These two strategies differ from chase strategies not only because either the workforce or output rate is held constant but also because anticipation inventory, backorders, and stockouts are added to the list of possible capacity alternatives.

When a level strategy uses the first method, maintaining a constant *workforce level*, it might consist of not hiring or laying off workers (except at the beginning of the planning horizon), building up anticipation inventories to absorb seasonal demand fluctuations, using undertime in slack periods and overtime up to contracted limits for peak periods, using subcontractors for additional needs as necessary, and scheduling vacation timing to match slack periods.

Even though a constant workforce must be maintained with this first level strategy, many aggregate plans are possible. The constant workforce can be sized many ways. It can be so large as to minimize the planned use of overtime and subcontractors (which creates considerable undertime) or so small as to rely heavily on overtime and subcontractors during the peak season (which places a strain on the workforce and endangers quality). Thus, the advantages of a stable workforce must be weighed against the disadvantages of the other alternatives allowed, such as increased undertime, overtime, and inventory.

When a level strategy uses the second method, maintaining a constant output rate, it allows hiring and layoffs in addition to the other alternatives of the first level strategy. The output rate can be level even if the workforce fluctuates, depending on the set of alternatives that is used in the strategy. The key to identifying a level strategy is whether the workforce or output rate is constant.

mixed strategy A strategy that considers and implements a fuller range of capacity alternatives and goes beyond a "pure" chase or level strategy.

MIXED STRATEGIES. Used alone, chase and level strategies are unlikely to produce the best acceptable aggregate plan. Improvements are likely by considering plans that are neither pure level nor chase strategies. The workforce (or output rate) is not exactly level and yet does not exactly match demand. Instead, the best strategy for a process is a **mixed strategy** that considers and implements a fuller range of capacity alternatives and goes beyond a pure chase or level strategy. Whether management chooses a pure strategy or some mix, the strategy should reflect the organization's environment and planning objectives. For example, for the municipal street repair department, which faces seasonal demand shifts and needs an ample supply of unskilled labour, possible strategies include varying the workforce level, reducing overtime, and eliminating subcontracting.

THE PLANNING PROCESS

Figure 12.2 shows the process for preparing aggregate plans. It is dynamic and continuing, as aspects of the plan are updated periodically when new information becomes available and new opportunities emerge.

DETERMINING DEMAND REQUIREMENTS

The first step in the planning process is to determine the demand requirements for each period of the planning horizon using one of the many methods that we have already discussed. For staffing plans, the planner bases forecasts of staff requirements for each workforce group on historical levels of demand, managerial judgment, and existing backlogs for services. For example, a director of nursing in a hospital can develop a

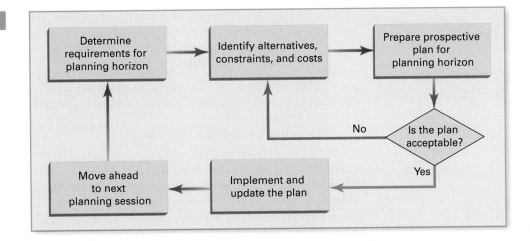

FIGURE 12.2

The Process for Preparing Aggregate Plans

direct-care index for a nursing staff and translate a projection of the month-to-month patient census into an equivalent total amount of nursing care time—and, thus, the number of nurses—required for each month of the year.

For production plans, however, the requirements represent the demand for finished goods and the external demand for replacement parts. The planner can derive future requirements for finished goods from backlogs (for make-to-order operations) or from forecasts for product families made to stock (for make-to-stock operations). Sometimes distributors or dealers indicate their requirements for finished goods in advance of actual orders, providing a reliable forecast of requirements from those sources.

IDENTIFYING ALTERNATIVES, CONSTRAINTS, AND COSTS

The second step is to identify the alternatives, constraints, and costs for the plan. We presented the capacity alternatives used in aggregate plans earlier, so we now focus on constraints and costs.

Constraints represent physical limitations or managerial policies associated with the aggregate plan. Examples of physical constraints might include training facilities capable of handling only so many new hires at a time, machine capacities that limit maximum output, or inadequate inventory storage space. Policy constraints might include limitations on the amount of backordering or the use of subcontracting or overtime, as well as the minimum inventory levels needed to achieve desired safety stocks.

Typically, many plans can satisfy a specific set of constraints. The planner usually considers several types of costs when preparing aggregate plans:

1. *Regular-time costs.* These costs include regular-time wages paid to employees plus contributions to such benefits as health insurance, dental care, employment insurance, and retirement funds and pay for vacations, holidays, and certain other types of absence.

2. *Overtime costs.* Overtime wages are typically 150 percent of regular-time wages (50 percent premium), exclusive of fringe benefits. Some companies offer a 200 percent rate for working overtime on Sundays and holidays.

3. *Hiring and layoff costs.* Hiring costs include the costs of advertising jobs, lower productivity, interviews, training programs for new employees, scrap caused by the inexperience of new employees, and initial paperwork. Layoff costs include the costs of exit interviews, severance pay, retraining remaining workers and managers, and lost productivity.

4. *Inventory holding costs.* Inventory holding costs include costs that vary with the *level* of inventory investment: the costs of capital tied up in inventory, variable storage and warehousing costs, pilferage and obsolescence costs, insurance costs, and taxes.

5. *Backorder and stockout costs.* As discussed earlier, the use of backorders and stockouts involves costs of expediting past-due orders, costs of lost sales, and the potential cost of losing the customer's sales to competitors in the future (sometimes called loss of goodwill).

PREPARING AN ACCEPTABLE PLAN

The third step is to prepare the aggregate plan. Developing an acceptable plan is an iterative process; that is, plans may need to go through several revisions and adjustments (see Figure 12.2). A prospective, or tentative, plan is developed to start. A production plan with monthly periods, for example, must specify monthly production rates, inventory and backorder accumulations, subcontracted production, and monthly workforce levels (including hires, layoffs, and overtime). The plan must then be checked against constraints and evaluated in terms of strategic objectives. If the prospective plan is not acceptable for either of those reasons, a new prospective plan must be developed.

IMPLEMENTING AND UPDATING THE PLAN

The final step is implementing and updating the aggregate plan. Implementation requires the commitment of managers in all functional areas. The planning committee may recommend changes in the plan during implementation or updating to balance conflicting objectives better. Acceptance of the plan does not necessarily mean that everyone is in total agreement, but it does imply that everyone will work to achieve it. Once implementation is underway, management can begin the planning process again.

PREPARING A PLAN WITH SPREADSHEETS

Here we use a *spreadsheet* approach that involves adopting a planning strategy, identifying alternatives, developing a plan, comparing the developed plan to other plans, and finally modifying the plan or strategy as necessary, until we are satisfied with the results. We demonstrate this approach by developing three aggregate plans: the first using a chase strategy, the second using a level strategy, and the third using a mixed strategy. For service or manufacturing companies where inventory is not possible, the level strategy is usually adjusted using overtime or undertime to reduce the number of employees.

After a planning strategy has been stated and plan developed, it is evaluated by use of a spreadsheet. One part of the spreadsheet shows the *input values* that give the demand requirements and the capacity alternative choices period by period. Another part shows the *derived values* that must follow from the input values. The final part of the spreadsheet shows the *calculated costs* of the plan. Along with qualitative considerations, the calculated cost of each plan determines whether the plan is satisfactory or whether a revised plan should be considered. When seeking clues about how to improve a plan already evaluated, we identify its highest-cost elements. Revisions that would reduce these specific costs might produce a new plan with lower overall costs. Spreadsheet programs make analyzing these plans easy for developing sound aggregate plans.

CHASE STRATEGY

Consider the chase strategy that adjusts workforce levels as needed to achieve requirements without using overtime, undertime, subcontractors, or inventory. This chase strategy can result in a large number of hiring and layoffs. However, many employees, such as college students, prefer part-time work. With this chase strategy, the workforce level row is identical to the requirement row, with no overtime in any period.

EXAMPLE 12.1	*A Chase Strategy with Hiring and Layoffs*

The manager of a small heating equipment manufacturer must determine how many part-time workers to maintain on the payroll. The workers are usually recruited from the surrounding agricultural region. To begin, the manager divides the next year into six time periods, each two months long. Each part-time employee can work a maximum of 20 hours per week on regular time.

Workforce requirements are shown as the number of part-time employees required for each time period at the maximum regular time of 20 hours per week. For example, in period 3, an estimated 18 part-time employees working 20 hours per week on regular time will be needed.

	TIME PERIOD TOTAL						
	1	2	3	4	5	6	Total
Requirement*	6	12	18	15	13	14	78

*Number of part-time employees.

Currently, 10 part-time clerks are employed. They haven't been subtracted from the requirements shown. Constraints on employment and cost information are as follows:

1. The size of training facilities limits the number of new hires in any period to no more than 10.

2. No backorders are permitted; demand must be met each period.

3. Overtime cannot exceed 25 percent of the regular-time capacity (i.e., five hours) in any period. Therefore, the most that any part-time employee can work is 1.25(20) or 25 hours per week.

4. The following costs can be assigned:

Regular-time wage rate	$4000 per time period at 20 hours per week
Overtime wage rate	150 percent of the regular-time rate
Hiring	$1000 per person
Layoff	$500 per person

5. Each part-time employee produces 50 products per period, at a variable cost of $500 per unit. Inventory carrying cost is 4 percent per two-month period.

SOLUTION

OM Explorer can be used to assist with the calculations for developing an aggregate production plan and exploring the cost implications of different capacity alternatives. Tutor 12.1 deals with the simple situation with five periods. Solver-Aggregate Planning with spreadsheets covers more complex plans. The input values are the *requirement*, the *workforce level*, *undertime*, and *overtime* for each period. The workforce level might be expressed as the number of employees, but the requirements and inventory are expressed as units of the product. However, relationships between the requirements and capacity alternatives must account for these differences.

To simplify input, the OM Explorer spreadsheets require a common unit of measure for all values, such as requirement and workforce level. So we must translate some of the data prior to entering the input values. Perhaps the easiest approach is to express the requirements and reactive alternatives as *employee-period equivalents*. If demand requirements are given as units of product, we can convert them to employee-period equivalents by *dividing* them by the productivity of a worker. For example, if the demand is for 750 units of product and the average employee produces 50 units in one period, the demand requirement is 15 employee-period equivalents.

This translation from product units to employee-period equivalents also applies to the initial inventory or backorders at the beginning of period 1, if they are given as product units. To convert the spreadsheet results back to product units, we simply *multiply* employee-period equivalents by the productivity rate. For example, an ending inventory of 20 employee-period equivalents would translate back to 1000 units of product, or 20 × 50.

The first row of derived values is called *productive time*, which is that portion of the workforce's regular time that is paid for and used productively. In any period, the productive time equals the workforce level minus undertime. The hires and layoffs rows can be derived from the workforce levels. In this example, the workforce is decreased for period 1 from its initial size of 10 employees to 6, which means that 4 employees are laid off. The next period, 6 employees are hired, bringing the total workforce level to 12, to match the demand requirement for that period. Similar adjustments are made to the workforce to mirror each period's demand requirement.

The chase strategy, illustrated in Figure 12.3, was developed using OM Explorer Solver: Aggregate Planning. The $329 500 cost of this plan is considerably above the basic regular-time costs because of the frequent hiring and layoffs, which add $17 500. Reducing frequent workforce adjustments provides a lower-cost solution.

FIGURE 12.3

	1	2	3	4	5	6	Total
Requirement	6	12	18	15	13	14	78
Workforce level	6	12	18	15	13	14	78
Undertime	0	0	0	0	0	0	0
Overtime	0	0	0	0	0	0	0
Productive time	6	12	18	15	13	14	78
Inventory	0	0	0	0	0	0	0
Hires	0	6	6	0	0	1	13
Layoffs	4	0	0	3	2	0	9
Costs	1	2	3	4	5	6	Totals
Productive time	$24 000	48 000	72 000	60 000	52 000	56 000	$312 000
Undertime	$0	0	0	0	0	0	$0
Overtime	$0	0	0	0	0	0	$0
Inventory	$0	0	0	0	0	0	$0
Hires	$0	6 000	6 000	0	0	1 000	$13 000
Layoffs	$2 000	0	0	1 500	1 000	0	$4 500
Total cost	$26 000	54 000	78 000	61 500	53 000	57 000	$329 500

Decision Point   The manager, now having a point of reference with which to compare other plans, decided to evaluate some other plans before making a final choice, beginning with the level strategy.

LEVEL STRATEGY

One possible level strategy, which uses a constant number of employees that will satisfy demand during the planning horizon, is determined by taking the total annual requirements and converting that into a constant production rate. By doing so, the workforce level will not change, except possibly for hiring or layoffs at the beginning of the first period if the current and desired constant workforce levels do not match. For many manufacturing and service organizations, the level strategy can lead to considerable build up of inventory or backorders, if permitted.

EXAMPLE 12.2	*A Level Strategy with Inventory*

As an alternative, the manager wants to develop a staffing plan with a level workforce, so as to avoid hiring and layoffs after the year has begun. Inventory can also be stored to satisfy later demand.

SOLUTION

For this particular level strategy, the manager begins by finding the number of part-time employees at 20 hours per week needed to meet the annual requirement.

$$w = \frac{\text{Total requirement}}{\text{Number of planning periods}} = \frac{78}{6} = 13 \text{ workers}$$

A 13-employee staff size exactly matches the total annual requirement with production on regular time.

Similar to Example 12.1, the OM Explorer spreadsheets require a common unit of measure for inventory cost. To calculate the employee-period equivalents, we again use workforce productivity and the holding interest rate per period. Recall that each employee can produce 50 units per period, the inventory carrying rate is 4 percent per period, and the variable cost is $500 per unit. Thus, the equivalent inventory holding cost is $50 \times 500 \times 0.04 = \$1000$ per employee-equivalent per period.

The complete plan, developed using OM Explorer Solver: Aggregate Planning, is shown in Figure 12.4. The $335 000 cost of this plan is somewhat higher than using the chase strategy. The spreadsheet shows that most of the cost increase results from the high inventory carrying cost.

FIGURE 12.4

	1	2	3	4	5	6	Total
Requirement	6	12	18	15	13	14	78
Workforce level	13	13	13	13	13	13	78
Undertime	0	0	0	0	0	0	0
Overtime	0	0	0	0	0	0	0
Productive time	13	13	13	13	13	13	78
Inventory	7	8	3	1	1	0	20
Hires	3	0	0	0	0	0	3
Layoffs	0	0	0	0	0	0	0
Costs	1	2	3	4	5	6	Totals
Productive time	$52 000	52 000	52 000	52 000	52 000	52 000	$312 000
Undertime	$0	0	0	0	0	0	$0
Overtime	$0	0	0	0	0	0	$0
Inventory	$7 000	8 000	3 000	1 000	1 000	0	$20 000
Hires	$3 000	0	0	0	0	0	$3 000
Layoffs	$0	0	0	0	0	0	$0
Total cost	$62 000	60 000	55 000	53 000	53 000	52 000	$335 000

A related alternative is to use some overtime during the peak month, so as to reduce the total inventory that must be stored in the preceding months. For example, if the workforce is reduced to 12 employees (total annual regular-time capacity is 12(6) = 72), overtime is needed in periods 4, 5, and 6 as inventory from periods 1 and 2 fills the requirement for period 3. However, this change increases the total cost to $338 000 and so is rejected.

Decision Point Having found that level strategies are worse than the chase strategy, the manager decided to formulate some mixed strategies that keep more of the elements of the chase strategy.

MIXED STRATEGIES

The manager of the manufacturing firm in Example 12.1 might find even better solutions with a mixed strategy, which varies the workforce level or output rate somewhat but not to the extreme of a chase strategy. She might also consider a fuller range of capacity alternatives, such as vacations, subcontracting, and even customer service reductions (increased backlogs, backorders, or stockouts).

EXAMPLE 12.3	*A Mixed Strategy*

As a third alternative, the manager wants to develop an aggregate production plan that includes changes in the workforce size, as well as the use of inventory to satisfy later demand. As before, backorders, stockouts, and subcontracting are not permitted.

SOLUTION

Figure 12.5 summarizes a mixed strategy for a manufacturer that varies the workforce and uses inventory. The plan calls for expanding the workforce in periods 2 and 3, reducing the workforce in periods 5 and 6, and holding inventory in periods 1, 2, and 5.

FIGURE 12.5

	1	2	3	4	5	6	Total
Requirement	6	12	18	15	13	14	78
Workforce level	10	11	15	15	14	13	78
Undertime	0	0	0	0	0	0	0
Overtime	0	0	0	0	0	0	0
Productive time	10	11	15	15	14	13	78
Inventory	4	3	0	0	1	0	8
Hires	0	1	4	0	0	0	5
Layoffs	0	0	0	0	1	1	2

Costs	1	2	3	4	5	6	Totals
Productive time	$40 000	44 000	60 000	60 000	56 000	52 000	$312 000
Undertime	$0	0	0	0	0	0	$0
Overtime	$0	0	0	0	0	0	$0
Inventory	$4 000	3 000	0	0	1 000	0	$8 000
Hires	$0	1 000	4 000	0	0	0	$5 000
Layoffs	$0	0	0	0	500	500	$1 000
Total cost	$44 000	48 000	64 000	60 000	57 500	52 500	$326 000

We know it is a mixed strategy because (1) neither the workforce nor output rate matches the requirements as with a chase strategy (note that inventory varies from one period to the next) and (2) neither the workforce nor output rate is constant as with a level strategy.

Decision Point Given the lower total cost, along with the relatively small change in the level of the workforce, the manager favoured the mixed strategy.

MANAGERIAL CONSIDERATIONS

Although a series of capacity plans can be tried and compared to find the best plan, managers also can use a variety of mathematical techniques and software packages to assist with meeting particular management objectives. For example, Supplement I, "Linear Programming," on the Student CD-ROM shows how to formulate different aggregate planning and scheduling problems as linear programming models—and how to solve them once modelled. In their simplest form, the models allow management to minimize cost, subject to meeting demand, given the costs of capacity alternatives.

Spreadsheets also routinely include extra software modules that assist with optimizing against particular criteria determined by management, such as minimum cost (e.g., Excel has an add-in module called "Solver"). The aggregate production plan illustrated in Figure 12.5 is the minimum-cost alternative, given the manufacturer's costs and constraints.

Although such techniques can be useful in developing sound aggregate plans, they are only aids to the planning process. As you have seen, the planning process is dynamic and often complicated by conflicting objectives. Analytic techniques can help managers evaluate plans and resolve conflicting objectives, but managers—not techniques—make the decisions. As a result, the minimum-cost plan might only serve as a guide or benchmark against which to compare alternatives that more effectively balance other customer- and operations-related objectives, such as flexibility and risk.

IMPLEMENTING THE AGGREGATE PLAN

After arriving at an acceptable aggregate plan, management must implement it by disaggregating the plan—that is, breaking it down into specific products, workstations, and dates. The next chapter further details the process of disaggregating the plan into specific requirements for resources and materials. A final critical step is to develop detailed schedules for managing customer orders, equipment, and personnel. Scheduling generates a specific timetable that assigns particular resources to specific tasks.

workforce scheduling
Developing a timetable that determines when employees work.

operations scheduling
Developing a timetable that assigns jobs to machines or workers to jobs.

Two basic types of scheduling are used: **workforce scheduling**, which determines when employees work, and **operations scheduling**, which assigns jobs to machines or workers to jobs. In many services, like that described for Air New Zealand in the Managerial Practice, managers work with employees to develop their workforce schedules. Workforce scheduling is crucial, because measures of performance such as customer waiting time, waiting-line length, utilization, cost, and quality are related to the availability of the servers. Operations scheduling is equally crucial, because many other performance measures, such as on-time delivery, inventory levels, operations throughput time, and cost and quality, relate directly to the scheduling of each customer order or production lot.

SCHEDULING IN MANUFACTURING

Operations scheduling focuses on how best to use existing capacity, taking into account technical production constraints. One input to an operations schedule is the master production schedule, which details the dates and amounts of production for specific final products (see Supplement K, "Master Production Scheduling," on the Student CD-ROM). The process structure has important implications for scheduling (see Chapter 2, "Process Management"). Tasks in a project or small batch process are difficult to schedule, because of the variability in customer order routings and the continual introduction of new jobs to be processed. In contrast, with a line or continuous flow process, tasks are easier to schedule, because the facility uses a common flow pattern through the system. Often scheduling involves determining when to end the production of one specific product and start the next (i.e., batch size). Regardless of the environment, scheduling mistakes can be costly in either situation.

For small batch processes, several jobs (e.g., open orders for components) must often be processed at one or more workstations. Typically, a variety of tasks can be performed at each workstation. If schedules are not carefully planned to avoid bottlenecks, waiting lines may develop. For example, Figure 12.6 (page 411) depicts the

MANAGERIAL PRACTICE
Building a Schedule for an Airline

How important is scheduling to an airline company? Certainly, customer satisfaction regarding on-time schedule performance is critical in a highly competitive industry such as air transportation. In addition, airlines lose a lot of money when expensive equipment such as an aircraft is idle. Flight and crew scheduling, however, is a very complex process. For example, Air New Zealand (www.airnz.com) has 8000 employees and operates 85 domestic and 50 international flights daily. Scheduling begins with a five-year market plan that identifies the new and existing flight segments that are needed to remain competitive in the industry. This general plan is further refined to a three-year plan and then put into an annual plan where the flight segments have specific departure and arrival times.

Next, crew availability must be matched to the flight schedules. From the crew's point of view, it is also important to satisfy as many crew requests and preferences as possible. There are two types of crews—pilots and attendants—each with its own set of constraints. Pilots, for example, cannot be scheduled for more than 35 hours in a seven-day week and no more than 100 hours in a 28-day cycle and must have a 36-hour break every seven days and 30 days off in an 84-day cycle. Sophisticated optimization models are used to design generic minimum-cost tours of duty that cover every flight and recognize all the constraints. Each tour of duty begins and ends at a crew base and consists of an alternating sequence of duty periods and rest periods with duty periods including one or more flights. The tours of duty are posted and crew members bid on them within a specified period of time. Actual crew rosters are constructed from the bids received. The roster must ensure that each flight has a qualified crew complement and that each crew member has a feasible line of work over the roster period.

Periodic refresher training for pilots in a B747 simulator is just one example of specific activities that must be built into detailed flight crew rosters.

Scheduling does not end with the definition of the flights and crew rosters. Daily disruptions such as severe weather conditions or mechanical failures can cause schedule changes to crews, pilots, and even aircraft. Customers expect a fast resolution of the problem, and the company needs to find the least-cost solution. In the airline industry, the aggregate planning and scheduling process can determine a company's long-term competitive strength.

Sources: David M. Ryan, "Optimization Earns Its Wings," *OR/MS Today*, April 2000, pp. 26–30; "Service Scheduling at Air New Zealand," *Operations Management in Action Video Series* (Upper Saddle River, NJ: Prentice-Hall, 2000).

complexity of scheduling a manufacturing process. When an order is received for a part, the raw materials are collected and the batch is moved to its first operation. The arrows show that batches follow different routes through the manufacturing process, depending on the product being made. At each workstation someone must determine which order or batch to process next, because the rate at which each arrives at a workstation often differs from the rate at which the workstation can process them, creating a waiting line. This is a dynamic environment, with new batches entering the manufacturing process at any time. Such complexity puts pressure on managers to develop scheduling procedures that will efficiently handle the production stream.

FIGURE 12.6

Diagram of a Manufacturing Process

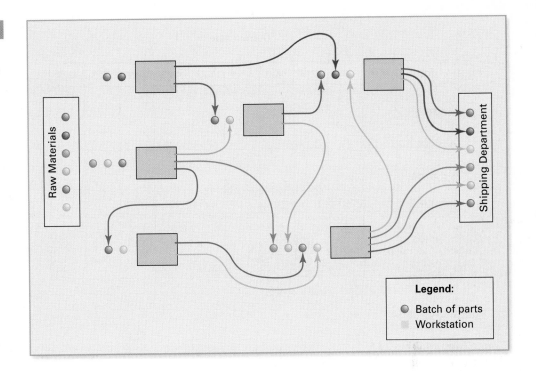

GANTT CHARTS

Here we introduce the problem of scheduling by presenting a traditional manual tool for scheduling called the Gantt chart. (For more on the performance measures and specific scheduling approaches used in manufacturing, see Supplement J, "Operations Scheduling," on the Student CD-ROM.)

The Gantt chart, which we introduced in Chapter 3, "Managing Projects," can be used as a tool for sequencing work on machines and monitoring its progress. The chart takes two basic forms: the activity progress chart and the machine chart. Both types of Gantt charts present the ideal and the actual use of resources over time. The *progress chart* graphically displays the current status of each batch or order relative to its scheduled completion date. For example, suppose that an automobile parts manufacturer has three orders under way, one each for Ford, Honda, and BMW. The actual status of these orders is shown by the shaded bars in Figure 12.7; the lines indicate the desired schedule for the start and finish of each order. For the current date, April 21, this Gantt chart shows that the Ford order is behind schedule, because operations has completed only the work scheduled through April 18. The Honda order is exactly on schedule, and the BMW order is ahead of schedule.

Figure 12.8 shows a *machine chart* for the automobile parts manufacturer. This chart depicts the sequence of future work at the two machines and also can be used to monitor progress. Using the same notation as in Figure 12.7, the chart shows that for the current date of April 21, the Honda order is on schedule at the grinder, because the actual progress coincides with the current date. The BMW order has finished at the lathe, which is now idle. The plant manager can easily see from the Gantt machine chart the consequence of juggling the schedules. The usual approach is to juggle the schedules by trial and error until a satisfactory level of selected performance measures is achieved.

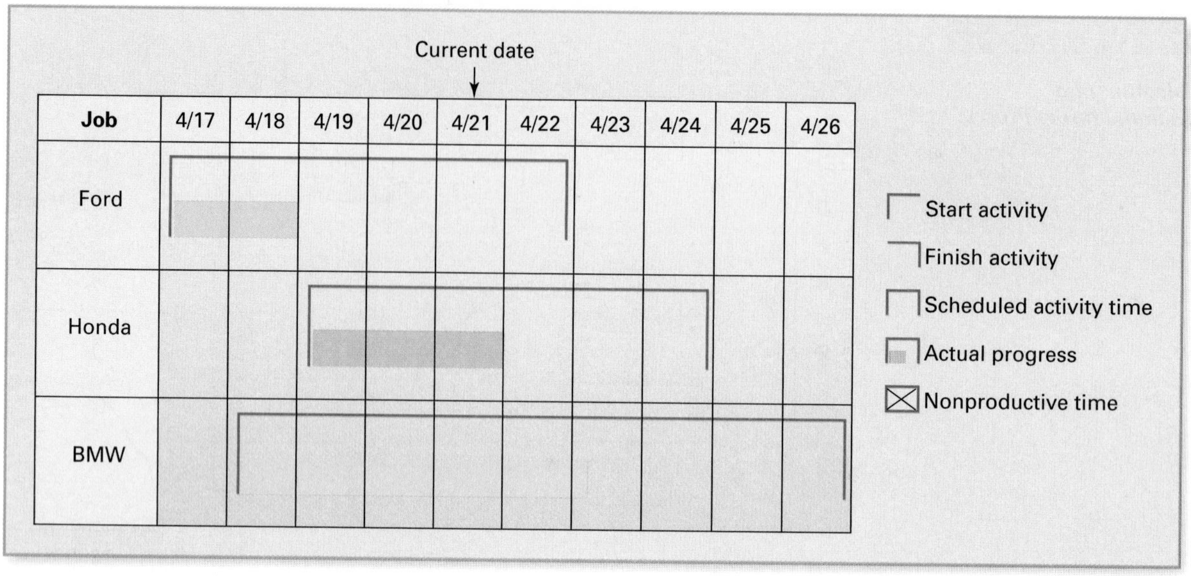

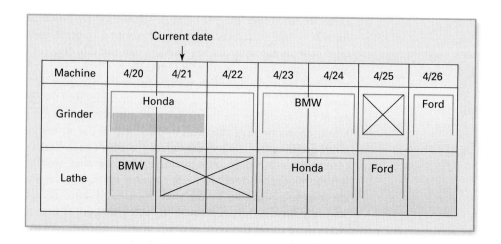

FIGURE 12.7

Gantt Chart of Job Progress for an Auto Parts Company

FIGURE 12.8

Gantt Chart for Machines at an Auto Parts Company

SCHEDULING IN SERVICES

One important distinction between manufacturing and services is that in service operations, demand often is less predictable. Customers may decide on the spur of the moment that they need a hamburger, a haircut, or a plumbing repair. As noted earlier in the chapter, scheduling customers using appointments, reservations, and backlogs is one way to adjust demand to encourage specific arrival times and definite times of service. With this approach, capacity remains fixed and demand is levelled to provide timely service and better utilize capacity.

A second distinction is that service operations cannot create inventories to buffer demand uncertainties. Thus, capacity, often in the form of employees, is crucial for service providers. In this section, we discuss various ways in which worker scheduling systems can facilitate the capacity management of service providers.

SCHEDULING THE WORKFORCE

A scheduling system for workers is necessary to specify the on-duty and off-duty periods for each employee over a certain time period, as in assigning postal clerks, nurses, pilots, attendants, or police officers to specific workdays and shifts. This approach is used when customers demand quick response and total demand can be forecasted with reasonable accuracy. In these instances, capacity is adjusted to meet the expected loads on the service system.

Recall that workforce schedules translate the staffing plan into specific schedules of work for each employee. Determining the workdays for each employee does not in itself make the staffing plan operational. Daily workforce requirements, stated in aggregate terms in the staffing plan, must be satisfied. The workforce capacity available each day must meet or exceed daily workforce requirements. If it does not, the scheduler must try to rearrange days off until the requirements are met. If no such schedule can be found, management might have to change the staffing plan and authorize more employees, overtime hours, or larger backlogs.

CONSTRAINTS. The technical constraints imposed on the workforce schedule are the resources provided by the staffing plan and the requirements placed on the operating system. However, other constraints, including legal and behavioural considerations, also can be imposed. For example, Air New Zealand, described in the Managerial Practice feature, is required to have at least a minimum number of flight attendants on duty at all times. Similarly, a minimum number of fire and safety personnel must be on duty at a fire station at all times. Such constraints limit management's flexibility in developing workforce schedules.

The constraints imposed by the psychological needs of workers complicate scheduling even more. Some of these constraints are written into labour agreements. For example, an employer may agree to give employees a certain number of consecutive days off per week or to limit employees' consecutive workdays to a certain maximum. Other provisions might govern the allocation of vacation, days off for holidays, or rotating shift assignments. In addition, preferences of the employees themselves need to be considered.

One way that managers deal with certain undesirable aspects of scheduling is to use a **rotating schedule**, which rotates employees through a series of workdays or hours. Thus, over a period of time, each person has the same opportunity to have weekends and holidays off and to work days, as well as evenings and nights. A rotating schedule gives each employee the next employee's schedule the following week. In contrast, a **fixed schedule** calls for each employee to work the same days and hours each week.

rotating schedule A schedule that rotates employees through a series of workdays or hours.

fixed schedule A schedule that calls for each employee to work the same days and hours each week.

DEVELOPING A WORKFORCE SCHEDULE. Suppose that we are interested in developing an employee schedule for a company that operates seven days a week and provides each employee two consecutive days off. In this section, we demonstrate a method that recognizes this constraint.[1] The objective is to identify the two consecutive days off for each employee that will minimize the amount of total slack capacity. The work schedule for each employee, then, is the five days that remain after the two days off have been determined. The procedure involves the following steps:

- *Step 1.* From the schedule of net requirements for the week, find all the pairs of consecutive days that exclude the maximum daily requirements. Select the unique pair that has the lowest total requirements for the two days. In some unusual situations, all pairs may contain a day with the maximum requirements.

---

[1]See Tibrewala, Philippe, and Browne (1972) for an optimizing approach.

If so, select the pair with the lowest total requirements. Suppose that the numbers of employees required are:

Monday	8	Friday	7
Tuesday	9	Saturday	4
Wednesday	2	Sunday	2
Thursday	12		

The maximum capacity requirement is 12 employees on Thursday. The pair having the lowest total requirements is Saturday–Sunday, with 4 + 2 = 6.

● *Step 2.* If a tie occurs, choose one of the tied pairs, consistent with provisions written into the labour agreement, if any. Alternatively, the tie could be broken by asking the employee being scheduled to make the choice. As a last resort, the tie could be broken arbitrarily. For example, preference could be given to Saturday–Sunday pairs.

● *Step 3.* Assign the employee the selected pair of days off. Subtract the requirements satisfied by the employee from the net requirements for each day the employee is to work. In this case, the employee is assigned Saturday and Sunday off. After requirements are subtracted, Monday's requirement is 7, Tuesday's is 8, Wednesday's is 1, Thursday's is 11, and Friday's is 6. Saturday's and Sunday's requirements do not change because no employee is yet scheduled to work those days.

● *Step 4.* Repeat steps 1–3 until all requirements have been satisfied or a certain number of employees have been scheduled.

This method reduces the amount of slack capacity assigned to days having low requirements and forces the days having high requirements to be scheduled first. It also recognizes some of the behavioural and contractual aspects of workforce scheduling in the tie-breaking rules. However, the schedules produced might *not* minimize total slack capacity. Different rules for finding the days-off pair and breaking ties are needed to ensure minimal total slack capacity.

EXAMPLE 12.4   *Developing a Workforce Schedule*

Amalgamated Parcel Service is open seven days a week. The schedule of requirements is:

Day	M	T	W	Th	F	S	Su
Number of employees	6	4	8	9	10*	3	2

The manager needs a workforce schedule that provides two consecutive days off and minimizes the amount of total slack capacity. To break ties in the selection of off days, the scheduler gives preference to Saturday–Sunday if it is one of the tied pairs. If not, she selects one of the tied pairs arbitrarily.

SOLUTION

Friday contains the maximum requirements (designated by *), and the pair S–Su has the lowest total requirements. Therefore, employee 1 is scheduled to work Monday–Friday. The revised set of requirements, after scheduling employee 1, is:

Day	M	T	W	Th	F	S	Su
Number of employees	5	3	7	8	9*	3	2

Note that Friday still has the maximum requirements and that the requirements for S–Su are carried forward because these are employee 1's days off. These updated requirements are the ones the scheduler uses for the next employee.

The unique minimum again is on S–Su, so the scheduler assigns employee 2 to a M–F schedule. She then reduces the requirements for M–F to reflect the assignment of employee 2.

The day-off assignments for the remaining employees are shown in Table 12.2. In this example, Friday always has the maximum requirements and should be avoided as a day off. The schedule for the employees is shown in Table 12.3.

TABLE 12.2 *Scheduling Days Off*								

M	T	W	Th	F	S	Su	EMPLOYEE	COMMENTS
4	2	6	7	8*	3	2	3	S–Su has the lowest total requirements. Reduce the requirements to reflect a M–F schedule for employee 3.
3	1	5	6	7*	3	2	4	M–T has the lowest total requirements. Assign employee 4 to a W–Su schedule and update the requirements.
3	1	4	5	6*	2	1	5	S–Su has the lowest total requirements. Assign employee 5 to a M–F schedule and update the requirements.
2	0	3	4	5*	2	1	6	M–T has the lowest total requirements. Assign employee 6 to a W–Su schedule and update the requirements.
2	0	2	3	4*	1	0	7	S–Su has the lowest total requirements. Assign employee 7 to a M–F schedule and update the requirements.
1	0	1	2	3*	1	0	8	Three pairs have the minimum requirement and the lowest total: S–Su, M–T, and T–W. Choose S–Su according to the tie-breaking rule. Assign employee 8 a M–F schedule and update the requirements.
0	0	0	1	2*	1	0	9	Arbitrarily choose Su–M to break ties because S–Su does not have the lowest total requirements. Assign employee 9 to a T–S schedule.
0	0	0	0	1*	0	0	10	Choose S–Su according to the tie-breaking rule. Assign employee 10 a M–F schedule.

TABLE 12.3 *Final Schedule*								

EMPLOYEE	M	T	W	Th	F	S	Su	TOTAL
1	X	X	X	X	X	Off	Off	
2	X	X	X	X	X	Off	Off	
3	X	X	X	X	X	Off	Off	
4	Off	Off	X	X	X	X	X	
5	X	X	X	X	X	Off	Off	
6	Off	Off	X	X	X	X	X	
7	X	X	X	X	X	Off	Off	
8	X	X	X	X	X	Off	Off	
9	Off	X	X	X	X	X	Off	
10	X	X	X	X	X	Off	Off	
Capacity, C	7	8	10	10	10	3	2	50
Requirements, R	6	4	8	9	10	3	2	42
Slack, $C - R$	1	4	2	1	0	0	0	8

Decision Point With its substantial amount of slack capacity, the schedule is not unique. Employee 9, for example, could have Su–M, M–T, or T–W off without causing a capacity shortage. Indeed, the company might be able to get by with one fewer employee because of the total of eight slack days of capacity. However, all ten employees are needed on Fridays. If the manager were willing to get by with only nine employees on Fridays or if someone could work one day of overtime on a rotating basis, he would not need employee 10. As indicated in the table, the net requirement left for employee 10 to satisfy amounts to only one day, Friday. Thus, employee 10 can be used to fill in for vacationing or sick employees.

COMPUTERIZED WORKFORCE SCHEDULING SYSTEMS. Workforce scheduling often entails myriad constraints and concerns. In some types of firms, such as telephone companies, mail-order catalogue houses, or emergency hotline agencies, employees must be on duty 24 hours a day, seven days a week. Sometimes a portion of the staff is part-time, allowing management a great deal of flexibility in developing schedules but adding considerable complexity to the requirements. The flexibility comes from the opportunity to match anticipated loads closely by using overlapping shifts or odd shift lengths; the complexity comes from having to evaluate the numerous possible alternatives. Management also must consider the timing of lunch breaks and rest periods, the number and starting times of shift schedules, and the days off for each employee. An additional typical concern is that the number of employees on duty at any particular time be sufficient to answer calls within a reasonable amount of time.

Computerized scheduling systems are available to cope with the complexity of workforce scheduling. For example, L.L. Bean's telephone service centre must be staffed with telephone operators seven days a week, 24 hours a day. The company uses 350 permanent and temporary employees. The permanent workers are guaranteed a minimum weekly workload apportioned over a seven-day week on a rotating schedule. Temporary staff works a variety of schedules, ranging from a full six-day week to a guaranteed weekly minimum of 20 hours. The company uses a computer program to forecast the hourly load for the telephone service centre, translate the workload into capacity requirements, and then generate week-long staffing schedules for the permanent and temporary telephone operators to meet these demand requirements. The program selects the schedule that minimizes the sum of expected costs of over- and understaffing.

AGGREGATE PLANNING AND SCHEDULING ACROSS THE ORGANIZATION

Aggregate planning is meaningful throughout the organization. First, the aggregate planning process requires managerial inputs from all of a firm's functions and must reconcile sometimes conflicting needs and objectives. Marketing provides inputs on demand and customer requirements, and accounting provides important cost data and the firm's financial condition. One of finance's objectives might be to cut inventory, whereas operations might argue for a more stable workforce and for less reliance on overtime. Second, each function is affected by the plan. An aggregate plan puts into effect decisions on expanding or reducing the size of the workforce, which has a direct impact on the hiring and training requirements for the human resources function. As an aggregate plan is implemented, it creates revenue and cost streams that finance must deal with as it manages the firm's cash flows. Third, each department and group in a firm has its own workforce. Managers of its processes must make choices on hiring, overtime, and vacations. Aggregate planning is an activity for the whole organization.

Schedules are also a part of everyday life, whether the business is a railroad, computer manufacturer, or hospital. Schedules involve an enormous amount of detail and affect every process in the firm. For example, product, service, and employee schedules determine specific cash flow requirements, trigger the billing process, and initiate requirements for the employee training process. The order-fulfillment process depends on good performance in terms of due dates for promised products or services, which is the result of a good scheduling process. In addition, when customers place orders using a Web-based order-entry process, the scheduling process determines when they can expect to receive the product or service. Certainly, regardless of the discipline, schedules affect everyone in a firm.

CHAPTER HIGHLIGHTS

- Aggregate plans (production plans or staffing plans) are statements of strategy that specify time-phased production or service rates, workforce levels, and (in manufacturing) inventory investment. These plans show how the organization will work toward longer-term objectives while considering the demand and capacity that are likely to exist during a planning horizon of only a year or two. In manufacturing organizations, the plan linking strategic goals to the master production schedule is called the production plan. In service organizations, the staffing plan links strategic goals to the workforce schedule.

- To reduce the level of detail required in the planning process, products or services are aggregated into families, and labour is aggregated along product family lines or according to the general skills or services provided. Time is aggregated into periods of months or quarters.

- Managerial inputs are required from the various functional areas in the organization. This approach typically raises conflicting objectives, such as high customer service, a stable workforce, and low inventory investment. Creativity and cross-functional compromise are required to reconcile these conflicts.

- The two basic types of alternatives are capacity and demand. Capacity alternatives take customer demand as a given. Demand alternatives attempt to change the timing or quantity of customer demand to stabilize production or service rates and reduce inventory requirements.

- Two pure, but generally high-cost, planning strategies are the level strategy, which maintains a constant workforce size or production rate, and the chase strategy, which varies workforce level or production rate to match fluctuations in demand.

- Developing aggregate plans is an iterative process of determining demand requirements; identifying relevant constraints, alternatives, and costs; preparing and approving a plan; and implementing and updating the plan.

- Although spreadsheets, linear programming, and other software tools can help analyze complicated alternatives, aggregate planning is primarily an exercise in conflict resolution and compromise. Ultimately, decisions are made by managers, not by quantitative methods.

- Scheduling is the allocation of resources over a period of time to accomplish a specific set of tasks. Two basic types of scheduling are workforce scheduling and operations scheduling.

- Gantt charts are useful for depicting the sequence of work at a particular workstation and for monitoring the progress of customer orders in the system.

- Capacity considerations are important for scheduling services. If the capacity of the operating system is fixed, demand alternatives such as appointments, reservations, and backlogs can be used to level demand. If service is determined by labour availability, workforce scheduling may be appropriate.

- A workforce schedule translates a staffing plan into a specific work schedule for each employee. Typical workforce scheduling considerations include capacity limits, service targets, consecutive days off, maximum number of workdays in a row, type of schedule (fixed or rotating), and vacation and holiday time.

CD-ROM RESOURCES

The Student CD-ROM that accompanies this text contains the following resources, which allow you to further practise and apply the concepts presented in this chapter.

- **Discussion Questions**: Three questions raise important considerations in layoff costs, workforce variability, and a company's responsibilities to a community.

- **Cases**:

  - *Memorial Hospital*: What nurse staffing plan do you propose?

  - *Food King*: What schedule do you propose for stockers and baggers?

- **Experiential Exercise**: Use the *Memorial Hospital* case as an in-class team experience.

- **OM Explorer Tutors**: OM Explorer contains four tutor programs that will help you learn how to implement basic level and chase strategies (five periods), various staffing strategies, and workforce scheduling.

- **OM Explorer Solvers**: OM Explorer has five programs that can be used to solve general aggregate planning problems with spreadsheets, production planning with the transportation method, and workforce scheduling.

- **Extend LT**: *Scheduling Vehicle Repair at Precision Autobody*. While the shop had an excellent reputation for quality, significant improvements were needed to better schedule customer delivery of repairs.

- **Supplement I**: *Linear Programming*. See how linear programming problems can be solved and how both aggregate planning and scheduling problems can be modelled.

- **Supplement J**: *Operations Scheduling*. Read about various scheduling approaches in job shop and flow shop environments.

SOLVED PROBLEM 1

The Cranston Telephone Company employs workers who lay telephone cables and perform various other construction tasks. The company prides itself on good service and strives to complete all service orders within the planning period in which they are received.

Each worker puts in 600 hours of regular time per planning period and can work as many as 100 hours overtime. The operations department has estimated the following workforce requirements for such services over the next four planning periods:

Planning period	1	2	3	4
Demand (hours)	21 000	18 000	30 000	12 000

Cranston pays regular-time wages of $6000 per employee per period for any time worked up to 600 hours (including undertime). The overtime pay rate is $15 per hour after 600 hours. Hiring, training, and outfitting a new employee cost $8000. Layoff costs are $2000 per employee. Currently, 40 employees work for Cranston in this capacity. No delays in service or backorders are allowed. Use the spreadsheet approach to answer the following questions:

a. Develop a level workforce plan that uses only the overtime and undertime alternatives. Maximize the use of overtime during the peak period so as to minimize the workforce level and amount of undertime.

b. Prepare a chase strategy using only the workforce adjustment alternative of hiring and layoffs. What are the total numbers of employees hired and laid off?

c. Propose an effective mixed-strategy plan.

d. Compare the total costs of the three plans.

SOLUTION

a. The peak demand is 30 000 hours in period 3. As each employee can work 700 hours per period (600 on regular time and 100 on overtime), the level workforce that minimizes undertime is 30 000/700 = 42.86, or 43, employees. The level strategy calls for three employees to be hired in the first quarter and for none to be laid off. To convert the demand requirements into employee-period equivalents, divide the demand in hours by 600. For example, the demand of 21 000 hours in period 1 translates into 35 employee-period equivalents (21 000/600) and demand in the third period translates into 50 employee-period equivalents (30 000/600). Figure 12.9 shows one solution using the "level strategy" option of Tutor 12.4.

FIGURE 12.9

Starting workforce	40	Regular-time hrs per worker	600
Regular-time wages	$6 000	Max overtime hrs per worker	100
(per worker per quarter)		Overtime rate ($/hour)	$15
☑ Employees paid for undertime		Cost to hire one worker	$8 000
		Cost to lay off one worker	$2 000

Level Strategy ▼

Required staff level   43

	Quarter				
	1	2	3	4	Total
Requirement (hrs)	21 000	18 000	30 000	12 000	81 000
Workforce level (workers)	43	43	43	43	172
Undertime (hours)	4 800	7 800	0	13 800	26 400
Overtime (hours)	0	0	4 200	0	4 200
Productive time (hours)	21 000	18 000	25 800	12 000	76 800
Hires (workers)	3	0	0	0	3
Layoffs (workers)	0	0	0	0	0
Costs					
Productive time	$210 000	$180 000	$258 000	$120 000	$768 000
Undertime	48 000	78 000	0	138 000	264 000
Overtime	0	0	63 000	0	63 000
Hires	24 000	0	0	0	24 000
Layoffs	0	0	0	0	0
Total Cost					$1 119 000

b. The chase strategy workforce is calculated by dividing the demand for each period by 600 hours, or the amount of regular-time work for one employee during one period. This strategy calls for a total of 20 workers to be hired and 40 to be laid off during the four-period plan. Figure 12.10 shows the "chase strategy" solution that Tutor 12.4 produces.

FIGURE 12.10

Starting workforce	40	Regular-time hrs per worker	600
Regular-time wages (per worker per quarter)	$6 000	Max overtime hrs per worker	100
		Overtime rate ($/hour)	$15
☑ Employees paid for undertime		Cost to hire one worker	$8 000
		Cost to lay off one worker	$2 000
Chase Strategy ▼			
Required staff level	---		

	Quarter				
	1	2	3	4	Total
Requirement (hrs)	21 000	18 000	30 000	12 000	81 000
Workforce level (workers)	35	30	50	20	135
Undertime (hours)	0	0	0	0	0
Overtime (hours)	0	0	0	0	0
Productive time (hours)	21 000	18 000	30 000	12 000	81 000
Hires (workers)	0	0	20	0	20
Layoffs (workers)	5	5	0	30	40
Costs					
Productive time	$210 000	$180 000	$300 000	$120 000	$810 000
Undertime	0	0	0	0	0
Overtime	0	0	0	0	0
Hires	0	0	160 000	0	160 000
Layoffs	10 000	10 000	0	60 000	80 000
Total Cost					$1 050 000

c. The mixed strategy plan that we propose uses a combination of hires, layoffs, and overtime to reduce total costs. The workforce is reduced by 5 at the beginning of the first period, increased by 8 in the third period, and reduced by 13 in the fourth period. Switching to the general-purpose Aggregate Planning with Spreadsheets Solver for this mixed strategy, and hiding any unneeded columns and rows, we get the results shown in Figure 12.11. The Solver can evaluate any aggregate plan that is proposed. Its format is much the same as that for Tutor 12.4, except that the data in the top half of the spreadsheet (above the cost data) are expressed as employee-period equivalents rather than as hours.

FIGURE 12.11

Solver - Aggregate Planning with Spreadsheets

Enter data in yellow-shaded areas.

☑ Employees Paid for Undertime

	1	2	3	4	Total
Requirement	35	30	50	20	135
Workforce level	35	35	43	30	143
Undertime	0	5	0	10	15
Overtime	0	0	7	0	7
Productive time	35	30	43	20	128
Hires	0	0	8	0	8
Layoffs	5	0	0	13	18
Costs	1	2	3	4	Totals
Productive time	$210 000	180 000	258 000	120 000	$768 000
Undertime	$0	30 000	0	60 000	$90 000
Overtime	$0	0	63 000	0	$63 000
Hires	$0	0	64 000	0	$64 000
Layoffs	$10 000	0	0	26 000	$36 000
Total cost	$220 000	210 000	385 000	206 000	$1 021 000

d. The total cost of the level strategy is $1 119 000. The chase strategy results in a total cost of $1 050 000. The mixed-strategy plan was developed by trial and error and results in a total cost of $1 021 000. Further improvements to the mixed strategy are possible.

SOLVED PROBLEM 2

The Food Bin grocery store operates 24 hours per day, seven days per week. Fred Bulger, the store manager, has been analyzing the efficiency and productivity of store operations recently. Bulger decided to observe the need for checkout clerks on the first shift for a one-month period. At the end of the month, he calculated the average number of checkout registers that should be open during the first shift each day. His results showed peak needs on Saturdays and Sundays.

Day	M	T	W	Th	F	S	Su
Number of employees	3	4	5	5	4	7	8

Bulger now has to come up with a workforce schedule that guarantees each checkout clerk two consecutive days off but still covers all requirements.

a. Develop a workforce schedule that covers all requirements while giving two consecutive days off to each clerk. How many clerks are needed? Assume that the clerks have no preference regarding which days they have off.

b. Plans can be made to use the clerks for other duties if slack or idle time resulting from this schedule can be determined. How much idle time will result from this schedule and on what days?

SOLUTION

a. We use the method demonstrated in Example 12.4 to determine the number of clerks needed.

	DAY						
	M	**T**	**W**	**Th**	**F**	**S**	**Su**
Requirements	3	4	5	5	4	7	8*
Clerk 1	Off	Off	X	X	X	X	X
Requirements	3	4	4	4	3	6	7*
Clerk 2	Off	Off	X	X	X	X	X
Requirements	3	4	3	3	2	5	6*
Clerk 3	X	X	X	Off	Off	X	X
Requirements	2	3	2	3	2	4	5*
Clerk 4	X	X	X	Off	Off	X	X
Requirements	1	2	1	3	2	3	4*
Clerk 5	X	Off	Off	X	X	X	X
Requirements	0	2	1	2	1	2	3*
Clerk 6	Off	Off	X	X	X	X	X
Requirements	0	2*	0	1	0	1	2*
Clerk 7	X	X	Off	Off	X	X	X
Requirements	0	1*	0	1*	0	0	1*
Clerk 8	X	X	X	X	Off	Off	X
Requirements	0	0	0	0	0	0	0

*Maximum requirements.

The minimum number of clerks is eight.

b. On the basis of the results in part (a), the number of clerks on duty minus the requirements is the number of idle clerks available for other duties:

	DAY						
	M	T	W	Th	F	S	Su
Number on duty	5	4	6	5	5	7	8
Requirements	3	4	5	5	4	7	8
Idle clerks	2	0	1	0	1	0	0

The slack in this schedule would indicate to Bulger the number of employees he might ask to work part-time (fewer than five days per week). For example, clerk 7 might work Tuesday, Saturday, and Sunday, and clerk 8 might work Tuesday, Thursday, and Sunday to eliminate slack from the schedule.

PROBLEMS

1. The Barberton Municipal Division of Road Maintenance is charged with road repair in the city of Barberton and surrounding area. Cindy Sarker, road maintenance director, must submit a staffing plan for the next year based on a set schedule for repairs and on the city budget. Sarkar estimates that the labour hours required for the next four quarters are 6000, 12 000, 19 000, and 9000, respectively. Each of the 11 workers on the workforce can contribute 500 hours per quarter. Payroll costs are $6000 in wages per worker for regular time worked up to 500 hours, with an overtime pay rate of $18 for each overtime hour. Overtime is limited to 20 percent of the regular-time capacity in any quarter. Although unused overtime capacity has no cost, unused regular time is paid at $12 per hour. The cost to hire a worker is $3000, and the cost to layoff a worker is $2000. Subcontracting is not permitted.

   a. Find a level workforce plan that allows no delay in road repair and minimizes undertime. Overtime can be used to its limits in any quarter. What is the total cost of the plan and how many undertime hours does it call for?

   b. Use a chase strategy that varies the workforce level without using overtime or undertime. What is the total cost of this plan?

   c. Propose a plan of your own. Compare your plan with those in parts (a) and (b) and discuss its comparative merits.

2. Bob Carlton's golf camp estimates the following workforce requirements for its services over the next two years.

Quarter	1	2	3	4
Demand (hours)	4200	6400	3000	4800

Quarter	5	6	7	8
Demand (hours)	4400	6240	3600	4800

Each certified instructor puts in 480 hours per quarter regular time and can work up to 120 hours overtime. Regular-time wages and benefits cost Carlton $7200 per employee per quarter for regular time worked up to 480 hours, with an overtime cost of $20 per hour. Unused regular time for certified instructors is paid at $15 per hour. There is no cost for unused overtime capacity. The cost of hiring, training, and certifying a new employee is $10 000. Layoff costs are $4000 per employee. Currently, eight employees work in this capacity.

   a. Find a level workforce plan that allows for no delay in service and minimizes undertime. What is the total cost of this plan?

   b. Use a chase strategy that varies the workforce level with minimal undertime and without using overtime. What is the total cost of this plan?

   c. Propose a low-cost, mixed-strategy plan and calculate its total cost.

   If total demand is the same, what level of production rate is needed now?

3. Management at Davis Corporation has determined the following demand schedule (in units).

Month	1	2	3	4
Demand	500	800	1000	1400

Month	5	6	7	8
Demand	2000	1600	1400	1200

Month	9	10	11	12
Demand	1000	2400	3000	1000

An employee can produce an average of 10 units per month. Each worker on the payroll costs $2000 in regular-time wages per month. Undertime is paid at the same rate as regular time. In accordance with the labour contract in force, Davis Corporation does not work overtime or use subcontracting. Davis can hire and train a new employee for $2000 and lay one off for $500. Inventory costs $32 per unit on hand at the end of each month. At present, 140 employees are on the payroll.

a. Prepare a production plan with a level workforce strategy. The plan may call for a one-time adjustment of the workforce before month 1.

b. Prepare a production plan with a chase strategy that varies the workforce without undertime, overtime, and subcontracting.

c. Compare and contrast the two pure-strategy plans on the basis of annual costs and other factors that you believe to be important.

d. Propose a mixed-strategy plan that is better than the two pure-strategy plans. Explain why you believe that your plan is better.

4. The Flying Frisbee Company has forecast the following staffing requirements for full-time employees. Demand is seasonal, and management wants three alternative staffing plans to be developed.

Month	1	2	3	4
Requirement	2	2	4	6

Month	5	6	7	8
Requirement	18	20	12	18

Month	9	10	11	12
Requirement	7	3	2	1

The company currently has ten employees. No more than ten new hires can be accommodated in any month because of limited training facilities. No backorders are allowed, and overtime cannot exceed 25 percent of regular-time capacity in any month. There is no cost for unused overtime capacity. Regular-time wages are $1500 per month, and overtime wages are 150 percent of regular-time wages. Undertime is paid at the same rate as regular time. The hiring cost is $2500 per person, and the layoff cost is $2000 per person.

a. Prepare a staffing plan utilizing a level workforce strategy. The plan may call for a one-time adjustment of the workforce before month 1.

b. Using a chase strategy, prepare a plan that is consistent with the constraint on hiring.

c. Prepare a low-cost, mixed-strategy plan.

d. Which strategy is most cost-effective? What are the advantages and disadvantages of each plan?

5. The Twilight Clothing Company makes jeans for children. Management has just prepared a forecast of sales (in pairs of jeans) for next year and now must prepare a production plan. The company has traditionally maintained a level workforce strategy. Currently, there are eight workers, who have been with the company for a number of years. Each employee can produce 2000 pairs of jeans during a two-month planning period. Every year management authorizes overtime in periods 1, 5, and 6, up to a maximum of 20 percent of regular-time capacity. Management wants to avoid stockouts and backorders and will not accept any plan that calls for such shortages. At present, there are 12 000 pairs of jeans in finished goods inventory. The demand forecast is as follows:

Period	1	2	3
Sales	25 000	6 500	15 000

Period	4	5	6
Sales	19 000	32 000	29 000

a. Is the level workforce strategy feasible with the current workforce, assuming that overtime is used only in periods 1, 5, and 6? Explain.

b. Find two alternative plans that would satisfy management's concern over stockouts and backorders, disregarding costs. What trade-offs between these two plans must be considered?

6. Gerald Huang manages the Michaels Distribution Centre. After careful examination of his database information, he has determined the daily requirements for part-time loading dock personnel. The distribution centre operates seven days a week and the daily part-time staffing requirements are:

Day	M	T	W	Th	F	S	Su
Requirements	6	3	5	3	7	2	3

Find the minimum number of workers Huang must hire. Prepare a workforce schedule for these individuals so that each will have two consecutive days off per week and all staffing requirements will be satisfied. Give preference to the pair S–Su in case of a tie.

7. Cara Ryder manages a ski school in a large resort and is trying to develop a schedule for instructors. The instructors receive little salary and work just enough to earn room and board. They do receive free skiing, spending most of their free time tackling the resort's notorious double black diamond slopes. Hence, the instructors work only four days a week. One of the lesson packages offered at the resort is a four-day beginner package. Ryder likes to keep the same instructor with a group over the four-day period, so she schedules the instructors for four consecutive days and then three days off. Ryder uses years of experience with demand forecasts provided by management to formulate her instructor requirements for the upcoming month:

Day	M	T	W	Th	F	S	Su
Requirements	7	5	4	5	6	9	8

a. Determine how many instructors Ryder needs to employ. Give preference to Saturday and Sunday off. *Hint:* Look for the group of three days with lowest requirements.

b. Specify the work schedule for each employee. How much slack does your schedule generate for each day?

8. The mayor of Black Creek, wanting to be environmentally progressive, has decided to implement a recycling plan. All residents of the city will receive a special three-part bin to separate their glass, plastic, and aluminum, and the city will be responsible for picking up the materials. A young city and regional planning graduate, Janet Sanchez, has been hired to manage the recycling program. After carefully studying the city's population density, Sanchez decides that the following numbers of recycling collectors will be needed:

Day	M	T	W	Th	F	S	Su
Requirements	12	7	9	9	5	3	6

The requirements are based on the populations of the various housing developments and subdivisions in the city and surrounding communities. To motivate residents of some areas to have their pickups scheduled on weekends, a special tax break will be given.

a. Find the minimum number of recycling collectors required if each employee works five days a week and has two consecutive days off. Give preference to S-Su when that pair is involved in a tie.

b. Specify the work schedule for each employee. How much slack does your schedule generate for each day?

c. Suppose that Sanchez can smooth the requirements further through greater tax incentives. The requirements then will be 8 on Monday and 7 on the other days of the week. How many employees will be needed now? Find the optimal solution in terms of minimal total slack capacity. Does smoothing of requirements have capital investment implications? If so, what are they?

Additional applications of production-planning problems may be found in Supplement I, "Linear Programming," on the Student CD-ROM.

9. The Bull Grin Company makes a supplement for the animal feed produced by a number of companies. Sales are seasonal, but Bull Grin's customers refuse to stockpile the supplement during slack sales periods. In other words, the customers want to minimize their inventory investments, insist on shipments according to their schedules, and will not accept backorders.

Bull Grin employs manual, unskilled labourers, who require little or no training. Producing 1000 kilograms of supplement costs $830 on regular time and $910 on overtime. There is no cost for unused regular-time, overtime, or subcontractor capacity. These figures include materials, which account for 80 percent of the cost. Overtime is limited to production of a total of 20 000 kilograms per quarter. In addition, subcontractors can be hired at $1000 per thousand kilograms, but only 30 000 kilograms per quarter can be produced this way.

The current level of inventory is 40 000 kilograms, and management wants to end the year at that level. Holding 1000 kilograms of feed supplement in inventory per quarter costs $100. The latest annual forecast is shown in Table 12.4.

Use the spreadsheet approach to find a good production plan and calculate its cost.

10. The Cut Rite Company is a major producer of industrial lawn mowers. The cost to Cut Rite for hiring a semiskilled worker for its assembly plant is $3000 and for laying one off is $2000. The plant averages an output of 36 000 mowers per quarter with its current workforce of 720 employees. Regular-time capacity is directly proportional to the number of employees. Overtime is limited to a maximum of 3000 mowers per quarter, and subcontracting is limited to 1000 mowers per quarter. The costs to produce one mower are $2430 on regular time (including materials), $2700 on overtime, and $3300 via subcontracting. Unused regular-time capacity costs $270 per mower. There is no cost for unused overtime or subcontractor capacity. The current level of inventory is 4000 mowers, and management wants to end the year at that level. Customers do not tolerate backorders, and holding a mower in inventory per quarter costs $300. The demand for mowers this coming year is:

Quarter	1	2	3	4
Demand	10 000	41 000	77 000	44 000

TABLE 12.4 *Forecasts and Capacities*

	PERIOD				
	Quarter 1	Quarter 2	Quarter 3	Quarter 4	TOTAL
Demand (kilograms)	130 000	400 000	800 000	470 000	1 800 000
Capacities (kilograms):					
Regular time	390 000	400 000	460 000	380 000	1 630 000
Overtime	20 000	20 000	20 000	20 000	80 000
Subcontract	30 000	30 000	30 000	30 000	120 000

Two workforce plans have been proposed, and management is uncertain as to which one to use. This table shows the number of employees per quarter under each plan:

Quarter	1	2	3	4
Plan 1	720	780	920	720
Plan 2	860	860	860	860

a. Which plan would you recommend to management? Explain, supporting your recommendation with your own production plan.

b. If management used creative pricing to get customers to buy mowers in nontraditional time periods, the following demand schedule would result:

Quarter	1	2	3	4
Demand	20 000	54 000	54 000	44 000

Which workforce plan would you recommend now?

11. Little 6, Inc., an accounting firm, forecasts the following weekly workload during the tax season:

	DAY						
	M	**T**	**W**	**Th**	**F**	**S**	**Su**
Personal tax returns	24	14	18	18	10	28	16
Corporate tax returns	18	10	12	15	24	12	4

Corporate tax returns each require four hours of an accountant's time, and personal returns each require 90 minutes. During tax season, each accountant can work up to ten hours per day. However, error rates increase to unacceptable levels when accountants work more than five consecutive days per week.

a. Create an effective and efficient work schedule.

b. Assume that Little 6 has three part-time employees available to work three days per week. How could these employees be effectively utilized?

REFERENCES AND FURTHER READINGS

Andrews, B. H., and H. L. Parsons. "L. L. Bean Chooses a Telephone Agent Scheduling System." *Interfaces*, November/December 1989, pp. 1–9.

Armacost, R. L., R. L. Penlesky, and S. C. Ross. "Avoiding Problems Inherent in Spreadsheet-Based Simulation Models—An Aggregate Planning Application." *Production and Inventory Management*, vol. 31 (1990), pp. 62–68.

Ashton, James E., and Frank X. Cook, Jr. "Time to Reform Job Shop Manufacturing." *Harvard Business Review*, March/April 1989, pp. 106–111.

Browne, J. J., and J. Prop. "Supplement to Scheduling Routine Work Hours." *Industrial Engineering*, July 1989, p. 12.

Buxey, G. "Production Planning and Scheduling for Seasonal Demand." *International Journal of Operations and Production Management*, vol. 13 (1993), no. 7, pp. 4–21.

Dillon, Jeffrey E., and Spyros Kontogiorgis. "US Airways Optimizes the Scheduling of Reserve Flight Crews." *Interfaces*, September/October 1999, pp. 123–131.

Fisher, M. L., J. H. Hammond, W. R. Obermeyer, and A. Raman. "Making Supply Meet Demand in an Uncertain World." *Harvard Business Review*, vol. 72 (1994), no. 3, pp. 83–93.

Heskett, J., W. E. Sasser, and C. Hart. *Service Breakthroughs: Changing the Rules of the Game*. New York: The Free Press, 1990.

Lesaint, David, Christos Voudouris, and Nader Azarmi. "Dynamic Workforce Scheduling for British Telecommunications plc." *Interfaces*, January/February 2000, pp. 45–56.

Port, Otis. "Customers Move into the Driver's Seat." *Business Week*, October 4, 1999, pp. 103–106.

Ryan, D. M. "Optimization Earns Its Wings." *OR/MS Today*, vol. 27 (2000), no. 2, pp. 26–30.

Sipper, D., and R. Bulfin. *Production: Planning, Control, and Integration*. New York: McGraw-Hill, 1997.

Tibrewala, R. K., D. Philippe, and J. J. Browne. "Optimal Scheduling of Two Consecutive Idle Periods." *Management Science*, vol. 19 (1972), no. 1, pp. 71–75.

Voet, M., and P. Dewilde. "Choosing a Scheduling Package." *APICS—The Performance Advantage*, November 1994, pp. 28–31.

Vollmann, Thomas E., William Berry, and D. Clay Whybark. *Manufacturing Planning and Control Systems*, 4th ed. Homewood, IL: Irwin Professional Publications, 1997.

13 Resource Planning

Across the Organization

Resource planning is important to:

- **accounting,** which coordinates the payments to suppliers and billings to customers with the resource plan.
- **finance,** which plans for adequate working capital to support the schedules generated in the resource plan.
- **human resources,** which determines the implications of the resource plan on personnel requirements.
- **management information systems,** which must identify the information requirements of managers and the information that can be generated from the resource plan.
- **marketing,** which makes reliable delivery commitments to customers.
- **operations,** which is responsible for inventories and the utilization of the resources required by the firm's processes to meet customer demand.

Learning Goals

After reading this chapter, you will be able to:

1. distinguish between independent and dependent demand and their differences when planning for the replenishment of materials.
2. explain the logic of material requirements planning, how it can be used to plan distribution inventories, and how to schedule the receipt of materials to meet promised delivery dates.
3. identify the key outputs from the resource planning process and how they are used.
4. provide examples of the effective use of manufacturing resource planning and its benefits to various functional areas of the firm.
5. discuss resource planning for service firms.

What do Wrangler or Lee jeans, Timber Creek khakis, Vanity Fair underwear, Healthtex clothes for kids, Jantzen bathing suits, and JanSport backpacks have in common, other than that you can find them in diverse retail outlets such as The Bay, Wal-Mart, and university bookstores? One-hundred-year-old VF Corp. (www.vfc.com), a US$5.5-billion-a-year company in Greensboro, North Carolina, and the world's largest apparel producer, manufactures all of these products and many more. VF's sales had been flat and management initiated a drive to focus its key business processes on identifying and fulfilling customer needs. Moreover, VF's 14 divisions were operated as independent entities—each with its own purchasing, production, marketing, and computer systems—adding to cost. The restructuring resulted in five "coalitions": Jeanswear, Intimates, Playwear, Knitwear, and International Operations and Marketing.

Data on demand for products such as backpacks and outdoor equipment are important inputs for VF's ERP system.

The coalitions need to work together to take advantage of common resources. However, resource planning across such a complex environment poses major challenges. To establish the critical information links between the coalitions, VF decided to install a modified version of SAP's Enterprise Resource Planning (ERP) software specifically designed for apparel and footwear manufacturers as the core integrating system. However, VF also decided to use the *best of breed* implementation strategy, which allowed VF to choose the best applications modules from any vendor or retain some of its own legacy systems. For example, the heart of the ERP system has only four modules: order management, production planning, materials management, and finance.

However, each coalition has its favourite applications from other vendors that have to be included. Intimates uses one vendor's system to cut product design costs and another to optimize materials utilization and assembly-line space. Information is then fed back to the core ERP production planning module. VF's own customized software tracks production in the plants, using information from the production planning, order management, and materials management modules, and then reports back to the core system for the fine-tuning of production plans. Finally, VF has also developed a "micro-marketing" system that forecasts the need for a specific size and colour of particular products, such as Wrangler jeans for the beginning of summer at a particular Wal-Mart store.

Key modules for resource planning in the new system are material requirements planning and capacity planning. The material requirements planning system uses forecasts from the sales and demand planning module to determine the purchase quantities and delivery dates for supplies and materials such as leather, fabric, or linings; the production of finished goods such as jeans, backpacks, or shirts; and the manufacture of assemblies such as shoe soles or bootlegs. The output from material requirements planning can be used by the capacity planning module, which facilitates the planning for critical resources such as skilled employees or specialized equipment to support their production plans.

VF has had a great start but has a long way to go. Jeanswear was the first to completely implement the common systems platform, and Intimates is the next to go online. VF has spent more than US$100 million on the new system, which is not unusual for complex environments such as this one.

Source: Eryn Brown, "VF Corp. Changes Its Underware," *Fortune*, December 7, 1998, pp. 115–118; "SAP Consumer Products for Apparel & Footwear," July 2000; VFC press release, "VF Corporation Launches First Large Scale Apparel Industry-Specific SAP Solution," May 31, 2000.

The VF Corporation demonstrates that companies can gain a competitive edge by integrating processes through an effective operations information system. Maintaining an efficient flow of materials and services from suppliers and managing internal activities relating to materials and other resources are essential to a profitable operation. Operations management ensures that all resources needed to produce finished products or services are available at the right time. For a manufacturer, this task may mean keeping track of thousands of subassemblies, components, and raw materials. For a service provider, this task may mean keeping track of various materials, supplies, and time requirements for many different categories of employees and equipment.

We begin this chapter with a discussion of material requirements planning (MRP), which is a key element of many enterprise resource planning (ERP) systems. We discuss the important concept of dependent demand and all the information inputs to MRP that are used to generate the reports needed for managing manufacturing and distribution inventories as well as other resources. We also devote an entire section to resource planning for service providers and demonstrate how the concept of dependent demands can be used to manage supplies, human resources, equipment, and financial resources. Resource planning techniques are important elements of ERP systems for manufacturers as for well as for service providers (see Chapter 11, "Managing Technology").

OVERVIEW OF MATERIAL REQUIREMENTS PLANNING

material requirements planning (MRP) A computerized information system developed specifically to aid in managing dependent demand inventory and scheduling replenishment orders.

Material requirements planning (MRP)—a computerized information system—was developed specifically to help companies manage dependent demand inventory and schedule replenishment orders. MRP systems have proven to be beneficial to many companies. In this section, we discuss the nature of dependent demands and identify some of the benefits that firms have experienced with these systems.

DEPENDENT DEMAND

dependent demand The quantity required is a function of the demand for other items produced or held in inventory.

parent Any item manufactured from one or more components.

component An item that may go through one or more operations to be transformed into or become part of one or more parents.

To illustrate the concept of dependent demand, let us consider a bicycle produced by Rocky Mountain Bicycle, a fast-growing manufacturer of high-performance bikes, with its operations in Vancouver, B.C. Demand for a final product such as a bicycle is called *independent demand*, because it is influenced only by market conditions and not by demand for any other type of bicycle produced or held in inventory (see Chapter 6, "Inventory Management"). Management must *forecast* that demand on the basis of a variety of market factors. For bicycle models in higher demand, management might decide to hold some inventory at the manufacturing plant to speed delivery. However, another alternative is to keep many of the items used to make completed bicycles in inventory, including frames, wheels and wheel rims, handlebars, and pedals. Each of these items has a **dependent demand**, because the quantity required is directly related to the demand for completed bicycles. Operations can *calculate* the demand for dependent demand items once the production levels for bicycles are established. If a bicycle of a particular style needs two wheels, then 20 completed bicycles need $20(2) = 40$ wheels. Statistical forecasting techniques aren't needed for these wheels.

The bicycle, or any other good manufactured from one or more components, is called a **parent**. The wheel is an example of a **component**—an item that may go through one or more operations to be transformed into or become part of one or more parents. In turn, each wheel is assembled from subcomponents, including a tire and a rim. For complex products, the list of components can be very lengthy, with many components made from other subcomponents. In addition, the wheel might have several different parents, because it might be used for more than one style of bicycle.

The parent–component relationship can cause erratic dependent demand patterns for components. Suppose that every time inventory falls to 10 units (a reorder point), an order for 20 more bicycles is placed, as shown in Figure 13.1(a). The assembly supervisor then authorizes the production of 40 wheels, along with other components for the finished product; demand for the wheel is shown in Figure 13.1(b). So, even though customer demand for the finished chair is continuous and uniform, the production demand for wheels is "lumpy"; that is, it occurs sporadically, usually in relatively large quantities.

FIGURE 13.1

*Lumpy Dependent
Demand Resulting
from Continuous
Independent Demand*

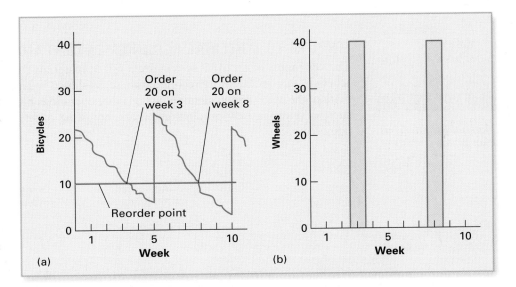

Managing dependent demand inventories is complicated, because some components may be subject to both dependent and independent demand. For example, operations might need 40 wheels for new bicycles, but Rocky Mountain Bicycle can also sell replacement wheels for old bicycles to retail dealers. This practice places an independent demand on the inventory of wheels. Material requirements planning can be used in complex situations involving components that may have independent demand as well as dependent demand inventories.

BENEFITS OF MATERIAL REQUIREMENTS PLANNING

For years, many companies tried to manage production and delivery of dependent demand inventories with independent demand systems, but the outcome was seldom satisfactory. Instead, because an MRP system recognizes dependent demands, the use of MRP enables businesses to reduce inventory levels, utilize labour and facilities better, and improve customer service. These successes are due to three advantages of material requirements planning.

1. Statistical forecasting for components with lumpy demand results in large forecasting errors. Compensating for such errors by increasing safety stock is costly, with no guarantee that stockouts can be avoided. MRP calculates the dependent demand of components from the production schedules of their parents, thereby providing a better forecast of component requirements.

2. MRP systems provide managers with information useful for planning capacities and estimating financial requirements. Production schedules and materials purchases can be translated into capacity requirements and dollar amounts and can be projected in the time periods when they will appear. Planners can use the information on parent item schedules to identify times when needed components may be unavailable because of capacity shortages, supplier delivery delays, and the like.

3. MRP systems automatically update the dependent demand and inventory replenishment schedules of components when the production schedules of parent items change. The MRP system alerts the planners whenever action is needed on any component.

INPUTS TO MATERIAL REQUIREMENTS PLANNING

The key inputs of an MRP system are a bill of materials database, master production schedule, and an inventory record database, as shown in Figure 13.2. Using this information, the MRP system identifies actions that operations must take to stay on schedule, such as releasing new production orders, adjusting order quantities, and expediting late orders.

FIGURE 13.2

Material Requirements Plan Inputs

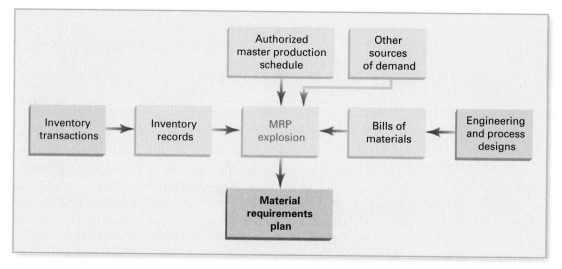

An MRP system translates the master production schedule and other sources of demand, such as independent demand for replacement parts and maintenance items, into the requirements for all subassemblies, components, and raw materials needed to produce the required parent items. This process is called an **MRP explosion**, because it converts the requirements of various final products into a *material requirements plan* that specifies the replenishment schedules of all the subassemblies, components, and raw materials needed by the final products.

MRP explosion A process that converts the requirements of various final products into a material requirements plan that specifies the replenishment schedules of all the subassemblies, components, and raw materials needed by the final products.

BILL OF MATERIALS

The replenishment schedule for a component is determined from the production schedules of its parents. Hence, the system needs accurate information on parent–component relationships. A **bill of materials (BOM)** is a record of all the components of an item, the parent–component relationships, and usage quantities derived from engineering

bill of materials (BOM) A record of all the components of an item, the parent–component relationships, and usage quantities derived from engineering and process designs.

usage quantity The number of units of a component needed to make one unit of its immediate parent.

and process designs. In Figure 13.3, the BOM of a simple ladder-back chair shows that the chair is made from a ladder-back subassembly, a seat subassembly, legs, and leg supports. In turn, the ladder-back subassembly is made from legs and back slats, and the seat subassembly is made from a seat frame and a cushion. Finally, the seat frame is made from seat-frame boards. For convenience, we refer to these items by the letters shown in Figure 13.3.

All items except A are components because they are needed to make a parent. Items A, B, C, and H are parents, because they all have at least one component. The BOM also specifies the **usage quantity**, or the number of units of a component needed to make one unit of its immediate parent. Figure 13.3 shows usage quantities for each parent–component relationship in parentheses. Note that one chair (item A) is made from one ladder-back subassembly (item B), one seat subassembly (item C), two front legs (item D), and four leg supports (item E). In addition, item B is made from two back

FIGURE 13.3

Bill of Materials for a Ladder-Back Chair

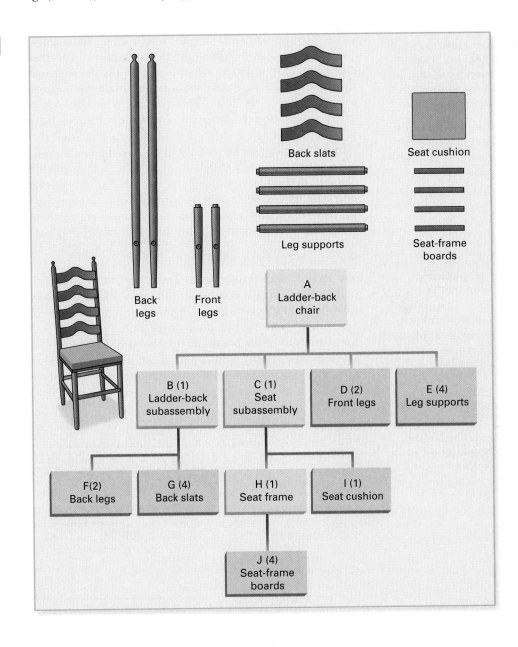

legs (item F) and four back slats (item G). Item C needs one seat frame (item H) and one seat cushion (item I). Finally, item H needs four seat-frame boards (item J).

Four terms frequently used to describe inventory items are end items, intermediate items, subassemblies, and purchased items. An **end item** typically is the final product sold to the customer; it is a parent but not a component. Item A in Figure 13.3, the completed ladder-back chair, is an end item. Accounting statements classify inventory of end items as either work-in-process (WIP), if work remains to be done, or finished goods. An **intermediate item** is one such as B, C, or H that has at least one parent and at least one component. Some products have several levels of intermediate items; the parent of one intermediate item also is an intermediate item. Inventory of intermediate items—whether completed or still on the shop floor—is classified as WIP. A **subassembly** is an intermediate item that is *assembled* (as opposed to being transformed by other means) from *more* than one component. Items B and C are subassemblies. A **purchased item** has no components, because it comes from a supplier, but it has one or more parents. Examples are items D, E, F, G, I, and J in Figure 13.3. Inventory of purchased items is treated as raw materials in accounting statements.

A component may have more than one parent. **Part commonality**, sometimes called *standardization of parts* or *modularity*, is the degree to which a component has more than one immediate parent. As a result of commonality, the same item may appear in several places in the bill of materials for a product, or it may appear in the bills of materials for several different products. For example, the seat assembly in Figure 13.3 is a component of the ladder-back chair and of a kitchen chair that is part of the same family of products. The usage quantity specified in the bill of materials relates to a specific parent–component relationship. The usage quantity for any component can change, depending on the parent item. Part commonality increases volume and repeatability for some items—which has advantages for new product introduction, process design, and quality—and helps minimize inventory costs. Today, with the need for greater efficiency in all firms, part commonality is used extensively.

MASTER PRODUCTION SCHEDULE

The second input into a material requirements plan is the **master production schedule (MPS)**, which details how many end items will be produced within specified periods of time. It breaks down the aggregate plan (see Chapter 12, "Aggregate Planning and Scheduling") into specific product schedules. Figure 13.4 shows how an aggregate plan for a family of chairs breaks down into the weekly master production schedule for each specific chair type (the time period can be hours, days, weeks, or months). Here the scheduled quantities are shown in the week they must be released to the plant to start

end item The final product sold to a customer.

intermediate item An item that has at least one parent and at least one component.

subassembly An intermediate item that is *assembled* (as opposed to being transformed by other means) from *more* than one component.

purchased item An item that has one or more parents but no components because it comes from a supplier.

part commonality The degree to which a component has more than one immediate parent.

master production schedule (MPS) A part of the material requirements plan that details how many end items will be produced within specified periods of time.

FIGURE 13.4

Master Production Schedule for a Family of Chairs

	April				May			
	1	2	3	4	5	6	7	8
Ladder-back chair	150					150		
Kitchen chair				120			120	
Desk chair		200	200		200			200
Aggregate production plan for chair family	670				670			

final assembly so as to meet customer delivery promises, based on the MPS. The chair example demonstrates the following aspects of master scheduling:

1. Total quantities of all end items, that is, ladder-back, kitchen, and desk chairs, in the MPS must equal those in the aggregate production plan. This consistency between the plans is needed because of the capacity and economic analysis done earlier to develop the best aggregate plan.

2. Production quantities must be allocated efficiently over time. The specific mix of chair types—the amount of each type as a percentage of the total aggregate quantity—is based on historical demand and marketing and promotional considerations. The planner must select lot sizes for each chair type, taking into consideration economic factors such as production setup costs and inventory carrying costs.

3. Capacity limitations, such as machine or labour capacity, and other resources, such as storage space and working capital, differ between chair styles. These factors must be taken into account when setting the timing and size of the production quantities.

The MPS is then used by the MRP system to determine the timing and quantities of components needed. Further details of how to develop the MPS are contained in Supplement K, "Master Production Scheduling," on the Student CD-ROM.

INVENTORY RECORDS

inventory record A record that shows an item's lot-size policy, lead time, and various time-phased data.

Inventory records are the final input to MRP, and the basic building blocks of up-to-date records are inventory transactions (see Figure 13.2 on page 430). Transactions include releasing new orders, receiving scheduled receipts, adjusting due dates for scheduled receipts, withdrawing inventory, cancelling orders, correcting inventory errors, rejecting shipments, and verifying scrap losses and stock returns. Recording such transactions is essential for maintaining the accurate records of on-hand inventory balances and scheduled receipts necessary for an effective MRP system.

The **inventory record** divides the future into time periods called *time buckets*. In our discussion, we use weekly time buckets for consistency with our MPS example, although other time periods could as easily be used. The inventory record shows an item's lot-size policy, lead time, and various time-phased data. The purpose of the inventory record is to keep track of inventory levels and component replenishment needs. The time-phased information contained in the inventory record consists of (1) gross requirements, (2) schedule receipts, (3) projected on-hand inventory, (4) planned receipts, and (5) planned order releases. We illustrate the discussion of inventory records with the seat subassembly, item C, shown in Figure 13.3 on page 431. It is used in two products: a ladder-back chair and a kitchen chair.

gross requirements The total demand derived from *all* parent production plans.

GROSS REQUIREMENTS. The **gross requirements** are the total demand derived from *all* parent production plans. They also include demand not otherwise accounted for, such as demand for replacement parts for units already sold. Figure 13.5 shows an inventory record for item C, the seat subassembly. Item C is produced in lots of 230 units and has a lead time of two weeks. The inventory record also shows item C's gross requirements for the next eight weeks, which come from the master production schedules for the ladder-back and kitchen chairs (see Figure 13.4). If both types of chairs were produced in the same week, these quantities would be added together. The seat subassembly's gross requirements exhibit lumpy demand: operations will withdraw seat subassemblies from inventory in only four of the eight weeks.

FIGURE 13.5

*Material Requirements
Planning Record for
the Seat Subassembly*

Item: C						Lot Size: 230 units		
Description: Seat subassembly						Lead Time: 2 weeks		

	Week							
	1	2	3	4	5	6	7	8
Gross requirements	150	0	0	120	0	150	120	0
Scheduled receipts	230	0	0	0	0	0	0	0
Projected on-hand inventory 37	117	117	117	−3	−3	−153	−273	−273
Planned receipts								
Planned order releases								

Explanation:
Gross requirements are the total demand for
the two chairs. Projected on-hand inventory
in week 1 is 37 + 230 − 150 = 117 units.

The MRP system works with release dates to schedule production and delivery for components and subassemblies. Its program logic anticipates the removal of all materials required by a parent's production order from inventory at the *beginning* of the parent item's lead time—when the scheduler first releases the order to the shop.

SCHEDULED RECEIPTS. Recall that *scheduled receipts* (sometimes called *open orders*) are orders that have been placed but not yet completed. For a purchased item, the scheduled receipt could be in one of several stages: being processed by a supplier, being transported to the purchaser, or being inspected by the purchaser's receiving department. If production is making the item in-house, the order could be on the shop floor being processed, waiting for components, waiting in queue, or waiting to be moved to its next operation. According to Figure 13.5, one 230-unit order of item C is due in week 1. Given the two-week lead time, the inventory planner released the order two weeks ago.

projected on-hand inventory An estimate of the amount of inventory available each week after gross requirements have been satisfied.

PROJECTED ON-HAND INVENTORY. The **projected on-hand inventory** is an estimate of the amount of inventory available each week after gross requirements have been satisfied. The beginning inventory, shown as the first entry (37) in Figure 13.5, indicates on-hand inventory available at the time the record was computed. As with scheduled receipts, entries are made for each actual withdrawal and receipt to update the MRP database. Then, when the MRP system produces the revised record, the correct inventory will appear.

Other entries in the row show inventory expected in future weeks. Projected on-hand inventory is calculated as:

$$\begin{pmatrix} \text{Projected on-hand} \\ \text{inventory balance} \\ \text{at end of week } t \end{pmatrix} = \begin{pmatrix} \text{Inventory on} \\ \text{hand at end of} \\ \text{week } t-1 \end{pmatrix} + \begin{pmatrix} \text{Scheduled} \\ \text{or planned} \\ \text{receipts in} \\ \text{week } t \end{pmatrix} - \begin{pmatrix} \text{Gross} \\ \text{requirements} \\ \text{in week } t \end{pmatrix}$$

planned receipts Orders that are not yet released to the shop or the supplier.

The projected on-hand calculation includes the consideration of **planned receipts,** which are orders not yet released to the shop or the supplier. In any week, there will never be both a scheduled receipt and a planned receipt. In Figure 13.5, the planned receipts are all zero. The on-hand inventory calculations for each week are:

Week 1:	37	+	230	−	150	=	117
Weeks 2 and 3:	117	+	0	−	0	=	117
Week 4:	117	+	0	−	120	=	−3
Week 5:	−3	+	0	−	0	=	−3
Week 6:	−3	+	0	−	150	=	−153
Week 7:	−153	+	0	−	120	=	−273
Week 8:	−273	+	0	−	0	=	−273

In week 4, the balance drops to –3 units; this indicates that a shortage of 3 units will occur unless more seat subassemblies are built. This condition signals the need for a planned receipt to arrive in week 4. In addition, unless more stock is received, the shortage will grow to 273 units in weeks 7 and 8.

PLANNED RECEIPTS. Planning for receipt of new orders will keep the projected on-hand balance from dropping below zero. The planned receipt row is developed as follows:

1. Weekly on-hand inventory is projected until a shortage appears. Completion of the initial planned receipt is scheduled for the week when the shortage is projected. The addition of the newly planned receipt should raise the projected on-hand balance so that it equals or exceeds zero. It will exceed zero when the lot size exceeds requirements in the week it is planned to arrive.

2. Projection of on-hand inventory continues until the next shortage occurs. This shortage signals the need for the second planned receipt.

This process is repeated until the end of the planning horizon by proceeding column by column through the MRP record—filling in planned receipts as needed and completing the projected on-hand inventory row. Figure 13.6 shows the planned receipts for the seat subassembly. In week 4, the projected on-hand inventory will drop below zero, so a planned receipt of 230 units is scheduled for week 4. The updated inventory on-hand balance is 117 (inventory at end of week 3) + 230 (planned receipts) − 120 (gross requirements) = 227 units. The projected on-hand inventory remains at 227 for week 5, because there are no scheduled receipts or gross requirements. In week 6, the projected on-hand inventory is 227 (inventory at end of week 5) − 150 (gross requirements) = 77 units. This quantity is greater than zero, so no new planned receipt is needed. In week 7, however, a shortage will occur unless more seat subassemblies are received. With a planned receipt in week 7, the updated inventory balance is 77 (inventory at end of week 6) + 230 (planned receipts) − 120 (gross requirements) = 187 units.

FIGURE 13.6

Completed Inventory Record for the Seat Subassembly

Item: C Description: Seat subassembly							Lot Size: 230 units Lead Time: 2 weeks	

	Week							
	1	2	3	4	5	6	7	8
Gross requirements	150	0	0	120	0	150	120	0
Scheduled receipts	230	0	0	0	0	0	0	0
Projected on-hand inventory 37	117	117	117	227	227	77	187	187
Planned receipts				230			230	
Planned order releases		230			230			

Explanation:
Without a new order in week 4, there will be a shortage of 3 units: 117 + 0 + 0 – 120 = –3 units. Adding the planned receipt brings the balance to 117 + 0 + 230 – 120 = 227 units. Offsetting for a two-week lead time puts the corresponding planned order release back to week 2.

Explanation:
The first planned order lasts until week 7, when projected inventory would drop to 77 + 0 + 0 – 120 = –43 units. Adding the second planned receipt brings the balance to 77 + 0 + 230 – 120 = 187 units. The corresponding planned order release is for week 5 (or week 7 minus 2 weeks).

planned order release
An indication of when an order for a specified quantity of an item is to be issued.

PLANNED ORDER RELEASES. A **planned order release** indicates when an order for a specified quantity of an item is to be issued. We must place the planned order release quantity in the proper time bucket. To do so, we must assume that all inventory flows—scheduled receipts, planned receipts, and gross requirements—occur at the same point of time in a time period. Some firms assume that all flows occur at the beginning of a time period; others assume that they occur at the end of a time period or at the middle of the time period. Regardless of when the flows are assumed to occur, we find the release date by subtracting the lead time from the receipt date. For example, the release date for the first planned order release in Figure 13.6 is 4 (planned receipt date) − 2 (lead time) = 2 (planned order release date). Figure 13.6 shows the planned order releases for the seat subassembly.

PLANNING FACTORS

The planning factors in an MRP inventory record play an important role in the overall performance of the MRP system. By manipulating these factors, managers can fine-tune inventory operations. In this section, we discuss the planning lead time, the lot-sizing rule, and safety stock.

PLANNING LEAD TIME

Planning lead time is an estimate of the time between placing an order for an item and receiving it in inventory. Accuracy is important in planning lead time. If an item arrives in inventory sooner than needed, inventory holding costs increase. If an item arrives too late, stockouts or excessive expediting costs (or both) may occur.

For purchased items, the planning lead time is the time allowed for receiving a shipment from the supplier after the order has been sent, including the normal time to place the order. Often, the purchasing contract stipulates the delivery date. For items manufactured in-house, the planning lead time consists of estimates for:

- Setup time
- Process time
- Materials handling time between operations
- Waiting time

Each of these times must be estimated for every operation along the item's route.

LOT-SIZING RULES

A lot-sizing rule determines the timing and size of order quantities. A lot-sizing rule must be assigned to each item before planned receipts and planned order releases can be computed. The choice of lot-sizing rules is important, because they determine the number of setups required and the inventory holding costs for each item. We present three lot-sizing rules: fixed order quantity, periodic order quantity, and lot-for-lot.

fixed order quantity (FOQ)
A rule that maintains the same order quantity each time an order is issued.

FIXED ORDER QUANTITY. The **fixed order quantity (FOQ)** rule maintains the same order quantity each time an order is issued. For example, the lot size might be the size dictated by equipment capacity limits, as when a full lot must be loaded into a furnace at one time. For purchased items, the FOQ could be determined by the quantity discount level, truck-load capacity, or minimum purchase quantity. Alternatively, the lot size could be determined by the economic order quantity (EOQ) formula (see Chapter 6, "Inventory Management"). Figure 13.6 illustrates the FOQ rule. However, if an item's gross requirement within a week is particularly large, the FOQ might be insufficient to avoid a shortage. In such unusual cases, the inventory planner must increase the lot size beyond the FOQ, typically to a size large enough to avoid a shortage. Another option is to make the order quantity an integer multiple of the FOQ. This option is appropriate when capacity constraints limit production to FOQ sizes (at most) and setup costs are high.

periodic order quantity (POQ) A rule that allows a different order quantity for each order issued but tends to issue the order at predetermined time intervals.

PERIODIC ORDER QUANTITY. The **periodic order quantity (POQ)** rule allows a different order quantity for each order issued but tends to issue the order at predetermined time intervals, such as every two weeks. The order quantity equals the amount of the item needed during the predetermined time between orders and must be large enough to prevent shortages. Specifically, the POQ is:

$$\begin{pmatrix} \text{POQ lot size} \\ \text{to arrive in} \\ \text{week } t \end{pmatrix} = \begin{pmatrix} \text{Total gross requirements} \\ \text{for } P \text{ weeks, including} \\ \text{week } t \end{pmatrix} - \begin{pmatrix} \text{Projected on-hand} \\ \text{inventory balance at} \\ \text{end of week } t - 1 \end{pmatrix}$$

This amount exactly covers P weeks' worth of gross requirements. That is, the projected on-hand inventory should equal zero at the end of the Pth week. The POQ rule does *not* mean that operations must issue a new order every P weeks. Rather, when an order *is* planned, its lot size must be enough to cover P successive weeks. One way to select a P value is to divide the average lot size desired, such as the EOQ (see Chapter 6, "Inventory Management"), or some other applicable lot size, by the average weekly demand. That is, express the target lot size as desired weeks of supply (P) and round to the nearest integer. See Solved Problem 2 on page 452 for a detailed example of the POQ rule.

lot-for-lot (L4L) A rule under which the lot size ordered covers the gross requirements of a single week.

LOT-FOR-LOT. A special case of the POQ rule is the **lot-for-lot (L4L)** rule, under which the lot size ordered covers the gross requirements of a single week. Thus, $P = 1$, and the goal is to minimize inventory levels. This rule ensures that the planned order is just large enough to prevent a shortage in the single week it covers. The L4L lot size is:

$$\begin{pmatrix} \text{L4L lot size} \\ \text{to arrive in} \\ \text{week } t \end{pmatrix} = \begin{pmatrix} \text{Gross requirements} \\ \text{for week } t \end{pmatrix} - \begin{pmatrix} \text{Projected on-hand} \\ \text{inventory balance at} \\ \text{the end of week } t - 1 \end{pmatrix}$$

The projected on-hand inventory combined with the new order will equal zero at the end of week t. Following the first planned order, an additional planned order will be used to match each subsequent gross requirement. See Solved Problem 2 for a detailed example of the L4L rule.

COMPARISON OF LOT-SIZING RULES. Choosing a lot-sizing rule can have important implications for inventory management. Lot-sizing rules affect inventory costs and setup or ordering costs. The FOQ, POQ, and L4L rules differ from one another in one or both respects. We can make the following three generalizations:

1. The FOQ rule generates a high level of average inventory because it creates inventory *remnants*. A remnant is inventory carried into a week that is too small to prevent a shortage. Remnants occur because the FOQ does not match requirements exactly. For example, according to Figure 13.6 on page 436, the stockroom must receive a planned order in week 7, even though 77 units are on hand at the beginning of that week. The remnant is the 77 units that the stockroom will carry for three weeks, beginning with receipt of the first planned order in week 4. Although they increase average inventory levels, inventory remnants introduce stability into the production process by buffering unexpected scrap losses, capacity bottlenecks, inaccurate inventory records, or unstable gross requirements.

2. The POQ rule reduces the amount of average on-hand inventory because it does a better job of matching order quantity to requirements. It adjusts lot sizes as requirements increase or decrease.

3. The L4L rule minimizes inventory investment, but it also maximizes the number of orders placed. This rule is most applicable to expensive items or items with small ordering or setup costs. It is the only rule that can be used for a low-volume item made to order.

By avoiding remnants, both the POQ and the L4L rule may actually *introduce* instability by tying the lot-sizing decision so closely to requirements. If any requirement changes, so must the lot size, which can disrupt component schedules. Last-minute increases in parent orders may be hindered by missing components.

SAFETY STOCK

An important managerial issue is the quantity of safety stock needed. It is more complex for dependent demand items than for independent demand items. Safety stock for dependent demand items with lumpy demand (gross requirements) is valuable only when future gross requirements, the timing or size of scheduled receipts, and the amount of scrap are uncertain. Safety stock should be reduced and ultimately removed as the causes of the uncertainty are eliminated. The usual policy is to use safety stock for end items and purchased items to protect against fluctuating customer orders and unreliable suppliers of components, and to avoid using safety stock as much as possible for intermediate items. Safety stocks can be incorporated in the MRP logic by scheduling a planned receipt whenever the projected on-hand inventory balance drops below the desired safety stock level (rather than to zero, as before). The objective is to keep a minimum level of planned inventories equal to the safety stock quantity. Figure 13.7 shows what happens when there is a requirement for 80 units of safety stock for the seat assembly using a FOQ of 230 units. Compare these results to Figure 13.6 on page 436. The net effect is to move the second planned order release from week 5 to week 4 to avoid going below 80 units in week 6.

Inventory Record for the Seat Subassembly Showing the Application of a Safety Stock

Tutor: FOQ, POQ, and L4L Rules								
FOQ Rule						Lot Size		230
						Lead Time		2
						Safety Stock		80
	1	2	3	4	5	6	7	8
Gross Requirements	150	0	0	120	0	150	120	0
Scheduled Receipts	230	0	0	0	0	0	0	0
Projected On-Hand Inventory 37	117	117	117	227	227	307	187	187
Planned Receipts	0	0	0	230	0	230	0	0
Planned Order Releases	0	230	0	230	0	0	0	0

OUTPUTS FROM MRP

Material requirements planning systems provide many reports, schedules, and notices to help managers control dependent demand inventories, as indicated in Figure 13.8. In this section, we discuss the MRP explosion process, action notices that alert managers to items needing attention, and capacity reports that project the capacity requirements implied by the material requirements plan.

MRP EXPLOSION

MRP translates, or *explodes*, the master production schedule and other sources of demand into the requirements for all subassemblies, components, and raw materials needed to produce parent items. This process generates the material requirements plan for each component item.

An item's gross requirements are derived from three sources:

1. MPS for immediate parents that are end items

2. Planned order releases for parents below the MPS level

3. Other requirements not originating in the MPS, such as the demand for replacement parts

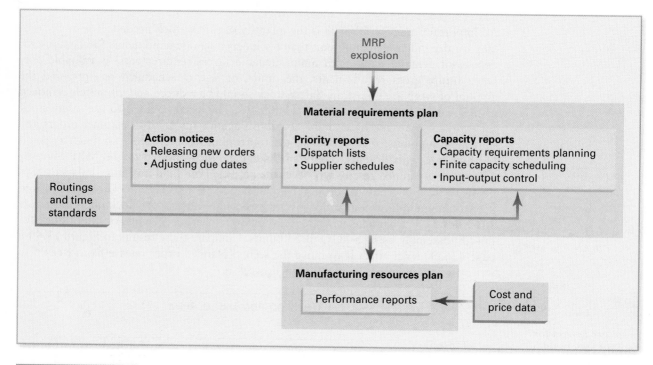

*Material Requirements
Planning Outputs*

Consider the seat subassembly (item C) for which we have developed the inventory record shown in Figure 13.6 on page 436. The seat subassembly requires a seat cushion and a seat frame, which in turn `needs four seat-frame boards. Its BOM is shown in Figure 13.3 on page 431. How many seat cushions should we order from the supplier? How many seat frames should we produce to support the seat subassembly schedule? How many seat-frame boards do we need to make? The answers to these questions depend on the inventories we already have of these items and the replenishment orders already in progress. MRP can help answer these questions through the explosion process.

Figure 13.9 shows the MRP records for the seat subassembly and its components. We have already shown how to develop the MRP record for the seat subassembly. We now concentrate on the MRP records of its components. The lot-size rules are an FOQ of 300 units for the seat frame, L4L for the seat cushion, and an FOQ of 1500 for the seat-frame boards. All three components have a one-week lead time. The key to the explosion process is to determine the proper timing and size of the gross requirements for each component. When we have done that, we can derive the planned order release schedule for each component by using the logic we have already demonstrated.

In our example, the components have no independent demand for replacement parts. Consequently, in Figure 13.9, the gross requirements of a component come from the planned order releases of its parents. The seat frame and the seat cushion get their gross requirements from the planned order release schedule of the seat subassembly. Both components have gross requirements of 230 units in weeks 2 and 5, the same weeks in which we will be releasing orders to make more seat subassemblies. In week 2, for example, the materials handler for the assembly department will withdraw 230 seat frames and 230 seat cushions from inventory so that the assembly department can produce the seat subassemblies in time to avoid a stockout in week 4. The materials plans for the seat frame and the seat cushion must allow for that.

Using the gross requirements in weeks 2 and 5, we can develop the MRP records for the seat frame and the seat cushion, as shown in Figure 13.9. For a scheduled

| FIGURE 13.9 | *MRP Explosion of Seat Assembly Components* |

Item: Seat subassembly
Lot size: 230 units

Lead time: 2 weeks	Week							
	1	2	3	4	5	6	7	8
Gross requirements	150	0	0	120	0	150	120	0
Scheduled receipts	230	0	0	0	0	0	0	0
Projected inventory 37	117	117	117	227	227	77	187	187
Planned receipts				230			230	
Planned order releases		230			230			

Usage quantity: 1   Usage quantity: 1

Item: Seat frames
Lot size: 300 units

Lead time: 1 week	Week							
	1	2	3	4	5	6	7	8
Gross requirements	0	230	0	0	230	0	0	0
Scheduled receipts	0	300	0	0	0	0	0	0
Projected inventory 40	40	110	110	110	180	180	180	180
Planned receipts				300				
Planned order releases			300					

Item: Seat cushion
Lot size: L4L

Lead time: 1 week	Week							
	1	2	3	4	5	6	7	8
Gross requirements	0	230	0	0	230	0	0	0
Scheduled receipts	0	0	0	0	0	0	0	0
Projected inventory 0	0	0	0	0	0	0	0	0
Planned receipts		230			230			
Planned order releases	230			230				

Usage quantity: 4

Item: Seat-frame boards
Lot size: 1500 units

Lead time: 1 week	Week							
	1	2	3	4	5	6	7	8
Gross requirements	0	0	0	1200	0	0	0	0
Scheduled receipts	0	0	0	0	0	0	0	0
Projected inventory 200	200	200	200	500	500	500	500	500
Planned receipts				1500				
Planned order releases			1500					

receipt of 300 in week 2, an on-hand quantity of 40 units, and a lead time of one week, we need to release an order of 300 seat frames in week 4 to cover the assembly schedule for the seat subassembly. The seat cushion has no scheduled receipts and no inventory on hand; consequently, we must place orders for 230 units in weeks 1 and 4, using the L4L logic with a lead time of one week.

Once we have determined the replenishment schedule for the seat frame, we can calculate the gross requirements for the seat-frame boards. We plan to begin producing 300 seat frames in week 4. Each frame requires 4 boards, so we need to have 300(4) = 1200 boards available in week 4. Consequently, the gross requirement for seat-frame boards is 1200 in week 4. Given no scheduled receipts, 200 boards in stock, a lead time of one week, and an FOQ of 1500 units, we need a planned order release of 1500 in week 3.

The questions we posed earlier can now be answered. The following orders must be released: 300 seat frames in week 4, 230 seat cushions in each of weeks 1 and 4, and 1500 seat-frame boards in week 3.

ACTION NOTICES

action notice A computer-generated memo used by inventory planners to make decisions about releasing new orders and adjusting the due dates of scheduled receipts.

Once computed, inventory records for any item appearing in the bills of materials can be printed in hard copy or displayed on a computer screen. Inventory planners use a computer-generated memo called an **action notice** to make decisions about releasing new orders and adjusting the due dates of scheduled receipts. These notices are generated every time the system is updated. The action notice alerts planners to only the items that need their attention such as those items that have a planned order release in the current period or those that need their due dates adjusted because of changes to parent item schedules or the availability of raw materials and components. They can then view the full records for those items and take the necessary actions. An action notice can simply be a list of part numbers for items needing attention. Or it can be the full record for such items, with a note at the bottom identifying the action needed.

CAPACITY REPORTS

By itself, the MRP system does not recognize capacity limitations when computing planned orders. That is, it may call for a planned order release that exceeds the amount that can be physically produced. An essential role of managers is to monitor the capacity requirements of material requirements plans, adjusting a plan when it cannot be met. In this section, we discuss two sources of information for short-term decisions that materials managers continually make: capacity requirements planning reports and finite capacity scheduling reports.

capacity requirements planning (CRP) A technique used for projecting time-phased capacity requirements for workstations; its purpose is to match the material requirements plan with the plant's production capacity.

CAPACITY REQUIREMENTS PLANNING. One technique for projecting time-phased capacity requirements for workstations is **capacity requirements planning** (CRP). Its purpose is to match the material requirements plan with the plant's production capacity. The technique is used to calculate workload according to work required to complete the scheduled receipts already in the shop and to complete the planned order releases not yet released. This task involves the use of the inventory records, which supply the planned order releases and the status of the scheduled receipts; the item's routing, which specifies the workstations that must process the item; average lead times between each workstation; and the average processing and setup times at each workstation. Using the MRP dates for arrival of replenishment orders for an item to avoid shortages, CRP traces back through the item's routing to estimate when the scheduled receipt or planned order will reach each workstation. The system uses the processing and setup times to estimate the load that the item will impose on each station for each planned order and scheduled receipt of the item. The workloads for each workstation are obtained by adding the time that each item needs at a particular workstation. Critical workstations are those at which the projected loads exceed station capacities.

Figure 13.10 shows a capacity requirements report for a lathe station that turns wooden table legs. Each of four lathes is scheduled for two shifts per day. The lathe station has a maximum capacity of 320 hours per week. The *planned* hours represent labour requirements for all planned orders for items that need to be routed through the lathe station. The *actual* hours represent the backlog of work visible on the shop floor (i.e., scheduled receipts). Combining requirements from both sources gives *total* hours. Comparing total hours to actual capacity constraints gives advance warning of any potential problems. The planner must manually resolve any capacity problems uncovered.

FIGURE 13.10

Capacity Requirements Planning Report

Date:				Week: 32		
Plant 01 Dept. 03: Lathe Station						
Capacity: 320 hours per week						
	Week					
	32	33	34	35	36	37
Planned hours	90	156	349	210	360	280
Actual hours	210	104	41	0	0	0
Total hours	300	260	390	210	360	280

Explanation:
Projected capacity requirements exceed weekly hours of capacity.

For example, the CRP report shown in Figure 13.10 would alert the planner to the need for scheduling adjustments. Unless something is done, the current capacity of 320 hours per week will be exceeded in week 34 and again in week 36. Requirements for all other time periods are well below the capacity limit. Perhaps the best choice is to release some orders earlier than planned so that they will arrive at the lathe station in weeks 32, 33, and 35 rather than weeks 34 and 36. This adjustment will help smooth capacity and alleviate bottlenecks. Other options might be to change the lot sizes of some items, use overtime, subcontract, offload to another workstation, or simply allow backlogs to occur, with the associated late delivery.

FINITE CAPACITY SCHEDULING. In large production facilities, thousands of orders may be in progress at any one time. Manually adjusting the timing of these orders with the use of spreadsheets or wall-mounted magnetic schedule boards is virtually impossible. The best solutions—those that meet the MRP schedule due dates and do not violate any constraints—may never be identified, because of the time needed to explore the alternatives. A useful tool for these situations is a **finite capacity scheduling (FCS)** system, which is an algorithm designed to schedule a group of orders appropriately across an entire manufacturing plant. Using resource constraints, part routings, available capacity, shift patterns, and workstation scheduling rules, the system determines the priorities for orders (see Supplement J, "Operations Scheduling," on the Student CD-ROM).

To be effective, the FCS system needs to be integrated with MRP. The MRP system can download the orders that need to be scheduled, but the FCS system needs much more than that. An FCS system operates at a finer level of detail than MRP and needs to know the status of each machine and when the current order will finish processing, the maintenance schedule, the routings, the setup times, machine speeds and capabilities, and resource capacities, for example. The FCS system uses that information to determine actual, realistic start and end times of jobs and uploads the results to MRP for subsequent replanning. The FCS system provides a more accurate picture than MRP of when the orders will be completed, because MRP uses estimates for job waiting times in job lead times, does not recognize capacities when making the materials plans, and often uses aggregated time buckets (e.g., weeks). If these realistic completion times conflict with the MRP schedule, it may have to be revised and the FCS system rerun. Many companies are using advanced planning and scheduling (APS) systems that link their FCS and MRP systems to their ERP and supply chain management systems (see Chapter 12, "Aggregate Planning and Scheduling").

LINKS TO FUNCTIONAL AREAS

The basic MRP system has its roots in the batch manufacturing of discrete parts involving assemblies that must be stocked to support future manufacturing needs. The focus is on producing schedules that meet the materials needs identified in the master production schedule. When managers realized that the information in an MRP system would be useful to functional areas other than operations, MRP evolved into a second generation system, **manufacturing resource planning (MRP II)**. MRP II is a system that ties the basic MRP system to the company's financial system and other resources, as depicted in Figure 13.11. MRP II enables managers to test "what-if" scenarios by using simulation. For example, managers can see the effect of changing the MPS on the purchasing requirements for certain critical suppliers or the workload on bottleneck work centres without actually authorizing the schedule. In addition, management can project the dollar value of shipments, product costs, overhead allocations, inventories, backlogs, and profits by using the MRP plan along with prices and product and activity costs from the accounting system.

The focus of MRP II was internal; the next-generation software, enterprise resource planning (ERP), extended beyond the firm to improve the planning and monitoring of external production decisions. ERP integrated external supply chain relationships, including both suppliers and customers. Information for the ERP system is drawn from a central database and is used by managers in manufacturing, purchasing, marketing, finance, accounting, and engineering. Reports from the system help managers develop and monitor the overall business plan and recognize sales objectives, manufacturing capabilities, and cash flow constraints. Suppliers and customers also can access production schedules to better plan their own production and delivery schedules. Although the benefits of improved information flows and planning from ERP extend far beyond those of just materials planning, MRP still remains a central element.

---

finite capacity scheduling (FCS) An algorithm designed to schedule a group of orders appropriately across an entire shop.

manufacturing resource planning (MRP II) A system that ties the basic MRP system to the company's financial system.

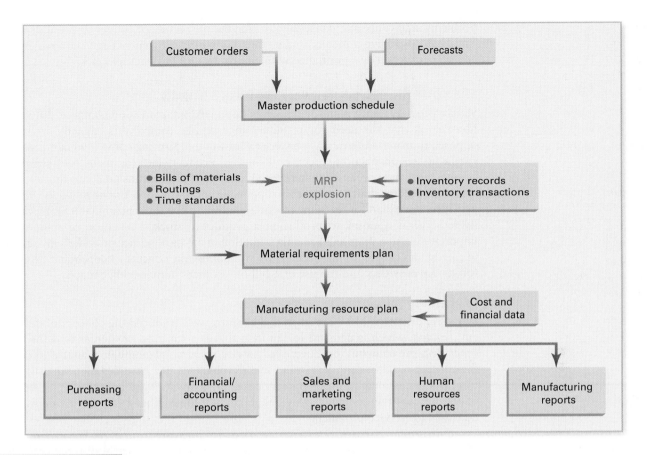

FIGURE 13.11

Overview of a Manufacturing Resource Planning System

MRP AND THE ENVIRONMENT

Consumer and governmental concern about deterioration of the natural environment has driven manufacturers to re-engineer their processes to become more environmentally friendly. Disassembly and recycling of base materials is becoming more commonplace, and products are being designed for a fate other than disposal at the end of their useful lives. Despite these improvements, manufacturing processes often produce a number of wastes that need to be properly disposed of. Wastes come in many forms, including the following:

- Effluents such as carbon monoxide, sulphur dioxide, and hazardous chemicals associated with the processes used to manufacture the product
- Materials such as metal shavings, oils, and chemicals associated with specific operations
- Packaging materials such as unusable cardboard and plastics associated with products or purchased items
- Scrap associated with unusable product or component defects generated by the manufacturing process

Companies can modify their MRP systems to assist them in tracking these wastes and planning for their disposition. The type and amount of waste associated with each item can be entered into its bill of materials by treating the waste much like you would a component of the item. When the master production schedule is developed for a product, reports can be generated that project the amount of waste that is expected and when it will occur. Although this approach requires substantial modification of a firm's bills of materials, the benefits are also substantial. Firms can identify their waste problems in advance and consequently plan for the recycle or proper disposal of them. The firms also have a means to generate any formal documentation required by the government to verify compliance with environmental laws and policies.

RESOURCE PLANNING FOR SERVICE FIRMS

Service providers must plan for resources just as manufacturers do. A major difference, however, is that the need for resources in a service company is capacity-driven, as opposed to material-driven. We have seen how manufacturing companies can disaggregate a master production schedule of finished products into the plans for assemblies, components, and purchased materials, which in turn can be translated into the needs for resources such as staff, equipment, supporting materials, and financial assets. Service providers must plan for the same resources; however, the focus is on maintaining capacity to serve as opposed to producing a product to stock. Utilization of resources is important because materials are only a fraction of a typical service provider's investment in capital and people. In this section, we will discuss the concept of dependent demands for service providers and the use of a bill of resources in managing capacity.

DEPENDENT DEMAND

When we discussed MRP earlier in this chapter, we introduced the concept of *dependent demand*, which is demand for an item that is a function of the demand for some other item the company produces. For service resource planning, it is useful to define the concept of dependent demand to include demands for resources that are driven by forecasts of customer requests for services or by plans for various activities in support of the services the company provides. Here are some other examples of dependent demands for service providers.

RESTAURANTS. Every time you order from the menu at a restaurant, you initiate the need for supporting materials (uncooked food items, plates, and napkins), staff (chef, servers, and dishwashers), and equipment (stoves, ovens, and cooking utensils). Using a forecast of the demand for each type of meal, the manager of the restaurant can estimate the need for resources. Many restaurants have "specials" on certain days, such as fish on Fridays or prime rib on Saturdays. Specials improve the accuracy of the forecast for meal types and typically signal the need for above-average levels of staff help.

AIRLINES. Whenever an airline schedules a flight, there are requirements for supporting materials (meals, beverages, and fuel), staff (pilots, flight attendants, and airport services), and equipment (plane and airport gate). Forecasts of customer patronage of each flight help determine the amount of supporting materials and the type of plane needed. A master schedule of flights based on the forecasts can be exploded to determine the resources needed to support the schedule.

HOSPITALS. With the exception of the emergency room, appointments, a form of master schedule for specific services, generally drive the short-term need for health-care resources in hospitals. Forecasts of requests for various services provided by the hospital drive the long-term needs. When you schedule a surgical procedure, you generate a need for supporting materials (medicines, surgical gowns, and linens), staff (surgeon, nurses, and anesthesiologist), and equipment (operating room, surgical tools, and recovery bed). Hospitals must take care so that certain equipment or personnel do not become overcommitted. That is why an appointment for a hernia operation is put off until the surgeon is available, even though the appropriate operating room, nurses, and other resources are available.

HOTELS. The major fixed assets at a hotel are the rooms where guests stay. Given the high capital costs involved, hotels try to maintain as high a utilization rate as possible by offering group rates or special promotions at certain times of the year. Reservations, supplemented by forecasts of "walk-in" customers, provide a master schedule of needs for the hotel's services. When a traveller makes a reservation at a hotel, a need is generated for supporting materials (soap and towels), staff (front desk, housekeeping, and concierge), and equipment (fax, television, and exercise bicycle). The Managerial Practice feature illustrates resource planning in the hotel industry.

MANAGERIAL PRACTICE
Resource Planning at Starwood Hotels & Resorts Worldwide

Starwood Hotels & Resorts Worldwide (www.starwood.com) is the largest hotel and gambling company in the world, with more than 650 hotels and resorts in more than 70 countries worldwide. It owns international hotel chains such as Sheraton Hotels, CIGA Hotels, Four Points Hotels, and The Luxury Collection, which includes the St. Regis in New York, the Prince de Gaulle in Paris, the Hotel Gritti Palace in Venice, and the Hotel Imperial in Vienna. It also owns Caesar's Palace in Las Vegas and other casinos in Cairo, Egypt, and Atlantic City. More than 50 million travellers a year visit Starwood's properties.

Resource planning at a company such as Starwood is complex, not only because of the size of the business but also because of the variety of its holdings. As in any service environment, resources such as employees, equipment, and supplies must be managed so as to ensure that the needs and expectations of the customers are met. Information technology can help by providing the means for centralized information flows while allowing decision making to take place at the most appropriate level. An important concept for resource planning in services is *dependent demand* for key resources. Starwood makes use of that concept in two ways. First, Starwood's reservation system builds profiles of its customers' preferences so that they can be better served each time they stay at a hotel or resort. For example, the profile would include information such as whether they like a feather or foam pillow, what types of newspapers they like, whether they want a low floor or a high floor, if they want suites, or even if they have a disability. The profile is used at the time a reservation is made to estimate the requirements for various types of rooms and locations, newspapers, pillows, and any other resource affected by the customer's preferences. Such a capability provides a "customized" experience for every guest.

Second, Starwood plans to link its worldwide reservation system to its property management system for resource plan-

A concierge for the Hotel Gritti Palace greets customers: a rowing team. This hotel is one of many properties of Starwood Hotels & Resorts Worldwide that faces complex resource planning issues.

ning at a particular property. The property management system schedules staff and housekeepers and projects requirements for the food-preparation department. Given expected occupancies for weeks in advance, property managers can plan for the needed resources to make their customers' stay enjoyable.

The ERP system Starwood uses for managing the resources of this worldwide enterprise has a centralized database and common modules, including Payroll, Accounts Payable, General Ledger, and Fixed Assets, from Oracle, as well as some legacy systems. Given the enormity of this application, various parts of the enterprise will be phased into the integrated system over time.

Source: Adapted from: David Baum, "Setting the Standard for Service," *Profit Magazine,* 1999, <www.oracle.com>.

BILL OF RESOURCES

The service analogy to the BOM in a manufacturing company is the **bill of resources (BOR)**, which is a record of all the required materials, equipment time, staff, and other resources needed to provide a service, the parent–component relationships, and the usage quantities. Given a master schedule of services, we can use the bills of resources to derive the time-phased requirements for the firm's critical resources, as we did for the inventory records in MRP.

A BOR for a service provider can be as complex as a BOM for a manufacturer. Consider a hospital that has just scheduled treatment of a patient with an aneurysm. As shown in Figure 13.12, the BOR for treatment of an aneurysm has seven levels, starting at the top (end item): (1) discharge; (2) intermediate care; (3) postoperative care—step down; (4) postoperative care—intensive; (5) surgery; (6) preoperative care—angiogram; and (7) preoperative care—testing. Each level of the BOR has a set of material and resource requirements and a lead time. For example, at level 6 shown in Figure 13.12(b), the patient needs 6 hours of nurses' time, 1 hour of the primary MD's time, 1 hour of the respiratory therapist's time, 24 hours of bed time, 3 different lab tests, 1 dietary meal, and 10 different medicines from the pharmacy. The lead time

FIGURE 13.12a

Bill of Resources for Treating an Aneurysm

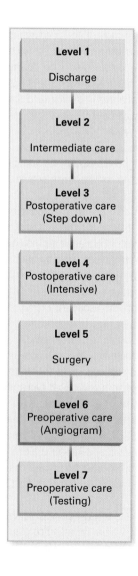

FIGURE 13.12b

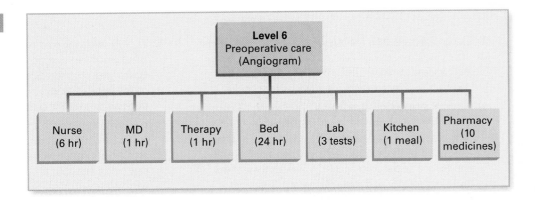

for this level is 1 day. The lead time for the entire stay for treatment of the aneurysm is 12.2 days. A master schedule of patient admissions and the BORs for each illness enable the hospital to manage their critical resources. Reports analogous to those we discussed for MRP II can be generated for the managers of the major processes in the hospital.

RESOURCE PLANNING ACROSS THE ORGANIZATION

Resource planning lies at the heart of any organization. We have seen examples of how traditional bricks-and-mortar organizations such as manufacturers, restaurants, airlines, hospitals, and hotels organize their resource planning efforts by utilizing integrated information systems that connect the organization's enterprise processes and functional areas.

But what about the so-called dot-coms, which rely extensively on Internet connectivity to customers and suppliers? They too have resource planning concerns that permeate the organization. For example, consider online grocers, who do not have the retail outlets and checkout counters their bricks-and-mortar competitors do. What resource planning must online grocers do? To be competitive in this service industry where profit margins are very small, the online grocer must make it easy for the customer to shop on the Internet, provide a wide variety of goods, and make sure the deliveries of groceries are on time and cost-efficient. To that end, Web pages must be designed to keep track of customers' preferences so that weekly shopping is easier and shoppers are apprised of specials and promotions that are sometimes keyed to the availability of goods in stock. The demand for goods at a warehouse is derived from the orders placed by customers at a Web site. Online grocers also must do the order picking, packing, and handling that customers normally do at traditional supermarkets either using manual labour or automated picking equipment. In addition, the delivery of customer orders is derived from the delivery time requested by the customers as well as the completion of the packing process. This operation needs a specialized delivery fleet, capable of moving perishable, bulky items over short distances. Finally, managers of an online grocer are also concerned with cash flow planning, which is derived from the timing between sales of groceries and payments to suppliers and employees. Dot-com companies have very important resource planning problems that affect all the major processes of the firm.

CHAPTER HIGHLIGHTS

- Dependent demand for component items can be calculated from production schedules of parent items in a manufacturing company. Dependent demands can be calculated from forecasts and other resource plans in a service company.

- Material requirements planning (MRP) is a computerized scheduling and information system that offers benefits in managing dependent demand inventories because it (1) recognizes the relationship between production schedules and the demand for component items, (2) provides forward visibility for planning and problem solving, and (3) provides a way to change materials plans in concert with production schedule changes. MRP has three basic inputs: bills of materials, the master production schedule, and inventory records.

- A bill of materials is a diagram or structured list of all components of an item, the parent–component relationships, and usage quantities.

- A master production schedule (MPS) states the number of *end items* to be produced during specific time periods within an intermediate planning horizon. The MPS is developed based on the aggregate production plan.

- The MRP is prepared from the most recent inventory records for all items. The basic elements in each record are gross requirements, scheduled receipts, projected on-hand inventory, planned receipts, and planned order releases. Several quantities must be determined for each inventory record, including lot size, lead time, and safety stock.

- The MRP explosion procedure determines the production schedules of the components that are needed to support the master production schedule. The planned order releases of a parent, modified by usage quantities shown in the bill of materials, become the gross requirements of its components.

- MRP systems provide outputs such as the material requirements plan, action notices, capacity reports, and performance reports. Action notices bring to a planner's attention new orders that need to be released or items that have open orders with misaligned due dates.

- Capacity requirements planning (CRP) is a technique for estimating the workload required by a master schedule. CRP uses routing information to identify the workstations involved and MRP information about existing inventory, lead-time offset, and replacement part requirements to calculate accurate workload projections. Finite capacity scheduling (FCS) determines a schedule for production orders that recognizes resource constraints.

- Manufacturing resource planning (MRP II), or more broadly, enterprise resource planning (ERP) ties the basic MRP system to the financial and accounting systems. Advanced systems integrate management decision support for all business functions.

- Service providers can take advantage of MRP principles by developing bills of resources that include requirements for materials, labour, and equipment.

CD-ROM RESOURCES

The Student CD-ROM that accompanies this text contains the following resources, which allow you to further practise and apply the concepts presented in this chapter.

- **Equation Summary**: All the equations for this chapter can be found in one convenient location.

- **Discussion Questions**: Three questions will challenge your understanding of the usefulness of MRP to all functional areas of a business and of how the principles of resource planning can be applied to service firms.

- **Case**: *Flashy Flashers, Inc.* Determine the requirements for materials and components in a practical setting and assess the implications for MRP implementation at an automotive electric component manufacturer.

- **OM Explorer Tutor**: OM Explorer contains a tutor program that will help you learn how to use the FOQ, POQ, and L4L decision rules for inventory lot-sizing decisions.

- **OM Explorer Solver**: OM Explorer has three programs that can be used to solve general problems involving single-item MRP inventory records, MRP records for multiple-level bills of material, and master production schedules.

- **Supplement J:** *Operations Scheduling.* Use this supplement to see how resource planning systems link to advanced planning systems in practice.

- **Supplement K:** *Master Production Scheduling.* Learn how to develop master production schedules and how customer due-date promises are linked to production schedules.

SOLVED PROBLEM 1

Refer to the bill of materials for item A shown in Figure 13.13.

FIGURE 13.13

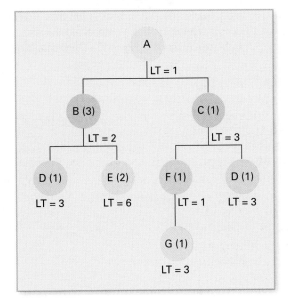

If there is no existing inventory, how many units of G, E, and D must be purchased to produce five units of end item A?

SOLUTION

Five units of G, 30 units of E, and 20 units of D must be purchased to make 5 units of A. The usage quantities shown in Figure 13.13 indicate that 2 units of E are needed to make 1 unit of B and that 3 units of B are needed to make 1 unit of A; therefore, 5 units of A require 30 units of E ($2 \times 3 \times 5 = 30$). One unit of D is consumed to make 1 unit of B, and 3 units of B per unit of A result in 15 units of D ($1 \times 3 \times 5 = 15$); plus 1 unit of D in each unit of C and 1 unit of C per unit of A result in another 5 units of D ($1 \times 1 \times 5 = 5$). The total requirements to make 5 units of A are 20 units of D (15 + 5). The calculation of requirements for G is simply $1 \times 1 \times 1 \times 5 = 5$ units.

The MPS for product A calls for the assembly department to begin final assembly according to the following schedule: 100 units in week 2; 200 units in week 4; 120 units in week 6; 180 units in week 7; and 60 units in week 8. Develop a material requirements plan for the next eight weeks for items B, C, and D. The BOM for A is shown in Figure 13.14, and data from the inventory records are shown in Table 13.1.

FIGURE 13.14

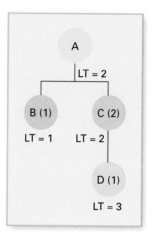

TABLE 13.1 *Inventory Record Data*

| | ITEM | | |
DATA CATEGORY	B	C	D
Lot-sizing rule	POQ ($P = 3$)	L4L	FOQ = 500 units
Lead time	1 week	2 weeks	3 weeks
Scheduled receipts	None	200 (week 1)	None
Beginning (on-hand) inventory	20	0	425

SOLUTION

We begin with items B and C and develop their inventory records, as shown in Figure 13.15 on pages 453 and 454. The MPS for item A must be multiplied by 2 to derive the gross requirements for item C, because of the usage quantity. Once the planned order releases for item C are found, the gross requirements for item D can be calculated.

Notice that an action notice would call for delaying the scheduled receipt for item C from week 1 to week 2. Other action notices would notify planners that items B and D have a planned order release in the current week.

FIGURE 13.15

Item: B
Description:

Lot Size: POQ (*P* = 3)
Lead Time: 1 week

		Week									
		1	2	3	4	5	6	7	8	9	10
Gross requirements			100		200		120	180	60		
Scheduled receipts											
Projected on-hand inventory	20	20	200	200	0	0	240	60	0	0	0
Planned receipts			280				360				
Planned order releases		280			360						

Item: C
Description:

Lot Size: L4L
Lead Time: 2 weeks

		Week									
		1	2	3	4	5	6	7	8	9	10
Gross requirements			200		400		240	360	120		
Scheduled receipts		200 →									
Projected on-hand inventory	0	200	0	0	0	0	0	0	0	0	0
Planned receipts					400		240	360	120		
Planned order releases			400		240	360	120				

(continued on next page)

FIGURE 13.15

(continued)

Item: D
Description:

Lot Size: FOQ = 500 units
Lead Time: 3 weeks

		Week									
		1	2	3	4	5	6	7	8	9	10
Gross requirements			400		240	360	120				
Scheduled receipts											
Projected on-hand inventory	425	425	25	25	285	425	305	305	305	305	305
Planned receipts					500	500					
Planned order releases		500	500								

PROBLEMS

1. Consider the bill of materials in Figure 13.16.

   a. How many immediate parents (one level above) does item I have? How many immediate parents does item E have?

   b. How many unique components does item A have at all levels?

   c. Which of the components are purchased items?

   d. How many intermediate items does item A have at all levels?

   e. Given the lead times noted on Figure 13.16, how far in advance of shipment is the earliest purchase commitment required?

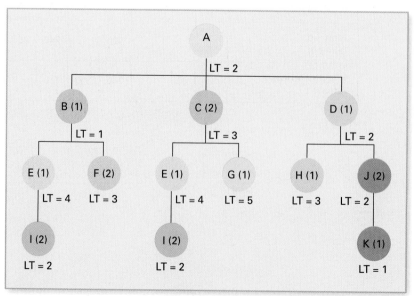

FIGURE 13.16

2. Item A is made from components B, C, and D. Item B is a subassembly that requires 2 units of C and 1 unit of E. Item D also is an intermediate item, made from F. All other usage quantities are 2. Draw the bill of materials for item A.

3. A milling machine workstation makes small gears used in a transmission gear box. As of week 22, the capacity requirements planning (CRP) report for the workstation revealed the following information. The planned hours for weeks 22, 23, 24, 25, 26, and 27 were 40, 60, 100, 120, 175, and 160, respectively. The actual hours for the same weeks were 90, 75, 80, 0, 0, and 0. Each of two machines at the workstation is scheduled for two shifts per day. The workstation has a maximum capacity of 160 hours per week. Does the CRP report reveal any problems at the workstation? If so, what are they and what should be done to correct them?

4. The partially completed inventory record in Figure 13.17 shows gross requirements, scheduled receipts, lead time, and current on-hand inventory.

   a. Complete the last three rows of the record for an FOQ of 110 units.

   b. Complete the last three rows of the record by using the L4L lot-sizing rule.

   c. Complete the last three rows of the record by using the POQ lot-sizing rule, with $P = 2$.

Item: M405-X
Description: Tabletop assembly

Lot Size:
Lead Time: 2 weeks

	Week									
	1	2	3	4	5	6	7	8	9	10
Gross requirements	90		85		80		45	90		
Scheduled receipts	110									
Projected on-hand inventory 40										
Planned receipts										
Planned order releases										

FIGURE 13.17

5. The partially completed inventory record in Figure 13.18 shows gross requirements, scheduled receipts, lead time, and current on-hand inventory.

   a. Complete the last three rows of the inventory record for an FOQ of 50 units.

   b. Complete the last three rows of the record by using the L4L lot-sizing rule.

   c. Complete the last three rows of the record by using the POQ lot-sizing rule, with $P = 4$.

Item: Driveshaft							Lot Size: Lead Time: 3 weeks		
	Week								
	1	2	3	4	5	6	7	8
Gross requirements	35	25	15	20	40	40	50	50
Scheduled receipts	80							
Projected on-hand inventory 10								
Planned receipts								
Planned order releases								

FIGURE 13.18

6. The BOM for product A is shown in Figure 13.19, and data from the inventory records are shown in Table 13.2. In the master production schedule for product A, 500 units are needed in week 6. The lead time for production of A is two weeks. Develop the material requirements plan for the next six weeks for items B, C, and D. *Hint:* You cannot derive an item's gross requirements unless you know the planned order releases of all its parents.

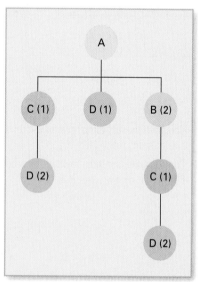

FIGURE 13.19

TABLE 13.2 *Inventory Record Data*			
	ITEM		
DATA CATEGORY	*B*	*C*	*D*
Lot-sizing rule	L4L	L4L	FOQ = 2000
Lead time	3 weeks	1 week	1 week
Scheduled receipts	None	None	2000 (week 1)
Beginning inventory	0	0	200

7. The BOMs for products A and B are shown in Figure 13.20. Data from inventory records are shown in Table 13.3. The MPS calls for 85 units of product A to be started in week 3 and 100 units in week 6. The MPS for product B calls for 180 units to be started in week 5. Develop the material requirements plan for the next six weeks for items C, D, E, and F. Identify any action notices.

TABLE 13.3 *Inventory Record Data*

	ITEM			
DATA CATEGORY	C	D	E	F
Lot-sizing rule	FOQ = 220	L4L	FOQ = 300	POQ ($P = 2$)
Lead time	3 weeks	2 weeks	3 weeks	2 weeks
Scheduled receipts	280 (week 1)	None	300 (week 3)	None
Beginning inventory	25	0	150	600

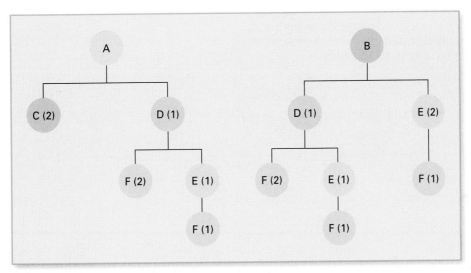

FIGURE 13.20

8. Figure 13.21 illustrates the BOM of product A. The master production schedule for product A calls for 50 units in week 2, 65 units in week 5, and 80 units in week 8. Item C is produced to make A, and to meet the forecast demand for replacement parts. Past replacement part demand has been 20 units per week (add 20 units to C's gross requirements). The lead times for items F and C are one week, and for the other items the lead time is two weeks. No safety stock is required for items B, C, D, E, and F. The L4L lot-sizing rule is used for items B and F; the POQ lot-sizing rule ($P = 3$) is used for C. Item E has an FOQ of 600 units, and D has an FOQ of 250 units. On-hand inventories are 50 units of B, 50 units of C, 120 units of D, 70 units of E, and 250 units of F. Item B has a scheduled receipt of 50 units in week 2.

Develop a material requirements plan for the next eight weeks for items B, C, D, E, and F.

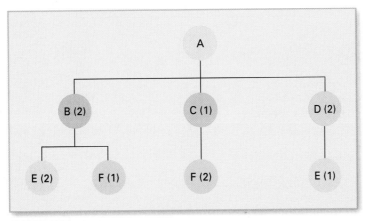

FIGURE 13.21

9. The following information is available for three MPS items.

Item A	An 80-unit order is to be started in week 3.
	A 55-unit order is to be started in week 6.
Item B	A 125-unit order is to be started in week 5.
Item C	A 60-unit order is to be started in week 4.

    Develop the material requirements plan for the next six weeks for items D, E, and F, identifying any action notices that would be provided. The BOMs are shown in Figure 13.22, and data from the inventory records are shown in Table 13.4. *Warning:* There is a safety stock requirement for item F. Be sure to plan a receipt for any week in which the projected on-hand inventory becomes less than the safety stock.

TABLE 13.4 *Inventory Record Data*

	ITEM		
DATA CATEGORY	**D**	**E**	**F**
Lot-sizing rule	FOQ = 150	L4L	POQ ($P = 2$)
Lead time	3 weeks	1 week	2 weeks
Safety stock	0	0	30
Scheduled receipts	150 (week 3)	120 (week 2)	None
Beginning inventory	150	0	100

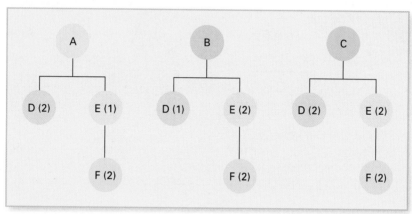

FIGURE 13.22

10. The BOM for product A is shown in Figure 13.23. The MPS for product A calls for 120 units to be started in weeks 2, 4, 5, and 8. Table 13.5 shows data from the inventory records.

    Develop the material requirements plan for the next eight weeks for each item. *Warning:* Note that item E has a safety stock requirement.

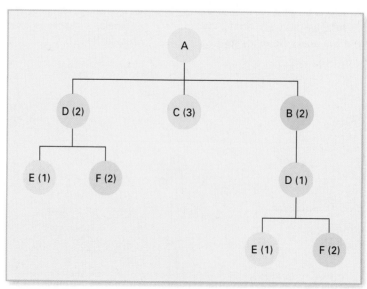

FIGURE 13.23

	ITEM				
DATA CATEGORY	**B**	**C**	**D**	**E**	**F**
Lot-sizing rule	L4L	FOQ = 700	FOQ = 700	L4L	L4L
Lead time	3 weeks	3 weeks	4 weeks	2 weeks	1 week
Safety stock	0	0	0	50	0
Scheduled receipts	150 (week 2)	450 (week 2)	700 (week 1)	None	1400 (week 1)
Beginning inventory	125	0	235	750	0

TABLE 13.5 *Inventory Record Data*

11. Develop the material requirements plan for all components and intermediate items associated with end item A for the next ten weeks. Refer to Solved Problem 1 for the bill of materials (Figure 13.13 on page 451) and Table 13.6 for component inventory record information. The MPS for product A calls for 50 units to be started in weeks 2, 6, 8, and 9. *Warning:* Note that items B and C have safety stock requirements.

	ITEM					
DATA CATEGORY	**B**	**C**	**D**	**E**	**F**	**G**
Lot-sizing rule	L4L	L4L	POQ ($P = 2$)	L4L	L4L	FOQ = 100
Lead time	2 weeks	3 weeks	3 weeks	6 weeks	1 week	3 weeks
Safety stock	30	10	0	0	0	0
Scheduled receipts	150 (week 2)	50 (week 2)	None	400 (week 6)	40 (week 3)	None
Beginning inventory	30	20	60	400	0	0

TABLE 13.6 *Inventory Record Data*

REFERENCES AND FURTHER READINGS

Blackstone, J. H. *Capacity Management.* Cincinnati: South-Western, 1989.

Conway, Richard W. "Linking MRP II and FCS." *APICS—The Performance Advantage*, June 1996, pp. 40–44.

Haddock, Jorge, and Donald E. Hubicki. "Which Lot-Sizing Techniques Are Used in Material Requirements Planning?" *Production and Inventory Management Journal*, vol. 30 (1989), no. 3, pp. 53–56.

Hoy, Paul A. "The Changing Role of MRP II." *APICS—The Performance Advantage*, June 1996, pp. 50–53.

Melnyk, Steven A., Robert Stroufe, Frank Montabon, Roger Calantone, R. Lal Tummala, and Timothy J. Hinds. "Integrating Environmental Issues into Material Planning: 'Green' MRP." *Production and Inventory Management Journal*, Third Quarter 1999, pp. 36–45.

Ormsby, Joseph G., Susan Y. Ormsby, and Carl R. Ruthstrom. "MRP II Implementation: A Case Study." *Production and Inventory Management*, vol. 31 (1990), no. 4, pp. 77–82.

Prouty, Dave. "Shiva Finite Capacity Scheduling System." *APICS—The Performance Advantage*, April 1997, pp. 58–61.

Ptak, Carol. *MRP and Beyond.* Homewood, IL: Irwin Professional Publications, 1996.

Roth, Aleda V., and Roland Van Dierdonck. "Hospital Resource Planning: Concepts, Feasibility, and Framework." *Production and Operations Management*, vol. 4 (1995), no. 1, pp. 2–29.

Vollmann, T. E., W. L. Berry, and D. C. Whybark. *Manufacturing Planning and Control Systems*, 4th ed. Homewood, IL: Irwin Professional Publications, 1997.

Wallace, Tom. *MRP II: Making It Happen.* Essex Junction, VT: Oliver Wight Ltd. Publishers, 1994.

Appendix: Normal Distribution

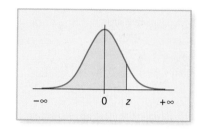

	.00	.01	.02	.03	.04	.05	.06	.07	.08	.09
.0	.5000	.5040	.5080	.5120	.5160	.5199	.5239	.5279	.5319	.5359
.1	.5398	.5438	.5478	.5517	.5557	.5596	.5636	.5675	.5714	.5753
.2	.5793	.5832	.5871	.5910	.5948	.5987	.6026	.6064	.6103	.6141
.3	.6179	.6217	.6255	.6293	.6331	.6368	.6406	.6443	.6480	.6517
.4	.6554	.6591	.6628	.6664	.6700	.6736	.6772	.6808	.6844	.6879
.5	.6915	.6950	.6985	.7019	.7054	.7088	.7123	.7157	.7190	.7224
.6	.7257	.7291	.7324	.7357	.7389	.7422	.7454	.7486	.7517	.7549
.7	.7580	.7611	.7642	.7673	.7704	.7734	.7764	.7794	.7823	.7852
.8	.7881	.7910	.7939	.7967	.7995	.8023	.8051	.8078	.8106	.8133
.9	.8159	.8186	.8212	.8238	.8264	.8289	.8315	.8340	.8365	.8389
1.0	.8413	.8438	.8461	.8485	.8508	.8531	.8554	.8577	.8599	.8621
1.1	.8643	.8665	.8686	.8708	.8729	.8749	.8770	.8790	.8810	.8830
1.2	.8849	.8869	.8888	.8907	.8925	.8944	.8962	.8980	.8997	.9015
1.3	.9032	.9049	.9066	.9082	.9099	.9115	.9131	.9147	.9162	.9177
1.4	.9192	.9207	.9222	.9236	.9251	.9265	.9279	.9292	.9306	.9319
1.5	.9332	.9345	.9357	.9370	.9382	.9394	.9406	.9418	.9429	.9441
1.6	.9452	.9463	.9474	.9484	.9495	.9505	.9515	.9525	.9535	.9545
1.7	.9554	.9564	.9573	.9582	.9591	.9599	.9608	.9616	.9625	.9633
1.8	.9641	.9649	.9656	.9664	.9671	.9678	.9686	.9693	.9699	.9706
1.9	.9713	.9719	.9726	.9732	.9738	.9744	.9750	.9756	.9761	.9767
2.0	.9772	.9778	.9783	.9788	.9793	.9798	.9803	.9808	.9812	.9817
2.1	.9821	.9826	.9830	.9834	.9838	.9842	.9846	.9850	.9854	.9857
2.2	.9861	.9864	.9868	.9871	.9875	.9878	.9881	.9884	.9887	.9890
2.3	.9893	.9896	.9898	.9901	.9904	.9906	.9909	.9911	.9913	.9916
2.4	.9918	.9920	.9922	.9925	.9927	.9929	.9931	.9932	.9934	.9936
2.5	.9938	.9940	.9941	.9943	.9945	.9946	.9948	.9949	.9951	.9952
2.6	.9953	.9955	.9956	.9957	.9959	.9960	.9961	.9962	.9963	.9964
2.7	.9965	.9966	.9967	.9968	.9969	.9970	.9971	.9972	.9973	.9974
2.8	.9974	.9975	.9976	.9977	.9977	.9978	.9979	.9979	.9980	.9981
2.9	.9981	.9982	.9982	.9983	.9984	.9984	.9985	.9985	.9986	.9986
3.0	.9987	.9987	.9987	.9988	.9988	.9989	.9989	.9989	.9990	.9990
3.1	.9990	.9991	.9991	.9991	.9992	.9992	.9992	.9992	.9993	.9993
3.2	.9993	.9993	.9994	.9994	.9994	.9994	.9994	.9995	.9995	.9995
3.3	.9995	.9995	.9995	.9996	.9996	.9996	.9996	.9996	.9996	.9997
3.4	.9997	.9997	.9997	.9997	.9997	.9997	.9997	.9997	.9997	.9998

Name Index

Subject Index

Note: f denotes a figure and *t* denotes a table.

CD ROM WITH
BOOK

DATE DUE	RETURNED

Photo Credits

← over 1 page

"AS IS" LICENSE AGREEMENT AND LIMITED WARRANTY

READ THIS LICENSE CAREFULLY BEFORE OPENING THIS PACKAGE. BY OPENING THIS PACKAGE, YOU ARE AGREEING TO THE TERMS AND CONDITIONS OF THIS LICENSE. IF YOU DO NOT AGREE, DO NOT OPEN THE PACKAGE. PROMPTLY RETURN THE UNOPENED PACKAGE AND ALL ACCOMPANYING ITEMS TO THE PLACE YOU OBTAINED THEM. THESE TERMS APPLY TO ALL LICENSED SOFTWARE ON THE DISK EXCEPT THAT THE TERMS FOR USE OF ANY SHAREWARE OR FREEWARE ON THE DISKETTES ARE AS SET FORTH IN THE ELECTRONIC LICENSE LOCATED ON THE DISK:

1. GRANT OF LICENSE and OWNERSHIP: The enclosed computer programs <<and any data>> ("Software") are licensed, not sold, to you by Pearson Canada Inc. ("We" or the "Company") in consideration of your adoption of the accompanying Company textbooks and/or other materials, and your agreement to these terms. You own only the disk(s) but we and/or our licensors own the Software itself. This license allows instructors and students enrolled in the course using the Company textbook that accompanies this Software (the "Course") to use and display the enclosed copy of the Software for academic use only, so long as you comply with the terms of this Agreement. You may make one copy for back up only. We reserve any rights not granted to you.

2. USE RESTRICTIONS: You may not sell or license copies of the Software or the Documentation to others. You may not transfer, distribute or make available the Software or the Documentation, except to instructors and students in your school who are users of the adopted Company textbook that accompanies this Software in connection with the course for which the textbook was adopted. You may not reverse engineer, disassemble, decompile, modify, adapt, translate or create derivative works based on the Software or the Documentation. You may be held legally responsible for any copying or copyright infringement which is caused by your failure to abide by the terms of these restrictions.

3. TERMINATION: This license is effective until terminated. This license will terminate automatically without notice from the Company if you fail to comply with any provisions or limitations of this license. Upon termination, you shall destroy the Documentation and all copies of the Software. All provisions of this Agreement as to limitation and disclaimer of warranties, limitation of liability, remedies or damages, and our ownership rights shall survive termination.

4. DISCLAIMER OF WARRANTY: THE COMPANY AND ITS LICENSORS MAKE NO WARRANTIES ABOUT THE SOFTWARE, WHICH IS PROVIDED "AS-IS." IF THE DISK IS DEFECTIVE IN MATERIALS OR WORKMANSHIP, YOUR ONLY REMEDY IS TO RETURN IT TO THE COMPANY WITHIN 30 DAYS FOR REPLACEMENT UNLESS THE COMPANY DETERMINES IN GOOD FAITH THAT THE DISK HAS BEEN MISUSED OR IMPROPERLY INSTALLED, REPAIRED, ALTERED OR DAMAGED. THE COMPANY DISCLAIMS ALL WARRANTIES, EXPRESS OR IMPLIED, INCLUDING WITHOUT LIMITATION, THE IMPLIED WARRANTIES OF MERCHANTABILITY AND FITNESS FOR A PARTICULAR PURPOSE. THE COMPANY DOES NOT WARRANT, GUARANTEE OR MAKE ANY REPRESENTATION REGARDING THE ACCURACY, RELIABILITY, CURRENTNESS, USE, OR RESULTS OF USE, OF THE SOFTWARE.

5. LIMITATION OF REMEDIES AND DAMAGES: IN NO EVENT, SHALL THE COMPANY OR ITS EMPLOYEES, AGENTS, LICENSORS OR CONTRACTORS BE LIABLE FOR ANY INCIDENTAL, INDIRECT, SPECIAL OR CONSEQUENTIAL DAMAGES ARISING OUT OF OR IN CONNECTION WITH THIS LICENSE OR THE SOFTWARE, INCLUDING, WITHOUT LIMITATION, LOSS OF USE, LOSS OF DATA, LOSS OF INCOME OR PROFIT, OR OTHER LOSSES SUSTAINED AS A RESULT OF INJURY TO ANY PERSON, OR LOSS OF OR DAMAGE TO PROPERTY, OR CLAIMS OF THIRD PARTIES, EVEN IF THE COMPANY OR AN AUTHORIZED REPRESENTATIVE OF THE COMPANY HAS BEEN ADVISED OF THE POSSIBILITY OF SUCH DAMAGES. SOME JURISDICTIONS DO NOT ALLOW THE LIMITATION OF DAMAGES IN CERTAIN CIRCUMSTANCES, SO THE ABOVE LIMITATIONS MAY NOT ALWAYS APPLY.

6. GENERAL: THIS AGREEMENT SHALL BE CONSTRUED AND INTERPRETED ACCORDING TO THE LAWS OF THE PROVINCE OF ONTARIO. This Agreement is the complete and exclusive statement of the agreement between you and the Company and supersedes all proposals, prior agreements, oral or written, and any other communications between you and the company or any of its representatives relating to the subject matter.

Should you have any questions concerning this agreement or if you wish to contact the Company for any reason, please contact in writing: Permissions, Pearson Canada Inc., 26 Prince Andrew Place, Toronto, Ontario, M3C 2T8.